Track and Field Omnibook

**4th Edition
Revised and Updated**

Ken Doherty, Ph.D.

tafnews

**Book Division of
Track & Field News**

FOURTH EDITION

Published by Tafnews Press
Book Division of Track & Field News, Inc.
P.O. Box 296, Los Altos, CA 94022 USA

Standard Book Number 0-911521-14-3

Printed in the United States of America.

Cover photos: L-R, Nawal El Moutawakil, by Charles Shaffer;
Alonzo Babers, by Claus Andersen; Mike Tully, by Diane Johnson.

Cover design by Jon Peters.

CONTENTS

TO THOSE YOUNG MEN AND WOMEN*

WHO run and jump and throw
    Primarily because doing so is innate,
        Organically beneficial, and fun;

WHO compete with, not against, others;

WHO do their utmost to win,
    Not as the main thing,
        But to enjoy the struggle for victory, and
        To motivate the day-after-day-after-day training—
            The greater its demands,
            The greater the personal growth and fulfillment;

WHO honor the basic tenets of amateur sports—
    That mutual respect and fair play are essential—
    Fair play on the field, but equally
    Fair play off the field—
        Conformance to both intent and letter of the
        Governing Rules,
        Rejection of all unfair advantages;

That other life commitments—
    Studies, vocation, social obligations—
    Have first priority;

That participation in sports is therefore limited—
    Limited time-energy for training and competition,
    Limited personal commitment,
    Limited material rewards;

That professionals, however high their personal integrity,
    Are unfettered by such limitations—
        An unfair advantage that tends to corrupt
        Amateurs competing with them;

That material rewards, per se, provide no unfair advantage,
    But do reverse priorities, increase time-energy,
        promote hypocrisy, and prostitute higher values;

WHO, in summary, judge the worth of a fellow athlete,
    Not only by the level of performance, but also
    By conformance to the Rules,
        Rules often unenforceable and often violated
        By individuals, institutions and nations
            In their lust to win;

BUT ALSO, TO THOSE COACHES

WHO respect these tenets, and
    Seek actively to instill them in those
    That train under their guidance.

Ken Doherty, Pa.
Swarthmore,
Oct., 1934

*Adapted from Doherty, "To Those Olympians," OLYMPIC REVIEW, No. 178, International Olympic Committee, August 1982.

PREFACE

This OMNIBOOK holds that the major values of track and field relate to its developmental effects--on the millions of individuals, ages 6 to 60, active on a limited time-energy-commitment basis, the Amateurs. Public attention, as in the News Media, argues otherwise. Deploring widespread hypocrisy, some critics take an extreme view, "Someday there will be no distinction between so-called amateurs and so-called professionals....and the sooner the better."

But such views are shortsighted. In their focus on the Evil of hypocrisy, they have lost the full and long view. They have focussed so narrowly on the few hundred who attain World and National Ranking each year, and on the rights of the spectator to see the Best without restriction of any kind, that they are blind to the full realities of sport. The values of sports for spectators, at the Game and by way of the news media, are important, though I can't resist adding that such values were present at the gladiatorial contests of Rome and at the Sport Festivals of Hitler's Germany. But the greater values of our sport relate primarily to development, development of the individual and society. We can think of such development as a two-sided coin. We all accept the obvious upperside--development of the individual through competition and through planned programs of training to improve technique and performance. But even more crucial among sport values is the obscure underside, the off-the-field development inherent in the Rules of Conduct and Eligibility that even the Professionals find necessary, though at least-possible levels.

To keep this function clear, call it character development. Character is unchallenged and so, withers under a Dictatorship in which Rules are precise and rigidly enforced; as under an Anarchy that has no Rules at all. Character grows best when the Rules are sound and reasonable though impossible to state in unambiguous words. Character grows best when enforcement is carried out vigorously, but with loopholes here and there. Now conformance occurs mainly out of personal ethics, because one believes in the Rules. High ethical character allows no other choice, even when aware that others with lesser standards may not conform, and so gain unfair advantages of many kinds.

THAT's THE ESSENCE OF AMATEURISM--in sports and wherever Rules of Conduct occur. Shamateurism? Of course. It'll be with us as long as imperfect human beings are involved. Only an ideal? But ideals have power to change and improve, both individuals and society-- even when the words of ethics are far more common than their observance. But when ideals are rejected completely, whether out of disillusionment, impatience, apathy, or fear of scorn makes no difference, man's struggle upward toward maturity is lessened. That's true in every phase of life, and certainly in sports.

It is generally accepted that our Culture is suffering an overall breakdown--call it adjustment if you wish--in moral values. As would be expected, our sport is following such trends. But that's only at the top, on the surface. Underneath and supporting the entire sport structure are all those that take part, all those that run or jump or throw at any level of age or organization. The major values of our sport relate to these, not to the highly visible professional few; to the hundreds of thousands of college athletes, high school athletes, elementary school athletes, Masters' level athletes--male and female.

All such athletes are Amateurs in the clear and certain sense that they practice and compete within certain limits--limited time, limited energy, limited personal commitment, and very, very limited material rewards. Playing and training for the Game primarily because it's fun and beneficial.

All these athletes, students and workers alike, require off-the-field Rules. Such Rules will inevitably be general, with different meanings in different Cultures and languages, so that enforcement will vary widely. But therein lies the real challenge and uses of sport in a Democracy--to achieve a sound balance between the outer pressures of the Rules and the inner imperatives of believing in them and acting in accordance with belief. Hopefully and doubtfully, others will do the same.

As Baron de Coubertin wrote almost a century ago, "The most important thing in the

Olympic Games is not to win but to take part; the most important thing in life is not the triumph but the struggle."

ACKNOWLEDGEMENTS

Had Mrs. Nancy D. Johnson, Swarthmore, expert in manuscript planning and typing, not been available, this 4th edition would never have been even started. Each of the hundreds of line-drawings had to be put in place, with appropriate space allowance so as to relate to the text on that page. Then the words had to be typed around them--a miracle of patient planning and placing, especially when the immediate result, without change, is the finished product--no editing, no corrective type-setting, just direct litho-photography. The certainty that it would all be done so well and cheerfully, kept me sleeping more quietly, rising earlier and working later throughout a long summer in hot-humid suburban Philadelphia.

Ed Fox, Publisher, *Track & Field News*, Box 296, Los Altos, CA 94022, was most encouraging and helpful, especially in providing copies of the latest research and ideas from their many books and other publications, which made my job mainly one of selecting and editing.

Vern Gambetta, editor *Track Technique*, added to that valuable source many personal suggestions and materials not yet published, as well as books from abroad. His contributions to the Certification-of-Coaches movement have great potential for progress in United States track and field.

George Dales, longtime friend and editor *Track & Field Quarterly Review*, 1705 Evanston St., Kalamazoo, Michigan 49008, receives numerous articles for publication from here and abroad. All those he considered significant were quickly made available to me. Especially helpful over the years has been George's support of my "old-fashioned views" on amateurism, coaching ethics and an insistence on excellence in a context of sport as a second-priority activity in life.

Kevin McGill, hammer coach, Columbia University, New York, wrote all but the first three pages of Chapter 14, the Hammer Throw--an excellent piece of work to which he brought both enthusiasm and years of successful coaching.

Throughout this text there are scores of black-shirted figures illustrating techniques and related power exercises. They are the product of USSR artists from articles and books published by *Physical Culture and Sports*, Moscow. Their accuracy and simplicity are incomparable. The drawings in this 4th edition are greatly improved and sized to fit precisely by Steve Snow, Media Printing Service, Media, Pa.

I can't resist adding that a few more months will total four score years of life and about 75 of running and jumping and throwing. I still remember my mother's wooden clothes-pole with two nails in the end that fixed our pole plant in the sod and enabled us to clear miraculous heights--four feet or even more!--down to the turned-over-and-raked sod pit, in the true meaning of the word. Then to realize that today they still call that 3-foot cushion a pole-vault pit. I often wonder why words like "pit," "hard work" and "the Olympic Ideal" remain unchanged even when their meanings-in-action are just the opposite.

A. B. Krishnaswamy from Madras, India, sent me this heart-warming message:

Your book is my bible, a household name in my family. Every morning, when I get up from bed, my daughter will place your book by my side. I read two or three pages and then only start my daily physical exercise. I am fond of quoting from the beautiful and very high English by which you explain techniques.

That two-inch line implies a special nook that holds Lucile who, living her own full life throughout our 55 years together, has strongly encouraged this writing despite its demands on time-energy--hers as well as mine--and so helped me to help myself in so many mutually supportive ways. Our University of Michigan track men used to say it was all so much more worthwhile, if only to enjoy one of Lucile's excellent dinners, be privileged to wash her dishes, and then be invited back to talk with her of--who knows what or what not. What a great coach of young men she would have made!

Preface to the 3rd Edition

These opening paragraphs, commonly called a Preface, are equally an Epilogue, since they are written last in preparing this textbook for coaches-in-training for track and field. First, this is an epilogue of a full century of track and field development in performance; performance at all levels as shown in the Tables of Outstanding Performances for each event--world, college, high school, but most clearly in the great Olympic Games--from 1896 Olympic championships won at 36 feet 9½ inches in putting the shot, 10 feet 9½ inches in pole jumping, or 20 feet 10 inches in the long jump, to the 1968 Olympic long jump of 29 feet 2½ inches that many consider a "human ultimate."

Second, this is an epilogue of a century-long development by trial-error-success in better techniques and training methods. This is just as exciting a story as that of performance--a story of new ways of increasing the time-distance through which power is applied to the projected instruments--the shot, discus, javelin, hammer, or the human body itself; a story of better ways to greater power--basic, related, and simulative in both its strength and its velocity aspects; a story of greater speed through mastery of skill, relaxation, speed-power, and speed-endurance; and lastly, a story of greater endurance by training more days per year and years per career with a balanced concern for both quantity and quality training.

Third, this is an epilogue of development--painfully slow during the early decades-- in the sciences as they relate to both athletes and athletics. At first such research tended to focus on implements and "safe" mechanics. Neither coaches nor scientists had much understanding or interest in the others' problems or viewpoints. Coaches refused to allow their athletes to be tested in "dangerous" ways; scientists denied such dangers and, in any case, felt that the need to know had priority over the need to win. Until about the 1950s, useable research was in short supply and of doubtful quality.

Fourth, if I may be personal, this is an epilogue of my own half-century involvement in track and field: (1) as a mere dual-meet place winner whom 10 years of effort developed to two National Decathlon Championships and an Olympic bronze-medal; (2) as a track coach for over 30 years in high school and the Universities of Princeton, Michigan and Pennsylvania; (3) as an organizer of track and field meets--the Pennsylvania Relay Carnival, *The Philadelphia Inquirer* Games, the first (1959) USA-USSR dual meet in this country, and--most exciting--the 1935 "Jesse Owens Meet" in Ann Arbor, Michigan when he broke three world records and tied a fourth; and (4) as a writer of track and field textbooks beginning with *MODERN TRACK AND FIELD* in 1954. In looking back, those 20 years or more of writing have had their special uses not obtainable in any other ways. Writing requires concentrated thinking and a discipline of distractions just as severe as training for competition, and forces both an analytic and holistic approach to problems quite different from, and in some ways, superior to that of coaching.

Fifth, this is an epilogue of development in the organization of track and field. Of the many possible examples, consider the development of the Pennsylvania Relay Carnival from an informal get-together in May 1893 of Pennsylvania-Princeton 440-men to run a relay team-race with each man touching-off the next runner, to today's gigantic Carnival with some 140 events, not counting sections within races, some 6000 individual athletes representing over 500 schools and colleges, and requiring four days of competition. Or consider the Olympic Games in 1896 at which eight nations were represented--some unofficially--in such varied activities as mountain climbing, choral singing, dumbbell swinging, still-fishing, as well as track and field. Now, within only 20 Olympiads of four years each, that Grecian festive picnic has evolved to our Modern Mammoth Extravaganza with some 125 nations, 10,000 athletes trained year-round by coaches, scientists, physicians, in a score or more of sports.

A PREFACE

But more importantly--for you this is a preface to your own involvement in the challenging but frustrating world of track and field coaching. Such coaching demands the very best of you; it demands that you believe in the worthwhileness of what you are doing, that you concentrate your energies in terms of it and the boys you are trying to help, and that you set aside 101 other activities you'd like to do, and that are worth doing. But, no matter how demanding the work, small the results, or unappreciative the team members, the coach that puts the best of himself into his sport will get a comparable satisfaction out of it.

Murray Halberg dedicated his autobiography to: "The man I have cursed most on cold, wet winter days and thanked most on the victory dais--the man who has been my inspiration, guide, mentor and friend--Arthur Lydiard." Few express themselves so cogently; most never do so in any verbal way. But a coach knows whether or not he's given his best, and if he's wise, that's enough.

Second, this is a preface to a changed world of motivation--from locally centered to internationally derived; from play--the game for the game's sake--to work, the game for the reward's sake; from winning as a motivating force for training and personal development to winning as the main, indeed, the only end worth the arduous striving.

Be prepared in reading this OMNIBOOK for a confusing two-mindedness toward the time-energy-commitment that can properly be given to amateur sport. On the one hand I am certain that the greatest fun-joy-satisfaction emerges from the highest levels of struggle and risk. That's true in every field of human endeavor, physical, mental or spiritual. It's implied in the Olympic slogan, "higher-faster-farther," and confirmed in the assumption that all world records are made to be broken.

On the other hand, it is equally certain that all sports are encircled, occur within limits as fixed by the rules. The challenge is not how far we can project a 16# shot, but is how far we can put it in a fixed way from the narrow limits of a seven-foot circle. Increase or remove those limits and performance will improve, *but we have reached agreement on such limits and all conform without dissent.* In all sports at the non-professional level, there must be similar limits on time-energy-commitment that full-time students or workers can give to sports preparation and competition, and a social climate of integrity in conforming to those limits. That's a dilemma that future sportsmen will struggle to solve, though unlikely to ever resolve.

Third, this is a preface to the book itself. Above all else, and despite the 400,000 or so words, this book emphasizes the actions of track and field, and a coaching insistence on "learning by your doing, not by my telling." But as will be repeated many times, the apparently simple and natural actions at the highest levels of performance always lie at the far end of complex preparation--thoughtful analysis, careful organization, persistent practice--all of which culminate in a simple, unthinking flow of movement. Track and field is an art, with all the concentration of training and effort that goes into any art, if it is to be mastered and so become artless. That applies to competitive performance; it applies to competence in coaching.

BASIC VIEWPOINTS

The most basic concept of this third edition of the OMNIBOOK relates to what I like to call "the human uses of our sport." Not the use of our sport for institutional or national glory; not the use of our sport for private or group profit--that social cancer we must somehow remove or we all perish together. But the use of our sport for the betterment of individuals and humanity. Such use, as described in Chapter 3, requires a VITAL BALANCE as between expertise in working with persons and expertise in the techniques and methods of track and field. If this OMNIBOOK fails in advancing that Vital Balance, it fails. Period.

The first edition of this OMNIBOOK used Abraham Maslow's term, "holistic-analytic" to indicate its underlying approach to the problems of track and field. It assumed that sound understanding is always a two-phased process of analysis and synthesis, of discovering "parts" and clarifying relationships among many wholes. As examples, the essentials of training for endurance running were analyzed into 22 aspects, and the concept of relaxation was seen as having at least 10 ways to better understanding. But analysis inward was but one means to better understanding. The other, equally necessary as indicated by the unifying hyphen, looked outward toward the many relationships that lay the foundation, establish the motivation, determine the means for track and field, just as they do for all human activities. Nothing in nature is separate--not things, not mankind, not individuals, and certainly not the games they play. Gardner Murphy's tenet was accepted that "the only valid organism is the universe itself."

Throughout the OMNIBOOK, concern is expressed for the inter-relationships of track and field. Chap. 4 gives thumb-nail sketches of coaches of widely-varied attitudes and relationships, within the team and team family and outward with the sponsoring institution, the local community, the national organization, and with the international Olympic Games. In 1976, Lord Killanin of the I.O.C. stated that to accede to Canada's demand for the exclusion of Taiwan as the Republic of China would ultimately lead to the dissolution of the Games as a whole. In 1980, President Carter, with, in my judgment, a pitiful lack of understanding of the Olympic movement or concern for the longtime effects of what he did, decided that the United States and its allies should boycott the Moscow Games. On overall balance, the effect of this myopic action may be beneficial--to slow down or even reverse Olympic expansion. In one century we've reached a level of excess in our Modern Olympics that it took the Ancient Greeks a thousand years to gain--or should I write "lose."

The basic viewpoint I wish to emphasize is that sport emerges out of its social system, and can be separated from it only in a make-believe or as-if way. Nothing unusual in that; in fact, most of what we humans believe and say and do is based on make-believe. Our words--and so our assumptions--separate mind from body, a tree from earth and sun, an individual from society, Man from Nature. If we all, West and East, agree to believe it and act it, a single century could produce a workable separation of the Olympic Games from National drives for glory, or of college sports from College drives for glory. It could be done. Throughout man's history, his "common sense" has allowed him to separate the inseparable; in fact, scientific method is based on so doing. I repeat--it could be done, but don't hold your breath.

PART 1
The Human Side of Coaching

Brutus Hamilton (University of California at Berkeley, 1932-1965) was a coach of track and field but, much more, a coach of young men by way of track and field. Their personal development was his primary goal, not his personal record of success. He liked to win, was a tough competitor as an athlete and a coach. But winning was not an end in itself so much as a means of motivating the day-after-day training and anguish that lead to the primary goal of self-development. Such a view respects the off-the-track rules of sport, even though aware that they are often unenforceable and violated by one's rivals. We tend to think of most men as enclosed within the outline of their own skin. Hamilton's true skin was equally an inline of the many, many persons--in and outside of track and field, in and outside of sport, in and outside our national boundaries--with whom he established mutually supportive relationships. But most of all, his story is one of loyalty and respect for his boys and their almost mystical devotion to the man they still remember as "The Coach."

1

Clearly, the expression "coach of track and field" is a way of speaking, if not an actual mis-nomer. We are actually coaches (teachers) of young men and young women by means of the methods and techniques of track and field. But clear or not, the difference is enormous. The first focuses on mechanics and computers; the second, on understanding the individual, on personal relationships and on social responsibilities. Throughout its 28 Chapters, this OMNIBOOK empha-sizes the rapidly increasing complexity of our sport, especially as related to technology. But technology is only one side of the coaching coin; the other side relates to an even greater complexity, to what is called here "the human side of coaching"--coaching persons. Fifty years ago, "persons" was a simple word. It related to this individual, to this team, in this high school or college, in this community or college conference. Beyond such concerns there was little interest.

It's hard to realize how complex things are now unless we understand how simple it all was then. No real awareness of the Olympic Games, no professional sports other than baseball and "shamateur" tennis, no TV, no newspaper sports sections of consequence, no national sports maga-zines. Very few people were interested in sports; we had to plead for recognition and support, especially financial. We just had to keep things simple. No college scholarships or grants-in-aid. No recruiting budget. At the University of Michigan in 1940 our entire track budget, not counting salaries, was $5000. Train year-round? Nonsense, that would interfere with our summer jobs as Camp Directors or playground supervisors.

Whether we intended it or not, our World, West and East, has evolved into a sports-minded society. President Eisenhower warned us against the military-industrial complex with its winner-take-all viewpoints. He might better have called it a military-industrial-sports complex; for today, sports are as much in our national consciousness and over-emphasis as are the other two. Witness the take-over by Big Business of the 1984 Olympic Games (which has been called The God Bless America Games) in Los Angeles, now hailed as a model for future Games by virtue of the 150-million dollar profit derived from them--profit they say that will be used for the better organization of sports nationally and especially for the creation of more effective Olympic Sports Training Centers and National Sports Teams.

Have we really accepted the premise that national success in the Olympic Games is our major concern in coaching young men in college and high school? When, in the 1970s, our college-school track program became Olympics oriented, with such Olympic events added as the 400-meter hurdles, the 3000-meter steeplechase, the 5000-meter run, and similar events for women, few asked if such events are justified for full-time students of higher education.

When such corporations as AT&T, Ford Motors, Anheuser-Busch and Levis became "official sponsors" of the Olympic Games, few asked why; few asked what interest such sponsors had in furthering One World of Men by way of one world of sport. It was all so "successful." So why not?

Frankly, a quick overview of the 500 or more pages of this OMNIBOOK will reveal an apparent confusion of goals and motivations. On the one hand, we find the opening statement, "to those young men and women who run and jump and throw primarily because...it's fun" and the implication here and there that other life activities--school, vocation, service--should have first priority in time and energy and commitment. On the other hand, there also seems to be a demand for ex-cellence and an advocacy of more time, energy and devotion to ensure its attainment--all related to greater performance in the Olympics against Communist countries, as though they were the fulcrum of our efforts. Gradually we have adopted the view first advanced by Communist countries of "Periodization," with its assumption of year-round training and acceptance of hurt-pain-agony as the one and only path to achievement. It wasn't intended that way as the book was written. It just seeped its way in, filtered through the tissues as in osmosis. As Alan Watts wrote, "the in-line of our skin that encloses us is but the out-line of our social climate that surrounds us." We can't escape its influence whether it be its physical blessings or the pol-lution of its acid-rain or trash dumps or its "winning is the main thing."

In summary, the human side of coaching demands serious study, research and action. My gener-ation of coaches is long gone. We made some progress but mostly on the side of techniques and implements. But our world changed so fast as to surpass our understanding of what was at stake. Now it's up to you and your generation. It won't be easy, but a more vital balance can be achieved, one that places greater weight on the human side.

Chapter 1
THE DEVELOPMENT OF TRACK KNOWLEDGE

Careful consideration of the many problems and social forces influencing future progress in United States track and field leads to the conclusion that major advances during the coming decades will occur through a better understanding and use of the human side of coaching.

This does not suggest that training methods and techniques of track and field events will diminish in importance. Actually we are only beginning to understand and use the great potentials of the physical sciences. For example, physiology has consistently claimed that the number of fibers in an individual's muscle is a matter of heredity and not subject to increase. But a June 1984 article in *SPORTS ILLUSTRATED* states that Dr. William J. Gonyea of the University of Texas Health Sciences Center, Dallas, claims to have achieved "hyperplasia" (fiber increases) in cat muscle, thus supporting Bulgarian claims that they have gained similar increases through their intensive Olympic weightlifting program for boys (beginning at age 12) and men. Such extremes of training--for better or for worse--could revolutionize power training for all sports.

But a greater emphasis on the human side of coaching does suggest, especially now that Olympic sports have become so absorbed by the social forces of our world--political, industrial, governmental--that they no longer control their own destiny, and that unless our society can adopt policies of mutually supportive relationships, nation to nation, national policies to sports, sports to institutions and communities, what we may do on the technical side may be simply irrelevant.

Many considered it a plus for sports when American business decided to subsidize Olympic sports in every way, including research. Just as some thought it a plus when that great Evil, "hypocrisy," was removed by allowing direct payments in cash above the table, especially when this helped to equalize the advantages in time-energy for training held by the State-subsidized athletes of Communist Countries. But when these policies were adopted, forces were released that may never be drawn back into the bottle.

Now the human side of coaching has become so complex that none, neither sportsmen nor sociologists nor political leaders, understand or can offer valid solutions. But it is clear that this is the side, not the technical, that should concern us most and needs greatest emphasis, related research, and programs for everyday use. Prior to 1952, our goals in coaching were relatively simple and clear: this team for its own sake, this school, this balanced league or conference of comparable schools, this training program limited to about six months each year, this limited knowledge uncomplicated by scientific research.

But today, with all our vastly superior knowledge, we can scarcely glimpse its implications for our

Fig. 1.1. Minimal technique, facilities and performance in the shot put.

future. The Genie is out of the bottle and can't be put back. Our only hope lies in moving forward gradually, carefully, toward more and better on the technical side, but with all due respect for the inherent limitations of our human side.

THE DEVELOPMENT OF KNOWLEDGE RELATED TO TRACK AND FIELD COACHING. Earlier editions of this OMNIBOOK told a somewhat detailed story of the lethargic development of related knowledge for coaching track and field. Related literature was at first non-existent, then snail-pace slow in being published, and even slower in being accepted. This was true, not only for track and field textbooks, but even more so for books in physiology, biomechanics, sports medicine, social and individual psychology. Gradually they did become available, but not in language that could be understood by the coach, and not dealing with problems relevant to his work.

THE EARLY YEARS. During the early years, roughly 1870 to 1932, the local coaches had almost no ways of knowing what was being done, or what had been tried and discarded in other areas of the country. Performance was low-level, but knowledge of techniques or training methods was equally so. Today, it's impossible to comprehend how minimal these were. A few books had been published, such as ATHLETICS, London: The Badminton Library, 1904; or Michael Murphy, ATHLETIC TRAINING, New York, 1920, but there were no ways of publicizing these--no national magazines, no radio, no national meetings of any kind--so they had little influence.

Each coach had to experiment out of his own ingenuity. In many instances he repeated the errors that had been made at other schools, in other isolated areas, decades before. For example, I went to Western High School, Detroit, 1921-4. Our "coach" was excellent as a German Turnverein instructor. He knew much about high bars and horses and Indian clubs but he had never heard of a shift of the hands in the pole vault. I competed for the team in that event; best height, 7'6". Then I went to Detroit City College (now Wayne State). David L. Holmes was Director of Athletics and coach of four sports including football and basketball-- all with but three assistant coaches, none for track. He had an avid thirst for better methods and encouraged us to try this, try that, and keep on trying. He later gained national recognition for his starting blocks and hurdles, for his booklet of drawings, TRACK AND FIELD MOVIES ON PAPER, taken from his own films of champions, and for his development of five Olympic placewinners. During my four years, 1924-1927, we tried as many as a half-dozen different techniques in some events. In the discus, for example, we tried facing to the front and to the side, holding the discus behind the back with palm and discus up, spinning with one foot on the ground throughout the spin, hopping up-then-down to a low crouch, crouching throughout the turn, weaving the discus in a wave-like motion, throwing the discus at various planes from 20 to 45 degrees, pulling across the discus at release to give it more spin, and probably other woeful methods I have forgotten.

Similar, almost random, trials were made in each of the other field events. We threw the javelin as would any baseball-oriented American boy, with five or six easy steps and a hop. In the pole vault, we landed on sandy loam, about 12 inches above ground level. No wonder our first concern at takeoff was on turning over to ensure a safe landing.

In general, performances were consistent with such minimal techniques. In 1925, these per-formances won NCAA Outdoor Championships: high jump--6'2"; pole vault--12'4"; broad jump-- 25' 10 7/8" (world record); shot--50'; discus--148'4"; javelin--201'11"; hammer--150'1½"; mile--4:18.8; 2-mile--9:32.8. Small college and high school performances were scaled down accordingly. In 1925, the Indiana Conference Championships (DePauw, Wabash, Butler, Earlham, etc.) achieved these marks: high jump--5'9½"; pole vault--11'; shot--40'4"; discus--129'7½". The Pennsylvania Interscholastic Championships, 1925, brought forth: 12# shot--45'2"; (no discus or javelin); high jump--5'8¼"; pole vault--10'9"; broad jump--20'8½". Needless to say, California performances at all levels were superior to those listed here.

Time-energy For Training. The time-energy given to training and competition was as minimal as was performance and knowledge. Indoor track had few competitions and lacked facilities. The Big 10 Indoor Championships were first held in 1911, but there were no fieldhouses and few gyms that could be used. All indoor sports shared the one gym that most schools provided-- along with classes in physical education of course. If that gym had a track, it was about eight feet wide and designed for jogging, not racing. Track and field was mainly an outdoor sport and, east of California, that meant it began in late April and ended with the local Conference meet in late May--a six-week season. Few schools included the NCAA Championships (first meet, 1921) in their schedule. Is it any wonder that the number of hours per day, days

4

per week, and weeks per season given to training were very, very limited. In brief, we practiced one to two hours a day, three to five days a week, and started perhaps six weeks prior to our first meet, depending on when the frost was out of the ground. Distance runners could start earlier, but rain or snow on dirt surfaces or sandyloam landing pits are not helpful to jumping or throwing. Add to this that, since performance was generally low-level, most men doubled or tripled. In my own case, I divided my time--in training and competition--among some six events, simply because 21 feet in the broad jump or 150 feet in the javelin might score a point or two in a dual meet.

But in addition to these minimums in the potentially positive factors, there was a climate of negative attitudes that held back school sports. European schools had no such program and strongly doubted their values in Education. English schools and colleges enjoyed sports, but at what we would call an extramural level--no paid coaches, no gate receipts, no school subsidies or facilities. Even as late as 1954, the Oxford University track, on which Bannister ran the first mile under four minutes, was financed and maintained by Oxford students and their friends. Bannister had no coach, being convinced that "the athlete could be sufficient unto himself."[1]

Many American educators agreed with this view, pointing out that coaches at certain schools-- Steve Farrell, Michigan; Tom Keane, Syracuse; Keene Fitzpatrick, Princeton; Lawson Robertson, Pennsylvania, Jimmie Curran, Mercersburg Academy--had taken part in professional racing with its gambling, roping, fictitious names, and cheating in any way to ensure a purse. "Fine characters to teach American youth!" (I knew them all; four, personally; they were a joy to be with and no one who knew them questioned their integrity.)

<u>Taboos Against Exertion</u>. During the early years and continuing into the 1940s, when Coach Billy Hayes, Indiana, first brought us word of the hard training of the Swedish runners, Gunder Haegg and Arne Andersson, there was much greater concern for the dangers of overtraining and staleness than exists today, though today's training levels are two or three times as great in time and intensity. Each advancement in training methods or performance in distance running brought forth charges of "burning out," or of "cutting a boy's life short." The danger of developing an enlarged "athlete's heart" was assumed by most members of the medical profession. Certainly no one should train year-round. Three or four months of complete rest, along with two days of each week were mandatory. "Breaking training" was a much-hallowed custom. A respected physiology of exercise,[2] 1932, warned,

Too frequently the day of the last athletic contest of the season's schedule marks the beginning of a short period of jollification and riotous living....This has neither a physiological nor hygienic foundation....The detraining process should be as gradual as the training process if one wishes to avoid indigestion, constipation, faulty slouching posture and the other ills attendant upon a loss of muscular tonus.

Strength training was another taboo. Everyone knew that the greater one's strength, the lesser one's muscle quickness, and quickness was all-important. We had heard of Sandow and Hackenschmidt and knew what oxen they were. It wasn't merely weight-lifting that was taboo. Long canoe trips, bicycling, and heavy gymnastics were all discouraged. Swimming? It produced soft muscles. Hot showers? They sapped one's energies. Social dancing? Absolutely out! It distracted the mind, weakened the will, dissipated one's powers. Beer drinking? Unthinkable for college men--at least in the middle-west. I still remember my own sense of wrong-doing when, on coming to Princeton as assistant coach in 1929, I saw beer being served to team members, following the dual meet with Oxford-Cambridge.

<u>COMMUNICATION IN THE EARLY YEARS</u>. During the early years, only a few University and Club coaches had an acceptably sound understanding of training principles and techniques. But there were almost no ways by which such knowledge could be shared--almost no track clinics or publications. In the late 1920s, the New York Public School Athletic League did conduct and

---

[1]Roger Bannister, *THE FOUR MINUTE MILE*, New York: Dodd, Mead & Co., 1955, p. 208.

[2]A. G. Gould & J. A. Dye, *EXERCISE AND ITS PHYSIOLOGY*, 1932, New York: A. S. Barnes and Co., p. 388.

publish (hardcover) a series of lectures by coaches of the ICAAA, some of whom had competed as professionals in Europe and America in the 1880s and 90s. The Big Ten and other Conference coaches did get together at their championships for bull sessions following games of bridge or poker. But I know of no other meetings that could be called coaching clinics.

The very few meets at which coaches could observe better techniques tended to be local affairs. The Pennsylvania Relay Carnival began in 1895 and was a great aid to the spread of knowledge. But transportation was so time-consuming and fatiguing that it tended to be an Eastern college and school event. The ICAAAA (1876) looked on its championships as the National Championship, as its name (Intercollegiate Amateur Athletic Association of America) implies. Individuals and even teams from Southern Cal, Stanford, California, Michigan, Notre Dame and a few others did compete, and this provided some interchange of ideas. The NCAA Championships did not begin until 1922, at Stagg Field, Chicago. The National AAU Championships were of little interest to colleges and schools. Even the Olympic Games were of relatively little consequence; it's now hard to realize how little as compared with their present preeminence. Up to 1932, all Olympic Games had been held in Europe; only a few American coaches had seen them or learned from them. In fact, one could say that our National awareness of the Olympics did not really gain momentum until the 1932 Games at Los Angeles. Thousands of coaches and future coaches attended and derived a tremendous boost in knowledge and enthusiasm.

Perhaps an example of slow communications will help our understanding. In 1912 George Horine of Stanford set a world record of 6'7" in the high jump using a new technique that came to be known as the Western Roll. But a decade later, in the 1920s, Horine's style was little known nationally. Jumpers in the Eastern and Middle States were still using the 1895 Sweeney style or some variation of it. We heard rumors of the new Western style, that another Western-er, Beeson of California, had jumped 6'7¼". In 1923, Tom Poor of Kansas won the NCAA (6'3") with his own version of such a style. But not until Harold Osborne of Illinois cleared 6'8¼" and won the 1924 Olympic title did the style gain general acceptance. To make my point even stronger, Osborne claimed that he originated his own style with no knowledge of Horine or Beeson, having read only an article by Walter Camp on Alma Richards, the 1912 Olympic champion. Richards' "style" was to simply draw up his legs and hop over the bar, so that Osborne's claim to originality seems valid.[1] Even in the 1930s, some coaches were claiming technical superior-ity for the Eastern style as jumped by George Spitz (1933-6'8¼"), a full twenty years after Horine.

Now contrast this 20-year molasses-slow process with the explosive change that followed Fosbury's Olympic performance in 1968. Within a mere four years, his revolutionary Flop was known, analyzed, and largely adopted throughout the entire world. In 1973, only five years later, the International Track and Field Coaches Association, meeting in Madrid, devoted ten of a total of 23 technical papers to some aspect of the Fosbury Flop.

SPORTS MEDICINE AND TRACK AND FIELD. It is beyond the scope of this book to trace the history and uses of sports medicine as related to track and field. Its first emphasis as a movement and within the American College of Sports Medicine was on the medical aspects of sport--health and longevity effects, prevention and care of injuries, health effects of sports diets, drugs, training at altitude, and the like.

But growing awareness of the challenge from Communist countries, of their effective use of sports sciences, and of our need to greatly improve performance brought increasing pressures on sports medicine to broaden its scope and change its emphasis to more positive approaches.

---

[1] Harold M. Osborne, "Championship Competition," in THE HIGH JUMP, R. L. Templeton, editor, New York: American Sports Publishing Company, p. 153.

In 1976, the United States Olympic Committee (USOC) established a U. S. Olympic Training Center at Colorado Springs that included "a well appointed sports medicine complex." An M.D. with personal experience in track and field was put in overall charge of research. Respected scientists chaired various sections in such sciences as biomechanics, physiology, and psychology, all as they relate to improved performance in Olympic sports.

In the early stages of this program, athletes and coaches were brought to this Center for relatively brief periods for analysis of techniques, training condition, mental attitudes and the like. Follow-ups and return visits occurred. During Olympic years and in special cases, these could become extensive. A few individuals and teams could derive much of value.

But to make such a program fully effective among a dozen or more Olympic sports on a nation-wide basis is a very complex and expensive operation. Whatever program is developed at the National Training Center will be inadequate unless it becomes the means for coordinating research and training at universities and other Centers throughout the country. According to Charles Dillman, Ph.D., sports medicine coordinator for the 1980 Olympic ski team, the Soviet Union was 10 years ahead of the United States in its use of scientific sports research, spending some $8 million a year for that purpose.

PSYCHOLOGY AND TRACK AND FIELD. In the 1920s, courses in the psychology of education were available at many colleges. I sat through ten such graduate courses at the University of Michigan School of Education--psychology of learning, psychology of motor learning, psychology of the self, psychology of character, group dynamics--but unfortunately their combined direct use for coaching track and field could have been better acquired through ten one-hour sessions, if properly employed.

In 1926, Coleman R. Griffith[1] published his *PSYCHOLOGY OF COACHING*, oriented toward the team sports. But few track coaches heard of it and, if they had, would have ignored it as being of little practical use. "Who needs that stuff"?

Such lack of interest created a lapse of 25 years before another such text in the psychology of coaching, that by Lawther,[2] 1951, also pointed toward the more popular team sports. But in 1966, Ogilvie and Tutko,[3] *PROBLEM ATHLETES AND HOW TO HANDLE THEM*, did focus attention on track and field, its individual athletes, and importantly, on the track coach himself. The authors state the book was organized "with the coaches' needs as our primary concern."

Psychological investigations must provide the reliable data that will enhance and complement coaching skill. The role of the psychological consultant should be the systematic study of the problems with which every coach must deal when applying his technical knowledge.

A similar direct application to our sport was made in 1970 by Vanek and Cratty[4] in *PSYCHOLOGY AND THE SUPERIOR ATHLETE*, with sections on the evaluation and psychological preparation of the superior athlete. Another related psychology was by Tutko and Richards,[5] 1971, *PSYCHOLOGY OF COACHING*, in which they analyze the personalities of both coaches and athletes.

Despite these advances, it seems clear that the coaches of other countries assume a much

---

[1]Coleman R. Griffith, *THE PSYCHOLOGY OF COACHING*, New York: Charles Scribner's Sons, 1926, 213 pps.

[2]John D. Lawther, *PSYCHOLOGY OF COACHING*, Englewood Cliffs, N.J., Prentice-Hall, Inc., 1951.

[3]Bruce Ogilvie, Ph.D. and Thomas A. Tutko, Ph.D., *PROBLEM ATHLETES AND HOW TO HANDLE THEM*, London: Pelham Books Ltd., 1966, p. 10.

[4]Miroslav Vanek and Bryant J. Cratty, *PSYCHOLOGY AND THE SUPERIOR ATHLETE*, New York: The Macmillan Company, 1970, 212 pps.

[5]T. A. Tutko, Ph.D. and Jack W. Richards, *PSYCHOLOGY OF COACHING*, Boston: Allyn & Bacon, 1971.

greater value for Sports Psychology than we do in the United States. In 1984 the International Society of Sport Psychology had a total world membership of over 1600, many of whom were coaches.

THE SOCIAL PSYCHOLOGY OF BUSINESS MANAGEMENT. At first glance, coaching in educational institutions and management in private-profit business seem to have little in common as to either goals or methods. But when writing the first edition of this *OMNIBOOK* I became aware of important similarities, especially if we equate production with sport performance and profit with winning.

Intrigued by these similarities, I spent some months studying leading textbooks in business management, especially those taking a research approach to problems. In brief, the various theories of management fall into four classes, commonly called Theory X and Theory Y as developed by Douglas McGregor,[1] Rensis Likert's[2] principle of supportive relationships, and a broad spectrum of concepts related to General Systems Theory[3].

THEORY X--MANAGEMENT AS PRODUCTION-CENTERED. McGregor describes management under Theory X as traditional, production-centered, and authoritarian,

If there is a single assumption that pervades conventional organizational theory it is that authority is the central, indispensable means of managerial control....

(Such authority under Theory X) tends to rely on such control devices as rewards, promises, incentives or threats, and other coercive means, methods that are of limited value in motivating people whose important needs are social and egoistic....

So long as the assumptions of Theory X continue to influence managerial strategy, we will fail to discover, let alone utilize, the potentialities of the average human being.

Under Theory X, authoritarian business leadership is understood in terms of personal qualities or traits. The great Captains of Industry are assumed to have magnetic personalities or some undefinable charisma akin to occult powers, quite independent of the situation and other relationships.

As late as 1958, Robert McMurry,[4] of the Harvard Business School, called for a view of business as a "benevolent autocracy," with a "great man" at its head. He assumed a basic human need for security and direction from others. Only at the top of organizational structure was there room for a few dynamic leaders to direct the organization and its workers.

Under such assumptions, understanding leadership becomes primarily a process of analysis and use of traits. R. M. Stogdill,[5] after an extensive survey of the literature, concluded that leadership is associated with: (1) intelligence including judgment and verbal facility, (2) a reputation for related achievement, (3) emotional maturity including persistence and a drive for achievement, (4) social competence, and (5) a desire for socio-economic status. Innumerable related studies have been made, of course, but Stogdill's work indicates the trend.

Since the authoritarian managers under Theory X are production-centered, they naturally concentrated their efforts toward greater efficiency in work methods. This culminated in the

---

[1]Douglas McGregor, *THE HUMAN SIDE OF ENTERPRISE*, New York: McGraw-Hill Book Company, 1960.

[2]Rensis Likert, *NEW PATTERNS OF MANAGEMENT*, New York: McGraw-Hill Book Company, 1961, 97-118.

[3]Richard A. Johnson et al., "Systems Theory and Management," in Max S. Wortman, *EMERGING CONCEPTS IN MANAGEMENT*, New York: The Macmillan Company, 1969, 331ff.

[4]Robert N. McMurry, "The Case for Benevolent Autocracy," *Harvard Business Review,* Vol. 36, No. 1, January 1958, pp. 82-90.

[5]R. M. Stogdill, "Personal Factors Associated with Leadership: A Survey of the Literature," *Journal of Psychology,* Vol. XXV, January 1948, pp. 35-64.

"Scientific-Management School," as presented by Frederick W. Taylor,[1] that urged a science-oriented approach in all aspects of business related to production and profit. Workmen must be "scientifically" selected and trained for maximum outputs. (No mention was made of their personal goals or needs.)

THEORY Y--MANAGEMENT AS PERSON-CENTERED. In reaction to this use of science for only the work or production aspects of the managerial function, McGregor proposed his "Theory Y: the integration of individual and organizational goals." Actually there existed a 100-year background for this view, as in Robert Owen's (1825) emphasis on workers as human beings ("Vital machines") not as cogs in a machine; or in the work (1923) of George Elton Mayo[2] at the Western Electric Hawthorne plant from which he concluded that social-psychological factors determined workers' production more than did economic factors.

McGregor's Theory Y with its emphasis on the human side of business was a great advance over traditional views. He tended to assume that production and profit are the main goals of business enterprise, goals that generally take precedence over those of the individual member. But he concluded that when individual goals and procedures are integrated with those of the enterprise, men work harder and better, assume greater responsibility, do a better job of policing rules infractions, and therefore, sweet to the ears of industry, production and profit are increased.

McGregor analyzed 111 research studies of the nature of leadership and concluded it to be a special quality as had been widely held, but also a complex of relationships among the leader-followers-institution-social milieu, all of which are unique in any given situation and vary from one generation or culture to another. When such relationships are in opposition, as is usually the case under authoritarian leadership, interest and energy wane or may even become destructive. Methods of leadership that are mutually supportive of the enterprise and its workers produce gains in cooperation, effort and effectiveness in work output. He concluded that, in contrast to the technological excellence sought by those of the scientific management schools, "the major industrial advances of the next half century will occur on the human side of enterprise."

MANAGEMENT AS MUTUALLY SUPPORTIVE RELATIONSHIPS. In his award-winning book[3] of research on the problems of business management, Rensis Likert confirmed the work of McGregor in concluding that works at all levels of the business enterprise, top to bottom, are more productive and tend to increase profits when they feel the enterprise is centered in and organized under "a principle of mutually supportive relationships."

The leadership and other processes of the organization must be such as to ensure a maximum probability that in all interactions and all relationships with the organization each member will, in the light of his background, values, and expectations, view the experience as supportive and one which builds and maintains his sense of personal worth and importance.

The two words "view" and "sense" are specially significant, for Likert emphasizes that "it is how he (the worker) sees things that counts, not objective reality." The worker should believe that the mission of the organization is genuinely important and that he "contributes in an indispensable manner to the organization's achievement of its objectives. He should see his role as difficult, important, and meaningful."

CREATIVE MANAGEMENT. These theories of McGregor and Likert are strongly supported by the success experienced by Shigeru Kobayashi, personnel manager of Japan's great SONY Corporation,

---

[1]Frederick W. Taylor, *SCIENTIFIC MANAGEMENT*, New York: Harper & Brothers, 1947.

[2]George Elton Mayo, *THE SOCIAL PROBLEMS OF AN INDUSTRIAL CIVILIZATION*, in H. F. Merrill (ed.) *CLASSICS IN MANAGEMENT*, New York: American Management Association, 1960, pp. 21-25.

[3]Rensis Likert, *op. cit.*, 103ff.

as reported in his book, *CREATIVE MANAGEMENT*.[1] Here are some of his chapter heads--"More About the Joy of Work," "Everyone is a Manager," "True Education Within the Company," :Self-Imposed Rules and Regulations," "Work Can't Be Purchased with Wages," "Relationships Based on Trust."

As an example of procedures, Kobayashi says that SONY plants have no timeclocks to be punched or absentee reports controlled by management. If production falls off in a department, small "cells" of workers check on themselves for possible causes. Such viewpoints and methods seem amazing, feasible only where a climate of mutual trust and mutual respect between management and workers prevail.

As in American corporations, Kobayashi found that successful business leaders do possess "charisma." that he related to such personal qualities as courage (strong will, vitality, sense of responsibility and determination to complete assigned tasks), and what he called "gentleness," the capacity to understand and trust human beings even when they sometimes betray that trust.

I felt then that the Oriental way of thinking inherent in the Japanese mind might excel in creating a type of management centered about human beings; that the integration of this management with the scientific methodology we acquired from abroad might provide the basis for the management style of the future, not only in Japan but throughout the world.

Production and profit? Kobayashi agrees they are absolutely essential, but as the indispensable means to the end of greater service to the common good, not as the ultimate end of the enterprise on a purely economic basis. I have no way of knowing to what extent SONY practice corresponds with Kobayashi theory. But it is clear that his theory represents a new concept of the true ends of business enterprise, one that is in keeping with the gradually emerging General Systems Theory that is unifying so many areas of human knowledge.

THE MANAGERIAL GRID. In 1961, Robert R. Blake and Jane S. Mouton established Scientific Methods, Inc. as a means for improving business management methods and relationships. Their success has been remarkable. In 1975 over 75 of the top 100 industrial companies of the United States, as judged by *Fortune*, were clients; seminars were conducted in most of the States, as well as in some 40 other countries.

The key to this operation is the book, *THE MANAGERIAL GRID*,[2] an introductory study for managers prior to their attendance at a series of extended week-end seminars. In the first of these, managers of similar levels but from different companies study their common problems; in later sessions, managers of different levels from the same company seek mutual goals and helpful relationships. Many client companies have reported improved managerial effectiveness through these seminars and follow-up use of Grid methods.

In *THE MANAGERIAL GRID*, Blake and Mouton assign numerical values to various degrees of concern for (1) methods that are work-oriented (concern for production methods and profit), and (2) methods that are people oriented. A checkerboard grid was constructed, 9 x 9 squares in size, with "concern for people" rated on the vertical scale, and "concern for production" on the horizontal. Low concern was given a value of 1; high concern, 9. The authors identified five basic styles of managerial leadership:

9,1 The highly authoritarian manager with expertise and high concern for methods of production but little or no concern for people as persons.

1,9 The manager primarily concerned with getting along with people, though with little understanding or interest in their high-level capacities, and little

---

[1]Shigeru Kobayashi, *CREATIVE MANAGEMENT*, New York: American Management Association, Inc., 1971, p. 68.

[2]Robert R. Blake and Jane S. Mouton, *THE MANAGERIAL GRID*, Houston: Gulf Publishing Company, 1964, 338 pages.

concern for the problems of production.

9,9 The manager equally concerned and expert in the two areas of human relations and production. He seeks high output but through the medium of committed people having mutual respect, trust, and a realization of the interdependence of the enterprise and its workers.

5,5 The "compromiser," who balances moderate concern for production with moderate concern for human relations.

1,1 The manager who gets by with minimum effort and concern.

Of these five basic viewpoints, the 9,9 managerial style, with its integration of the goals and attitudes of business management with those of workers as both individuals and groups, was found to be most likely to ensure success of the enterprise, that is, highest-level production and profit.

SUMMARY. The job of coaching young men and women in the many events of track and field is both simple and very complex. It is simple in its sharp focus on doing--doing what needs to be done again and again, day after day; more running leads to better running. But it is very complex in several ways--complex, for example, in its need for up-to-date knowledge of modern techniques and training methods, as well as for understanding derived from the related sciences. It is also complex in its relationships with people--the individual athlete, the team, members of the sponsoring institution, alumni, local community groups, and the like.

Even today, a coach can get by--even do well--with simple tools and limited understanding. By recruiting high-level talent and working hard at the essentials for success, he can win even a national championship. But as with any art, the more one knows about its tools and methods, the greater one's chances for mastery and, most important, the greater one's satisfactions out of the work.

The development of track and field has followed such a gradual evolution. It began on a basis of local trial and error-success, with very limited knowledge of how others in other places had tried and succeeded. Such sciences as physics or physiology had no existence for the coach or athlete, just as "track and field" had no existence for the physicist or physiologist. The two disciplines of sport and science simply had no sense of relevance, one to the other. Around the 1920s, mutual awareness and co-operation flickered timorously here and there, but was largely ignored, if not scorned, by both sides.

As might be expected in a machine-minded society, first break-throughs came in the area of mechanical tools and methods--more scientifically designed starting blocks, hurdles, vaulting equipment, throwing implements. Following mechanics came biomechanics, then track-and-field mechanics. Physiology, as a more measureable and "respectable" science, came into relatively early use as compared with the "damn-fool fantasies" of psychology. Psychology evolved from arm-chair subjectivism through gestalt-organismic-field theories--always with considerable empirical tailoring to make them fit the practical situation. Branching out, psychology and its sister-science, social-psychology, became involved in the problems of business management with its theories of "X" and "Y" and "mutually-supportive relationships."

Business with its primary goal of personal profit seems far afield from coaching track and field. But its research into the basic problems of leadership has had far greater financial support as well as trained probing by superior intellects than could possibly be available to any sport, certainly to track and field. Such research has direct application to the problems of coaching-leadership in track and field, and leads to the conclusion that modern coaching requires scientific training on the human side of our sport at least as much as on the mechanical and "physical" side. Future progress in our sport demands mutual understanding, respect and cooperation between scientists and coaches. Gabe Korobkov, former Chief National Coach for the USSR, retired from coaching to do research at the National Sports Institute, Moscow, to help other scientists understand the facts of training and competition. Laboratory theories must be validated within the less controlled complex of practical sport situations, and if they stand the test, they safeguard the individual and improve performance. Otherwise they must be modified or discarded and more useful theories must be formed. Thus the spiral of sports knowledge and performance rises through cooperative efforts of theorists and practitioners.

Chapter 2
COACHING LEADERSHIP

Up to now we have almost entirely neglected the human-centered sciences: individual psychology, group dynamics, sociology, social psychology. We have claimed that their research had little relevance for track and field, and it's true that directly useable research has fallen far short of our needs. But Chapter 1 sketched all too briefly their uses in the hard-headed world of business management, and raised the important question as to whether such research has direct relevance to the problems of coaching management in track and field. In the remaining chapters of Part I, we shall try to interpret these insights into track and field terminology.

COACHING LEADERSHIP AS CHARISMA

Traditional viewpoints have tended to view the leader as the crucial element in the leadership process, an element that often takes the form of benevolent autocracy in which the Great Man assumes full control and responsibility. We have assumed a very limited capacity of ordinary human beings to take effective action on their own without undergoing great stress and anxiety. Their need for security is more basic than the need for adventure and self-realization, so that they tend to turn to the leader for direction and for safety within the well-structured organization he provides.

In keeping with these views, we tend to accept the Great Coach theory of success: behind every great athlete we expect to find a charismatic leader. For example, behind such Olympians as Ron Delany, Charlie Jenkins, Don Bragg, Marty Liquori, Don Paige and many more (22 in all), writer Skip Myslenski found the late Jumbo Elliott had such a reputation among his champions:

"He's an institution, an attraction," says Marty Liquori. "He's like the Liberty Bell." "The Liberty Bell, oh my God," says Jumbo Elliott, laughing heartily. "Old hat'd be more like it."

"It is a mixed bag, Jumbo Elliott's methods, an eclectic blend of showmanship, salesmanship, Irish wit, Irish blarney, parental care, parental disciple, instinct and know-how."

"Jumbo is always first-class in everything he does," says Marty Liquori. "He would never, never let us go second class, because we were the best. In fact, I sometimes think he dug into his own pocket to treat us as the best."

Because of its emphasis on the individual rather than on the team, coaching charisma in track and field is not as apparent as in the team sports. For example, Frank Dolson[1] quotes one of Notre Dame's football players as having this reaction to coach Ara Parseghian,

"You see him (the first time), you can't help but be impressed," this year's No. 1 quarterback, Rick Slager, said. "You know how he talks. It's a feeling he gives you. You know who's boss right off the bat. He's super-friendly, but you walk in his office,

---

[1]Frank Dolson, "And the Habit is Apparent at Notre Dame, *The Philadelphia Ainquirer,* October 6, 1975.

he's got a pad and pencil there and he starts talking. And you say, 'Oh boy...'
And you keep saying it. And thinking it. And feeling it.

"He was Ara Parseghian," Slager said. "He ran the team. There was a certain air about him that you'd have to say was hard to penetrate. And a certain excitement.

"He'd come into the locker room just before we came out. He'd become extremely, EXTREMELY, intense. He was super with his pre-game talks. Especially before the big games. You couldn't wait to play."

I can think of perhaps a score of such charismatic leaders among the track coaches I have known. But that's a surprisingly small number among the hundreds of other very successful coaches. These others, perhaps out of my own myopic viewpoint, just did not have the striking personal qualities implied by the word "charisma." Their style was of the quieter kind, more related to warm friendships and concerned teaching than to some magnetic drawing power. For example, Bob Giegengack, Yale coach for 30 years. One might say Bob had charisma--a constant need to verbalize eased by a delightful wit, self-confidence to the point of cockiness, a friendly and ready smile, and the respect of his peers that led to his selection as Head Track and Field Coach for the 1964 Olympic Team. Here is his attitude toward the training of Frank Shorter, 1972 Olympic Marathon Champion, while at Yale,

He really enjoyed those activities (skiing and a singing group), and that's the way it has to be with a kid at Yale....I'm certainly not permissive in workouts. But on the other hand I have to respect the right of someone else to disagree with me about the importance for him of doing this particular thing....Even if I had the power, I couldn't say, "Now this is what you're going to do. You're going to stop taking that course. You're going to be out here for practice...whether you like it or not, because you have a scholarship.[1]

Hardly the kind of attitude you'd expect from a strong leader, no matter how benevolent.

Under normal conditions, young men accept strong leadership eagerly. They want to believe in the coach and his program as long as certain goals are held in common. They expect and even seek discipline. Discipline is not a problem for disciples. When the Master demands training to the levels of hurt-pain-agony as did swimming authority Doc Counsilman of Indiana, they follow with few if any reservations, even take pride in having done so and in their "slave-driver" coach.

There is another view of charisma that leads to quite a different definition. Charisma emerges from a man's social environment as much as from his personal qualities of leadership-- two sides of one coin. A charismatic leader is a Master Violinist who inspires the audience and his orchestra associates alike, only if he is perfectly in tune with their playing.

During the decades after the Vietnam War, with its senseless search for military glory, and overall incompetency in national leadership, the younger generation lost its faith in the Establishment and in leadership at all levels. For example, in his autobiography, Vince Matthews, 1972 Olympic 400-meters champion, states their view clearly,[2]

One of the problems connected with organized sports in the United States is that it has become too coach-oriented. The coach has been pictured so often as a father figure that he has begun to believe in it himself. What he cannot rationalize is that society has changed many of its attitudes toward authority and sports and that athletes have changed as well. The athlete no longer accepts everything a coach says as instant fact and truth. He wants to know why he should accept it, why what one coach is demanding is any better than the doctrine preached by another coach.

---

[1]John Parker, THE FRANK SHORTER STORY, Mountain View, Cal.: Runner's World Magazine, 1972, p. 34.

[2]Vince Matthews with Neil Amdur, MY RACE BE WON, New York: Charterhouse, 1974, p. 265.

Actually, once a coach demonstrated he was competent and could be trusted, Matthews was more that willing to follow his lead. Resentful of the AAU rule that each club must have a coach, he and his teammates of the BOHAA (Boys Over the Hill Athletic Association) reluctantly chose Charlie Turner as their coach, but later credited him for much of their improvement in training organization and performance.

CHARISMA AS ENTHUSIASM. The art of coaching is partly a transfusion of the coach's enthusiasm, energy, confidence with the life stream of his athletes. Almost without exception, the biographies of great athletes tell how their coach inspired them, put backbones into their wishbones, gave them courage to begin, and then to keep on trying despite so many discouragements.

But a coach is enthusiastic, not merely out of an effervescence of animal spirits, but from a deep knowledge and feeling for the many aspects of his sport--the men and the action. Such a coach lives track and field, thinks, feels, acts, talks it. The more he becomes involved and absorbed in the sport, the more it expands him, opens up new channels to knowing more, and-- our main point here--lends an enthusiasm to his teaching that is hard to resist.

I would be hard pressed to decide whether it's more vital that this book should give you the facts of field and track, or whether its words should fire your enthusiasm until it fires you to go on the field and find out for yourself. Actually, knowledge and enthusiasm are two aspects of one coaching essential; lacking either, effective coaching is diminished. Men fail in coaching because they do not know enough about the job but also because they are not sufficiently enthused about what they do know.

The minute you become aware of a sense of dullness toward your coaching, take a sharp look-- not at what's wrong with the sport, but at yourself. It is you that are losing your shine, not the team members, not the sport. It is you that needs polishing, whether by way of a vacation, or from some new insight gained from seeing a record performance, or from exposing yourself to the enthusiasm of other coaches at a clinic, or from reading an inspirational book. Above all, remind yourself that enthusiasm and work grow on the same stalk, gain strength from each other. When enthusiasm lags, concentration on some new phase of your job may restore it.

CHARISMA AS AN OUTGROWTH OF HARD WORK. A coach that plans for success adopts a policy of persevering work--for his team members, but even more crucial, for himself. It takes a dauntless spirit of resolution to get up at 6 A.M., as so many successful coaches have done throughout their coaching careers, just to ensure an early morning workout for a dozen or so boys. It takes tenacity to study the mechanics of field events with no background in the terminology. It requires strength of purpose to make the rounds, trying to discover vacation jobs for team members that allow them to run early mornings or late afternoons. Only diligence and patience can arrange team trips so that every detail is covered satisfactorily. It takes endless persistence to get top performance out of a boy who does many things well--in different sports, but also in social affairs, or in school dramatics or music, and enjoys doing them all.

There are no elevators in the Track and Field Hall of Fame. To get to the top floor one has to step up each stair, one by one by one. Some say that recruiting is an easy escalator to the top. Not today; the competition there is just as tough as on the field. And even after you get good prospects by recruiting, you've got to work hard to make them great.

When the whole man is absorbed, fully wrapped up in what he is doing, there is no work. Work implies exertion to produce an extrinsic outcome or reward, but when you're engrossed in interesting work, only the work itself matters, not the reward. It becomes play. I'm reminded of the comment attributed to Babe Ruth, though I can't imagine the Babe saying it, "What a fraud--to be paid for doing what I'd enjoy doing for nothing."

We wrote above of unremitting continuous work. We all get fired up to work hard at times. When 15 seniors leave the team, we really scurry to fill their places. But truly effective coaching is continuous. William James, America's greatest practical psychologist, explained in his essay, *The Energies of Men,* what every distance runner knows, that all demanding work brings us, sooner or later, to a fatigue point--usually physical and mental and either acute or chronic--at which we want to quit. Soon we're sure we can't go on any longer. But we discover that if we keep on doggedly, with brief intervals of recovery and re-creation, we move up to a new level of energy. We discover untapped reservoirs of energy deeper than we had thought possible. Every coach knows this, but tends to know it only for his distance runners and weight men. Few realize it applies equally to his own coaching energies. A Kansas track man spoke warmly of Coach Bob Timmons: "He just plain cares about the guys, and if he drives us hard, if he cuts the blood out of us, why he cuts the blood out of himself too. You go by that Field House any night at 11, and you'll see the light on in his office. He's a hell of a little guy."

For the past 40 years or more, I've watched certain teams, college and high school, establish a high success record. They seem to have the secret for winning. But then things change; they're on the losing end. I've talked with their coaches, and often find a man who has lost his drive to succeed. He's lost his enthusiasm, his belief in what he's doing, or in his school or town. Perhaps these have really gone down hill, but often the real change is in the coach. He thought he had it made. "Anyway, life is too short. I'm missing so much. I'm going to enjoy things for a while." This is the same kind of talk that so many champions give when they quit as their best years are just beginning. I could name hundreds. Each coach must realize it applies to himself as well as to his athletes.

LEADERSHIP ENHANCED BY RELATED SCIENCE.
So many, in lectures and books, insist that leadership is an Art; that is, an ephemeral quality that some persons have and others do not, a quality difficult to define, a sixth sense of insight or understanding by which a "natural" leader KNOWS just what to say or do at that most teachable moment. The lecturers speak of personality, inborn authority, innate self-confidence, voice, charisma. There, I've just bitten my own toe. For charisma is precisely what was selected first in this Chapter to describe leadership.

True, leadership can be validly described as an Art. But no true Art is purely intuitive, not if carried beyond mere beginnings. Even the Fine Arts are based on careful analysis, even serious research, of their principles and methods. One would search long to find a modern book on the Art of Leadership in business management that is not based "on major findings of an intensive research program."

So with leadership in coaching. Coaching leadership assumes a certain aptitude for meeting the demands of the job, an innate authority of figure or voice or piercing eye, that leads others to say, "What he is speaks so clearly and cogently I hear every word he says."

But there is also an authority of facts, of facts based on scientific research that induces follower-ship at least as effective as that based on charisma. True, there are certain inborn qualities of leadership that some coaches have, others do not. But many equally essential qualities can be acquired, can be trained in ways consistent with research findings just as can the aptitudes of distance runners and high jumpers.

Turn to Chapter 19 and read a scientific approach to distance running by David L. Costill, Ph.D. Turn to Chapter 7 on high jumping and try to imagine our bar-clearances of 7 feet 10 inches or so without the science that created our running surfaces and landing mounds or that is now quantifying the strength, power, velocity, relatedness factors that today make up optimal training. True, high jumpers are born--witness Zhu of China. But they're also made--witness so many others and, hopefully, Zhu in the future.

So with leadership in coaching.

In the decathlon, our performance is measureable, can be given a number value. Unfortunately it's not that simple as related to our character. Over the years we have erected strong defenses to protect our ego, especially in its areas of possible weakness. We believe in the adequacy of our present qualities, and are slow to attempt, or may even resent, change. Unconsciously, we fear possible failure if we attempt better ways of behavior that are not our ways and with which we do not feel comfortable. For example, we may agree that we tend to be cautious and even uncertain in making decisions. But we'd rather continue in that pattern than undergo the risk of pushing ourselves to faster and firmer decisions. The right way feels wrong to us; the wrong way, right. Why then seek improvement?

But that's like the straddle-style high jumper for whom the flop style feels wrong until he has practiced and practiced until it becomes his way and feels right. Of course he has a coach; you don't, and that makes a great difference.

Every beginning coach should make a critical assessment of his range of personality and coaching style. The crucial word in that sentence is "range." Each "trait" always has a + or - sign indicating a flexibility or range of educability or usefulness. This seems obvious as stated here but it's hard to apply to ourselves as coaches. We rarely ask clearly defined questions of this kind about ourselves. And when such questions are asked, we tend to give vague answers.

We might feel sure that "I like boys." If you think you do, try putting your attitudes to a critical test by checking your reaction to twelve types of athletes, as listed by Ogilvie and Tutko (1966, 18). They provide a four-degree scale including deeply resent, slightly resent, slightly unconcerned, and completely unconcerned. If you're honest, you'll find in each instance a range of possible reaction; if you're analytical, you'll often be unable to answer, at least in a reliable fashion. You'll feel a very wide range of possible response depending upon an infinite variety of situations and individual differences.

Despite such difficulties, you will undoubtedly conclude from such a test that you do tend to react favorably to one type of athlete and negatively to another. Note the "tend to." How narrow and fixed is that tendency? How wide and flexible? Here is the key to improvement of your coaching assets. Quite possibly your attitudes are the result of your home community attitudes, or of the attitudes of your parents, or of your own coach you admire so much. *But there is a range within which these can be improved.*

We have used attitudes toward boys as our example. But the same range-of-potential approach can be taken toward such coaching attributes as self-assuredness, knowledge of track and field, personal experience in track and field, level of energy and enthusiasm, sense of humor, speaking voice and diction, or level of expectancy of competitive performance.

COACHING LEADERSHIP AS MUTUALLY SUPPORTIVE RELATIONSHIPS

As Rensis Likert concluded from his study of leaders in Business Management, success depends as much on what one can do for others--help them in any way, related or seemingly unrelated-- as on what they can do for you: what Likert called, *"mutually supportive relationships."*

So with coaching track and field. The life history of any coach, successful or not, can be predicted or told later in terms of the degree to which his inter-personal relationships are mutually supportive: relationships with the team or its individual members; relationships with his institution and its administration and faculty; with his community; with such "feeder" groups as lower-level schools, alumni, clubs; relationships with fellow coaches and with track and field organizations, local, state, national and international. Mutually supportive relationships is a potent phrase, useful in so many areas of life, and vital to success in coaching.

What might be the mutually supportive relationships between the college coach and a number of high school coaches? The latter provide prospective team members and prestige-getters to the college coach. In return, his effectiveness in developing those prospects to their highest potentials is the greatest satisfaction the high school coach can be given.

Support can be just saying "thanks," or giving credit publicly at banquets. Coaching aids are supportive. A coach may be scientifically trained in biomechanics and physiology and understand their applications on the track and field. He may be entirely competent in technique, but that is only one side of the coin. I know of no coach, past or present, including the recruiter and employer by way of scholarships or material payments, who maintained success over a long career who failed to ensure such mutual helpfulness throughout all his personal relationships, as a way of life.

It is important to add that this way of life has equal potency at the high school level. A high school coach who fails to give support to his athletes, his fellow-teachers, the community--in fact, the wide world of track and field athletics--is unlikely to succeed for long, either in victories won or in the respect of others.

In summary, and it's impossible to over-emphasize the point, the extent and nature of relationships with others is at least as crucial to coaching success as is knowledge of track and field methods and techniques. It will therefore be the primary concern throughout the remainder of this and the following Chapters in Part I.

ROLES OF THE COACH

The actual roles of the track and field coach are so numerous and complex as to defy definite analysis, and certainly are beyond the scope of this book. But the following summary may stimulate thinking and discussion. Actually we should add to our heading the words "in our American society today," with emphasis on the word "today." Coaching roles are constantly changing, through influences from within and outside sport, along with our changing culture. In my generation, the role of the coach was about what he made it; few questioned his authority to do so. But not all cultures take such a view. I shall never forget my sense of being put down, even humiliated, when Lou Montgomery and I, as head coaches, attended the Penn-Cornell, Oxford-Cambridge banquet in London. We were seated at a rear table with the English coaches and were never recognized at any time during the evening. In contrast, in Finland and Europe generally, student coaches and athletes rise respectfully when the head coaches enter the lecture hall.

During recent decades the traditional roles of the coach have been seriously questioned, just as have so many other aspects of the so-called Establishment. Tomorrow the coach may interpret his roles from quite a different frame of reference to that presented here.

OVER-EVALUATION. The real value of a coach for improved performance, especially at the individual level, is easily over-estimated and over-stated. As I have observed great athletes that have developed under other coaches as well as under my own teaching, I've often felt that we coaches merely create helpful situations and a few pushes toward self-development. What they accomplish emerges mainly out of themselves, out of their own powers of muscle and heart and self-discipline and persistence. After three or more years of coaching a great athlete, a coach tends to acquire an attitude that now he has the secret. Whatever the coach says is quickly understood and becomes effective. Only after the athlete is gone does the coach realize clearly that the secret went with him. Brutus Hamilton was a most effective coach. But he often insisted that his greatest value lay in not interfering with the normal progress of his boys.

THE COACH AS TOILER. The word "toiler" was chosen deliberately as meaning one who engages in fatiguing, emotionally stressful, and even arduous work for long hours day after day after day. The job has so many aspects, all of which contribute or are even essential to success, that the days are simply not long enough to do a fully effective job. How well I remember my own experiences as a first-year coach when, coming home on the train from Chicago after the end-of-the-year Conference Championships, we reviewed our losses through graduation, assessed our chances for the coming year, and made plans effective immediately to improve those chances. It's a year-round vocation, regardless of the school calendar or pay checks.

Over the years, I've heard so many comments, "One thing I'll say about Coach so-and-so, he may drive his men hard, harder than I think he should, but he drives himself just as hard; he's always on the job." When Ara Parseghian retired after 25 years as head football coach, he was quoted as saying, "I was physically and emotionally drained. I knew I had to get out. I also knew I won't be able to stay away for good. I'll want back. But I need some time to get myself back together, and time is one luxury our business doesn't provide."

Woody Hayes, Ohio State's winningest football coach, was known to everyone as a workaholic, one who worked on weekends of course but also on all holidays in and out of season. He was said to have originated the present vogue for delivery truck pads in which he could grab a quick nap when on his way to recruiting or speaking appointments. Even a heart attack reduced only a little his time on the road. At one interview he estimated he had been away from home over 200 nights during the past year.

Of course, that's football, and fortunately the public pressure on track coaches is not nearly so great as that on football coaches. But the inner urge to succeed is just as great, and the demand for work just as crucial for success.

Even in those high schools and small colleges where coaching is an extra assignment for which a few hundred dollars extra are paid, the self-respecting coach will find himself forced to study hard to gain the required knowledge, to use many off-the-job hours in getting to know his protégées better, to eat many a warmed-over supper in order to complete the workout of the late-lab athlete, and even slip out to the track during a free period to emphasize a point or two with a twice-a-day shot-putter.

THE COACH AS TRAINER. In its early years, our sport was mainly related to running, not so much to the field events; and improvement in running was mainly related to discipline: discipline by daily exertion, by maintaining a restricted diet, by avoiding all the vices of living that sapped the energies and weakened the will. And so track coaches became trainers--men who disciplined their charges. When an athlete broke the training rules, he was subject to discipline, perhaps to cutting from the team.

Later, this concept of the coach became confused when track coaches also acted as "trainers" for the football and basketball teams, one who supervised calisthenics and the conditioning of the team, along with giving rubdowns (an almost daily ritual with talented athletes) and caring for injuries. Such trainers had great power and prestige, sometimes taking players off the field when the head coach wanted them to stay.

Gradually, such "training" work became specialized and full time, requiring knowledge of Sports Medicine and approval of the Medical profession, well beyond the scope of a track coach. Perhaps Ducky Drake of UCLA, coach of Olympic Champion Rafer Johnson and other greats, was the last of the combined track coach-trainer. In 1972 he found it necessary to retire from coaching so as to continue as full time trainer for all sports.

THE COACH AS PLANNER. The track coach tends to assume primary responsibility for making plans, both team and individual. He alone knows the entire set-up: training and competition, team and individual, on and off the track, at home and on trips, etc. Much as he may insist that he is but one member of the team, and that his plans are team plans, the necessity for getting the job done, and done well, tends to put major planning in the hands of the coach.

THE COACH AS EXECUTOR. The sources of basic team policy are many: tradition within the sport of track and field, school tradition, school administration, alumni and community enthusiasts, and then of course the team and the coach. Regardless of how team policies are reached, the paid coach in America tends to be the primary executor of policy. He is paid to get things done. It must be added that in America the coach is paid to get things done in such a way as to best ensure winning. As one educator said recently,

I have found that 99 percent of all communities want you to win. True, they also want you to build character, promote rules of amateurism and good sportsmanship, and be a worthy leader whom young Americans should follow, but they want you to win. They believe in character education; they employ guidance counselors, principals, teachers to build such character, and certainly they do not want the coach to tear it down, but they want him to win.

But each season and each team develops its own views and problems as related to basic policy. In trying to solve such problems, the coach must often tread lightly in executing policy and shift to the role of arbitrator-mediator. An arbitrator is empowered by others on both sides of the issue to analyze the facts and make a final decision. A mediator brings all related persons and facts together and by contrivance or toughness keeps them together until they reach agreement.

THE COACH AS RECRUITER. It's rather surprising that someone has not written a full-size book revealing the wide variety of methods and viewpoints of recruiting, with special emphasis on its positive aspects. For, contrary to common usage, recruitment as a means of ensuring a constant supply of fresh talent, can have a legitimate place in both school and college sports. Every effective coach must be a recruiter in one way or another. Even those coaches who declare that they never seek the athlete, that the athlete must come to them for help, do recruit by means of the reputation that success has created, or perhaps by way of the disciples that follow them. No one could accuse Coach Ted Haydon of being a recruiter in the sense of seeking out and subsidizing talent for his Chicago Track Club, but he was an outstanding recruiter by way of the nation-wide reputation he slowly acquired as a sound coach unselfishly interested in the welfare of his boys.

What is basically wrong with the concept of hard-sell recruiting? First, within the institution, it reduces the opportunities of members of the regular student body to participate in sport and so gain the valuable developmental training and competitive experiences of sport. Second, among institutions organized into conferences of associations to provide fair play among individuals of comparable talent and attitudes toward sport, recruiting upsets the normal balance of winning and losing. Each recruiter assumes all others are at least bending the rules and so feels justified in bending them even further to make sure he's getting a fair shake. But even more fundamental, hard-sell recruiting adopts the goals of business management that production and profit are primary and so subverts the educational goals of higher education.

The most flagrant example of this in the entire history of college track and field occurred at the University of Texas at El Paso. In 1973, UTEP's coach was fired for excesses in recruiting and promotion. But in 1980, his successor, Ted Banks, won the NCAA Indoor Team Title by recruiting athletes from seven countries--Kenya, Sweden, Nigeria, South Africa, Jamaica, Bermuda and Tanzania. These men scored 64 of UTEP's winning total of 72. What's wrong with such a program? Two important things: First, the opportunity to participate had been taken from regular members of the UTEP student body; second, the principle of fair play had been violated--at least two of these men were over 28 years of age, and others were well over the usual age of college students. In 1984, the UTEP administration cut back its track program.

It's hard to argue against the thesis that such hard-sell recruiting is inherent in our competitive industrial-military culture. Educational institutions are necessarily supportive of the ways and ethics of the culture that creates them. In a business-oriented society, "educational" becomes interpreted as vocational training; "ethics" as those of the business community. Small wonder that recruiting of the so-called student-athlete takes on the stench of automobile sales procedures with their emphasis on the bottom line of private profit.

But education in our society is not entirely vocational training within the business ethic. Some schools and colleges still emphasize a truly liberal education; and all have departments and faculties that try to inculcate broader horizons and an ethic somewhat higher than that of the marketplace. For such schools, the geographical radius of recruiting should be roughly that of the regular student body, not as a rule to be policed but as a common-sense approach to the problem. Even better, recruiting would occur at home, from within the regular student body. Intercollegiate sports programs would now become extramural.

Utopian? Unrealistic? Of course. But not because the idea is unsound; not because some rigid human nature makes our present system inevitable. On the contrary, these ideas are unrealistic only in a business culture that follows McGregor's Theory X--authoritarian, self-serving, profit-centered. To the extent that growing environmental and social problems force business and its training institutions to adopt a Theory Y approach, such ideas can gain common acceptance and usage. Now winning in sports, like profit in business, will still be essential, but winning, not as the only end, not as the main end, not as the end at all; rather as the means of motivating what Coubertin called, "the struggle of life"--the hard training, the sacrifice of ease and fun that are essential for both improvement and satisfaction in sports, as in any worthwhile work.

How would such a principle work in practice? Study the operation of the University of Chicago Track Club under Ted Haydon, as outlined in this OMNIBOOK. Their gate receipts and donations are the means to greater service to more track and field athletes of wide-ranging talents and backgrounds. Winning and record-breaking emerge out of numbers and opportunities for practice and competition, not out of recruitment or intense training directly related to winning. As a second example, the Board in Control of Athletics (faculty-controlled) at the University of Michigan has as a basic principle allocated gate receipts to improvement of inter-collegiate sports facilities but only if a like amount were spent on recreational facilities for all students.

But the most soundly-based example of this mutually-supportive principle of which I know that at the city of Medford and the state of Oregon under the 30-year leadership of Bob Newland and Bill Bowerman, as outlined in this OMNIBOOK. In a nutshell, these two men assumed the many phases of the Medford Public Schools sports system and of the State of Oregon sports system were many phases of one system. To develop successful track and field at the State University level or at the Medford High School level required well-organized programs at all sublevels-- the junior high schools and elementary schools. Meetings were held to discuss common problems and goals. Out of those a track and field handbook was prepared under the leadership of the high school coach, Bob Newland, that provided (1) the gist of sound coaching methods, (2) track and field records at all levels from grade schools up, (3) selected textbook references, and (4) a free copy of a leading textbook. Clinics were held. High School (and later, University) coaches and athletes were available to help beginners at all levels. By such methods, not only was motivation increased, but commonly-held coaching procedures were ensured. Now the elemen-tary-school coach feels that his role is a challenge to him and of some importance to the entire Medford sports system. If the high school athlete wins, at least three coaches feel they were of some help, however small. In keeping with this attitude, their continuing card-file is of special value. As an athlete progressed in school, his personal file with all relevant infor-mation, including each coach's comments, progressed with him.

And as Bill Bowerman, the originator of the Medford system, moved up to the University at Eugene, these views and procedures tended to move with him. No wonder the city of Eugene is often called the distance-running and jogging capitol of the United States, and certainly its most enthusiastic track and field city. All-in-all, a sound grass-roots recruiting system mutually supportive of itself and all its subsystems.

If this soft-sell approach to recruiting is still not clear, try contrasting the Medford or Chicago approaches with that at any one of all too many Universities that pluck the athlete out of his home-school environment, transport him to a "foreign" milieu, exchange his talents for something of monetary value, with scarcely a nod to the home helpers. Even when they receive "first-class treatment throughout," as is claimed by the Villanova champions, one has an impres-sion of good-business procedures- not of a developmental educational system.

THE COACH AS SALESMAN. Every coach, if he is to be effective, must be a salesman. Some will protest this statement on the basis that selling implies an exchange of goods of monetary value. Unfortunately, this is what actually happens at some colleges. But my use of the word "salesman" was intended to imply persuasion, inducement, encouragement, cooperative exchange and the like. Such salesmanship is warranted in any situation.

Certain key questions arise. What is he selling? Himself or his program, institution, situation? What sales methods is he using? True, each coach-situation is unique and so each sales approach will be similarly unique. But there must be some answers that have broad impli-cations. I think of the head college coach who followed a two-step approach with all prospec-tive athletes. First, the assistant guided the prospect through all parts of the campus and student life that interested him. He thereby gained detailed answers to all questions. But most important, the head coach also spent some time alone with the prospect. Why? "Because I love this school. I believe in it and what it does for its individual students and all those associated with it. Somehow I must convey a portion of that love and belief to this prospect." Such a combination of selling the mind and the heart would be hard to improve.

Though written over 45 years ago, Dale Carnegie's HOW TO WIN FRIENDS AND INFLUENCE PEOPLE,[1] with its strong emphasis on cooperation is still relevant today and not far removed in its views from Rensis Likert's principle of mutually supportive relationships. Carnegie's pre-scription was simple--be like Charles Schwab, the genius in executive management selected by

---

[1]Dale Carnegie, HOW TO WIN FRIENDS AND INFLUENCE PEOPLE, New York: Simon & Schuster, 1936.

Andrew Carnegie to manage his financial empire. Schwab knew how to get men to do what he wanted them to do while thinking it was primarily their idea to do it. His secret, according to Dale Carnegie, was an enormously winning smile, a smile claimed to be "worth a million dollars." Schwab made men feel important, the "deepest urge in human nature," according to Carnegie. He extended lavish praise, offered hearty approbation, talked about things the listener was interested in, let them feel new ideas were their ideas, evidenced genuine interest in them as persons. All this made them feel important. And somehow this ennabled the smiler to sell his program and product.

The first question that arises relates to the sincerity and integrity of this approach. Does one smile out of sheer good spirits and good will, or is it an obvious mask related to the need to sell? An insincere grin doesn't fool anyone; in fact, we resent it. In a true salesman, the smile must come from within, from a deep-seated belief in the enterprise and the product, and from a genuine interest in the welfare of other people.

We must keep in mind that Dale Carnegie believed in the business enterprise he was selling; his was salesmanship within and for the system. Without such a genuine belief, his program was based merely on William James' teachings that we can acquire attitudes of mind by acting *as if* we actually feel a certain way. We can learn to feel happy simply by smiling *as if* we are happy. Furthermore, people are quite willing to believe in such smiles, if only out of their great need to be smiled at and so be made to feel important.

With whom does the coach have the relationship of salesman? To athletes of course--present, past, and future. Since future athletes are unknown individually, one must maintain close relationships with all the coaches, near and far, who will be developing them. On this point consider again the Medford, Oregon organization. But also mutually supportive relationships must be maintained with the school administration, with interested members of the community, with parents, even with rival coaches; in short with the entire track team family. The more broadly based, the more effective it will be.

I think of Joe Paterno, the Penn State football coach, who over the course of years has established a solid reputation for personal integrity, pride in his profession of coaching, and personal concern for the general betterment of his charges. Everyone--the communications media, other coaches, the man on the street--speaks well of him and his program. That's real salesmanship, and in the long run the most successful.

THE COACH AS FATHER FIGURE. Some coaches tend to elicit warm emotional feelings from their boys and to respond in kind. In fact, as I try to assess the many coaches I have known, a large percentage had this quality; some more, some less. Among the more outstanding were Tom Jones of Wisconsin, Emil Von Elling of NYU, Don Mollenauer of Mt. Lebanon High School, Pa., Billy Hayes of Indiana, Bob Giegengack of Yale, and Brutus Hamilton of California at Berkeley. But that's a personal reaction with little validity. Another coach would present a quite different list. But all would have in common a primary concern for the boy.

If you do not genuinely enjoy being with young athletes, stay out of coaching. To want to help them is not enough; to be fascinated by the mechanics of track and field is not enough. Genuine friendliness is an essential requirement. Every profession has its special requirements, special conditions, atmosphere, problems. The coach has to feel relaxed and "at home" when travelling with the team, should be one of the team members in laughter and gaiety, while still maintaining their respect and the proper coach-athlete relationship on the field. Without that warmheartedness, without such a sense of mutual enjoyment, there may be victories and record performances, but there is not likely to be the inspiration, zest, and deep satisfaction so essential to great coaching.

Some successful coaches are known as strict disciplinarians. But you'll find that somewhere, someway--on the track or at off-hours--such taskmasters will establish their place in the hearts of their boys. The coaches that fail altogether to be heart-centered are seldom effective and--hopefully--do not remain long in the profession.

Oh, it's not all cream and sugar. There'll be times when you'd like to wipe out the lot of them. There'll be "teams" that just never are able to work or feel together. When the going gets rough, they'll get rough with each other. There'll be men that seem to hate you, and whom you'll--not hate--but at least be glad when they graduate. There'll be times when you feel you're only a policeman, or worse, a spy. But if you like boys, they'll usually buoy you up, infect you with enthusiasm and energy, amaze you with "impossible" performances, and even--now and then and hesitantly--credit you with having been of some small help in some unimportant way. But that'll be compensation enough. I am reminded of Kahlil Gibran's comment that when a true leader dies, the people will say, "We did this thing ourselves."

Quite obviously, an effective coach knows the what and how of his boys' living as they relate directly to track and field. That's his job. But how broadly does he define the word "direct-ly?" Many a boy has withdrawn entirely from track and field because of girl problems, study problems, draft-board problems. How can a coach, with perhaps a hundred boys on his squad, find time and energy for all this, when there's hardly enough time for coaching on the field and for the important demands of coaching clinics, professional improvement, community services, and all the rest? He can't, of course, not really, and yet somehow he does.

Somehow he does maintain personal contact. He realizes the need in all men for recognition and some degree of commendation. He trains himself to look for what is well done--or at least well tried--and finds sincere ways of expressing his appreciation. There is an artless art of such expression, of knowing how an athlete feels, of what is important to him, and what words he will accept--and reject. "Art" because it can be learned; "artless" because it must never seem contrived.

When a disappointed Jerry Siebert returned to California after placing sixth in the Tokyo 800 meters, a letter awaited him from his coach, Brutus Hamilton,

I was never more proud. Knowing something of your condition, [Jerry competed despite illness] I was surprised you ran at all, and I'm not altogether certain that you should have run, but the fact that you did run, and ran well, will always be a source of great pride to your old coach.

Contrived? Insincere? From some coaches it might have seemed so; from Brutus it was as in-character as ham and eggs in a Western breakfast.

Track and field competition and training is a profound experience in which self-doubt and elation, discomfort and joy, numb despair and wild hope, arduous work and surging energy, are all jumbled together. The insensitive "it's-a-job" coach assumes that the outward action is all that is happening to a boy, and reacts only to the hard facts of the situation. But the coach that likes boys, and knows out of his own experiences and his own related emotions what they feel inside the facts, somehow conveys his empathy to the boy, perhaps without saying a word.

Of course, as Ryan[1] pointed out, the father symbol can have a negative influence. To the extent that the boy's father was over-dominant and restrictive, the boy may resent and resist the teachings of the coach, especially when a coach's analysis of a boy's technique becomes, in the boy's mind, a job of surgery on himself personally.

THE COACH AS RELIEVER OF ATHLETE RESPONSIBILITY. The coach plays a very important role in relieving the athlete of the burden of responsibility for planning and making decisions that quite often he is neither ready nor willing to make. This is obviously true for beginning athletes but also for those of long experience at high-performance levels. Dolson tells of George Young's difficulties[2],

The ulcers struck again in 1967, a year before the Mexico City Olympics, and George went through an agonizing summer trying to decide if his track career was over. Maybe he simply couldn't take the strain anymore....He had to do something to reduce the pressure. Anything...

The solution hit him. He had a friend in Silver City...a math instructor and a

---

[1]Frank Ryan, "Some Aspects of Athletic Behavior," *NCTCA Clinic Notes*, 1955, 1.

[2]Frank Dolson, *ALWAYS YOUNG*, Mountain View, Cal.; *World Publications*, 1975, p. 152.

knowledgeable track coach. If George could lean on Jim Fox, maybe the mental strain wouldn't be so great.

"I realized one of my big mental problems...was I would devise workouts for myself, then I wouldn't complete them because I'd think maybe they weren't that good," he said. "Or maybe they were too hard. I felt if I could get him to train me through the mail this would take a lot of the worries off me"....

He followed those workouts religiously--and, more important, unquestioningly--for close on two years. "It did take a lot of pressure off me"...(and he attained) the greatest shape of his life.

Unfortunately, what began as mere helpful relief has gradually become self-righteous power. The coach and sports administrators generally now tend to take such power of decision for granted, quite apart from its uses for the athlete. Eric Fromm, in his *Escape from Freedom*, describes the strong tendency for people to escape from the burdens of responsibility when freedom creates confusion and anxiety, by delegating crucial powers to their leaders, especially to those authoritarian leaders who promise the most at the least cost. Usually, such delegation occurs gradually, in little ways, with little awareness of final implication. But once gained, authority tends to assume an inherent right, and defends itself for its own sake, without regard to the original intent of the people.

This is what has occurred in American sports generally, though to a lesser degree in track and field. As I review this tendency in the light of my own long experience as a coach, I realize with a sense of almost shock the degree to which I assumed this role of the coach. I can't imagine anyone accusing me of being dictatorial in my relations with others; my failings would be on the other side of the scale. And yet, I did make so many decisions--our schedule of meets, our use of college vacation periods, who should make trips, who would room with whom, what would we wear, what would we eat, when would we come and go--with little or no consultation with the individuals involved. It just never occurred to me, nor to all the other coaches doing the same thing, that there was a better way to do it. Nor, with rare exceptions, do I remember that team members ever questioned my right to make such decisions or suggested improvements. That was the way it had always been done. But after Vietnam, attitudes tended to be reversed. As one phase of the revolt against the Establishment and all authority, athletes began to assume individual freedom and doubted the coach's right to make decisions, even when they related to team organization and spirit.

SUMMARY. This discussion of coaching roles is intended, not to advocate this or that role, but to help you understand the varied roles that the track coach in America is expected to play. But if the material is accepted without critical analysis of its applications for your coaching situation and for you specifically as a person, it may delude far more than it helps.

A coach must assess the whole situation--the community, the school, the sports traditions, the athletes, and especially himself--very critically. To a degree he can mould and discipline himself in the roles that are most likely to prove effective. To a degree he can select and train assistants who will strengthen those roles in which he is weak. But in any case and with no exceptions, the roles of the coach and the needs of the situation must somehow mesh, must somehow fit together so as to operate effectively.

GROUP DYNAMICS IN TRACK AND FIELD. Track and field is often described as an individual sport in which competition among individuals predominates, and the team wins if each individual does his isolated best. Usually the organization of the team is low-level. Meetings are irregular, usually for factual rather than morale reasons. Often team members travel to meets separately, and may not even meet together prior to competition. Some coaches succeed by collecting an aggregation of self-centered stars whose contribution to the team is entirely one of scoring points. For such coaches, group dynamics would be of little use.

But when, as in most successful operations, the emphasis is on the team as being, not merely more than, but other than the sum of its individual members, or when the team is felt to comprise the local community and student body, as well as the athletes and coach, then group dynamics becomes a crucial concern.

The word "dynamics," derived from the Greek, means the forces acting in any given field. As related to human groups, it suggests the motivating or driving forces that operate within and upon groups. As a concept for research and related use, it came into acceptance in the 1930s, primarily through the insights and work of Kurt Lewin (1935, 1951). Lewin was impressed by society's need for a more scientific approach to understanding the problems of groups and their relation to individual members: how they are formed, how they function and change, what relationships exist between members, how leaders are chosen, how different leadership methods affect group actions as well as individual actions, and many more.

Once again lack of space cuts off adequate treatment of the subject, but the following summary may be of value, not at all as statements of finality; rather as ways of looking at things, ways of stimulating thought and discussion, ways to be balanced with opposite conclusions.

1. The holistic concept of the organism-in-environment is basic to a sound understanding of the problems of track coaching. We easily accept the statement that the human organism adapts the environment to itself; we must learn to accept just as completely that the environment as a truly indivisible whole adapts the human organism to itself. For example, the problems of coaching 50 years ago contrast with present-day problems: Then winning was generally considered secondary to academic success and we assumed limitations on time-energy-devotion to sports. Today sports tend to adopt the assumptions of Big Politics-Big Business that "winning is not the main thing, it's the only thing." Fortunately this attitude is not so prevalent as the media proclaims it to be.

2. A track team is a dynamic social group. That group may be loosely organized; it may be a mere aggregation of recruited individuals. Such individuals may never see each other except at competitions, and perhaps not even then. But even such a "team" has a dynamic force. A track team always stands for something. That something, whether strong or weak, influences the behavior of its members. How and to what degree that influence occurs is a function of the team family in its widest sense, as well as of its leadership.

3. A track team is a constantly changing and very flexible organization. In any one year, different kinds of meets call for different competitors, different in both number and events. In different years, team members and even the coach may change. At different institutions situated in different environments, attitudes and customs vary greatly. I suppose only personal experience can make one realize the full significance of this statement. I coached for equally long periods at the Universities of Michigan and Pennsylvania. Though the same principles of coaching were used, the applications of those principles were disturbingly different.

But teams vary, not only in the closeness of their internal organization, but also in the scope of those who share team goals and methods. We have advanced the concept of the team family which, as at Harvard or California, might extend to the 50 states of the Union. Or to suggest an extreme example, in the sport of rowing, a Harvard crew can progressively represent its University at Poughkeepsie, northeastern United States at the final Olympic tryouts, and the nation as a whole at the Olympic Games.

4. If a track team is to be a truly effective group, its members (athletes, coaches, trainers, managers, and the loyal family of followers) must have a strong sense of togetherness, of belonging to one group and sharing its common goals. Our team, not my team; our training rules, not his rules; our team success, not my winning record as a coach. This principle does not preclude separate individual goals but when the team is the focal concern, individual goals should lead toward, not away from the common goal.

5. A track team judges the worth of its coaching member in terms of his contribution to team goals and values. That he is an authority in the sport, that he is a valued contributor to state and national coaching circles, that his research or his writings have gained wide recognition, that he has been honored as an athlete or coach, all these may be happily accepted as one may rejoice in the success of a friend, but they will be valued as they serve directly the purposes of the team and its members.

6. The greater the awareness that team goals contribute to the furtherance of individual goals, the greater and more helpful the influence that the team and its coach can exert on its individual members. The team and its members are two aspects of one reality; neither should preclude the other. Just as the individual should further the team, so the team should further

the goals of its individuals. Within this two-way pattern of operation lies the high art of coaching.

7.   In attempts to improve the behavior, attitudes, or feelings of team members, the more relevant those improvements are to actual performance on the track and field, the greater the influence that the team and the coach can exert. Consider the relative importance in terms of performance of (1) time and energy on the field, (2) training conduct off the field, (3) length and neatness of hair, (4) clothing on campus and on trips, (5) attitudes toward social problems, (6) problems of sports amateurism. The wise coach focuses on essentials in his efforts to influence the behavior of team members, recognizing that what is essential is often doubtful.

8.   Information relating to behavior must be shared openly with all team members that might be affected. It is essential to keep the channels of communication open. One of the first consequences of mistrust and hostility is the loss of free communication about the problem-producing tension. As communication slows, hostility increases.

9.   In seeking to maintain mutual respect and discipline, the coach will be less concerned with inflicting punishment for defiance of "my rules" than with creating conditions by which the team and its members will discipline themselves for breaking "our rules."

10.   The effectiveness of pressure for change is greatest when it comes from within the group; it thereby creates a shared perception of need, method, and degree of change.

11.   Different styles of leadership bring forth different styles of aggressive behavior from any given group (team) or from its individual members.

12.   Individuals must be valued equally. Equality of opportunity is a critical issue today, both in society as a whole and in the track team. We now recognize this as it applies to race, color, or creed. But it also applies to differences in talent. For example, treatment of star athletes as special persons is likely to disrupt team morale and to ostracize those athletes. Most champions prefer leaders that treat them as regular members.
Nelson (1967, 35) gives an excellent example of this in Coach Timmons' treatment of Jim Ryun. Even when Jim returned to the East High School squad after the Tokyo Olympics, he was treated as just "one of the boys" in his conformance with team rules and training schedules. All boys followed the same basic training schedule, but those of higher ability ran each phase faster or longer.

MOTIVATIONAL PATTERNS IN COACHING.   One of the more respected theories of human motivation was developed by the late Abraham H. Maslow.[1] He suggested that human needs can be categorized within five levels or hierarchies, as follows:

        5--Need for self-actualization (development, growth, creativity, self-realization, achieving the higher levels of one's potential energies and talents)
      4--Ego needs (both self-esteem as indicated by feelings of competence, capacity, power, adequacy; and esteem of others as indicated by recognition, respect, prestige, status)
    3--Social needs (friendship, love, belongingness, team membership)
  2--Safety needs (freedom from possible injury or excessive pain, social security--vocation, finances, student status, religion, an orderly society)
1--Physiological needs (food, water, shelter, activity, sleep, sexual fulfillment, and the like)

---

[1]Abraham H. Maslow, *MOTIVATION AND PERSONALITY*, New York: Harper & Row, Publishers, Inc., 1954, pp. 81-106.

203401

Once a lower-level or more basic need is satisfied, it loses its potency as a motivating force. "Man lives by bread alone only as long as he has no bread." Then the next higher level of need becomes operative. Such theory does not suggest an actual separation of these levels of need. A level does not require 100 percent satisfaction before the next becomes potent. Usually we are partially satisfied-unsatisfied at each level at any given time. For instance, Maslow suggests an average citizen satisfaction of perhaps 85 percent in physiological needs, 70 percent in safety needs, 50 percent in social needs, 40 percent in ego needs, and 10 percent in self-actualization needs.

In studying Maslow's five levels of need, a track and field coach will reach several conclusions: (1) The three top levels (self-actualization, esteem, belongingness) are most related to sports motivation. (2) However, they have lowest priority if the more basic needs are unsatisfied. (3) If finances or student status are in jeopardy, they become dominant as motivators, and the higher levels are diminished or inoperative. (4) Most important, as Likert made clear, satisfaction-unsatisfaction must be measured, not only by actual conditions, but by attitudes and feelings. They determine what is acceptable, even more than do the realities of the situation.

MOTIVATIONS AND COACHING ASSUMPTIONS. On the basis of much related research in industry, we can conclude that the assumptions a coach makes about human nature and its reaction to any difficult task will have a greater effect on his way of coaching and the reactions of his boys than can all his technical skills in planning, directing, coercing and rewarding.

According to Douglas McGregor[1] the authoritarian approach (Theory X) to business management has ignored a great weight of contrary scientific research in its acceptance of basically unsound assumptions:

1. The average human being has an inherent dislike for work and will avoid it if he can.

2. Most people must therefore be coerced, controlled, given extrinsic rewards, directed and threatened with punishment to get them to put forth adequate effort toward the achievement of organization objectives.

3. The average human being prefers to be directed, wishes to avoid responsibility, has little ambition, and wants security above all.

4. Wages are a sufficient motivating force for effective work.

Having made these basic assumptions, management then proceeds to construct situations, procedures and motivations that are consistent with them. It takes away control and responsibility and so finds that workers are irresponsible. The results "prove" the validity of the original assumptions. To round out this circular thinking, such Theory X management uses this "proof" as evidence that its kind of management is best for production and profit and should be supported.

It ignores the possibility that different basic assumptions and related procedures might have brought out quite different responses and greater production and profit. McGregor concludes that management's views of human nature as related to work are of greater significance in the effects on worker response, and so on production and profit than are management's skills, however expert, in the techniques of production, planning, and controlling.

We can assume a similar relationship between coaching assumptions and athlete performance. Perhaps the most obvious example of this was the great success and failure of Mihaly Igloi during the 1960s in this country. Igloi had highest-level expertise in the technology of training for endurance running and a sound background of success in his handling of Iharos, Roszavolgyi and Tabori in Hungary. But his military background induced him to exert complete control and direction of all aspects of training and competition. "It's your job to run; I'll do all the rest." He had success as long as his runners relaxed and followed instructions. His breadth of knowledge of all aspects of running was prodigious. But he failed when

---

[1] Douglas McGregor, *THE HUMAN SIDE OF ENTERPRISE*, New York: McGraw-Hill Book Company, Inc., 1960, pp. 33-49.

self-esteem caused his men to seek a greater degree of freedom and self-control.

In contrast to the authoritarian approach, McGregor[1] used research in sociology and business management to construct his Theory Y with its more realistic assessment of the motivations of workers. When the proper climate of human relations has been established and basic needs satisfied:

1. Effort in meaningful work is as natural as play and rest.

2. Man will exercise effective self control and direction in work whose objectives have his full commitment.

3. Commitment to objectives enhances the effects of extrinsic rewards for achievement.

4. Under proper conditions, the average worker learns, not only to accept, but to seek responsibility.

5. Success of the business enterprise is most fully assured when workers feel that their personal goals are integrated with those of the enterprise.

Almost all coaches agree in general with such an approach to motivation in track and field. But most still feel that the coach knows best and should exercise some degree of benevolent autocracy. Their problem becomes one of granting certain kinds and degrees of control, giving and seeking cooperation, meeting the more basic levels of need of team members, granting fair treatment and ample rewards in return for successful performance, but always maintaining the reins of control in their own hands.

McGregor favored clear communication of objectives with as much self-direction and self-control as is feasible. However, after serving as president of Antioch College, he wrote:[2]

Before coming to Antioch...I believed that a leader could operate successfully as a kind of advisor to his organization. Unconsciously, I suspect, I hoped to duck the unpleasant necessity of making difficult decisions, of taking responsibility for one course of action among many uncertain alternatives, of making mistakes and taking the consequences. I thought that maybe I could operate so that everybody would like me--that good human relations would eliminate all discord and disappointment. I could not have been more wrong.

He concluded that, even among wise and good men, effective leadership cannot ignore its inherent role as initiator, decision-maker, and executor. Things must get done and effective leadership must lead the action. The questions remain as to how this is accomplished and with what patterns of motivation.

ATTITUDES ARE CRUCIAL. Both McGregor and Likert emphasized that attitudes toward working conditions were at least equally important as the actual conditions of work. McGregor wrote of "the climate of relationships" within the managerial enterprise. "The climate is more significant than the type or personal style of leadership."[3] Similarly Likert wrote,[4]

It is how he sees things that counts, not objective reality. Consequently an individual member of an organization will always interpret an interaction between himself and the organization in terms of his own background, experience and expectations.... In order therefore to have an interaction viewed as supportive, it must be of such a

---

[1]Ibid., pp. 47-48.

[2]Douglas McGregor, LEADERSHIP AND MOTIVATION, Cambridge: The M.I.T. Press, 1966, p. 67.

[3]Ibid.,p. 134.

[4]Rensis Likert, NEW PATTERNS OF MANAGEMENT, New York: McGraw-Hill Book Co., 1961, p. 102.

character that the individual himself...sees it as supportive.

The crucial factor then is the attitudinal climate within which interactions occur. That climate can be a function of local traditions, of the present situation, of the coach himself, or of all taken together. But it is the attitude that counts. High altitude in itself detracts from running performance. But it becomes an asset when attitudes use it as a stimulus to greater performance. Who would have thought that the hot, humid climate and lack of running tradition of the state of Florida could have developed the 1972 Olympic marathon champion, Frank Shorter, as well as a half-dozen or more other excellent distance men? Attitudes must have been influential.

In the 1930s, the University of Chicago withdrew from the Big Ten Athletic Conference and reduced greatly its commitment to the major sports. Conditions for track and field certainly seemed unfavorable. But a few decades later, primarily through the attitudes and energies of Coach Ted Haydon and his fellow-workers, there emerged the University of Chicago track club and program, in my judgment, the most significant development for the improvement of United States track and field of the past fifty years.

I remember with some regret but much satisfaction the limited training conditions of my own track career at Detroit City College (now Wayne State University) in the 1920s; no indoor facility except the college class-room corridors and women's gym when and if they were finished with it; no outdoor facility except the Detroit Recreation Department track on Belle Isle, six miles from school. No hot showers; no training room or trainer; no locker in which to leave one's track clothes overnight; a seldom-brushed or watered cinder track; jumping pits that we often spaded ourselves. But we had no basis for comparison; so far as we knew such conditions were quite normal. And in any case, the boundless enthusiasm and energy of Coach David L. Holmes would have soon quieted any team members inclined to gripe. We just made the most of what we had and thought nothing of it. In fact I could make a strong case in arguing that I won two National Decathlon titles because of those "handicapping" conditions, not despite them. Such conditions meant our squad was small so I competed in every event in which I might score a single point, some times as many as seven events in a dual meet. We developed a toughness and resiliency that were of great help later in the decathlon.

The primary factor is how the coach and the team members perceive and interpret the situation. Such attitudes may be quite unrelated to the actual situation and emerge out of the individual's innate optimism or negativism, or out of a reaction to one seemingly unimportant aspect of the situation to which the individual has a strong bias for or against. Such biases are of all kinds: the provincial attitudes of the student body, of the local townspeople, or of one's roommate; the size and atmosphere of the town; the religious or social conservatism of one's associates; the food and sleeping conditions; or to shift the focus, the extent to which the coach reminds the athlete of his own father or of a former coach. All the ingenuity of an expert leader of men may be unable to establish a mutually supportive relationship if the athlete is personally hostile out of his own preconceptions.

GOALS (ENDS AND MEANS). Success in coaching comes in so many forms and by way of so many methods that a summary is not feasible. But one way to a successful beginning--however "successful" is defined--includes a detailed listing of goals and the means of their attainment, all in order of priority.

Such a plan helps to create a charisma of wholeness and integrity as related to the coach, his relationships and methods. Others know where he stands, what he believes in. He's all-of-one-piece, so to speak. He follows what can be called a hierarchy-of-value system in which lesser values are judged, and decisions made, as they relate to the first-priority value. Having a basis for judgment, decisions--even those of vital importance--can be made quickly, surely and soundly.

Of the coaches described in Chapter 4, Jumbo Elliott of Villanova University was the most successful in terms of world-level champions in media events--Olympics, invitational indoor meets, ICAAAA championships, Penn Relays. Judged by this goal--though restrained by his "genuine interest in the welfare of his boys," as described by his own Olympic champion, Charlie Jenkins--Elliott evidenced a one-value system of goals, not only as a coach but as a man. He was a winner in whatever caught his interest and energies. He was a big winner in his earth-moving machinery business, a winner in golf and among its followers, a winner as fund-raiser for his University, a winner in his Church and Community relationships--all within socially accepted rules of the game though interpreted "realistically" by a competitive market-place standard. From his first year as a coach, Elliott knew where he wanted to go, and followed a clear road map of how to get there.

Within a competitive industrial society such as the United States is today, the Elliott-Villanova example is most likely to gain media recognition and social approval. A different example of mutually supportive ends and means can be found, all too rarely, within institutions and communities that focus their primary objectives on what can be called a liberal education: development of well-rounded individuals toward a better society. I think of my present home-town, Swarthmore (Pa.) High School. During the past half century, over 90 percent of its students have gone on to colleges with high-level academic requirements. Its winning record in all sports has been excellent, but winning was only a means to a more important end--a well-rounded education.

Of the college coaches I have known, Brutus Hamilton, University of California at Berkeley (1932-1965), best exemplified such a broader-based and less-controlled system. Note that when winning is the goal, the individual must adjust to the system; when education is the goal, the system in all its phases tends to adjust to the multiple demands of each unique individual--a much more difficult task. Hamilton's goals were clearly centered on his many boys. His biographer, Lawrence J. Baack, makes that clear time after time. Above all else, he was an educator, a teacher, a worker with college students. Winning was important, but as a motivator toward excellence, not at all as an end in itself. Though chosen as United States Head Olympic Coach, he once valued his leadership "as refraining from interference with the normal progress of the boys." Idealistic? Impractical? Read Chapter 4 and make up your own mind. For me, I have never known a man with such well-integrated goals or well-ordered approach to life-- within himself, his university family, or with his much-respected boys.

Elliott and Hamilton differed widely in the basic orientation of their goals. But they were alike in that they lived well-ordered lives, followed well-ordered goals, used well-ordered means in seeking those goals. Both were fortunate to coach in universities and communities whose ends and means were supportive of their own. Had they exchanged social environments, both would have been misplaced, less successful, and much less satisfied.

In contrast to these examples of success and well-ordered planning, think of the descriptive phrases one tends to use for the unsuccessful coach: lack of organization, inability to plan, disoriented as to the attitudes and mores of other persons or related institutions, an uncer-tainty of mind and action, a man with problems, lacking in self-confidence. Such a man has goals; in fact he undoubtedly suffers from an excess of goals, centripetal goals that lead away from center at almost any tangent.   Or such a man may be well-integrated within him-self as to his ends and means, but finds he's not at all on the same wave length with his institution and community. His goals in the various phases of coaching are not their goals. Their conception of the ways and means of sport just doesn't tune in with his methods. Result--failure and all that goes with it.

At first thought, the problem of integrating one's goals would seem to be much easier for a coach in such planned societies as the USSR or East Germany. There sport is openly regarded as an arm of government and party policy. Sport and those that take part in sport tend to be a means to a one-value system of Communist success. Whatever problems may arise; whatever decisions must be reached, can all be related to that one pre-eminent goal.

THE DYNAMICS OF INDIVIDUALITY. Only in recent years have there been serious scientific efforts to discover the infinite ways in which individuals vary from each other. Though his concern was not for sports, Roger J. Williams (1956, 1967) has contributed greatly to our understanding in this important field. At least three of his conclusions are of practical use to coaches:
1. Both structurally and functionally, individuals are uniquely different in all aspects of their being. Only lack of sufficiently sensitive measuring devices prevents full documen-tation. We accept the statement that no two fingerprints are identical, and use the fact in practical ways. In supporting his assumption that similar variability is present in all struc-tures and functions, Williams gives numerous examples of anatomical variations in heart, stomach, liver, colon, respiratory tract, hand and face nerve patterns, blood composition, and many more; as well as functional variations in nutrition.

2. To speak of normal persons has its uses. Actually, there are no entirely normal persons, or better, no persons that are within the range of normality in all structures and functions. Williams gives many examples of abnormal organs and systems in normal people, and suggests that all of us have such abnormalities. Such deviation helps us to understand the so-called peculiarities of athletes. For example, in studying the characteristics of marathon runners, Ernst Jokl[1] and others have reported that though one might describe the typical marathon runner in various aspects of body size, weight, heart action, age, intelligence, blood chemistry, etc., many men evidence characteristics that must be considered deviates from the normal. In each case, success is achieved through compensating factors, including training, which bring balance and effectiveness to the whole.

3. The common practice of classifying individuals under group names and programs is necessary--necessary to understanding, to communication of ideas, and to overall organization. But the moment such categories are used in actual practice, specific individuality becomes a crucial consideration. Williams gives the example of the important uses of norms and types as they relate to human eye structure and function. But application of such knowledge requires the services of an expert oculist to prepare glasses precisely ground to the precise needs of the individual eye. The same basic approach must be made to the problems of track and field. Examples will be given from three areas: nutrition, heat-humidity, altitude.

a. NUTRITION. We tend to assume that a well-balanced diet is fully adequate for every "normal" athlete. We assume that there is a natural "wisdom of the body" that will select what it needs and can do so adequately for all the high-level needs of sport. But Williams cites experiments that support his thesis that "(1) each human individual has quantitatively a distinctive pattern of nutritional needs, (2) from individual to individual, specific needs may vary several fold, and (3) important deficiencies may exist that have not been discoverable clinically by observing acute outward symptons."

b. HEAT-HUMIDITY. In 1959, in the USA-USSR dual meet in Philadelphia, the four competitors in the 10,000-meter run were assumed to be of similar ability and condition. But performance varied greatly--one man finished strongly, one dropped out, and two were widely separated at various stages of the race. This great variation in performance was brought about by one factor in the situation: their varying capacities to run under the conditions of 85 degree temperature and 78 percent humidity. The winner, Desyatchikov, held up well, though obviously affected. Bob Soth had some spectators in tears as he fought for several laps in the weird, high-stepping and backward-leaning style of a man undergoing heat exhaustion. He finally dropped and was helped from the track. Pyarnokivi showed similar signs of collapse but stayed on the track to the finish. Truex, more experienced than Soth, slowed down as he felt the effects of heat, then came on with a thrilling sprint at the finish. In summary, their race patterns were specific to their reactions to heat and humidity, not to their over-all conditioning and ability.

c. ALTITUDE. The Mexico City Olympic Games provided numerous examples of specific reactions to high altitudes. Quite obviously, training at altitude improved response to it. But though in some instances the kind and amount of training seemed identical, actual performance in the Games was specific to each individual. Some were able to adapt more readily than others.

SUMMARY. Men are both alike and uniquely different. Our common humanness and our biochemical individuality are two sides of one coin; which side we focus on depends on the purpose and situation. As we focus on alikeness, we construct training systems, well-balanced diets, programs of competition, team goals, or patterns of attitudes ahd behavior. As we focus on uniqueness, we must adapt these systems and goals and attitudes to the special needs of the individual. The art of coaching includes both aspects. But since a coach can adopt the plans and methods of others the real art of coaching is one of individual application.

---

[1] Ernst Jokl, M.D., "Response of Body to Distance Running," *The Amateur Athlete,* Feb. 1955, p.24.

Chapter 3
COACHING — PERSONS AND MECHANICS

Strictly speaking, there can be no track and field coaches, only coaches (teachers) of young men and women in the training methods and techniques of track and field, and in mutually supportive relationships with many other persons. To say it differently, effective coaching requires a balance--a vital balance--between expertise in working with persons and expertise in the technology of our sport (Line A-D, Figure 3.1).

In its review of the development of track and field knowledge, Chapter One made clear that during our first 100 years serious study was related perhaps 90 percent to the technology side of this vital balance, only about 10 percent to the human side. Consider the time-energy devoted to physiology, anatomy, kinesiology, biomechanics, and especially engineering as related to facilities and equipment. Now contrast the paucity of serious time-energy directed toward the improvement of mutually supportive human relationships in track and field coaching.

The concept of mutually supportive relationships, so basic to the human side, is complex and needs research just as much as does biomechanics or physiology. From such relationships each member gains and derives satisfactions, not as the prime mover (coach, organizer, management) decides, but as each member feels and determines his own best interests-needs-goals-values. That's the major difference between autocratic and democratic leadership.

Coaches vary from aardvark to zygote in both the "who" and the "how" of such relationships. Chapter 4 will illustrate this. But all successful coaches have been effective--somehow, someway-- in working with people. It is the intent of this Chapter to use the graph of Figure 3.1 as a first effort toward a more analytic study of the human side of coaching. It seeks the meanings of individual squares suggesting individual coaching styles. But the crucial purpose is to emphasize those styles that lie along the line (A-D, Figure 3.1) of vital balance between the human and the technological sides.

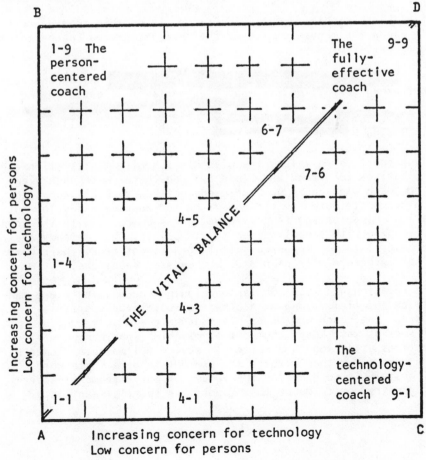

Fig. 3.1 The Vital Balance (line A-D) between expertise in technology and in working with numerous and varied persons. Horizontal lines show increasing concern for technology (training methods, techniques and the related sciences); vertical lines, increasing concern for persons.

Effective coaching seeks a balance between the two, as in the squares 4-3, 4-5, 7-6, 6-7 that lie along the A-D balance line. Only as we approach the fully effective coach (9-9) is there integration of both at highest levels.

31

VALUES AND LIMITATIONS OF A COACHING GRAPH

The primary purpose and value of this graphic approach is to urge the importance of clarifying goals and the means for achieving them. It is not to describe precisely modelled ways of coaching to be emulated by the coach-in-training. If certain coaching styles, such as a 1-9 or a 9-1 style, are highlighted, they are intended only to suggest basic patterns among an infinity of possible patterns by which coaches can develop what Douglas McGregor called "managerial climates," or what Rensis Likert called "mutually supportive relationships".

To form any useful theory, such as attempted here, the relevant words and viewpoints must be clearly defined so that explanations and understandings can be on an intelligent basis. But such definitions are arbitrarily in support of theory assumptions. The more precise the definitions, the greater the apparent clarity but also the actual delusion. Real situations are not so readily packaged. Real coaches just cannot be squeezed into such neat squares as outlined in a grid. No real-life coach conforms precisely to any description of a 1-9 or 9-3 coaching method. Each coach is uniquely and infinitely himself, just as each athlete-team-school-situation is uniquely and infinitely itself. Each is beyond precise description.

But patterns of coaching can be discerned; climates of relationships can be distinguished. To understand those patterns and relationships enables the coach-in-training to choose better patterns for himself and thereby develop a better product of both coach and athlete. He and his coaching situation will establish the precise "what" and "how" and "how much" in choosing between concern-for-persons and concern-for-sport-methods-and-techniques.

THE 1-9 COACHING STYLE

The coach that follows a 1-9 style is described as having a low-level concern for the sport of track and field in terms of maximum performance and winning, and so of the many ways these are brought about: training methods, techniques, equipment and facilities, competitive program and all the rest. In contrast, his highest-level "9" rating indicates a high concern for his boys. But the nature of this concern is limited by his lack of personal enthusiasm and commitment to his sport, and his low esteem for his job as a coach. This means his concern for athletes-as-persons is more for their goodwill and approval than for their full development through the challenges and hardships of track and field training and competition.

COACHING RELATIONSHIPS IN THIS STYLE. As pointed out by McGregor, leadership in any social situation is always a relationship among the many elements of that situation: the coach-athlete-institution-community-culture, in a variety of ways.

In his relations with his boys, the 1-9 coach thinks of himself as a friend, as an educator, as one who educes performance rather than compelling it, who is primarily interested in the health and character values of sport. For such a coach, losing is no disgrace, in fact, has character-building uses of comparable value to those of winning: "One of the essentials of sport is to be a good sportsman in losing."

Such a coach will have mutually supportive relationships with his school administration and community members only if their objectives for track and field are consistent with such viewpoints. Then they will ask, not how much winning he has achieved, but how much his approach and method of program organization has contributed to the education and character development of his boys. His assumption of a low value for sports participation as compared with the academic phases of school life is in keeping with school-community viewpoints. His demands are few and easily met. His boys are never late for supper or too fagged to eat or do their homework. His training program does not interfere with plans for weekends or vacations.

What schools would seek a close relationship with such a non-winning coach? There are many high schools and colleges where track and field along with other non-spectator sports is simply not a matter of major concern. The coach who keeps his charges reasonably content, who keeps them busy in a recreational sort of way, keeps them out of mischief and in no way disruptive to the community, often retires after long and faithful service following a dinner at which the principal, the team, and even a few team mothers are present to give forth words of praise. To denigrate this coaching style is to question the values of our intramural sports programs so highly praised in our country, or to doubt that "sport for sport's sake" is a worthy motivation.

On the other hand, if a 1-9 coach finds himself in a school or community more typical of what American attitudes are presumed to be--develop character but win; educate but win; have fun but win--his coaching relationships will be much less mutually supportive and his job as coach much less secure. He will never be given a coach-of-the-year award. The news media will totally ignore his program. His community will not point with pride or attend the home competitions. In summary, such a 1-9 coach without supportive relationships will have to go it alone, finding his satisfactions in the pleasant, low-tension associations with those of his boys that have similar low-keyed ambitions in his sport.

CONCERN FOR ATHLETES AS PERSONS IN THE 1-9 STYLE. The concern of the 1-9 coach for his athletes as persons is based on a low estimate of their energy and talent capacities. He assumes limited vital energies and, if training and competition for track and field make copious demands, the energies and enthusiasm for the more primary purposes of education, academic studies, will be lessened and even insufficient. He believes time-energy for studies is vital and that he can serve his role best by a policy of non-interference with such study. He assumes that high pressures for winning and record-breaking work against high performance as students.

He therefore is non-authoritarian in his coach-athlete relations. His job is to help them help themselves in the ways and at the stress-levels they seem to prefer. Likert emphasized "a feeling of supportive relationships," as being even more crucial for the achievement of goals than their actual presence. The 1-9 coach is so concerned about how his boys feel toward him and his work assignments that he is inclined to be over-cautious and to expect a lower level of training even if that means a lower level of performance.

The 1-9 coach is invariably likeable. He is interested in his boys' life problems. He coaches by gentle persuasion, by giving reasons for his methods, and by sugar-coating such unpleasant requirements as cannot be avoided. He tries to distinguish between what the athlete does that is unsatisfactory and what he is as a person; the former can be criticized; but loyalty to the latter is never suspect. In return, of course, he expects personal loyalty from his boys and is deeply disturbed when such loyalty is not given.

The 1-9 coach may be emotionally upset about losing; hard not to in our win-centered culture. But he protects his boys. "You made a great effort. That's what really counts--in track and in life. Being a good loser is just as important as winning. Don't let it bother you. We'll do even better next time. Congratulations."

Such a coach assumes that his boys want to do well, do try to make their best effort. He seldom blames them for not trying, and would certainly defend them from any charge of quitting. Such charges would create personal antagonisms, and reduce his effectiveness as a coach and friend.

A 1-9 coach seldom has written or precisely stated rules of training off-the-track. He expects his boys to act as they know they should simply because he believes they are well-intentioned. He prefers that whatever training rules are operative should be set up by the team and policed by the team. If he is forced to discipline a team member, he does so on behalf of the team, not because "my rules are broken" or "my authority is challenged." He avoids checking on his boys and punishing them, and thus avoids resentments and team divisiveness such actions might bring forth.

COACHING METHODS IN THE 1-9 STYLE. The leadership approach of the 1-9 style coach tends to be by consensus, not by personal authority. He says, "This is our team or your team, never my team." High team morale is a focal concern, but "high" should be interpreted at the level of having fun while playing the game more than as the high morale required of high-risk adventure.

The 1-9 coach provides opportunities--movies, books, clinics--by which team members can see and learn sound methods and techniques, but allows them to choose or reject without coercion from him. Encouragement and having fun are major concerns. He's adept in informal conversations, at joking and telling stories, and quick with an understanding smile and pat on the back--an altogether charming fellow. When vaguely defined rules are not followed, he tends to assume the offender will straighten himself out, with only a gentle reminder from the coach that he's always ready to be helpful if asked.

Though anxious to get along with everyone, including school and community critics, the 1-9 oriented coach tends to reject pressures for winning and record-breaking that go beyond the wishes and best interests of his boys. His endurance training program is therefore at energy-pain levels generally considered acceptable and healthful, but avoids--and resents the practice when done by other coaches--any demand for time-energy-pain that might be considered excessive.

For the most part, teaching techniques will not be the forte of the 1-9 coach. More experienced team members will be expected to teach beginners, or, if available, the assistant coach is given this assignment. The head coach would tend to stay in one spot on the track where he could work with numbers of men rather than serving the time-consuming needs of field-event athletes.

GOALS IN THE 1-9 COACHING STYLE. Perhaps the most important function in the coaching enterprise is related to goals. What are we trying to accomplish in this sport? How high can we climb in the time and under the conditions allowed us? What demands on our time-energy-commitment do such goals require? What other interests must be curtailed, even eliminated? All this needs to be done specifically and clearly, and it is vital to know how such general goals are to be sought. Ends are almost meaningless unless we know the specific means. In fact, ends and means are inseparable--two aspects of a single process.

The primary goal of the 1-9 oriented coach is to get along with people--with his administrative superiors, with his community, with his peers in the coaching profession, and above all, with his boys on the track team. He seeks an integration of goals with each of these groups by working within their self-chosen goals. To impose, coerce, or even strongly induce goals of his own preference on others would be personally out of character and worrisome.

Team goals and individual goals would be considered helpful, even essential to everyone's success, but these should be goals reached by consensus: challenging but within rather easy grasp, so as to gain team support with a minimum of argument and discord.

Depending on the situation, a 1-9 coach would probably emphasize dual meets with local schools having a similar viewpoint for sport. Dual meets are non-controversial, are ignored by the news media, are low-tension affairs--for the team members and the coach. Such a coach is unlikely to develop individual star athletes; they require an expertise in methods and techniques he does not have. Further they tend to be disruptive within the team, require special attention, special equipment, special meets in which they can get equal competition. In contrast, dual meets can be won by encouraging large numbers of boys to participate, by keeping them happily interested with no painful demands or competitive tensions. Being local, they cost little, so that large numbers can be handled on a low budget and without disruption of administrative routines. The coach's superiors are likely to be satisfied, even though not enthusiastic or bursting their chest buttons with pride.

Team and individual goals can be high under even a 1-9 coach, depending on the ambition and energy of the team, of the team captain or even of some local enthusiast. Team meetings could be held at which goals could be agreed on well above those the 1-9 coach might choose on his own. Success could follow, success that might carry over into next year and the year after. School and community enthusiasm might be aroused and even an expectation of winning created. Since the 1-9 coach wants, above all else, to get along with people, he can join in wholeheartedly. But not as a genuine forerunner.

MANAGING CONFLICT IN THE 1-9 STYLE. Disagreements and conflicts within the team family disclose the basically weak position of the 1-9 coach. His overriding concern for the good opinions of others makes quick and stern decisions too upsetting to face. His disparagement of winning as an all-or-nothing goal puts him at odds with many strong voices in the community. His lack of knowledge and expertise in track and field, the thing for which his athletes should respect him, diminishes whatever self-esteem he may have. As a result he tends to avoid all direct confrontation in the early stages of opposition, and then appeases or compromises when it can no longer be avoided.

If the 9-1 coach tends to suppress conflict, the 1-9 coach tries to smooth it over, to get along with whoever or whatever is causing it, to talk it over as a reasonable man, and not to fight anyone for any reason. Under such a coach, important issues are seldom settled. An outwardly friendly attitude prevails but important grievances continue on to surface later when conditions worsen.

SUMMARY. In summary, the 1-9 oriented coach is highly concerned with human relations, but in only a partial way. He wants to get along with them as they are, more than pushing them toward what they can become. He has a low estimate of student-athlete energies and willingness to accept discomfort and hardship--in track and field as well as life in general. What is drained away in one area diminishes what can be done in other areas.

The 1-9 coach tries to help the development of his boys, but within the limits of their own estimates and their own sentivity to the pains of fatigue and day-after-day-after-day training. Enjoying the game is more important than peak performance.

Like the 9-1 and 9-9 coach, he also wants to win, but not at high cost; in fact, not at any cost that his boys or his friends might consider excessive. If, by way of illustration, we refer to the Dedication of this OMNIBOOK, page iv , the 1-9 coach would be greatly concerned about the avocational nature of amateur, that is, school-college sports. He would respect the first priority of student work (studies), make time-energy demands within what was left over, and would not wish to interfere in any way with their requirements. Within those limits, the 1-9 coach might urge an athlete's best efforts but lacks the interest or expertise in training methods and techniques that would make such efforts successful in the larger fields of competition.

THE 9-1 COACHING STYLE.
In the symbol, "9-1" the hyphen is important as indicating a relationship--perhaps of balance, perhaps of imbalance--between two complex tendencies. How that relationship is developed, within what climate of attitudes and feelings, is the crux of any given coaching style.

The two competing tendencies in the 9-1 style are (1) a primary concern for winning performance and its rewards, and (2) a low concern for athletes as persons, with all the wide-ranging conflict of interests and energies that the word "persons" implies. The excessive need to win makes of this coach an exacting taskmaster in training for endurance and strength, often an expert in event techniques, facilities, equipment, or in whatever improves performance and the chances of winning, with special emphasis on the recruitment of outstanding talent.

The overall climate of relationship between the 9-1 coach and his athletes tends to be one of opposition and even distrust. He assumes they will work at levels below his needs, and so must be driven or given material rewards of some kind if they are to measure up. He assumes they will break his training rules if given a chance, and so contrives checks and punishments to ensure conformance. He believes their goals as persons with many interests beyond sport are inevitably detrimental to highest performance and winning, and so must be set aside.

The successful 9-1 coach knows the importance of motivation for both competition and training. If he does so begrudgingly at least possible levels, he can be classified as a true 9-1 coach. On the other hand, if he is aware of modern research in industry that concludes a high concern for persons is the best way of increasing production and profit, he may treat his athletes on a first class basis, give them the best of everything, but all for the primary end of winning. Should he relax, discover the satisfactions of helping athletes achieve their own personal goals apart from track and field, he would then be classified as a 9-3 or 9-5 coach. Once again, we remind ourselves that we are interested in describing general patterns of behavior, not in pigeonholing individual coaches.

COACHING RELATIONSHIPS IN THE 9-1 STYLE. The need for a supportive surround is just as important for this as for any style of coaching. But since our culture tends to accept the preeminence of winning as a goal, such supportive relationships are easy to establish. Even where a school or community has no tradition or awareness of such winning viewpoints, a 9-1 coach can usually discover a few enthusiasts to further his winning ways. Once the values of success become apparent by way of the news media and town talk, supporters will multiply amazingly.

In fact, the 9-1 oriented style of coaching may initiate its program by seeking first the support of community and other outside groups and individuals for a greatly expanded program of track and field. This year's team may be neglected so that coaching energies can be more profitably employed. At the college level this takes many forms: improving the local facilities, equipment and home-meet program, raising funds with which more attractive away-meets can be attended, securing scholarships, finding low-energy high-pay jobs, increasing booster-club funds for supplementary financial help, enrolling bird dogs in the broadest possible recruiting fields to help flush out the quarry; all this of course within the written rules of the governing body, though with more concern for getting caught than for observing the spirit of the rules, and all for the purpose of recruiting talent.

At the high achool level, the coaching style would be the same, though limited by the much more restricted supervision and scope of operation. In some areas, recruiting athletes from junior high schools and from nearby school districts is becoming almost as excessive as in college ranks. Highly talented athletes are absolutely essential to the goal of winning of the 9-1 coach. Their development by means of the participation of hundreds of prospective athletes is a far-too-slow and uncertain process. Neither the coach nor his backers can be so patient. He therefore recruits talent, by paying for it in whatever ways are required. Having paid them--within the rules of course--he can and does make demands on the time-energy-devotion they give to his sport.

The crux of the coach-athlete relationship in the 9-1 style is therefore the exercise of authority by the coach and obedience by the athlete. Until his reputation for success is firmly established, until his athletes feel that first-class rewards will be certain to follow first-class performances, such a demand for obedience may be met reluctantly and even with resistance. Failure in the early years, for whatever reason, may nullify the entire project. Bitterness is sure to follow--against failure and against the dictatorial coach that produced it. Today the local newspaper announced the firing of a high school football coach in mid-season who had demanded much from his team, the school and the town. At first he won, beat the perennial league winner and was carried high on shoulders off the field. But the next few years things went awry--injuries occurred to crucial men, some said through overwork; the coach was misquoted; his critics were loud; things got pretty nasty. He could walk onto the field or scratch his ear and the crowd would boo. After all, the local booster club had to maintain its self respect. When he loses, the 9-1 coach has no friends. But once success is assured everyone prospers and is more than willing to go along with the authoritarian mode. However, the 9-1 coach is unlikely to experience personal friendship with rival coaches, because his urge-to-win makes the field of play a battleground and his excessive recruiting and demands for maximum training create resentment as being unfair and illegal. Unwritten codes may lead his rival coaches to hide all open resentment and bitterness but few would interpret their smiles as genuine warmth of feeling.

CONCERN FOR ATHLETES AS PERSONS IN THE 9-1 STYLE. Under 9-1 coaching, athletes are regarded as instruments of winning in meets that gain public attention. Regardless of how well he may treat them or reward them for their work they are but the means to the coach's goal of personal success. He values them as athletes and will help them in every way he can as long as their athletic talents contribute to his goal. Whatever he may seem to do for them as persons should be suspect.

If running more miles or at greater intensities more days per week and more weeks per year will produce faster competitive performance, more wins and records and greater public attention, the 9-1 coach will demand it, with little or no concern for the needs of non-sport interests and activities. Time-energy-commitment to anything other than track and field is resented as interference with the all-out commitment to sport, allowed only if required or necessary.

His concern for beginners and non-talented team members is nil, even negative, as they expect him to give them coaching time that might better be used with more productive members. If the school program requires dual meets in which second and third places are helpful, he may tolerate these incompetents, but since they were not recruited and have no scholarships they are independent and not inclined to accede to his more extreme demands.

THE TEAM CONCEPT WITHIN THE 9-1 STYLE. Under the 9-1 style of coaching, the most valid definition of "the team" is an aggregation of individuals drawn together by the coach for a common purpose. The coach is the producer and promoter of the team, outside and not a member of it. If morale is good, reference is to the coach and the team; if morale breaks down, to the coach versus the team. In both cases the team captain serves primarily an honorary role and a sort of go-between for the coach and the team.

Traditionally this has been the role of the captain in colleges and schools. Coaches who believed in the importance of team morale tried to influence as best they could the selection of each year's captain, so as to ensure a man supportive of team tradition and of the coach's policies. Quite often the captain was the coach's agent for preventing or settling disagreements. He received special privileges including dinners at the coach's home. All quite innocent of course, and in keeping with tradition. Up to about 1960 few had questioned that tradition.

Under such a 9-1 coaching style, the team as a group would have little organization, few meetings, and low team morale. Traditionally, two meetings a year were sufficient: the end-of-the-year team banquet and the get-together for the team picture after voting for next year's captain. In fact, where dual meets are minimal and athletes travel to invitational meets separately, as was the custom in the East when the Madison Square and Boston Gardens dominated the indoor season, track teams have no opportunity to get together before or after competition. On one occasion during the early indoor season, I, as coach, actually introduced one runner to the other three members of a relay team after they had reached the Garden! He had practiced separately and travelled on the train separately.

CONCERN FOR PERFORMANCE AND WINNING IN THE 9-1 STYLE. Success of the 9-1 style, both in college and high school, depends primarily on the recruitment of outstanding talent. But outstanding talent, if it is to be developed to its highest levels, requires highest-level methods of training and event techniques. The 9-1 coach must therefore train himself to become expert in these and all other phases of track and field, if he is to be fully effective.

Not only has the 9-1 style of coaching produced some of our most successful coaches as judged by national individual and team championships, record-breaking, Olympic champions, and the like, it has also produced some of our highest authorities as to methods and techniques from both a scientific and practical standpoint. The urge to win may be the primary motivating force, but it has often led to genuine creativeness that has made important contributions to our sport.

GOALS (ENDS & MEANS) IN THE 9-1 STYLE. The all-consuming goal of the 9-1 coach is clear: victory in meets that draw attention to the accomplishments of my boys, my team, my school and myself. The "my" is not an exaggeration insofar as he rates a lowest possible "1" in his concern for others. If the "my" is less blatant, if it takes the form of "our" even occasionally, then he rates a 9-2 or even higher.

The point has been made that the practical nature of goals, as of leadership, depends on relationships; on the kinds of spectator-oriented meets that are available, on the attitudes of the school administration, the alumni, the community, the news media. Ordinarily, the coach's devotion to winning gives him a wide base of support, for our competitive private-enterprise system, the coach and the athletes requires the athletes to support the system, regardless of their personal goals. Some kind of compensation is therefore essential, and so the prevalence of scholarships as reward and the threat of their withdrawal as punishment. The 9-1 style tends to produce a business-enterprise climate focussed on production and profit for the enterprise.

But in recent years, the financial support so essential to the 9-1 college coach has been gradually withdrawn. Greatly increased expenses have caused college administrators to concentrate their resources among the income-producing sports, of which track and field is rarely one. If this trend continues, the path of the 9-1 coach will lead to something less than his goal of personal glory.

MANAGING CONFLICT IN THE 9-1 STYLE. Just as the 9-1 coach tends to be authoritarian in his high concern for performance and winning, so is he authoritarian in his handling of conflicts between himself and team members or among team members. Whatever interferes with the primary goal of winning and attention-getting performance must be dealt with decisively.

In a recruited-team situation in which the coach has the power to withdraw scholarships, serious disagreements are not tolerated. In a non-recruited situation, as in most high schools, the tradition of coaching authority may allow this same dictatorial way of settling disputes. In a more democratically-oriented school or college, the 9-1 style must learn to be flexible, conceding a setback or two in order to maintain its basic position of dominance.

The overall climate of relationships in this style tends to make all differences personal.

37

The coach must prove himself right and all others wrong; the others tend to react similarly. Any mistake or defeat produces an emotional reaction and the least hint of criticism is taken personally. The 9-1 coach has a low tolerance for human frailty. Arnie Sowell of Pittsburgh was potentially an all-time Great in world half-miling, the probable winner of the Olympic Championship. Even today, I can hear with a feeling of distaste the "chewing out" that his coach gave him following a bad preliminary race in the Nationals. Arnie was sent home immediately with no chance to even see the finals. I've often wondered what he would have done under a 9-9 coaching style, a style that the Pitt coach would have considered "soft" and "pampering."

THE 9-9 COACHING STYLE
The salient feature of the 9-9 style of coaching leadership lies not so much in the charisma of the man, important as that is, as in the mutually supportive relationships he establishes among all sectors of the team family. Four viewpoints are inherent:

1. The vital energies of men are far more capable of development to higher and broader levels of daily energizing than is commonly realized. When energy development is by gradual increments of stress, daily work at the higher levels of one's potential energies requires no more hours of sleep and rest than does lower-level work, and need not interfere with the time-energy-commitment given to other activities.

2. Integration of the goals, means and attitudes of the various members of the track family is essential; all can achieve their goals best by attitudes and efforts that are mutually supportive.

3. Highest-level performance and winning at both the individual and team levels are important, even indispensable, but important as means to seeking the educational or developmental goals of the athlete and the institution, not as the dominant ends of sport.

4. For a coach to extend full respect and concern for others, he must first have achieved full respect and esteem for himself. Modern psychologists (Erich Fromm, Abraham Maslow, Gardner Murphy and many others) are in agreement on this point. In fact, Maslow[1] makes it an essential element in his description of what he calls self-actualizing people.

THE ENERGIES OF MEN. In 1904 William James wrote the essay, *The Energies of Men*, which, after numerous reprints,[2] has become the classic statement on the subject:

Compared with what we ought to be, we are only half awake. Our fires are damped, our drafts are checked. We are making use of only a small part of our possible physical and mental resources....

But the very same individual, pushing his energies to their extreme, may in a vast number of cases keep the pace up day after day, and find no reaction of a bad sort, so long as decent hygienic conditions are preserved. His more active rate of energizing does not wreck him; for the organism adapts itself, and as the rate of waste augments, augments correspondingly the rate of repair....

Stating the thing broadly, the human individual...energizes well below his maximum as well as below his optimum.

The history of track and field in our world over the past century discloses a gradually developing realization of the truth of James' insights, though undoubtedly to extremes of energizing well beyond those James would have deemed sustainable by normal human beings. In my personal experience over the past 50 years, each generation has used the same words to express a common feeling: "Track coaches can properly demand this level of time-energy-commitment from their boys. But no more than this level! To expect more is to jeopardize studies, social duties and health." But within that same generation some coach-athlete has demonstrated

---

[1] Abraham H. Maslow, *MOTIVATION AND PERSONALITY*, New York: Harper & Row, 1954, pp. 199-260.

[2] John J. McDermott, *THE WRITINGS OF WILLIAM JAMES*, New York: The Modern Library, pp. 671ff.

higher levels were quite attainable without additional sleep and rest, and without unreasonable interference with other activities. In the 1920s I remember Pennsylvania's Lawson Robertson's condemnation of Stanford's Dink Templeton for "burning out" his runners. In the 1930s Charlie Hoyt of Michigan had adopted Templeton's level of energizing but now was criticizing Billy Hayes of Indiana for his work schedules of greater mileage and intensity of training than ever before. Today, Hayes' program would be thought inadequate. In 1983, a Polish training program for the shot put recommended 5-7 hours of related training on one day each week.

My main point is that this rise in acceptable energizing applies, not just to track training, but to life in general. The rate of restoration increases along with the rate of use. If training increases are carefully gradual a college or high school boy of will and enthusiasm can take part successfully in the most rigorous of sports such as running or swimming, have time for studies, and live a normal student life with several hobbies on the side. Just yesterday on TV I watched an All-Conference college football player as he practiced the piano preparing himself for a concerto concert in New York City. He had played the piano and some form of football since he was five years old. To do both, along with studies and other activities was his way of life, certainly nothing to get excited about. "I'd be bored if I wasn't busy all the time. No, I don't feel I have unusual talent or vitality. It's just that I started early and got the habit."

That is the crux, and the excellence, of the 9-9 coaching style. Such a coach conveys to the athlete a high expectation of excellence in all phases of his life, not just in athletics. He knows that the main dangers of stress arise from the negative emotions: self-doubt, fear of failure, worry, inability to "burn away" by physical activity the wastes of stress; and in trying to do too much too soon, before the person is prepared to properly handle such a high level of stress. Such a coach accepts Hans Selye's warning[1] that the vital energies of men are limited and, once depleted, cannot be restored, but is quietly sure that careful and wise use of modern training methods will not encroach on such dangerous levels. The purpose of every training program is to develop powers of recovery greater than the training stress and so increase resistance to competitive stress. A coach would be a fool to provide stresses for which the athlete is unprepared and so result in negative returns. A 9-9 coach carefully and scientifically, insofar as feasible, measures out his dosages of stress to ensure the fulfillment of his high-level expectations.

THE PRINCIPLE OF INTEGRATION. The third principle underlying the 9-9 coaching style is that of integration: the organization of the conditions of competition and training so that the efforts of the coaching enterprise as a whole and those of its individual members are integrated and mutually supportive. The special meaning of this principal in the 9-1 and 1-9 styles of coaching has been described as workable only if the individual members conform to the system; as, in industry, workers conform to the goals of business enterprise for greater production and profit.

In the 9-9 coaching style, integration takes on a new dimension: a dimension of freedom between equals, or better, of freedom within the restraints of inter-dependence of the many parts of one entity. We might call that entity, "the track team family," including the culture-community-school-coach-athletes. Since each of the members of any interdependent relationship must accept a degree of restraint in the full achievement of goals, major conflict is likely to arise unless all members feel that on balance and in the long run this is the best way. Once the restraints are accepted by everyone (especially the coach and his supporters), inter-personal tensions relax and a climate of freedom of action and attitude prevails.

Such an integration between equal partners in a common enterprise implies that the lower level needs (physiological-safety-social) of Maslow's hierarchy are acceptably taken care of and that concentration on the higher levels of esteem (self-esteem and esteem of others) and self-actualization (working toward one's potentials) can become paramount to all members of the team family. To the school, this means that winning is important, but important as a means to the ends of better education and greater service to the educational needs of its members, in and out of school. To the individual athlete, this means that he can achieve his goals best by working with the coach and within the school sport system. Mutual support would

---

[1]Hans Selye, THE STRESS OF LIFE, New York: McGraw-Hill Book Co., Inc., 1956, 324 pages.

be inherent in the situation; suspicion that one was being used by the other for selfish purposes just wouldn't be in the air.

Achieving such integration is not primarily a matter of precise tactics or special methods. These will vary greatly with the overall situation (cultural and institutional), the team, and the coach. The importance of the attitudes of all concerned cannot be over-emphasized: they must all seek diligently to establish a spirit of mutual trust, respect, and confidence.

THE COACH-AS-PERSON IN THE 9-9 COACHING STYLE. Crucial to the 9-9 coaching style is the fourth concept that a coach can extend full concern for others insofar as he has achieved full respect for himself. At first thought, this seems to suggest narcissism and excessive self-concern. But in his fascinating booklet, THE ART OF LOVING, Erich Fromm makes clear that,

Whoever is capable of giving of himself is rich; the more he is able to give, the richer he becomes....But in giving he cannot help bringing something to life in the other person, and this...reflects back to him....It is clear that respect (for others) is possible only if I have achieved independence: if I can stand and walk without needing crutches, without having to dominate and exploit anyone else.[1]

Men having such self-respect tend not to worry about themselves or about the basic needs of safety, shelter, esteem from others or belongingness that, according to Maslow, are common to men generally. Their overall orientation is positive and optimistic--toward more and better and greater challenges, with little or no anxiety about all the negatives that might occur. All my life I have idolized Robert Falcon Scott and his companion, Edward Wilson, who starved and froze to death following their desperate attainment of the South Pole in 1912. Despite the deep disappointment of finding that the Norwegian, Roald Amundsen, had beaten them to the Pole, Scott's last diary notes expressed no rancor against his bad luck, or against those who had failed to establish food depots for their return; rather, a calm acceptance of the situation and deep admiration for the "everlasting cheerfulness and courage" of his companions. "We have decided to die naturally in the track....We could have got through had we neglected our sick."

This may seem an extreme example, somewhat far afield from track athletics, but it makes the point clearly. Once full commitment is made to the task and to others, concern for one's own selfish interests is no longer operative. Almost any biography of a track coach or athlete illustrates the point. Self-esteem? Of course, more than most humans. Great achievement would be almost unthinkable without a belief in oneself. But with it, a selflessness or unconcern for self that makes it possible to focus outwardly on the goal and on others.

COACHING AUTHORITY IN THE 9-9 STYLE.
If it is to be effective, the 9-9 style of coaching entails authority; without authority, both leadership and program will founder. But such authority tends to be indirect or as symbol of some higher authority. Among those relevant to track and field we can cite: (1) authority of tradition and institution, (2) authority of team agreements, (3) authority of commitment to excellence, and (4) authority of coaching competence.

In contrast to the 9-1 style, such authority is not authoritarian. The authority of the 9-9 coach seldom requires unquestioning obedience, and even then it is to the situation, not to the coach. It derives its force more from the climate of felt relationships--mutual trust and purpose--than from fear of punishment.

This does not imply approval of the British tradition of centering authority in the team captain, with the coach in a mere advisory capacity, a sort of "help-if-asked" function. This not only rejects authority-as-person but also as representative. Much as though, in our courts of law, we were to reject all authority of the judge, even though it be as symbol of the higher authority of law and order.

Nor does it suggest approval of the 1-9 coaching style in which a "soft" or "laissez-faire" relationship is present. The disciplines of arduous training and high-level competitive

---

[1]Erich Fromm, THE ART OF LOVING, New York, Harper & Brothers Publishing, 1956, p. 28.

performance must be maintained; it's inherent in the sport and in the employment of a coach to do a job. Minimal coaching authority is not a workable alternative to authoritarianism. Decisions must be made, often immediately without waiting for group approval. The Chapter 2 story of McGregor's experience as new president at Antioch makes that clear. But always within the climate of mutual trust or of mutually supportive relationships inherent in the 9-9 style.

THE AUTHORITY OF TRADITION AND INSTITUTION. Man's basic urge toward adventure and risk-activity is in conflict with his basic need for safety. Almost inevitably he seeks solutions by way of the leader, especially the leader who impels him to efforts beyond his own self-confidence, and also assumes a major share of the responsibility for defeat.

In the 1930s, the Pennsylvania State High School Athletic Association sought to reduce both coaching authority and pressures for winning by removing the coach entirely from the playing bench. But many complaints--of the weight of over-responsibility on the boys and of incompetence as related to winning--soon forced them to reverse their action.

The point here is rather obvious and needs little further discussion. Under normal conditions (the 1960-70 tendency to question all authority was quite abnormal)men seek guidance when they enter into new endeavors for which they lack competence. Those who guide them soon acquire a reputation of authority. Their followers must trust that authority, whatever its source, if they are to succeed in their enterprise.

Only when there is betrayal of that trust--as in the Vietnam war, or in the use of University research by those supporting that war, or in the exploitation of college athletes to serve the ambitions of college administrators or coaches--does revolt occur against such authority.

THE AUTHORITY OF TEAM AGREEMENTS. We use the word "team" in the sense of the greater team family. For the establishing of proper conduct is a function of many persons over a long period of time. Such persons include past team members, sports administrators both within and outside the sponsoring institution, parents, members of the local community, and of course the team and coach. This year's team cannot make its own rules exclusive of social tradition. However, once the agreements of such a team family have been established, once they have been discussed, understood, modified perhaps, and accepted by the members of this year's team, they then should take on an authority that is firm and binding. Agreements as to conduct both on and off the field must be adhered to strictly; fairly of course, but without exceptions for special or most-talented members.

Those who punish rule-breakers do so, not to satisfy some unfulfilled need in themselves to rule over others, nor to further their selfish goals; they are merely the agents of the authority of agreements made to achieve the goals of the team, and of its individual members.

THE AUTHORITY OF COMMITMENT TO EXCELLENCE. Every commitment to a program of personal development exacts a loss in personal freedom. Freedom to do one's best in any activity requiring effort assumes, on the one hand, concentration, and on the other, the discipline of all other activities and attitudes that would interfere or distract.

Such discipline is based on an acceptance of authority, though it be only the athlete's freely chosen training schedule. Such a schedule demands that certain work must be done when it needs to be done whether one feels like doing it or not. It has an authority that denies freedom to do as one pleases. Almost every biography of great track or field champions warns that if training is to be successful, it must be adamant in its essentials.

In his biography of Jim Ryun, Nelson describes a situation that illustrates this problem,

During winter (in Jim's high school junior year), State rules did not permit the coach to be with the boy, so Jim came to Timmons in the swimming pool.

All I could do was offer advice and he had to do the approaching....

Once he came to me and I could tell he was down in the dumps. It was the off season and he had been out running in the dark, in the snow and ice and rain, all by himself. There

weren't any other runners out, day after day like that, and it hurt him. And I could see he was beginning to wonder if it was worth it. And I told him, 'Jim, I'm not going to fight you on this. If this goal--the four-minute mile--isn't worth enough to get out and work day after day, then just forget about it. Nobody should browbeat you into achieving anything, as great as the goal may be...But I don't want you to come back at the end and tell me that if I had made you work you could have made it.'

THE AUTHORITY OF COACHING COMPETENCE. Of a thousand evaluations by outstanding athletes of their coaches, the most common adjectives would undoubtedly relate to personal integrity, respect, esteem or trust. But behind the aura of personal worth can be found the persuasive force of competence, what might be called the authority of successful experience.

Faced with such authority, men needing discipline become disciples; the problem disappears. I'm reminded of the comment, "What you've done speaks so clearly, no words are needed." Eamonn Coghlan once said of his coach, Jumbo Elliott, "I feel he coaches and treats his athletes the same way he does his business. He runs a high-class business and he deals with us as high-class athletes...There's no bull. Everything is very honest."

Such authority requires years, including early years in which failure is as frequent as success. Certainly that was true in Elliott's career.

GOALS IN THE 9-9 COACHING STYLE. In his award-winning research on better ways of business management, Rensis Likert studied the nature of highly effective groups in and out of business. Quite clearly their most important characteristic related to goals--clearly stated, long-time and immediate, accepted by common agreement, mutually supportive of the group and its members, challenging but achievable, and requiring the cooperation of all members.

Each member accepts willingly and without resentment the goals and expectations that he and the group establish for themselves. The anxieties, fears, and emotional stresses produced by direct pressure from a boss (authoritarian)...are not present. Such groups seem capable of setting...goals high enough to stimulate each member to do his best but not so high as to create anxieties or fear of failures....Mutual help is an important characteristic.[1]

Clearly, the 9-9 style of coaching must place great emphasis on this goal-centered approach, and give careful consideration to each of the following items.

Setting Goals--Mutually Agreeable and Supportive. Research on the goal-insight approach to coaching track and field is lacking. But related research in social psychology and in business has been extensive. For example, Kurt Lewin concluded from his classic experiment in group dynamics that methods by which the group (including members and leaders) reached its own decisions for changing group behavior were from two to ten times as effective as was a lecture exhorting change. Again, in industry, Hemphill found that the setting of clearly defined goals, not for, but WITH individual workers was the most effective of all devices for increasing production.

Effective coaching will try in many ways to hold team goals, individual goals, and the coach's goals in common, as inseparable aspects of a single complex of goals. Higher authority and long-established traditions may fix the schedule of meets, the budget, facilities, even attitudes within and toward the sport. To this extent, the framework of team goals is already established. But within this framework, team members should feel that they and the coach, working together, have decided what emphasis shall be placed on what meets, how daily practice will be related to that emphasis, what "off-the-field" training rules shall be established and how they shall be policed, how leadership within the team will be organized, how individual differences between team members or between team members and the coach will be resolved, and many other team-centered problems.

Such goal setting WITH the team need not require many long meetings or discussions. Far

---

[1]Rensis Likert, *op. cit.*, p. 168.

better that it emerge out of a sound institutional tradition in sports, and out of sound coach-athlete relationships over the years. Then the fewer the words, the better. Once a climate of mutual empathy and trust surrounds the team family, only a few details need to be agreed on. On the other hand, never take the team's understanding and acceptance of past traditions for granted. During the past decade the very word "tradition" has been moot.

The Integration of Team Goals with Individual Goals. Effective track teams plan programs that provide opportunities for high-level performances by both the team and its individual members. Dual meets and multi-school championships tend toward the first; invitation meets toward the second. But some coaches such as Bill Bowerman, Oregon, used dual meets to serve both purposes. He began by maintaining a large squad of competitors. He then discouraged doubling whenever it might interfere with best-possible performance in the athlete's specialty. "I don't believe there is any danger of physical damage but psychologically I don't think it's a good thing."[1]

THE COACH HELPS THE INDIVIDUAL SET HIS OWN GOALS. Nelson[2] quoted Bob Timmons, who coached championship teams in both high school and college, that the goal-insight system was the most important aspect of his coaching,

Very few noteworthy achievements come about by happenstance. They're accomplishments of thorough planning, determined sacrifice, genuine effort, and continuing hard work, all of which are given direction and purpose by the use of goals. The backbone of our program is in the establishment of goals. We believe that every boy must have a season and a career goal for his event....

Nothing was permitted to hinder their progress toward their goals. To us early season losing wasn't of great concern if the effort is good; and winning isn't good enough unless the performance is the best possible under the circumstances.

Of course, the athlete's belief in the competence and integrity of the coach is absolutely essential. Nelson writes,

When, six months after starting training, Jim ran a mile in 4:26.4, Timmons approached him, smiling and excited, "Jim, you've got a chance to run the mile under four minutes in high school."

The high school record was 4:08. Jim was 15 years old.

Jim's reaction: "Coach, crazy!" And it might have been such. But Timmons had already coached San Romani, had kept accurate records, and could prove that Jim had done better than Archie at the same age and level of experience.

At times, especially with beginners, the coach must lead strongly,

There were times when Timmons talked very straight to Ryun. If it were to take pressure, Timmons would apply it--and Jim accepted it. Later Jim said, "When we started, I wasn't sold on the idea at all. But as time went on and I began to see what the hard work would do, then I began to understand what Timmie was doing." It was tough work.

But ultimately, the athlete has the final veto; only he can decide whether to run or not to run,

"He has to sacrifice," Timmons says, "just the same Spartan life by his own decision. I don't threaten him or force him. I feel that he ought to become the best miler in the world, but it doesn't matter how we outsiders feel. It's all up to Jim. He does the work; he gets the credit. He should make the decisions about himself. He has to decide if he wants to go to the top of the world himself."

---

[1] Joe Henderson, "A Coach and a Tradition," Los Altos, Calif.: *Track & Field News*, I June, 1968, p. 21.

[2] Cordner Nelson, "The Jim Ryun Story,"Los Altos, Calif.: TAFNEWS Press, 1971, pp. 8-44.

A Planned Time and Place. Reaching agreement as to team and individual goals cannot be left to chance or for the right moment to arrive. For the team, it is a group process that requires a regularly scheduled time and place. This allows informal prior discussions so that agreement in most instances is reached by consensus, not by factional argument and majority rule. Certainly, in the 9-9 style, agreement on goals is not gained merely by acceptance of the coach's statement of goals. But in any case, a climate of mutual trust and respect is essential.

Similarly, the setting of individual goals must have a time and place, even though unscheduled. All too often, the coach's office is not convenient to students. All too often the coach has "important work to do," and students hesitate to interfere. All too often the coach lives far off campus so that evening discussions are at least difficult. Brutus Hamilton had a custom of going early to the field, sitting in the first row of the stand away from technical coaching, and waiting for team members to come to him. He told me he had found this one of the best ways of setting up a relaxed one-on-one situation, away from the action-centered practice field, and open to frank discussion of whatever problems the athlete might have on his mind--personal or otherwise. Hamilton's excellent assistant coach, Al Ragan, was always on the field for coaching techniques.

Is the Goal Worth Its Cost? From time to time doubt arises in the mind of every athlete--great and not so great--as to whether the planned goals are really worth their cost in effort and agony and denial of other worthwhile activities or pleasures. Every biography provides examples. George Young was one of the toughest in maintaining his goals during 20 years of running, including four Olympic Games, despite the demands of full-time teaching, of a wife and family, and of a physical environment somewhat adverse to running. His duties required early-morning workouts, usually at 6 so as to be at school on time.

George Young may have been lonely on those early-morning runs through the desert, but he wasn't alone. There were coyotes and lizards and, above all, there were rattlesnakes....Although he never got bitten, the possibility was always there, and he couldn't help thinking about it at times....

The winter was the worst because it would still be dark when he completed his workout and that, he said, "was kind of demoralizing--knowing everyone else was still asleep....[1]

Some times George felt, "This hasn't been a sport for me. It's been an obsession. I'm beginning to feel guilty about the time away from my two kids. I've only been fishing once with my little boy. It's been four years since I took Shirley to a movie.[2]

Was it really worth it? Throughout a full score of years, George Young maintained adamantly that it was, and at the end he was deeply regretful that he could no longer continue. But within that adamancy there were many times of self-doubt and even anxiety, as was indicated by his constant battle with bleeding ulcers. "Hereditary," he said, but we can be sure heredity was aggravated by circumstances.

The important point to be made here is that every coach should be aware of this uncertainty, especially in the minds of beginners and the less-talented, so as to provide the encouragement and proper viewpoint. Is what you're doing today satisfying? Then we need not worry about what might happen next month or next year.

Goals Must be Realistic. I remember one fine prospect who was determined to make the American Olympic team. I encouraged such a goal--one never knows--but as something for the future, three years or even seven years from now. But to the boy it was a daily obsession. The value of each practice and of each competition was judged by its furtherance of his Olympic prospects.

---

[1]Frank Dolson, *ALWAYS YOUNG*, Mountain View, Calif.: World Publications, 1975, p. 138.

[2]*Ibid.*, p. 10.

He was frustrated at his slow progress. His frustration developed into a complex of difficulties. In the end, it was hard to say whether he quit or was requested to leave the team.

Such boys seldom disclose to the coach the hows and whys, or even the goal itself, for fear he may deride them. And therefore the coach will often be at a loss to understand what is going on in the boy's mind. When such a long reach for achievement exceeds the runner's ability to grasp it, his continuing sense of failure may block even those performances that he can do. His goals take on an emotional value far in excess of their real importance; emotion creates tensions which, directly and indirectly, hold him back.

He may blame himself for his failure. He may blame others. He is quite likely to blame the coach, especially if the coach puts forward more reasonable goals, but goals that the boy feels are empty of challenge or will delay his progress toward the goals *he* thinks are really important.

Such cases of over-evaluation of unsound goals are seldom simple. Solutions are likely to be difficult. One or two suggestions based upon my own errors more than my successes might be of interest: (1) be personally concerned about the athlete but not personally involved in his frustrations; (2) try to help the athlete define his problems clearly and matter-of-factly; and (3) help him to keep both the problems and their solutions at the simplest level possible. The tendency of a frustrated athlete and an interested coach is to dig deeper than the situation requires. If attention can be concentrated upon doing well today and tomorrow--and enjoying it--for its own sake, the problem will be well on its way toward solution.

Which reminds us to return to Bob Timmons' statement that "every boy must have a season and a career goal for his event." And we might add, a goal for this week's competition and this day's practice and this work-time-distance. Unless the boy understands and accepts these goals whole-heartedly, his energies in seeking them will be diminished.

High-Level Goals Require Gradual Increments of Effort. The assumption of striving for excellence inherent in the 9-9 coaching style depends on gradual increments of effort. That is, the goal is external--a championship to be won, a record to be achieved. But the means to that goal lies within, in the gradual development of muscle and heart and self-confidence and will, by which progress occurs. A gradual approach to effort is best when related to the entire career of the athletes, most unlikely within our three-stage school system with dissimilar and separated coaching at each stage. Henry Marsh, America's greatest steeplechaser, said, "Bill Bowerman's greatest strength as a coach is his ability to hold you back as he brings you forward." Which reminds me of Bowerman's oft-quoted admonition, "If you can't carry on a conversation when doing mileage work, you're running too fast."

Goals as Commitment. The Dedication of this OMNIBOOK praises those athletes who, within the limitations of time and energy placed by their higher-priority commitment to the studies, vocation or other services, "strive to their utmost to raise performance ever higher, faster, and farther." But we must balance this with the earlier statement on the potentially abundant energies of men with its assumption that, under supportive conditions and motivations, the everyday student-athlete can do all this and all that too, both at high levels. Average men have reservoirs of energy that far surpass common assessments of their capacity.

Unfortunately, few people agree with this concept that we can strive to our utmost in more than one area of action. The time-energies spent here take away from the time-energies properly spent elsewhere. They fail to realize that the rate of restoration increases along with the rate of use. The 4:00-minute miler needs no more hours of sleep and rest than does the 5:00-minute miler. Nevertheless, many a well-balanced individual with potential in track and field is turned away by this "over-emphasis" on dedication to sport. Brian Mitchell suggests that we distinguish between a dedicated attitude and a dedicated life. To dedicate one's life to track and field would be foolish; life has far greater potentials than that. But we can take an attitude of utmost dedication to our sport within its proper merits, without excluding or suppressing the other phases of life.

Following Dave Roberts' world-record pole vault at 18'6½", Jon Hendershott[1] quoted him,

"Actually, my No. 1 priority this year wasn't vaulting--and it still isn't. I've been studying awfully hard in grad school, and I'm applying to medical school. School has been a full time job and I'm trying to vault well, which is also a full-time job. I guess I'm kinda burning the candle at both ends, but it has worked out."

Indeed, for he earned all A's last quarter in school--and his achievements in the other we already know about.

Of course such a multiple commitment must come primarily from within. Most persons acquire it during the first years of life from the climate of action and attitude in their home-community-school. If it's not there, neither the stick nor the carrot can create it. But an effective 9-9 coach can do much to nourish and encourage its development.

ACHIEVED GOALS DESTROY INCENTIVES. When goals are underestimated or when performance exceeds all expectation, it is very difficult to maintain incentives. Perhaps the most amazing example of this was Bob Beamon's superhuman performance (29' 2½") in the 1968 Olympic long jump. No jumper had ever done even 28 feet. His superlative leap brushed aside several decades of normal progress and cleared a distance to be expected in the 1980s or later. It overwhelmed everyone, and Beamon most of all. For several years he trained and competed, but never approached such an effort, and probably achieved less than he would have without it.

Somewhat similarly, Dick Fosbury gained his goal of being Olympic champion high jumper during his college junior year, four years sooner than planned. After two years of almost no jumping, he was quoted as saying,[2]

One of my problems was that I went too high in the Olympics. When I jumped 7' 4¼" I exceeded my goal for the year by a couple of inches. That threw me off. I was sort of lost for a while as far as my mind was concerned. I had nowhere to go. Now that I've been completely away from competition for a while I'm starting over again. I can set a goal again, and come close to it, working up gradually.

PERSONAL EXPERIENCE IN THE 9-9 COACHING STYLE. The 9-9 coaching method assumes that young athletes will reach toward the highest levels of performance and so into the highest levels of training energies and the so-called "agonies" inherent in them. (Actually, the idea of "agony" is the invention of the less developed or ill-trained; sound training develops defenses against the feelings of exhaustion as much as against the physical aspects.)

It is therefore very important that the 9-9 coach should have had personal experience in the many aspects of track and field--in both competition and training. Possessing such a knowledge out of muscle spindles and pain endings, a coach can inflict fatigue pains without uncertainty or sense of guilt or fear of harm to his pupil. As Lydiard said to Peter Snell at the Rome Olympics, "Throw up if you feel like it. You'll feel better for it. But then, go ahead and take your workout." No hint of concern or suggestion of easing the work that needed to be done. Insensitive? Yes, from a layman's or inexperienced point of view. But Lydiard had trained for and run the marathon. He knew by personal experience that sometimes insensitivity to discomfort is the only means of impelling a man beyond what he believes possible. As such it can be proof, not of harshness, but of deep personal concern, in contrast to the false concern of allowing the less painful way that leads to lesser performance and a lesser person.

Seb Coe's father/coach, Peter Coe, was tough in his training demands on his talented son:

---

[1] Jon Hendershott, "Roberts gets his Record and Then Some," *Track & Field News*, September, 1975, p. 4.

[2] "Dick Fosbury Looking for 68 Spark," *Track & Field News*, 1 February 1971, 7.

"I want to know...that you're liberated from the fears. The biggest fear...is that of your own inadequacy and until you can learn to run (in front) from gun to tape with a total commitment, to talk about tactics is rubbish....But it does make me angry when people suggest that I don't know the effects of training sessions because I was never an athlete."

Just after the War, Peter had been a passionate cycler. "Not a day went by that P. Coe did not train hard, or a week-end go by without a long ride that sometimes lasted all day."[1] That is, he first knew from within himself what he was demanding from his son.

Perhaps America's greatest coach of distance runners was Billy Hayes of Indiana. I've never heard that Hayes was a competitive distance runner but he had a muscle-nerve feeling for running that his many greater champions seldom if ever questioned. He was the first of our coaches to spend several summers in Scandinavia where he watched and listened to runners and coaches along the woods paths at Swedish Vålådalen or Finnish Vierumäcki until he knew in his bones the higher levels of what could be done. It was that bone certainty that gave Coach Hayes the authority that impels acceptance.

<u>MOTIVATION IN THE 9-9 COACHING STYLE</u>. The pattern of motivation inherent in this method of coaching is that of McGregor's Theory Y as stated in Chapter 2, "Motivations and Coaching Assumptions." Challenging work is as natural and enjoyable as play or rest. Once committed, men (including boys and girls) will exercise a considerable degree of self-direction in their work. The satisfaction of work well done is more satisfying than the rewards that sometimes attend it. External controls and the threat of punishment are mainly necessary under the assumptions of Theory X.

Examples of this approach are innumerable. Most track Greats tend to be self-dependent and in some real measure, self-coached. This is clearly shown in Frank Dolson's biography of George Young,[2] America's first distance runner to compete in four Olympics. During those 16 years, George was almost entirely self-driven. Whatever he received in the way of recognitions and awards was quite secondary to his own need to come up to his own expectations in running. Along similar lines, Brutus Hamilton wrote to the mother of Don Bowden, first American to better four minutes for the mile,[3]

My only disagreement with Don has been in the amount of work that he should do. I usually have to chase him off the track each afternoon because he always wants to do one more straightaway or one more lap. Even this week, after his great effort of Saturday, he still wants to do more than I think he should....

Perhaps no track and field man ever developed himself as close to his maximum potentials as did Bill Toomey. During four years of college track, he was an NCAA non-place-winner in the long jump and 440. In 1969 he was Olympic Champion and world-record holder in the decathlon, a truly amazing development. Frank Dolson, sports columnist of *The Philadelphia Inquirer*, told it this way,[4]

Bill Toomey has done a good many unbelievable things. Over a five-year period he completely rebuilt his body, changing himself from a 165-pounder with pretty good speed into a 195-pounder with blazing speed. His "secret" was dedication. From the day he first set his sights on becoming an Olympic decathlon man to the moment he climbed the victory platform in Mexico City, he let nothing stand in the way of his "impossible dream."....

---

[1] Tony Ward, "Modern Coaching--Different Methods, Different Men," *Track and Field Quarterly Review*, Fall, 1983, pp. 9-12.

[2] Frank Dolson, *ALWAYS YOUNG*, Mountain View, Calif: World Wide Publications, 1976.

[3] Lawrence J. Baack, *THE WORLDS OF BRUTUS HAMILTON*, Los Altos: Tafnews, 1971, p. 19.

[4] Frank Dolson, "Bill Toomey Tells Young People what Winning is All About." *Family Circle*, July 1969, p. 60.

From 1964 through 1968, Bill trained daily. He ran, worked with weights, and did all the things a decathlon man has to do to become No. 1. Except for his family and friends, nobody noticed....It would have been very easy for Bill to give up his Olympic dream.

"The hardest thing is getting out there every day," Bill says, "It's so simple to find something else to do. Your body tells you, 'Forget it; don't work out today.' Your mind says, 'Do it!'"

Bill's mind won.

The 9-9 coaching style can and does accept scholarships and other material rewards within its system, if given and controlled by the regular scholarship faculty of the college. But as Maslow has made clear, the man whose lower-level needs of food-shelter-safety are satisfied is no longer motivated by those needs. In terms of inciting greater efforts on the track or field, scholarships, once granted, are ineffective. Without them, of course, the athlete might not be in college at all. But only in the 9-1 style, where the coach can give and take away, does fear of loss make them a factor in performance.

THE 9-9 COACHING STYLE ENCOURAGES THE ATHLETE'S SELF-DEPENDENCE.

Many related research studies in business and industry (Hollander and Hunt, 1963, 506ff) support actual experience in track and field that development will proceed more rapidly if the individual athlete is critical of his own goals, of his own training methods and techniques, and of his own tactics in competition. On the basis of their work with track athletes and coaches, Ogilvie and Tutko recommend,

An open reception on the part of your athletes; not an uncritical acceptance, but a measured, thoughtful involvement in your counsel. The athlete retains his integrity as an individual but allows new knowledge or theories to blend with his preconceived notions or past....experiences....Remember that you are always planting seeds.... It will not be until the athlete actually feels in a personal way the significance of your words or instruction that true learning has occurred.

Coaches disagree on the extent of such thinking and self-criticism by their athletes, depending on their concepts of the coach-athlete relationship. A few take the attitude, "I'll do the thinking; you stick to doing what I tell you," and produce record performances and winning teams. But as a group, successful performers in track and field tend to be intelligent, self-dependent men, given to critical analysis of situations, techniques, and methods, especially as these apply to themselves.

Looking back from 1984, I realize that one of my greatest joys in coaching was working with Charles Fonville who, considering methods and attitudes of the 1940s, achieved as close to perfect technique in the shot put as has any man. Time after time he came to me saying, "Coach, I've been thinking about that problem we discussed last week. I think this will work." And then he'd execute, with almost no practice, the very point we had not been clear about.

I once asked Parry O'Brien why he wasted so much time working alone and with only one shot. His answer, "Coach, doing it this way gives me time to think about what was wrong with the last effort and what will be right in the next." Some months before the actual event occurred, Gunder Hägg predicted in Sweden that though many men were trying, Roger Bannister would be the first to break the four-minute "barrier" in the mile, not because he possessed the greatest physical powers, but because he approached the problems of training and self-analysis intelligently and with clear concentration upon what such an effort required.

Of course, individuals differ in the benefits they can derive from such self-dependent thinking. Assuming maturity, the greater the intelligence, the more likely good effects will result. Lacking maturity, defined as self-confidence and self-control, to be "thoughtful and critical" of one's own methods can lead to doubt and lack of direction. Some successful athletes seem to adapt themselves best to the rigors of training when they put themselves--body and mind--in the hands of a respected coach. By giving over the mental-emotional stresses of both training and competition, such men tend to relax more, sleep better, enjoy their food more, and perform better.

MANAGING CONFLICT IN THE 9-9 STYLE. During the 1960s and early 70s a spirit of revolt against the Establishment was in the very air we breathed. The authority of anyone who could in any way be representative of the System was open to challenge--and often was challenged. And this carried over from the political and military spheres to that of education and sport. The Princeton University track team voted in midseason to stop the year's competitive schedule in protest of the Vietnam war and the Kent State killings--and had their way.

Many a longtime track coach who had ruled his situation--autocratically perhaps but kindly and without dissent ("It never occurred to me to do otherwise")--found himself beleaguered from all sides. Some 9-1 coaches, firmly established through long success, resisted hard, fired team members for insubordination, and are still coaching. Others were deeply hurt and chose early retirement, long before their years of effective coaching were gone.

On balance, the total result of this conflict against authority was on the plus side. It called into question a full spectrum of problems that had been hidden. And out of it emerged a better understanding of what I have called "the human side of the coaching enterprise." In those colleges and schools where the overall climate of attitude was in keeping with the 9-9 style of coaching, that is, where the goals and attitudes of the institution-coach-athletes were integrated and mutually supportive, there was relatively little difficulty. At Princeton, for example, Ken Fairman, Athletic Director, supported quite readily the vote-to-quit of the team. "They're dropping out because they no longer feel a 100 percent commitment to sports; their hearts are no longer in the game. After all, they always have a veto; they're not hired by us to compete."

The 9-9 style does not prevent conflict. In some ways, its emphasis on freedom and openness stimulates it. But it does so in healthful ways. It does not avoid direct confrontation; it welcomes it as the best means of making the issues clear and open. Since personal authority is not at stake in this style, loss of authority is not feared. Nor is the strong need to get along with people at any cost, that characterizes the 1-9 style, evident here.

Conflict tends to arise from off-the-field conduct. What is the image our track team wishes to convey to others--to other students on campus, to the public when we travel, to the news media if they become interested? Are we fully committed to excellence in our off-the-field efforts just as on the field? What time and energy does this allow for having fun? What kind and degree of fun? How do we travel to meets? Separately? How do we dress on trips and in hotel lobbies? What hotels do we stay in?

In many situations, these are questions for which the athletes feel no concern. They're glad to have such unimportant details settled without any effort on their part. "Give me a quiet place, a good bed, food I like, and a fair chance to compete; that's all I care about." But in other situations, the least hint of neglect, of discrimination, of changing the rules and customs, of restricting individual rights or habits, can become issues leading to revolt and direct confrontation.

The more open the door and the mind of the coach to the suggestions and disagreements of team members, the more open their attitudes to consult with him. The potential conflict is now met at its weakest point--before it congeals or gathers its forces. Discussions now relate to solving problems, not to suppressing persons. Time consuming? In the short run, yes. But in the long run, definitely time and energy saving. One needs to be convinced of that. Otherwise it's so much easier to avoid confrontation now; so much easier to put it off, make do, compromise.

As I look back on my own coaching career, I remember so many instances of person-to-person conflict and one of coach-to-team conflict in which early open discussion would probably have avoided hostility. I can think of various excuses--the long distance from campus to coach's office, the endless demands on a coach's time, the chip-on-the-shoulder attitudes of some youth--but the core of the trouble was failure to establish a sufficient climate of mutual trust and personal concern, the key to the 9-9 style.

Every team operation requires control. In his autobiography, Vince Matthews told of what I consider to be excessive demands by a dozen or so of America's top track and field champions. On the one hand, they wanted the benefits of Olympic and inter-nation team competitions; on the other, they demanded complete individual freedom to arrange their own tours, set their own wage demands, follow their own training and life styles.[1] With such attitudes by team members, not even the most expert coaching leadership could achieve a sound team operation.

A team is not a mere aggregation of individuals. A team has a character of its own that is more than and other than the sum of its individual members. The purpose and goal of the team must be pursued even though this diminishes individual freedom and the pursuit of individual goals. In the long run this will be more than balanced by individual benefits from team efforts--successful or not.

The team must work together to get its job done, and primary responsibility for that work rests with the coach. That's the demand of the school administration and the demand of all that are worthwhile team members. Obviously, the 9-9 coach will seek control first by democratic means as advocated throughout this section. But he must be clear that control, one way or another, must be achieved or the entire enterprise will founder.

COACHING PERSONS AND MECHANICS--A SUMMARY

This graphic approach seeks to improve our understanding of the job of coaching by dividing it into two aspects: one related directly to persons and inter-personal relationships; the other to the methods and techniques of track and field training and performance. In life and on the field, these are inseparable. But distinguishing between them, as in a graph, implements clearer understanding, deeper analysis, and a more sound balance of coaching emphasis between the two.

The major concern of Part I of this OMNIBOOK is with coaching leadership and its mutually supportive relationships with other persons within and outside the track team family; that is, with those aspects of coaching that lie along the vertical axis of the Figure 3.1 graph. The major concern of the remainder (Part II) of the OMNIBOOK is with track and field mechanics and training systems--those evaluated along the horizontal axis of the graph. Both aspects are essential to coaching. However, to simplify and shorten the discussion, these latter concerns were largely ignored throughout this Chapter 3, thus forcing contrasts between the different coaching styles primarily on the basis of differing attitudes as related to persons. Obviously, both the 1-9 coach and the 9-1 coach are fictional, actual non-entities. Teachers teach students by way of this or that course of study. They must challenge, and students must react, must do something positive and developmental. To merely "sit under" a lecturer, to cause no disturbance, would be utter failure of teaching. In that sense, the 1-9 coach fails completely when he does everything for persons but requires nothing by way of responsive action-- challenging action that demands sacrifice in time-energy and acceptance of hurt-pain-agony as a way of sports training--as of life. Similarly, the 9-1 coach with his exclusive concern for training methods and techniques is imaginary only. To totally ignore persons, to cut off all mutually supportive relationships would be totally destructive. Only some approximation of the 9-9 coach is worth striving for.

In the past, both textbooks and lecturers at coaching clinics have dealt almost exclusively with methods and techniques. But coaches have found the problems of persons, both within and outside the team, to be both more common and more complex. Much more sound research must be done in this area; we've hardly begun to take it seriously. This material is only a beginning. There's a great need for a full-sized volume on coaching persons in track and field.

To make best use of this graphic approach, we must go back to the work of Douglas McGregor and Rensis Likert with their emphasis on climates of mutual trust and mutually supportive relationships, not only within the track team, but among the many other groups that relate to the coaching enterprise--the institution, community, team family and extending to the entire culture. When these are in conflict, the enterprise is diminished.

As a final and crucial point, we must be constantly aware that the graphic use of precise numbers, such as 9-3 or 5-7, is merely a convenience or tool to further analysis and communicate ideas. No coach or coaching style can be circumscribed to precisely. These numbers are value symbols; if valid they may simulate life values but no more than that. Neither humans nor human operations can be squeezed into any mathematical symbol.

[1]Vince Matthews with Neil Amdur, *MY RACE BE WON*, New York: Charterhouse, 1974, hardcover, 396 pp.

Chapter 4
TRACK AND FIELD COACHES OF INTEREST

These thumb-nail sketches of coaches have a number of uses. First, they serve as examples of the various coaching styles indicated in the Coaching Grid from 1-9 to 9-1 to 9-9. No one of these coaches can be fitted into any one pigeonhole; humans are far too elusive and variable for that. Second, class discussions of the general area of the Grid into which these coaches fall should (1) bring clearer insights into the principles of coaching given in Chapters 2 and 3, and (2) suggest the wide range of coaching styles that have proved successful. Third, these sketches should indicate the many ways you can modify and improve your own coaching style. We change our basic attitudes and behavior in small ways and with great reluctance. But, with time and persistence, they can be modified. So with our coaching styles. It's probably easier to change oneself than to change one's coaching situation.

BRUTUS HAMILTON--UNIVERSITY OF CALIFORNIA, BERKELEY (1932-1965)

It has been my good fortune to be with Brutus Hamilton at many coaching clinics, dual meets, and championship meets. He was inherently impressive--impressive of figure and face and voice and attitude and way of speaking and, most important, of personal and coaching success. What other track coach had been National Decathlon champion, Chief U. S. Olympic coach, Director of Athletics, Dean of Students, and coach of many world and Olympic champions?

But along with all this, he had a clear quality of selflessness, both in his life and in his coaching. No one could question that he got things done, but by his own charisma which impelled others to help themselves, without leaning on him except for inspiration and a direct answer when asked. No one could accuse Brutus of pushing his own weight around. I was with him in 1956 as we were about to enter the Los Angeles stadium for the final Olympic trials. He was chief Olympic coach. At the last moment he discovered he had left his ticket at home. He could have pushed himself into the stadium easily. Everyone knew him. Certainly I could have identified him to the ticket-taker. But he quietly went to the ticket-seller and bought himself a seat!

I was with him in India in 1954 among coaches whose technical knowledge was at least doubtful if not non-existent. During three weeks of coaching, Brutus's strongest admonition was "Look within yourselves for your answers. India has an infinite capacity for good coaching. Believe in it. Work in terms of your own Indian way of life. Adapt Western techniques and details to yourselves. For your sports future lies within you, not in acquiring the secrets of coaches from other countries, no matter how successful those secrets may have been for them."

This was Hamilton's approach when teaching other coaches, but also when coaching his own athletes. He seldom urged a point of view, and never dictated, "Do it my way." Certainly he could never be accused of over-coaching, at least as it applies to teaching techniques. His knowledge of techniques, based on his own experience, was sound. But he evidenced that knowledge in his coaching, not so much by authoritative direction as by suggestion, by asking questions in such a way that the right answers became evident, by encouraging thoughtful analysis and discussion among his athletes, by presenting himself as a resource expert to whom they might come for help in their efforts to help themselves.

At the time of his retirement, Harry O. Bain wrote in the *California Monthly*,

the story of Brutus Hamilton, ...a man whose life has been stamped with rare idealism, with love of sport, not for the sake of winning alone, but for the will to strive, to compete. Even more it is a tale of loyalty and love for his athletes and their almost mystical devotion to the man they remember as 'The Coach.' Brutus' allegiance to his athletes is a constant in an often unbalanced athletic world where premiums are set on winning. To blame a beaten athlete, or criticise an official's judgment publicly is unthinkable to the Hamilton character . . . .

But Brutus' concern for the athlete goes beyond physical and academic welfare. To him each boy is special, whether he is a world class competitor or a 'little man' whose efforts never pay off in points or records. In Brutus' eyes his athletes are equals. One spring night in 1956, when the great Don Bowden became America's first sub-four-minute miler . . . Brutus was literally swarmed by well wishers in the stands. On the track where the two mile was about to start was another of Hamilton's athletes, a runner far below Bowden's stature, but a boy gifted with great team spirit and desire to excel . . . . Brutus slipped quietly away from the jubilant crowd, saying simply, "I must be there to tell Val how he looked at the finish." . . .

There is a wide streak of humor in Brutus Hamilton. An inveterate letter writer, his prose fairly glitters with wit, and some of his best shots are aimed at his own head. In 1952, after coaching the U. S. Olympic team to a resounding success at Helsinki, Brutus summarized his contribution "as refraining from interference with the normal progress of the boys."

Shortly after Brutus' death in December, 1970, Dave Maggard wrote the following paragraphs for Track & Field News.[1] Maggard was captain of a Hamilton-coached California track team and was highly recommended by Hamilton to succeed himself as head coach.

Brutus Hamilton was a unique human being. A scholar, philosopher, poet and gentleman, Brutus could have excelled in whatever profession he had chosen. A man of keen intellect, I think he may have been the most articulate man the sport has ever known.

Without a doubt, Brutus was ahead of his time as far as coaching was concerned. Rapport with his athletes was excellent. Respect was mutual. There were times when he drew criticism from his colleagues for not being a tougher taskmaster. Some even felt he did not care about winning. Nothing could have been further from the truth. A great athlete during his competitive days, he was a winner in every respect. None of his athletes were pampered or coddled. Care about them he did but exploiting an athlete never entered his mind. The athlete competed because he had the desire to excel, not because he was being coerced. Brutus could be disturbed by the spoiled athlete--the type who complained that the world owed him a living.

Brutus felt there was one real reason for being part of the team--the athlete had to have the desire to be the best. He could guide an athlete as far as he cared to go toward excellence. Winning was the name of the game--but not at all costs. Not at the cost of sacrificing ideals. He had an excellent understanding of the student-athlete and problems he might encounter along the way. His emphasis was placed on getting an education-- getting through the University and preparing for life. He looked on his athletes as men who could take lessons from athletics for later years. The carry-over values can be great. Many of those he coached continued to improve even after graduation, due mostly to the acquisition of a solid background and the love of competition. His idea of the athlete standing on his own two feet lends to this continued success.

Team morale on Brutus' teams was just great. Not a forced, rah-rah type of enthusiasm but a quiet, sincere dedication. Foolishness and frivolity were not a part of the man's character. Having fun and enjoying what you were doing seemed to exemplify his coaching philosophy. Brutus' long experience and great knowledge gave him a quiet confidence. His enthusiasm for life and sport was almost indescribable--so mellow, yet inspirational. Seldom did he raise his voice either during a meet or practice. A warm handshake or pat on the back with a complimentary remark made it all seem worthwhile. He was a great stabilizing influence. "Keep things in proper perspective" was a common phrase for Brutus. I once heard him say to a young aspiring sophomore, "This is your first race for California, make yourself proud of the association." Or just before an important meet, he might say, "Don't underestimate your competitor, honor him with your best performance." . . .

Shortly after I had taken my first job at the high school level, I received a letter

---

[1]Dave Maggard, "So Mellow, Yet Inspirational," Track & Field News, 1 February 1971, 14.

from Brutus. Many of the things he said then I feel reflected not only his coaching philosophy but also his wonderful sense of humor.

"Coaching track will always be rather a personal coach-athlete relationship....Some coaches know all the techniques except they forget to tell their boys to get there first. They become so form conscious that they invariably forget to win. Form is, of course, important and essential but it should never stick out." ...

Forrest Beaty, now a medical student, relates the manner in which Brutus had recruited him. Forrest was being wined and dined by many colleges all over the country. He was somewhat surprised when his recruiting luncheon was at Fenton's ice cream parlor. Brutus' approach was most refreshing and Forrest ended up at California.

Archie Williams, 1936 Olympic 400-meter gold medalist and world record holder,.... now a teacher in Marin County (near San Francisco), said he often asks himself, "What would the coach want me to do?"

Don Bowden, first American to run the mile below four minutes, talked of Brutus' ability to get the athlete ready at the right time. "Any coach can work an athlete hard but only the great ones know when to ease off."

Lon Spurrier, former world record holder in the 880, tells of the times when Brutus was always there to share the blame for poor performances but never around to accept credit for the athlete's great performances.

The list continues on and on--all influenced by the greatness of Brutus Hamilton.

In my judgment, Brutus was unique among United States track coaches in the great breadth of his activities, his interests, his track and field contributions, and his tolerance of others-- an authentic 9-9 leader. He was a respected Major in the Army Air Corps[1] but I knew him to be a strong advocate of peace among all men of One World, a man cited for "his idealism, sensitivity, light-heartedness, beauty and wisdom." (Strange words to ascribe to a winning coach of a major track college.) He was a second-team end on Walter Camp's 1921 All-American football team, a forward on the National AAU Championship basketball team for the Kansas City Athletic Club in 1923, National decathlon and pentathlon champion and Olympic Games silver medallist in 1920, but along with all that, an excellent student at the University of Missouri specializing in English poetry and prose. Baack wrote[2]

"This did not mean that athletics dominated his life at the University. On the contrary his first love was probably literature and history. As he once wrote, 'one of the dearest and most inspiring friendships of my life' was with John Rutledge Scott, Professor of Elocution at Missouri. 'I made hundreds of trips from the Delt house to his home (a four-mile walk, going and coming) and literally sat at his feet for four years.'"

Brutus was Director of Athletics at the University of California, 1946-1955, with all the problems of big-time sports promotion and alumni relations that job entails, but was also Dean of Men, 1944-1946, Track Coach, 1932-1965, Chairman of the NCAA Track Rules Committee, 1955-1965, and one must add, instructor of English literature and history at Westminster College, Missouri, 1924-1929. This latter interest stayed with him. His wife, Rowena, wrote me that "He always found time to read--very often poetry. He had a wonderful memory and could quote poetry by the hour."

He was an avid fisherman, for love of quiet and the out-of-doors, and also was known through-

---

[1]"He did this because he was very patriotic in a quiet sort of way and because as he said, 'If I'm going to work with boys the rest of my life, I've got to know what they've been through.'" Lawrence J. Baack, *THE WORLDS OF BRUTUS HAMILTON*, Los Altos: *Tafnews*, 1975, p. 14.

[2]*Ibid.*, p. 10.

out Berkeley as "the gentle caretaker of the birds at Edwards Stadium." He once posted a notice that, prior to leaving Berkeley for a long trip, he had weighed each bird very carefully, "Woe to all persons...if one gram is missing from any one bird. Mr. Hamilton is ordinarily a very peaceful man, but he wishes to remind...(you) that he knocked out Benny Herring in the second round of a scheduled four-round bout for the Regimental Light-Heavyweight Championship in World War I. BEWARE!"

Brutus also had a lifetime love affair with the harmonica--always in his travel case or pocket. I remember well the closing festivities of our three-week coaches' clinic at Patiala, India, at which each person was expected to do his thing. Brutus was the hit of the evening with "Turkey in the Straw," the California Bear Fight Song, but most movingly, with "Shenandoah."

To confirm the great variety of friendships that Brutus maintained, he was a close friend of rival coach, Dink Templeton of Stanford, for whose place as an athlete on the 1920 Olympic team he had fought vigorously. To me, Templeton was the opposite of Hamilton--explosive, restless, at least outwardly a tyrant, crudely profane and increasingly alcoholic; somehow they found much in common. But Brutus was also a kind friend of the "Dear Good and Gracious Lady" who owned the flower shop in Berkeley.

No description of Brutus Hamilton would be complete without inclusion of two helpers. The first, Rowena Hamilton, his wife during 44 years. At Brutus' retirement dinner, I had the sharp impression that it was equally in recognition of her many contributions. That seems an exaggeration, but athlete after athlete spoke so warmly, even emotionally, of her personal concern, her ever-present smile, her well-loaded dinner table, or of her help in solving some personal problem for which only such a woman could have empathy and sound suggestions. In one letter Rowena wrote to me, "I have always been grateful that Brutus was in a profession I could share. It was great to know the athletes and their girls--what they thought and what they wanted to be. When an athlete was hurt, both Brutus and I worried and lost sleep." The Hamiltons were clearly a two-person coaching staff.

But there was another important member of that staff, Al Ragan, California's assistant track coach for over 45 years, 1927-1974. Of-one-piece with Brutus, Ragan extended the emphasis on fundamentals and "keeping things simple," so inherent in Hamilton's coaching. He told Ted Brock[1] that "Brutus believed in a very basic approach too. With an athlete he'd take one thing at a time. Keep watching. Keep watching. Sometimes I think the kids didn't realize how much they were being coached. He and I stayed quite close to them, in their work, their academics, their talk of the future."

There you have it all in a nutshell--"He and I (and Rowena) stayed quite close to them." We tend to assume that a coach is restricted to the outline of his own skin. But if the research of McGregor and Likert has any meaning at all, his skin is also an inline of the persons and the devices and the climate of supportive relationships a coach establishes about him, which, working all together, gain their mutual goals.

This sketch neglects entirely Hamilton's attitude toward recruiting--in brief, one that extends a warm welcome to the boy as a worthy member of the California student body, as well as an athlete. His letter[2] to "Woody" Covington of Compton High, the 1958 California State High School mile champion, illustrates this attitude perfectly, but our lack of space allows quotation of only one-half:

I am pleased that you have sent your transcript to the University for evaluation. Your marks thus far completed show that you should have no difficulty meeting the stern entrance requirements here, provided, of course, you continue your excellent work during your last high school semester. This I know you shall do.

You now face three major decisions. First, the university which you wish to attend;

---

[1]Ted Brock, "Al Ragan: The Stuff of Permanence," Los Altos: *Track & Field News*, 1 June 1972, p.30.

[2]Lawrence J. Baack, *op. cit.*, p. 29.

second, the profession which you wish to follow; and, third and finally, the girl with whom you wish to share your life. I refuse, of course, to have anything to do with this latter decision in any case. However, I might say in passing that there is no dearth of charming, brilliant and high charactered girls on this campus, should you decide to cast your lot with us, and should you evidence an interest in such distracting items.

For the most part, I coach by indirection. I like to coach men without their realizing they are being coached. I want them to enjoy running and not make a grim business of it....

But a coach can only point the way. Inspired performances must come from deep within the boy himself. We work hard on the mental side and try to get a boy to realize and achieve his potential.

But coaching is something more than a craft. We follow a general pattern but no two men are worked exactly alike. Insofar as possible, we follow the rule of a certain voice teacher who was once asked what method she used in teaching her pupils. She replied, "I have twenty-five students. I use twenty-five different methods." So, if you asked me exactly how you would be coached, I couldn't tell you. I can tell you, except for the above generalities, only after I've had a chance to study you and work with you...

JAMES (JUMBO) ELLIOTT -- VILLANOVA UNIVERSITY (1936-1981)

Skip Myslenski's article, "The 40-year Odyssey of Jumbo Elliott," appeared in the April 13, 1975 issue of *The Philadelphia Inquirer,*

In a time of too many spurious copies, one James Francis Elliott exists as an original,...a kaleidoscopic blend of coach, counsellor, celebrity, dictator, entertainer, hustler, genius, magician and father confessor....

"Yeah, Jumbo is just Jumbo," says miler Eamonn Coghlan, who runs for him now. "He influences a lot of people, but nothing influences him."

"Jumbo is so complex I don't think he understands himself," says Tom Donnelly, who ran for him in the late Sixties. "I don't mean that in a derogatory sense, but it seems like he's always pre-occupied, things are always off-handed, he's off in the distance somewhere. But of course what he says always works out."

"He's an institution, an attraction," says Marty Liquori, who ran at the same time as Buerkle. "He's like the Liberty Bell."

"The Liberty Bell, oh my God," says Jumbo Elliott, laughing heartily. "Old hat'd be more like it."

He began in 1936, barely 22 years old, recently graduated and earning $135 for a year as both trainer and track coach. As a student he himself had run not unimpressively (he still holds the school's 600-yard record), captained the golf team, scheduled meets (golf on Friday, track on Saturday) and often accompanied football coach Harry Stuhldreher to Penn, where they would watch and learn from Billy Morris, the Olympic trainer. He received an appointment to West Point (at the time you could graduate from college then compete four more years for the Academy if you entered before July 1 and were not yet 21), stayed eight months, then returned to begin his career.

For 40 seasons now he has cajoled, tended, directed and ministered to various Villanova track teams. He has coached 22 Olympians, 217 IC4A champions, 61 AAU champions, 52 NCAA champions, 14 world record holders...He has made Penn Relays a personal showcase for his runners, dominated Eastern track since the war, earned the admiration of most all and been denied an Olympic coaching position only because he refuses to play the political game....

It is a mixed bag, Jumbo Elliott's methods, an eclectic blend of showmanship, salesmanship, Irish wit, Irish blarney, parental care, parental discipline, instinct and knowledge. "I think the big thing is he takes a genuine interest in the boys in terms of their welfare," says Charlie Jenkins, who won a gold medal at the 1956 Olympics. "You know, it's hard to fool kids nowadays, and when you find someone like Jumbo who is genuinely interested, you respond. And when you respond to Jumbo, who's an excellent coach, you can't help but come out good."

"He really doesn't create a coach-athlete relationship the same way other coaches do," says Eamonn Coghlin. "I feel he coaches and treats his athletes the same way he does business. He runs a high-class business and he deals with us as high-class athletes. He doesn't worry you about all the bull, busting records, being in the top 10, that crap. It's just run your race, do your job that day then move on to the next race. There's no bull. Everything is very honest."

"If he's anything he's a salesman," says Marty Liquori. "He knows how to handle people, how to sell things and he teaches you how to be quick on your feet, how to think on your feet. He realizes the big thing is psychological and is a master at getting you psyched up, getting you mentally prepared. Then by the time you're a senior you have Jumbo's philosophy, so even if he isn't around for a month, you still have that feeling in the air. You have a feeling that just doesn't let you be anything but a winner."....

Too, he is the successful businessman, wealthy, refined, tasteful, the chief executive of Elliott & Frantz, Inc., dealers in heavy equipment. He lives on the Main Line, drives a Cadillac (he received the first 1975 model shipped to Philadelphia), belongs to the selective Squires Country Club, wears custom-made suits and shoes (the latter from England, where the company has a mold of his feet) and plays golf with Bob Hope, Andy Williams, Mike Douglas, Perry Como and Cardinal Krol. Indeed, he helped found a country club in Florida in partnership with Hope and William Ford III and vacations there for two weeks each March....

When they compete at the NCAA Indoors they stay at the Ponchartrain, Detroit's best hotel; other teams stay at Howard Johnson's. When he was recruiting Billy McLoughlin he took him, Liquori, Dave Patrick and Frank Murphy to Mama Leone's on a Friday night; he ignored the long line, claimed reservations he didn't make, demanded a table immediately and received the best in the restaurant.

"Jumbo is always first class in everything he does and that's important," says Liquori. "He would never, never let us go second class because we were the best. In fact, I think he even sometimes dug into his own pocket to treat us as the best.

"This may be the most important thing about him, his being a first-class guy. Most of us want to be first class sooner or later and there's no better way than to associate with someone who is. And traditionally the winners go first class, the losers go second class. So it's all part of his plan to convince us that we're the best. Oh, we might run some bad races, but that's just a temporary thing, the cream will always come to the top. And we're the cream."

Rain falls on this Tuesday afternoon, so Jumbo Elliott moves his team through its routine quickly before Villanova's old, cinder track turns soft and treacherous. That completed, he ambles up to a second-floor office in the fieldhouse, greets his visitor, then turns his attention to the others in the room. There is a word, a smile, a joke for everyone....

During the talk he will laugh often...when he learns what others have said about him, when he realizes what his visitor has heard of him...."I just don't know, I just don't know," Jumbo Elliott says, slowly shaking his head. "I think you have to communicate with them. I think you have to control them. I think I know what basically is the way to train, that they're all individuals and that they're all different...

"Everybody is handled in an individual way. I couldn't treat Brian McElroy like Dick Buerkle like Marty Liquori, they're each different. I don't like to dominate them, but I do dominate them to the point that I control them. For example, if someone would come out with a workout in his head, it could be anything, well, I've been doing it so much that they'll do what I want them to do but in a way that they think that they're doing what's exactly in their head.

"What I like to have them feel is that at the end of four years they know as much about track as I do and that they can go on a track and run and that they're masters of the situation, that they don't have to wait for a coach to say you ran that first quarter three-tenths of a second too fast and carry on to these extremes like some coaches in the past have done. I feel that's ridiculous....

In summary, Jumbo Elliott's coaching can be described with reasonable validity as that of a man well-trained in Business Administration at Villanova University, and working wholehearted-ly within the values and methods of traditional business management and Dale Carnegie's *HOW TO WIN FRIENDS AND INFLUENCE PEOPLE*. Forced to supplement the $135 he received from Villanova for his first year of coaching, he became a salesman of heavy earth-moving machinery (somehow that's in keeping with his style), and there learned--the hard way--the best methods of selling his product and himself.

He followed this two-way vocational pattern throughout his career. It was far from easy, with many failures and frustrations in early coaching and sales endeavors. But gradually he acquired a more relaxed and self-confident attitude and a sound formula for success in his rapidly expanding sales business and his coaching: (1) Sell a first-class product. (2) Work within the Business, Church and Social System; believe in its ethic, assume its attitudes and ways of getting along, praise it and don't knock it. (3) Work hard at your selling; concentrate your energies so that all distracting and interfering influences are eliminated. Enjoy your golf and your coaching for their own sakes but conduct them in ways that will further your success in business and social life. (4) All aspects of selling should be done with integrity though without qualms as to the more delicate aspects of integrity; balance conscience with effectiveness, sincerity with making the right impression. (5) Demand high-level effort and performance from your associates and helpers but in return give them first-class compensations; by working hard together, first-class rewards for all--for them and for yourself--will be assured. (6) Show yourself and your product, whether machines or athletes; don't waste time-energy in non-productive showcases. (7) Study carefully the consequences of what you do and what you say; work to make those consequences productive. (8) In summary, analyze and understand what is effective and what is not effective, what secures public recognition and what the public ignores; concentrate on the essentials of success, disregard the non-essentials, shun the hindrances.

One suspects that Jumbo had studied--studied carefully--the various books of Dale Carnegie and Norman Vincent Peale (at least in his emphasis on positive thinking, if not in his Protestant theology). Jumbo may well have simulated the big smile and out-going manner of Charles Schwab, the steel magnate so much admired by Carnegie. He had an easy-going joviality in meeting people, especially those he respected and (I suspect) felt he needed. He took pride in his ability to make many friends and influence them toward acceptance of his programs and himself.

Certainly he attained success--success in business as attested by the 100 or more persons he employed and the six-figured gross income, and success in track coaching as attested by 22 Olympians and 217 IC4A champions--two parts of one Whole.

Was all this coldly deliberate? Was it a carefully planned use of a successful track and field program to advertise and make valuable contacts for a profitable business, Elliott & Frantz Sales? Jumbo would deny it--vehemently, and all but his severest critics would agree with him. Note that his athletes (Coghlin, Liquori, Jenkins) spoke of his integrity. "There's no bull; everything is honest." But Jumbo openly admitted such a business value of his talents in golf--one of the best ways of making effective contacts with potential buyers, friends of Villanova track and, not least, the higher echelons of society. At various times he urged his assistant coach, Jim Tuppeny, to take up golf for similar reasons.

But all would agree that the Elliott track program was a close adjunct to the machinery sales business, and was conducted with similarly effective managerial methods and policies. Certainly he used his track eminence to gain friends and helpers, bulldozing track promoters into giving what he needed. I have a built-in reaction against human bulldozers of all kinds. Frankly, Jumbo and I seldom agreed on anything. When I was director of the *Philadelphia Inquirer Games*, Jumbo insisted that he must have some 35 or more tickets for his friends and the upper hierarchy at Villanova. I, just as adamantly, refused, "I'll treat you fairly-- just as I do every other college coach in the Philadelphia area, and none of them even ask for tickets!" But Jumbo won, I discovered later, by going upstairs to higher *Inquirer* personnel.

Above all, Jumbo was hardworking, never idle. His daily schedule found him at the sales office--early of course. If out of the office, a bleeper system kept him in constant touch with phone calls related to either track or saleswork. He was usually at the Villanova track from three to six P.M. His assistant coach took care of the early or late comers. He was home most evenings but was busy on the telephone--with track and business--until late in the evening.

What were the essentials of the Elliott program of track and field? First, he emphasized competitions that had spectator appeal; minimized those that did not. Second, he and his assistants recruited first-class athletes--mostly runners since these fitted best into the chosen competition. The more mature runners of Ireland, Scotland, England accepted his invitations to become student-athletes gladly, especially after his masterful job in helping Ron Delany rise to the 1956 Olympic 1500-meter championship--perhaps a score of them altogether. But he also had remarkable success with more local talents such as Charley Jenkins and Marty Liquori and such early unknowns as Pat Traynor and Dick Buerkle.

Third, acceptance of his authority and his hard-work training programs. In the early years this took the form of demands, and acceptance was not always easy since there was no proof of his effectiveness. Those were rough years, rough on Jumbo and rough on at least some of his athletes. But with the gradually acquired aura of success and competence, his dominance became less obvious. "I've been doing it so much (successful coaching) that they'll do what I want them to do but in a way that they think they're doing exactly what's in their own heads." Gradually the team attitude became, "Go along with Jumbo; he'll treat you right and your personal success will be certain." Once such general acceptance was attained, everyone prospered. The burden of doubt was removed from the runners' shoulders; they were more relaxed in training and in competition; high spirits, joking even poking fun at the coach became part of the training atmosphere, though never publicly to the detriment of coaching authority.

Fourth, work with each athlete as an individual, treat him fairly, make him no promises you will not fulfill, conduct all aspects of his relationship to your program on a first-class basis, show him off to the public in a first-class way. I first became aware of Jumbo's men through their expensive Villanova sports jackets, their clean overall appearance, their relatively sophisticated manner when meeting the public and especially the news media. Ron Delany, with his delightful Irish brogue and wit, Charlie Jenkins and Marty Liquori were perfect examples of this. Not only did they sell the Elliott public; equally important, they sold other first-class prospects on the advantages of running in the Elliott track program.

And finally, eliminate inner and outer conflicts by co-ordinating the track program with other life activities and interests. For the track-team members, balance the demands of strenuous training with those of academic and some measure of social life. For Elliott, co-ordinate all interests and activities--track and field, business, home, golf, social life--so that they all contribute to the main life goal--success within Elliott's assessment of the System.

WILLIE WHITE--BERKELEY (CA) HIGH SCHOOL, 1966-1984[1]

A strong high school team of either men or women is nothing surprising. Berkeley High has had those, the men taking the California State title last year, while the women grabbed the honor in 1974 and '76.

But this year, coach Willie White's Yellowjacket squad may well be the finest overall team in prep history. A sweeping statement? Perhaps, but try some of these stats on for size:

Three Berkeley individuals lead the prep lists in their events.
Berkeley relay teams pace the country in 4 events, the 4 x 200 (1:25.1) and sprint medley
   (3:21.1 HSR) for men and the women's 4 x 100 (45.9) and 4 x 200 (1:38.1).
Four other Berkeley individuals appear, or have appeared, in our Top 10 lists in 1981.
Three other Berkeley relay teams make the lists--men's 4 x 100 (41.2) and 4 x 400 (the
   No. 2 All-Americans last year off their 3:10.42 (3:12.9 so far in '81) and the women's
   4 x 400 (3:49.6).

[1]This article was written by Keith Conning, teacher of Consumer Economics and Business Law at Berkeley High School, prep editor of *California Track & Running News*, and of the *NorCal Running Review*. It first appeared in *Track & Field News*, June '81, then updated as of Sept. 1984.

What's up in this college town, the home of UC Berkeley? The prominence of Berkeley High
is made up of equal parts of the atmosphere of BHS itself and the influence of Coach White
and his three assistants, Aaron Ward, Arno Brewer and Sonia Williams. Willie has coached at
Berkeley since 1966. A Cal graduate, he was a world-class sprinter 2 decades ago. He ranked
4th in the world in the 100 in 1957, 10th in '58, contributed a leg to Cal's World Record sprint
medley (3:18.8, '58) and placed 6th in the '60 Olympic Trials 100.

Voted 1980 Coach Of The Year by the California Interscholastic Coaches Association, White
feels that his powerful 1981 team really was born at the '79 California State meet. "We
caught many a cinder from Dave Mack of Locke High in Los Angeles," he says. "Three of our
current seniors were sophomores then and they remember finishing 7th in the mile relay."

One of the keys to the women's program is the Berkeley East Bay Track Club (BEBTC)
coached by White in the summer. "Athletes like Sherifa Sanders and Sharon Ware joined the club
when they were 10 years old," explains White. "During the last 2 years the whole group has
worked together and has been unselfish. You must give up some of your individuality, even
forego your specialty, for the team. Attitude in track & field is the key thing."

While White demands much from his athletes, in listening to them speak of their coach, it
is clear that he gives back plenty. Says Pete Richardson, Berkeley's record-setting 800-me-
ter runner, "Coach White is not only an excellent coach, he also knows you as a person. He
is like a father to the track team. If I have any problems I can go to him. At a track
meet, Mr. White can sit down and enjoy the meet because he has prepared us to take responsibility. Other coaches have to run around and keep after their athletes."

Johnny Langerston was a 2:01 half-miler during 1980; he attributes his improvement this year of 1:53.7 to White, the team and self-pride. "I look to Mr. White as a father,"
he says. "He knows when something is wrong. Our team is like one big family. Everyone has
pride in accomplishing their goals." Adds Charles Clewis, a 48.2 quarter-miler, "Mr. White
understands what we are going through, since he has been there himself."

Being on a team with other top-class athletes is also an inspiration to many of the athletes; the old idea of "success begets success." Says Kenny Robinson, brother of 800 Olympian
James Robinson, "I like being on this team. We always practice together and I want to work hard
in every practice." Unlike many prep teams, Berkeley practices at 7:30 each morning, men and
women. The team runs on Cal's superior facilities; Berkeley High's own track is so old it
doesn't even have its own lane markings.

Richardson continues, "The team relationship among the athletes is strong. You've got to
want it, and we all want success. I attribute all my success to hard work and good concentration." Walter Murray, also a wide receiver in football, compares: "On the track team, you're
never totally by yourself. Our competition is ourselves. In football, I felt alone." Says
hurdler Robyne Johnson, "Being on this team allows you to compete against some of the best competitors in the state. It makes you want to run. Our competitiveness carries over to the class-
room. We all take many of the same classes and we actually compete in class."

Berkeley's excellent academic program has been another factor responsible for the development of the school's strong track program. Inter-district transfer rules allow students from
out of the city proper to attend Berkeley High. But they often attend for BHS's academics,
as much as for athletics. So the ingredients are many and varied, probably as many as the
young athletes involved. But the constants are White and the school's academic program. That's
not to say there haven't been hitches in the Berkeley success story. The relay teams have been
plagued by dropped batons at innopportune moments--as in the women's team not making the state
finals for 6 straight years.

But those are small detours compared to the overall success of White's program at Berkeley.
In 1981, Berkeley High won State team titles for both men and women, the first time in California Interscholastic track and field. For 1982 and 1984, following the loss of many seniors
on the 1981 team, the men's program required rebuilding. Not at all an easy task in view of
the withdrawal of the University's facilities for practice, and the necessity of using those
of Berkeley High--no jumping pits and a track in very poor condition. But in 1984, they finished second with 31 points, and seemed well on their way up again.

In 1982, Berkeley High men won the State title without winning a single first place, a tribute to Coach White's emphasis on balance and numbers. In 1983, the women won their third-straight team title. In 1984, White became head women's coach at Cal State U. Hayward.

TOM TELLEZ--UNIVERSITY OF HOUSTON (1976-----).

Along with his success in working with such Greats as Carl Lewis and Mike Tully, Tom Tellez is best known as one who has brought a more scientific approach to the problems of coaching track and field. The following article was written for publication here by David E. Morey,[1] a decathlete who sought Tellez' help at Houston in 1982.

It's a hot day in Houston. A spring breeze blows the stiff dry grass on Robertson Stadium. Back and forth strides 50-year old Tom Tellez. The Houston coach moves from athlete to athlete, standing patiently with his arms crossed, wearing long pants that seem out of place in the Texas sun. He eyes a discus thrower. Shaking his head he enters the ring himself and spins with grace, hips whirling him to the front as he releases an imaginary platter.

A vaulter calls and Tellez's tanned face turns. The vaulter skies over the cross-bar but it doesn't matter. He looks to the coach as if realizing his fate is part of Tellez's nod or scowl. Everyone looks, as if their fates too are part of his judgment. The critique is bellowed across the field. The focus returns as Tellez pretends to hold his imaginary discus. Tom Tellez is one of track's gurus. Ultimate technician, purveyor of perfect movement, a scientist come to sport. He is widely recognized as one of the nation's best and has twice been on the Olympic coaching staff.

But whence does an Olympic Coach come? Well, there was a California summer...
...the young Tellez, a JC student, was teaching swimming. Suddenly, the California native unconsciously began to "evaluate movement--I tried to analyze the moves myself and feel what was the best feeling. I had no background in biomechanics, it was just a feeling." The feeling convinced him he was meant to teach. He began with 5-year-olds: "It became an obsession with me to teach kids better things or learn the methods sooner than normal. I knew I'd found my niche. I think my personality lent itself to teaching. I knew we have a lot of teachers in our family." While others read the same books and took the same "Ed-Psych" courses--formal, sometimes platitudinous how-to-teach schemes--most couldn't get it across. Tellez could.

"I would not let a kid leave without learning to swim," he remembers. It was amazing. Parents began bringing 5-year-old Johnny or Susan to the pool. They'd given up after a string of failed swimming courses and frustrated teachers. Soon Johnny and Susan splashed with the best of them. Tellez's approach was far from unique. "Coaching by the seat of the pants," he explains. "I was still groping. I always felt I had a good eye for movement; I knew what looked right." But now he began questioning the wisdom passed out at clinics: "I went out and tried it and they weren't right. They all talked about the athlete they had, and what that athlete did."

Something was amiss, and one day it hit Tom like a javelin. After 3 years of JC coaching he had been convinced he knew as much as most. Working with a high jumper on the straddle, Tellez was told by an assistant coach (who happened to be a physics major) that he was wrong. Dead wrong. The lead arm shouldn't thrust under the bar. Newton's Laws say it's opposite and equal reaction. They argued. Tom's ego was hurt. "I asked myself, 'What the heck's going on? Have I been cheating the athlete?'" He went back: "I read Newton's Laws. I read everything--Dyson's The Mechanics of Athletics, John Bunn's Scientific Principles of Coaching. I went back to every Research Quarterly ever written. I went back to physics and math. At first I couldn't make heads or tails of it."

But he pored over the journals and their equations, now convinced that coaches had the wrong perspective in beginning with the athlete, not the laboratory. "We were taking the genius athlete and copying him," he realized.

---

[1] David E. Morey is a former All-American decathlete and IC4A Champion who competed on numerous United States National teams. He spent 1982 training under coach Tellez in Houston, and is currently Foreign Affairs advisor to U.S. Senator John Glenn.

For years he watched films. He wrote a Master's thesis, The Cinematographic Analysis of the Shot Put. He measured, plotted and figured velocities, vectors and angles. He filmed from the top, back and side. "After a while I thought, 'Where have I been?' There was a big gap: the coaches doing only an adequate job and the researchers who couldn't coach. We had to get these closer together, bridge the gap." His coaching life has been built along such a bridge, one which carried him to Fullerton CC, 8 seasons as a UCLA assistant (during which time the school won 4 NCAA titles) and the last 6 years at Houston.

In the summer of 1979, a lanky 17-year-old perked up as Tellez neared. It was long jump prodigy Carl Lewis, fresh from a national High School Record, and getting ready to enter Houston in the fall. He was already a superstar, but when he first stepped onto campus it was back to ground zero.

"When I was being recruited in high school, Coach Tellez told me a lot of things I couldn't even imagine were involved in long jumping," Carl explains. "I had to learn from the beginner's point where most would learn." First, Tellez convinced Lewis he must switch from the simplified hang style to the technically superior double hitch-kick. The second task was to get him to leave the board correctly. Other coaches stressed a long, almost lunging, last stride. Tellez convinced him that he'd sail smoothly off a shorter last step. Now Lewis hits the narrow board at perhaps 27mph; his foot snaps down and he "attacks" the air, double hitchkicking his way into the sport's history.

"Everything he has done has been based on a mechanical principle," Tellez points out. "Based on horizontal velocity, vertical velocity, movements in the air. We've broken it up and worked a little bit on all of them. As soon as he put them together I knew he was going to go far."

One imagines Tellez proving theorems with chalk on a blackboard. Even at a track meet he can look misplaced, almost professorial. But he motivates. "He can stress competitiveness at the same time as technique," says 200-7 discus thrower Rick Meyer. "He trains the athlete to be a competitor in his own eyes; to be his own competitor rather than his coach's."

Says former vault WR claimant Mike Tully, "He's the best technical coach in the United States; the best I've ever seen or talked to." Confirms 17-6 vaulter Charlie Brown, himself an aspiring coach, "I decided to take 2-3 years out of my life to serve an apprenticeship. I pick out an event a day and follow him around. He's the best."

"I think every educator has a responsibility to give the student the best. And that's what I want to give them, and try to give them. The teachers you remember most are the ones that brought the subject to life. Man, they made it interesting. They just made the stuff come alive. They knew their subject so well. They understood the scientific principles behind it. But then they simplified it and explained it so clearly. That's what I'd like to do."

BUD WINTER -- SAN JOSE STATE UNIVERSITY (1940-1970).
The following paragraphs were all written by Dick Drake[1] for Track & Field News,

Bud Winter has an ego. Not a bloated one, mind you, but should the occasion arise, he can tell quite a success story in 25 years at San Jose State. He has aided the careers of 15 Olympic participants, including three gold medallists and a half dozen world record holders (with about 25 records). Winter's success with sprinters is world renowned.
"Bud is a remarkably different coach," says Dr. Bruce Ogilvie, a foremost sports psychologist..."They tend to be well organized aggressive, tough-minded...and conservative, especially in politics, economics and religion.
"Bud's value system is not directed toward these conservative dimensions. He's much more open; he's a laissez-faire sort of guy....On those aspects of track which Bud considers important, he is obsessed and totally committed. But through it all, he remains

[1]Dick Drake, "Laissez-Faire Winter," Track & Field News, 11, June 1969, 1.

open, flexible, and willing to explore. He has been a great innovator....

"Bud describes his approach as 'common sense.' While he's not given to over-reaction, he has a strong sense of fairness to guide him in making judgments. 'We get the job done by kidding and cajoling the athletes along. If purple vitamin milk will make them run faster, then we give it to them. But open communication remains the most important element in our coaching. The greatest technician won't be more than a fair coach if he can't impart his knowledge and feelings. There are occasions to be firm but a common sense approach is definitely the answer to all problems.'

Bud is obsessed with track," comments Ogilvie, "In his total commitment, he is living in an insular world. He doesn't let other things intrude very much. Perhaps this is what it takes to be exceptional. His approach is intuitive. He gets a feeling and carries it through. He really doesn't think beyond the strategy of the moment. But Bud can focus down on the unique individual aspects of a performance. It's as though he has some special insight, and he communicates this with high confidence and emotional commitment."

Art Simburg, close observer of the San Jose track scene, elaborated, "Bud is constantly observing and commenting on an athlete's style and method. He zeroes in on special problems, and gets the athlete to think about what he is doing. At the Olympics, Tom Smith hadn't seen Bud until one day he walked up in his hunting cap, fishing shirt and hush puppies. Tom wanted to laugh. But the feeling all turned to inner warmth because he knew that Mr. Knowledge with the special scret would have the answers. He went through the high knee drills and his rhythm came back. And Tom felt confident again."

Bud is at his best in a one-to-one personal relationship. And it's this intense personal interest in individuals and his drive to help and be loved by all his athletes that leads him to spread himself thin. On the surface he appears disorganized. The clutter of papers on his desk and in his car support this conception. Little details don't bother him if they're not directly related to an individual athlete. . . .

Says Ogilvie, "Bud would be an extremely difficult man to work under. As much affection as I have for him, I could never work on a team with him as assistant coaches do. Of all his creative skills, organization is the most difficult for him to come by. He has a chaotic approach. Even if he eventually does get the job done, he spreads himself all over the place. He simply cannot delegate responsibility.

"Loyalty is extremely important to Bud, and the violation of this trust breaks him up. He can't understand it, and yet in his relationships with people he does tricky things, and does not realize why they may not respond to his ideas as innovations. I have seen sophisticated young men like Tommie Smith and John Carlos smiling about being taken in. I would say that there is a humorous, gentle disrespect for Bud."

Bud relies heavily on gimmickry, key phrases, tricks and clever motivating forces to get his job done. And for the most part they seem to be effective. He is interested in the unusual, and perhaps this explains why he will permit more differences than most coaches. His gimmickry is probably most useful with the young, unsophisticated athletes, according to Ogilvie. Imagine the psychic effect as he communicates his 'Rocket Sprint Start' or his 'Jet Sprint Relay Pass.' . . .

And then there's the matter of motivation. Bud challenges his athletes with 'Get something out of the coach.' He posts on the bulletin board the marks athletes must achieve to win milkshakes from the coach. Each time an athlete improves a San Jose State school record he is entitled to a German chocolate cake which Bud's wife bakes at the end of the season.

Bud's involvement in activities and organizations, and his inventiveness are impressive. He was responsible for creating the State Department track tours of goodwill throughout the world; Ogilvie credits Bud with being the first coach in America willing to let Ogilvie 'tamper' with his athletes. "Until then, everybody said, 'Oh God, I wouldn't let a headshrinker near the club.'" He was instrumental in creating, developing and testing the track surface we now know as Tartan. His four books on sprinting and high jumping have been top sellers at Track and Field News. He has a color film on sprinting that has been widely *distributed. He was the organizer of the first International Coaches Clinic at Berkeley, California, 1956. He has conducted clinics in India, Burman, Rumania, Ceylon, Finland, Sweden, and Denmark.*

TOM BOTTS -- UNIVERSITY OF MISSOURI (1945-1972).
The following article concerning Coach Tom Botts of Missouri appeared in the Kansas City *Star*, February 1, 1972:

It fits the Tom Botts way of doing business that he will retire before a light flashes on a computer, signifying that his working years have run out. The man who has been the head track coach at Missouri for 27 seasons will call it a career this spring because he-- not somebody else--thinks it is the right thing to do.

There is no pressure on Tom Botts--not from the university administration, not from Sparky Stalcup (the athletic director), not from Tiger alumni. Tom Botts is a happy man, a man at peace with his world. And he is a healthy man--one issued top-quality equipment by the Good Lord, one who has taken care of what the Lord gave him. He neither looks nor acts nor feels his 67 years.

If he followed the accepted course, he would stay on for another three years. But he says, "For the good of all concerned, I think it's time to change. I felt it was time to drop out last year, but I did want to coach one year in the new field house." He says it apologetically, almost as if it were an admission of selfishness.

Then he adds, "And I'll say it is a disappointment that I didn't coach there. (Construction still is not completed.) But I made up my mind last fall that I would step out before I'm forced out. And I'll enjoy watching athletic events in the new facility."

His Day Starts Early and Ends Late.
Botts says he is just as willing to work as ever, which means he arrives at Brewer Field House (to go through his daily 2-mile run-jog workout) while the rest of the city sleeps and stays until after most have called it a day. He says, "Coaching is no great strain on me. The only thing I notice is that the hurdles are getting a little heavier-- and I want to carry my share."

This also fits Tom Botts. Never has he asked more of his athletes than he was willing to give. He coaches by example, not by demand. As Bob Teel, the M.U. assistant since 1961 and the man who will replace Botts, puts it: "He believes in a minimum training program, hoping the athlete will go beyond it. Now his minimum isn't easy--but Coach won't drive anybody. He thinks the athlete must push himself."

And it works. Missouri has fielded good track teams under Tom Botts--winning the league outdoor title four times, the indoor crown four times, the cross-country championship twice. The Tigers even took the national indoor title in 1964. No one appreciates winning more than Botts, so championship squads rank high on his good-memory list.

But when Tom Botts lists the greatest track accomplishment by M.U. during his time at the helm, he goes to a 4-man squad winning the 1964 Texas Relays team trophy. And he didn't see it. Teel took the four to Texas; Botts stayed home for a dual meet.

There have been great track men in these 27 seasons, men who exemplified what Botts values so highly, those who combined attitude and performance. He doesn't like to name names--beyond Robin Lingle, Dick Ault and Teel--because there might be an omission. But he does want this on the record: "Some I remember most fondly have not been great performers." That means attitude ranks first with Botts, just as getting an education ranks above getting a spot on the track team.

He Goes Beyond Coaching.
What it all means is this: Tom Botts is more than a coach. He is an honest man, a genuinely humble man, a genuinely good man. As one of his former standouts put it: "He didn't stop at showing us how to run. He showed us how to live."

Perhaps the best expression of Bott's imprint on his pupils is this: In 1966, when

Botts completed his 25th season at M.U. (and that included three years as an assistant), his former athletes came back to M.U. to honor him. There were 120 contacted, and 93 responded--with spoken tribute, with money enough to buy him a new car. That stunned those in the university's business school, those who know a 2 percent response to a solicitation is average and that a 20 percent reply is the ultimate. For Botts, it was better than 75 percent.

And when Botts showed up at a cocktail party before that dinner in his honor, men in their 40s put down cigarettes and drinks. They didn't want to disappoint him. And one who dropped his smoke was a former high jumper who had been dismissed from the squad--for smoking just before a meet in which his sure points could have been the difference between winning and losing.

It is a stern code that Tom Botts follows. Unfortunately, it is one that many consider out-of-date. It is one that will not let him knock any fragment of the collegiate athletic system--not even recruiting that rubs against his grain.

It is a code so strict he will not follow the accepted pattern for retired coaches, writing a book. As he says, "I would not want to impose my ideas on anyone."[1]

The Dedication in the printed program of the 1954 National AAU Championships held in St. Louis, Missouri was to Tom Botts. It read (in part and with my own minor changes--JKD) as follows:

> A Coach of men through excellence in techniques and methods,
> A gentleman proud to be in the coaching profession,
> A Christian who knows no substitute for principle,
> "And when we youngsters reach the evening of our day,
> And gray a little or bald a bit, we still will say,
> 'There was a man!
> A man who coached the right way to run and jump and throw
> While practicing his own right way to live.'"

WILLIAM J. "Bill" BOWERMAN--UNIVERSITY OF OREGON (1947-1973), MEDFORD HIGH SCHOOL (1933-1947)
ROBERT "Bob" NEWLAND--MEDFORD HIGH SCHOOL (1947-1957), NORTH EUGENE HIGH SCHOOL (1957--)

I have placed these two coaches, Bill Bowerman and Bob Newland, under one heading deliberately, not that they were alike in personality, but that together they formed a unified coaching system, a system that involved all the essential subsystems of local community, lower-grade schools, state-wide feeder groups; all with mutually helpful relationships and a complete absence of hard-sell recruiting.

Both men had charisma, though in quite different ways. Bill Bowerman was big and impressive: a rough-hewn outdoors face, well over six feet tall, large bones and frame, a low-toned, slow-speaking voice. One tended to listen when he spoke, to believe what he said, and to do without question what he advised doing. Prefontaine, the great long distance runner of the early 70s so tragically killed before reaching his potential, was once quoted as saying, "I'll never forget the first time I met him. I felt like I was talking to God. I still do."

This all suggests authority, and rightly so. But Bill always considered himself a teacher and instructor, not a director of men. In fact he actually discouraged reference to himself as coach, in reaction to his own unfortunate experience as an athlete with an authoritarian coach. In the preface to his textbook, COACHING TRACK AND FIELD (title probably chosen by his publisher), he uses the words "teacher" or "teacher-coach" 10 times; "coach" only three times. For example, he writes, "I am proud to be a teacher and to be associated with a group of men and women who, on the whole, love youngsters and do not care a whoop if their critics...cause them to be underpaid, underestimated, and overworked."

Bowerman was a major with the 10th Mountain Division during World War II that fought so successfully in Italy, and somehow that fits. As does his love for the out-of-doors in all

---

[1]Dick Wade, "Talk of the Times," Kansas City Star, Feb. 1, 1972.

its aspects. His ranch-style home is on 70 acres of a mountain above the McKenzie River, a great terrain for fishing and hunting, and incidentally for hiking and running. In summary, the man, his personal and coaching experience, his life style were all of one piece, of one well integrated whole.

His coaching success was great, both in high school and college. Prior to Bill's coming, the University of Oregon track team record was only fair; for example in 1946 they scored no points in the NCAA Championships. Under Bowerman, Oregon won the NCAA team title in 1962, 1964, 1965, and was second in 1961 and 1967. Small wonder he was selected as Head Track and Field Coach for the 1972 Olympic team. Things did not go smoothly at Munich. Not only was the international situation chaotic, a number of our own athletes[1] felt strongly that they could skipper their own boat, and Bill as ship's captain, was not one to hold the steering wheel lightly. In Oregon his benevolent authority during some 40 years of coaching had been accepted without question. But these Olympians challenged everything. Bill spoke out bluntly and openly, and that didn't endear him to these athletes or to the top brass of our Olympic staff. For a while the water was rough but Bowerman maintained control and in the end the respect of most everyone.

But when trying to judge Bill Bowerman's stature as a coach, one tends to think first of his total surround or system, of the Oregon environment--physical and social, much as one does when judging the great running tradition of Finland. The Oregon country is varied in terrain, consistently cool, a perfect set-up for the fartlek type of training that Bowerman emphasizes. The town of Eugene is nuts about running. I once stopped at a gas station there, whose attendant expressed more enthusiasm and personal concern for the track team than those in other states do for football or basketball. And this enthusiasm extends throughout the state of Oregon. Eugene is called "the jogging capital of the world," the initiator of the present American jogging craze.

When the total situation is positive, effective coaching and winning come easily and naturally, with few of the high pressure methods and inducements so often used in more negative situations. Joe Henderson[2] makes this point very clear:

Bowerman wouldn't admit to having any "secret method" of turning out distance men... He talks openly about his methods and there's little new or startling about them. It's clear that the man and the total distance environment at Oregon are as responsible as the training methods for one of the longest-running success stories in track.

It begins with recruiting--but not the high pressure kind of selling so commonly associated with college athletics. Bowerman neither likes it nor seems to need it. "I'm opposed to all-out recruiting," he says, "I don't like to get into the rat race. If I hear from someone I know, or preferably, if an athlete will write to me, I will do my best to interpret the University of Oregon's educational opportunity and athletic objectives to him....Of the present team, of the 21 who now make the U.S. (best performance) charts, only four ever appeared among the high school listings."

Once in school, the athletes become submerged in an atmosphere of infectious distance running enthusiasm. It's present in their coach who logs several miles of jogging himself each day. They're surrounded by a throng of talented team-mates. They're in a community with thousands of run-for-fun-and-fitness addicts. The newspapers, radio, and TV devote an extraordinary amount of space and time to track. In brief, the Oregon runners feel important and appreciated....

Runner Kvalheim tells about his training. "I think one of the secrets of Oregon's success in distance running is the way we enjoy our training together as a group of buddies. In the fall and winter, we take off every Sunday for a long run up in the mountains or down at the beach, having a lot of fun although training hard. After the run we often drop by Bill's house up on the hills to get served juice by Mrs. Bowerman. Bill is putting

---

[1] Read Vince Matthew with Neil Amdur, *MY RACE BE WON*, New York: Charterhouse, 1974, p.303ff.

[2] Joe Henderson, "A Coach and a Tradition," *Track & Field News*, 1 June 1968, 20.

a lot of emphasis on the importance of fartlek runs. This way of training makes the whole thing more pleasant than running intervals day after day on the track."

But as first stated, Bill Bowerman's story is only half told if confined to his own person. Beyond any coach I have known, his was one of mutually supportive relationships, of cooperation with and help from so many persons. For example, Bob Newland.

Bob Newland. During the Bowerman era, Medford High won four State High School team titles. During Bob Newland's ten years, Medford won nine team firsts and one second. How? The Bowerman tradition of success had a strong carry-over. Hard work on a year-round basis was accepted by the boys, the school and the community. But most important, Newland practiced organization in all its aspects.

Organization within the school. Every boy in the physical education classes was screened by use of the John Core 5-Star Test. The school paper emphasized track items. A bulletin board included a "Profile of Champions" with pictures and comments on team members--varsity and JV. A trophy case showed track records--school, state, national. During the noon hour, track films (Olympic and national) were shown. The track squad ran between 65 and 80 with everyone encouraged to stay with the sport. Faculty joined townspeople as officials at track meets. Service clubs sponsored meets such as the Kiwanis Relays and the Lions Invitational. In response to related questions, Bob Newland wrote me that,

Our home was open at all times to our athletes, and they frequently dropped in for conversation or a pre-meet meal. We considered them a part of our family and so we were able to discuss problems openly and in general enjoy one another. The athletes get to feel the coach is interested in them personally apart from athletics. As Bill Bowerman said so often, "Remember you are a student first, an athlete second."

Organization among Feeder Schools. This was the primary reason for Medford's success. Newland believed the foundation of the high school track program was based on that within the Medford Public School System. He began by meeting and reaching agreement among all public school teachers interested in track. To encourage as many youngsters as possible to compete, grade school competition was divided into three classes--A, B, C--on an age-height-weight scale. To further uniform methods, a respected track textbook was given free to each grade school and junior high coach, along with a 31-page brochure, TRACK AND FIELD-THE MEDFORD SYSTEM. This was a manual on how to create interest, discover prospects, organize a program, conduct track meets, with a hint as to recommended methods and techniques. Most important, this manual was officially issued by the Medford Public Schools System with an Introduction by the Medford Superintendent of Schools. This added authority to its teaching values. Track clinics began at the 5th-grade level. On call, "star" high school track men would be sent to a grade or junior high school to work with the young athletes; this was found very effective.

Another valuable device was a card-file system whereby the grade school coach started a card for each athlete giving all vital information including performances and personal evaluations by the coach. These cards were passed along as the athlete progressed in school, and gave important background information, especially if a coach wanted to check out why an athlete had failed to report for track.

North Eugene High School. When Newland came to North Eugene High School in 1957 as vice-principal, he was asked to continue being active in track and field. He immediately re-established his close relationship with Bill Bowerman and, working together, they started their age-group all-comers summer track program that became the model for the United States Track Federation's National Age-Group Program.[1] This had the strong support of the University of Oregon and the Oregon Track Club. Newland wrote me,

While the Oregon Track Club did help all high school track programs in the area, that was not its full intent. We wanted to enlist community support for the University track and field program as well as provide a great physical fitness and fun program for the Greater Eugene community.

---

[1] Bob Newland, "Organizing Summer Track Meets," *USTCA QUARTERLY*, Vol. 64, No. 3, 1964 and Vol. 67, No. 2, 1967.

That first summer, 1957, they had five two-day meets with about 75 athletes at each meet. In 1975, between 500 and 600 competed in the program. Oregon Track Club athletes *and their wives* (most important!) did most of the officiating. But prominent people also help, as when the Mayor of Eugene officiated the high jump and Dick Fosbury put up the cross-bar.

"At first," says Newland, "we had age-group divisions like six-and-under, 7-10 and 11-13, but that was too wide a spread. All the older kids were winning. Since we wanted to encourage as many as possible, we narrowed the grouping to two years. That meant lots more ribbons which pleased everybody. Even Dyrol Burleson, Olympic 1500 place-winner, came up for his ribbon....

Thursday meets are a wonder to behold--swarms of children running, jumping, putting the shot; swarms of parents with stopwatches on the field, grinning maniacally or shouting themselves hoarse from the bleachers....

During the girls' four-and-under race, the shouting from the stands is tremendous. Then the leader stops one foot from the finish, shyly unwilling to break the string.[1]

Add to this summer-long program a series of all-comers long-distance runs called Butte-to-Butte, of which there are many in the area, with 300 or more competitors, and we begin to understand what Newland and Bowerman mean by trying to establish wide and warm relationships.

I have said nothing of Bob Newland's leadership as personal charisma. That's not the word unless we can define charisma in terms of long hours and hard work. Add to his full-time job as vice-principal and track coach, the following activities: Director National Collegiate Track Championships--1962, 1964, 1972. Assistant Manager U.S. Olympic Team, 1976. Director National AAU Track Championships, 1971. Director Portland Indoor Invitational, 1961-1972. Track and Field Chairman Oregon AAU, 8 years. Track and Field Chairman, USTFF, 6 years. Director U.S. Olympic Final Trials, Eugene, 1972. Guest Lecturer, First International Track & Field Coaches Association Clinic, Berkeley, Cal., 1956. President Oregon High School Teachers Association, President University of Oregon Dads' Club, 1970.

Small wonder that Bob wrote me,

Coaching hours are hard to measure. When you aren't writing letters to outstanding coaches and athletes for information, making up workouts for individual athletes, publicizing your program, writing lesson plans for classes, instructing classes, we may be assisting in either football or basketball. Sometimes it seems the day never ends. Many times in the winter months I did not get home until 9 or 10 in the evening.

WAYNE VANDENBURG--UNIVERSITY OF TEXAS EL PASO (1967-1972).
Under the head of "Fastest Super-Mouth in the West," Bert Nelson (*Track & Field News*, 1 June 1972, 20) wrote the following concerning Wayne Vandenburg,

To use his favorite word, Wayne Vandenburg is a "super" promoter. The young coach at the El Paso campus of the University of Texas may, in fact, have no peers among track and field coaches when it comes to promoting their sport.

It wasn't long after he entered college coaching, as assistant coach at the University of New Mexico in 1965, that Vandy started making a national reputation. A virtually non-stop talker, he soon became known as the fastest mouth in the west. Soon it was realized that a lot of knowledge backed up the flow of words and Wayne was recognized as one of the country's best informed experts on the subject of high school track and field. Track & Field News' far-reaching string of prep correspondents occasionally failed to come up with details of schoolboy athletic feats that Vandenburg could rattle off without pause.

It wasn't long before that knowledge and that gift of gab were put to practical use. Recruiting it was called, and it seemed he was born for the game. He got his chance to

---

[1]Bobbie Conlan Moore, "A Fever Running Through the Streets," *Sports Illustrated*, August 23, 1974, p. 26.

prove it early, being named head track coach of the University of Texas at El Paso.

To some it must have seemed an early end of a promising career. Texas El Paso was nowhere as a track school. Remotely located on the high desert in the western tip of Texas, UTEP wasn't likely to appeal to many hotshots from the rest of the sprawling state, let alone to the sophisticates of either coast. Money was scarce. Team support was close to non-existent. And the physical facilities were less than super.

Was Vandenburg worried? Not to listen to him. No sooner was the job his than he un-abashedly admitted "my goal is to win an NCAA title." The laughter could be heard from Los Angeles to Eugene to Philadelphia, but it was doubtful the brash 25-year-old was listening. He was too busy talking--and recruiting.

A short two years later the laughter abruptly ceased. The impossible had happened. UTEP had its NCAA title. Villanova, winner for the past three years, surrendered its cross-country throne to the Texas upstarts. But it wasn't really a Texas team, for of the seven runners three were Australians and a fourth was English. That's capital R Recruiting, and from then on Wayne Vandenburg has been recognized, and feared, as the equal if not the superior of the country's track recruiters.

There are those who say Vandy recruited a little too hard. His early track squads were hastily patched together congregations which included unknown frosh, transfers from other schools and second-chance drop-outs. There were some who probably shouldn't have been in college and some who definitely weren't suited for UTEP. The predictable result was trouble and El Paso had it. There was an official NCAA reprimand and a number of athletes, headed by superstar Bob Beamon, departed.

Pausing only long enough to digest his lesson, a mellowing, maturing Vandenburg began to build on a more solid base. UTEP became firmly established as a track power on the basis of two fifths and a sixth in the NCAA outdoor meet and a second indoors. This year, the Miners, whose coach actually is talking a little less and listening more, have a real shot at the big bauble. They have a fast, deep sprint squad capable of scoring well in five events, a double-threat in Fred DeBernardi, and a lot of others who could get in the money, including, believe it or not, two hammer throwers.

Hammer throwers in El Paso? You bet. And in that unlikely situation is found two of the keys to Vandenburg's success. Peter Farmer hails from far away Sydney, Australia, one more proof of Vandy's unquestioned recruiting ability. But it takes more than recruit-ing to take a 19-year-old freshman from 195-6 to 220-plus in one season. Or to take the other ball-and-chainer, Pryor Nunn, from the 130-feet he threw last spring as a newly converted discusman to the 195-footer he is today.

But the greatest coach in the world is helpless without material and recruiting long has been known as the name of the US collegiate game. And that is where Vandenburg excels. Of the 48 names in the 1972 press book, only 12 are from Texas, including seven locals from El Paso. Seven foreign countries furnish 14 athletes, including six from Australia alone. New York and California contribute seven and six squad members and the rest are scattered among five other states. That is indeed super promotion.

But super promoter Wayne Vandenburg hasn't earned the title on recruiting alone. To his everlasting credit, he cares, really cares, about track. It's a love with him. And he promotes it.

Item. He's the only track coach I know to have his own TV program "The Wayne Vandenburg Track Show" is aired for a half-hour weekly.

Item. UTEP put up only half the $120,000 cost of the new Tartan track. So Vandy pro-moted the rest. They got an eight lane Tartan track, complete with field event run-ups.

Item. It takes help to dig up that kind of money, and the additional funds needed for grants and other expenses. So Wayne promoted the El Paso Amateur Track & Field Associa-tion and the El Paso Track & Field Officials' Association, which is a division of the former. The latter group has 117 men, each of whom not only bought a handsome uniform at $85 each and worked to become competent officials, but gave their time and energies to promoting track in the El Paso area.

Item. A first-class team deserves first-class competition, and so the 6-2, 200-pound coach put together (an extensive) 1972 home schedule, beginning Feb. 26 and ending May 22...

Item. Such a schedule deserves fan support, requiring promotion. So two large, color posters...were printed by Coors Beer and distributed to 1100 Coors' outlets. El Paso Natural Gas came through with 12,000 folders....Two local gas chains contributed 5000 bumper stickers. Television stations produced 20-, 30-, and 60-second spots over an eight week period and radio did its part. All hammered away at the "Debut '72" theme.

Item. There was no judges stand. So when Wayne spotted some airplane loading ramps no longer needed by El Paso's new terminal, the result was inevitable and the highly suitable stand is in action today....

Item. Not content with a "super facility" he touts as one of the best in the country, Vandy has complete plans for $108,000 worth of electric scoreboard and electronic timing capacity and is on his way to promoting it.

Item. There is more to track than intercollegiate competition and, wanting the best, the hard-working coach created the El Paso Invitational last year. Nearly blown out of the stadium by a dust storm the natives still brag about, Vandy was undeterred. This year the weather was great, the field was super, and the crowd was disappointingly small. The meet took a bath that could cost as much as $10,000. But the true promoter never quits, and within hours Wayne was vowing to come back with another super winner.

Item. Attracting class athletes to an invitational meet, particularly when it's in far-off El Paso, is a promotional art in itself. So Vandenburg laid on the hospitality and provided prizes the likes of which may not have been seen in this country. To the winner went AM-FM cassette recorders, while second placers got AM-FM digital clock radios, and third-placers won AM-FM transistor pocket radios. Each placer received a pair of double-knit slacks. And all took home unique El Paso Invitational plaques. Created by Tiny Barcena, a former track coach and active member of the booster club, the plaques are works of art and would be more than satisfactory prizes themselves. An 11 inch casting featuring the Aztec sun calendar is mounted on a hand carved wooden base 16 inches in diameter. Together, they emphasize the cultural blend that exists in El Paso, the largest American city on the Mexican border. The prizes were promoted, of course. Each event sponsor paid $150 for the privilege, items were purchased at wholesale or less and one sponsor, Chico's Tacos to be exact, came through with a cool $1000.

How and why does this friendly, enthusiastic father of two do it? The question is answered in the UTEP press book: "The secret to Vandenburg's success is work, and here's how he reflects on the subject: 'I like a situation where you never get caught up, no matter how hard you work. So you go at it as hard as you can, as long as you can. You achieve results, but you're never really satisfied, because you know you could have always done more.' He's a high pressure, constant motion man who lives and dies track."

Never stopping, never satisfied, Vandy is even now preparing his talented squad for that NCAA challenge, winding up the finishing touches on a recruiting campaign that already has a flock of goodies headed for Vandytown, planning landscaping for the stadium, and, undoubtedly, working on a super promotion or two.

There is a sequel to this. In November 1972, Vandy[1] was fired by the UTEP athletic director for flagrant violations of university authority and rules. In 1975, UTEP, under its new coach, Ted Banks, won the NCAA team title in indoor and outdoor track as well as cross-country. No school had ever done that before. In 1980, UTEP won the NCAA indoor title with a record 72 points. Sixty four of these were scored by men from seven foreign countries, most of whom

---

[1]"Successful El Paso Coach Vandenburg Fired," *Track & Field News*, Box 296, Los Altos, Cal., 19422, December 1972, p. 27.

were over 21 years of age; two over 27. It seems clear that Vandenburg's excesses in promotion were really quite in keeping with UTEP's belief in winning as the main, if not the only, end.

EDWARD M. "Ted" HAYDON--UNIVERSITY OF CHICAGO TRACK CLUB (1950--).

Ted Haydon's primary qualification as a "coach of unusual interest" is his role as originator, organizer, money-raiser, locker room supervisor, track and pit raker, program editor, father confessor, and--oh yes--coach, humorist and good friend of the University of Chicago Track Club.

That's both a unique and important qualification. In various talks and papers,[1] I have described his program--one that allows non-college athletes of any age or sex or talent to have the advantages of college facilities and coaching for year-round training and competition--as the most significant of the past 50 years in its potential for improvement of our national program of track and field. Why was it so significant? In brief, because this was the first longtime effort to successfully combine our shamefully weak club program with our outstanding school-college program--all at little extra cost to the latter.

Bill Jauss of *The Chicago Tribune* tells the story,[2]

Pick out almost any time in Ted Haydon's 25 years as coach of the University of Chicago Track Club. You're sure to find evidence of the resiliency and the droll sense of humor that make Haydon one of the best liked and most respected persons in sport.

Go back, for example, halfway in the 25-year UCTC history. Haydon's purely amateur runners were being hassled then as pawns in the selfish, senseless power struggle between the two grand poo-bahs of amateur sport.

The Amateur Athletic Union (AAU) and the U. S. Track and Field Federation, an arm of the National Collegiate Athletic Association (NCAA), each told Haydon that his athletes would be barred from competition unless their group--and only their group--sanctioned Haydon's track meets.

Haydon, you must understand, never has been terribly impressed with sanctions or unions or federations or associations. Instead, this white-haired, red-faced, Canadian-born, South Side-reared 62-year-old ex-social worker simply works hard so that the greatest number of people--regardless of sanction, sex, skin color, or speed--can run or jump in his meets....

During the AAU-NCAA "alphabet war" in the 60s, Haydon recalled, during an interview, he had to "get tough" when neither of the factions saw much humor in his unsanctioned "practice meets." "We told both of them," Ted said, "that we, not they, had exclusive sanction to the territory between 56th and 57th and between University and Greenwood. And that our sanction body was 'R.F.F.'" Haydon pronounced "R.F.F." like a dog snarling at a door-to-door peddler: "Rrrrooofff!" The initials stand for "Run for Fun."

Ken Doherty, respected director of the Penn Relays and ex-coach at Michigan, spoke precisely about Haydon last Sunday when, at the UCTC Silver Anniversary dinner, he said that Haydon's "Run for Fun" philosophy and his university's permitting outsiders to run for its club represent "the most significant work of any track coach in the U.S.....and the most significant development in amateur sport in 50 years."

Think of sports as we know them. Imagine how things would change if others dropped their win-at-all-cost, recruit-at-all-cost policies and replaced them with the Haydon-Chicago plan.

Chicago is a school where no candidate is cut from a varsity squad. Haydon conducts a club program where no athlete gets recruited or paid and even a superstar such as the half-mile record holder, Rick Wohlhuter, may be asked to pay part of his expenses to a meet.

_____

[1]Ken Doherty, "A Better Future for United States Track and Field," *USTCA Quarterly*, June 1966, 39-47.

[2]Bill Jauss, "The Man Who Keeps the UCTC Running," *The Chicago Tribune*, January 23, 1975.

In 1950, Haydon quit being a volunteer coach and full-time social worker and succeeded Ned Merriam, his old college track coach. He also welcomed postcollege Maroons who still wished to compete....

The UCTC breakthru came in 1954 when miler Lawton Lamb, an Illinois grad training with the club, asked Haydon: "Can I run for this club even tho I didn't go to Chicago?" Haydon relayed the question to his athletic director, T. N. Metcalf, who answered: "Why not."...Drop in at one of the 30 to 40 meets a year at the University of Chicago. You see black and white, Jew and gentile. Male and female. Young and old. Bearded and clean-shaven. Intellectual and barely literate. Champion and plodder.

"We do not discriminate," Haydon said years ago, "against anyone on the basis of race, creed, or talent." Author Hal Higdon, still a competitive distance runner at 40-plus, has told the delightful story of Sam Ash. Sam (like "Murphy the Milkman") walked into the fieldhouse one day and announced to Haydon that he was a miler. When Ted asked how fast Sam ran the mile, he pondered and replied, "oh, 4 or 4½ minutes." Sam Ash, Higdon recalls, probably never broke six minutes. But one time Sam found himself in a race against five class milers including Coleman, Ted Wheeler, and Higdon. Ash finished sixth and dead last, of course. But they awarded medals in this meet to the first six finishers. "Coach," medal winner Ash told Haydon the next day, "that was the proudest moment of my life."

Open to all? You'd better believe it. Higdon once questioned Haydon about the sign painted on the stately Gothic walls of old Bartlett: "Power to the Gay Jocks." First came Haydon's familiar smile. Then, "there's nothing to prevent homosexuals from having a wholesome interest in sports, is there?" Haydon looked up from the notes he'd just taken. "Our group," he said, "is just like a natural gang. It starts somewhere," he said. "It ends somewhere. But you're never sure just where. You can't say 'these are the athletes.' Or, 'these are the officials.' Or 'these are the contributors.' Because we all do each thing."

Haydon withdrew from a file cabinet the current (loose, of course) budget of the track club. It's up $10,000 from last year to $32,000. Home meets took in only $927. In the midst of the "alphabet war," meet receipts were just $300, suggesting why the AAU and NCAA ignored Ted's jiving them. The club, Haydon explained, breaks even because scores of ex-Olympians and Murphy the Milkmen contribute to it. Nearly 80 percent of the expenses ($25,000 last year) went to sending athletes to meets.

Haydon's phone jangled. This time it was a Peoria high school coach expressing some "concerns" about the upcoming weekend meet. "...Just come up Saturday. I'll guarantee you there will be athletes your people can beat. And I'll guarantee, no matter how good they are, your athletes will be beaten by some others..." Haydon listened, then smiled. "...What's that? Oh, 'our neighborhood' here? Well, I've heard some bad things about Peoria, too. No, just park in the street. Nobody will bother you."....

If Haydon sometimes wears a dazed look, his duties as coach of the undergraduate Maroons and the club sometimes take 16 hours a day.

In some unfathomable fashion, in that shipwreck office of his, Haydon handles the budget, travel plans, and correspondence for UCTC. After dark, he has shivered, turned flashlight on stopwatch, and cried out interval times to circling club runners (Olympians and Sam Ashes alike).

"If Ted was paid double time for overtime," says Maroon Athletic Director Wally Hass, "he would be a multimillionaire." Haydon is rich in wealth a bankbook cannot measure. He's helped coach U. S. Olympic teams in Mexico City and in Munich in 1968 and 1972. He holds the respect of hundreds of past and current Maroon and UCTC athletes.

During the past century, our school-college track program has been supreme among the many Olympic nations in providing the essentials of success--facilities, coaching, training and competitive program. But that program covers only the years between about 12 and 22. Beyond those years we have provided almost none of the essentials--no facilities, very inadequate coaching, and a competitive program restricted to only a few hundred of the best athletes.

When we realize that these essentials of the school-college system are largely unused during the hours of the day (evening), weekends, and months of the year (summer) when those with jobs would most like to use them, it seems only common sense that they should be made available as was done by Ted Haydon and the University of Chicago. Add the fact that other successful Olympic nations in Europe and the Soviet Union center their sports programs around the club concept in which people engage in organized sports as long as they feel it's worth doing--any age from 6 to 60. Add finally the keystone of Haydon's approach--Run-for-Fun, and we have a sound formula for a rebirth of track and field in this country. Only long tradition with its fear of what might happen in the way of added costs and misuse of facilities stands in the way.

But the over-25-year UCTC program has effectively demonstrated it can be done--in a large-city college within a less-than-desirable residential area, with an actual enhancement of the college program, and at minimal additional cost to the college administration. How was this done?[1] In all-too-brief summary: (1) An emphasis on numbers--numbers of club members and competitors in club meets. In 1975 the UCTC had 200 members of both sexes and from ages 11 to 53. (2) No formal recruiting of track stars. Welcome those that join of their own free will, provide full opportunities for training, for coaching, and for year-round competition, and the stars will be happy to join. For example, by 1976 the UCTC held the world record for the two-mile relay (7:10.4) and had won six out of seven AAU Indoor Championship two-mile relays (1969-1975), using such Greats as Rick Wohlhuter and Lowell Paul. (3) Organize many meet competitions--indoors and outdoors, winter-spring-summer, as well as some six cross-country runs in the fall--a total of 30 or more with from 150 to 600 competitors in each meet. (4) Emphasize number and needs of athletes, not number or needs of spectators. In 1974 total gate receipts for over 30 meets was under $1000. Pay no expenses to star athletes competing in UCTC-sponsored meets. Welcome but otherwise ignore the news media. (5) Keep the UCTC yearly budget low. Until 1970 it was kept below $10,000, but rose in 1975 to $30,000. Raise money for this budget from (a) contributions by friends of the UCTC--44 percent; guarantees for athletes' expenses from large-meet directors--34 percent; entry fees for UCTC meets--10 percent; gate receipts--3 percent; other--9 percent. Contributions by friends included several hundred small gifts but also a few larger gifts by such organizations as the Mayor Daley Youth Foundation.

True, there has been only one Ted Haydon. True, it requires a near-genius in dedication and energy, in achieving an acceptable organization of meets and schedules within an apparent chaos, in maintaining patience and good humor despite endless frustrations and small irritations, in making-do with less, and in solving all the problems inherent in any attempt to open elitist doors to the many. Perhaps only a very few coaches will be able to equal Haydon's program. But most school-college coaches can exert enough influence one way or another to start such a club program and gradually increase its scope as attitudes and conditions permit. Not only would such a national program upgrade our Olympic performances; even more important it would allow many thousands of young and old to gain the benefits of year-round training and competition in track and field.

Oh, by the way--hardly worth mentioning though when you're speaking about Ted Haydon--Ted was Assistant Olympic Coach at both Mexico City and Munich, was Head Coach for the Russian and Polish meets abroad in 1975, and was inducted into the National Track and Field Hall of Fame, 1975, "for long and outstanding service to United States track and field." When congratulated for such honors, Ted always grins away his embarrassment with some such remark as "Yes, I guess it was a lot of hard work I enjoyed but it took Rick Wohlhuter's world records to bring all this attention, and that was all his doing, not mine."

One further important point. Jauss wrote, "his duties as coach...sometimes take 16 hours a day." Sixteen hours! How much time did that leave Ted to fulfill his other obligations to his home and community? When I wrote Ted's wife, Goldie Haydon, about this, she replied,

Ted is home evenings after 8 o'clock, except for occasional meetings. Sundays he is home except for 4-7 o'clock when he goes to the fieldhouse for team workouts and for high school athletes to have a chance to run on a track instead of in the high-school hall. Holidays and vacation periods he has daily workouts, except that in the summer

---

[1]Ted Haydon, "Starting a Track and Field Club," NCTCA *Quarterly*, 1960, p. 13.

I feel it is good to get away to Michigan for a change, where we have no telephone. But we return to Chicago for meets.

When we have a family date or dinner occasionally, Ted's assistant coach substitutes at practice. He pays his own assistant because the University had to cut down.

Preparations for meets are done by us at home. Ted has no secretary so I help him with stuffing-mailing-sealing-stamping letters. I also pin medals on ribbons and help prepare the judges' record cards, etc. Ted has the use of two rooms for all this. He has a typewriter and copier. We do a great deal of telephoning at home.

Much of our social life is with people involved in the program, and all of it has to be planned around the year's schedule. Occasionally we have athletes staying overnite, as do others from our own club; all join in to help out with meet preparations when needed.

For all-day meets (afternoon and evening), I usually have four buffet suppers a year for the coaches, since there are few suitable places to eat near the University.

All this takes time, lots of work, honesty and real interest. The reward is satisfaction in being able to contribute to others' lives, and the fun of creating something worthwhile.

That says it all. Wait, not quite; I must add that Goldie's letter indicated a typewriter badly in need of repair and a ribbon badly in need of replacement. And that takes care of those who wail that their budgets just won't permit a Chicago Club plan at their school.

GARY WINCKLER -- FLORIDA STATE UNIVERSITY, (Women's Track and Field, 1982----)
In June 1984, Florida State University won its first-ever Women's NCAA track and field title, a great tribute to the organizational ability of Gary Winckler, then in only his third year at FSU. But let *Track & Field News*[1] tell the story,

"People talk about how precarious it is to depend on sprinters, but I can't see that as being any more precarious than depending on distance runners," said Florida State's Gary Winckler as the meet began to rev up. "Our sprinters are experienced and know what to expect."

Pure speed doesn't hurt either, and the Tallahassee lassies showed plenty of it as they won both relays and all three sprints. The 4 x 100 title went to Michelle Finn, Marita Payne, Brenda Cliette and Randy Givens. For the 4 x 4 the order was Janet Davis, Cliette, Givens and Payne. All scored well individually, too, Givens winning the 100 and 200 (Cliette runner-up on both occasions), Payne capturing the 400 (with a 3rd in the 200), Finn taking 4th in the 100 and 9th in the 200 and Davis copping 6th in the half-lapper. That fearsome fivesome thus combined for 129 points, just enough to beat Tennessee's 124.

Before Winckler's arrival, no track and field team from FSU had finished in the top 50 teams in the NCAA title meet. But in 1981 (Gary was assistant coach), and 1982, FSU finished third; in 1983, second; and as above, in 1984, first. Winckler was assistant women's coach at Oregon State prior to joining the staff at FSU. During three seasons at Oregon, he helped build the program from 10 to a roster of 45, demonstrating his continuous emphasis on numbers and team balance. In addition to publishing numerous articles, especially those emphasizing planning and the concept of "Periodization" as basic to optimal organization, Winckler has somehow found time to function as Associate Director with Vern Gambetta of the TAC National Coaching Certification Program.

In contrast to the other ten coaches in this Chapter through whom we have highlighted personal and group relationships, this story of Gary Winckler will seek to develop his views on program planning. All available information indicates that his "mutually supportive relationships" have been strong, warm and vital to his success in coaching. Nor should we ignore his being able to employ two full-time assistant coaches: Al Schmidt, coach of distance running

---

[1]*Track & Field News*, July 1984, p. 24.

and FSU's recruiting coordinator; and Malcolm Coomber, former British A.A.B. senior coach, who is now working for his master's degree in motor behavior at Florida State--all in all, a capable and science-oriented staff.

But the unique aspect of Coach Winckler's work, the aspect that best justifies his inclusion in this Chapter on "coaches of special interest," is his emphasis on planning--planning in a holistic sense but equally, planning of all phases and details of his work. The following paragraphs are both digested and excerpted from personal letters, from publications, but especially from the multigraphed sheets he prepared for his own squad members.

From a letter.

As a basic premise, I believe very strongly in "Planned Performance Training" or periodization. I feel one of the most overlooked areas in sprint coaching within the United States is that of training the proper energy systems. For example, there are many "good" sprint coaches who never train the alactic-anaerobic energy systems of their athletes in the early preparation part of the training year. The only time these athletes use these energy systems is when they compete. This leads in turn to higher injury potentials as well as lower performance results. What I have attempted to do this year in particular is draw up a training plan where each component of training (eg, speed, speed endurance, etc.) is distributed by volume with weighted variance and sequenced throughout the meso and microcycles of the training year so as to complement the training of other components.

From the 1984 squad instruction sheets.

The beginning of another training year is once again upon us. Hopefully each of you has taken some time to evaluate the past year, to rest, and to catch for yourselves greater visions for the year ahead.

The training year outlined in the coming pages is based upon the supposition that we have all grown a year older, accomplished higher levels of achievement during the past year than before, and, most important, are now anxious to embark upon a well planned assault on yet higher levels of excellence in personal growth and athletic achievement. In the absence of this supposition none of us can grow and the efforts we put forth this year as athletes and coaches would result in disharmony. We must all keep in mind that TRAINING is not just what you do on the field but is a life style composed of methods of eating, sleeping, relaxing, personal health care, physical work, and mental preparedness working in concert together. Training is stressful. The body must adapt to stress. Do not limit yourselves in dealing with this stress and you will not become disappointed. To quote Norman Cousins in his book ANATOMY OF AN ILLNESS, "What is important is the knowledge that human beings are not locked into fixed limitations. The quest for perfectability is not a presumption or a blasphemy but the highest manifestation of a great design."

Training.

It is well accepted that talent is a large factor in determining ultimate potential. However, how one trains determines how successful you become in achieving that potential. There does not exist any one or best way to train, but there do exist principles which must be adhered to if training is to become effective.

The basic laws in training which must be obeyed in devising any training program are:

1) Specificity--"You are what you train to be". Adaptation is brought about by placing desireable stresses upon the athlete. Adaptation is specific to a stressor and the affect of a stressor is specific to an individual athlete.

2) Overload--It is necessary to provide a progressive increase in intensity and extent of loadings or stressors for the body to reach a higher level of adaptation.

3) Reversibility--When intensity or extent are reduced, the level of adaptation brought about by overload will decline. In general, the quicker the gains the quicker the losses; the slower the gains, the slower the losses.

Other key characteristics to any training program are that it be:

1) Systematic--Carefully combining all the components of training into a system.

2) *Sequential*--Dividing the training year into specific phases each building upon the previous one to achieve a peak level of fitness and preparation at the desired time.

3) *Progressive*--Building upon what has been previously accomplished.

4) *Variational*--Avoiding monotony (without confusing the issue with too many extraneous activities and ideas).

5) *Imitational*--Simulates mentally and physically the conditions of competition with regard to terrain, time of day, type of facility, length of competition, etc.

The Plan. "When a man does not know what harbor he is making for, no wind is the right wind." Planning is the start of control and consistency. It brings the future into the present so that you can do something about it today. Let's begin by first dividing our training into the...components of training which we will need to blend together to devise our plan.

Maximum Strength--The greatest force the neuromuscular system is capable of exerting in a single maximum voluntary contraction.

Elastic Strength--The ability of the neuromuscular system to overcome resistance with a high speed of contraction. This is accomplished through the coordination and involvement of reflexes and the elastic and contractile components of muscle.

Strength Endurance--The ability to withstand fatigue. It is characterised by the high ability to express strength over long time periods. For example, 400H, 400m, 800m - 3000m are all events requiring a high degree of strength endurance.

Basic Endurance--The ability to carry out a given amount of work during a prolonged period of time without deterioration in the quality of such work.

Mobility--The capacity to perform joint actions through a wide range of motion.

Speed--Moving a limb, part of the body's lever system, or the whole body with the greatest possible velocity. Speed can be improved through short duration work at 90-100% maximum intensity.

Special Endurance--Competition specific endurance work special to the event. Work is of very high intensity with long recoveries between a small number of repetitions.

Speed Endurance--The ability to produce high qualities of speed performance despite the presence of high oxygen debt and lactic acid buildup.

Technique--The capacity to perform an event with the most efficient biomechanical application under conditions of high physical intensity and mental and physical stress.

Recovery--Allowing the body to recover from training bouts.

The Training Year

Probably one of the most neglected facets of training athletes in sports is the area of organization of the training year into progressive phases designed to get the best performances from all athletes during the biggest competitions. The term given for describing such organization is PERIODIZATION. Periodization has three primary objectives:

1) To prepare the athlete for achievement of optimal performance improvement.
2) To prepare the athlete for a climax to the competitive season, (eg NCAA or TAC Nationals).
3) To prepare the athlete for the...major meets leading up to the championship event.

The above is only a summary of Winckler's introduction to his planned program. Details have been deleted. The remainder of his 37-page squad instructions spell out precise ways by which this process of "Periodization" is to be implemented.

LeROY T. WALKER, Ph.D.,--NORTH CAROLINA CENTRAL UNIVERSITY (1945-1978).
A most remarkable story--that of LeRoy T. Walker, a story of a Black boy growing up in segre-
gated Atlanta, Georgia in the 1930s, long before the Whites' social shackles had been loosened,
a Black boy who, within a ten-year span from 1971-1982, received national honors at the highest
possible level including (1) Head Coach U.S. Olympic Track and Field, 1976; (2) the Luther B.
Gulick Award, 1982, "the highest honor the American Association of Health, Physical Education
and Recreation can give to one of its members"; (3) Chancellor of his own North Carolina
Central University, and (4) the Encyclopedia Britannica Achievement-in-Life Award, 1977. To
these honors can be added induction into nine Track and Field Halls of Fame and seven wide-
ranging honors and awards listed at the end of this sketch.

It's a story worthy of a book-size biography that might well be sub-titled, "A Study in
Supportive Personal Relationships." The word "supportive" is in itself remarkable. How can
it possibly describe an Atlanta, Georgia Black boy of the 1930s who attended Benedict College
in Columbia, South Carolina, at that time non-accredited, all-Black, with an enrollment of
less than 1000. A Black boy who, despite his Magna Cum Laude academic status at graduation,
was placed on the "waiting lists" of the White medical schools he sought to enter; and then
waited--and waited--and waited--to no avail. In 1945 he began coaching at all-Black North
Carolina Central College which lacked prestige in track and field even more than it lacked
finances and facilities for practice. Later Walker recalled "the day in 1948 when NCC was
running in the Washington Evening Star Games. In the sprints we had to take two athletes with
the same shoe size simply because we only had one pair of shoes between them--perhaps the only
time in history when one pair of shoes won two first places while being worn by two persons."

He also recalled the desperation of coaching Olympian Lee Calhoun, and baton-passing among
the fine sprinters that made up his championship (4 x 100y) relay teams--all with "impossible"
facilities. But he found Bob Chambers, Duke track coach, most supportive so that "occasionally" they worked out on the Duke track with hurdles champion, Joel Shankle.

Out of all that and much more of the same or worse, one would expect discontent, resentment,
bitterness and, in 99.9 percent of other Black boys of Walker's era, would have found it. But
by some magic of upbringing or innate character, Coach Walker was genuinely supportive of all
those with whom he came in contact--supportive not in the "get-by" sense of doing others' work
for them but of encouraging and challenging others to do their own best-possible work. Somehow he was able to set aside his own feelings and preferences so as to better understand other
persons' viewpoints and to be helpful in terms of other persons' needs. Somehow, as one man
judged Walker's work on a committee of Consultants to the U.S. Olympic Committee, he became
"a healer of differences" between the various factions fighting for recognition and control.
Somehow, as another said of his success in organizing the 1978 USA-USSR track meet in Durham,
"He put everyone to work and they enjoyed it and were proud of what they had done."

That's a rare quality--to some extent innate by virtue of physique and face and voice and
inner calmness, but also acquired through years of making more out of less, of being constantly
surrounded by family and friends that were mutually supportive, firm-handed, even strictly
disciplined, but kind in their inter-relationships, of being self-dependent but also enjoying working with others.

In other words, as Walker wrote to me, of having "learned from my mother, brothers and
sisters at a very early age the meaning of the four D's--Discontent (with the statue quo),
Dedication, Devotion to task, and Discipline." And apparently all of this, in Walker's mind,
as related to working with and for people.

My first contacts with Coach Walker occurred when he brought his track team from NCCU to the
Pennsylvania Relays in the late 1950s. As a new Director, I sought a more democratic approach
by way of coaches' meetings. Frankly, it wasn't a very practical idea. The largest track meet
in the world required precision in all its operations and immediate solutions when problems
arose. But 50 coaches meeting together tended to have 50 viewpoints. Arguments required time;
strident voices required patience. Gradually, I became aware of one well-controlled and im-
personal voice coming through the others with unbiased suggestions that gained acceptance,
that of LeRoy Walker. Later we compromised by replacing the general meeting with a coaches'
committee, on which of course was Walker.

In 1968 we recognized Walker's supportive actions as well as the success of his teams at the Carnival--12 sprint relay championships and 8 individual titles including those of Norm Tate, 1964, and Larry Black, 1972, as "most outstanding athlete"--by making him Honorary Referee of the Carnival.

Inevitably, in 1969, he became the working referee where he has served ever since under the present Carnival Director, James Tuppeny. A largely thankless job--no citations, no newspaper articles--no laudatory statements in the printed Program, not even full travelling expenses. But many tough decisions to make that, either way, hurt and even lost friends. In 1983, a controversy arose between Arkansas and hometown favorite, Villanova. Could Arkansas switch its 220-440 men between trials and final. Penn Relay policy said, "No;" the NCAA Rules Book said nothing against it. So, though local fans were irate, Walker ruled in favor of Arkansas. He listened to both viewpoints, consulted with unbiased others, then ruled calmly, quickly and decisively with no further discussion. May all referees do as well! Just now I phoned Director Tuppeny, "Will LeRoy be asked to serve again in 1985?" "Yes, of course, and for 1986 and the year 2000 if we're all still around."

As a coach, Walker enjoyed remarkable success, especially when we realize NCCU's relatively small student body, its lack of success prior to Walker's coming in 1945, and very limited track and field facilities. Eight of his men earned places on U.S. Olympic teams (1956-1984), of whom Lee Calhoun was Olympic 110m hurdles champion twice--1956, 1960. (In addition, Walker coached numerous Olympians as Olympic coach for Ethiopia, Israel, Jamaica, Trinidad and Kenya-- all prior to his selection in 1976 as Head Coach U.S. Olympic Track and Field.

But through it all, and I think this is the true measure of his accomplishment, Walker's primary influence was on the man, even more than on the athlete. In a taped radio interview, Lee Calhoun, later head coach at Yale University, said of him, "When I first came to Coach Walker in 1955, I wanted to be a high jumper; I did not want to be a hurdler. But he was pretty demanding in those early days, so I hurdled and soon learned to like it. But first he demanded that I be a better student, and I did that, and liked it. He'd say, 'It's all very simple. Whatever you try to do, go out and do your best at it. I will give you a program you can live by; although it may hurt you, it won't kill you; it will give you many a night of pain and aches but in the end you will be the better for it.'"

In a similar interview, Norm Tate, class of '64, stated, "I see him now and I just light up. When he first started coaching he was more dominant, even demanding. But now he's a lot looser; he's mellowed a lot." To which Walker laughed, "I don't know about being mellower, but I do listen to them a lot more and if they're saying things relevant to what's going on in this new world, well, I listen, or try to listen. I guess I was demanding in those early years, but I only demanded 1½ to 2 hours of practice, and sometimes we'd just take time off and do nothing--when exams came along and that sort of thing. But in all those years, on all those teams, we had only a dozen or so that failed to get their college degrees."

Sprinter Larry Black made even clearer the same point, "Of all the records we now have at NCCU, the most important thing that Dr. Walker explained to us was--You are here for two reasons: academically was first and track and field was second. If we didn't do our work, we didn't run. But I love the man!"

The activities described here up to this point would normally be enough for one man, certainly enough to justify inclusion in this group of track and field coaches of interest. But, though coaching track was a primary love for Walker, it was but one phase of a much broader career; in fact, much more broad than can be listed here. Between 1960-1964 he was President of the Central Intercollegiate Athletic Association; from 1971-1974, Commissioner of the Mid-Eastern Athletic Conference. From 1960-1969 he served the U.S. State Department as Educational Specialist with the Peace Corps, including Director of Program Planning and Training for the African Continent, and in 1980, 1981, 1982, Sports Consultant to the People's Republic of China.

Continuous with all that, Dr. Walker was head of the Department of Health and Physical Education at NCCU, attended national meetings regularly, served on various committees, and in 1979 was elected as National President of AAHPERD. That's an enormous organization, with many diverse personalities drawing attention; not even a Head Olympic Coach rises so high except on a basis of direct service and time-energy. The prestigious Gulick Award was made in 1982.

Consistent with his Ph.D. and high academic stature, Walker authored numerous articles in physical education and track athletics, as well as four successful books: *A MANUAL IN ADAPTED PHYSICAL EDUCATION*, Piedmont Printers, Durham, NC, 1961; *PHYSICAL EDUCATION FOR THE EXCEPTIONAL STUDENT*, William C. Brown Co., 1963; *CHAMPIONSHIP TECHNIQUES IN TRACK AND FIELD*, Parker Publishing Co., 1969; *TRACK AND FIELD FOR BOYS AND GIRLS*, The Athletic Institute, 1983.

One further bit of insight into Walker's character. In preparing for this sketch, a score or more of sources were used, including letters to me from him, a dozen speeches about him, and eight citations of his career. In none of these is there any mention of money or personal material gain. Opportunities were surely there. I think of others in similar situations who retired well-to-do. It seems clear that Walker's interests just do not lie in that direction.[1]

At my request, Coach Walker mailed this personal statement, for whatever need it might fill,

Success is a journey, not a destination. An absolute belief in this axiom has influenced my life in general, my coaching career, and has provided the basis for my interpersonal relationships with professional colleagues and the athletes with whom I have been associated for nearly four decades.

My parents and immediate family did not have the slightest clue that I would become a coach. As a matter of fact, I was groomed to become a physician. I lived across the street from a physician-family, a husband and wife team, during my early childhood in Atlanta, Georgia. I admired them both and wanted to be like them when I grew up. Furthermore, the wife of my coach at Benedict College was a Head Nurse at Waverly Hospital in Columbia, South Carolina (which was located only two blocks from the college) and often permitted me to visit the hospital operating rooms.

If all medical schools had been opened to Blacks when I finished college as a Magna Cum Laude graduate, I would have been accepted instead of being placed on various medical school "waiting lists." The waiting became long and longer, and finally led me to enter a second-choice profession which would permit me to work with people-- Health and Physical Education. In time, I gained my Master's from Columbia University and my Ph.D. from New York University.

Add to these the lessons I learned from my two early-youth idols, coach Frank Forbes, Morehouse College, and Charlie Clark, one of Morehouse College's greatest athletes, and founder of the Community Youth Club of which I was an active member. These men conducted sports in ways that emphasized (1) the value of a Spartan approach--sternly disciplined and keeping things simple; (2) the rewards of hard work; (3) the importance of a wholesome respect for an opponent while, at the same time, doing all that is fair, to win; (4) to recognize success as achieving some personal improvement; and (5) to be certain that winning at any cost is not worth the price one must pay in lessened self-respect.

I am certain that these principles, as well as those taught me by my own family, entered into my coaching and were important factors in the great development made by the fine athletes whose lives I have touched. Certainly I was inspired by their accomplishments, and felt that they would respond to ever-higher levels of motivation. Great demands on them placed greater coaching demands on me--a combination that quickened the pace of the journey and made it so much more fun.

HONORS
1971: The City of Durham Distinguished Service Award
1971: Kiwanis International Distinguished Service Award
1972: AAHPERD Honor Award
1974: North Carolina--Governor's Ambassador of Good Will Award
1976: O. Max Gardner Award for Contribution to the Welfare of the Human Race
1978: Encyclopedia Britannica Achievement-in-Life Award
1982: The President's Council on Physical Fitness & Sports Silver Anniversary Award
1982: AAHPERD Highest Honor: The Gulick Award

[1]P.S. This material was mailed (Sept. 1984) to Chancellor Walker at NCCU, and handwritten approval came from L.A. airport as he was en route to Tokyo as "Head Coach and Chief of Mission for the U.S. team" competing against the USSR, Japan, East Germany, Great Britain, etc.

WHY THESE COACHES? Reviewing the styles of these eleven coaches has been, for me at least, absolutely fascinating. I knew, personally, all but three of them--Vandenburg, White and Tellez. As a group their accomplishments were tremendous. But why these coaches, out of scores of others. Frankly, the first reason is that their stories had already been printed and were easily available. But beyond that, they were chosen because their differences in person and environment form a broad spectrum of coaching styles and relationships, one that will enable a student of the human side of coaching to analyze and understand.

These coaches were not chosen as models to be imitated or shunned as you may judge their relative merits, or from whom you may select certain traits or tricks by which to win friends, much as Dale Carnegie plucked out Charles Schwab's "prodigiously winning smile" as being his secret device for getting others to do what he wanted them to do.

Nor were these coaches chosen as examples of coaching personalities and ways of operating to be analyzed and judged as fitting within a 9-3 or 3-9 pigeonhole. In the first place, that can't be done; the infinity of attitudes and actions of any man can never be compressed into even a flexible pigeonhole. On the other hand, this process of analyzing and judging, of arguing differences and clarifying agreements should lead to a better understanding of the coaching enterprise and a clearer feeling of the general direction and attitude each student will take in trying to become a more effective coach.

Each student-coach will choose his own path, of course. But on one principle, such prolonged discussions should produce clarity and agreement. The coaching enterprise is not centered within a person, whatever his charisma or knowledge or experienced expertise may be. Rather the coaching enterprise is a relationship among that person and all the other persons within what I have called the team family--team members, administration and faculty of the school or college, the local community, the alumni and bird dogs, the entire track world at home and abroad. A coach always functions within such a complex of relationships.

When we evaluate any given coach we need to ask who he was and what he accomplished, but equally crucial, within what team family, what social milieu, what cultural system and sub-systems did he operate. Use Jumbo Elliott and LeRoy Walker as examples. Both were very successful and respected coaches. Elliott was a business man, a millionaire salesman of earth-moving machinery, an occasional golf partner of Bob Hope, a student of Carnegie's *HOW TO WIN FRIENDS AND INFLUENCE PEOPLE*, a Catholic in a large-city Catholic University for which he was chairman of alumni fund-raising. In one long sentence, a certain climate of mutually supportive relationships is made clear.

LeRoy Walker also achieved much--Head Olympic Coach, winner of the AAHPERD Gulick award, Educational Specialist for the Peace Corps, Chancellor of his University. But the climate of his relationships was so different from that of Elliott. Walker's early life was as a Black in a Southern White community. He accepted sports and physical education as a "second-choice profession which would permit me to work with people." Money was neither a goal in itself nor a means to such a goal. His personal relationships gradually became as world-wide as those of any man ever in any sport.

Which of these eleven coaches presents a pattern that might influence your hopes and plans for the future?

Chapter 5
THE HUMAN SIDE OF COACHING

All agree that the job of coaching is one of personal and public relations at least as much as of training methods and event techniques. But strangely, we tend to assume that only the latter requires special analysis and study. Apparently the former can be mastered by some innate charismatic quality or adequately learned while on the job. Actually, the investigation in this OMNIBOOK of the human side of coaching is but a beginning, a mere hint of what should and can be done in the future. We hope full textbooks and college courses related to the human side of coaching in all sports will soon be available, as they now are in Eastern Bloc countries. In recent years (1984), a few articles have appeared such as James O'Brien, "The Role of the Coach--a Holistic Point of View;" an excellent review for track and field. But they are limited in both scope and number.

Even though this is a mere beginning or hint, the previous four chapters do attempt to make clear the nature of the problem. Chapter 1 traced the gradual development of track knowledge and related college courses, and led to a study of methods of business management. Of special interest were Douglas McGregor's "management as person-centered," and Rensis Likert's "mutually-supportive relationships" as between persons and groups. Chapter 2 summarized theories on the nature of leadership and the many roles that coaches must play in performing the various facets of their job. Chapter 3 emphasized the importance of striving for a vital balance between expertise in the technology of track and field and expertise in working with persons. A coaching grid was devised by which the problems of balance could be analyzed more precisely--needless to say, with only limited validity. Chapter 4 selected a dozen track and field coaches whose personalities and methods covered a wide range of coaching potentials-- from all-out recruiting of talent for winning to a genuine concern for the development of athletes as persons. The two approaches can occur together but tend to be mutually exclusive.

Throughout all four chapters, special concern was expressed for the importance of compatibility and unity between the coach and his social surround--goals, means, methods, attitudes. The main focus of these can be at any square within the coaching grid, or at any point along a wide range of possible coaching attitudes and actions. But if effective work is to be done, the many parts must dovetail and provide <u>mutually</u> <u>supportive</u> relationships.

For the most part, the term, "social surround" was defined at the local level--all those persons and groups with whom every coach has direct contacts. But there is a greater social sphere within which all United States coaches function and by which they should be judged-- what is often called "the system"--our modern business-centered society with its belief in competitiveness as a primary and unalterable instinct, its worship of winning and of material gains as an almost divine right of winners.

This idea of a social surround out of which we absorb our ideas-attitudes-beliefs is difficult, even impossible, to comprehend fully. We understand how we are taught specifically this or that. But not how beliefs and attitudes become infused so early and continuously in life. It isn't teaching so much as a process of osmosis, a subconscious seepage through the skin, not merely through the eyes and ears and brain. No better example could be found than the flag-waving fervor now being displayed at the 1984 Olympics at Los Angeles.

A 1978 East German textbook for track and field coaches makes a major point of these views,[1]

The coaches of the Athletic Association of the GDR will only be able to accomplish the tasks set them if they are dedicated to their profession, if they have acquired a high standard of political and professional knowledge, educational skill, and if they are distinguished by socialist convictions, habits and qualities so they can set an example to their athletes by their political thoughts and actions. The coach is an official of the workers' state according to his social calling....
(Then on a later page)--*They are to be educated in the love and faith of the working class, its party and our state. When our athletes are convinced that the victory of socialism is the main task of our era, they will fight even more passonately and consistently for the improvement of their athletic performance.*

Extreme? Utter nonsense? Applicable only to a Marxist-Leninist society, but not to our own? Definitely yes, in terms of the details of what is believed and taught. But definitely not so, in terms of the principle of individual-group unity. Although we scorn such mawkish expressions of social duty and loyalty, we tend to be unaware that our system has its own compelling ways of ensuring conformity with what it considers essential.

We use certain names to describe our society--"Capitalism," "Science and Technology," "Materialistic," "Business-oriented." Such names imply certain basic assumptions--private enterprise, work for material gain more than for satisfactions inherent in the work, analysis into separate things more than synthesis toward wholeness, individualism that views society as an aggregate of separate individuals--all confirming competitiveness as a primary instinct in human nature, and winning for material gain as a main goal in sports, as in life generally.

Can we be certain that these assumptions are any less extreme or nonsensical than those of the East German textbook? These assumptions are among those that such leading social analysts as Erich Fromm, Karen Horney, Renee Dubos or Lewis Mumford describe as "dehumanizing," "Neurotic," "alienating," and "destructive of self and society."

Over many years we have gradually accepted the custom of calling ourselves track and field coaches. That seems an innocent habit, one that distinguishes us from football or swimming coaches. And it is, unless--and here's the catch--unless such a focus on the medium obscures our real goal, the human goal. It's not innocent at all; it's downright dangerous if we begin to think and act as though techniques-methods-performance-winning are our REAL goals; the youngsters we work with, only the tools for reaching those goals.

Bill Bowerman, longtime coach at Oregon and 1972 United States Head Olympic Coach, hated the very word, "Coach," and refused to answer when called by such a title. His early experience as an athlete led him to relate "Coach" to dirty tactics in recruiting, to promotion more than education, to using sports and athletes to satisfy the lust for winning. In the preface to his textbook, *COACHING TRACK AND FIELD*,[2] he wrote,

I am proud to be a teacher and to be associated with a group of men and women who, on the whole, love youngsters and do not care a whoop if their critics...cause them to be underpaid, under-estimated, and overworked.

Bill was a tough competitor--as an athlete and a coach. He battled hard to win; in fact, won three NCAA team titles while at Oregon. But his main emphasis, and his great contribution to United States track and field related to the many thousands that he encouraged to take part.

All this leads up to the point that, if such assumptions are really inherent in our business-oriented society, those coaches who follow the ways of winning-as-the-main-goal are its natural offspring, entirely worthy of the high praise and material rewards that such a culture grants to loyal disciples that embrace its teachings and follow its ways. In contrast, those

---

[1]Gerhardt Schmolinsky, *TRACK AND FIELD*, Berlin: *Sportverlag*, 1978, pp. 30ff.

[2]Bill Bowerman, *COACHING TRACK AND FIELD*, Boston: Houghton Mifflin Co., 1974, 400 pages.

that deny such teachings and seek other and better ways are likely to be rewarded only with discouragement, general alienation, and even loss of their jobs.

The important point to be gained relates to understanding the scope of the problem, to awareness of the vital importance of knowing just where you-as-coach stand in relation to your own social surround--in America, but more precisely in Philadelphia, or Ames, Iowa; in El Paso, Texas or Eugene, Oregon. If such relationships among you-team-school-community are mutually supportive, you're likely to achieve success, along with such rewards as that kind of success warrants, from cold cash to deep personal satisfaction. When such compatibility of ends and means is lacking, the end result is likely to be a sense of personal isolation, anxiety, and little accomplishment--for you, your school, and your athletes.

Our great society is not monolithic, all of one kind. Its varied communities and institutions do provide opportunities for work motivations other than those of business. An intelligent young coach will face the issue squarely--to find a school-community whose ends and means for sport are compatible with his own, or to mold his own attitudes and methods to conform with those that surround him. Otherwise success will come hard, however success be defined. Both Villanova's Jumbo Elliott and Berkeley's Brutus Hamilton enjoyed great success, though quite differently oriented. There is a choice.

CERTIFICATION OF TRACK AND FIELD COACHES. One of the most important aspects of improving United States track and field at all levels, as related to both the human and the technical side, is that of the certification of coaches. Certainly no aspect has been so widely neglected. Primarily this has occurred through lack of a national consensus--and certainly of program--as to the place of sports in our educational and social system.

At the college and club levels, no qualifications are needed, other than convincing local employers that their concept of what the job requires will be fulfilled. During its 50-year history, the College Track Coaches Association has prepared no formal Statement as to the level of competency needed to coach our sport. During its 100-year history, our national governing body, the National AAU, took no position on the matter. Anyone with the will, energy and means could organize and coach a club team.

As a result of such a lack of nation-wide policy, many entirely unqualified persons have coached our sport--unqualified on both the technical and the human side. We've had great coaches--the best in the world--great coaches of techniques and methods, beloved educators of young men and women. But such great coaches have emerged almost by chance, out of trial-and-error guided only by the assumption that whoever can do it well, can coach it; and whoever can coach well enough to win is a fit person to teach in institutions of higher learning. For instance, the 1980 Charter of the newly-formed TFA/USA contained 17 detailed statements of purposes and objectives. Number 15 was "to train and certify competent track and field officials." But no such specific statement related to track and field coaches. Apparently their competency was of lesser concern.

At the high school level a similar lack of national consensus is present. But at this level, studies of the problems of certification have been made for many years, and a few States have actually adopted requirements, however minimal. Among the better published statements for high schools is that by Samuel Adams, Washington State University,[1]

Requiring certification of all interscholastic athletic coaches would be a major step forward for the coaching profession and interscholastic school sports. If sports are educational, it is logical that specific criteria be established for high school coaches just as there are special requirements for other special areas of education--driver's education, vocational education, counseling, speech therapy, and special education....

The need for more qualified coaches that had been accentuated by more participation by both boys and girls in sports in secondary schools since the late 1960s became acute with Title IX.

---

[1] Samuel Adams, Ph.D., "Coaching Certification: The Time is Now," Mobile, Ala.: *United States Sports Academy News*, Vol. 3, No. 4, Sept. 1979, p. 1. (The excerpt given here is not complete.)

Administrators of secondary schools had historically relied upon physical educators to handle the coaching responsibilities. The problem inherent in the increase in participation in sports is the lack of teaching positions related to coaching positions. For example, in a typical high school of 1,000 students there are approximately 20-25 coaching jobs for 10 boys' sports. In this same school there are usually two to three fulltime men physical education and health education teachers. Even with each man coaching three sports, only nine of the 20 positions are filled. Personnel from other teaching and district positions have had to be utilized, many of them without any form of professional training. This same staffing problem is now facing girls' sports. Therefore, there is a dire need for professional training for coaching personnel from the other areas of education. Following the 1972 Olympic Games the United States Sports Academy sent out a series of surveys in an attempt to evaluate the credentials of people in coaching. Results indicated that over 70% of the coaches in schools don't have a physical education major; over 65% don't even have a P.E. minor; and over 50% have never competed in sports themselves. ......

However, the task is not the formulation of a certification program but realization that it is needed now. Only a few states have moved into certification. In 1976 45 states, Puerto Rico, and the District of Columbia had no specific certification requirements for coaching; however, most of them require that a coach be a certified teacher. Only six states have minimum certification requirements for coaching in addition to teachers certification. These states are Minnesota, Nebraska, Iowa, Wyoming, Pennsylvania, and South Dakota. Only three of these states, Iowa, Nebraska, and Minnesota have additional coaching certification requirements for physical education majors. All of these coaching certification programs are sub-minimum with the exception perhaps, of the requirement for women coaches in Minnesota, which could be considered minimum.

In the Winter 1981 issue of *Track Technique*, editor Vern Gambetta's lead editorial declared, "Let's Certify Coaches."

Over the past 12 years there has been a steady decline in the success of American track and field athletes at the international level....What is the reason for our decline? It is the failure of the established coaches and sports administrators to place a proper emphasis on development at the lower levels of the sport--i.e., in junior high and high school. It is at this level--during an athlete's formative years--that the best coaching should be provided. Instead, coaching during this stage tends to be a shot in the dark, a hit and miss approach that fails to provide for maximum development.

After reviewing many athletes' training programs I have come to the conclusion that many athletes are achieving success in spite of their coaching, not because of it. The following are common American coaching pitfalls:

One: the tendency to blindly copy the technical and training methods of current record holders on the assumption that because they are the best, they must have the best technique.

Two: many coaches tend to teach only what they were taught or what worked for them as athletes. They fail to revise and update technique and training.

Three: the techniques of successful coaches are used whether or not they are appropriate for the athlete at another level of development. What works for a college level athlete is often very inappropriate for a beginning high school athlete.

Four: in our country a coach can receive recognition just by being successful at recruiting top level athletes. This has been termed by the sardonic British as "poaching," rather than coaching.

What then is the solution? Part of it lies in the proper balance between art and science in coaching. Most of our top coaches have tended to be artists more than scientists. That is, they coach more on feeling and tradition, rather than scientific principles. Their methods will not achieve consistent success in today's high technology world of international sport.

Coaches must recognize that there are physiological, biomechanical and psychological principles that cannot be ignored. These principles should form the foundation of coaching. The coach should know the physiological effects of a particular type of running workout or the mechanical effect of a change in technique. Once the principles are understood, the art of coaching assumes its importance in the application of these principles. It is up to the coach to apply the spirit, the enthusiasm, and motivation to make the science work. The art without the science is like a ship without a rudder.

The establishment of a comprehensive coaching certification program, with specific requirements for coaches at all levels will ensure a proper foundation and balance between art and science. There are many models of successful certification programs that we could adapt to our system. The most successful track and field nations in the world have all implemented their type of programs--the U. S. is the sole exception.

Certification should be required of all track and field coaches. Particular attention must be given to the proper training of the coaches who will be working with the athletes during their formative skill learning years.

Then, at long last, the recently formed National Governing Body for track and field, TAC (The Athletics Congress) established a program of certifying coaches "that structures and professionalizes coaching development in a systematic manner."[1]

"The certification program guarantees that each coach will possess a specific body of knowledge. This eliminates confusion and controversy and insures continuity as the athlete progresses through the system. The program also guarantees that all coaches are working within the framework of sound educational, physiological, and psychological principles.

THE PROGRAM

The certification program is comprised of three levels. Each of these three levels has the following three components:

1. *Sports Science:* Each level includes extensive instruction in sports science in order to provide a scientific basis of understanding for the rational development of technique and training programs.

The sport science portion has been developed by the American Coaching Effectiveness Program (ACEP) and the National Certification Committee. It encompasses the disciplines of sport psychology, biomechanics, physiology, pedagogy and sports medicine. The fundamental premise is that to be an effective coach in today's technological society, it is necessary to have a firm grasp of sport science and its relationship to track and field.

2. *Technical-Event Specific:* Event Specific instruction is progressive in nature--that is, each level covers the events in greater depth and detail than the previous level.

Level I covers all events in an elementary manner, emphasizing rules, teaching progressions and general fundamentals.

Level II focuses in on two event groups of the coach's choice with more depth and technical analysis.

Level III focuses in on a single event group with great detail and depth.

3. *Practical:* This component refers to the time spent coaching athletes. Minimum standards of practical experience are set for each level.

CERTIFICATION LEVELS

Level I--Local Coach

Goal: To give coaches a basic understanding of coaching methods involved in Track & Field events. This will be integrated with an elementary knowledge of sports science as it applies to coaching.

Qualification: Certification at Level I qualifies one to coach all events at the junior age group, club, junior high school or high school level.

Eligibility: a) Must be at least 20 years of age; b) Must show evidence of having worked with a club or school team for a minimum of one year or be a Physical Education or Coaching major or minor at an accredited college or university.

Requirements: a) Attend regional coaching school; b) Pass objective test with a minimum score of 80%. This test will cover event-related and sports science subjects.

Level II--Regional Coach

Goal: To give coaches more advanced knowledge in a narrower range of events. This will be related closely to advanced sports science concepts and training principles.

Qualification: a) Certification qualifies one to coach all events at the senior age group, club, high school, and collegiate level; b) With an additional ten hours of instruction as a

---

[1]"TAC National Coaching Certification Program," *Track Technique*, 85, Summer '83, pp. 2729. Vern Gambetta, Director, Coaches Certification Program. The Athletic Congress, 90 120th St., Indianapolis, Indiana, 46206.

lead instructor the Level II coach is qualified to teach a Level I coaching school.

Eligibility: a) Must have completed requirements for Level I and coached at that level for a minimum of three years; b) Must attend TAC Certification School(s) which include at least 10 hours of instruction in each of two broad event groups: (20 hours total) Sprints and Relays, Hurdles, Endurance Events, Jumps, Throws, and Multi Events. Ten hours of instruction in sports science is required. (30 hours total of instruction)

Requirements: a) Pass objective test covering material in the chosen event groups and sport science subjects. The minimum passing score is 80%; b) Submit an actual training program for two events from the respective event groups which have been used by the candidate's athletes.

Level III--Senior Coach

Goal: To give coaches comprehensive knowledge in a specific event or event group, including sport science and Training Theory.

Qualification: Certification at this level qualifies one to coach at the collegiate level and to be eligible for selection as a coach of a national team.

Eligibility: a) Must have coached a minimum of ten years with a recognized school or club program; b) Must have three years experience at Level II; c) Must be actively coaching; d) Must have demonstrated unique coaching and administrative abilities by having completed at least two of the following: 1) Development of a strong age group or club program; 2) Development of a school program that has gained national recognition; 3) Successfully promoted Track & Field by active involvement in developing meets and clinics.

Requirements: a) Must attend a coaching school with a curriculum containing advanced sports science and training theory; b) Must attend coaching school with a curriculum containing material in chosen events or event groups; c) Must submit an original paper on technique or training in one event in the chosen event group and must submit a detailed training program in that event; d) Must have an oral interview with the TAC Certification Committee to discuss event related and sports science topics appropriate to this level; 3) Must show a high degree of expertise in one of the major event groups: Sprint/Relays, Hurdles, Endurance Events, Throws, Jumps, Multi-Events.

COACHING SCHOOLS

The first Level I coaching schools will be held beginning in January 1984 at various sites throughout the country."

PART 2
Coaching Field Events

The above medal was submitted for use as the official Olympic medal
by sculptor R. Tait McKenzie of the University of Pennsylvania in 1928
when the currently-used Olympic medal was adopted. It shows all the
field events and is therefore depicted here to introduce this section.

Chapter 6
TRAINING FOR FIELD EVENT POWER AND FLEXIBILITY

The evolution of power in field events can be said to have come full circle in the past 30 or so years, though of course at a much higher level of both understanding and performance.

(1) Up to 1950, complete reliance on training for better technique and, with many exceptions, increased velocity in all phases of each event.

(2) From 1950 to about 1970, an extreme emphasis on the strength factor (power equals strength x velocity) through lifting heavy weights, especially the Olympic lifts.

(3) During the past decade, a more balanced concern for technique-strength-power-velocity, especially in ways that relate specifically to the muscle groups and movements of each event.

(4) A phase that tends to close the circle of technique-strength-technique though, I repeat, at a higher level: both experience and sports research have established that an "increase in absolute strength can have a negative influence on movement speed and explosiveness of muscle. This does not mean that the importance of absolute strength should be underestimated. Rather that it should be considered within the actual movement pattern within its requirements in training time-energy, and within the values of strength for a particular event in all its phases."[1]

During the 1950s an almost 90 percent emphasis was placed on maximal strength in the large muscles of the torso, legs and arms, with only minor concern for skill. Such shot-putters as Otis Chandler (Stanford), Stan Lampert (NYU) and the great Parry O'Brien (USC) lifted maximal weights as might an Olympic weightlifter, especially the basic three--the power clean, the bench press and the squat. World records soared to 65'10" (William Nieder, Kansas, 1960--a devotee of the basic three.)

Unfortunately, over 30 years later, we still suffer from that delusion. In training for field events, we still say and write "strength training" or "weightlifting" as not only the basic program supporting all others--which it is--but as a valid and sufficient concept to use when describing such training. It is our contention here that "power" with its inclusion of a range of action from strength to velocity is a much more valid term.

A major part of our present-day confusion lies in our failure to accept the tenet so emphasized in the science of general semantics that "the word is not the thing," that words such as "strength" are just that--words, abstractions, devices for communication that serve as symbols of the actual quality or action. In fact, the word "strength" is used in a wide variety of meanings: strength of muscle, strength of character, strength to endure, strength of taste or of odor, of which no two meanings are at all the same.

It makes a significant difference if a training system assumes that strength and power and velocity and skill are separate entities rather than strength-power-velocity-skill abstracted out of a continuous spectrum of movement. As an analogy, we might consider the relationships among the colors that emerge when sunlight is passed through a prism. We name them and use them--red, yellow, blue, violet AS IF they are separate entities, but such use should be within the context of the continuum out of which we abstracted them. Colors are ways of

---

[1] Juri Verhoshanski, "Specific Training for Power," Moscow: Legkaya Atletika.

analyzing and understanding sunlight. Or, as a second analogy, we can take "still-life"--
note the self-contradiction--sequence photos of human movement. To do so is entirely valid
and very useful, as long as we maintain awareness of the continuous life-movement from which
they were "stilled."

To define muscular strength as might a dictionary, as "the contractile power of muscles
as a result of a single maximal effort," and muscular power as "work done per unit of time"
leads as much to confusion and misuse as to clarity. Equally confusing, however, is to fail
to distinguish at all between the two terms, and so to use them interchangeably. Strength,
power, velocity can be defined, and used in ways and systems that are consistent with such
definitions, but always as positions along a continuum of action.

But more in point, strength as related to putting the shot is not the same word as in
throwing the hammer; and, most important, demands a training program uniquely fitted to the
unique requirements of that event. This is true even more if related to the discus or javelin.
And yet, even among our scientists, let alone our coaches, we find research programs and
training programs that fail almost entirely to distinguish significant differences and assume
the word "strength" applies in similar ways to all.

Leading to even greater confusion are those writers that assume everyone knows what is
meant when they write the word "strength" or the word "power." Those in the science of
general semantics call this "an uncritical assumption of mutual understanding." As when the
fabled six blind men understood mutually that an elephant was--who could doubt it--an elephant. They had been told that an elephant was "a large five-toed mammal with a nose elongated into a prehensile trunk." They knew the meaning of those words or thought they did,
until actually chancing on such a mammal, each took hold of a particular part of the elephant's
anatomy. Now, for one, an elephant was a "rope;" for another, a massive leather-like column.
They still used the old word "elephant" and assumed the others defined it as they now did--a
rope, a column, a wall--an uncritical and invalid assumption.

So with our use of the word "strength," and so with the related training program we
construct. Our thinking is somewhat clearer if we keep in mind the formula (power equals
strength x velocity) but even this is too vague. The questions remain--just how much
strength, how much velocity.

One solution to this problem is to make use of the method called indexing: the use of
numbers to identify and distinguish things or ideas. The method has been used for centuries, as in assigning numbers to houses, to books or cars or towns, as with zip codes. But
indexing also relates to quantities, as occurs in algebra. Algebra uses superscripts
(exponents) as in A equals X^2Y^3. Now we understand more clearly the nature and value of A and
the precise quantity of X and Y that form it. Similarly the science of chemistry uses index
devices called subscripts as when assigning H_2O as the formula for water. Now we understand
precisely that water requires two parts of hydrogen to one part of oxygen, much more precisely than if--as is now done when dealing with the formula for power--we had simply
written, "water is made of hydrogen and oxygen."

To use such indexing devices in sports research and writing would certainly clarify our
meanings, and someday we shall do so, just as we now accept such indexing terms as Metveyev's
"Periodization" with its macrocycles, microcycles and the like. Ten years ago we would have
called them mere scientific jargon of no value for practical coaching. But today such precise quantifying of time-energy ennables a Sergey Bubka to say, after clearing 19 feet $3\frac{1}{2}$
inches in June, 1984, "Speaking simply, I'm benefitting from the enormous background training
I have done for the Olympic Games. In a little more than a month, I will enter the optimal
phase of my condition, and then I should be able to approach 6m (19'8$\frac{1}{4}$")"--which he did.

To make a beginning with such devices, would we not be clearer in our mutual understanding
if we acquired the habit of using exponents, and for example, wrote a formula on a ten-point
scale for training power for shot putting as strength^6 velocity^4 (S^6V^4), and that for javelin
throwing as strength^4 velocity^6 (S^4V^6).

All this does not diminish the values of strength training. We assume that strength is
basic to all actions requiring power, and that weightlifting is a basic means of acquiring

such strength, *but only within the time-energy limits as needed for optimal training for a particular throwing or jumping event.*

As another example, we might write a formula (S^6V^4) in early season training for shot-putting, whereas the formula for late season training might place a greater emphasis on velocity with a lesser emphasis on strength, as in S^4V^6 or even S^2V^8. Now the meaning is more sharply defined and we can assume a mutual understanding that is closer to reality and to valid use.

Only closer, but far from close enough. Precisely, in action, what does the exponent "4" mean. Somehow we must identify its meaning in terms of what we do, in terms of weight-lifting, plyometrics, circuit training and precisely how these relate to the implements and the movements of each significantly different event.

Even more precisely, though now we risk the confusion of over-analysis, if we intend the exponent to relate to weightlifting, we might write "Strength$^{bench\ press}$--6 x 80%M." If to plyometrics, we'd write, "Strength$^{30"box}$--drop-rebound M."

Complex? Of course, but only as our training is increasingly complex. And certainly our thinking and our words would be so much clearer, our training programs so much more precisely related to the demands of each event and the needs of each individual. Keep in mind that Zhu, world-record holder in the high jump (1984--7'10") was 6'4" tall, weight only 152#, and had had but one year (once a week) of lifting light weights with a PR squat (1RM) of 275#. What are his precise needs for strength when seeking to develop power for jumping even higher?

Keep in mind that velocity of motion--of a human body or an instrument--is the true goal; strength is but the means to that goal. Also that in the continuum of the formula for power (from "pure" strength at one extreme to "pure" velocity at the other) maximal weightlifting, basic as it is, lies far to the left.

In summary, to name our programs, "strength training" is to indicate a primary concern for but one phase of a wide range of action contained in the more comprehensive term, "power training;" just as "velocity training" relates to the opposite phase of that range. In contrast, "power training" connotes the entire range, including strength and velocity, and so-- the difference is significant--is the more valid term to use.

Most regretfully, especially to the author, this insight came only after the text as a whole was completed; actually it was called back from the editor for last-minute inclusion-- too late for its consistent use in this volume. Perhaps later toilers in the field will refine and expand its use.

A BRIEF REVIEW OF RELATED RESEARCH.
Major credit for first stating the principle of progressive overload in building strength is given to Thomas De Lorme in reporting (1945) his work rehabilitating the wounded from World War II. He originated such expressions as "progressive resistance exercises" (PRE) and "repetition maximum" (RM). By the first, he proposed that an optimal increase in strength comes by gradually increasing the resistance against which that muscle-group moves. By the second, he meant the maximum number of times a given weight can be lifted. For example, a weight that can be lifted only six times with maximal effort is indicated as 6RM. In his early work, De Lorme used from 7 to 10 sets with 10 repetitions per set, but concluded later that from 20 to 30 repetitions brought greater strength development.

A second important source of research knowledge of the progressive overload principle was the work of Hellebrandt[1] and Houtz. Among their conclusions were (1) the amount of work done per unit of time is the critical variable on which continuous development depends; (2) determination not to reduce the rate of working when the stress imposed seems insuperable is a crucial element in overload training; (3) strength and endurance increase together when

---

[1] F. A. Hellebrandt and S. J. Houtz, "Mechanisms of Muscle Training in Man; Experimental Demonstration of the Overload Principle." in CLASSICAL STUDIES ON PHYSICAL ACTIVITY, ibid., 288-304.

repetitive exercise is performed against heavy resistance; (4) the rapidity with which work overloads increase the power capacity suggests that changes in the central nervous system are important aspects of training development.

During the past decade, a flood of related research has been reported from the United States, the USSR, East and West Germany, England and Canada, much of which has been published in such Journals as *Track and Field Quarterly Review,*[1] and *Track Technique,*[2] and in such texts as *THE THROWS,* edited by Jess Jarver.[3]

From a review of such research. H. Harrison Clarke[4] drew nine conclusions from which, in my own words, these are relevant:

(1) A variety of PRE programs have not been significantly different in improving muscular strength, including (a) two-thirds maximum strength twice weekly; (b) 2RM for six bouts three times weekly versus 6RM for three bouts three times weekly; (c) 10RM for three bouts twice weekly versus the same but three times weekly; (d) three sets of 7RM versus four sets of 5RM versus five sets of 3RM, and (e) three sets of 10RM versus three sets of 5RM versus three sets of 3RM; in all three programs, weight loads are increased five pounds weekly.

(2) In PRE, when training for six, nine and 12 weeks, three sets each session produced greater improvement in strength than when doing one or two sets.

(3) Superior strength development occurs when using 10RM if (a) each of the 10 repetitions is adjusted progressively to 1RM; that is, a maximal load for each lift is ensured by allowing for fatigue effects, and adjusting the load to a maximal or near-maximal effort. This method was found to be more developmental than the usual 10RM regimen.

(4) Clarke reviewed one study that concluded--when bench presses were performed at fast, moderate and slow speeds, no significant differences in strength development were found, *provided the load employed was maximal in all cases.* This suggests training time can be saved by using faster rates.

The first conclusion to be drawn from this great abundance of research and variety of strength training systems is that all forms of progressive overloads lead to increases in strength, at least in their early stages. Not all in equal measure, nor to equally high levels, but all are helpful. In the 1950s and 60s, Olympic weightlifting was the only program; one that achieved remarkable development in competitive performance. Today, there is a great confusion of programs, both between and within each country of the Olympic world, many of which are promoted as being the best or even the only road to greatest performance.

To provide in this limited textbook space a clear understanding of even the gist of such programs is most difficult if not impossible. Not only because of their widely varying concepts and methods, but even more by doubtful translations, by the special jargon of each author and by the unclear meanings some authors give to such basic concepts as "strength" and "power." In fact, by their failure to understand the underlying concept of words as abstraction as stated at the beginning of this Chapter.

It therefore seems that greatest service to the reader can be made by my own assimilation

---

[1]*Track and Field Quarterly Review,* edited by George G. Dales, 1705 Evanston, Kalamazoo, Michigan, 49008.

[2]*Track Technique,* edited by Vern Gambetta, TAFNEWS, P.O. Box 296, Los Altos, CA, 94022.

[3]Jess Jarver, *THE THROWS,* TAFNEWS, P.O. Box 296, Los Altos, CA., 94022, 1980.

[4]H. Harrison Clarke, "Development of Muscular Strength and Endurance," *President's Council of Physical Fitness and Sport Research Digest,* Series 4, No. 1, 1974; extracted by Jess Jarver, editor, *THE THROWS,* TAFNEWS, 1980, p. 9.

of the many programs by using basic words and methods with consistent and clear meanings, by avoiding repetition of ideas and methods that are basically the same but which each author states in his own unique way, and by using my own judgment in re-phrasing what each writer intended to say. I regret my own inability to do this without misunderstanding and error.

CONCEPTS RELATED TO POWER TRAINING.

Progressive overload, as first stated by Thomas De Lorme, is one that increases progressively and gradually the resistance to muscle contraction beyond its normal uses. Such overloads result in a breakdown of muscle tissues, especially protein. During the following rest period (36 or more hours), "supercompensation" reconstructs the muscle and improves its protein, thus making the muscle stronger and often larger (hypertrophy).

Progressive Resistance Exercises (PRE), as related to strength, are those that lift heavy weights with few repetitions in a program that gradually increases its intensity over weeks or months of training. When weights are maximal (only one contraction can be made without intervening rest) the expression, "one repetition maximum" (1RM) is used. If as many as six repetitions can be made, then 6RM is indicated.

Dynamic Contractions, also called isotonic (some tonus), refer to muscle tension with movement. This may be "concentric"--the contracting muscle shortens and bones move closer (toward the "center"); for example, the "up" phase of the biceps curl. Or it may be "eccentric" (not centered), in which muscles lengthen through external resistance; for example, the "down" phase of the biceps curl.

Dynamic (isotonic) Training is usually carried out by the use of barbells (weights) with submaximal loads that can be lifted a number of times. These weights provide constant resistance throughout the full range of motion, but have varying effects as the angle of pull of muscle-tendon on bone changes. For example, in the biceps curl the strongest angle of the elbow is 110 degrees; the weakest, 180 and 40 degrees. This means that a maximum load (1RM) will tax the muscle maximally only at the weakest angles, and submaximally (about 50 percent) at 110 degrees.

Static contractions, also called isometric (same length) refers to muscle tension without movement; that is, when resistance equals or is greater than muscle contraction. Maximal static contractions for 5-10 seconds will strengthen a muscle. However, these tend to be localized, or even confined to the muscle fibers active during contraction at that joint angle. Maintenance of a single position during the hammer turns and, to a lesser extent, in the discus turns, are examples of static contractions. But almost all field event and speed running contractions are dynamic (involve movement), isometric training tends to be used for specific needs, whereas major emphasis is placed on dynamic (isotonic) training.

Isometric Training. The isometric craze of the 60s has now receded to its proper level, as reported by its original research workers--Theodor Hettinger, E. A. Muller, F. M. Henry and others. Actually these men were not concerned with sport or work so much as with greater knowledge--the nature of muscle development, of a minimal developmental load, and the like. They chose isometric contraction because it met the needs of science for validity and reliability. Today, after years of field experience, we realize that isometric training is useful primarily in research; only secondarily in the cautiously derived insights such research can provide for dynamic training. Among such insights are the following:

1. There is no doubt that isometric muscle training, performed daily, and with greatest possible intensity and frequency, will result in an increase in isometric muscle strength.... But if the muscle strength is intended for performing certain tasks in labor or sport, isometric training probably is rather worthless. This is because the obtained isometric strength apparently cannot be transferred directly to other forms of activity.

2. Well-controlled studies show no significant correlations between the strength gains from isometric and dynamic training programs. In part this results from the unreliability of dynamic strength measurements. It also suggests that conclusions from one such program should be used very cautiously as related to the other.

3. Static strength gains occur very quickly when a muscle's present strength is a small

percentage of its potential strength, but occur very slowly as muscle strength approaches its maximum. Gains usually range from one to ten percent per week, but some investigators have reported gains in beginners of as much as 73 percent per week for static training, and 168 percent for dynamic training.

Isokinetic Training makes use of a machine that uses variable resistances to ensure a constant speed of movement and an optimal taxing of the muscle throughout the full range of movement. That is, as the muscle length changes from about 40 to 180 degrees, (press), the machine's resistance changes in direct proportion to the force exerted by the muscle.

Plyometric Training uses exercises that prestretch the muscle (amortization or negative phase) so as to increase the kinetic energy developed in the following positive contraction. That is, a high-velocity movement is enhanced if preceded by a movement in the opposite direction. Exercises used in this type of training consist of depth jumps from benches 30-40 inches high, to develop the leg-torso muscles; but also of heavy weights suspended from the ceiling that pre-stretch the shoulder girdle muscles (amortization phase) just before they are projected forward by the arm muscles (acceleration phase).

FUNDAMENTALS OF POWER TRAINING

All progressive resistance exercise (PRE) systems are developmental: not to the same degree, nor in the same way, but all (PRE) do have a positive effect. This dictum has special significance for the young athlete, during the early stages of a training program, or whenever muscles are weak, for whatever reason. It applies not only to strength training, but equally to endurance and skill, in both the physical and mental-emotional aspects of their development.

Improvements in strength-power were greatest for all related sports events in the 1950s, when a simple program of weightlifting was first used to improve performance. During that decade, almost any exercises against progressively greater resistances would have been effective. Only later, when the limits of such a narrow program were realized, did we turn to related power training, plyometrics and the like.

Basic Strength Work (BSW) is Essential. High-level strength, especially of the large muscles of the torso, legs and arms, is a requirement that underlies all maximal performances in field events. This is not to say that maximal ("pure" or "absolute") strength should be sought as an end in itself, from which highest-level performance will be a certain outcome. Such extremes of BSW are wasteful of both time and energy and, as previously quoted from Verhoshanski, can actually have a negative influence on movement speed and explosiveness of muscle. This BSW phase should comprise about 10-20 percent of the year's schedule of work, with greater emphasis during the early weeks, lesser in the competitive season, but maintained in some measure throughout.

Starting Weights. Assuming the all-round conditioning program has been of sufficient length and gradually developed, starting weights should be those that can be lifted about 20 times without strain. After several sessions with satisfactory recovery, increase the "overloads" (loads greater than this athlete's normal) gradually to ensure proper recovery and avoid injury.

Repetitions. Authorities differ as to a specific number of repetitions that is optimal, once serious weightlifting is started. As a basic rule, Ryan[1] suggests three sets that can be done with eight reps, then increased, one rep at a time, to 12. Now increase the weight so that eight reps is a maximum, again gradually increasing the reps to 12. Ryan makes no claims of "this being the one and only way. It just seems to work well and is a good way to get started." With certain exercises, such as squats or heel raises, Ryan suggests more reps-- "probably 12 to 15."

---

[1]
Frank Ryan, *WEIGHT TRAINING*, New York: The Viking Press, Inc., 1969, p. 57.

Lukk,[1] of Estonia, reviewed related research and recommended a three-stage program: when medium weights will gain the intended purpose, eight to 10 reps are best; for heavy resistances, four to seven; for maximal or near-maximal resistances, one to three.

Taking a different approach, Miller[2] gives an example of progressions in repetitions in four exercises--split squats, front squats, knee-ups, and bench presses. After two weeks of gradual build-up with moderate weights, one of his athletes followed this program:

> The following four weeks he did eight sets of five repetitions. This first set was done with moderate weight and 7-12# were added with each set, hitting his maximum on the fourth or fifth set, and then trying to stay with as much weight as possible until eight sets were completed....On every repetition, every effort was made to explode... Admittedly the last repetition did not go very fast, but the nerves were being told to explode. Since we were striving for strength, we took a long rest (three to five minutes) between sets.

Sets. The number of sets in any given session varies in keeping with the time of year as related to competition, with the purpose of that particular session, and with the nature of each exercise. For example, when the purpose is focussed on basic strength, as distinguished from velocity and special movement patterns, the number of sets--as of repetitions--is usually kept low with ample rest periods between sets: three sets of 6-8 RM (Repetitions Maximum-- the maximal weight that can be lifted six to eight times.) But diaries of champions often disclose sessions in which six sets are used for cleans, snatches, and squats but only two sets for dead lifts and trunk twisting.

Hooks[3] seeks to develop both strength and velocity by sessions of three sets of ten, eight, and six reps each. In the first set of an over-head press, for example, the lifter presses ten times with a weight about 50% of maximum with concentration upon all-out speed of movement. On the second set, weight is added so that speed is reduced, even though maximum explosiveness is attempted; repetitions are reduced to eight. On the third set, the weight is further increased; the reps reduced to six. When ten reps can be done in the third set without straining, all three sets are increased by 20 pounds (larger muscles) or 10 pounds (smaller muscles).

Pickering[4] recommends the pyramid system as "the most favored of all systems." He suggests five sets with a decreasing number of repetitions from five down to two, and with increasing weights for each set (ten pounds for weaker muscles; 20 pounds for stronger ones). When two repetitions with a maximum weight can be done, the beginning weight with five reps is increased, and the series repeated until again two reps can be made with a heavier maximum weight.

W. Schroder[5] of West Germany recommends that, when doing sets, optimal local muscle recovery as well as training effects will be most certain by avoiding early fatigue. The recovery phase between sets should average from three to five minutes; its precise duration depends on the load used and the recovery rates of each individual athlete. For this reason, the most basic and beneficial exercises should be done early in the workout. Mobility and stretching exercises between sets aid recovery, but stretching of the muscle groups used in the preceding exercise should be avoided.

---

[1]T. Lukk, "Science and Throwing," *Track Technique*, #72, June 1978, p. 2307.

[2]Carl Miller, *HOW TO USE WEIGHT TRAINING FOR YOUR SPECIFIC SPORT*, self-published, p. 8.

[3]Gene Hooks, *APPLICATION OF WEIGHT TRAINING TO ATHLETICS*, Englewood Cliffs, N.J.: Prentice-Hall, Inc., 1962, pp. 24, 47.

[4]Ron Pickering, *STRENGTH TRAINING FOR ATHLETICS*, London: AAA, 1970, p. 51.

[5]W. Schroder, "A Summary of Strength and Power Development," translated in *THE THROWS*, edited by Jess Jarver, *Tafnews Press*, Los Altos, CA, 1980, p. 14.

The Basic Three. Jim Murray,[1] a leading authority on weight training, considers three exercises as being the most basic and developmental for strength in sports: the power clean, the bench press and the squat. Murray affirms that these three, in their simplest forms, are easily learned; in contrast to the complex techniques of such Olympic lifts as the snatch or the clean and jerk, but ensure the same development in strength in much less time for learning. In Murray's power clean, the barbell is lifted only to shoulder level. In the bench press the barbell is simply pushed upward until the arms are fully extended. Murray's squat is modified with the thigh line not lower than parallel with the floor at the start, and the torso erect at completion.

Fig. 6.1 ABC--Murray's basic three: A, The power clean; B, The bench (inclined) press; C, The squat.

As to repetitions and sets, Murray suggests that if a shotputter can power clean 220 pounds at 1RM as a limit, he might warm up by cleaning 135 pounds, then move up by 10-pound additions from 155 to 185-200 pounds. Five sets would be done for the first three lifts; three for the next one or two lifts; and two or one for the last two lifts. Similar progressions should be followed for the bench press and squat.

Murray recommends three sessions per week on alternate days--all three exercises in each session, but attempting personal best efforts only once a week in any given lift.

For a beginner, progression in strength (poundage lifted) will tend to be steady, perhaps for three or four months. But eventually improvement will slow, reach a plateau, or even retrogress. Before this happens, the athlete will do well to shift his approach to a more varied program as in the cycle system described by Murray, or as in Pickering's pyramid system previously cited, or as in circuit training as advocated by Loffler.

Related Power Work (S^4V^6--S^0V^{10}). The use of less-than-maximal resistances in movements that simulate those of the competitive event *should form the most significant phase of training for power*--strength x velocity (SV), significant in the sense of time-energy spent, planning, and positive outcomes.

The degree to which movements simulate those of the event is critical. Even a slight change in pattern will increase the load on certain muscle groups and decrease the load on others. It is this essential that has led to the use of 20# shots, over-weight discuses, and 4-5# balls for the javelin. Such light-weight loads develop power within the flow of muscle contractions that most closely simulate those of the actual event, a flow or pattern that is not feasible with heavier loads. Warning: When practicing for more perfect skill, no additional weights or resistances of any kind should be used. To do so is to change the pattern of skill in coordination, strength required and velocities of contractions; that is, to learn a significantly different skill.

The relative emphasis on strength as related to velocity is also important, as was made clear in the introduction to this Chapter. When resistances are heavy (S^8V^2) we speak of strength training; when light (S^4V^6), as in putting a 20# shot or throwing a weighted discus or javelin, we speak of power. When resistances are less than normal, as when putting a 12# shot or lightweight discus or javelin, then the velocity factor is dominant and we write S^0V^{10} or S^1V^9.

[1]Jim Murray, *WINNING WEIGHT TRAINING*, Chicago: Contemporary Books, Inc., 1982.

This principle of relatedness applies not only to movements but also to time-resistance patterns. For example the use of rubber cables while simulating the action of throwing the javelin or discus has been proved inefficient. As the rubber tightens, the resistance increases and slows the action; while in the actual throw, the velocity of the implement shows a linear increase.

PLYOMETRICS--DEPTH JUMPS AND RELATED REACTIVE CONTRACTIONS.

The explosive events of jumping, throwing and sprinting demand dynamic power rather than "pure" or ultimate strength; explosive power with emphasis on related movements and on the velocity phase of the formula (power equals strength x velocity). Weightlifting is essential to power training but much research has confirmed that plyometric exercises provide a valuable tool.

Plyometrics use "forced" stretching such as occurs in jumping down from a box (depth jumping), which increases the reactive contractions (stretch reflex) of related muscles. The faster muscles are forced to lengthen, the greater the reactive tension they exert. Such plyometric training acts as a "shock" on the central nervous system, forcing it to work at a higher rate which stimulates more muscle fibers to contract than could occur in a non-reactive exercise.[1]

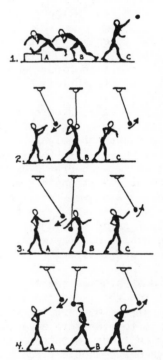

According to Gambetta[2] the research basic to depth jumping was done in the Soviet Union as early as the mid to late sixties. Since then, in growing volume, researchers have explored many of its aspects. For example, in their 1970 *TEXTBOOK OF WORK PHYSIOLOGY*, Astrand and Rodahl reported research that confirmed the values of the stretch reflex for power: "An unattached unstimulated muscle is at its equilibrium length, and the tension is zero....Normally, when attached by its tendons to the skeleton, the muscle is under slight tension, since it is moderately stretched (resting length). Measurements of the tension developed by the stimulated muscle show that tension is maximal when the initial length of the muscle at the time of stimulation is about 20 percent above the equilibrium length (1.2 to 1)."

But the plyometric principle relates not so much to stretching per se as to the intensity and immediacy of the stimulus-response. For example, in the discus throw, the discus arm is held back on partial stretch during the turn. As the left foot lands at the front of the circle, an explosive clockwise action of the hip-shoulder places the related muscles on stretch so as to stimulate immediate reactive contractions for the throw. A similar stretch reflex (myotatic reflex) should occur in the shot, javelin and hammer throw, as well as in the sprint start.

A further example of the uses of plyometrics relates to the jumping events. Recent studies in the USSR have found that during the eccentric (yielding) phase, the power needed to prevent excess flexion of the joints is significantly greater than that required during the concentric (push-off) phase. If such flexion is controlled, then the reactive push-off is more likely to be more effective, much as a rubber ball returns to its normal state.

Fig.6.2. Plyometric exercises for throwing events. (1) Depth jump for reactive response in power leg in shotputting. (2,3, 4) Plyometrics for reactive response in torso-shoulder girdle-triceps of throwing arm for (2) shotput, (3) discus throw, and (4) javelin throw.

---

[1]Russ Polhemus, et al, "The Effects of Plyometric Training with Ankle and Vest Weights on Conventional Weight Training for Men," *Track and Field Quarterly Review*, Vol. 80, #4, 1980, p. 59.

[2]Vern Gambetta, "Plyometric Training," *Track and Field Quarterly Review*, Vol. 78, #1.

Consensus from such studies is that:

(1) Power development as in weightlifting is essential but insufficient; that training of the powerful contractions of joint extensions as occurs in the squat or bench press is not enough.

(2) In plyometric exercises the main concern is for the intensity, immediacy and velocity of the reactive response. This makes clear the great values of depth jumps from boxes of varying heights in which the muscles that resist yielding are loaded optimally and so stimulate immediate response at maximal velocities in the opposite direction.

Boxes for Plyometrics as in Depth Jumping. For lack of agreement among researchers no optimal height for plyometric boxes can be given. In practice, varied heights are used; for the young or untrained, lower boxes are preferred. Most experienced athletes use varied heights in accordance with the intended outcomes.

Miller and Power[1] reviewed the related research. Asmussen and Bonde-Peterson found that optimal results are obtained from jumping down from a height of 40 cm (16"); others, (Katschajov et al) found that 80 cm (32") was optimal. Verhoshanski (1967) concluded that jumps from heights greater than 110 cm (41½") are counter-productive. But Dursenev obtained optimal results from heights of 320 cm (about 10 feet!), though admitting that such jumping over time was "without desire and sometimes only under pressure from the instructor."

But on one point related to depth jumping there is definite agreement. Both research and experience have found that the extraordinary forces in plyometrics tend to produce high-stress reactions from tendons and muscles--certainly fatigue and all too often injury. The following precautions are warranted:

(1) A related power-training program should precede plyometric exercises.

(2) Plyometrics should be introduced gradually; first, easy bounding, then higher bounds for distance of heights. Depth jumps should come later.

(3) Plyometric boxes should, at first, be at lower heights--30 inches or less. Some Russian researchers[2] used "maximal" height boxes (2.8 to 3.2 meters) and obtained greatest increases in strength. But the stresses of such jumps would be prohibitive for all but the highly trained.

(4) Consensus is that depth jumping with weighted vests, belts or sand bags is especially stressful and should be done with great caution. Furthermore, such weights tend to emphasize strength as contrasted with the velocity factor in developing power; to that extent their values are limited.

Most studies therefore conclude that depth jumping should be followed by ample time for full recovery, and certainly should be followed by work of a different kind that might aid recovery. Easy jogging is of special value. For beginners, one session per week is sufficient; for the more advanced, two sessions per week. A highly stressful depth jumping session tends to temporarily slow nerve-muscle reactions so that as much as eight to ten days of recovery should precede important competition.[3]

Variety in Plyometrics. We have emphasized that plyometrics include a great variety of exercises limited largely by the inventiveness of program organizers. Since restricted drills during year-long training tend toward boredom, special effort should be made to provide variety in all ways--implements, kind of movements, degree of stress, and so forth. Continuous motivation is essential.

---

[1]Brian P. Miller and Sean L. D. Power, "Developing Power in Athletics Through the Process of Depth Jumping," *Track & Field Quarterly Review*, Vol. 81, #4, pp. 52-54. This review of research related to depth jumps is of special value and should be given serious study.

[2]L. I. Dursenev, "Strength Training of Jumpers," *Track & Field Quarterly Review*, Vol. 82, #4, p. 53.

[3]Jim Santos, "Jump Training: A Method for All Events," *Track & Field Quarterly Review*, Vol. 82, #4, p. 51.

Depth Jumps using boxes of various heights from 12" to 40".

1) *Box to ground, then leap vertically.* For high jump, emphasize takeoff leg but also use other leg, then both legs to ensure balanced development.

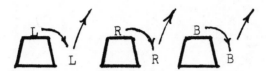

2) *Box to ground, then leap more horizontally.* For long jump, emphasize takeoff leg; for triple jump, each leg.

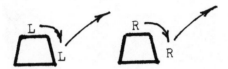

3) *Ground to box then leap vertically.* Vary this by taking several strides before the box.

4) *Ground to box, then leap as in horizontal jumps.* Vary legs as in items 1) and 2). Vary this by taking several strides before the box.

5) *Box to ground to box, etc.* Use 2 or 3 or more boxes. Use boxes of varying heights. Change legs as in 1) and 2); or alternate legs as in triple jump.

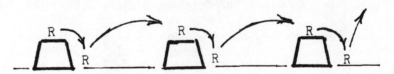

6) *Repeated hopping over bench laterally.* Use both legs, or each leg, or alternate legs. Emphasize height of each hop or reaction velocity.

Hurdle plyometrics
1) Using hurdles of various heights, 3-4 feet apart, hop from both legs, or from takeoff leg, or for balanced development from opposite leg.

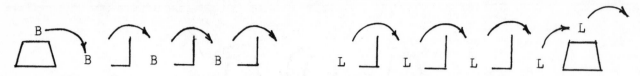

Stadium Steps
1) Hop up one or two stadium steps (or benches) at a time; a) hop from both legs; b) hop from a single leg, especially the takeoff leg. Safety suggests avoidance of hopping down the steps.

Repetitive Jumps
1) From modified squat position, bound high. Bound from both feet, or from each foot. Bound explosively as high as possible; or as high-far as possible. A relatively soft surface, such as grass, is helpful to avoid injury.

Stretch-reflex for Throwing Events
For illustrations, see Figure 6.2.

Twisting Depth Jumps for Throwers.
To simulate rotational action of discus and hammer, and final drive of all throws, use partial-twist action from box or ground; rotate 90 degrees or 180 degrees or as much as 360 degrees on each jump.

PLYOMETRICS BIBLIOGRAPHY.
Plyometrics have such great potential and wide application, much of which is relatively unexplored. A brief bibliography from easily available journals seems justified. In addition to those previously cited, these will prove of value:

Bosco, Carmelo, Ph.D., "Physiological Considerations of Strength and Explosive Power and Plyometric Exercises," 1982 Conference on Planning for Elite Performance, published by CTFA/ACA, 355 River Road, Vanier, Ontario, Canada, K1L 8C1

Fritzsche, Dr. Gunter, "Power Exercises for Young Athletics," in Jess Jarver, THE JUMPS, Los Altos: Tafnews Press, 1981, pp. 19-22.

Gambetta, Vern, "Plyometric Training," TAF Coaching Manual, West Point, NY: Leisure Press, 1981, pp. 27-28.

Jarver, Jess, "Specific Power in Jumping (A Summary of Plyometric Exercises)", THE JUMPS, ibid, pp. 24-26.

Mann, Ron, "Plyometrics," Track & Field Quarterly Review, Vol. 81, #4, 1981, pp. 55-61.

Moynihan, Patrick S., "Plyometrics: Training and Exercises," Track & Field Quarterly Review, Vol. 83, #4, 1983, pp. 52-59.

Verhoshanskiy, Yuriy, "Depth Jumping in the Training of Jumpers," Track & Field Quarterly Review, Vol. 82, #4, 1982, p. 60.

Verhoshanskiy, Yuriy, "Specific Training for Power," in Jess Jarver, ibid, pp 9-11.

Wilt, Fred, "Plyometrics," Track Technique, #63 and 64, 1976, pp. 1992, 2024.

Wolcik, Mike, "Power Development for Jumpers," Track & Field Quarterly Review, Vol. 83, #4, 1983, pp. 47-51.

Circuit Training. Circuit training has been used in both power and general physical fitness training for over 40 years--in the United States and abroad. I first observed its use in 1940 when training Navy recruits for WWII at the University of Michigan. In keeping with the purpose of the training program, a series of from three to a dozen stations are set up in a gym, organized so as (1) to be simple and easily learned; (2) adjusted to the age and performance levels of participants; (3) be reliable in measuring progress; (4) within the full circuit, to exercise all related muscle groups; (5) to alternate fatiguing work and rest of each muscle group; and (6) to ensure a rapid shift within a set time (perhaps as little as 30 seconds) from one station to the next.

Perhaps its greatest value lies in the proficiency by which it provides power training for large numbers of athletes within a relatively short time: from 40 minutes (8 exercises, duration 90s, recovery 60s) to as little as 10 minutes (3 exercises, duration 15s, recovery 30s).

A circuit-training method that requires maximal performance at each station produces time requirements that vary with each individual and so, to inefficient use of group time. It has its values, depending on goals and available time. But most coaches, such as Dr. Hans-Peter Loffler[1], East Germany, prefer a fixed time in which each station is completed. Loffler suggests two of many possible circuits:

Circuit 1. (For early training with emphasis on trunk, arm and leg muscles):

(1) Sit-ups with feet supported (abdominals);
(2) Two-legged takeoff jumps over a rope (legs and feet);
(3) Trunk lifts in prone position with feet supported (back);
(4) Push-ups (arm extension);
(5) Jump and reach (leg extensions);
(6) Pull-ups in half-hanging position (arm flexors).

As a circuit for more advanced training, Loffler suggests the exercises shown in Fig. 6.3.

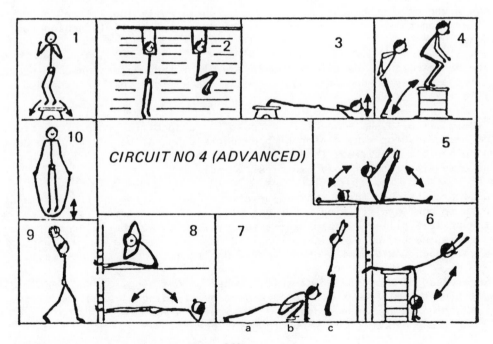

Fig. 6.3. Advanced Circuit as drawn by Loffler.

---

[1]Dr. Hans-Peter Loffler, East Germany, "Young Athletes and Strength," reprinted in THE THROWS, edited by Jess Jarver, Tafnews Press, Los Altos, CA, 94022, 1980, p. 29.

Brent McFarlane[1], Canadian National Hurdles Coach, provides a simplified approach by first stating the principles underlying circuit training--specificity, overload and reversability. Specificity suggests that "the load on a muscle must be specific to the fitness of the athlete and his/her event needs." Overload implies that "gains in strength occur when muscles are progressively overloaded"....(as in examples McFarlane provides.) Reversibility--"if specificity and overloading decline, so will the athlete's strength."

"Our purpose here is...to develop strength-endurance and to link this with developing power. Basically, strength gains result from using a resistance in one of the following five methods:
1. Body weight as a resistance (push-ups, sit-ups);
2. Using a falling body weight as a resistance (depth jumping, hurdle hops, bounding... special strength);
3. Weight as a resistance (Olympic weights, Nautilus, isokinetic resistance, cybex);
4. Weighted objects while simulating specific skills (weight vest, sandbags, ankle weights, weight shoes); and
5. Using a resistance to a specific event movement (cables, towing, accelerator, computerized harness).

SPECIFICITY

Circuit A--Pillar
Abdomen--sit-ups (bent knee)
Back--good mornings
Abdomen--chin-ups
Back--forward arches
Abdomen--jackknife (bent knees)
Back--chest raises

Circuit B--Ankle/Pillar
Ankle--toe raises (in, out, straight)
Pillar--sit-ups (feet up on box)
Ankle--ankle hops (low)
Pillar--twisting sit-ups
Ankle--skipping (with rope)
Pillar--bicycle (feet in front)
Ankle--trippling (low ankle drives)

Circuit C--Legs/Pillar
Legs--half-squats (arms in front)
Pillar--chin-ups
Legs--running on the spot
Pillar--leg raises
Legs--lunges

Circuit D--Ankle/Arms
Ankle--hop sideways (in circle)
Arms--clap push-ups
Ankle--walk (hop), toe in and out
Arms--speedball (punching bag)

"What do the above circuits have in common? How might they be designed to prevent injuries? How specific are they to an individual's needs? How might they be expanded to further develop specificity?

"Each of these circuits has a specific purpose for a specific group of muscles. The endless choice of exercises for many different body parts can best be designed to meet individual needs, including ankles, feet, legs (adduction, flexion, extension), pillar (abdomen, back), arms (flexion, extension), total body exercises (complex).

"All circuits are designed to prevent injuries but can be used on alternate body parts if an injury occurs to one specific area. For example, if the hamstring is injured, work can continue on the ankles, pillar and arms while rehabilitation on the injured area occurs. The choice of exercises, number of exercises, specific muscle groupings and movement patterns required are left to each individual's needs (based on strengths and weaknesses.)

"OVERLOAD. Regardless of the type of circuit, number of exercises or the specificity, the development of strength only comes with progressive overloading of a muscle group. The physiological adaption to increased work loads basically allows the original load to become an underload" and the enhancement of strength gains occurs.

"Simply, the quantity can be increased by increasing the reps using time (15, 30 or 45 seconds) to do a specific number of exercises or increasing the number of exercises; the

---

[1]Brent McFarlane, "Simplified Circuit Training," *Track Technique*, Vol. 88, Spring 1984, p. 2797.

number could be 60 or more.)

"The quality can be increased by decreasing reps and doing them faster or by adding a resistance to a set number of exercises (weight vest, ankle weights.)

"Density can be altered by increasing or decreasing the recovery between exercises or sets....How might power be developed using circuit training? The answer lies with special strength (plyometrics, depth jumping activities) being introduced into circuits. Once a strong base of total body fitness with specific emphasis on the lower leg and pillar has been completed, then circuits of 8 to 12 exercises, alternating an exercise for the body with one using special strength are introduced.

"Repetitions may start at 4 and build to 10 but must be done fast and safely for all leg exercises. Body exercises may vary but will always be more than 10 (possibly 100s) reps. Exercises should be changed every 6 weeks but not the sequencing or muscle groups.

"Legs--hurdle hops (5H, double leg hops)
 Body--clap push-ups
 Legs--box jumps (2'3½", 1 contact jump)
 Body--sit-ups (knees bent)
 Legs--squat jumps, etc. (10-12 exercises)

"REVERSIBILITY. If an athlete expects gains in strength, then the principles of specificity and overloading must be adhered to, or strength gains will drop off. Keeping records of increases and testing every 3 or 6 weeks are important to help set loads."

ORGANIZATION OF TRAINING FOR POWER.
This section on organizing a program of training for power for any given event or athlete cannot and does not presume to be complete or even adequate. Such modern training is complex with its gradations from basic to related to specifically imitative, gradations that vary with each event and each unique individual. Such a complete approach requires a separate, full-size textbook, or at least a full section in a book on the jumps or the throws as was attempted by Jess Jarver.[1]

Present-day efforts at organization of training, both here and abroad, tend to be based on the work (Periodization) of Mateyev as explained in Chapter 16, in which he divides the full year into segments appropriate to need and relatedness. At this point, that discussion should be reviewed.

However, it's necessary to remind ourselves that all such European and Soviet sports programs are organized within a club system, not a school-college system. Such clubs assume year-round training that varies in intensity with the sports schedule of competition, but very little in relation to the school schedule. Even more critical, an athlete often trains throughout an entire career under a single coach. Though those of outstanding talent are likely to be moved to special training centers, perhaps in a different city, where coaching experts of Olympic quality can give them highest-level attention. Such multi-year--even lifetime-- coaching by a single expert produces a more serious, even professional approach--professional in the sense of a career, not necessarily of financial rewards.

We should therefore be wary of swallowing whole the methods proposed by East German or USSR trainers. For example, Michael Yessis[2], Editor of the *Soviet Sports Review*, writes
 To get some of these answers on how to train (for strength) most effectively, we must turn to science, as it is now pervading all aspects of weightlifting and

---

[1]Jess Jarver, THE JUMPS (1981) and THE THROWS (1980), *Tafnews Press*, Box 296, Los Altos, CA 94022.

[2]Michael Yessis, Ph.D., "Recent Trends in the Development of Strength," *Muscle and Fitness*, December, 1980, and reprinted in *Track & Field Quarterly Review*. Vol. 83, #1, 1983, p. 55.

weight training. First and foremost is that a good training program is year-round.
Perhaps--if such science is balanced by good judgment as to what is best for the individual,
and perhaps--if "year-round" is interpreted within a sound school-college program in which
sports performance is a secondary concern, secondary to progress toward a more worthwhile
career than professional sports, whether for personal profit as in our country, or for service
to the State as in Communist countries.

Long-time Planning. Even within our school-college program of coaches that change with
each educational level, there should be a unified, or at least consistent plan for training
each athlete. What is done today and next month should be based on what was done a year ago
and what should ensure progress toward successive years.

Just as technique is acquired gradually during an entire career, so should maximal
strength and related power be expected to develop and be emphasized in training. For young
athletes, the expression "maximal loading" should be interpreted as less-than-maximal (60-
80%). Only more mature and experienced athletes should attempt all-out heavy loadings
(85-100% maximal).

Record Keeping. It follows from this approach that some form of record keeping must be
maintained by both the coach and athlete. Carried to extremes, this can become a chore,
consuming more time than it's worth. But, in all cases, enough detail must be available to
carry out intelligent organization from year to year. In strength training, for example,
type of exercise, loadings, repetitions, sets, and allowance for recovery are essential. No
better way can be used to ensure continued motivation and optimal progress in performance.

Variety in Training Routines. Variety in all phases of the training program is essential
to good planning. Such variety maintains enthusiasm and motivation, but also ensures development of all related muscle groups, as well as full recovery and neuromuscular growth.
Peter Tschiene's excellent review[1] of power training among top throwers in West Germany and
the USSR is primarily a statement of the necessity for continuous variety: variety in work-
rest periods; variety in loads per exercise, per day and in total lifted in a given number of
days; variety in muscle structures and patterns of movement; variety in simulation of exercise
to the movement of the projected event. As one example, he cites these monthly changes in the
weight training of Dieter Moser, West German shotputter: Preparation period 1: November--3
sessions per week, submaximal (85%); December--5 times weekly, extensive (60%); January--3
times weekly, submaximal (85%); February--5 times weekly, extensive (60%); Preparation period 2:
March-April--3 times weekly, intensive (75-80%); May--4 times weekly, maximal (90-95%); Competition period 1: June--twice weekly, intensive (75-80%); July--once weekly, maximum in
'pendulum' training (West German Championships); Competition period 2: August--once weekly,
submaximal (80%); September--'pendulum' training for Olympic Games.
Tschiene also reported a year-round plan by USSR Master Coach V. Kuznyetsov that divided
the year into three interwoven periods: basic strength work (BSW), diversified conditioning
(DC) and specialized power work (SPW). For the hammer and javelin Kuznyetsov recommended
the following interwoven proportions: BSW--10-20%; DC--20-30%; SPW--50-60%. Similar proportions should be valid for other throwing events and, modified, for the jumping events.

Individual Differences in Power Training. Individuals differ in all aspects of developmental training. Study after study reports that "individuals react to exercise in a manner
unique to themselves," or that "great individual variations occur under the same experimental conditions." True, men are more alike than they are different, and the same basic
principles of training apply to all individuals. But the specific blend of training factors
that is optimum for any one individual is always unique.

1. Individuals differ in their responsiveness to heavy resistances in strength training.
Some are innately heavy muscles; others, light muscled. Some, generally slow, others, generally
fast. Even with outwardly equal physiques, two individuals may differ greatly in both natural
strength and velocity of muscle contractions.

---

[1]Peter Tschiene, *Track Technique*, Vol. 52, pp. 1642-1654. (Though written in 1972, this
article by a National Coach of West Germany is of present-day value for all throwing events.
Examples are drawn from diaries of great performers.)

2. Individuals differ in the pattern of strength-velocity-coordination in different parts of the body. One individual may be superior in the movements of his arms but inferior in those of the legs, or vice versa. For example, de Vries states that "this specificity extends even to the type of task and the direction of movement...Is has been shown...that speed is 87 or 88 percent specific to the limb. Even within the limb, speed is 88 to 90 percent specific to the direction of movement." (Keep in mind that "speed" is not a separate entity but a way of looking at "power," and that what is said of one relates to what can be said of the other.)

3. As a generality, we tend to assume a 1:1 ratio between muscle cross section and its absolute strength. Individuals differ, of course, in such scross sections. But Morehouse points out, "there are repeated observations that exercised muscle can increase in size, but not in strength," as witness the "body beautiful" of the muscle pumper.

4. Very important: Individuals vary widely in the relative lengths of the bony levers of the body, as also in the effectiveness with which these levers function at various angles.

5. Individuals also vary greatly in what can be called "willed control" of strength. For example, Ikai[1] and Steinhaus concluded, "Our findings appear to support the thesis that in every voluntarily executed, all-out maximal effort, psychologic rather than physiologic factors determine the limits of performance." Such psychologic inhibitions, or lack of them, vary infinitely with each individual's unique environmental influences.

Bruce Jenner had his weight-training eyes opened when, in 1975, he shifted from his kingpin role at Graceland college to San Jose where the Big Boys--Feuerbach, Wilkins--were training,

> *I'd always thought I was strong, but very soon I found out different. The first time I went to the weight room at the YMCA...I did a few squats and thought I was real hot stuff. Then along comes Maren Seidler, a woman shot-putter, and she outsquats me like it was nothing at all. A girl‡....It made me realize how underdeveloped I was, how much further I had to go, seeing all these guys so much better than I was.[2]*

This list of five areas of individual differences is merely suggestive. Roger J. Williams' life-time studies[3] led him to conclude that just as our fingerprints are individually unique, so are all aspects of our structures and functions.

SAFETY IN TRAINING FOR POWER

Even with trained supervision and careful organization of strength training, there is always danger of injury from overloading skeletal-muscle systems when doing power exercises. On beginning a weight-lifting program, strength develops rapidly; young boys and girls become enthusiastic; they attempt weights beyond their readiness, or use techniques that place over-strain on points of skeletal weakness.

Injuries, as in all aspects of strenuous sports, will occur. The all-important responsibility of both the coach and the weight-room supervisor is to make certain that the risk of injury is minimal. When it occurs--and it will occur--they each should feel they took all precautions to avoid it. I know all too well! Even now after more than 30 years, I get a tight feeling in my throat whenever I think of Charlie Fonville, world-record holder in the shot put, 1948. "The American most likely to win a gold at the London Olympics," he failed to make the U.S. Olympic team because of a lower-back injury while practicing the shot. No weight-lifting, of course, in the 1940s, but 10,000 repetitions of putting a 16# weight is a power exercise that can put all related structures on strain. Note that the shotputting action is identical to that of the lower figure in Figure 6.4. We weren't aware of that in 1948, but the bone-and-joint medics were, and we should have been.

---

[1]Michio Ikai and Arthur Steinhaus, "Some Factors Modifying the Expression of Human Strength," in Steinhaus, *ibid.*, p. 137.

[2]Bruce Jenner and Phillip Finch, *DECATHLON CHALLENGE*, Englewood Cliffs, N.J.:Prentice-Hall Inc., 1977, p. 72.

[3]Roger J. Williams, *BIOCHEMICAL INDIVIDUALITY*, New York: John Wiley & Sons, 1956, 215 pp.

Gunter Fritzsche[1], of West Germany, summarized the pros and cons of safety in weightlifting, the gist of which is as follows:

1. "The coach should continuously inform young athletes of the danger of premature tests of strength."

2. "Particularly important is the all-around development of the youngster in his early years." "Barbell work should not be performed until after the 13th year."

3. "There is basically no difference in teaching weight training to boys and to girls. However, because of less power, initial poundages for females should be 10-15% less."

Youngsters of widely different ages and abilities should work out separately. Supervision and teaching can then be more precisely fitted to both knowledge and capacity.

4. An all-round conditioning program, one that ensures good muscular development of the torso (medicine balls, sandbags, bars, etc.), should precede weight lifting.

5. "Correct lifting technique is particularly important...Correct motions should first be learned with unweighted bars."

Fig. 6.4--Movements that tend to cause injury.

6. "The objective for each training session must be carefully thought out and well understood by all."

7. Adequate warmup, both general and specific, must precede each exercise. As to possible dangers of heavy-weight training programs in general, Fritzsche cites the work of Falameyev and Lukanov, USSR, "Exercises with weights cause no particular changes to the spine but actually favorably influence its structure in that weight training develops a supportive 'corset of muscles.'"

8. Until both the supervisor and the youngster are sure of what can be handled without strain, weights should be lifted easily; repetitions, low so that the last lift on the last set involves sub-maximal effort; and progressions from week to week, gradual.

Consistent with Fritzsche's warnings are the recent recommendations of Russian researchers. When seeking power through depth jumping, an emphasis on increased heights of boxes, hurdles and the like produces more rapid power increases than does the use of weighted vest, belts, or sandbags. The latter have produced all-too-prevalent injuries to related joints, tendons and muscles, and so should be introduced into the program very gradually.

---

[1]Gunter Fritzsche, "Safety Factors in Weightlifting," *Track Technique*, #64, June 1976, p. 2025. Translated by G. A. Carr from *Leichtathletik*, #7, 1975.

FLEXIBILITY FOR TRACK AND FIELD

A well-designed program of flexibility based on stretching exercises can be an important factor in preventing injuries, as well as in improving performance. In simplest terms, flexibility relates to the range of movement within a joint or series of joints. For some joints, such as the elbow or knee, the bony structure fixes the limits of this range. But for most, as in the ankle, wrist or hip, the range of motion depends on more stretchable tissues: (1) muscles and their fascial sheaths; (2) connective tissue including tendons, ligaments, and joint capsules; and (3) the skin. Related research has established that, of these factors, resistance to extension arises almost entirely from the fascial sheaths that closely bind muscles and muscle-fiber units. It is these fascial sheaths that are the primary concern of a program of flexibility exercises.

Herbert deVries,[1] after a careful survey of related research, identified two types of flexibility: static--a measure of range of motion; and dynamic--a measure of a joint's resistance to motion. In his study of static flexibility, deVries distinguished between two methods: (1) ballistic--the usual calisthenic exercises such as trunk rotators, benders and lifters, or leg and arm lifters. Antagonists are stretched by contraction of the agonists, and vice versa, in bobbing or bouncing movements. (2) Static stretching methods, not unlike the static positions (*asanas*) of Hatha yoga. Joints are locked for a period of time so as to extend muscles and connective tissues maximally.

DeVries found that both methods made significant and similar gains in flexibility, but concluded that the static stretching method has three distinct advantages: (1) less danger of injury by over-extension; (2) lower energy requirements; and (3) in contrast to ballistic stretching, it seems to relieve muscle soreness, not cause it.

Cyril Carter[2] prefers the word, "suppling"--bending easily without strain or breaking--as used in ballet and gymnastics. He suggests ballistic movements during the warm-up phase, with emphasis on complete relaxation; then moves toward the extremes of a joint's range of motion, again with a first concern for relaxation. In many instances this relaxed stretch can be held for as long as 30 seconds.

The main principle governing this type of suppling is that...the athlete should never use his own muscular strength to force a joint beyond its "natural" range... The natural reaction of a training muscle, when encountering a sudden forceful movement, is to tighten up...to prevent injury to the joint. This counters the intent to stretch and lengthen (supple) the muscle and ligaments, and often causes small tears...in the muscle.

In all exercises for suppling the emphasis is on relaxation of the limb to be worked on. Therefore, whatever position is being practiced, the athlete must attempt to go to the extremes of his range and stay, relaxed, for a period of time. It is the number of times,...together with the length of time spent in such positions, that determines just how supple (and how quickly) one is likely to get. The only effort is (that) required for relaxing.

Suppling is an all-round (two-way) process....It is of little use suppling in one direction without spending an equal amount of time suppling in the opposite direction. Example: if one requires suppling of the hamstrings for the lead-leg action in hurdling, one must also supple the opposing muscle (the quadriceps) on the same leg.

(Carter's exercises are similar to those described here, though with a greater emphasis on

---

[1]The views stated in this section have been drawn primarily from Herbert A. deVries, *PHYSIOLOGY OF EXERCISE FOR PHYSICAL EDUCATION AND ATHLETICS*, Dubuque, Iowa: Wm. C. Brown Co., Publishers, 1974, Chapter 22--Flexibility.

[2]Cyril A. Carter, "Suppling: the Myth of Mobility Exercising," *Track Technique*, #73, Fall 1978, p. 2329.

BASIC FLEXIBILITY EXERCISES

Basic Flexibility Exercises. Most of these exercises can be done by both the ballistic and static stretching methods as described by deVries. However, the work of all three investigators reviewed here confirms that major emphasis should be placed on the static (suppling) method. In most instances, the ballistic method is better used when warming up.

complete relaxation and on the length of time positions are held. He ends his article as follows:)

Remember that (suppling) is a long and slow process (often painful but not injurious), in which the emphasis is on relaxation, not on activity. If you feel any sharp or sudden pain, stop immediately. Take your time and persevere for, just as the results are slow, so too are they certain and safe.

Consistent with these findings, Croce[1] and DiPaolo selected 32 static exercises (positions) that stretch the various joints and muscles that incur greatest stress in sports. Joints are gradually extended toward their maximal range of motion. Positions are held for from five to ten seconds, then repeated three to five times, with complete relaxation between.

To avoid muscle soreness and possible injury from over-stretching, the authors emphasize (1) such warm-up exercises as easy calisthenics, jogging-in-place and rope skipping, and (2) gradual increments of stretching during first movements. Among their recommended exercises, the following seem of special value for track and field:

Head to Floor--Sit with legs straddled wide; keeping legs straight with hands grasping lower legs loosely, bring forehead slowly forward toward and eventually to the floor. Repeat with increase of leg spread. Muscles stretched--trunk extensors, groin, hamstrings.

Knees to Floor--Sit with soles of feet together; use hands to pull heels maximally toward crotch; lean forward, using elbows to push knees down to floor. Muscles stretched--groin.

Heels to Buttocks--Lie prone; keeping chin on floor, grasp both ankles; slowly pull heels to buttocks. Muscles stretched--quadriceps. (As an extension of this exercise, lift chin and pull knees from floor; then rock forward and back.)

Palms to Floor--Stand with feet together; keeping knees straight, bend slowly forward until the palms touch the floor. Muscles stretched--hamstrings, trunk extensors.

Head to Floor--Stand with feet spread about 3-4 times shoulder-width; keep knees straight; hands should grasp lower legs to aid forward bend bringing head to the floor. Muscles stretched--hamstrings, trunk extensors, groin.

Calf Stretch--Stand with feet about four feet from wall, extended palms on wall; keeping entire body straight and heels on floor, slowly lean forward using arms for support. Muscles stretched--calf, ankle plantarflexors.

Prayer Stretch--Place palms of hands together in front of chin at shoulder level; raise elbows maximally. Muscles stretched--wrist flexors. (To stretch wrist extensors, reverse this exercise with backs of hands together; pull elbows down.)

---

[1] Pat Croce and Matt DiPaolo, *STRETCH YOUR LIFE*, C & D Publications, Box 447, Springfield, Pa., 19064, 1980, paperback, 48 pps. A completely illustrated guide to static stretching exercises.

Note: Excellent discussions of both the theory and practice of suppling can be found in: (1) David E. Martin and Marc Borra, "Understanding Flexibility for Track & Field Athletics," *Track Technique Annual*, 1983, edited by Vern Gambetta, *Tafnews Press*, Los Altos, CA 94022, 1983, p. 55; and in
(2) Sally Seavy, "Reciprocal Inhibition in Stretching," *Track Technique*, Vol. 81, Fall 1980, p. 2570.

Dick Fosbury, pioneer of the flop style of high jumping.

Chapter 7
THE HIGH JUMP

In contrast to the single-line approach of the other jumping events, the 180-degree area in front of the running-high-jump crossbar is unrestricted. During the past 100 years of trying to jump higher and higher, men have run down or curved across each of those 180 degrees, and each variation has produced its own unique technique--in the run, in the gather and spring, and in the method of clearing the bar. In this last phase alone, we can distinguish at least eight different styles, as will be described in a later section.

Actually, the method of clearing the bar is not at all the crucial phase of jumping high. Geoffrey Dyson, the English expert in biomechanics, estimated that this phase contributed only about ten percent to the height obtained as compared with 90 percent from what he called "spring"--vertical velocity at takeoff. Dwight Stones (WR--7'7¼", 1976) confirms this, "The approach run-up for me is very important--80 percent or more of overall execution of the jump."[1] It follows that any attempt to understand the development of technique in the running high jump must consider, not only the various styles of clearing the bar, but even more important the diverse patterns (direction, length, velocity and method) of both the run and the conversion of forces during the takeoff.

But first, a discussion of certain concepts that are basic to jumping high whatever the technique.

Fig.7.1. Tamara Bykova, USSR, clearing 2.03m (6'8") indoors, Mar.6, 1983, an indoor world record. Tamara was 24 years old and USSR high jump champion, 1980.

[1]Dwight Stones, *THE HIGH JUMP BOOK*, by David E. Martin et al, TAFNEWS PRESS, 1982, p. 19.

TABLE 7.1

OUTSTANDING PERFORMANCES -- HIGH JUMP

OLYMPIC CHAMPIONS -- MEN

Date	Record		Name	Affiliation	Age	Hgt.	Wgt.	Style
1948	6'6"	1.98	John Winter	Australia		6'4"		Eastern
1952	6'8¼"	2.04	Walt Davis	Texas A&M	21	6'8½"	190	Western
1956	6'11½"	2.16	Charles Dumas	Compton	19	6'1½"	179	Straddle
1960	7'1"	2.17	R. Shavlakadze	USSR	27	6'1¼"	183	Straddle
1964	7'1 7/8"	2.19	Valeriy Brumel	USSR	22	6'1½"	175	Straddle
1968	7'4¼"	2.25	Richard Fosbury	Oregon St.	21	6'4"	183	Flop
1972	7'3 3/4"	2.24	Juri Tarmak	USSR	26	6'4"	161	Straddle
1976	7'4½"	2.26	Jacek Wszola	Poland	19	6'3"	168	Flop
1980	7'8 7/8"	2.36	Gerd Wessig	E. Germany				
1984	7'7¼"	2.32	D. Mogenburg	W. Germany	22	6'7"	172	Flop

OLYMPIC CHAMPIONS -- WOMEN

Date	Record		Name	Affiliation	Age	Hgt.	Wgt.	Style
1972	6'3¾"	1.91	Ulrike Meyfarth	W. Germany	16	6' ¼"	154	Flop
1976	6'4"	1.93	Rosie Ackermann	E. Germany	24	5'9"	130	Straddle
1980	6'5½"	1.97	Sara Simeoni	Italy	27	5'9¼"	151	Flop
1984	6'7½"	2.02	Ulrike Meyfarth	W. Germany	28	6'2"	154	Flop

PERFORMANCES OF SPECIAL INTEREST -- MEN

Date	Record		Name	Affiliation	Age	Hgt.	Wgt.	Style
1887	6'4"	1.93	W. Byrd Page	U. of Penn.		5'6 3/4"		Mod scissors
1895	6'5 5/8"	1.97	Mike Sweeney	Xavier A.C.		5'8¼"		Eastern
1912	6'7"	2.01	George Horine	Stanford		5'11"		Western
1917	6'9½"	2.07	Clint Larson	Brig. Young	25	5'9½"		On back
1924	6'8¼"	2.04	Harold Osborn	Illinois	25	5'11½"	178	Western
1932	6'6"	1.98	Jim Stewart	So. Cal.	23	6'3"		Straddle
1936	6'8 3/8"	2.04	Kalevi Kotkas	Finland		6'6"		Eastern
1936	6'9 3/4"	2.08	Dave Albritton	Ohio State	23	6'3"	176	½D-Straddle
1941	6'11"	2.11	Les Steers	Oregon	24	6'1"	190	Straddle
1956	7' 5/8"	2.15	Charles Dumas	Compton	19	6'1½"	179	Straddle
1960	7'3 3/4"	2.24	John Thomas	Boston U.	19	6'4 3/4"	187	Straddle
1963	7'5 3/4:	2.29	Valeriy Brumel	USSR	21	6'1½"	175	Straddle
1984	7'7½"	2.32	Dwight Stones	L.Beach St.	28	6'5"	175	Flop
1984	7'10"	2.38	Zhu Jianhua	China	21	6'4"	152	Flop

PERFORMANCES OF SPECIAL INTEREST -- WOMEN

Date	Record		Name	Affiliation	Age	Hgt.	Wgt.	Style
1978	6'7"	2.01	Sara Simeoni	Italy	25			
1983	6'7"	2.01	Louise Ritter	USA	25	5'10"	132	(US record)
1984	6'8 3/4"	2.04	Tamara Bykova	USSR	26	5'10"	189	(WR)

HIGH SCHOOL LIST -- BOYS

1983	7'6"	Dothel Edwards	CS, Athens, GA
1983	7'4¼"	James Lott	Refugio, TX
1983	7'4¼"	Maurice Crumby	Bal, San Fran. CA

HIGH SCHOOL LIST -- GIRLS

1983	6'2 3/4"	Lisa Bernhagen	WR, Hailey, ID
1983	6'1½"	Mary Moore	Issaquah, WA
1983	6'1"	Tonya Mendonca	MW, Vis. CA

BASIC CONCEPTS IN LEARNING TO JUMP HIGH.

(1) Major concern in learning to jump high should be placed on related power training, on the pattern of run-gather-takeoff-flight angle, and on the techniques of bar clearance--in that order of learning time and training emphasis.

These three phases are not merely inter-related but are three aspects of one whole, never to be thought of or practiced as separate, unrelated actions.

(2) An early emphasis on related power training is essential to highest jumping and to prevent injury. Ecker states that "top-level high jumpers exert a force against the ground that is as much as four times their body weight."[1] Such force requires great power (strength x velocity) in the takeoff leg (torso, thigh, knee, lower leg, ankle, foot), and great power in the lead leg to aid the upward drive. Further, the rapid acceleration-deceleration of the run-gather place great strain on related muscles and tendons, strain that tends toward injury unless prevented by power training, as well as by a gradual approach--never too much too soon.

(3) Major concern in learning to jump high should be to increase upward velocity at takeoff by developing an optimal run, gather and flight angle. Upward velocity and flight angle determine the height to which the jumper's center of mass rises. Such a run pattern must be consistent with the method of clearance but should be given primary emphasis in early learning.

Tom Tellez, University of Houston, writes that the greatest asset of the flop style lies in its fast approach, rapid change of direction and takeoff from the outside foot. These combine to produce powerful eccentric and reflex contractions in the quadriceps of the takeoff leg, and so greater vertical force.

"Once the jumper leaves the ground, he will have established the parabola of the center of mass. This parabola cannot be changed. The only thing that the jumper can do is to move his arms and legs around the center of mass for bar clearance. This is why 90 percent or more of coaching should be done on the run and takeoff."[2]

(4) The greater the velocity of the run, the greater its potential for jumping high, assuming horizontal velocity is effectively converted upward. As an example of this principle, I think of an indoor game my grandson has. By pulling a rod, a steel spring is compressed. Its release shoots steel balls horizontally against an upward-curved slope, hopefully into holes at various heights and increasing value. The more the spring is compressed, the greater its power-velocity, as well as that of the ball, on release, and the higher the ball is projected into the air.

In this game, the upward slope converts horizontal force upward. In human jumping, the body is self-propelled; there is no curved slope, but the principle is the same. In fact, in 1957 Yuri Stepanov set a world record at 2.16 (7'1") wearing an "inclined-plane shoe" with a thick sole in the takeoff shoe; this in turn produced the present rule fixing the thickness of the sole at 13mm. In other words, jumping high requires a method of gather-takeoff that simulates the curved-slope or inclined-plane concept.

(5) *The greater the velocity of the run, the greater its tendency to shorten the time during which force can be exerted against the ground during the takeoff phase,* and so to decrease the impulse (force x time) upward. Note that this is the negative aspect of concept #4. There is no benefit in a faster run if a man lacks the power or technique for using it. Dyson suggests that each jumper and each jumping style has a "critical speed beyond which takeoff efficiency can be impaired." That is, if the height of present jumping is important, a jumper should use a running velocity that is relative to his present related muscle power and conversion technique. In the past, this has meant that, lacking power training and effective conversion technique, men have tended to slow their run.

Today we understand that the negative effects of faster running is only a tendency that allows a range of possible use, not a fixed value. It follows that in early season or with

[1] Tom Ecker, "High Jump Takeoff," *The Athletic Journal*, March 1975, p. 18.

[2] Tom Tellez, "The Flop,", *Track and Field Quarterly Review*, Vol. 82, #4, 1982, p. 43.

beginning jumpers the run should not be slowed to ensure critical speed. Instead, primary concern should be to gain greater power in the related muscles, and better techniques to increase the duration of force against the ground, techniques that are inherent in the flop style.

(6) Impulse = Force x Time. Other things being equal, the greater the time that force is applied upward, the higher the center of mass is propelled. This concept has many implications, and we are still discovering better ways of making it more effective. During the last few strides the center of gravity must be lowered, thus compressing the muscle springs, and providing more time for the application of force.

Recent research has shown that on higher jumps, the takeoff foot is on the ground for a shorter length of time. This is only an apparent contradiction to this concept #6. Highest level jumpers have greater muscular power that gives them greater quickness in all the related aspects of the jump; their time factor is therefore shorter. Given equal power (quickness) the technique that lengthens the time in which force is applied will exert a greater vertical impulse.

(7) Rotational movements seeking an efficient clearance style are of two kinds--direct and indirect. Direct rotation occurs while the jumper is still in contact with the ground, when a force in any given direction produces an effect in that same direction--leaning forward produces a forward rotation; to the inside, an inward rotation, and so forth. Since its direction of force is always to one side or the other of the line of flight of the center of gravity, direct rotation diminishes vertical force, and so the height reached by the center of gravity.

Indirect rotation occurs after contact with the ground has been lost, and so has no detrimental effect on vertical force or the height reached by the center of gravity. Now movement of the extremities has an action-reaction effect. A left-ward thrust of the right arm turns the torso to the right; a downward thrust moves it upward. An upward lift of the head lowers the torso; a lowering of the torso tends to lift the extremities.

In general, effective jumpers seek maximal vertical impulse with minimal direct rotation, and achieve efficient clearance by way of indirect rotation. Attempts to coach direct rotation in the Flop by emphasizing an inward eccentric drive of the lead knee tends to increase rotation directly and diminish the vertical thrust of the takeoff leg.

(8) Improved technique and higher jumping are acquired together; each aids the other. A higher height of the bar forces a more vertical effort and also allows more time for the movements of indirect rotation and clearance.

(9) To provide maximal upward force, the lead leg must accelerate maximally during the first 90 degrees of its upward swing while the takeoff foot is still on the ground. Once takeoff is completed, such acceleration cannot add to the jumper's velocity. Since a flexed lead leg can drive upward more quickly, and so contributes more force in the brief time the foot is against the ground, it is so used in the Flop and Dive-Straddle styles. In the Straddle, the great concern for vertical force allows more time in which a

Fig. 7.2. Aspects of the flop clearance.

straighter (longer) lead leg can contribute greater angular momentum and upward pull to the body. But in every style, early maximum acceleration of the lead leg's forceful upthrust is crucial.

A SUMMARY HISTORY OF THE RUN.

Over the past century of high jumping we have gradually learned to run faster and make more effective use of the potential values of such speed. But this is an over-simplification of what actually happened. It was no straight-line development; each generation of jumpers had advocates of a somewhat longer-faster run, and other advocates of a forceful spring with emphasis on only the last three or four strides of the run.

THE RUN IN THE EASTERN STYLE. Prior to about 1940, most of those favoring a faster run followed some variation of the Eastern style. Such a run was inherent in the style with its outside-foot takeoff and forceful swing-up of the inside leg.

Mike Sweeney (N.Y.A.C., 1895, 6'5 5'8'') was the first major jumper to achieve a full layout from an outside-foot takeoff. In fact, his achievement was so startling that for many years men spoke of the Sweeney style (Figure 7.4a) much as we now do of the Fosbury Flop. Not until some years after the Horine style came to be called the Western Roll was Sweeney's style called the Eastern.

> *Sweeney started his run in the middle of the runway (about 75 feet back), and swung slowly towards the right edge of the cinder track, turning sharply to the left at an exactly fixed point. He then took three strides as rapidly and with as much force as he could compel. This brings his left foot on the take-off, and gives his body a sort of twist that aids greatly in getting over the bar.[1]*

There's no evidence that Dick Fosbury ever read that 1896 quotation, but it's a striking instance of history repeating itself, for his run, though from the opposite side, was remarkably similar to that of Sweeney.

One variation of the Eastern style, that used by Clint Larson (1917, 6'7''; 1924, 6'9½'' exhibition), made an even greater use of speed in the run. Larson described his clearance (Figure 7.5) as ''a face-upward, back-to-the-bar position'', and wrote that,

> *I feel certain that I ran farther and faster than any other high jumper of my time. I gave particular attention to the practice of sprinting and under favorable conditions could cover the 100 yards in 10.2 seconds. I believe that my jumping ability is due to speed and direct co-ordination of action from the time I start the run until I land on the other side of the bar....I ordinarily cover a distance of from 12 to 14 feet....from takeoff to point of landing.[2]*

As with Murphy, Larson's words might have been taken from a talk by Dwight Stones (''I consider speed in the run as of primary importance'') but we must deduct heavily for 1920 conditions (soft surfaces for run-up and takeoff, heavy shoes with two-spiked heels, no power training) when we interpret the meaning of ''speed'' in action. In any case, this emphasis on a forceful run gradually faded as the Eastern style lost favor.

THE RUN IN THE WESTERN ROLL. The Western Roll and its variations had a built-in tendency to slow the run so as to ensure a maximum spring and efficient clearance style. Its inventor, George Horine (1912, 6'7''), described his run,

> *I used a short preliminary run--actually a walk--except for the last three or four steps....I never measured my run and never marked my takeoff.[3]*

---

[1] *TRACK ATHLETICS IN DETAIL*, compiled by Editor of *Harper's Round Table*, New York: Harper & Brothers Publishers, 1896, p. 56.

[2] Clinton Larson, ''Larson on High Jumping,'' in R. L. Templeton, *THE HIGH JUMP*, American Sports Publishing Co., 1926, p. 125.

[3] George Horine, ''My Development of the Western Roll,'' in R. L. Templeton, *THE HIGH JUMP*, ibid., p. 109.

Harold Osborne (1924, 6'8¼"), with his own back-to-the-bar version of the Western Roll (Figure 7.7b) was very exact in his way of running but gained little momentum,

I measure my approach with a great deal of care, allowing 24 feet between my takeoff and first check-mark, and 12 feet to the second mark. I take three steps to the middle mark and four more to the takeoff--about three feet from the crossbar. I approach from an angle of about 45 degrees and use a long easy bounding step, a little faster than a dog trot. On the last step I "settle" for the spring, then swing the outward leg up and over the bar with considerable force.[1]

THE RUN IN THE STRADDLE STYLE. In its early stages, Straddle-style jumpers followed the minimal speeds in the approach and in amount of practice as established by Horine and Osborne. But Les Steers (1941, 6'11") changed this. Of course power training was unknown at that time. But Steers partially offset this by gradually increasing, during a 12-year career, his ability to jump many times at high heights day-after-day-after-day, probably more than has ever been done in jumping history. Bowerman[2] states that Steers often "jumped twice a day, sometimes taking 20 to 30 jumps on the morning of a meet as a warm-up." Steers said that he ran without any special emphasis on speed, but actually he ran much faster than his contemporaries.

As a spectator-coach, I was greatly impressed by the potential value of Steers' running velocity. In 1953, in the first edition of *MODERN TRACK AND FIELD*, I wrote:

It is my considered opinion that a man can learn to use greater speed at the takeoff than has heretofore been used, and that some means of suddenly "bracing" against horizontal momentum can be acquired....The jumper will have Les Steers' ability to take work, developed through years of effort, and will have Clint Larson's speed and gather up to the bar. Only by combining the two will the best-ever performance be forthcoming.[3]

Unfortunately, most coaches and jumpers did not agree and Steers' methods met strong resistance. In 1956, the Olympic Champion, Charles Dumas, first man ever to clear seven feet, reduced the run to its minimal values. From an angle of 43 degrees, he took eight strides to the takeoff, almost walking the first few and accelerating rapidly only on the last three, much as Harold Osborne had done in 1924.

In my judgment, the longer-faster runs of today were originated by the great Swedish jumpers of the 1950s. In 1954, at the Swedish National Championships, I watched Bengt Nilsson's efforts to become the first to clear seven feet. He used a 13-stride run in which the last seven or eight accelerated to give great force at takeoff. Though jumping Dive-Straddle style, Nilsson used a two-arm upward thrust as an aid to converting that force vertically, a method that was first copied by the Russians and later, by the jumping world.

Valeriy Brumel. The most perfect development of all aspects of the Straddle style came through the work of Valeriy Brumel, USSR, 1963, 7'5 3/4". (I have a strong inclination to write the name as Brumel-Dyatchkov, since the influence of this great National Coach of High Jumping was so vital to Brumel's success.) Perhaps their greatest contribution was that they contrived the means for making a fast run of practical use in increasing upward force. Their method had at least four aspects: (1) a related power training program, (2) a forward-upward thrust of both arms that delayed the rise of the center of weight during the spring, (3) a "settling" of the body during the last three strides, and (4) as an effect of these, an actual increase in the speed of the run.

How fast did Brumel run? Certainly faster than any world-rank jumper prior to 1960, with the possible exception of Larson, whom I never saw. He took seven strides plus three or four preliminary steps, with full acceleration on the first stride beyond his checkmark, a total

---

[1]Harold M. Osborne, "Championship Competition," in R.L.Templeton, *THE HIGH JUMP,*p. 162.

[2]William J. Bowerman, *COACHING TRACK AND FIELD*, Boston: Houghton Mifflin Co., 1975, p. 171.

[3]J. Kenneth Doherty, *MODERN TRACK AND FIELD*, Englewood Cliffs, N.J.: Prentice-Hall, Inc., 1953, p. 376.

run of 50 feet. During one of the great dual competitions (1962) in Madison Square Garden between Brumel and John Thomas (1960, 7'3 3/4"), several coaches found he averaged 2.15 seconds from his deep checkmark to takeoff. Dyatchkov reported that Brumel's speed at the next-to-last stride was 15.65 mph.

THE RUN IN THE FLOP STYLE. The Flop style of high jumping is best understood in all its phases if it is related to the Eastern style--more specifically, the Sweeney-Larson version of the Eastern style. Fosbury began jumping scissors-style in grade school. His high school coach tried to teach him the Straddle, but in one meet, age 16, he reverted to the Scissors with a back layout. At first his body angle was about 45 degrees to the crossbar but by his senior year he had rotated to the full 90 degrees during clearance. Without coaching, Fosbury found that he could run faster and faster up to his takeoff, with little tendency to decelerate during the last few strides.

Since Fosbury, the majority of great jumpers have adopted his style, and all have run at speeds greater than those generally used in the Western or Straddle. Dwight Stones (1973, 7'7¼") said repeatedly that the key to his jumping lay in speed, speed and more speed--"the faster I run, the higher I can jump." It seems clear that, not only is this an innate feature of the style, but the use of a curved approach during the last few strides also has special values. The natural lean into the curve and back from the takeoff foot balances centrifugal force and prolongs the compression of the body springs that Brumel contrived only with special techniques and long practice. This, added to the outside-foot takeoff and inside knee thrust upward, somehow makes the style more tolerant of limited leg strength, limited leg spring, and even limited skill.

This is confirmed by the clearance (June, 1984) of 7' 10" by Zhu Jianhua of China who, according to his Coach, Hu Honfei, had no formal weight training until 1984, and even then, once a week with relatively light weights. His PR squat (single rep) was a mere 275#.

Fig. 7.3. Dwight Stones: "As I turn from the first five straight-line steps, I am running at about 75 percent of maximal speed."

A SUMMARY HISTORY OF STYLES OF BAR-CLEARANCE.
Each champion tends to have his own unique way of clearing the bar. For example, though they both jumped "Western," Osborne (1924, 6'8¼", Fig. 7.7b) lay parallel with the bar and on his back, whereas Horine (1912, 6'7", Fig. 7.7a) was across the bar and on his side. (Osborne claimed his style was original and that he knew nothing of the Horine style.) Similarly, Brumel differed from Thomas, and Stones differed from Fosbury. On this basis, there have been as many styles as there have been champions. But among these individually unique thousands, we can validly distinguish nine bar-clearance techniques: the Scissors, the Modified Scissors (Page, 1887), the Eastern Cut-Off (Sweeney, 1895), the Eastern Trail-Leg Lift (Oler, 1914), the Eastern Back-to-the-Bar (Larson, 1917), the Western Roll (Horine, 1912), the Straddle (Stewart, 1930), the Dive-Straddle (Cruter, 1938), and the Flop (Fosbury, 1968).

THE SCISSORS AND MODIFIED SCISSORS. Every schoolboy knows the natural style of springing with the torso erect and the legs "scissoring"--first the inside leg upward, then the outside-- over the bar. Fosbury says he started jumping that way, and all that followed was a modification. Using only a slightly backward layout, W. Byrd Page, 5'6 3/4" tall, was the first (1887, 6'4") to achieve widespread recognition for this style. Almost a century of improvement of all kinds (techniques, practice methods, power training, equipment, facilities, motivation and mind-set) have added only about 14 inches to Byrd's achievement, the smallest relative gain in any field event.

THE EASTERN STYLE. Mike Sweeney (1895, 6'5 5/8") changed the Page method of lowering the heavy shoulders by reducing the high throw of the second leg, pulling it under the lead leg (the cut-off) and landing on it.

Sweeney's record lasted 17 years but his technique was gradually improved by such men as H. F. Porter and Wesley Oler who whipped the almost straight takeoff leg as high and forcefully as possible while twisting the shoulders down and in the opposite direction, then brought it down quickly for the landing, facing the bar (See Figure 7.4b).

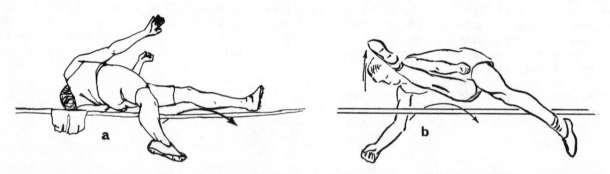

Fig. 7.4a. Eastern Cut-off Style. Drawn from actual jump by Mike Sweeney in setting 1895 world record of 6'5 5/8" that lasted 17 years.
Fig. 7.4b. Eastern Style with straight-leg vertical lift, as jumped by George Spitz (NYU, 1933, 6'8¼").

Oler, who held the schoolboy record in 1912, 6'3 5/8", considered the lift derived from the two-leg upward drive as most significant,[1]

The lead leg should be kicked up with all possible force and high above the head.... As the function of this leg is about over, the rear leg provides the upward action called the lift, accomplished by driving the leg up with every bit of force at one's command. The knee of this leg is slightly bent and the toe of the foot is turned out almost to 90 degrees....The paramount importance of the lift cannot be overemphasized...the maximum height the jumper attains will be governed by the amount of lift he is able to develop.

This Eastern trail-leg lift style persisted for many years, despite its tendency to a higher center of gravity during clearance. Throughout the 1930s, almost all the jumpers in the Eastern states and in other countries of the world used the Eastern style. In 1933, George Spitz of NYU cleared 6'8¼"; in 1936, Kalevi Kotkas of Finland, 6'8 3/8". In 1948, John Winter of Australia used the Eastern in winning the London Olympic title.

THE EASTERN BACK-TO-THE-BAR STYLE. Though very different in his method of spring and clearance, Larson's face-up, back-to-the-bar style (1917, 6'9½" exhibition) is best understood as a variation of the Eastern style. Larson (Fig. 7.5) described his method this way,[2]

---

[1]Wesley M. Oler, Jr., "Four Essentials of High Jumping," in R.L.Templeton, *op.cit.*, p. 143.

[2]Clinton Larson, "Larson on High Jumping," in R.L.Templeton, ibid., p. 127.

The last step before the spring upward is an extra long one. I drop into a low crouching position, so that I can get force to kick the right leg upward as high as possible. I...then spring upward with the left leg. In this way I get a double force....

As I approach the top of the crossbar, after the takeoff, I am in a sort of sitting position and when I reach my highest elevation, I shoot my legs straight out, "bob" my hips and throw my shoulders backward for a complete layout. At this time my body is parallel with the ground and forms practically a straight line....As the upper body clears the bar, I whip my right arm downward as sharply as possible, so that I land on my right leg and right arm.

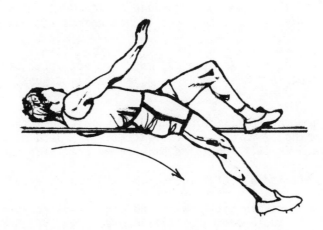

Fig. 7.5. Eastern Style by Clint Larson (1917, 6'9½" in exhibition).

THE FOSBURY FLOP. Though out of chronological order, the Flop belongs here from a technique standpoint, following Sweeney and Larson, and not following Brumel or Matzdorf. Roy Blount tells the story,

Then, in the course of a momentous meet when Fosbury was 16, he reverted to the scissors. As a straddler he had never jumped higher than 5'4". Scissoring he went higher and higher--and a strange thing began to happen. "As the bar got higher, I started laying out more," he recalls, "and pretty soon I was flat on my back."...

Fig. 7.6. The Flop Style by Dick Fosbury (1968 Olympic Champion, 7'4¼").

By his junior year, Fosbury's back was intersecting the bar at a 45 degree angle and he was clearing a little more than six feet. By the end of his senior year he had just about attained the pure 90-degree-angle Flop.[1]

Fosbury's ultimate clearance style will be described in detail later, but can be quickly understood by studying Figure 7.6.

THE WESTERN ROLL.   In 1912, George Horine of Stanford startled the high-jump world, and the Sweeney advocates in particular, by taking off from the inside foot, clearing the bar at 6'7" in a side-to-the-bar position, and landing on the takeoff foot (Figure 7.7a).   Horine wrote how it happened,[2]

I was forced into the "Western" form through an accident....As the available grounds were only 12 feet wide...we had to place the standards (to one side-J.K.D.) and leave them there.

I had always jumped scissors fashion off my left foot...The other boys...were using the same style except that they took off from the right foot, running from the left side....

So I had to run from the left side, though taking off from the left foot as before. This was the beginning of my new form....(At first I) used a straight (almost 90-degree) run and then in 1912 I changed back to my left-side run....

Within a week...I cleared 5 feet 9 inches and a few days later made 6 feet 1 inch.

The Western Roll gained both nation-wide and world-wide acceptance with begrudging slowness.   On the West Coast, Eddie Beeson of California (1914, 6'7 5/8") demonstrated it was no trick style.   But Eastern advocates claimed the Roll was a dive and not a true jump.   A new rule required the head to precede both feet over the bar and not be below the hips at the moment of clearance.   Even after Harold Osborne(1924, 6'8¼") of Illinois proved the Roll was not a West-Coast monopoly, critics were unconvinced.   In 1924 the cross bar rested on 3" pegs projecting from the side of each standard.   They said Osborne actually depressed the bar, pushed it against the standard, then rolled around it, gaining an unfair advantage by never achieving the true bar height.   First, one new rule placed the crossbar as it is today.   Then, after much quarreling and elimination of great jumpers for fouling (for example the famed Babe Didrickson at the 1932 Olympics), the rules on clearance were simplified--"a jumper must take off from one foot."

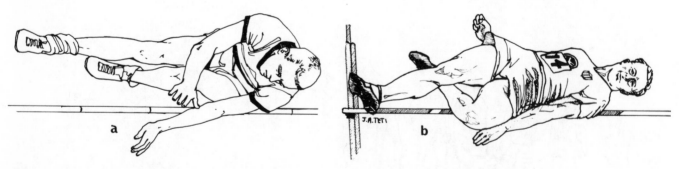

Fig. 7.7a.   Western Roll as jumped by George Horine (1912, 6'7", World Record).
Fig. 7.7b.   Western Roll by Harold Osborne (1924, 6'8¼", World Record).

---

[1]Roy Blount, Jr., "Being Backward Gets Results," *Sports Illustrated*, Feb. 12, 1969.

[2]George Horine, "My Development of the Western Form," in R. L. Templeton, *op. cit.*, p. 109.

<u>THE STRADDLE STYLE</u>. According to Dean Cromwell, Jim Stewart (USC, 1930, 6'6'') "was the first outstanding athlete to use the belly roll successfully in major competition." Cromwell gave a tongue-in-cheek explanation of its origin,[1]

Jim picked up the belly roll so quickly that I asked him if he had ever tried it as a youngster. He said that he had been raised on a ranch and had needed considerable agility at the fences whenever the cattle went rampaging. At first he took the barbed wire fences with the scissors high jump form, but he found this dorsal clearance both destructive for the seat of his trousers and unpleasant anatomically. Finally, he said, since the cattle didn't get any more peaceful and the fences didn't get any lower, he was forced to use the technique of the belly roll, for with this form he could hold down the barbed wire as he rolled over it. I never believed Jim's yarn either.

The changeover from the Roll to the Straddle also occurred gradually. Most Rollers, such as Les Steers (1941, 6'11''), felt that the Straddle created a tendency to dive and so lose vertical force during the takeoff. They continued to practice the Roll and in competition shifted to the Straddle only at highest heights. The first Straddler to achieve a world record was Dave Albritton (1936, 6'9 3/4'') who, surprisingly, combined a very fast, though short approach with a modified dive position over the bar.

During the 1940s and later, many coaches and jumpers were greatly concerned about vertical lift and the negative effects of diving. In part this was caused by the controversy between Eastern stylists and Western Rollers. But we should also be aware that some of these jumpers were well over six feet tall and attempting heights only a little above eye level. Diving "down" to the bar was a natural tendency and easily exaggerated. In contrast, our present-day heights of over seven feet provide time-distance to concentrate on vertical force and then, later, on bar clearance. Effective technique is easier when the bar is higher.

As a result, runs were shortened and slowed and great emphasis was placed on a forceful upward thrust of a straight lead leg as shown by Charles Dumas in Figure 7.8.

Fig. 7.8. The Straddle Style by Charles Dumas (1956 Olympic Champion, 7' 5/8''); though just out of high school, he was the first man to clear seven feet.

By the year 1960, perhaps 99 percent of jumpers were using some variation of the Straddle. To my knowledge, Gene Johnson (1962, 7' ½'') was the first and possibly the last Roller to clear seven feet.

---

[1]Dean B. Cromwell, *CHAMPIONSHIP TECHNIQUE IN TRACK AND FIELD*, New York: McGraw-Hill Book Co., Inc., 1941, 207.

THE DIVE STRADDLE. As might be expected, the Dive Straddle evolved with and emerged out of the Straddle, for actually they are variations of a single technique. In 1936, Dave Albritton took off perhaps five feet from the line of the bar and "dove" forward-up in setting his world record. A Dive-Straddle? Perhaps, though he held his head and right shoulder well up during clearance. I'm inclined to credit Gil Cruter (Colorado, 1938, 6'8½") with being the first to use a valid Dive-Straddle. In 1938 his style was criticized as emphasizing diving more than jumping high; actually his clearance was very similar to that of modern Dive-Straddlers, 40 years later.

But as a deliberately coached method, the Dive-Straddle emerged primarily out of Sweden. Between 1952 and 1961, at least four Swedish jumpers (Svensson, Dahl, Nilsson and Petterson) all used a pronounced dive while attempting world-ranked heights. Between them they contributed two important innovations. First, a longer, faster and more forceful run. Pettersson, for example, took 15 strides with increasing speed throughout. Second, they acquired a means for converting that running force upward by using what we now call a two-arm thrust, along with a flexed lead leg whose shortened lever drove more quickly and forcefully upward.

The next great Dive-Straddler (Yuri Stepanov, USSR, 1957, 7'1¼") was more famous for his "inclined-plane" takeoff shoe than for his world-record. At that time, the rules ignored sole thickness. A sole 3/4" thick enabled Stepanov to make more effective use of a faster run. A year later his record was approved, but sole thickness was set at one-half inch.

Fig. 7.9. Dive Straddle

Summary. In the third edition (1980) of this OMNIBOOK, equal space was given to describing the Straddle style and Flop style. Approximately equal numbers of high-level jumpers were then using each style. Highest jumps with the Straddle had been made by Yashchenko, USSR, (7'7 3/4", 1977) and with the Flop by Wessig, West Germany (7'8 3/4" in the 1980 Olympic Games) only a one-inch difference. Further, as late as 1979 USSR's National Coach of high jumping, Vladimir Dyatchkov, predicted that "both the Straddle and the Flop techniques will be used in the future."

However, each new year finds an increasing use of the Flop, certainly by world-level jumpers, and also by those at lesser levels, including colleges and high schools. The recent clearance (June, 1984) of 7'10" by Zhu Jianhua of China--with almost no benefit of power training--makes clear that 8 feet is not far in the future. Eight feet! Only the cost of safe landing mounds deters total acceptance. This OMNIBOOK edition, therefore, gives major space and detailed explanation only to the Flop style.

A caution, however. During each period, (Eastern, 1850-1936; Western, 1912-1936; Straddle, 1930-1980; Flop, 1968--) the advocates of that style were convinced it was the ultimate method to follow. Who knows but that sometime soon, some school boy such as Dick Fosbury will run up to the bar as did Clint Larson (1917, 6'9½" exhibition), take off from the outside foot as he and Fosbury did, lead with the inside leg in a more powerful drive than is now done in the Flop style, and clear the bar somewhat as did Larson (Fig. 7.5).

With modern year-found power training and the use of optimal velocity in the run, who knows how high Larson, or we today, might jump? Since he landed on his feet, there was no danger of injury, and no need for low-financed schools to buy high-priced landing pits. Why not jump Straddle with the same feet-first landing? Because Larson's style in its run, gather and takeoff is consistent with the Flop, and would lead easily to the latter when and if conditions warrant.

We have traced a 100-year history of style changes in the high jump--Eastern, Western, Straddle, Flop, each with a humber of variations. It would be unwise if we assume that now at last the ultimate technique has been found in the Flop.

ESSENTIALS OF TECHNIQUE IN THE STRADDLE STYLE[1]
As with all field events, the essentials of technique in the Straddle style must consider the whole action. All early actions--precise length of the first stride, body lean, direction and velocity--set the foundation and directly affect the vertical drive in later phases of the jump.

THE RUN IN THE STRADDLE STYLE
It must be emphasized again and again that the run is at least as crucial a phase of high jumping as is clearance technique. The run comes first, and so develops the potential force, the degree of relaxation, and the means of converting horizontal power upward. If the run is too short or too long, too slow or too fast, from an unuseable angle, or with mechanically unsound position of the body and its parts, the height of the jump will be diminished. A sound run which moves effectively into the conversion phase of the takeoff is the foundation of a sound jump.

DIRECTION OF THE RUN
In the straddle style, the angle of the run as related to the crossbar has varied among world jumpers from 43 to 28 degrees. Dumas, with a short, slow approach, ran at 43 degrees; Thomas, medium speed, at 37; Brumel, at faster speed, 28. Yashchenko, with his dive-straddle style, ran fastest of them all at 35 degrees.

Usually, the greater the angle at which one runs, the greater the awareness of the bar. This awareness tends toward a more vertical takeoff, but also toward a slower run and/or a distant takeoff. In contrast, the lesser the angle, the easier it is to get a close takeoff but the greater the tendency to lean in to the bar and dive along it.

Beginning jumpers are usually instructed to run at 40-45 degrees, as this induces a more vertical jump and a free swing of the lead leg straight ahead along the line of the run. This is enhanced if the bar is imagined as being well above the head. But a coach or jumper would be justified to begin at a theoretically sound angle--say 30 degrees--and then work in terms of the strengths and weaknesses of that angle.

LENGTH OF THE RUN
The run should be long enough to enable the jumper to build up optimum velocity *before*--we emphasize--before the transition stage of converting horizontal momentum upward, that is, before the last three steps. Dyatchkov advocates seven to nine steps. Brumel used seven measured steps but added three or four more preliminary steps from about 50 feet out.

Actually, length and speed of the run are inseparable. If the speed, for whatever reason, is slow, there is no point in a run of more than seven strides. But if the speed of the run is fast, as it must be for highest heights, seven strides from a fixed point is hardly enough to acquire speed smoothly before the transition to the conversion phase of the run and takeoff.

SPEED OF THE RUN
In principle, the optimal speed of a maximal high jump must be very fast, limited only by the developed power and skill by which a jumper converts such speed upward. As world-champions acquire greater power and related skill, the speed of their run-ups will be increased.

Dyatchkov favored "a rapid increase in speed from the starting point, with a gradual decrease of acceleration in speed at the end of the run-up."....Note that he says a "decrease in acceleration," not an actual decrease in speed. There is no slow-down, only a shift of attention from greater speed to a smooth use of speed. Velocity "reaches its maximum at the next-to-last step."

----

[1]A more detailed discussion of all phases of the Straddle Style--training and technique-- was included in the third edition (1980) of the OMNIBOOK. Readers with special interests should look there.

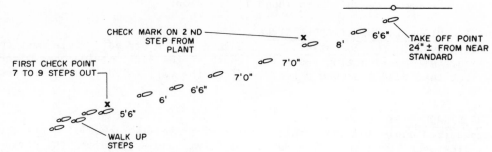

CHECK MARK ON 2 ND
STEP FROM
PLANT

FIRST CHECK POINT
7 TO 9 STEPS OUT

TAKE OFF POINT
24" ± FROM NEAR
STANDARD

6'6"

8'

7'0"

7'0"

6'6"

6'

5'6"

WALK UP
STEPS

Fig. 7.10 -- Diagram of run and checkmarks as used by Valeriy Brumel. Acceleration of the run began at the first checkmark.

THE TRANSITION PHASE

Dyatchkov and his Soviet jumpers have proved beyond all doubt that relatively great velocity in the run up can be used effectively to increase the height of the jump. As in all jumping--and throwing--such velocity must not be dissipated gradually; it must be maintained until the last moment--even increased--then converted forcefully, quickly, and smoothly.

THE TAKEOFF

The takeoff should be understood, not as the instant at which the foot leaves the ground, but as a flow of movement of the pelvis through the takeoff leg, the reaction to compression, and the forceful drive upward. The change in action of the takeoff leg from resistance and absorption of shock to that of exploding upward must occur instantly and with great force. Both power and great skill are needed.

THE LEAD LEG

The most powerful lead leg is one that swings through in a definitely flexed position (to increase acceleration of the swing), then straightens quickly as it swings up to the 11 o'clock position as shown in Figure 7.11.

Such an explosive thrust requires great power, and much related power training of those specific muscles, usually neglected, that drive the lead leg toward the vertical.

Note in Figure 7.11 that though the lead thigh is well above the horizontal, the takeoff foot has just left the ground. This is both unusual and helpful from an increased force standpoint. The higher the leg can swing while the takeoff foot can still apply a reactive force against the ground, the greater its effectiveness. (This applies to the upthrust of the arms also.)

A lead leg that remains flexed lacks the inertia of Dumas' straight leg, but more than compensates: (1) by greater velocity in the preceding run, (2) by its shorter lever that speeds the upward thrust of the leg, and (3) by its effective use in gaining the "through-a-window" clearance of Yashchenko.

Fig. 7.11--A straight lead-leg by Charles Dumas. First high jumper to clear 7 ft., 1956.

CLEARANCE OF THE BAR. Once contact with the ground is broken the angle of flight is fixed and the total rotary momentum of the body cannot be slowed or speeded up. However, the actual speed of rotation can be increased by shortening the arms and legs around the body's frontal axis, just as do ice skaters in their spins. This principle is of great value when the jumper wishes to speed up the actions of clearing the bar, as occurs in the early flexion of the

Fig. 7.12. Valeriy Brumel, USSR; 1964 Olympic high jump champion, 7'1 7/8"; 1963 world-record holder 7'5 3/4". Modified Straddle style.

THE WHOLE ACTION

The running high jump is just that--one action; one run-gather-takeoff-clearance-landing. From the standpoints of technique and training, all phases of that action are crucial. For 50 years or more we thought of high-jumping technique as related only to bar-clearance, but since Les Steers (1941, 6'11") and especially since the Dyatchkov-Brumel duo, the run-and-gather have been emphasized, precisely analyzed, and given special power-and-skill training.

The problem is to put it all together in one all-out flowing movement--in competition! There's the crux. It's a whole man that jumps, not just a body. If a man is to do his best, his energies cannot be drained away by thought of the details of technique, or by doubt as to what he can do. To do his best, he can have only one focus of mind and technique--running-and-jumping HIGH! When Yashchenko tried 7'8½" (2.35) after his world-record 7'7 3/4", he said afterwards "It was not really a test as such. For me, the height did not exist as a barrier or limit."

trail leg.

Second, any movement--up, down, or around--on one side of the center of gravity produces an equivalent "opposite" movement on the other side. An upward counterclockwise lift of the trail leg both produces and is increased by a downward clockwise thrust of the "opposite" head-shoulders-arms. Geoffrey Dyson once demonstrated this principle very dramatically by standing on a turnstool that moved freely on ballbearings. When he thrust his arms-shoulders clockwise, his legs-feet rotated counterclockwise. This is of crucial importance in attempts to clear the bar with the trail leg.

Fig. 7.13 A-B-C. Three variations of trail-leg clearance.

ESSENTIALS OF TECHNIQUE IN THE FOSBURY FLOP.

The most conspicuous feature of the Fosbury style is its method of clearance with the back to the bar, hence its name. But its most valuable asset lies in its style of run and method of converting the high velocity of that run into upward force. Tom Tellez writes,[1]

> *The greatest asset of the flop...lies in the powerful eccentric muscular contractions that arise out of a fast approach and sudden change of direction. The resistance to centrifugal force and linear force developed in the arc run of the flop forces the quadriceps of the jumping leg into more flexion resulting in more vertical lift. Once the jumper leaves the ground he will have established the parabola of his center of mass. This parabola cannot be changed. The only thing that the jumper can do is move his arms and legs about the center of mass to aid bar clearance. This is why 90 percent of coaching should be done on the run and takeoff.*

In keeping with this "new" emphasis, most of this discussion of Flop techniques will be related to the run-conversion phase. To re-state what Dwight Stones has said repeatedly-- "clearance is merely the follow-through phase of a proper run and takeoff; it's no problem--a natural outcome of the style."

THE RUN. A consistent, relatively high-velocity run is both inherent in the Flop style and absolutely necessary for highest jumping. Four phases of such a run warrant special

---

[1]Tom Tellez, "The Flop," *Track and Field Quarterly Review*, Vol. 82, #4, 1982, p. 43.

attention--its pattern, its velocity, its length--but of special import to the Flop, the consistency with which all phases are performed. With earlier styles, the run was slow enough to allow variations; jumpers could "feel" their way. In contrast, the high-speed Flop requires precision in all its phases.

✳ <u>CONSISTENCY IN THE APPROACH</u>. Even before discussing the technique of the run, it is important to emphasize that consistency in all phases of the run--its pattern, length, velocity, conversion curve, length of strides--is absolutely essential to maximal heights in the jump. Such consistency can be achieved only by many--I almost wrote, "endless"--repetitions, especially during the pre-competitive season. Such repetitions are often without attempting to clear a bar, but only as one practices the full action of the run-and-jump can mastery of high jumping technique be assured.

Pat Reid, one of Canada's foremost high jump coaches, spent much time in Europe studying European methods. He writes,[1]

> *The rhythm (of the run) is critical. Europeans spend hours in winter perfecting their running skills--tall, relaxed, upright, hips slightly forward...not sprinting, but high-jump-approach running. Sprinting, then high jumping, tends to cause too much initial forward lean...*

✳ <u>PATTERN OF THE RUN</u>. The J approach to takeoff has now gained general acceptance among world-class high jumpers. For example, most jumpers use five strides during the curved run-up to the bar, preceded by five or more strides on a straight line vertical or near-vertical to the bar.

But the most critical concern in the run pattern is that it be done precisely the same way every time-- the same "mental" preparation before the start, the same preliminary actions before the first step, the same strides on the vertical phase and on the curve--all become automatized so the jumper can concentrate on the leap upward.

Usually three markers are used: (1) the starting point, (2) a point on a straight line, vertical to the crossbar, that marks the beginning of the curve, and (3) the base of the right standards. (This assumes a jump from the left foot.) John Tansley[2] contends that "focussing on the bar or the top of the standard produces excessive backward lean, especially as the bar gets higher."

Dwight Stones, a master of technique, described his run pattern this way.[3] *Some jumpers like to walk into their run. I prefer to step back with my right foot, and then...use it to push me into my run. For the first steps, I accelerate rapidly, then maintain momentum during the first steps of the curve. I use my arms...I think of them as contributing 50 percent to velocity. For the second five steps, I lean into the turn, maintain speed, and then increase it (for me this begins with the seventh step), with a conscious drive of the arms. The length of the final step is shorter, not deliberately, but as a natural effect of body balance during the upward drive.*

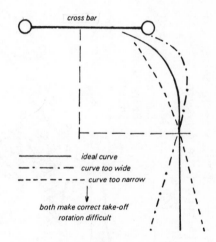

cross bar

——————— ideal curve
— · — · — curve too wide
— — — — — curve too narrow

both make correct take-off rotation difficult

Fig. 7.14. Three run patterns as drawn by Jess Jarver, *THE JUMPS*, Los Altos, CA, TAFNEWS PRESS, 1981, p. 29.

---

[1]Pat Reid, "European Approach to the High Jump," *Track Technique Annual*, 1983, p. 97

[2]John Tansley, "The Flop Run-Up," *Track and Field Quarterly Review*, Vol. 81, #4, 1981, excerpted from John Tansley, *THE FLOP BOOK*, L.K. Publications.

[3]This description is derived from Stones' comments in David E. Martin, *THE HIGH JUMP BOOK*, Los Altos, CA, p. 21, but amended to further brevity.

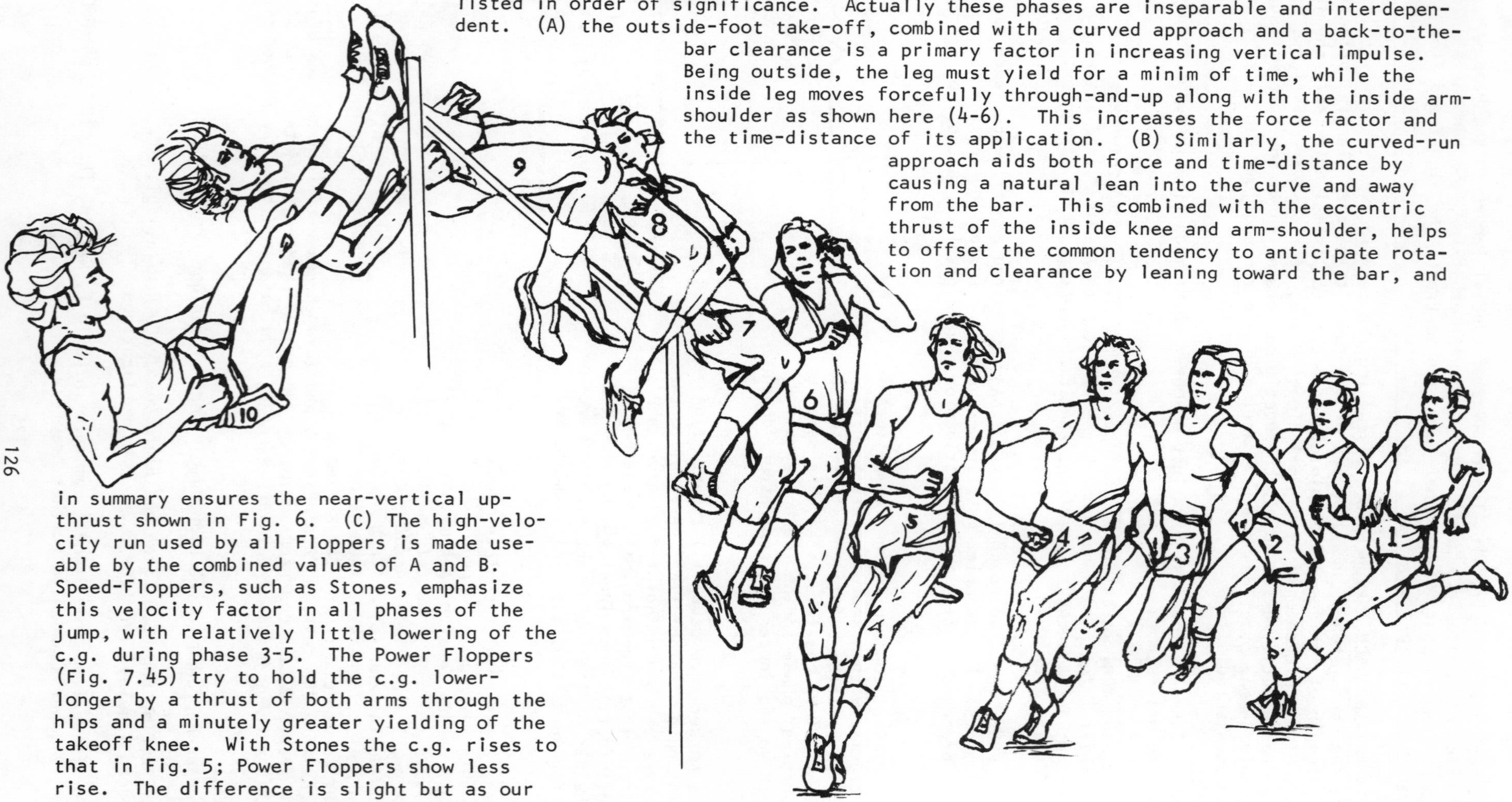

Fig.7.15. Speed Flop by Dwight Stones (1976, 7'7", world record; 1984, 7'8" US record.) Superiority of the Flop style can be attributed to four phases: (A) an outside-foot takeoff, (B) a curved-run approach, (C) a high-velocity run, and (D) method of bar-clearance, listed in order of significance. Actually these phases are inseparable and interdependent. (A) the outside-foot take-off, combined with a curved approach and a back-to-the-bar clearance is a primary factor in increasing vertical impulse. Being outside, the leg must yield for a minim of time, while the inside leg moves forcefully through-and-up along with the inside arm-shoulder as shown here (4-6). This increases the force factor and the time-distance of its application. (B) Similarly, the curved-run approach aids both force and time-distance by causing a natural lean into the curve and away from the bar. This combined with the eccentric thrust of the inside knee and arm-shoulder, helps to offset the common tendency to anticipate rotation and clearance by leaning toward the bar, and

in summary ensures the near-vertical up-thrust shown in Fig. 6. (C) The high-velocity run used by all Floppers is made useable by the combined values of A and B. Speed-Floppers, such as Stones, emphasize this velocity factor in all phases of the jump, with relatively little lowering of the c.g. during phase 3-5. The Power Floppers (Fig. 7.45) try to hold the c.g. lower-longer by a thrust of both arms through the hips and a minutely greater yielding of the takeoff knee. With Stones the c.g. rises to that in Fig. 5; Power Floppers show less rise. The difference is slight but as our grasp of technique improves will become increasingly significant. In general it seems one of $(velocity_8 + time\text{-}distance_7 = height_{15})$ as compared with $(velocity_7 + time\text{-}distance_8 = height_{15})$. But Stones' 1976 $height_{18}$ (7'7") suggests that his velocity factor might be valued as high as 11. It will take a decade however before the final tally is recorded. (D) The method of bar-clearance is listed last as a matter of relative significance in height cleared. In one way it is merely a follow-through of the preceding actions. Stones says "It just happens. No problem at all." On the other hand, Stones extends his bar-clearance all the way up-and-over--no quitting at the top, no tension of muscles that reduce quickness, as occurs too often with lesser jumpers.

Pat Reid[1] reports that, as of 1982, European jumpers such as Simeoni, Mogenburg and Wessig (all former world record holders) were using more of a "jog-into-it," or moving start; that is, eight or nine precise strides preceded by three or four "preliminary" strides to get up optimal speed smoothly. The rhythm of the approach is critical; the best jumpers are almost perfect in their consistency.

To ensure precise foot placement, some jumpers locate the turn mark exactly. For example, Mel Embree, Harvard (7'2¼") used a tape laterally to mark 15'1" and at right angles to the cross-bar 26'1". He started six running strides from the turn mark. "This allows me to set my starting point so I will be relaxed to the turn mark, and able to drive my last four jumps consistently on every jump."

Velocity of the Run. Emphasis during the straight-line strides should be on maximal, but controlled, acceleration. Fosbury's coach, Bernie Wagner of Oregon, once said, "Fosbury approaches the bar faster than any previous jumper; it is an inherent part of the Flop style." Dwight Stones has said repeatedly, "The key to my jumping more effectively lies in using more speed-speed-speed. I have yet to see a Flopper who runs slowly."

Tang Lei[2] reports that a fast approach was the primary factor in Zhu's technique in clearing 7'10", 1984, new WR. Using 10 strides (5 straight, 5 curved), he "builds up max. speed to the last stride, and his record for 30m sprint from stationary start is 3.59 sec."

One method of judging horizontal velocity is to time from touch-off on first step to touch-down at the takeoff. This can be done accurately for any given jumper (Pat Reid reports from 2.5 to 3.5 seconds) and so is of value in measuring consistency. But this is of less value when comparing the velocity of one jumper with that of others—methods of running vary too much.

Fig. 7.16. The Run-Up in the Flop Style. Excerpted from Jess Jarver, THE JUMPS, ibid, p. 29.

Run Length. The run should be long enough to ensure optimal velocity prior to the first strides of the conversion curve. "Optimal velocity" is not fastest-possible velocity, but is that speed that enables the jumper to gain fastest-useable velocity during the next-to-last stride before takeoff. Fosbury ran a curve from his first step 42'6" from the crossbar extended, using eight strides; Stones took ten strides from 65 feet out; Tom Woods, 8 strides from 56 feet; and other seven-foot jumpers, eight to 11 strides from 55 to about 70 feet out. (During the indoor season, jumpers must be prepared to shorten both the length of run and the lateral location of their starting point so as to adjust to the limited space of indoor facilities.)

The Conversion Curve. In the J pattern of run, the radius of the conversion curve is of great importance. A longer radius with its more gradual curve can either lessen centrifugal force and so decrease its potential values for vertical force, or it can utilize greater velocity in the run without decreasing vertical force. A shorter radius has the opposite potential effects. Given a fixed velocity, a "sharper" curve creates greater centrifugal force, tends toward a greater lean into the curve and back of the takeoff foot, and so a longer time in which force can be applied against the ground during takeoff. As jumpers improve their technique and clearance height, they tend to increase running velocity and decrease the radius of the conversion curve, but this is only a tendency that varies from man to man. Frank Ryan[2] reports Stones as saying,

---

[1]Pat Reid, ibid., p. 97

[2]Tang Lei, National Research Institute of Sports Science, China, "Three Keys to Zhu's World Record Jump," *China Sports*, Vol. 16, 1984.

[3]Frank J. Ryan, Ph.D., "The Fosbury Flop with Dwight Stones," *Scholastic Coach*, March 1976, p. 24.

During the first five strides I work on establishing rhythm and, at the same time, develop velocity. From the sixth step on, I go toward the curve. While running in the curve I try to maintain or even increase my speed. At this stage I can feel the pull of centrifugal force and I lean into what would be the center of the circle.

Length of the Final Strides. Normally, the length of the final strides will be a natural consequence of the pattern and technique of the approach. Analysis by the use of movies usually finds the next-to-last stride is longer; the last stride, shorter but this varies with the style of jump and the individual jumper, and so need no special coaching emphasis. In fact, attention directed to such differences is more likely to disrupt coordination than to help it.

Placement of the Takeoff Foot. Jumpers and coaches now seem generally agreed that the takeoff should be from a point directly out from the near standard. This ensures clearance of the bar at its lowest point, relates the takeoff point to a fixed and easily seen object, and most important, produces a landing on a safe foam-rubber mound. Otherwise, men tend to slide along the bar and end up on the hard apron, more than slightly bruised.

To be most effective, the line of placement of the takeoff foot should balance two concerns--alignment with the curve of the final strides, and facilitation of rotation during takeoff. Coach Wagner states[1] that Fosbury's foot was placed at 15 degrees to the crossbar. Stones tried to plant his foot parallel with the crossbar. Wszola (WR 2.35m, 7'8½'', 1980) said, "My footplant varies from 15 to 28 degrees away from being parallel to the crossbar, depending on my changing physiology from one competition to another, and from one jump to another." That's a wide variation, not to be expected in a world-record jumper, but still within the range of great jumping.

To be most effective, placement of the takeoff foot should be in line with the curve of the final strides, with body weight on the outside of the foot--thus maintaining the inward lean into the curve and optimal time-force against the ground. The takeoff foot should not aid rotation; that comes from the upper body and inside leg.

A short-radius curve tends to lessen the angle of foot placement; a wide radius, to increase it. In both cases, a straight-ahead placement and vertical thrust take precedence over rotation. Wagner says Fosbury "does not twist his spikes in the takeoff surface," though how that is determined from synthetic surfaces is hard to imagine. Actually a curved approach would produce a slight rotation of the foot from outside heel to inside big toe, during which the line of foot-placement would swing as much as five degrees.

Little or no coaching of these points is needed if the principle is understood and carried out effectively. But inexpert jumpers do tend to anticipate rotation in all takeoff movements, including rotation of the takeoff foot. In contrast, men with excellent technique as well as those attempting heights well above their standing height have a longer time in which to achieve rotation, and so can concentrate on jumping high with a minimum of rotation-- takeoff foot, lead knee, right shoulder and all.

SPRING. Strange as it may seem, high jumpers are not necessarily able to jump high, certainly not if we use the Sargent jump-and-reach test as our criterion. For years coaches have used performances in the latter event to discover prospects for high jumping, but the correlation between high jumping and the Sargent jump is apparently not high. Both Fosbury and Stones denied exceptional ability in the latter. In one interview[2] Stones said that "Al Feuerbach (260-pound shot putter) can easily out-jump me in the standing-jump test." This seems incredible. Donald Chu[3] found supportive evidence at the 1975 Olympic Development Camp at Indiana University.

---

[1] Berny Wagner, "The Fosbury High-Jump Style," *Track & Field Quarterly Review*, Vol. 75, No. 2, Summer, 1975, p. 111.

[2] John Tansley, "How They Train--Dwight Stones," *Track Technique*, No. 55, March 1974, p. 1757.

[3] Donald A. Chu, personal letter to me dated January 13, 1976.

At the Camp one of the tests for high jumpers and shot putters was the jump-and-reach test. The shot putters had a higher mean jump-and-reach than the high jumpers. Matzdorf had the best mark for the high jumpers--32 inches, but the best shot putter went three inches higher--35 inches. Everyone went "zonkers" thinking how high the high jumpers would go when they acquired the leg strength of the weightmen. But they were ignoring task specificity. High jumping is specific to the special skills of the run-conversion-spring-clearance.

Franklin Jacobs (Flop style, 1978, 20--5'8''--150#). The all-time master of "spring" was undoubtedly Franklin Jacobs, Fairleigh Dickinson University, who at age 20, set an indoor world record of 7'7¼''. Jacobs was 5'8'' tall, a difference of 23½'' as between head and clearance heights. This was an amazing achievement, comparable in its superhuman quality to Beamon's 29' 2¼'' in the long jump. A rather careful examination of the record discloses no other jumper with more than a 17-inch difference: Brumel--16¼''; Stones--14¼''; Yashchenko--15¼''; Mogenburg--12''. Jacobs ignored his shortness and emphasized the positives of greater relative explosiveness in lifting his lighter weight (150#) as compared with the 170 pounds or more of other jumpers. (Yashchenko weighed 183#).

It follows that spring is specific to each method of jumping high. In contrast to the jump-and-reach, the high jumper runs prior to jumping, takes off from only one foot, and uses special techniques to exert a force against the ground greater than that supporting his weight. In the Flop style, spring is initiated by a faster-than-usual run that ends with a short-radius curve and a sudden change of direction from horizontal to vertical. The faster run tends to

Fig. 7.17. Dwight Stones, U.S. record-holder, 7'8''.

Fig. 7.18. Zhu Jianhua, China, World record-holder, 1984, 7'10''

shorten durations of force during the spring but the Flop style compensates by increasing force-time through (a) an outside-foot takeoff, (b) a lean into the curve and lowering of the c.g. during the last few strides (called by some the "settle"), (c) a momentary bracing of the takeoff leg against horizontal force, and follow-up "yielding" as occurs in the exercise called depth jumping, (d) a quick acceleration of the arms and lead knee during takeoff that, by action-reaction, increases force against the ground, and (e) a vertical thrust by the takeoff leg with minimum loss of force to rotation and clearance.

Dyson emphasizes the value of early forceful acceleration of the arms and lead leg in increasing thrust against the ground. The greater that acceleration the greater the vertical-force reaction. "Ideally, the free leg and arms should be moving at their maximum velocity at the instant of takeoff, for their acceleration afterward cannot add to the athlete's vertical velocity."[1]

In the Straddle style, a straight lead leg aided vertical thrust and clearance. In the Flop style, both the direction and the force of upward thrust are aided by emphasizing a flexed leg that does not allow the foot to swing forward of the knee. If the foot does swing forward it tends to carry the c.g. along the bar and slows the accelerated drive of the knee Dyson considers essential. The line of the thigh rises very little above the horizontal, then drops down to gain clearance simultaneously with the takeoff leg.

In contrast, the arms are free to punch vertically and early while the takeoff foot is still flat on the ground, and with maximum force. They are effective in increasing ground thrust only as long as there is ground contact, but their ballistic follow-through over the head does aid the later clearance of the hips and legs.

All this assumes, and it's a critical assumption, that the related takeoff leg muscles have sufficient power (strength x velocity) to react to such great force. Only progressive and related strength training can provide the power required by the bracing-yielding and explosive reaction of these movements.

In summary, spring in the Flop style is the resultant of skill during the conversion strides, accumulated force against the ground, and vertical impulse (force x duration.)

Acquiring Rotation. If there is a potential "problem" as related to rotation in the Flop style, it comes from over-emphasis by the athlete and by the coach. As a rule of thumb, it

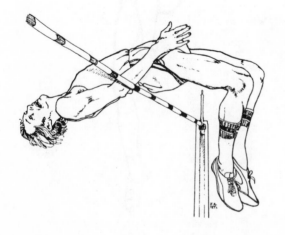

Fig. 7.19a. Dwight Stones

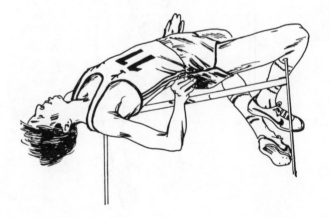

Fig. 7.19b. Zhu Jianhua

[1]Geoffrey H. G. Dyson, *op. cit.*, p. 145.

needs minimal direct coaching. If the jumper has watched other Floppers and gained a muscle-nerve feel of the technique, and if he has made a sound approach to the takeoff, the specific movements of rotation tend to be learned naturally, without special emphasis. If we analyze a slow-motion movie of the Flop, we abstract certain counter-clockwise movements (left-footed Flopper)--a slight rotation of the takeoff foot, an away-from-the-bar thrust of the lead knee, a slight swing of the inside shoulder and head. But such details of rotation will usually evolve naturally if the jumper observes other Floppers and gets a feel of the whole movement.

The primary value of the lead knee lies in its explosive and early thrust vertically, increasing the force against the ground. The athlete should have a sense of keeping such actions (including the arms) in close to the c.g., so as to increase their velocity and mini-mize rotation. Beyond that, the less coaching of details the better. Provide good examples by way of competitions and movies, then let the jumper work out his own details. Fosbury developed his style in his own back yard without benefit of coaching.

CLEARANCE. To the spectator, the method of clearance in the Flop style is its most spectacular feature--hence its name. Cameramen commonly catch the moment of buttocks-clearance when it appears certain the legs can never be lifted above the crossbar. But, strange as it may seem, clearance like rotation, occurs quite naturally *if the Flopper is aware of the crossbar as each part approaches it*. As Stones says, "it just happens." As the head-shoulders clear the bar they lift, both to see the bar and to prevent landing on the head. As the hips clear the bar and the head lifts, the hips drop. As the hips drop, the legs lift. It's as natural and simple as that. Similarly, the forceful thrust of the lead knee produces a wide spread of the knees, slows rotation, and aids both the arch and clear-ance of the legs.

The Power Flop. Men differ of course in all aspects of high jumping--velocity of the run, the gather, use of the arms and legs during the takeoff, the clearance. They are never pre-cisely of this kind or that. At the same time, some men tend to follow a certain way of jumping that can be distinguished from another way. In that sense, Speed Floppers can be distinguished from Power Floppers in ways that make a difference in both technique and train-ing. Keeping in mind the formula (power equals strength x velocity), Power Floppers tend to emphasize the strength factor in their approach to jumping; Speed Floppers, the velocity factor.

Fig. 7.20. The Power Flop showing a somewhat flat-footed approach in which the center of mass is lower by several inches than in the Speed Flop.

In keeping with such views, Prof. Nikolai Ozolin,[1] USSR, described two variations in the run-up and takeoff, both "requiring an increase of horizontal speed in the run-up in order to impart greater energy into the takeoff leg. In the first, (the Power Flop), the takeoff leg is placed further forward and the angle of backward body lean is increased. This places a much greater load on the muscles of the support leg and usually a greater bending of the leg. This requires greater strength if the takeoff is to be effective.

In the second variation (the Speed Flop, which Ozolin considers more efficient--KD), *horizontal speed must provide sufficient kinetic energy to the takeoff leg to react in the shortest possible time and with optimal effect. To achieve this, the foot cannot be as far forward, the backward body lean must be less, the support leg less bent, and the takeoff phase shorter.*

Though these statements were made by Ozolin in relation to the Straddle--style jump, they also relate with equal validity to the Flop.

Pat Reid, in an unpublished article (June 1984), "Speed Floppers and Power Floppers," makes clear those differences that seem significant:

SPEED FLOP	POWER FLOP
Approx. approach velocity of 7.7-8.4 m./sec.	Approx. approach velocity of 7.0-8.0 m./sec.
Approx. approach length of 8-9 strides	Approx. approach length 10-12 strides
Approx. takeoff time of .13-.18 sec.	Approx. takeoff time .17-.21 sec.
Approach run on the toes until last (plant) step.	First half of the approach on toes, second half flat footed and even on heels, incl. plant.
Usually controlled, fast, single arm action in the last 2 steps & takeoff.	Usually sustained wide <u>double</u> arm action with arms very active on takeoff.
Small loss of velocity in the last step (plant), body c. of g. stays relatively forward and high.	Greater loss of velocity in the last step (plant), body c. of g. sinks more and is back, or on top of plant foot, usually not forward!
Usually further away from the bar on takeoff.	Usually slightly closer to the bar on takeoff.
Usually less arm and leg action, in the air.	Usually more active in the air with the pulling up of the trail leg (heels to buttocks) and more active arm movements.
In discussions, world class speed floppers tend to refer to body lean, angle of takeoff, head position, arm position--components ABOVE the waist. (Components of <u>Direction</u>).	In discussions, world class power floppers tend to refer to fast placement, straight plant leg, trying to get the trail leg foot coming through higher and faster, the exaggerated knee drive components <u>BELOW</u> the waist. (Components of <u>Propulsion</u>).
Trail leg (after takeoff) seems to automatically come up (level to buttocks) close to the body automatically and very quickly.	Trail leg (after takeoff) tends to be slow and has to be forcefully (consciously) pulled up (heel to buttocks) to continue the activity that <u>results</u> in the back "arch."
Tend to see less "head throwing." Jumpers tend to look down the bar for feedback	Tend to see more "head throwing," no feedback of seeing anything. Looking down the

[1] Nikolai Ozolin, "The Mechanics of the High Jump Take-off," *LEGKAYA ATLETIKA, USSR*, and also translated by Jess Jarver, *THE JUMPS*, Los Altos, CA: *Tafnews Press*, 1981, pp. 36-39.

more naturally.

Important--Usually have low body weights, and tend to do less weight training.	Usually have higher body weights, and tend to do more weight training.
Do a lot of speed work (enjoy it).	Usually do less speed work (don't enjoy it as much).

HOW TO BEGIN.

Appendix A examines in detail the basic methods for improving motor skills. Here we need only suggest examples of how these apply to jumping high. How, for example, does the principle of whole-part-whole learning function in practice? Obviously, the whole jump of the beginner is of a low order which then progresses by gradually more complex wholes (whole$_2$--whole$_3$--etc.) to levels of complete mastery. The all-important concern is that each whole should be basically sound in terms of the next and, of course, the ultimate technique. Saying it differently, a high-jump coach must establish learning priorities; the actions and forces that contribute most to jumping high should be learned first, not as separate parts or progressions which, added together later will form a whole, but always on a whole-part-whole-part-whole basis.

Consistent with this principle, beginners in the high jump should use the scissors style. In that way they learn the highest-priority essentials first--jumping high from a preliminary run. In jumping scissors style efficiency of clearance is not a concern; attention can be concentrated wholly on jumping high. Soon, the beginner will crouch a little prior to takeoff. He may speed up his last three or four strides or emphasize their force against the ground. As this occurs, a checkmark at the point where these strides begin will be helpful in improving consistency of strides and fixing an effective point of takeoff. At first the beginner will feel his way to that checkmark, but the need for consistency and smoothness will soon produce a starting mark about five strides beyond. He now has the primary essentials of a sound high jump--a consistent approach and a vertical jump. Up to this point, the coach has said nothing about clearance style. The torso remains upright.

Speed of the run should at first be natural and uninstructed, though a casual suggestion to take it easier or move a little faster may not confuse the jumper. Similarly, little attention should be called to the run pattern. But gradually, the jumper should become aware of the potential value of the run-up for applying force against the ground and jumping high. Once he realizes that 90 percent of jumping high lies in this phase, and not in the more obvious and more talked-about phase of clearance efficiency, he is well on the road to sound learning.

As soon as the talented beginner shows interest in continuing with the high jump, his attention should be shifted to related power training.

POWER TRAINING FOR THE HIGH JUMP.

The running high jump is essentially a velocity event--velocity in the approach, velocity in the transition steps, velocity in the upthrust from the ground, in the throw of the arms, of the arch and upward lift of the legs. But velocity is directly intermeshed with strength (power equals strength x velocity), and is generally assumed to be maximal only if preceded by an extensive program of strength training both basic and related.

V. Nedobivailo[1] reported a 1983 research program on the relative values for high jumpers of related strength-power exercises: (1) related exercises that exerted 30-50 percent of maximal strength, and (2) related exercises that exerted 70-90 percent of maximal strength. Both programs, conducted over a four-week period, produced beneficial results. The first (16-18 percent), especially among those lacking the speed factor in power; the second (17-19 percent), especially among those lacking the strength factor in power. But the most positive effects were gained by those athletes who combined both heavy and light exercises.

On the other hand--and the point demands careful attention--prior to Zhu's amazing jump of 7'10" in June 1984, "he had formal weight training for only one year consisting of only

---

[1]V. Nedobivailo, "Weight Training for High Jumpers," *Track Technique*, Vol. 87, Winter 1984, p. 2785.

light weights, only once a week. His PR squat (single rep) is a mere 275 pounds." Either Zhu is the proverbial exception that proves the rule, or our power training must undergo an overhaul.

Pat Reid[1] of Canada reviewed the European approach to training for the high jump and found similar emphases,

In West Germany, we trained with Dragan Tancic, the national jumps coach. They use weights for specific strengthening of weak areas, but more so for total body toughening. Rather than strictly emphasizing leg strength in jumpers for instance, equal amounts of time are spent on lateral (trunk) pelvic girdle strength, low back strength and strength in the positions the athlete is in when performing the event. They use free weights and assume ranges of motion that are event-specific; i.e., high jumpers do toe raises on the take-off foot with a weight plate under one arm, with the other leg bent at the knee similar to a take-off position (Fig. 7.22). The exercises are specific to the force application positions so that when an athlete is trying a performance exceeding his/her previous best the limiting factor won't be an injury to these key areas.

Another example is toe raises on an incline board or step-ups on wooden ramps, etc.-- very simple, very applied, very effective. Lastly, Europeans adjust weight programs so that heavy cycles flow into speed cycles, (fast reps, medium weights), and they aren't so concerned about big max's, like boasting a 700 lb. half squat or 400 lb. bench press.

As far as women in the weight room in Europe they are introduced to it early, and aren't inhibited by the folklore that women can't push big weights. European women are very strong and it is not uncommon to find 16-year-olds doing ¼-squats and half squats with over 200 and 300 pounds.

RELATED POWER EXERCISES

---
[1] Pat Reid, *ibid.*, 1983, p. 95.

RELATED POWER EXERCISES

PLYOMETRICS FOR THE HIGH JUMP
The nature and values of plyometric exercises have been adequately described in Chapter 6, "Training for Field Event Power." But if carefully selected and loaded in keeping with high jump actions and needs for power, they are of special, even essential, value for the high jump.

How today's coaches use them in their training program will be indicated in a later section. But one aspect requires emphasis--that of relatedness, specific relatedness--the more imitative of high jump stresses and movements, the greater the value.

We have repeatedly emphasized that the greatest stress during a running high jump occurs in the last strides and the yielding phase just prior to the upward leap. This phase demands related plyometric training through exercises that closely simulate those high-stress actions. As examples:

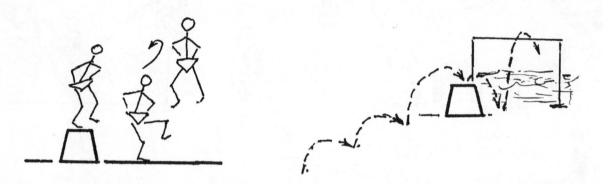

Fig. 7.21a. Related plyometrics. Depth jump from box of various heights. Note hands on hips to reduce effects of arm-drive. Rebound upward as in Flop style--back to bar.

Fig. 7.21b. After 2-3 strides to box of various heights, arms free. Depth jump from box, then rebound over crossbar as in Flop style.

Once again, a caution. Franz von Arx[1] warns that, "while there is little doubt that depth jumps have excellent training effects, there is also little doubt that these exercises can lead to joint, tendon and spinal injuries." Such warning is supported by Jess Jarver[2] who recommends that progress be gradual and preferably by a slow increase in the height of the platform, and not by the use of increasing weights. Beginners and young jumpers should prevent injury by (1) a developmental program of strength training, and (2) by repeated bounds and hops from soft surfaces--mats or grass. Maximal development of related power? Yes, but not too much too soon.

[1]Franz von Arx, "Power Development in the High Jump," *Track Technique*, #88, Spring 1984, p. 2818.
[2]Jess Jarver, *THE JUMPS*, Los Altos, CA: Tafnews Press, 1981, p. 26.

PLANNING A HIGH JUMP TRAINING PROGRAM
A well-balanced program of training for the high jump should meet four basic needs:

(1) A related power (strength x velocity) program designed to enable the jumper to both withstand and use effectively the great forces inherent in converting horizontal velocity to vertical lift. A related weightlifting program that emphasizes legs and torso is essential but should be supplemented by both plyometrics and circuit training.

(2) High jumping to improve technique--of special importance for younger jumpers.

(3) A program of related exercises that improve flexibility, agility, and control of the body while in the air.

(4) A program of sprint running to increase running speed and endurance as related to high jumping. Distance running for fun with others can be helpful but is not directly relevant to jumping high.

No detailed training program can be given that will meet the needs-ability, competency, time schedule for training, competitive schedule, injury proneness--of more than one jumper. The coaching journal *Track Technique*, has even abandoned its series, "How They Train," because of athletes' tendency to copy without modification. But the basics of training are essential to everyone--coach and individual athlete alike.

From a lengthy article on basic training for high jumpers by Dragan Tancic, West German National High Jump Coach, Jess Jarver[1] excerpted the following:

Horizontal Jumps: (1) Bounding up to 40m. (2) Hopping (single leg) up to 20m. (3) Standing 5-hops (left and right). (4) 5 hops from a 6-to 7-stride approach (left and right). (5) Standing triple hop (left and right). (6) Standing long jump.
Vertical Jumps: (1) Double-leg hurdle jumps (height 30-42", 6-7m apart). (2) Single-leg hurdle jumps (height 30-42", 6-7m apart). (3) Vertical jumps from a 4-stride approach. (4) Jumping on and off gymnastic boxes (24-42"). (5) Jumping up flights of stairs, jumping uphill, depth jumps.
Technique Imitation. (1) Straight run-up bunched jumps over the bar (40" to maximum). (2) Curved run-up scissor jumps over the bar (40" to maximum).
Sprinting. 40m from a flying start (maximum speed). (2) 100m accelerations. (3) Starts. (4) Uphill sprints.
Running. (1) Tempo runs over 150 to 400m. (2) Technique specific runs: a. Curved accelerations, slalom runs. b. Run-ups, changing to increased stride frequency.
Strength. (1) Abdominal and back exercises. (2) Leg exercises (full squats, half-squats, leg presses, leg machine).
Specific Strength. (1) Split jumps with a load. (2) Full squats against the clock. (3) Squat jumps with a load. (4) Lead leg exercises.
Technique. 1. Run-up development (first part, accelerating part, full approach). (2) Take-off development from shortened and full run-ups.
Others. (1) Mobility exercises. (2) Games. (3) Psychological training. (4) Sauna, massage.

These views by Tancic are supported by Pat Reid's[2] findings from personal visits with European coaches:

The European schedule includes hurdle hopping early in the year, a jumps decathlon early in the season, then moving to small boxes and double leg takeoffs and landings, then, in the precompetition period, moving to single-leg work and reducing the time of the exercise from fifteen minutes down to about eight minutes. The higher box work is left to triple and long jumps.

Volume, progression and intensity is built into this schedule like this:

[1]Jess Jarver, *Track Technique*, #82, Winter 1981, p. 2627.

[2]Pat Reid, *Track Technique Annual*, 1983, p. 98.

Sept/Oct.:   hurdles and two-feet work--45 minutes, 2 times a week.

Nov/Dec: hurdles and one-foot work--45 minutes, 2 times a week.

Jan/Feb: hurdles and one-foot work--15 minutes, 2 times a week.

Mar/Apr: hurdles and one-foot work--8 minutes, 2 times a week.

May/Sept: hurdles and one-foot work--15 minutes, once a week.

    These are done in sprint spikes, *not* in flats, and *done on a carpet on top of synthetic surfaces.* If done directly on a synthetic surface, athletes will have shin splints within three weeks.

Training for the High Jump by Don Chu[1]

A training program for high jumpers, devised by Don Chu, Ph.D. of Cal-State U. at Hayward, distinguishes two main phases: (1) basic and related strength training, and (2) high jumping for technique, endurance and maximal height. On a year-round basis, the first is given about 50 percent emphasis; jumping for technique, about 25 percent; the remainder on related activities including jumping for endurance and height.

Strength Training.

    A. Maximal Loading Base Period (Quantitive work--July-September).

        This is an early pre-season period. During this time the jumper does a great volume of lifting, usually measured in total pounds (or kg). A larger number of sets and repetitions at moderate weight are utilized--i.e., 4-6 sets of 10-15 repetitions at 60-70% of maximum.

    B. Power Development Period (October-January)

        During this phase, emphasis is placed upon the maximal amount of weight which can be moved during a specific time, usually one second. This is the Russian "optimal load" concept, used to enhance faster movement response. Lifting is interspread with jumping drills-bounding and box drills-twice a week, usually Monday and Friday.

    Example:

Half-squats	8 box jumps
1 set x 6 reps @ 80%	1 set x 8 @ 70%
optimal load (O.L.)	1 set x 10 @ 60%
1 set x 8 reps @ 90%	8 in-depth jumps
8 single-leg hops (each leg)	1 set x 5 @ 100%
1 set x 5 @ 100%	
1 set x 4 @ 110%	

    Exercises Used:

Half-squat		Snatch
Inverted Leg Press	Power-clean	Squat-Jump

---

[1]Don Chu, "Training Methods for Jumpers,"*Track & Field Quarterly Review*, Vol. 80, #4, 1980, p. 27.

Train three times per week--M-W-F. (No jump training on Wed.)

C. Power Transfer Period (February-April)
    These exercises are more specifically related to the jumping movements. They should be carried out at maximal speed.

    Do 4 sets x 5 repetitions at maximal intensity (85-95% of single RM):
        Double-legged jumps with barbell   Inverted leg press
        Single-legged jumps   Shoulder and biceps curl
        Bounding split squats

D.Transition Phase-Preparation for Major Competitions.
    This consists of two weeks of circuit training. Set-up 6-7 stations. Do 40-50% of single RM-30 seconds work, 15 seconds rest. 3 circuits.

E. Power Retention Phase.
    This helps to maintain gains made earlier, and is used during late season championship meets. One day per week. 4 sets x 6 repetitions for major muscle groups.

High Jump Work-Outs
    Three types of high jump work-outs are used to emphasize different aspects of the training program.

A. Technique.
    This is the commonest type of session, usually done twice a week. The bar is set 6 inches below the jumper's maximum jump. 15-18 jumps are taken. Adequate rest is taken between jumps so that the jumper can be fresh and go all-out with each jump. The bar is raised 1-2 inches after the first few jumps, if all is going well. The jumper must concentrate on the specific points to be stressed in the technique during this type of session.

B. Endurance.
    This is aimed toward taking many jumps during a session--up to 30 when the athlete is well-trained. Start the bar 8 inches below best jump attained. Clear 3 times at this height, and raise the bar by 2 inches. Repeat this process until the jumper has missed twice--then lower the bar by one inch and clear.

C. Maximal Height.
    Take 12-15 jumps at the jumper's lifetime best. Continue to jump regardless of whether the bar is cleared. Stress concentration on each jump. Try to relax and allow technique to remain and carry the athlete over.

    Some kind of high jumping occurs during all five phases of the year's training. High jumping for technique occurs about as follows: Phase A--once in 2 weeks; B--2 per week; C--2 per week; D--1 or 2 per week; E--1 per week. When power training and high jumping occur on the same day, jump first. High jumping for technique and for either endurance or maximal height are done on separate days. During the A-B, Power Development Periods (July to January), high jumping for technique occurs uncertainly, perhaps once in two weeks.

PREPARING FOR THE BIG MEET

Many a championship in the high jump is lost through failure to be prepared for the unexpected--
rain, cold, wind, or the long delays of competition. One of the better attempts to cover all
such happenings was made by Pat Reid,[1] National Coach for Jumping, Ontario Canada, who prepared
his jumpers for the 1984 Olympics by observing in detail just how the jumps in the 1983 World
Championships, Helsinki were conducted--length of time spent at each height and for the total
competition, number clearing each height, heights required for qualifying and placing, and
the like.

"Planning so an athlete's program results in a personal best on a given day is a difficult
task. The plan itself is not hard to design. The most difficult part is altering the components of the plan as the year unfolds.

"One of the athletes I coach is my wife Brigitte, who made the '84 Olympic Games qualifying
standard of 1.90 metres in high jump. She has to qualify at the Olympic trials in June, but
we're concerned with a much more serious objective--getting the best performance possible in
the Olympic final. To arrive at a performance objective for the 1984 Olympics in women's high
jump, we turned to the results of the world championships a year earlier in Helsinki. Under a
national coach/technical observer project conceived by Gerard Mach, national program director
of the Canadian Track and Field Association, a number of track and field coaches were at Helsinki to observe and prepare programs for their athletes who are preparing for the 1984 Olympics.

"My task at Helsinki was two-fold: (1) to analyze the technical complexities unique to
the high jump at this international level; (2) to weave these findings into a realistic yearly
program pointing toward the Olympic final this summer.

"Table I contains performance data of the women's world championship high jump final.
Interpretations of these statistics are based on my coaching experience.

"OBSERVATION 1--Ten heights were attempted by the gold medallist. Only five heights were
attempted by nine of the 18 finalists.

"INTERPRETATION 1--To be in the top half of the final results, an athlete should jump five
heights. Training should ensure large height increments of 5cm (2").

"OBSERVATION 2--It took 20 minutes to complete the opening height of 1.75 metres; 24 minutes to complete 1.80; 35 minutes for 1.84; 27 minutes for 1.88; and decreasing times for the
remaining heights, such as 11 minutes for 1.95 metres.

"INTERPRETATION 2--While it took three hours to complete the final (at 10 heights), it
only took 96 minutes to complete the first four heights. This means athletes have to be prepared to warm up, get mentally prepared, jump and stay in control while waiting approximately
30 minutes between successive heights. First-attempt clearances become critical. Events with
long delays between jumps should be built into the preparation phase of the athlete's training
program.

"OBSERVATION 3--Over the first five heights, there were 115 attempts. Of the 55 successful
clearances, 37 were first attempts, and 13 second attempts. There were only five third attempts.

"INTERPRETATION 3--At this level, very few athletes have technical flaws which cause them
to struggle with second and third attempts. They jump cleanly until they are eliminated. Very
clearly, athletes have to concentrate on first attempt clearances.

"OBSERVATION 4--In the final, athletes passed (elected not to jump) 11 times at the opening height and only once at the second to last height of 2.01 metres. This pass was made by
the silver medallist in a desperate effort to win.

"INTERPRETATION 4--Passing heights is a strategy used in most domestic and national meets.
However, at this level, with such large height increments, passing is eliminated.

---

[1]Pat Reid, "Preparing to Peak When it Counts," *Coaching Review*, Ottawa: Coaching Association
of Canada, Vol. 7, May-June, 1984, pp. 19-22.

"OBSERVATION 5--There is tremendous consistency between the finalists' season bests before the world championships and their results in Helsinki. All 18 finalists had jumped 1.88 before Helsinki. Twelve jumpers had made 1.92 metres (nine repeated it in the final), seven had made 1.95 (five repeated it), six had made 1.97 (four repeated it), three had cleared 1.99 (two repeated) and one had cleared 2.01. This she repeated to capture the gold medal.

"INTERPRETATION 5--There wasn't a single athlete in the final who jumped higher than she had in competition prior to the world championships. Even the gold medallist tied her seasonal best in the final. All 17 other jumpers jumped less than their individual seasonal best (from 1-18 centimetres less.)

"In discussing this with many of the finalists, it became clear they'd had to jump so high in the qualifying round two days earlier (1.90m) that it took too much out of them. Only half of the field could come back and jump at least that high in the final. Clearly, jumpers have to train at very high levels on successive two day periods to prepare for Los Angeles.

"The above observations were the key points noted of the final. A similar analysis was done of the qualifying round. The single most relevant statistic was that only jumpers who had achieved the "A" Olympic standard (1.90m) prior to the worlds, qualified for the final. (The same situation was true for the men's event and their 2.26 m. "A" standard.)

"RECOMMENDATIONS AND CONCLUSIONS. There are characteristics of world championships and Olympic Games that are clearly different from national-level events normally available for Canadian athletes preparing for Los Angeles. These characteristics have to be woven into pre-Olympic training. The "academically" prepared plan of an athlete's training is simply too simplified for this level of preparation....

"Based on observations at the women's high jump final in Helsinki, the following recommendations can be made to a woman looking to place eighth or in the top half of the field in the 1984 Olympic final. Although there are other factors to consider, this athlete must:

1) be prepared to jump 1.90 metres at 11:40 a.m. and return to jump 1.92 metres around 4:10 p.m. the next day.
2) be able to make four or five consecutive heights on first attempts.
3) be able to compete in meets of very high calibre in the preparation period. Three meets must last 1½-2 hours.
4) have cleared 1.90 metres in competition at least once prior to the Olympics.
5) focus on jumping heights like 1.88 and 1.92 metres in competition and not focus on simply "winning" (at lower heights).
6) seek competitions (or stage them) where the bar will be raised by large increments (e.g., 1.80, 1.85, 1.90, 1.95).
7) prepare for the August climate of Los Angeles and detail their personal peaking program, taking into account their strength-to-body-weight ratio. Athletes tend to over eat in Olympic villages and since the high jump is an anti-gravity event, this can mean certain failure.

"Numerous other factors must be analyzed and built into the training program. Clearly, the message is that the coach should review the characteristics of their events, no matter what they're preparing for."

Heights	1.75m	1.80m	1.84m	1.88m	1.92m	1.95m	1.97m	1.99m	2.01m	2.03m
Time Factor (3 Hrs)	20 min	24 min	35 min	27 min	16 min	11 min	9 min	5 min	5 min	14 min
No. of Attempts (145)	8	24	29	34	20	11	9	3	2	5
No. of Competitors (18)	18	18	18	16	9	5	4	2	2	2
Clearance Attempts First 41	6	13	11	5	2	1	1	1	1	0
Clearance Attempts Second 17	1	4	3	2	3	2	1	1	0	0
Clearance Attempts Third 6	0	1	2	2	0	1	0	0	0	0
Passes (12)	11	0	0	0	0	0	0	0	1	0
No. Competitors Over this Height Pre-Worlds (18)	18	18	18	18	12	7	6	3	1	0

Table 1: Statistical break-down of the women's high jump final in the 1983 world championships.

World record holder and 1983 world champion Sergey Bubka of the Soviet Union./Photo by Diane Johnson.

Chapter 8
THE POLE VAULT

A BRIEF HISTORY OF EQUIPMENT
The development of techniques and performances in the pole vault is so intimately related to equipment and facilities that a preliminary summary of the latter seems desirable.

THE VAULTING POLE. In the earliest competitions, the pole was of either ash, hickory or spruce, and had an iron device at its tip--a three-inch tripod with three spikes weighing, one author said, 25# but more likely much less, or an iron cup with a single iron spike. Between 1900 and 1915, tape-wrapped bamboo gained general acceptance--at first with a spiked end, then, as a stopboard and takeoff box were introduced, with a wood plug in the hollow end-section.

At the back of Michael C. Murphy's COLLEGE ATHLETICS, probably printed in 1909, A. G. Spalding advertised various track and field impedimenta, including pictures of three single-spiked vaulting poles: (1) a "thoroughly seasoned" spruce pole, 8 to 16 feet long, at $3 to $7 each; (2) a hollow spruce pole "considerably lighter than the solid poles, and the interior is filled with a special preparation which greatly increases the strength and stiffness," of similar lengths at a cost of $8 to $10 each; and (3) a bamboo pole "thoroughly seasoned, tape wound at short intervals, and fitted with special spike," 16 feet long, $7 each.

With a plug, a medium-sized bamboo pole weighed about 5½ pounds. In the 1930s, an aluminum pole was tried that weighed about the same, but lacked the flexibility of bamboo. Somewhat heavier but more flexible steel poles came from Sweden to the United States in the late 1940s but broke easily after several abrasions from falling. Fiberglass poles became available just after the war. For each pole, it took about ten years to gain acceptance.

THE TAKEOFF BOX. Prior to 1900, there was no one place for planting the iron spike of the pole; any spot the vaulter preferred was acceptable. But by the 1912 Olympic Games at Stockholm, a small depression and stopboard were allowed. In his 1914 book for coaches, Mike Murphy stated "the plank in the ground should be at least six feet in length. It is sunk 12 inches in the ground leaving an edge of about two inches above ground. In front of the plank is dug a small hole (4 to 6 inches in depth) so that the force of the pole as it strikes the ground will be against this plank."[1] This "hole" was gradually widened at its front end to become a slideway. Schulte's POLE VAULTING[2], 1927, contains a picture of Frank Foss (1920 Olympic Champion, 13'5") with just such a stopboard and dirt slideway, but also an article by Harry Hillman describing a "take-off box" of wood, very similar in size to that used today. In contrast, even as late as 1926, our National AAU Rules Book stated as a first choice, "Any competitor shall be allowed to dig a hole not more than one foot in diameter at the takeoff, in which he shall plant his pole. A wooden box or stopboard sunk in the ground may be allowed." (Specifications followed.) I should add that use of the stopboard and box made an iron-spiked pole a liability, and so produced round ends on the bamboo poles as well as on the diminishing ash and spruce. As a later and probably final improvement, the wooden takeoff

---

[1]Michael C. Murphy, ATHLETIC TRAINING, New York: Charles Scribner's Sons, 1914, p. 109.

[2]Henry F. Schulte, POLE VAULTING, New York, American Sports Publishing Co., 1927, p. 166.

TABLE 8.1

OUTSTANDING PERFORMANCES -- POLE VAULT

OLYMPIC CHAMPIONS

Date	Record	Name	Affiliation	Hgt.	Wgt.	Grip*	Time 100y	Run	Comments
1896	10'10"	Wm. W. Hoyt	NYAC		*Grip height is here				Ash Pole
1900	10'10"	Irving Baxter	NYAC		measured from top of				Bamboo
1904	11'6"	C.E.Dvorak	Michigan		the upper hand to the				
1908	12'2"	E.T.Cooke	USA		tip of pole				
		A.C.Gilbert	Yale						
1912	12'11½"	H.S.Babcock	USA						
1920	13'5"	F.K.Foss	Chicago						
1924	12'11½"	Lee Barnes	USC	5'8"	150	12'4"		115'	
1928	13'9½"	Sabin Carr	Yale	6'1"	168				
1932	14'2"	William Miller	USC						
1936	14'3¼"	Earle Meadows	USC	6'1"	160	13'2"	10.4	115'	
1948	14'1¼"	Guinn Smith	Calif.	6'2"	170	12'11"	9.8	125'	Bamboo Pole
1952	14'11¼"	Bob Richards	Illinois	5'10"	160	13'7"	10.0	115'	Steel Pole
1956	14'11½"	Bob Richards	Illinois						
1960	15'5"	Don Bragg	Villanova	6'3"	192	13'10"	10.2	125'	Steel Pole
1964	16'8 3/4"	Fred Hansen	Rice	6'	167	15'0"	10.2		Fiberglass
1968	17'8½"	Bob Seagren	USC	6'	175	15'2"	9.8	130'	Fiberglass
1972	18' ½"	W. Nordwig	E.Germany	6'½"	160	15'4"	10.8m	126'	Fiberglass
1976	18' ½"	T.Slusarski	Poland	5-10"	168	15'7"			
1980	18'11½"	W. Kozakiewicz	Poland	6'1-3/4"	185	16'0"	11.0		
1984	18'10¼"	Pierre Quinon	France	5'10-3/4"	161				

WORLD-RECORD PERFORMANCES OF SPECIAL INTEREST

Date	Record	Name	Affiliation	Hgt.	Wgt.	Grip	Time	Run	Comments
1887	11'5"	Hugh H. Baxter	NYAC	6'1"		(Ash Pole)			First over 11'
1904	12'1½"	Norman Dole	Stanford			(Bamboo)			First over 12'
1912	13'2¼"	M.S.Wright	Dartmouth			"			First over 13'
1927	14'0"	Sabin Carr	Yale	6'1"	168	"			First over 14'
1942	15'7 3/4"	C. Warmerdam	Fresno St.	6'1"	165	"	10.2	140'	First over 15'
1960	15'9¼"	Donald Bragg	Villanova	6'3"	192	13'10"	10.2	125'	Best ever steel
1962	16' 3/4"	John Uelses	U.S.Marines	6'0"	168	14'0"			First over 16' indoors
1962	16'2"	Dave Tork	U.S.Marines	5'8"	150				First over 16' outdoors
1963	17' 3/4"	John Pennel	N.E.La.	5'10"	170	14'10"	9.8	145'	First over 17'
1970	18' ¼"	C.Papanicolaou	Greece	5'11½"	168	15'10"	10.0	134'	First over 18'
1976	18'7¼"	Earl Bell	Kansas St.	6'3"	170	15'9"			Banana pole
1976	18'8¼"	Dave Roberts	Fla.T.C.	6'2½"	185	16'0"	9.7	138'	Banana pole
1980	18'8 3/4"	Mike Tully	U.S.	6'2"	181	15'10"			
1983	19'1"	P.Quinon	France	5'10-3/4"	161				
1983	19'1½"	T.Vigneron	France	5'11 3/4"	147				
1984	19'3½"	Sergey Bubka	USSR	6'	165				
1984	19'4¼"	T.Vigneron	France	5'11"	157				
1984	19'5 3/4"	Sergey Bubka	USSR	6'0"	165				

BEST PERFORMANCES -- HIGH SCHOOL

Date	Record	Name	Location	Hgt.	Wgt.
1969	17'4 3/4"**	Casey Carrigan	Orting, WA		
1972	16'4"	Craig Brigham	So. Eugene, OR		
1974	16'8¼"	Mike Tully	Long Beach, CA		
1978	17'4¼"	Anthony Curran	Encino, CA		
1979	16'6"	Greg Duplantis	Lafayette, LA		
1980	17'5¼"**	Joe Dial	Marlow, Okla.	5'8½"	131#
1983	17'½"	Doug Fraley	Clovis, W. Fresno		

**National High School record

box, which tended to rot and break with use, was changed to one of metal or other all-weather materials as done today.

THE LANDING PIT. First landings from the vault were undoubtedly made on unaltered grass. Turned-over sod is little softer and less level, and so was improved by uneven stages in this country and abroad by using, first sandy loam, then sawdust with sandy loam, and later shavings. Pits tended to be ground-level, though men were allowed to pile up the material in the center of the pit. But gradually they were raised. Hillman's 1926 article, just mentioned, advocated "For indoor vaulting a pit, two feet high, can be constructed on the floor and filled with sawdust, with mattresses arranged against sides of pit and on bottom underneath the sawdust." Very quickly, such construction was moved outdoors. Writing in 1940, Dean Cromwell complains[1] of European vaulting pits "as soft to land on as a cement sidewalk" and strongly recommends "a generous pile of wood shavings" both deep and wide. Shavings were supplanted in the late 1950s by huge mounds of loose foam rubber, and they, in the 60s, by the wonderfully soft though most expensive polyurethane now in use.

THE RUNWAY. If not over-used and properly cut, rolled and watered, a grass runway gives excellent footing, and did so throughout the early years. With heavy poles and short runs, no one cared for more than level footing. Even when cinder-loam and clay-loam runways were constructed, runs of more than 50 feet were unusual. Mike Murphy's 1914 book[2] for coaches suggests "Two checkmarks--six and twelve ordinary paces from the plank," less than 60 feet in all. But lighter poles and realization of the value of greater run velocities rapidly increased runway lengths to 100 and even more feet. Present-day synthetic runway surfaces were not introduced until the 1950s.

A BRIEF HISTORY OF TECHNIQUE
The early development of vaulting with a pole had a multiple ethnic origin, with each nation contributing to the event out of its own unique customs and viewpoints. The Germans and those they influenced used pole jumping as a gymnastic and physical-culture exercise; the English, Scottish and Irish used it as a competitive event in their athletic games that "have been one of the chief characteristics of both town and country life in 'Merrie England' as far back as chronicles will reach."[3]

First printed mention of pole jumping seems to have been made in Germany--in Johann Basedow, A BOOK OF METHODS, 1774, a complete system of primary education, in which he proposed leaping with a pole as an exercise in his "naturalistic" approach to German physical culture. But in Johann Guts Muth's GYMNASTICS FOR THE YOUNG, 1793, a full section was given to vaulting, with drawings and a detailed explanation of vaulting mechanics. Heavy wooden poles were used, forcing a slow and probably short run. Crossbars two or three feet higher than the vaulter's head were cleared.

In contrast to this formalized approach in Germany, jumping with a pole in England evolved out of the natural terrain, the long-held customs of beagling and crosscountry running, and the centuries-old tradition of competitive sports and pastimes. As one might expect, no one kind of pole nor one style of jumping was used, and just who did what with which is not at all clear. In my 1954 search for the facts, I received a letter from Harry Askew, track coach at The Royal Liberty School, England, who spoke with the son of Edwin Woodburn who held the record of 11'7" in 1874. "The son attributes the growth of pole vaulting in Ulverston to the fact that men following the beagles took a pole with them to jump over the many stone walls (about five feet high), and so keep up with the hunt. Since there were many such limestone walls enclosing tiny fields, this explanation seems most plausible." Askew added that beagling (hunting with hounds) on foot is still done in some parts of England. For such a purpose, one can assume that any stout pole, with or without a metal point, and any technique would be used that brought the pole on the far side of the wall, or watery ditch for that matter, so as to be carried to the next obstacle.

---

[1]Dean B. Cromwell, CHAMPIONSHIP TECHNIQUE IN TRACK AND FIELD, New York: Mc-Graw-Hill Book Co., Inc., 1941, p. 181.

[2]Michael C. Murphy, op. cit., p. 113.

[3]Montague Shearman, ATHLETICS AND FOOTBALL, London: Longmans, Green and Co., 1889, p. 4.

Without giving his sources, the English coach and writer, F. A. M. Webster, tells a different version of the Ulverston story,[1]

The method employed by the Ulverston men was unique, and for years the world's record holders came from that small town. Their poles were of ash or hickory, long and heavy, and shod at the lower end with a tripod of iron, forming a three-inch triangle. The weight of the pole necessitated a wide separation of the hands and a slow run-up. At the end of the approach run the tripod was planted some three feet in front of the cross-bar. The athlete then allowed his body to swing up and began to climb. The upper hand was shifted a foot up the pole and the lower hand brought up to it. The climbing continued until the pole had passed the vertical position. As it began to fall forward, the athlete drew up his knees and went over the bar in a sitting position, a last backward push preventing the pole from following through to remove the bar.

The Ulverston method obtained until 1889. The American athletes contended that the performances of Ray and Stones were nothing but acrobatic balancing feats, requiring neither strength nor endurance, and a new rule was passed prohibiting the athlete from shifting the grip of the upper hand and from placing the lower hand above the upper hand after the feet have left the ground. About this time too, several men suffered death by impalement, through their wooden poles snapping transversely, and the pole vault began to disappear from the programmes of British school sports.

The most authentic source for the early development of United States vaulting is from the article by Hugh H. Baxter,[2]

Up to 1879, American pole vaulters used various styles, all of them crude and unscientific. The upper grip on the pole was in all cases at least 3 feet higher than would be used by a modern pole vaulter for the same height. Some carried the thumb of the right hand up, and that of the left hand down, and all pulled with the upper hand alone, using the lower hand simply as a prop.

In 1879, W. J. Van Houten of the Scottish-American Athletic Club, New York, won the American championships with 10'4 3/4", using the same style as the record holders of today except that he did not have some of the fine points which have developed in recent years. He knew nothing about the shift, but being a very light man and using a very light pole he was able to carry it with both hands close together, thus obtaining the two hand pull which is the essential difference between the new and old styles and mainly accounts for the difference in records....

It is impossible to say just when or where the Van Houten style of pole vaulting returned and came into general use, but it is certain that R. G. Clapp of Yale used it when he made a record of 11' 10!" in 1898, and all subsequent records were made in practically the same style.

A BRIEF HISTORY OF PERFORMANCE

With increased use of lighter weight, more flexible and less dangerous bamboo poles, longer and faster runs, combined with a shift of the lower hand during takeoff, achieved greater upward velocity and higher heights. From 1904 to 1912, five world's records were made, beginning with Norman Dole's first-over-12 feet vault of 12' 1½" when winning the 1904 Olympics, and ending with Marcus Wright's 13' 2¼" at the 1912 Games, the first vault over 13 feet.

---

[1]F. A. M. Webster, *ATHLETES OF TODAY*, London: Frederick Warne & Co., 1929, p. 228.

[2]Hugh H. Baxter, "An Historical Contribution from an Early Champion," in Henry F. Schulte, *POLE VAULTING*, New York: American Sports Publishing Co., 1927, p. 172.

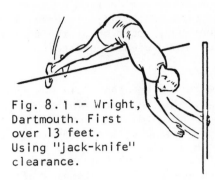

Fig. 8.1 -- Wright, Dartmouth. First over 13 feet. Using "jack-knife" clearance.

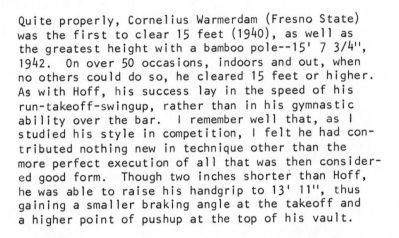

Fig. 8.2 -- Hoff, Norway; first over 14 feet (professional). Using fly-away clearance.

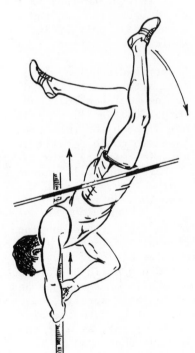

Fig. 8.3 -- Warmerdam, Fresno State; first over 15 feet. Using bamboo pole.

The "man's ultimate height" of 14 feet was not cleared officially until 15 years later (1927) by Sabin Carr (Yale). But the real innovator and influence of this period was Charles Hoff of Norway who cleared 13' 11 3/8" as an amateur, then 14 feet on various occasions as a professional. Hoff was a champion decathlon performer, 6'3" tall, and had run the 100 under ten seconds. The ease and speed of his run, high handgrip (12' 10"), free swing-up and quick flyaway and up from the pole, in contrast to the usual delayed release, opened up new potentials for the event.

What had been, up till then, a trick event for gymnasts, became a single-action jump and swing with a pole for tall sprinters and high jumpers with strong shoulders. In the next few decades, it was realized that the primary problems of vaulting were related to velocity rather than to strength and bar-clearance techniques.

Quite properly, Cornelius Warmerdam (Fresno State) was the first to clear 15 feet (1940), as well as the greatest height with a bamboo pole--15' 7 3/4", 1942. On over 50 occasions, indoors and out, when no others could do so, he cleared 15 feet or higher. As with Hoff, his success lay in the speed of his run-takeoff-swingup, rather than in his gymnastic ability over the bar. I remember well that, as I studied his style in competition, I felt he had contributed nothing new in technique other than the more perfect execution of all that was then considered good form. Though two inches shorter than Hoff, he was able to raise his handgrip to 13' 11", thus gaining a smaller braking angle at the takeoff and a higher point of pushup at the top of his vault.

In general, pole flexibility was not a major concern in these years, though Nikolai Osolin (USSR, 1939, 14' 1¼"), and Sueo Ohe (Japan, 1937, 14' 3¼"), with their 135-pound body weights and slender 4 3/4-pound bamboo poles, did demonstrate the uses of pole flexibility.

Then came the metal poles (aluminum-magnesium alloys and steel) with their false claims of "Lifetime durability" and "no need to transport your own poles to meets!" Their weights varied, of course, but averaged slightly heavier than the bamboo poles--about six pounds. The aluminum poles were lighter but very rigid; the best Swedish steel poles were relatively flexible but heavy. Ganslen (1970, 20) states that the steel poles of heavier men, such as Donald Bragg (192#) did bend 2-2½ feet out of line, but reacted very quickly in straightening. With such a pole, Bragg held a handgrip of 13'10" and cleared 15'9¼" for a world record and all-time high with a metal pole.

Introduction of the fiberglass pole brought about the most controversial and exciting change in both technique and performance since vaulting began. First used in the early 1950s, it was not fully effective until the 1960s. Its opponents said performance was now the effect of a machine's catapult action, but gradually all agreed that its main value was in its flexion at takeoff that (1) eased the jarring shock at the moment of pole plant, with reduced slipping of the hands; (2) it allowed a smoother and more gradual change of direction from horizontal to vertical, with less loss of momentum; (3) it permitted higher handgrips, and so a higher body position at the top of the vault; and (4) its extension aided greater upward momentum during the push-up.

Fig. 8.4. Bragg, Villanova. Best ever with steel pole - 15'9¼"

The first world record made with a fiberglass pole was in 1961--George Davies, 15'10¼". Within the next five years (1962-1967), fiberglass vaulters dominated the event with 15 new world-record performances. For the first time in this century, the record left the U.S.A. with Finland's Pentti Nikula at 16'2½", June 1962. In 1964 Fred Hansen raised the record to 17'4", then won the Tokyo Olympics at 16'8 3/4". Bob Seagren (17'5½"), Pennel (17'6 3/4"), Paul Wilson (17'7 3/4"), Seagren (17'9") and Pennel (17'10¼") each held it briefly, but again the record moved abroad, this time to Greece with Chris Papanicolaou in a first-over-18 feet (18'¼", 1970).

In 1972, Seagren and Kjell Isaksson of Sweden cleared 18'4½" on the same day in April but Seagren upped this in June to 18'5 3/4". In 1980, the record was held by Dave Roberts (18'8¼") of the Florida Track Club. In 1981 Thierry Vigneron (5'11½", 157#), France, cleared the first-ever height of 19 feet (19'¼"): then two years later, weighing, according to *Track & Field News*, ten pounds lighter, increased this to 19'1½".

A human ultimate? Not at all! In March 1984, the World Champion Sergey Bubka (6', 165#, 20 years old) cleared 19'1½" from a board runway, using a heavy pole (Olson called it "a cannon") 16'8 3/4" long and holding his upper hand 16'6" on the pole, a foot above other vaulters. Three months later (July 1984) he upped this to 19'4¼". His goal--to win the 1984 Olympic pole vault (sadly denied by the politicians and militarists) and to clear six meters (19'8")--entirely possible.

Fig. 8.5. Bubka, USSR, clearing 19'4¼", July 1984.

The running pole vault is a whole movement without separable parts. It has phases of action--the run-transition-takeoff-swingup-pullup. But these are words, devices of understanding and communication, valid for analysis only if it leads back to synthesis and wholeness of action.

We all remember the frustrated centipede who, when asked "which leg came after which, lay distracted in the ditch and knew not how to run." But coaches sometimes forget that applies equally to athletes. I once knew a coach who took this advice to heart and refused to coach details of technique. "Competitive spirit is the main thing; never mind the details. Have fun. Will yourself over the bar. Beat the other guy. Make up in determination what you may lack in technique."

That's carrying wholeness too far and denying the values of whole-part-whole-part-whole learning, in which each new whole is at a higher level--higher in understanding and higher in performance. Without analysis of the details of technique and without practice related to those details, coaching would be ineffective. But be sure the dissection is only of the action; not, as with the centipede, of the man in ways that lead to distraction, uncertainty and frustration.

ESSENTIALS OF SOUND TECHNIQUE[1]

It is sometimes argued that vaulters differ so much in
the details of technique, it is useless to speak of the
essentials of form. Give a man a pole, a place to work,
a few fundamentals and leave him alone. This attitude
is very much in error. Men are much more alike in
every way than they are different. Within a range of
tolerable variation, the biomechanics of vaulting are
the same for everyone.

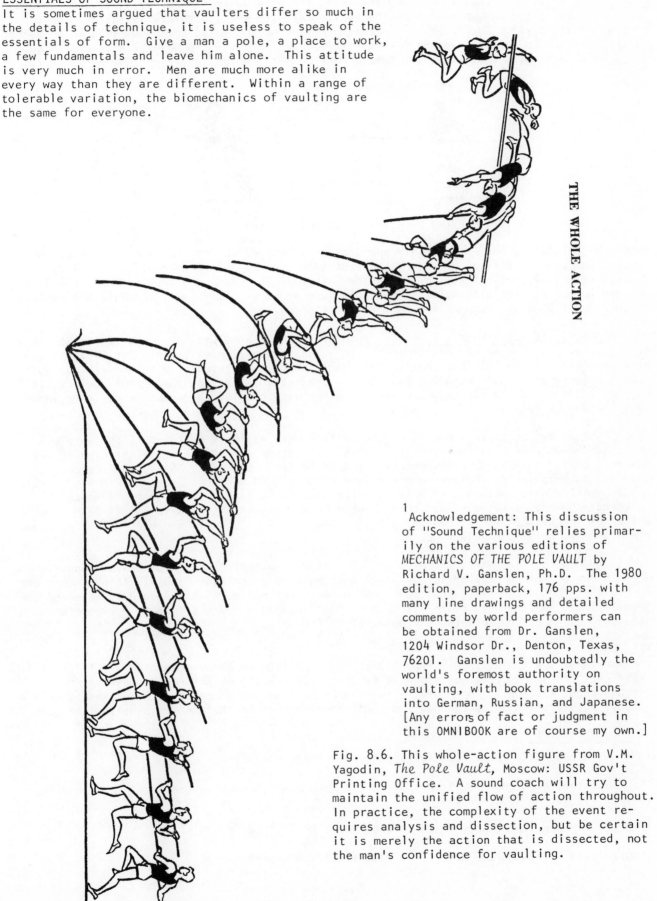

THE WHOLE ACTION

[1] Acknowledgement: This discussion
of "Sound Technique" relies primarily on the various editions of
MECHANICS OF THE POLE VAULT by
Richard V. Ganslen, Ph.D. The 1980
edition, paperback, 176 pps. with
many line drawings and detailed
comments by world performers can
be obtained from Dr. Ganslen,
1204 Windsor Dr., Denton, Texas,
76201. Ganslen is undoubtedly the
world's foremost authority on
vaulting, with book translations
into German, Russian, and Japanese.
[Any errors of fact or judgment in
this OMNIBOOK are of course my own.]

Fig. 8.6. This whole-action figure from V.M.
Yagodin, *The Pole Vault*, Moscow: USSR Gov't
Printing Office. A sound coach will try to
maintain the unified flow of action throughout.
In practice, the complexity of the event requires analysis and dissection, but be certain
it is merely the action that is dissected, not
the man's confidence for vaulting.

HOLDING THE POLE. Men vary in the way they hold the pole during the run-up. To aid forward
lean, some carry the pole hip-high on the horizontal with the tip pointed straight down the
runway. (Fig. 8.7A). To offset the increased weight of the pole, the hands tend to be placed
farther apart. To ease the weight of the pole, others lift the tip nose-high or even higher
(Fig. 8.7B) and swing the tip to the left a foot or more (assuming a right-handed vaulter.)

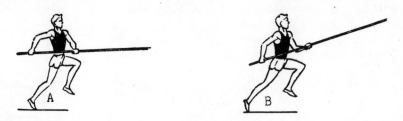

Figs. 8.7A and 8.7B. Varying pole levels during the run.

Such a high pole-tip must be smoothly and gradually lowered during the later stages of the run
so that the pole is horizontal during the last four strides before takeoff. (Fig. 8.8).
This is essential if acceleration during the last four strides and a very fast plant and takeoff are to occur. For all vaulters, the pole must be held quite steady and relaxed; certainly
it should not be swung forward and back during the run.

Height of the Upper-Hand Grip on the Pole. Grip height is usually measured from the top
of the upper hand to the tip of the pole. In a 1983 discussion at the Mt. Sac Relays Clinic,
A. Krzesinski,[1] former National Polish Pole Vault coach, suggested as a rule-of-thumb that
such a hold be at "double standing height plus one meter"; that is, a six-foot vaulter might
hold at 15 feet. Obviously he was speaking of one with considerable experience; a beginner
would hold much less.

A USSR study[2] concluded that 15 of the world's-best vaulters averaged 15'8" (4m 80cm) in
their handholds when clearing highest heights, an average difference of height cleared over
handhold of 43". In 1979, when Roberts set a WR 18'8¼", he held at 15'7", a difference of
only 37¼". Kozakiewicz (Poland) won the 1980 Olympic gold medal and set a WR 18'11½", while
holding 16'2 3/4" on a 16'4 3/4" pole, a difference of 40 3/4". But Vigneron (France)
achieved a pushup of between 45½" to 47½" when he set his WR 19'2¼" with a 16'4 3/4" pole
while holding between 15'11" and 16' 3/4".[3] Clearly, if--a big "if"--other factors are equal,
the higher we hold, the higher we go.

Sergey Bubka, 1983 World Champion at Helsinki, undoubtedly changed world-vaulting sights
when in March 1984 he cleared 19'1½" while holding a 16'9" pole at "roughly 16'6", about one
foot higher than did his rivals. Bubka was 6 feet, 165 pounds, and was said to have run the
100m in 10.3. Afterwards, Billy Olson said, "He's probably going to change everyone's
strategy. I've already ordered new poles at 17 feet."[4]

THE RUN.
The length of the run will vary from 100 to 150 feet (30m to 45m), depending on, first, the
experience and second, the overall ability of the vaulter. In 1984 world-class vaulters
average about 130 feet. In theory, a run should be long enough to allow a relaxed start and
gradual acceleration so as to ensure maximal speed one stride before the plant of the pole.

[1]Andrzej Krzesinski, *Track Technique*, #86, Fall 1983, p. 2734.

[2]V. Mansvetov, "Contemporary Technique in the Pole Vault," *Track & Field Quarterly Review*,
Vol. 79 #1, Spring 1979, p. 14.

[3]"PV Grips: Hang Them High," *Track & Field News*, April 1984, p. 75.

[4]"Bubka Wins First 19-foot Battle," *Track & Field News*, March 1984, p. 1.

Actually, the vaulter should think of increasing his velocity into the plant; certainly there can be no decrease and no out-of-line actions during the plant.

Running with a long pole at maximal speed is a most difficult feat and requires much drill. The vaulters' arms are restricted so as not to be used as in normal sprinting. The long pole feels heavy, creating tension in related muscles, all of which changes the "feel" of the action considerably from that of normal running. All drills to improve such running should be done with the pole, or certainly should closely simulate that action.[1]

Various methods of securing check marks are used. We suggest getting away from the pole vault runway to a surface where stride marks can be seen. An observer can note the seventh, and later the 23rd stride. After measuring, these marks can be transferred to the vault runway. Since such trial runs are free of all tension, they are likely to prove accurate. Stick to them for a while until certain they are incorrect. Eventually, of course, adjustments will probably be made.

CHECK MARKS. Most world-class vaulters use only a single check mark at the start of the run. But less experienced men need more assurance for the various phases of the run. For example, Coach Aubrey Dooley, former champion vaulter, recommends[2] as many as five checkmarks: (1) a starting mark; (2) a first-stride mark to ensure the vaulter starts the same way every time; (3) a mark two-thirds down the runway

Fig. 8.8--Sergey Bubka, USSR, in later stage of run, lowering pole for the plant. Bubka is using a 16'9" pole and holding at 16'6".

by which both the coach and vaulter can check precise striding; (4) a mark four strides from the plant to emphasize acceleration into the pole shift; and (5) a mark to indicate the take-off. All such marks should be related to the same foot--the left for a left-footed takeoff.

RUN VELOCITY. The faster a vaulter can sprint down the runway, other things being equal, the faster he will leave the ground. The faster he leaves the ground, the higher he can hold on the pole. The higher he holds on the pole, the higher he can vault. It's as simple as that.

That is to say, natural sprinting ability is essential to highest vaulting and an aid in vaulting at any height. Bubka (6' 165#--19'1½") is reported to have run 100m in 10.3sec. But natural speed is not enough; velocity while running with a long, relatively heavy pole requires repeated drilling on greater speed, both without and with vaulting.

Typical answers by outstanding vaulters: "I build speed all the way down the runway." "I try to gain my speed as soon as possible, then drive into the box." "Gradual build-up, maintaining speed in the middle of the run, then driving strides at the end." "Slowly pick up speed, then blast." "Slow start, gradual acceleration, then really accelerate 4-5 strides from plant."

---

[1]Alexander Malyutin, "Running with the Vaulting Pole," *Track Technique*, Vol. 81, Fall 1980, p. 2596.

[2]Aubrey C. Dooley, "Pole Vaulting Technique," *Track & Field Quarterly Review*, Spring 1979, p. 15.

Jan Johnson[1] says "There's too little training for running speed and jumping ability. These two items have more to do with...success in vaulting than any other criteria."

The Transition Phase. From the standpoints of degree of difficulty and effective vaulting, this transition phase is the most crucial in the entire vault. If it is effective, body momentum is maintained, even increased, and the later phases of the vault are relatively simple. The transition phase of the run begins about four strides from takeoff. Full velocity has been gained; the mind shifts from running speed to the smooth transfer of momentum (mass x velocity) to a pendulum pole whose point is fixed in the vault box. First, the pole must be shifted forward and up (Fig. 8.9). Second, the body's center of gravity lowers a little during the transition strides, much as does a long jumper before takeoff. Ganslen (1980, 20) writes, "But the vaulter must relax the last few strides and run in flat-footed as he prepares himself for the spring from the ground." Third, the flexible pole must be bent by the combined actions of the arms and the forward force of the body. All of this in ways that merge and flow into one another with a minimum loss of kinetic energy and, at the end, a maximum height of the center of gravity.

Planting the Pole. The vaulter has three concerns during the planting of the pole: (1) to maintain and even increase momentum, (2) to cushion the shock of stopping horizontal momentum so as to convert as much kinetic energy as possible upwards, and (3) to establish good balance for the remainder of the vault.

Fig. 8.9. The pole plant occurs smoothly, unhurriedly during the last three or four strides.

During the plant, the vaulter should try to drive forward into a strong spring-off that will aid the momentum of the pendulum swing of the pole. The body drops down just a little; the foot-plant is lower, though not on the heel until the final stride. The pole plant should occur smoothly during the last four strides of the run; certainly not during the last two strides which tends to hurry and discoordinate the action. An article from the West German publication Leichtathletik[2] describes the action in detail:

"Third last stride (left)--The pole is brought forward with the front end aiming for the right hand corner of the box.
Second-last stride (right)--The pole end reaches the box while the pole is moved in a straight line upwards. The right hand's fist should come into the vision of the athlete (this ensures that the shoulder axis remains square to the runway).
Last stride (left)--The right arm is extended fully upwards. The direction of the takeoff is forward-upward (about 45°). Hips are brought forward and the shoulder action remains square to the runway."

[1]Jan Johnson, "The Problems Holding Back American Pole Vaulters," Track Technique, Vol. 87, Winter 1984, p. 2770

[2]"Pole Vaulting," Track Technique, #83, Spring 1981, p. 2659, translated from Leichtathletik, West Germany.

The faster the last four strides before takeoff, the faster the plant-takeoff is likely to be. There should be no emphasis on a gather-jump at the takeoff; rather it should be a smooth forward-upward stride as occurs in the triple jump.

In discussing technique of the pole vault, Krzesinski[1] stated that the pole must be in front of the vaulter's face throughout the takeoff, and emphasized strongly that the lower arm should not be straight or rigid; it should be allowed to bend with only enough tension to aid the bend of the pole. Keep the hips back during the swing phase; bend the pole by "pressing with the chest." "He explained the drop of the knee at takeoff, which characterizes many European vaulters, as a means to lower the center of gravity and so, to a smoother bend of the pole."

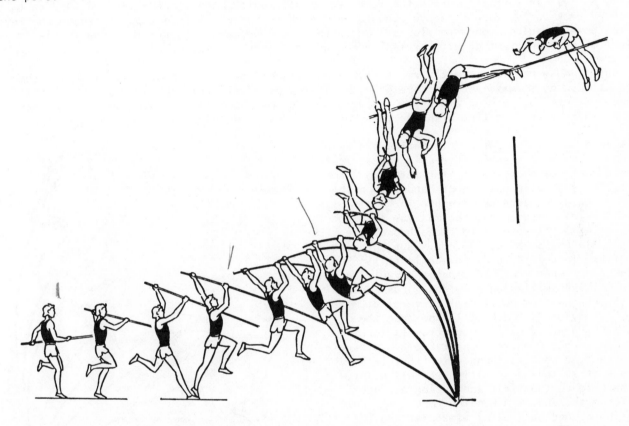

Fig. 8.10--Dave Roberts (1979 world record--5.70m, 18'8¼"). Best 100y--09.7. Top-hand grip-- 16'; "One should hold as high as he can...to reach maximum height." Handspread--18"; "As close as possible to facilitate storing (circular) momentum into the pole....a wide spread kills the swing." Pole plant--"Begin plant 3-4 steps from box. Push both hands forward at 45 degree angle forward and upward one step from box." Takeoff--"I drive the lead leg forward and down toward the box to aid swing with both legs straight and nearly together." Rock back-- "Delay the rock back as long as possible to maintain forward motion, especially with high grip." Delay of pull-up--"Keep arms straight, don't pull on pole....Most of delay should be in swing." (All quotes from Ganslen, 1980, pp. 106-117.)

[1] Andrzej Krzesinski, op.cit., p. 2734.

The Point of Takeoff. Vaulters using stiff poles tended to take off with the toe of their shoe on a point reached by a plumb line from the top of their upper hand. Flexible-pole vaulters tend to place their foot closer to the vault box. In Mansvetov's study previously cited, all 15 champion vaulters--(best heights from 5.20m (17'1½") to 5.70m (18'8½"))--had a takeoff point under the top hand, varying from 10cm (4") to 80cm (31"). Most were at about 13 inches. World-record holder (1979) Roberts was at 16 inches.

The Swing-Up (First Phase). The swing-up is a continuing phase of the spring-off, having validity only in words, not in action. It continues the forward action but begins to shorten the lever of the body pendulum and thus speed its swing-up. The rate at which this lever is shortened is a crucial point, and great vaulters do differ in this respect. Some do it relatively early. They tend to drive the lead leg up with quick knee flexion (Fig. 8.10), to lift the head back early, focus the eyes upward, and arch the back. This action lengthens the lever of the pole pendulum, tends to slow its momentum, but does gain an early increase in the height of the center of gravity, relative to the grip on the pole.

But it must be timed exactly right or, as happens so often with beginning vaulters, the hips will swing forward ahead of the pole, will slow pole velocity, and probably stall the vault. Expert vaulters do emphasize the upward drive of the lead knee but they counteract this by holding the head in line with the torso and the eyes focussed straight ahead.

Pole Bend During The Swing-up. During the swing-up and rock-back, the flexible pole has at least four advantages over the stiffer metal and bamboo poles. (1) It allows a higher handgrip on the pole which gives greater leverage in bending the pole. We can assume that the maximum straight-line grip is the same as that reached by the metal-pole users--about 14 feet. But the bend of the flexible pole extends this grip to 15'6" or even higher when measured along the vaulting pole. (2) Pole flexion provides a cushioning of the change from horizontal to vertical momentum. Study of Fig. 8.6 will show that the center of gravity of the body travels forward in a flat upward curve after takeoff. A steel-pole vaulter who has changed to fiberglass speaks of a sinking sensation at this point, comparable to that felt when using a rubber cable on the end of a hanging rope. (3) Pole flexion creates a greater time-distance for execution of the second phase of the swing-up, or rock-back as some prefer to call it. At the start of the swing-up, the distance of the center of gravity from the crossbar is significantly greater than when using a stiff pole. There's more room for movement. On the other

Fig. 8.11. Takeoff and full swing-up.

hand, the pole straightens with great quickness, so that the time factor is very limited. (4) The bend of the pole stores kinetic energy to be released at the last instant, in the so-called catapult effect, and thus increases the effectiveness of the pull-up along the straightening pole.

The Swing-Up (Second Phase) The second phase of the swing-up, often called the rock-back, acts primarily to shorten the body pendulum *but involves no upward pulling by the arms*. The bend of the pole is still increasing; in fact, greater body flexion during the rock-back increases pole flexion. Any pull-up during this phase could use only the inertia of a moving five-pound pole and so would greatly reduce momentum.

The takeoff (left) leg catches up with the right. The fixed, though relaxed, arms provide the fulcrum of the body lever. By rapid flexion of the hips and knees, the long axis of the body is shortened and the swing of the body pendulum is speeded up. The effect of this action on the pole pendulum is to move its center of weight (its bob if we think of a clock pendulum) away from the pole point and so to slow down its upward swing. It is therefore crucial to an effective vault that the rockback be delayed till just the right instant (Fig. 8.11).

Fig. 8.12. The rockback, also called the rollback or swingup.

The overall orientation of the vaulter during this rockback phase is upward "toward the sky" (Abada), or "toward the tip of the pole" (Nordwig), or "I just swing and try to get my feet as high as possible" (Isaksson). Many vaulters speak of the "feel" of pole bend and adjust their actions to it. Beginners that extend the feet toward the crossbar tend to swing under it, but experts acquire an orientation to the crossbar and adjust in terms of it. For all vaulters, pole extension carries the body toward the crossbar; no effort toward it is needed.

Any so-called waiting or "hang" in the vault should be related to the swing, certainly not to the rockback. This is crucial. All the developed momentum of the run and takeoff, all the conserved momentum of the swing and shortening of the body pendulum centers within the aggressive actions of the rockback and pullup-pushup. During the rockback the action is not to delay but to increase velocity of the c.g. upward. The kinetic energy of the straightening pole is now greatest so that shortening the body pendulum has the least negative effects. Once the trail knee rises above the level of the hands, the forceful pull lifts the body in perfect timing with the "catapult" extension of the pole. Some vaulters offset a tendency to turn too soon by emphasizing the pull of the lower hand and upward extension of the trail leg.

During the pull-turn-pushup, the feet should be kept together, with the turn being made through the c.g. or longitudinal axis of the body, that is, with a minimal transverse axis, thus improving body control as related to clearing the crossbar.

The Pullup-Turn-Pushup. As is implied by the hyphens, this is one continuous action, with no hint of hesitation between. This is the crucial instant when, if all the previous actions have been in good balance and full force, the vaulter explodes upward. Its effect might be compared to that of the finger-wrist action in the shot or javelin, a gathering culmination of force behind the projectile which, in this case, is the vaulter himself.

The pull-up does not begin as the pole starts to straighten; this would be too soon and would work against upward velocity. Rather, it begins an instant later when the pole is nearly straight and the pull-up can be along the pole with its base firm in the vault box (Fig. 8.12). By this time the center of body weight is close along the pole and to the source of power. The body pendulum is at its shortest and so gains its greatest rotational energy about the hands as well as being in a most efficient position for the final pull-push.

Ganslen (1980, 49) reminds us that the much-publicized catapult action of the pole during this phase has been greatly exaggerated. First, the direction of this pole force is more horizontal than vertical; second, this force is actually rather weak as related to the inertia of a 170-pound body. It is muscle power, more than pole power, that lifts the vaulter. But every little bit helps and the vaulter should make the most of it.

As with the pull-up, the turn should be delayed until the hips have lifted to or above the level of the hands. But then it occurs very quickly in coordination with the pull-up.

Fig. 8.13. Two views of the pull-up-turn-push-up.

The explosively forceful push-up should do just that--push the center of weight vertically up higher. This requires great power in the arm triceps and related muscles, and related power exercises should be done to develop the quick force with which this can be done. Certainly the push-up is not a weak pushaway of the pole that develops merely enough rotational force to ensure a proper landing. It should drive the heavy hips and legs, especially the right leg, UP; for that's what it is, a push UP as high and as explosively as possible.

CLEARING THE BAR. This description of the push-up establishes the method of clearing the bar. To be effective, any push-up must have a weight (in this instance, the hips and possibly right leg) to drive upward. Of course, some degree of arch over the bar is necessary to make a landing. Much as he might wish to do so, a vaulter cannot really push himself up into the sky.

But it should be clear that the hips should be close to the pole and above the hands until the hands have completed their push up from the pole. If such a style needs a name, it might be described as a lancet-arch style, one that reaches fully upward before starting its descent.

The expert vaulter will be much concerned about economy of clearance and will try to maintain his center of gravity at or even below the crossbar. But even then the push-up phase of the vault would have priority over economy of clearance. An emphasis on clearance style will tend to drop the legs too soon, before the hips have reached their potential height.

THE LANDING. Modern vaulting at high heights demands, not a pit, but a full three-foot high, foam-rubber mound. On such a buoyant surface a vaulter can land any which way without danger of injury. Most vaulters pull their legs quickly upward in an inverted pike position and land on their upper back.

HOW TO BEGIN

Just how a prospective vaulter should begin relates to many factors unique for each individual. There is no one way. But somehow, the beginner should acquire a mind-muscle feeling of the whole action. For example, by watching other vaulters, not merely with the eyes, as by allowing the feel of action to flow through his muscles as he watches. Slow-motion films are of special value for this.

There are respected coaches who feel that, before actually vaulting with a pole, a prospect will do well to establish a foundation of competence in related activities such as the related events of gymnastics.

In 1984, Jan Johnson,[1] coach at San Luis Obispo and 1972 Olympic bronze medal winner in the vault, wrote that lack of training in gymnastics was a primary cause of recent United States losses in the pole vault,

The fact that American pole vaulters get little or no gymnastics training is a problem. Next to sprinting speed, the single most important asset a vaulter can have is gymnastics expertise. Less than 2% of those vaulters attending my summer camps during the past 10 years have had any form of previous gymnastics experience. It also shows in our top athletes who often times show poor kinesthetic sense and control when compared to our gymnastically trained European competitors. These are items that can't be self-taught; it takes the experienced coaching of someone with gymnastics background for safe proper education.

As always, relatedness of learning is vital; major time should be given to those gymnastics events that most simulate the actions of vaulting--the swinging rope with rockbacks and climbing, high bar with pullups and over, acrobatics on mats and the trampoline, parallel bars, and the like--with special efforts throughout to perform movements that imitate those of vaulting. It may seem extreme but Fred Hansen used to tumble on the trampoline with hands held steadily in front of him as they would be held on the vaulting pole.

Drills to Improve the Phases of Action. Since, with such a complex event as the pole vault, it is impossible to learn the action as a "whole", emphasis in practice must be placed on learning phases. For example, Donald Knapp[2], Parkview High School, Rolla, Mo., uses a series of drills that simulate the various phases of the whole vault:

"Many athletes only practice the whole event, thereby ingraining many...*technique* faults. They spend many years working in frustration and vaulting well below their potential. The quickest improvements will come from development of the correct neuromuscular patterns utilized in pole vaulting. The athlete can develop these patterns through repetitions of drills. These drills are simulations of the different phases of the whole vault. The drills help the vaulter learn the correct body positions, and develop the feeling of motion through the phases....

"Many young pole vaulters make a quantum improvement (2 feet or more) in just one season, simply by learning to vault correctly. Hours in the weight room, doing speedwork, and training in the gymnasium don't make up for pole vaulting with proper technique. This extra training should be done, but not in place of technique work.

"We employ build-up drills to increase the skill level of our vaulters, and to increase the carry-over from one drill to the next. This allows more retention with less time spent overall. The whole pole vault is broken into five phases, with work practice on each phase in sequence for the athlete. Each athlete is evaluated in strength and weakness areas, with work on the weakness areas emphasized first. The 5 phases we use are:

"First Phase: Approach (Run, Check Marks, Pole Carry, Shift)
Running Drills. *Running Repeat Intervals.* 30, 40, 50, 60, 80, 100's with the pole; the number will vary depending on the part of the season.
    Goal--improve running rhythm, modified running endurance, technique and comfort of running with the pole, arm actions.

---

[1] Jan Johnson, op. cit., p. 2770.

[2] Donald Knapp, "Drills to Improve and Simplify the Pole Vault," *Track Technique*, #85, Summer 1983, p. 2699; and *Track & Field Quarterly Review*, Vol. 83, #4, p. 41.

"2. *Checkmarks Run.* Establish the takeoff distance from the box, beginning point, acceleration point, plant beginning marks. All runs may be done on the track, with or without a box or target.

    Goal--instill confidence, accurate placement of checkmarks; insure smooth build-up of the run.

"Second Phase: *Plant* (Plant, Takeoff)

1. *Shadow Plant.* Planting motion with an imaginary pole, may be stationary or moving. Emphasis is FORWARD and UP!
2. *Walking Plant.* Actual plant while walking; may use a regular pole or cut-off "stubby" pole. Emphasis is on maintaining balance during the plant.
3. *Stride Plant.* Intermediate to actual length run. Emphasis is on transition from the pole carry to planting; backward lean must be avoided, with no loss of approach speed.
       Goal--develop planting the pole properly. The pole plant must become automatic and consistent.
4. *Stubby Pole Plants.* Involves the use of a shortened, weighted end pole; the pole should be about 4 feet in length. Use this pole during sprint work. Emphasis is on proper running posture, arm carry, and planting, while maintaining top speed in the run.
       Note--use this pole on approach drills also.
5. *Towel Plant.* Use any length run. The vaulter uses planting motion and <u>Hits</u> a towel placed as a target on the floor or track. The vaulter can work on his run, takeoff, checkmarks, forward drive at takeoff (jump), going through the takeoff.

       Goal--the vaulter learns to use plant and run momentum to aid in actual takeoff, and he can see the accuracy of his checkmarks.
6. *Resistance Plant.* Use a normal or higher grip, 3 to 5 step run, *bend the pole* against the wall or in a real box. By resisting with the arms, the vaulter maintains body posture.
       Goal--this drill allows the vaulter to feel the pole bend, and learn to control the pole with the arms (especially the left elbow). Vaulters like this drill, and they try to over-bend the pole. DON'T overuse this drill.
   Live Box Drills--Use a free standing, smaller box with a carpeted or smooth bottom for sliding. This gives target orientation, and can be used with many drills, particularly drills #4, #5, #8, #9.

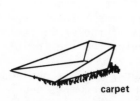

carpet

Live or free-standing box

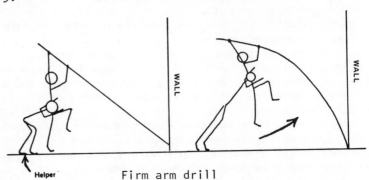

WALL

WALL

Helper

Firm arm drill

"Third Phase: *Penetration* (Takeoff, Swing)

1. *Live Box Takeoff.* Use of a free standing box. The vaulter may employ either regular or short run length. Vaulter goes through the takeoff while driving forward/upward from the ground. Keeping the arms rigid to maintain distance from the pole applies pressure through the pole to the free box (as in a real vault), and the box is pushed forward away from the vaulter. The vaulter semi-long jumps (may hold leg split) and lands standing. Check for alignment. Emphasis is on a proper run--plant--takeoff position (steps)--posture.
       Goal--teach continuation of takeoff and to drive off the ground into a pre-swing position.
2. *Bend Drill.* May use a normal or higher grip. The run is between 5 to 9 steps--the vaulter leaves the ground in a hanging, resisting position (he may lift his legs into a rockback). But the lack of speed does not give penetration, as the pole recoils the vaulter drops back to the runway. This is an <u>Advanced</u> drill, not for a beginner.
       Goal--to stimulate pole movement and the vaulter's motion at the early stages of

the vault. Teach the vaulter to stay down low taking off from the ground for penetration. Adjust to a new, and higher grip.

3. *Firm Arm Drill*. Use a flexible pole. The vaulter assumes the takeoff position, while a helping athlete pushes his shoulder forward into the vaulter's lower back. The vaulter is pushed forward and up, yet resists against the pole with his arms. The result is distance from the bent pole with the vaulter's arms extended, while the assisting athlete holds for a 15 second count. Additionally, the vaulter may swing his extended left leg and flexed right leg forward for a more strengthening effort. A high grip helps this drill to become effective. (This drill was adopted from Baytown South in Kansas City.)
   Goal--excellent strengthening exercise and position development.

4. *Hang Drill*. Use a short run, light pole, moderate grip. The vaulter takes off with a tall plant and maintains a "C" position while staying under the grip area of pole. There should be no flexion of the body or legs, the pivotal point is the shoulders. This is a total body hang on the right arm.

5. *Penetration Drill*. Use a long run with highest grip possible. This drill has 2 objectives:
   stay down--long body hang
   trail leg picked off the ground--holding the "C" as long as possible. This should help the vaulter move his grip area forward and upward before the legs swing up.
   Goal--develop a feeling for penetration by maintaining the "C" position, and lengthening the body during the swing. Increase the grip. The coach may assist by standing at the front of the pit and pushing the pole to the pit if the vaulter stalls out.

"Fourth Phase: Invert (Rollback, Extension)

1. *Right Knee Drill* (2 part drill)
   Leg Split Popup. The vaulter drives off the ground emphasizing a right knee drive and a straight left leg swing all the way to an invert, while maintaining at least 60 degree split between the legs.
   Knee and Shoulder Drill. As the body swings forward to parallel with the ground, the legs are above the body. The right knee should continue backwards till it is by the right shoulder, with the straight left leg along the pole. As the vaulter extends upward, his flexed right knee passes his right elbow but stays behind the pole. With the left leg straight along the pole, this will bring the hips to the pole directly above the shoulders.
   Goal--vaulter learns the timing of the swing to rockback, and is not premature. Learning to <u>hug</u> the pole and to rock all the way back. Most young vaulters don't do this.

2. *Popup*. (*Fundamental Drill*). Low grip, short run, stiff pole. The vaulter swings to an inverted position, with a straight right arm. However, to align himself vertically the vaulter must flex his left arm at both the wrist and elbow. The left elbow must be past the pole so that the head and shoulders are below the hips, all along the pole. The vaulter falls to the pit with the pole, he can check for extension and alignment. He may also have a distance point for landing.

3. *Extension Popups*. Regular popup motion to rockback; then as the pole attains vertical position, the vaulter extends vertically along the pole. If done correctly, upward force or momentum is increased. The action is similar to a gymnastic <u>kip</u>--if the vaulter is flexed at the hips and through the knees, with the legs behind the pole. This action should elevate the hips above the grip.

4. *Floor Drill*. The vaulter sits on a towel or something slideable on the floor, holding the pole at his side in the vault position. The pole tip should be against the wall. To begin, the vaulter leans backward, flexing the pole. As the pole recoils he lets his left arm flex-in past the pole, and extends his body. He may use a target on the floor to reach with the feet.
   Goal--vaulter learns to actively extend with the pole, and develop timing while maintaining the vertical position as the pole recoils.

"Fifth Phase--Finish

1. *Pull-Turn Drill*. Once the pop-up is mastered, vaulter may pull while in the air, raising hips past hands. As vaulter learns extension and correct pull technique, he may add a fast turn (along the pole) and land in the pit, face and stomach down on the mat.

2. *Double Bar Drill*. Total vault drill--involves use of two crossbars simultaneously. First bar is set approximately 2 feet below vaulter's best height. Second bar is set 3-4 feet above the first bar. The vaulter emphasizes early extension--attempting to kick off the

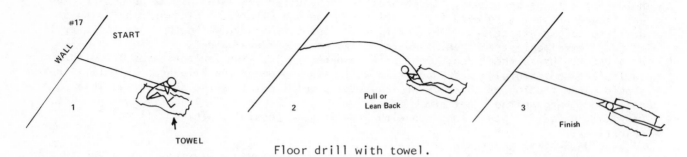

Floor drill with towel.

    top bar--and clear the lower bar.

       Goal--to learn to continue movement along the pole's vertical axis with body exten-
       sion, and to bring the arms into use to finish off the vault.

3. *Floor/Turn Drill* (20). Same as floor drill, but vaulter adds a pull-turn-push finish
to move himself further from the wall. The resistance of the floor adds to the delay
in the turn and is similar to the actual vault timing. This is a good strengthening drill.

4. *Standing Floor Drill* (21). Vaulter uses lean to bend the pole, but begins the drill from
a standing position. The vaulter then lifts his legs, becoming totally air-borne. With
the pole recoiling, he extends, pulls, turns, pushes and lands on his feet, with a good
push-off.

       Goal--strengthen and reinforce the fast, explosive finish of the vault.

5. *Pulley Drill* (22). Use a rope with a fixed hoop on one end, running through a short
(6 feet or less) pole on the other end. This should be about 18 feet long and can be
placed over the football goal posts. The rope must be short enough so the vaulter is on
his back-shoulders with feet in the hoop. The arms are extended to reach pole-rope.
From this semi-inverted position the vaulter pulls on the pole end, quickly going into a
total invert and finishes the vault action by turning and pushing rapidly in one motion.
By keeping pressure down on the pole end, the vaulter's feet are held up with the hoop
end. This enables the young vaulter to develop kinesthetic awareness for a position many
vaulters never achieve.

       Goal--vaulter learns to control upside-down position, and keep his feet elevated
during the critical finishing stages of the vault.

    "This set of drills is designed to help the developing pole vaulter learn his event with
proper technique. There are many other related areas of training: rope vaulting, gymnastics,
weight training, running, and vaulting itself. The ultimate aim is higher vaulting. Many of
these related areas strengthen, but fail to reinforce the neuromuscular patterns involved.
The drill system teaches concepts which lead to overall understanding of the event. This will
lead to better performances in this complex and demanding event."

COMMON FAULTS IN POLE VAULTING

    1. To use a pole that is too flexible and therefore breakable, dangerous, and expensive.

    2. To misuse a pole by allowing it to drop when vaulting, or to use it when the pole is
cold and the fiberglass brittle.

    3. To fail to achieve 95 percent maximal speed three strides before takeoff and then
drive forward on the last 3-4 strides.

    4. To fail to start the pole plant early so that the pole is in the box just before the
takeoff heel lands. The flexible pole tends to hide this fault but it is nevertheless a
crucial error.

5. During the pole plant to swing the pole forward out of line with the run and a vertical vault; the entire vault is then off balance.

6. To shift the hands too close so that they have little power in bending the pole and controlling the swing up.

7. To merely run-off at takeoff rather than to spring-off as does a long jumper. This is not a foot stamp but a compression-expansion of the springs of jumping.

8. At takeoff, to lift the eyes and head too soon, and so to cut the forward swing.

9. At takeoff, to fail to bring the lead knee up fast and forcefully.

10. To relax the lower arm so that the legs and hips swing ahead of the pole during the early phase of the swing up and so reduce pole velocity.

11. To fail to rockback with maximum force and velocity.

12. During the rockback, to look at the crossbar, rather than looking toward the upper tip of the pole.

13. To pull up too soon, before the pole is almost straight, and before the weight of the hips is above the hands.

14. To be more concerned for the method of clearing the bar than for making a maximum push upward off the pole.

POWER TRAINING FOR THE POLE VAULT

Before proceeding further, the reader is urged to review Chapter 6, "Training for Field Event Power," in which the concept of power is considered the all-inclusive term ranging from basic strength training to related power training to imitative power training to velocity training and on to improved technique of the actual event.

It also may be helpful to adopt the use of exponents as suggested there. That is, "power training" has a range of meaning from strength to velocity. Just where, along that range, can be more clearly written if we use exponents as in S^7V^3 as contrasted with S^3V^7 rather than by using descriptive words.

Third, it must be kept in mind that the running pole vault is the most complex of all field events requiring the running speed of a sprinter with the power and agility of an all-round gymnast, all in movements that are unique to pole vaulting.

It is obvious that power training for such an event must encompass a wide range of apparatus and exercises limited only by the genius of the coach-athlete contriving them and organizing them within a year-round program of development. For this, a review of Chapter 6 on planning field event training should be helpful.

Jan Johnson,[1] (18'½" and 1972 Olympic bronze medallist), suggested some 13 solutions to the present American recession in vaulting, among them: (1) A much greater emphasis on gymnastics that develop power and control in ways that simulate vaulting. (2) Increased development of sprinting and jumping ability. The relationship is simple--the faster you leave the ground, the higher you can hold...the higher you can hold, the higher the height you can clear. (3) Too much reliance on weight training as a cure-all. Overuse or misuse may be worse than no use at all. Much of weight training is non-related to vaulting; it takes up a great deal of time, and is seldom imitative of actions in the vault. (4) No vaulter can vault enough times to enable him to concentrate attention on each of its many phases.

Imitative drills and exercises (they go hand-in-hand with related gymnastics) are

---

[1] Jan Johnson, op. cit., p. 2770.

therefore a necessity. Jan Johnson further suggests that, since the American two-semester school system is unlikely to change, thus excluding summer practice from the schedule, the period when vaulting is best--summer camps for training vaulters should be established.

M. Kutman,[1] recommends a program of conditioning for pole vaulters that emphasizes gymnastics and trampolining as best developing specifically related power and vaulting techniques. He provides a series of "the most popular exercises....for vaulters at all performance levels."

CONDITIONING FOR POLE VAULTERS

ROPE

1. Climbing with the legs lifted above the grip with a slight upward stretching of the hip joint at each pull (A1).

2. Fast lifting of the legs during the hand on the rope from a short run-up (A2).

3. Hang and leg lift, assisted by a partner who pulls the rope tight (A3).

4. Hang and leg lift from a short run-up on a vertical rubber rope (B11).

5. The same exercise on a horizontally placed rubber rope (B12).

HORIZONTAL BAR

1. Leg lift between the hands from a short angular approach (C1).

2. Bar circle without touching it from a two-legged takeoff (C2).

3. From standing position, using a low bar, underswing with a forward dismount (C3).

4. Forward underswing with a turn into a hang position (C4).

5. Forward underswing with a push into a momentary handstand (C5).

RINGS

1. Forward swing with a pull into the half lever position (C6).

2. Upstart and push-up forward into planche(D7).

3. Upstart into handstand (D8).

4. Double-swing with a reverse somersault dismount (D9).

5. Forward swing with a turning dismount (D10) from a pike position at the backward swing.

PARALLEL BARS

1. Swing from front support into a handstand (D11).

2. Shoulder roll (D12).

3. Back lift-off from a hand below the bars (D13).

4. Swinging back lift from a hang below the bars (D14).

---

[1]M. Kutman, "Conditioning for Pole Vaulters," *Track & Field Quarterly Review*, Vol. 80, #4, 1980, pp. 50-51.

5. Low hanging pull to bent-arm extension (D15).

EXERCISES WITHOUT APPARATUS

1. Handstands and walking on hands (A4).

2. Handstand jumps down from a slightly elevated position (A5).

3. Push-ups in handstand, feet supported against a wall (A6).

4. Backward roll into a momentary handstand and the same exercise with a push-off over a low obstacle (A7).

5. Alternate jumps from a handstand to both feet and back into a handstand (B8).

6. Push-ups over a low obstacle (medicine ball) from a front lean, feet elevated and supported (B9).

TRAMPOLINE

1. From knees drop, forward leg lifts to back drops (E1).

2. Back drops with elevated legs (E2).

3. Back pull-overs into handstand from a back drop (E3).

4. Repetition bounces from sitting into pike position (E4).

5. Repetition bounces from back drops into elevated legs extended upward position (E5).

6. As the previous exercise with a turn in the air and landing on both feet (E6).

Before vaulters attempt the more complicated trampolining exercises they should concentrate on such simple routines as seat drops, back drops etc. It is advisable to perform trampolining exercises at the beginning of a training session because the exercises are physically not demanding but require strong concentration. Two or three trampoline workouts, lasting 30 to 40 minutes, are commonly used during the preparation phase of training.

THE ORGANIZATION OF PRACTICE
The overall organization of training and practice for the pole vault should follow the pattern established for all events in Chapter 16, in the development of basic strength, Chapter 6, and in the dynamics of skill, Appendix A.

Development in the pole vault should assume a year-round program,[1] for no event in track and field is so complex in its skill or so demanding in its need for related power, for running speed and speed-endurance, and for patience in continuing on despite the frustrations of slow progress and injuries of many kinds. But actual planning depends on the schedule of competition for each school. Assuming an indoor and outdoor season, planning should be made for four periods--fall preparation, indoor competitive period, spring preparation, outdoor competitive period, and, if feasible, a summer program of related activity.

Preparation periods have two phases. The first tends to be basic, emphasizing basic power, gymnastics, acrobatics, trampoline, sprinting, plyometrics and the like. The second phase shifts the emphasis (1) to similar activities but now they are specifically related to the muscle groups and movements of vaulting and (2) to the development of vaulting techniques by

---

[1]The program presented here is consistent with that of Jess Jarver, THE JUMPS, Los Altos: Tafnews Press, 1981, pp. 65-67, a softbound book (128 pages) that makes a sound and practical approach to the jumps--high, long, triple and the vault.

actual vaulting with a pole, using approach runs of different lengths--short, medium, full.

Throughout all such conditioning work, special care should be taken to prevent injury. In their attempts to closely simulate vaulting movements, men tend to lose all concern for safety--over-stretching, over-exerting, or ignoring landings. The trampoline has great potential for the vault; the hands can be held in vaulting positions while simulating vaulting movements in the air. But one of the great vaulters, Brian Sternberg (1966), an expert trampolinist, was paralyzed for life doing just such conditioning work.

Several weeks before indoor competition, the total volume of work should be reduced, especially in strength and slow-endurance work. The number of vaults over the bar with a short or medium run should be decreased; those with a full run, increased, with full rest-- perhaps two days--before important meets.

Following the indoor competition an active-rest period might include "safe" activities for fun and relaxation--swimming, volley ball, paddle ball, tumbling, whatever the athlete enjoys most.

The preparation period for the outdoor season would follow a pattern similar to that for indoors, but obviously developmental in selection of related activities and improved techniques. Each coach and each athlete will have his own unique approach, problems and solutions.

RELATED POWER EXERCISES

RELATED POWER EXERCISES

Use this approach in this exercise

[1]The black-shirted figures are excerpted from Nikolai G. Ozolin, *Modern System of Sports Training*, Moscow: USSR Gov't Sports Publishing Office, 1981.

1984 Olympic long jump champion and world record holder Anisoara Cusmir of Romania./Photo by Theo Van de Rakt.

Chapter 9
THE LONG JUMP

Up to about 1950 we thought of the long jump as a simple event--simply run down, take off, run in the air, land. That's the way Jesse Owens did it, and he was the greatest. He ran only 108 feet on a newly-laid grass runway. He did no related power training. When he jumped 26'8¼" it was his fifth event during two days of competition, with at least two more to go. The long jump was no specialty event, required very little practice for fear of injury, and was one part of getting more team points--along with the sprints and low hurdles. Today, computer-analysts and coaches judge such views as over-simplified, obsolete. The truth is somewhere in between.

A SUMMARY HISTORY OF PERFORMANCE AND TECHNIQUE

Long jumping has always been a natural part of man's everyday living as he cleared streams or fallen trees "at a bound," whenever the need was urgent. Certainly the mythology of every people tells stories of great feats of jumping from the Nibelungen tale of Siegfried's leap of 72 feet and more, carrying King Gunther with him beneath his Cloak of Darkness, to that of the Hindu monkey-god, Hanuman, who could clear oceans without use of the intervening islands. It was quite natural therefore that the long jump should be included in the Ancient Greek Olympics, though neither the high jump nor pole vault were contested. Gardiner's[1] carefully re-searched description of their methods is both interesting and instructive as it relates to modern jumping:

> *For the long jump a firm hard take-off was provided called the Threshhold. We do not know whether it was of wood or stone. In vase paintings the take-off is marked by spears stuck in the ground or by stone pillars similar to those used to mark the start of a race. . . . The ground in front of the take-off was dug up and leveled to a certain dist-ance. This was called the Skamma. "To jump beyond the skamma or the dug-up" was the pro-verbial expression for an extraordinary feat. Phayllus, the hero of a fabulous jump of 55 feet, is said to have jumped 5 feet beyond the skamma, and we are not surprised to hear from one commentator that he broke his leg in the performance. . . .*

> *The Greeks always used jumping weights, halteres, in the long jump. These jumping weights, which somewhat resemble and were probably the origin of our dumbbells, were made of metal or stone and varied in weight from 2 1/4 to more than 10 pounds. . . . The jumper with weights depends for his impetus partly on the swing of the weights, partly on the run. The run is short and not fast. . . . As the jumper takes off he swings the weights for-ward, so that in mid-air arms and legs are almost parallel. Before landing he swings them backwards, a movement which shoots the legs to the front and so lengthens the jump.*

Little is known of the true distances made by the Greeks, for they paid more attention to style than to records. But a few professional sprinters and jumpers in England during the 19th century used 5-pound dumbbells as a part of certain trick jumping acts. Gardiner appears

---

[1] E. Norman Gardiner, *ATHLETICS OF THE ANCIENT WORLD*, London: Oxford University Press, 1930, 144.

TABLE 9.1
OUTSTANDING PERFORMANCES -- LONG JUMP

OLYMPIC CHAMPIONS -- MEN

Date	Record		Name	Affiliation	Best 100y/m	Best High Jump
1936	26'5¼"	8.06m	Jesse Owens	Ohio State	9.4y	
1960	26'7½"	8.12m	Ralph Boston	Tenn A & I	9.7y	6'9"
1968	29'2½"	8.90m	Robert Beamon	USA	9.5y	6'2"
1972	27' ½"	8.24m	Randy Williams	USA	Triple jump	6'5"
1976	27'4.7"	8.35m	Arnie Robinson	USA	9.4y	
1980	28' ¼"	8.54	L. Dombrowski	E. Germany		
1984	28' ¼"	8.54	Carl Lewis	USA	9.93m	

OLYMPIC CHAMPIONS -- WOMEN

Date	Record		Name	Affiliation		
1964	22'2¼"(WR)	6.76	Mary Rand	GB		
1968	22'4½"(WR)	6.82	Viscopoleanou	Rum		
1972	22'3"	6.78	Heide Rosendahl	E. Ger.		
1976	22' ½"	6.72	Angela Voigt	E. Ger.		
1980	23'2"	7.06	T. Kolpakova	USSR		
1984	22'10"	6.96	Anisoara Cusmir	Rum		

PERFORMANCES OF SPECIAL INTEREST -- MEN

Date	Record		Name	Affiliation		
1928	26' 1/8"	7.93m	Silvo Cator	Haiti	(First over 26 feet)	
1935	26'8¼"	8.14m	Jesse Owens	Ohio State		
1965	27'43/4"	8.35	Ralph Boston	Tenn A & I	(First over 27 feet)	
1968	29'2½"	8.90	Robert Beamon	USA	(First over 28 & 29 ft.)	

PERFORMANCES OF SPECIAL INTEREST -- WOMEN

Date	Record		Name	Affiliation		
1980	22'113/4"	7.00	Jodi Anderson	Eugene, Or.	(American record)	
1983	24'4½"	7.43	Anisoara Cusmir	Rum	(World record)	

HIGH SCHOOL RECORDS

Boys

Date	Record		Name	Affiliation		
1979	26'8¼"	8.13	Carl Lewis	Willingboro, N.J		

Girls

Date	Record		Name	Affiliation		
1976	21.10.2"	6.78	Kathy McMillan	Raeford HS, N.C.		

to accept the statement of one of them that "J. Howard jumped 29 feet 7 inches at Chester in 1854" and that use of the weights "added at least 8 feet to his jump."

The McWhirters,[1] experts in great human feats, inform us that

The prospectus of the inaugural "Grand Annual Games" of 1860 at Oxford University invited entries for a "wide jump," though, when the programme came to be printed, the event was designated a "running long jump." The winner was Powell of Oriel with a "length of 17 feet 4 inches," which, incidentally was the same distance at which the first American championship was won 16 years later.

Of course, the conditions for jumping were then very poor. The pits were of turned over dirt and the first takeoff board was not used until 1886 when M. W. Ford reached 23' 2". During the next 15 years, the unofficial world's record was broken 10 times by three Irish and four American jumpers. The best of the Irish was Pat O'Connor who cleared the remarkable distance of 24' 11 3/4" in 1901, a record that held up for 20 years. Webster[2] states that O'Connor "did not use the hitch-kick but simply drew the knees up toward the chin."

The first jump over 25 feet was made in 1921 by Ed Gourdin of Harvard, who, after first beating the next Olympic champion, Harold Abrahams, in the 100-yard dash, leaped 25' 3" in the long jump. Pictures of Gourdin indicate that he also used a "float" style, with little leg action in the air.

---

[1] Ross and Norris McWhirter, *GET TO YOUR MARKS!*, London: Nicholas Kaye, 1951, 175.

[2] F.A.M. Webster, *ATHLETICS OF TODAY*, London: Frederick Warne & Co., Ltd., 1929, 215.

DeHart Hubbard, Michigan, cleared only 24'6" in winning the 1924 Olympic title, but the following year achieved 25' 10 7/8". Hubbard's style included a very short run of less than 100 feet, great acceleration, good height in the air (he was a six-foot high jumper), a single fast kick of the lead leg, and excellent forward placement of the feet in landing.

Three champions (Ed Hamm, Georgia, 1928--25'11 1/8"; Silvio Cator, Haiti, 1928--26 1/8"; and Luz Long, Germany, 1936--25'11") all used the "hang" style (Fig. 9.1), with its delayed hip and leg swing. At takeoff, they made a special effort to leap high with the chin and chest up, legs trailing. Just before landing, often too late, the legs swung forward-up, and the chin dropped forward-down.

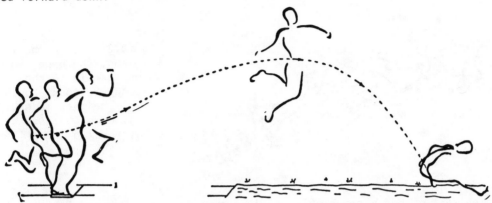

Fig. 9.1--The long jump, from movies of Silvio Cator, Haiti, first to clear 26 feet.

Then came the great Jesse Owens, Ohio State, with his 26'8¼" in 1935 that was to last for 25 years, the most long-lived of all track and field records. I was meet director of the Big Ten Conference meet in which Jesse not only made this record but also new world records in the 220 and the low hurdles, and a tie for the record in the 100, the greatest day any modern track man has even had. To bring the long jump in front of the spectators, we dug into the sod and installed a board and pit just one week before the event. The runway was on the old grass, cut short, watered and rolled.

Owens leaned forward on his one checkmark, only 108 feet from the board. That fact added to the grass runway meant he gained about 90 percent velocity at the board, as compared with today's 99 percent by best jumpers. At the takeoff he seemed to simply run off the board with no special effort to jump upward. In the air he used a simple one-leg swing, a natural movement for balance only. He had excellent leg extension on landing, legs almost straight at the knees, then bounced high and forward. It seemed clear that this "wasted" force might well have gone into greater height and so, distance.

Owens' long-jump practice consisted mainly of running through to make sure of strides and checkmarks. He was a great sprinter, trained on a minimum schedule of work as was the custom in 1935. To risk injury in long jumping would be foolhardy. Had Owens the use of today's perfect runways, had he had benefit of related power training, had he been able to practice the exact techniques of the gather and takeoff, who can say how far he might have jumped? His record might have lasted even beyond 1968 and Beamon's 29'2½"!

This is more a history of technique than of performance. Willie Steele, San Diego State (1948 Olympic gold; best jump--26'6"), slid off to the right during the landing, not straight forward. If done at precisely the right instant, this ennabled him to clear his buttocks; if too soon, his entire balance was out-of-line. Gregory Bell, Indiana (1956 Olympic gold; best jump--26'7"), a long jump specialist, used an excellent hitch-kick style (one and one-half strides in the air). Prior to landing, his feet were high, buttocks low and just clearing the sand as he tucked forward.

During the next decade, world long jumping was dominated by two men, Ralph Boston, Tennessee A & I (27' 4 3/4"--1965), and Igor Ter-Ovanesyan, USSR, (27' 4 3/4"--1967). In both cases great performance was the result of great natural ability plus mastery of individually different but quite orthodox styles. Both were fine decathlon prospects.

The styles of the two men were remarkably similar--long, fast approach runs, excellent height off the board, a single running stride in the air too smooth to be called a hitch-kick, excellent projection of the feet forward for the landing. Their follow-through after landing did differ, however. Boston tucked his chin forward-down between his legs, thus aiding the lift of his buttocks. In contrast, Ter-Ovanesyan rotated his hips to the right--usually beyond the break in the sand made by the heels (Fig. 9.2).

Fig. 9.2. As the heels touch the sand, the upper body-arms swing sharply to the right so that the buttocks touch-down beyond the mark made by the heels; a method used by the great Russian jumper Ter-Ovanesyan.

As a performer, Boston had a remarkable and long-time record. During six years (1960-66) he averaged 26'2 3/5" in 127 competitions, winning 115. Dick Drake[1] found that "a tally of Boston's best marks for each of the 10 decathlon events reveals would score 8045 points, fifth best in history." Among his best events were the high jump--6'9", high hurdles-- 13.7, triple jump--52'1½", 100 meters--10.5, pole vault--13'9", javelin--210'.

But in 1968, even Ralph Boston had to accept second ranking to the most shocking and perfect single performance in all field event history, that of Bob Beamon at Mexico City. Boston had dreamed of 28 feet, though it was over seven inches beyond his best. But Beamon ignored that mountain peak entirely and leaped all the way to a Mount Everest distance of 29' 2½". It was a perfect jump--perfect in the conditions in which it took place, perfect in the mechanics of action. *Track & Field News* (Oct/Nov 1968, 30) put it this way,

It was a rare jump indeed. But then, Beamon is a rare talent, and a combination of circumstances led him from a previous best of 27'4" to 29'2½". He was obviously fired up, his step was exactly right, his form bordered perfection, his speed (09.5 - 100y) came as a great asset, the runway was consistent and fast, the assisting wind read a maximum of 4.473 mph, the high altitude (7350 feet) provided reduced air resistance, and he put together perhaps the ultimate technical effort that all field event performers dream about but rarely realize.

In 1984 Carl Lewis is the greatest long jumper of all time with a dozen or more jumps over 28 feet, a best jump outdoors (7/24/82) of 28'9" and indoors (1/27/84) of 28'10¼". His technique will be discussed in detail later in this chapter, but the story[2] of his WR jump indoors is worth telling here.

It occurred at the Millrose Games. After five jumps, Larry Myricks led with his best-ever indoor jump of 27'6". On his final attempt, Lewis sailed past both Myricks and his own indoor World Record of 28'1" to break the sand at a startling 28'10¼".

The leap may have been intrinsically better than any recorded jump in history, all things considered, since it wasn't aided by a 1.89mps following wind (as was Lewis' outdoor 28'10¼"), nor by 7500 feet of altitude and a "2.00" aiding wind (as was Bob Beamon's 29'2½" in Mexico City).

---

[1]Dick Drake, "Ralph Boston: Super Giant, *Track & Field News*, November 1966, 11.

[2]"Lewis Surpasses Himself," *Track & Field News*, Feb. 1984.

Fig. 9.3. Carl Lewis, drawn by Dorothy Doolittle, Asst. Track Coach, University of Houston. On this jump, Lewis cleared 28'7 3/4", wind-aided, 1981.

Lewis' run is from a mark at 147'6", with a check-mark primarily for coaching purposes at 32'6" from the toeboard. Consistency in the first two-three strides in the approach is vital to an optimal jump. Lewis shows no change in sprinting mechanics--body angle, arm movements, center of gravity--until next to the last stride, and even there it is minimal. This stride is the longest--about 5 inches longer than the last stride.

The penultimate stride is actually where the jumper 'sets up' his takeoff. By slightly flexing the ankle, knee and hip joints, and planting the foot flat with a minimum loss of horizontal velocity, the jumper adopts a more erect position. This causes the hips to lower. Therefore, as the jumper leaves the penultimate stride, the hips rise, and rise continuously during the takeoff....

The greatest degree of flexion at the knee during Lewis' last stride is about 140 degrees (figure #8)....

Lewis uses a double hitch-kick. The takeoff foot circles twice....Once the jumper is in the air, nothing will change the parabolic path of the center of mass. Technique in the air aids the jumper's balance in the air and prepares him for an effective landing. The hitch-kick method can absorb and even counteract forward rotation to a small degree.... Delaying the extension of the legs as long as possible inhibits forward rotation. Therefore Lewis continues his cycling legs and arms to complete a double hitch-kick. Landing efficiency is increased when the distance between the heels and the center of mass is extended as far as possible....A common misconception among coaches and jumpers that failure to get the feet up high enough on landing is a sign of weakness in the abdominals. Actually it is the result of forward rotation. By bringing both arms forward (figs. 23-27) an equal and opposite reaction of the legs occurs. Thus, the landing point of the heels is extended.

It should be remembered that good technique in the air automatically follows a well executed (approach and) takeoff.

---

[1]Dorothy Doolittle, "The Long Jump--Demonstrated by Carl Lewis," *Track & Field Quarterly Review*, Vol. 82, #4, Winter 1982, p. 10-11.

Also printed in *Track Technique Annual*, '83, pp. 83-84.

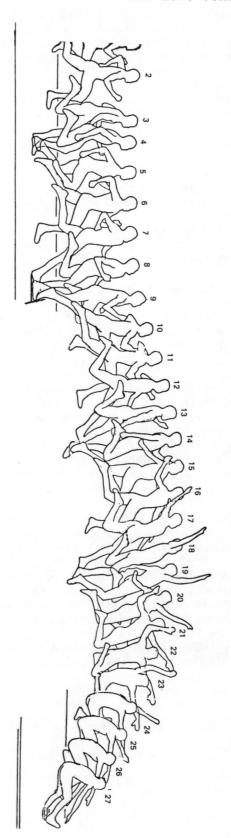

ESSENTIALS OF SOUND TECHNIQUE

The distance a man can long jump is strongly influenced by four "physical" factors: (1) the speed with which he can run about 40 yards, (2) the forward-up force he can apply against the takeoff board, (3) the time-distance and angle through which he can apply that force, and (4) the efficiency with which he can make a landing. Height in the air, so essential to distance is an effect of the first three factors. But psychological factors are also important; for example, dropping inhibitions against sprinting all-out and applying maximal force against the takeoff board. When Carl Lewis prepared for his jump of 28'10¼" indoors, he was told by his coach, Tom Tellez, to move his mark (152 feet) back one foot, then go-for-broke, at top speed, nothing held back--but relaxed. It worked!

THE RUN

The run in the long jump includes four aspects: length, speed, method (including the use of checkmarks), and what we call the gather.

THE LENGTH OF THE RUN. The run in the long jump should be the shortest distance in which a man can gain near-maximum velocity some four strides from the toeboard. Henry's[1] research on acceleration in sprinting is helpful,

> *The place at which a sprinter running a 100-yard dash reaches peak velocity . . . turns out to be a function of his speed, but is reached in almost exactly 6 seconds regardless of the speed if he is running at full effort. The runner will be within 1 percent of his greatest speed at 50 yards if he runs a 10.5 hundred, at 53.7 yards for 10 flat, 57.0 yards in case of a 9.5, and 60.6 yards in a hypothetical 9 flat. (Naturally these figures will vary slightly depending upon the characteristics of the individual.)*

These conclusions are drawn from sprinters who concentrate solely on all-out acceleration from their first movement. Long jumpers tend to be inhibited subconsciously (1) by the fact that they are jumpers, not sprinters, and (2) that speed must be tempered by the necessity of hitting the toeboard exactly right, as well as hitting the checkmarks on the way. Either of two conclusions is open: (1) the length of the run must be more than 200 feet (180 feet four strides from toeboard), or (2) long jumpers must be content with only about 95 percent maximum speed. Henry found that sprinters achieved 95 percent speed at about 66 feet, but for the reasons given, long jumpers would need a greater distance.

Related research by V. Popov, USSR, concludes, "to find the correct length of the run-up for each individual is extremely important, as a velocity loss of 0.1m/s before the takeoff represents an 8 to 10cm (3 to 4-inch) loss in the jumping distance."[2]

Actually, great long jumpers have varied in the length of their run from 108 feet to about 145 feet, using from 19 to 23 strides. The shortest of these was the 108-foot run of Jesse Owens (26' 8¼" - 1935), but Jesse began from a low crouch and attempted all-out acceleration from his first step. At the other extreme, such champions as Ralph Boston, Igor Ter-Ovanesyan, Willie Steele (26'6" - 1948), and Greg Bell (1956 Olympic champion - 25' 8½") used runs of over 140 feet. On his record 29'2½" jump (1968), Bob Beamon ran 130 feet. Lewis' jump of 28' 10¼" started from 152 feet.

---

[1]Franklin M. Henry, "Research on Sprint Running," *The Athletic Journal*, February 1962, 32.

[2]V. Popov, "The Long Jump Run-Up," *Track Technique*, Vol. 86, Fall 1983, p. 2708.

Assuming a certain degree of endurance and sprinting ability, even beginners should use a run of some such length; 19 or so strides are all too few in which to gain all-out relaxed velocity in time for the gather for the jump.

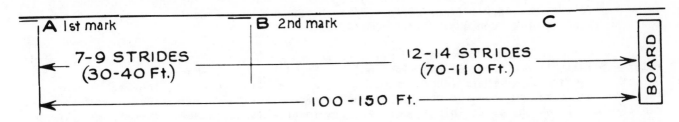

Fig. 9.4 -- Checkmarks and distances in the long-jump run.

THE SPEED OF THE RUN. In summary, a long jumper should accelerate and sprint as fast as he can within the limits of relaxation and readiness for the gather and precise takeoff. Dyson[1] has estimated that a jumper with great speed has only 5/36 second during which his take-off foot would be in contact with the board, only about one-half the time a high jumper uses. But this fact should not be used to argue for reducing speed, so much as for developing the speed-power and skill with which compression of the body springs and their reaction can be used effectively, in that brief instant. Such an approach is positive and in contrast to the negative assumption that the time factor is so limited that the speed of the approach must be equally so.

As long as a man is running relaxed, no concern for hitting the checkmarks and toeboard, or for providing more time in which to apply force against the board, should be allowed to decrease his speed. Assuming power and skill, the faster a man can run the farther he can jump.

On the other hand, despite this strong plea for greater speed, the distance actually jumped is a function of power and skill in jumping forward off the board, as well as of running speed. Boston broke Owens' 25-year old record though he could sprint only a "slow" :09.6 as compared with Owens' :09.4. But he could high jump 6' 9" as compared with Owens' 6 feet even. Another even more striking case is that of Rainer Stenius (Finland and Cal State at L.A.), who had a best time in the 100 of 10 flat and a best high jump of 5' 8", but long jumped 26' 9½" (1966). I heard Stenius talk before the USTCA coaches, and was greatly impressed that he used a full 40 minutes emphasizing the many aspects of skill in the gather and takeoff as well as the need for power in the particular muscles involved in these movements.

THE METHOD OF RUNNING. Three factors are crucial: velocity, relaxation, and exactness. We have already emphasized the first two, but exactness is of equal importance. A man must KNOW, must FEEL: in his muscles, in his mind, and in his heart, that he will hit just short of the front edge of the takeoff board *on every jump*. Actually, even with a master jumper, this won't always happen, but an occational failure will not disturb his calm assumption of a perfect run every time. Such a sense of certainty is the result of three requirements: (1) a positive mental attitude toward the run and its check-marks on the part of the coach and the jumper throughout all his practice and competition, (2) persistent and thoughtful practice using a whole-part-whole method, and (3) repeated and varied competitive experience.

Drake[2] reports that Ralph Boston fouled only seven times in 62 jumps taken in his most important competitions. He concluded that this was the result, not so much of endless practice, as of a positive mental attitude toward the situation. (I almost wrote the word "problem" but that's just the point--to think of fouling as a problem is to multiply its probabilities.)

---

[1] Geoffrey Dyson, *The Mechanics of Athletics*, London: University of London Press, 3rd edition, 1970, 152.

[2] Dick Drake, *op. cit.*

CHECKMARKS. The purpose of checkmarks is to make certain a precise placement of the takeoff foot on the toeboard. Having made certain of such precise placement, the jumper can concentrate on maximal velocity. Beginners will find two marks (A & B, Fig. 9.4) helpful, and even expert jumpers may continue to use them. But more than one mark tends to be a distraction that disrupts velocity. Assuming synthetic surfaces, those that have mastered the run use but one mark (A). Tom Tellez uses mark C (four strides from the board) as a coach's mark by which the coach, not the athlete, can analyze difficulties.

In fact, the very word "checkmark," valid as it may have been 50 years ago, is today a misnomer; at least in the sense of checking (holding back) velocity. Marks B and C might better be called go-marks, for their import is positive, a green light clearing the way in contrast to the checkmark's yellow light of caution and hesitation. For the well-trained long jumper, the run is one unit which, as training progresses, is invariably the same on every jump. The position of the feet at mark A is always the same; the forward lean, first step, and all succeeding steps are always the same; the degree of acceleration and the transitional final strides are always the same. Always the same in competition, and, as much as a sound approach to training can make it, always the same in practice.

Fig. 9.5. Jesse Owens who, from a run of 108 feet, on a grass runway, minimal practice of technique, no power training, set a 1935 WR of 26'8¼", unbroken for 25 years.

THE APPROACH STRIDES. Before the power training and plyometrics era, we used to coach the "gather"--a settling or lowering of the body's center of gravity during the last 2-3 strides before takeoff. "Relax, lower your arms, gather yourself for the leap upward. Drive upward, even though you lose a little forward velocity; height will more than compensate for it."

Today, height off the board is just as essential as it ever was. But the strength-velocity (S^4V^{10}) gained from related power exercises and related plyometrics, that are an essential phase of every legitimate long jumper's training, minimizes the need to gather. Or better, minimizes the time (number of strides) in which the "gather" occurs. Today's jumpers have enough related power to burst forward-upward on the final stride so smoothly that the drive for optimal height in the air is hardly noticeable to even a sharp observer.

It's not that the pre-power jumpers and their coaches were wrong in their approach; they just didn't have the tools to do the job.

Recent research[1] has emphasized the importance of the next-to-last "drive" step. Analysis of the action in three jumps by Beamon and Lewis discloses a powerful, even accelerating push-off from this penultimate stride into the takeoff stride, thus initiating a powerful acceleration of the free thigh that increases force against the board. This aids a high takeoff angle as well as horizontal velocity.

These views by Brady-Smith are supported by the East German scientists, K. Hempel[2] and H. Klimmer who conclude that emphasis on a longer next-to-last stride upsets the running rhythm, decreases velocity and leads to fouling. The critical factor is to maintain optimal speed without changing the rhythm of the run.

---

[1] Scott Brady-Smith, "The Drive Step--The Importance of the Push Off in the Penultimate Stride of the Long Jump," *Track Technique*, Vol. 87, Winter 1984, p. 2772.

[2] K. Hempel and H. Klimmer, "Last Strides in the Long Jump Run-up," *Track Technique*, Vol. 82, Winter 1981, p. 2040.

In conclusion, we should be clear that both velocity and a high-angled takeoff are essential to greatest distance. In the past, we over-emphasized jumping upward at a loss in velocity. Today, with no special attention to the relative lengths of the last three strides, we drive forward-up, or even up-forward off the board. Our intention is to accelerate forward but also to drive upward powerfully (s^2v9--see Chapter 6) if an optimal angle during the takeoff is to be gained.

Ultimately, the penultimate "drive" step should become an indistinguishable phase of the smooth transition of runup-takeoff.

A caution--for beginners or those inadequately training, such a unity of maximal velocity with optimal height is impossible. Verhoshanski[1] reports that two 22-foot jumpers on pre-training efforts were able to jump significantly farther using 3/4 speed during the approach than when using maximum speed. One might conclude that "coasting," or running at relaxed, controlled or optimal speed is better. But Verhoshanski concluded that these men lacked proper year-round training in both technique and related power to make a maximum-speed approach effective. Following such training, "the jumpers were able to jump confidently using maximum speed without any loss before the takeoff. Their performances improved significantly."

Fig. 9.6. Carl Lewis, as drawn by Dorothy Doolittle.[2] The penultimate stride (1-4) drives forward into the last stride (5-8). This drawing, perhaps mistakenly, indicates no lowering at all of the center of gravity. Certainly such lowering is less than that formerly obtained in the "gather." The upward drive of the c.g. is shown as occurring at the last instant. Lewis did secure excellent height in the air.

These findings are supported by the experience of Lynn Davies, Great Britain's 1964 Olympic Champion--26'5½". With a total run of 132 feet, Davies' checkmark "B" was only seven strides (54'6") from the board. During his early years of jumping, he tried to coast or gather for the takeoff. But in his later years when jumping his best, he tried to "change gears and sprint at the board." His coach, Ron Pickering[3] stated that "No longer does Lynn think of settling and sinking before reaching the board, but of really accelerating..." This change did not come easily or quickly but required months of related training.

Placement of the takeoff foot on the toeboard is shifted laterally inward a few inches to ensure a position directly under the c.g. where the takeoff leg can best apply its power upward, and body balance in the air can be best achieved. This tends to be a natural action for which coaching is only a distraction.

[1]Yuri Verhoshanski, "The Long Jump and Triple Jump Approach," in Fred Wilt, ed., *THE JUMPS,* Los Altos: *Track & Field News,* 1972, pp. 120-122.

[2]Dorothy Doolittle, op. cit., p. 10.

[3]Ron Pickering, "Coaching an Olympic Champion," *Royal Canadian Coaching Review,* Dec. 1967, p. 1.

THE TAKEOFF

By giving the takeoff a name, we tend to imply an entity that can be separated from other phases of the long jump. On the contrary, whether by word or action, the takeoff extends back to include the approach strides and forward to include the flight into the air. "Takeoff" is only a convenience of communication and understanding; if thought of in any separate sense, both are lost.

Keeping in mind, therefore, that the technique of the approach strides will determine the forces and movements of the takeoff, the latter can be discussed in three aspects: (1) yield-reaction to the takeoff board, (2) uses of the arms and lead leg during takeoff, (3) active extension off the board.

The same forces of yield-reaction discussed in the high-jump chapter are present in the long jump, but here the goal is distance rather than height, so that the yielding phase is minimal. Keep in mind that expert long jumping allows only about 0.12sec. for the complex movements during contact with the board. Dyson (1970, 152) estimated a contact time of 5/36ths as compared with 7+/36ths for the high jump. The yielding phase includes a follow-through of the lowered c.g. during the final stride; the foot placement is lower on the ball-heel; the ankle, knee and hip joints bend (yield) slightly; the lead arm thrusts forcefully forward-up, not simply "up" as formerly taught. If the yielding is too "soft," the joints will give way and the jumper will collapse into the near-end of the pit. If too "hard," and if the bracing of the takeoff leg has a significant braking effect, both velocity and distance jumped will be diminished.

As in high jumping, the uses of the arms and lead leg during the takeoff are primarily to increase the force of downward thrust of the takeoff leg against the board. During the first phase of takeoff, the forward-slightly downward thrust of the arms has the opposite effect; they help to cushion the momentary yielding phase and reduce pressure on the takeoff leg. But as the direction of arm and lead-leg force swings upward, their force of inertia is directed downward, increasing the load on the takeoff leg. Assuming the reactive power of this leg is adequate, the greater this downward force, the higher the jump.

Verhoshanski emphasizes the importance of precise timing of these related actions. With expert jumpers, maximum force from the lead arm and leg occurs at the end of the yielding or shock-absorbing phase and before the straightening action of the takeoff leg; beginners tend to start these actions earlier, before they can be effective. "In this detail lies the essential differences in the technique of a qualified jumper and a beginner."[1]

TAKEOFF ANGLE. Based on related research, Tom Tellez[2] concluded that (1) the faster a jumper is moving at takeoff, the smaller the takeoff angle is likely to be, but (2) the greater the height reached by the body's c.g. Most good jumpers achieve an angle of from 18 to 25 degrees; most poor jumpers get much more. If a jumper runs at a speed of 10s/100y and takes off at a 22-degree angle, he will jump 27'9"; if at a 24-degree angle, he could jump over 30 feet.

Fig. 9.7. Ralph Boston, 1960 Olympic champion.

[1]Yuri Verhoshanski, op. cit., p. 117

[2]Tom Tellez, "Long Jump," *Track & Field Quarterly Review*, Vol. 80, #4, Fall 1980, pp. 8-10.

ACTION IN THE AIR.
The purpose of all actions of legs-torso-arms while in the air is primarily to counteract forward rotation produced by the forward push of the takeoff leg, and thereby ensure an effective landing action.

Individuals vary considerably in the precise ways they perform these actions. We can describe the styles of three jumpers as being the hitch-kick, but that is not to say they are identical; each will have certain movements that are unique.

However, over the years, three styles have been identified. The first, the "sail," by which one simply lifts the legs and waits for the ground to come up, is ineffective and has been discarded. The second, the "hang" is shown in Fig. 9.8 with chest high, back arched, legs hanging together, then moving forward together to a "jack-knife" landing that, as shown in this Figure, is likely to be less effective than that gained in the "hitch-kick" style. Forward rotation is more difficult to control, so that buttocks tend to be high; heels, low.

Fig. 9.8. The "hang" style of long jumping.

The style-in-the-air preferred by almost all experts is the hitch-kick, a "run-in-the-air" or "cycling" style in which the number of strides varies with each jumper as a consequence of air-stride length and quickness as he/she seeks balance and an extended landing. Some excellent jumpers use one and one-half cycles; Carl Lewis uses two (the takeoff foot cycles twice). Geoffrey Dyson, mechanics expert, recommended two and one-half strides as best combining balance and an efficient landing. The precise number is not important. Fig. 9.9 (Greg Bell) shows the left lead leg swinging through one and one-half cycles. Bell was a long-jump specialist and was credited with a most effective method of long jumping.

Fig. 9.9. A hitch-kick style--one and one-half strides in the air. This sequence drawn from movies of Greg Bell, Indiana, 1956 Olympic champion - 25'8¼", best distance - 26'7", 1957.

THE LANDING.
The most effective method of landing allows maximal extension of the legs so that as they touch down, the heels are high as related to the buttocks; the buttocks are relatively low but just able to clear the sand as they reach the point of touch-down. For every inch the heels are held up, about two inches are gained in the jump. Ralph Boston, a great stylist, drove his chin-head forward-down between his legs at the last instant after touch-down, thus lifting the buttocks.

Geoffrey Dyson (1970, 157) advocates use of the arms,

Landing efficiency is increased in long jumping when, immediately before contacting the pit, the arms are behind the jumper, for he then adds to the horizontal distance between his Centre of Gravity and heels, and when he lands he can then throw the arms vigorously forward to assist the forward pivoting of his body, transferring momentum.

Fig. 9.10. An exaggerated but clear indication of the distance to be gained from an economical landing as contrasted with one in which the torso inclines forward causing the feet to drop.

Individuals vary as to the precise ways in which this is done. But five great champions (Bell, Boston, Ter-Ovanesyan, Beamon and Lewis) were alike in raising high the arm opposite whichever leg cycled forward, then swinging it forcefully down just before the landing (Figs. 9.3, 9.9). Fig. 9.10 shows two arms raised high, then forcefully down and well back, raising the buttocks--in this drawing, too soon. Bob Beamon, Fig. 9.11, was able to carry his feet very high as related to the buttocks just prior to landing.

PREVENTION OF INJURY IN THE LONG JUMP

In past decades, the long jump was considered the most dangerous of all jumping events in terms of strain of the leg muscles and tendons. Primarily this was due to lack of proper training. The event was dominated by sprinters who were too valuable to risk in practicing the jump but did take just enough jumps in meets to score the needed points. This led to a "kid-glove" attitude--a minimum of training work, and extremely little jumping. Despite his great record in competition, Jesse Owens was a typical example of such an attitude and practice.

Today, long jumping tends to be an event for specialists who train throughout the year in ways related to their specialty. The suggestions in Chapters 6 and 16 are just as valid for the long jump as for the high jump or shot put, especially as they relate to a toughening of tissues to prevent injury.

In summary, prevention of injuries is primarily a result of foresight in toughening the particular muscles and tendons on which long jumping places greatest strain. Some of the most important of these are the groin, the hamstrings, and the lower back muscles. Gradual overloading of these tissues in movements which imitate those of jumping

Fig. 9.11. Bob Beamon, 1968 Olympic Champion, 29'2½", the greatest single performance in all track and field history--the equivalent of 7'10½" in the high jump or 61'5 3/4" in the triple jump! This drawing is taken from a photo of the actual jump. The left leg seems to trail but is moving forward to a position similar to that of the right.

and sprinting can be very helpful in prevention. Most common of all injuries is that to the heel during the takeoff, especially when the area just behind the board is depressed. Modern synthetic runways make this injury less likely, but every long jumper should wear a heel cup, not merely after, but before injury occurs.

THE ORGANIZATION OF TRAINING.

Chapters 16, "A Modern System for Coaching Field Events" and 6, "Training for Field Event Power and Flexibility" provide a sound basis for planning a training program specific for the long jump and for this specific long jumper. To do much more than that is beyond this text and, in fact, is the responsibility of the coach-athlete in a specific situation. Only they know the what-when-how of this athlete's capabilities and schedule. The usual paragraphs on "How They (Lewis, Myricks, et al) Train" are not given. But a few summary comments may be helpful.

For all our great performances in competition, we in the United States have not taken the long jump seriously from a training standpoint. Most research and thinking has been done abroad in Germany, Yugoslavia, and the USSR. Ter-Ovanesyan of the USSR once wrote,

I am not afraid to tell you Americans that I have learned a lot from you and I wasn't ashamed to learn. Thousands of times I studied the movies of Jesse Owens' jumps. I tried to acquire the harmony of running form and speed which were peculiar to him and very much his own. From Bell I tried to learn the art of keeping balanced while in flight. From Bennett I wanted to learn his softness, from Shelby his impeccable landing. Boston forced me to see the takeoff in a new light. I commit no error when I say that I know the mistakes and strong points of these broad jumpers better than they know them themselves.

The three essentials of optimal long jumping are velocity in the run-jump, accuracy in the run-takeoff, and specifically related power in the jumping muscles. All three can be developed by carefully planned training.

Velocity in the run-jump is primarily an innate quality: without ability as a sprinter, a long jumper cannot go far. Not all sprinters, however talented, can long jump. But sprinting ability, from moderate to maximum, can be developed following the program recommended in Chapter 24. Lack of innate speed can be partially counter-balanced by improving the smoothness and height of the jump.

It is important that sprint training for the long jump be modified so as to relate directly to long jumping. Emphasis on sprints out of starting blocks is essential for sprinters, does develop power in sprinting muscles, but is not specific to long-jumping techniques. In the long jump, velocity off the toeboard is essential; velocity in starting is not.

Accuracy in the run-jump is achieved by many repetitions that duplicate long jumping as closely as is feasible. Danger of injury to muscles-tendons precludes many maximal efforts off the board. Most experts reserve such jumps for competition. But accuracy and confidence can be gained only by full run-ups and modified jumps off the board and into the pit. Beginners may start with three check-marks selected from natural striding away from the jump runway. But as confidence and mastery improve, the number of marks will be reduced.

Training related power should follow the schedules outlined in Chapters 6 and 16. But to emphasize the very important principle of relatedness, such exercises as shown here should be included. Gains are greatest from maximally explosive efforts, as from leaping upward from the ground following a box drop; or following the last of several multiple jumps from a five-stride run-up. Six to 8 repetitions are highly stressful so that full recovery is required before attempting a similar exercise. A full workout of such exercises should occur only once (beginners) or twice (well-trained) a week.

Verhoshanski's Approach to Training.[1] Verhoshanski made the obvious but unusual assumption that a jumper's inability to make effective use of a maximum-velocity approach was caused, not so much by some defect in technique or lack of related power, as by an irrational program of training. In particular, he assumed that learning is specific to the skill that is practiced, that if 75 percent of technique practice consists of short-approach jumps with emphasis on the takeoff, that specific skill is learned, with only a partial carry-over to jumping with a full-distance and maximum-velocity run. *Velocity of movement is as essential to the skill concept*

---

[1]Yuri Verhoshanksi, op. cit., p. 120.

as is the pattern of movement. The specific techniques of a 50-foot-approach jump are therefore quite different from those of a 130-foot-approach jump. *Somehow long jumpers must find
a training program by which they can practice the precise actions and velocities and powers
they use in competition.*

By-passing other needs of training including related power and flexibility, Verhoshanski
recommended the following year-round program for practicing technique, based on a competitive
season from May to September:

November-December. Goals: to improve sprinting technique; to improve the long-jump
approach rhythm emphasizing acceleration from the first stride. Means: many repetitions (at
least 8-10 times per session) of the full approach @ 3/4 effort without jumping. In these
runs, emphasize the approach phase by taking slightly faster and shorter strides. As physical
condition improves, add an easy takeoff-run through the pit to more closely simulate actual
jumping.

January-February. Goal: to master the techniques of increased speed throughout the
approach phase and takeoff. Means: many repetitions of the full approach as in the preceding
period. In these runs, 3/4 effort is still used during the early strides, but with maximum
speed during the approach strides. However, though these strides do increase in tempo, there
should now be no significant decrease in stride length. By concentrating on the specific
skills of power sprinting--explosive push-off by each foot, high knees, full leg extension,
forceful arm drive--the jumper gradually learns to drive through these approach strides and up
into the takeoff with increasing power. Practice should include a normal takeoff and action
in the air. The landing may be on one foot with a run-through beyond the pit, or with the
usual two-foot style into the pit. In summary of this period, all the specific techniques of
the approach phase of maximum long jumping are practiced, limited only by the 3/4 effort during
the early strides.

March-April. Goals: mastery of the techniques of maximum velocity throughout the run-
approach-takeoff. Means: repetitions of such maximum-velocity jumps in practice sessions. The
gradual six-month progression in velocity of jumping, augmented of course by related power
training and flexibility exercises, has now toughened the muscles and tendons to withstand the
strains of all-out jumping. Strains are always a danger, and all precautions should be taken
to avoid them, but basically the body is prepared and the danger is minimal.

May-September. Competitive period. Goal: perfection of the artless art of maximum long
jumping in which the details gradually fall away, as has happened at least once when Beamon
cleared 29 feet 2½ inches at Mexico City. Means: practicing the jump as a unified whole with
attention to its parts only as seems necessary.

In my judgment, Verhoshanski's approach to training for technique is a sound one; sound
in terms of basic motor learning and sound for the special problems of long jumping. Our
problem is to adjust this Russian time schedule to our own school-college schedule with its
indoor competitive season and tendency to lay off during the summer months. To hurry the
gradual increments of effort and strain so carefully planned by Verhoshanski would decrease
improvements of techniques and increase the dangers of injury. Where attitudes or competitive
schedules permit, competitive performance during the indoor season should be secondary to
proper training for the more important outdoor season.

RELATED POWER EXERCISES
LONG JUMP - - TRIPLE JUMP

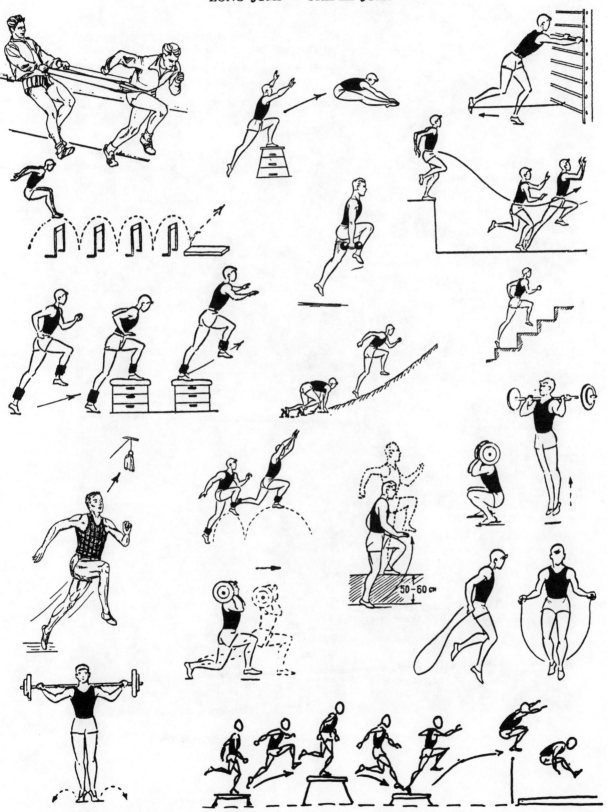

Al Joyner, 1984 Olympic triple jump champion./Photo by Kevin Morris.

Chapter 10
THE TRIPLE JUMP

The triple jump is a most challenging event. It demands great speed-precision-relaxation in the run; high-level power and resiliency in the yield-reactive phases of three jumps; good balance in the air; and an effective landing in the pit--all in all, one of the most demanding of all field events. Such demands call for longtime, gradual training for greater velocity in the run, for acquiring greater related power in the jumps, and for developing greater technical skill in putting it all together in a unified four-phased jump.

SUMMARY HISTORY OF TECHNIQUE AND PERFORMANCE

The evolution of technique in the triple jump can be summarized as having three phases: (1) that of changing emphases on the three jumps, (2) that of the use of related power training in developing the reactive or bounce power for each of the jumps, and (3) that of greater velocity in the approach run as well as within the jumps.

Pat Tan Eng Yoon[1] credits the Irish with having used an early prototype style of hopping twice, then jumping--an L-L-L-jump style, with the English adopting the present accepted method around the turn of this century. Quite naturally, the early jumpers thought in terms of each phase somewhat separately, and tended to emphasize first, the hop or first jump; then the final third jump; and more recently, the step or second jump. Today, the event is thought of as a single, undividable action, having various phases which must be emphasized within the total action so as to produce the greatest total distance.

One of the mysteries of our sport is why the triple jump was ever dropped from the American program, and why we waited until about 1962 before the event was restored on a full college schedule. Or why even today many State High School Associations do not sponsor it. Certainly it had a strong beginning here, for American athletes dominated the event in the first three Olympic Games. J. B. Connolly, Boston, won in 1896 with 45 feet; Meyer Prinstein, Syracuse, in 1900 and 1904, with 47' 4¼" and 47' even, despite the dropping of the event from the National AAU championship meet from 1893-1906.

Since then no American has ever won this event in the Olympic Games, though in 1911 Dan Ahearne of Ireland and later, the Irish-American AC, did jump 50' 11" which remained the world record until 1924. According to Richard Ganslen, the breakdown on Dan's jump was 20' -- 11'3" -- 19' 8", a ratio characteristic of early jumpers who took a relatively short step and emphasized the hop and jump.

Dan Ahearne's durability in a tough event was just as amazing as his record. He won the American championships on eight different occasions from 1910 to 1918, and in 1924, at something over 40 years of age, was still expert enough to represent America in the Paris Olympic games. Incidentally, his younger brother, Tim, won the 1908 hop, step, and jump event in the London

---

[1]Pat Tan Eng Yoon, "Research into the Hop, Step and Jump," *Clinic Notes*, NCAA Track Coaches Association, 1959, 16.

TABLE 10.1
OUTSTANDING PERFORMANCES--TRIPLE JUMP

OLYMPIC CHAMPIONS

Date	Record	Name	Affiliation	Hop	Step	Jump
1932	51'7"	Chuhei Nambu	Japan	21'0"	14'6"	16'2"
1936	52'5 7/8"	N.Tajima	Japan	20'4"	13'1"	19'1"
1948	50'7"	Arne Ahman	Sweden			
1952	53'2½"	A.F.da Silva	Brazil	20'4"	15'1"	17'9½"
1956	53'7½"	A.F.da Silva	Brazil			
1960	55'1 3/4"	Jozef Schmidt	Poland			
1964	55'3½"	Jozef Schmidt	Poland			
1968	57' 3/4"*	Viktor Saneyev	USSR	22'4"*	16'7"	19'10"
1972	56'11"	Viktor Saneyev	USSR	(*includes 8" takeoff before board)		
1976	57'8.7"	Viktor Saneyev	USSR			
1980	56'11 1/8"	Jaak Uudmae	USSR			
1984	56'7½"	Al Joyner	USA			

*Altitude -- 7350 feet

WORLD RECORDS OF SPECIAL INTEREST

Date	Record	Name	Affiliation	Hop	Step	Jump
1911	50'11"	Dan Ahearne	Eire	20'0"	11'3"	19'8"
1931	51'1 3/8"	Mikio Oda	Japan	21'4"	11'6"	18'3"
1935	51'9 3/8"	Jack Metcalfe	Australia	18'6"	13'6"	20'4"
1937	52' 3/8"	K. Togami	Japan	19'0"	14'0"	19'2"
1950	52'5 7/8"	A.F.da Silva	Brazil	18'1"	15'10"	18'6"
1951	52'6¼"	A.F.da Silva	Brazil			
1953	53'2 3/4"	L. Shcherbakov	USSR	19'8½"	16'3½"	17'2½"
1955	54'4"	A.F.da Silva	Brazil	20'7"	16'4"	17'5"
1958	54'5¼"	O. Ryakhovskiy	USSR	21'2½"	16'3½"	16'11"
1959	54'9½"	O. Fyedoseyev	USSR	21'4"	15'9 3/4"	17'7 3/4"
1960	55'10¼"	Jozef Schmidt	Poland	19'8¼"	16'5¼"	19'8 3/4"
1968	57' 3/4"	Viktor Saneyev	USSR	(altitude 7350')		
1971	57' 3/4"	Pedro Perez	Cuba	(sea level at Pan-Am Games)		
1972	57'2 3/4"	Viktor Saneyev	USSR			
1975	58'8½"	Joao Oliveira	Brazil	20'	17'7"	21'1½"

OUTSTANDING PERFORMANCES -- UNITED STATES

1981	57'7½"	Willie Banks	AW, Sacramento, CA (American record)

COLLEGE

1982	57'7 3/4"	Keith Connor	SMU	(Collegiate record)
1984	56'11½"	Mike Conley	Ariz.	(1984 NCAA winner)

HIGH SCHOOL

1978	53'4¼"	Sanya Owolabi	SH, No. Tarrytown, NY (HS record)
1984	52'0"	Joe Richardson	Pasadena, CA
1984	50'11¼"	Terrance Strong	Bakersfield, CA
1984	50'5½"	David Sanders	Bakersfield, CA

Olympics while Dan was trying to get settled after his emigration to America.

Following the world monopoly of the Ahearne brothers, men from Sweden and Finland won the event in the 1912 and 1920 Olympics, with jumps of 48' 5'' and 47' 7'' respectively.

JAPANESE DOMINANCE. But in 1928, Mikio Oda, (5' 6'' tall, weight--130#, best 100 yard time--about :09.9) began a 12-year world-dominance in the event for Japan. This was specially significant because many of the Japanese jumpers were slow as sprinters. Tan Eng Yoon reports that neither Oda, Tajima, nor Harada could break 11 seconds for 100 meters, though they all bettered 51 feet. But they did have great leg power and resiliency, acquired, some said, from the Japanese custom of sitting on the floor and using the power of crossed legs in rising. In any case, we know that they studied the event very carefully, emphasized a deeper knee-hip flexion and rebound on each jump, and a better balance of distance between the three phases of the jump. By 1932, their greatest natural athlete, Chuhei Nambu, combined excellent speed (100 meters--:10.5) with great jumping ability (world-record long jump--26' 2'') to gain the Olympic title and the world record at 51' 7''. In 1936, Japanese athletes won 1st, 2nd, and 6th at the Berlin Olympics, including Tajima's world record of 52' 5 7/8''. But the War destroyed all Japanese development in sports, and when they recovered, others had passed them by.

ADHEMAR da SILVA. Surprisingly, the next world champion, the fun-loving Adhemar da Silva, came from Brazil. Da Silva failed in 1948 at London because, he said, "I was so awestruck by the multitude of people that I forgot to warm up or anything else!" But in the years that followed, he forgot spectators in the sheer delight of jumping at any time and in almost any place in the world. First (1950, 52' 5 7/8''), he tied Tajima's record with the greatest series of jumps up to that time:

	HOP	STEP	JUMP	TOTAL
1.	18' 8 3/4''	14' 5 1/4''	16' 4 7/8''	49' 6 7/8''
2.	17'10 5/8''	15' 2 5/8''	18' 7/8''	51' 2 1/8''
3.	17' 8 1/4''	15' 3''	18' 2 1/2''	51' 1 3/4''
4.	18' 2 1/2''	15' 6 1/4''	18' 6''	52' 2 3/4''
5.	18' 2 1/2''	15' 8 5/8''	18' 7 5/8''	52' 6 3/4'' (foul)
6.	18' 1 3/8''	15'10 1/2''	18' 6''	52' 5 7/8''

The relative lengths of the hop, the step, and the jump warrant careful study for they are very similar to those of modern jumping. On a percentage basis, the three phases of his final record comprised 34.5 -- 30.1 -- 35.4 percent of the total effort, a very well-balanced performance, even by modern standards.

Then, at the 1952 Olympic Games at Helsinki, he set new world-records on three consecutive jumps with a final best of 53' 2 1/2''. He planned to retire, but when Shcherbakov of the U.S.S.R. beat his mark by one-quarter inch, he went into training again, with a new record of 54' 4''.

Once again he announced his retirement. But this time, according to his own telling, his wife agreed to present him with a third child if he would present her with another Olympic gold medal. Which, at Melbourne, he did; and which, in good time, she did. It was a boy!

SOVIET DOMINANCE. But individual efforts, even those as brilliant as da Silva's were being outshone by the mass athletics program of the Communist countries. The U.S.S.R. took this event very seriously, as being one that was relatively undeveloped in world competition. Coaches who specialized in this one event were appointed. Scientific studies were made. In 1961, these studies were summarized in a 214-page book on this event alone. All aspects were reviewed, past history, prevalent techniques, but especially, the outlook for the future. One table, for example, projected the probable performances of a 27-foot broad jumper, such as Ter-Ovanesyan or Ralph Boston. The result? Just over 59 feet! The world's record when the prediction was made was 55'10¼'' by Jozef Schmidt of Poland!

The Russian technique seemed to place great emphasis on the hop. Both Ryakhovskiy and Fyedoseyev cleared more than 21 feet, comparable to the efforts of Oda and Nambu of Japan back in 1928-1932. This great effort was maintained in their step (between 15'9'' and 16'3''), with least emphasis on the jump (16' 11" to 17' 7"). Perhaps their projection of an ultimate 59 feet influenced their methods; at least they used their momentum to a maximum degree on each phase, in the hope that some one at some time would have enough balance and relaxation to permit the momentum to continue into the last phase, the jump. Considering that none of their champions were even good sprinters or broad jumpers, their performances were truly remarkable.

THE POLISH METHOD. However, the next great break-through in performance and perhaps in method came from Poland, not the U.S.S.R. Just before the 1960 Olympic Games, Jozef Schmidt surpassed Fyedoseyev's world's record by more than a foot with 55' 10¼", in which the three phases were 35.2--29.4--35.4 percent of the total jump, a very well-balanced performance. Schmidt placed his emphasis where he was most capable--on velocity (best time 100 meters-- :10.5). By keeping his trajectory low on his first two jumps, he maintained momentum for a long third jump. His splits on his record jump were 19' 8 1/4" (relatively short), 16' 5 1/4" (relatively long), and 19' 8 3/4" (long). This came to be known as the Polish "flat" technique, and still has its advocates today. In its January 1984 issue, *Track & Field News* listed Zdzislaw Hoffman, Poland, (World Championships--57'2") as world's-best triple jumper.

MEXICO CITY. Schmidt's record lasted eight years, a long time in today's world. But in the eighth year, at the Mexico City Olympics (altitude - 7349 feet), it was broken not by one man, but by five. All related factors were on the plus side--altitude, wind, sunny weather, and the presence of the ten top triple jumpers on the all-time listings. Most competitors made personal-best records, topped by Saneyev's 57' 3/4".

LATER RECORDS. Great as 57 feet was in terms of past performances, it was some three feet short of our projected human ultimate of over 60 feet. As was soon demonstrated. In 1971, at sea-level, Pedro Perez of Cuba equalled Saneyev's distance, only to be outdone in 1972 when the Master, following his second gold at Munich, regained the world record at 57' 2 3/4".

The high altitude (low density air) of Mexico City that aided Saneyev's 57' 3/4" and Beamon's WR long jump of 29'2½", also contributed to the 1975 WR triple jump by Joao Oliveira (Brazil) of 58'8½"--as of July 1984, still unsurpassed. The three-jump breakdown of this great performance was 20' - 17'7" - 21'1½". As a matter of interest, if not great significance, this ratio is closest to that projected by Mikio Oda of Japan (35-30-35), with excellent balance as between the first and last jumps and a full second jump in between. Other than repeated sprints with weighted vest, Oliveira used a minimum of weight training. Even better jumps are undoubtedly forthcoming. Oliveira's time for 100m was 10.4. What if a Carl Lewis were to specialize in the triple jump? and were to compete at Mexico City. What then would be the world record!

ESSENTIALS OF TECHNIQUE
The objective in the triple jump, and we must be clear about it, is maximal distance beyond the toeboard. It is not height of the flight curve. It is not relative lengths of the three jumps. It is not velocity during the run that must be maintained throughout the jumps. It is jumping distance attained through optimal blending of these and other essentials.

A few years ago, almost exclusive attention by the theorists was on the relative lengths of the three jumps. Such lengths are very important; they do control the velocity-distance of succeeding jumps and the total distance. Today, attention tends to be focussed on velocity-- velocity in the run and in its conservation and "increase" during the three jumps.

Each of these is essential to maximal distance. But it is the blending, the fusion of these and all such essentials that ensures greatest distance. It is clear that, as with the long jump, the concept of velocity is the most critical. But all factors, including power as related to running, jumping and an efficient landing are vital.

BASIC SIMILARITIES BETWEEN LONG AND TRIPLE JUMPING. All aspects of the long jump have direct application to the triple jump, the run in all its phases including length, checkmarks, acceleration, takeoff and, of course, training. Such details are given in the long jump Chapter, and need no further discussion here, except to add that the two events are not identical, do have different emphases--jumping from each leg for example--and require training that is specific to those differences.

Fig. 10.1. THE WHOLE ACTION. The very complexity of the triple jump demands a rhythmic, smooth, unified approach. It is not three separate jumps as was implied by the English-American terms--hop, step and jump. Rather it is one action with three phases--actually four, counting the approach run.

Even in its beginner's stages, the triple jump, like the high and long jumps, is a challenging event that warrants inclusion in all programs from the elementary grades through college. Many variations can be used--from a stand or any length of run, or any combination of hops or steps, with a final jump into a pit or on to an indoor mat.

But though relatively simple at the beginner's level, mastery of the event is so difficult as to challenge full-time concentration for many years, and to require a carefully selected program of plyometrics and related power. Though it demands sprinting speed as much as does the long jump, few triple jumpers double in the sprints.

TRIPLE JUMP THEORY. Over 30 years or more, much research based on performances by world-level triple jumpers has focussed on each phase--velocity, height of the flight curve, related power requirements, relative lengths of the first jump with that of the athlete's best long jump, and especially on the relative lengths of the three jumps. Such theory is vital to progress. On the other hand, each jumper--beginner or expert--is unique in every way. It follows that he should not conform to theory. Rather, theory should be used as a guide by which he can develop his own style.

RELATIVE DISTANCES FOR THE THREE JUMPS. Table 10.1 gives us the actual distances for each of the three phases of the triple jump made during world-record performances. These are acceptably correct, though world statisticians do differ slightly on details. Needless to say, such measurements would be secondary to those of the official triple jump distance.

Our interest however, is for relative distances. These, and the resulting measurements for each phase of triple jumps of different lengths, are given in Table 10.2. Various coaches and researchers have advanced the merits of different ratios, such as the 6:5:6 or 10:8:9 ratios, which we have converted to distance percentages, since these provide a single basis for comparison.

1. 35-30-35 ratio. This was advanced in 1949 by Mikio Oda , the Japanese Olympic champion and coach. In seeking to improve the weak "step" phase of Japanese jumpers, Oda increased the step percentage as compared with the 37.5-25-37.5% they had used previously.

This revision consisted of injecting more speed into the three parts of the jump. In the past we ran about the same distance as in the running broad jump without attaching importance to speed and considering the balance and rhythm after the initial takeoff to be very important.

Thus in the new method we tried to increase the distance of the hop by relying on the speed of the run before the hop, one of the aims being not to overdo the hop (about 20 feet), and to land on the takeoff foot with a very deliberate stamp of the foot, and then to stretch the step over 15 feet. The objective is to extend the overall distance of the jump through speed, rather than by the rhythm of the jump. To do this one must hop lower than formerly and, moreover, one must move his legs quicker.

2. 37-30-33 ratio. In 1957 Pat Tan Eng Yoon[1] made a very exhaustive study of this problem at the world-renowned Loughborough Athletics Training School, England. He concluded his research by recommending Mikio Oda's percentages but also suggested a 37-30-33 ratio which places first relative emphasis on the step, second emphasis on the hop. This method intends that, when all the early phases of the triple jump have been mastered, sufficient momentum will have been maintained to achieve a long final jump. Yoon also suggested that beginners would do better with a ratio of 37-26-37. He agreed that this method de-emphasized the second phase, the step, and was unbalanced for the best performers.

Yoon's ratios were supported by Dietrich Gerner, Brazil, who is reported to have coached Adhemar da Silva for several years. He suggested that the combined distance for the first two jumps should double that for the third, but these figures were gained by averaging the results of past champions, not by reason of research in biomechanics--if such is possible. Such a formula produces a ratio between the hop and step of 5:4, almost identical to that obtained by Yoon.

3. 38-30-32 ratio. Vitold Kreyer[2] USSR National Triple Jump Coach and Olympic bronze medallist at both Melbourne and Rome, recommended this ratio, though with some flexibility as to the precise numbers. He found that beginners do well using a 38-27-35 ratio.

[1] Pat Tan Eng Yoon, "Research into the Hop Step and Jump," *Clinic Notes, National Collegiate Track Coaches Association*, 1959, 16-41.

[2] Gabor Simonyi, "Vitold Kreyer's Training for Soviet Triple Jumpers," *Track Technique*, #79, Spring 1980, pp. 2505-2508.

THE POLISH "FLAT"TECHNIQUE. The so-called "revolutionary" technique used by Jozef Schmidt of Poland in the 1960s was actually a return to the 1949 ideas of Mikio Oda of Japan, 1928 Olympic champion. Oda's emphasis on continuous velocity into and through the first jump and recommendation of a ratio of 35-30-35 was precisely that attained by Schmidt--1960, 1964 Olympic champion and a WR 55' 10¼" (19' 8¼"--16'5¼"--19' 8 3/4").

TABLE 10.2
ODA RATIO THEORY
35--30--35

Distance		35-30-35	Ratio
40	14'	12'0"	14'
42	14'8"	12'7"	14'8"
44	15'5"	13'2"	15'5"
46	16'1"	13'10"	16'1"
48	16'10"	14'5"	16'10"
50	17'6"	15'0"	17'6"
52	18'2"	15'7"	18'2"
54	18'11"	16'2"	18'11"
56	19'7"	16'10"	19'7"
58	20'4"	17'5"	20'4"

This low-angled technique puts no conscious emphasis on the "gather" that characterized early jumpers. There is a "settling" of the pelvis (c.g.) but this results from a low forward thrust of one or both arms. The difference seems minor but is significant in maintaining velocity, in shortening the first jump with a lengthening of the final jump that more than compensates.

Today, this low-angled "flat" technique, first advanced by Mikio Oda, has general acceptance with only minor individual variations.

Significance of Ratio Theory. Relative lengths of the three jumps are important to maximal total distance. On the other hand, Russian coaches[1] have concluded from years of experience that these relate to individual characteristics, tend to be well established during early learning and are very hard to change. It is therefore crucial that proper technique in all phases be learned as soon as feasible within the learning process. This is consistent with findings in learning other field events. Changes at a later stage can be made but not easily. Examples are cited of improved rhythms of jumping by the development of related power, and by persistent emphasis. At first, such improvements tend to relate to increased velocity-length of the first two jumps; later to a more evenly balanced distribution among the three jumps.

THE RUN. As with the long jump, maximal controllable velocity prior to the first-jump takeoff is the most necessary of all factors in achieving success in the triple jump. As with the long jump, such velocity requires a run-length of at least 120 feet with acceleration

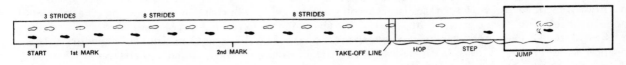

Fig. 10.2 A Triple-Jump Approach as drawn by Geoffrey Dyson, Track and Field Series, Chart #8, Canadian Olympic Training Plan. Use of checkmarks should follow that for the long jump in Chapter 8.

---

[1]J. Jeremin, V. Popov and V. Kreer, Soviet Union, "The Triple Jump Rhythm," published in Jess Jarver, THE JUMPS, Los Altos: Tafnews Press, 1981, pp. 126-128.

throughout, especially during the last 10-12 strides. For beginners this must be modified to perhaps 100 feet to help them concentrate on mechanics of the three jumps.

Velocity at the board is critical. But even a low-angled jump requires a slight relaxation and lowering of the center of gravity as the man prepares to jump, a small decrease in forward lean, and a lesser emphasis on acceleration. Stride mechanics do modify slightly; the last two strides are somewhat longer. But all of this is a natural effect of preparing for a high-velocity, low-angled takeoff, and needs no coaching.

THE TAKEOFF. The word "takeoff" is used broadly as including the range of action before and after taking off from the board or ground. It includes the "gather" (minimized in modern triple jumping but still significant), the slight lowering of the center of gravity, the low forward thrust of the arms (two or one), the inclination of the torso, and the upthrust of the lead knee.

Today's emphasis is on low-angled velocity, one in which the thrust of all forces is forward with just enough angular impulse to ensure maximal distance on the total distance, without over-emphasis on any one phase. Only on the last jump is there an effort to balance velocity with height in the jump, though again with distance as the single objective.

A 1982 study by Roger Milburn of two groups of triple jumpers of different levels of skill attempted to define factors that characterize skilled performance. It was concluded that "what distinguished the more highly skilled group of athletes was their ability to generate vertical (higher-angled--KD) velocity...with the least loss of forward speed." [1]

Fig.10.3. The takeoff--a forceful low-angled thrust forward.

The Double-Arm Action. In the early 1950s, the Swedish high jumpers introduced a two-arm upward drive during the gather and takeoff of the high jump. This was adopted and improved by the Russian high jumpers and their coach Dyatchkov, not so much because of the upward impulse given by the arms, as of the lowering of the center of gravity (the pelvis) aided by the swing of the extended arms as they came forward-downward.

Such a double-arm swing in the triple jump was first used by the Russian jumpers in the 1960s when they dominated the event, was soon copied by others, and today has general acceptance (Fig. 10.1). Of the three United States triple jumpers at the 1984 Olympics, Joyner and Conley used a forceful two-arm thrust during all three takeoffs; Banks used a one-arm style.

Simonyi[2] states that this double-arm action is of significant force value, not only in its own forward-upward drive but also in its effects on body flexion in increasing the time-distance in which leg force can be applied. As the rather extended arms come forward and downward (Fig. 10.4) they tend to keep the center of gravity low just an instant longer. The hips now ride flatly forward, thus delaying for an instant the upward extension of the legs and torso.

---

[1]Peter D. Milburn, "Triple Jump," *Track & Field Quarterly Review*, Vol. 82, #4, 1982, pp.16-18.

[2]Gabor Simonyi, op. cit., 1377.

Fig. 10.4. The technique of the two-arm thrust in the triple jump. Its values relate to keeping the pelvis low during the "settle," and to the upthrust at takeoff. It can be used on one, two, or all three of the jumps.

Torso Angle. Throughout the three phases of the run and three jumps, the slight forward lean of the body tends to remain stable, in keeping with today's emphasis on continuous velocity. Only as an increased effort to gain height occurs does this angle increase.

High Knee Thrust. As takeoff occurs in each of the three jumps, the knee of the lead leg thrusts forward and high, thighs at the horizontal, lower leg relaxed and pulled close to the upper leg as shown in Figs. 10.1 and 10.2. This difficult, "static" position of flexion of

Fig. 10.5. Willie Banks (1983 -- 56' 10") demonstrates the wide leg split and high knee of the lead leg so essential to an extended reach for distance on each jump.

the knee and at the hip joint is of utmost importance. Actually, it has a double movement. At takeoff, a wide split of the legs occurs; this decreases, then widens again as the jumper reaches out for increased distance and a forceful, reactive landing. Depth jumping is the most effective training exercise to develop this ability.

YIELDING-REACTIVE POWER. Expert triple jumpers are able to minimize the shock of a heel-ball-toe landing on each phase. The USSR coach, Verhoshanski[1], wrote of this action some 20 years ago as a "yielding-reactive force" for which he and others developed the training program of plyometrics and depth jumping.

Dyson (1978, 161) explains the problem in mechanical terms,

---

[1]Yuri Verhoshanski, "Jumping Downward as a Means of Training Jumpers," Moscow, USSR, *Legkaha Athletika*, September 1967. Translated by Dr. Michael Yessis, California State College.

The acute angle at which he lands tends severely to check his forward movement. To reduce this resistance, the expert triple jumper moves his leading foot back quickly immediately before landing to reduce its forward speed in relation to the ground, lands with the greatest practicable angle between his leading foreleg and the ground, and then "gives" at the hip, knee and ankle joints. Yet he must stress none of these movements at a cost, subsequently, to essential velocity of the action.

This "yield-reactive" power concept is also described as a stretch-reflex that includes eccentric-concentric contractions. "Yielding" stretches the powerful extensor muscles, much as occurs in a trampoline when stretched by body loading. This is the eccentric phase. Research has shown that such stretching of muscles induces a much more powerful concentric reaction than if no pre-stretching occurs. Further, and here muscles differ from trampoline action, the greater the velocity at which muscles are stretched, the greater the velocity-power of reflex action.

Therefore, to ensure full developmental effects, every valid training program must include such plyometrics as depth jumps with boxes, hurdles, with or without weights, with special emphasis on the velocity factor of power (strength x velocity), as is described on pages 181, 196-198.

Fig. 10.6. The First Phase (The Hop). Emphasis is on maintaining full velocity of the run so as to ensure maximal distances in the second and third phases. Forward lean of the torso-head is similar to that while sprinting. The drive for height is secondary, enough to pro-duce a flight angle of 15 to 18 degrees. (Draw line through centers of gravity of figures 1-3). In both the hop and step, the thigh gains a horizontal "position" that is often described as "waiting for the ground to come up" (figures 4-5). This produces a forward reach (figures 5-6), a slight yielding (flexion) of the knee-hip (figure 1 of the Step), a heel-first touchdown, and a powerfully reactive heel-ball-toe takeoff that thrusts the center of gravity forward-up into the second phase (the step).

This jumper uses a single-arm drive during the first two phases with a double-arm drive into and during phase three. Contrast this arm action with those shown in Figures 10.1 and 10.4.

Fig. 10.7 The Second Phase (The Step). All three theories as to the relative lengths of the three phases of the triple jump agree that this second phase should comprise 30 percent of the total distance: for 50-foot jumpers, 15 feet; for 45-foot jumpers, 13 feet six inches. An inevitable loss of forward velocity tends to lower slightly the flight angle. The forward angle of the torso (55-60 degrees), as shown in figure 2 must be maintained during the flight (figures 3-4).

Note the double-arm action in figures 5-6 that lowers the center of gravity (the yielding phase), the left leg extension and heel placement (figure 6)--all part of the forceful foot-leg drive forward-up during the final jump takeoff.

Fig. 10.8. The Third Phase (The Jump). The dynamics of this final jump phase are basically the same as for the long jump. Usually it is made from the same foot used "naturally" for long jumping, and so is consistent with all actions in the air that occur "naturally" in the latter. Note the important yield-reaction of hip-knee-foot shown in figure 6 of phase two and figures 1-2 of this jump-phase. This jumper is using a "hand" technique in the air, in contrast to the "hitch-kick" technique of Fig. 10.1, preferred by most theorists and expert jumpers today.

The up-over-and-down, double-arm thrust is here performed in excellent style. It drives the torso forward, aids the lowered head action between the knees, and helps the buttocks clear the sand just beyond the break made by the heels.

Willie Banks./Photo by Victor Sailer.

HOW TO BEGIN

The decision as to "How to Begin" depends so much upon the individual jumper--his age, ability, jumping experience, and related power training. The overall approach for all field events has been outlined in Chapter 16; that for the long jump, especially as related to power training, in Chapter 9. Those sections should be reviewed.

However, the following procedures for the triple jump should be considered for beginning jumpers:

1. <u>The Standing Triple Jump</u>. Practice three quick jumps from a standing start (either two feet on the line or the takeoff foot forward) R-R-L-jump and also L-L-R-jump. Encourage resilient ball-heel-toe landings and takeoffs. Emphasize forward velocity rather than height, and so develop a feeling for one unified effort with its three phases.

As boys develop proficiency, coach increasing height in the three phases--low on the first; higher on the second; highest on the third. A low first-phase jump is achieved by spending less time in the air, by not lowering the center of weight, by focussing the eyes and face forward and not up, and by continuing the natural swing of the arms. A highest third-phase jump is achieved by lowering the body weight through greater flexion of the takeoff leg (hip, knee, ankle) and rebounding explosively by lifting the eyes-head-chest upward, by dropping both arms down-back then driving them forward-up in rhythm with the lead leg. (Note--this two-arm drive is disruptive and, though mentioned, should not be emphasized.)

2. <u>Getting Checkmarks and Practicing the Run</u>. With our emphasis on the whole action and the crucial importance of the run, we feel it should be practiced early in the learning process. Follow the same methods as for the long jump, using a minimum hop-step-jump off the board. Take a positive approach; coach simple learnings before they become problems.

3. <u>Develop Related Power</u>. Follow instructions provided in Chapter 6, "Training for Field Event Power," with special attention to the section on plyometrics. Also use the exercises in this Chapter on related power and plyometrics.

4. <u>Target Distances and Ratios</u>. On a basis of 75 percent of best long jump, using the formula (3 x 75% of best long jump), establish a target distance for the triple jump. For example, 3 x .75 of 20 feet equals 45 feet. Then, using the recommended ratios of 35-30-35 shown in Table 10.3, place "target" marks in the board-to-pit area. Such efforts will lead to consistency, confidence and greater distances. Try to feel an evenly timed rhythm between jumps.

TABLE 10.3
TARGET DISTANCES AND RATIOS

Best Long Jump	Hop	Step	Jump	Total TJ Distance
18	14'2"	12'2"	14'2"	40'6"
19	15'0"	12'9"	15'0"	42'9"
20	15'9"	13'6"	15'9"	45'0"
21	16'6"	14'3"	16'6"	47'3"
22	17'4"	14'10"	17'4"	49'6"
23	18'1"	15'7"	18'1"	51'9"
24	18'10"	16'4"	18'10"	54'
25	19'7"	17'0"	19'7"	56'2"

5. <u>Competition for Fun</u>. Triple jump exercises are inherently competitive and fun. Any combination of hops, with or without steps or jumps, can be measured for distance. Heinz Rieger[1] reports a scoring system, commonly used in East Germany, which trains for greater speed-power in jumping. By scoring on a combined basis of distance covered and time required (Example--46-49 feet in 3.8 seconds), the jumper learns the crucial importance of forward velocity while still covering long distances. An approach run of seven rapidly accelerated strides is used. Note that each improvement in distance is achieved in a lesser time, which illustrates the importance of the velocity factor in gaining greater distance.

[1]Heinz Rieger, "Training for Triple Jumpers," (translated by Gerry Weichert), *Track Technique*, September 1964, 538.

TABLE 10.4

CLASSIFICATION OF SPEED-POWER IN JUMPING

Action	Class III	Class II	Class I	Master
Steps (RLRLR)	46'-49' (3.8s)	49'-59' (3.5s)	55'-62' (3.0s)	65'-75' (2.8s)
Hop-step-hop-jump	46'-49' (3.8s)	49'-59' (3.5s)	55'-62' (3.0s)	65'-75' (2.8s)
Hop (RRRRR or LLLLL)	43'-46' (4.0s)	46'-52' (3.8s)	52'-59' (3.3s)	65'-69' (2.8s)

POWER EXERCISES FOR THE TRIPLE JUMP

To emphasize the crucial importance of training for the long jump, we deliberately placed some 25 exercises for the long and triple jumps in that chapter. In addition to these more basic power exercises, the following should be of use in overloading the specific movements of the triple jump or in teaching its various skills:

1. Exercises to Teach Double-Arm Action.

Note: The above figures excerpted from the USSR publication, *Light Athletics*, 1965 #9.

Note in the above figures that the arms are flexed as they swing back-and-up. The time in which they do this when triple jumping is very limited, so that speed of movement is essential. Second, as they drive forcefully forward, they extend downward, thus aiding a flat forward movement of the pelvis, maintaining torso and leg flexion an instant longer, and so increasing the time-distance through which power is applied in the upward jump. This is especially crucial on the third, and to a lesser degree, the second jump.

Fig.10.9a & b. Two examples of depth jumping to develop the "yielding-reactive" power as described by Verhoshanski. Note in item 3 his distinction between different-height tables in developing either power or strength. This difference is significant.

196

2. <u>Exercises to Overload Jumping Power.</u>

Fig. 10.10. 2 x RRL, and 2 x LLR, then increase distances between boxes by 12"; repeat.

Fig. 10.11. 2 x RRL and 2 x LLR, then increase distances between boxes by 12"; repeat.

Fig. 10.12. 2 x RRL and 2 X LLR. From take-off to box 15'; then increase distance by 12".

Fig. 10.13. 2 x RRL, and 2xLLR. Absorb landing shock with knee and rebound to top of next box, then over a string for distance.

These illustrations show boxes or stands of very sturdy construction. They should be specially built with wide bases to prevent overturning and possible injury. Height--18 to 24 inches since this produces the proper knee flexion on the rise, as well as an overload on the descent.

Only four exercises are shown. However, a little imagination will produce any number of jump combinations. Rule of thumb--think of a specific movement in triple jumping and overload it. Use a weighted vest or belt when needed for overloading.

3. <u>Exercises to Develop Yielding-Reactive Power.</u> Verhoshanski[1] emphasizes the need for special exercises to develop the power of flexion-extension. It's more than resiliency, the ability to rebound, that is required. The ability to "give" just enough at the right instant, to yield to compression is equally important. To develop this two-phase power, Verhoshanski concluded after research that what he calls depth jumps are most effective. For example, he suggests jumping from a height of either .75 or 1.10 meters (30 or 43 inches), landing on both legs and bounding upward quickly and powerfully. Use of a cloth on a string above the head will motivate higher and higher jumps. To prevent injury and further relaxation, the landing should be made on "a thick elastic or felt cover (a gymnastics mat is not sufficient) resiliently on the forward portion of the foot. The angle of flexion in the knee joint should be optimal so as to soften the landing in the 'yield' phase and achieve a maximum reaction upward."

Verhoshanski warns that such depth jumping needs no overloading such as weighted vests. This would increase strength but slow down the speed of reaction and rebound. He also confirms the exact heights of the depth jumps. At 30 inches, maximum velocity in the yielding-reactive power formula (power = strength x velocity) is achieved; at 43 inches, maximum strength. Increasing table height changes the mechanics of the action so that the exercises tend to lose their meaning for jumping. (We must add that individual differences require a certain flexibility in Verhoshanski's figures.)

---

[1]Yuri Verhoshanski, *op. cit.*

The jumps are done in sets (2 x 10 reps at 30") plus (2 x 10 reps at 43"). Between sets do light running and relaxation exercises. Fatigue effects of these jumps are usually long-lasting. He suggests they be discontinued 10-14 days before important competition.

To prevent knee injury, gradual build-up exercises should precede depth jumping. Beginning jumpers should avoid depth jumps altogether until power training has developed the necessary toughness of tissues. In general, depth jumps are effective only when combined with other power exercises of a reactive-explosive nature.

THE ORGANIZATION OF PRACTICE

The triple jump is a most challenging contest in skill, in resilience in bounding high, not once but three times, in related power in the sense of both strength and velocity of movement, in endurance, and certainly in sprinting speed.

That's an impressive list of necessary qualities. It follows that the organization of a year-round and well-planned training program must be similarly impressive. Perhaps two of the 12 months can be allowed for recreation and renewal, but these should include vigorous activity along with the fun and rest. Of the ten that remain, organization will, as always, depend on the individual, his opportunities for practice, and his competitive schedule.

The overall plan for organization should follow that suggested in Chapter 16, and supplemented in Chapter 6 which review the problems of training for power. More specifically, however, we urge an early emphasis on learning the skill of triple jumping. It's fun to triple jump, even on the first attempt; there's none of the embarrassment or doubt that is inherent in the shot put, when weakness is exposed, or in the pole vault, when skill is lacking. Such early exposure build motivation for the long weeks of power training that lie ahead.

Table 10.5

YEAR-ROUND BASIC TRAINING PROGRAM[1]
(Victor Saneyev, USSR, 3-time Olympic Champion)

Month	10	11	12	1	2	3	4	5	6	7	8	9
Period-ization	PREPARATION PERIOD (I)				COMPETITION PERIOD (I)		PREPARATION PERIOD (II)		COMPETITION PERIOD (II)			TRANSITION PERIOD
Mon.	-Sprinting -Strength				-Rest		Technique -Sprinting		-Rest			-Ball game
Tue.	-Jump power				-Technique -Sprinting		-Jump power -Strength		-Technique -Sprinting			-Rest
Wed.	-Ball game (Active rest)				-Rest		-Rest		-Jump power -Strength			-Ball game
Thu.	-Rest				-Sprinting -Strength		-Rest		-Rest			-Rest
Fri.	-Sprinting -Strength				-Rest		-Technique -Sprinting		-Rest			-Ball game
Sat.	-Jump power -Ball game				-Warm ups		-Jump power -Strength		-Warm-ups			-Ball game
Sun.	-Rest				-Competition		-Rest		-Competition			-Rest

[1] Yukito Muraki, "A Study of Selected Prominent Jumpers," *Track & Field Quarterly Review*, Vol. 78 #2, Summer 1978, p. 38.

To achieve such a high level of related condition requires a well-planned year-round program. A rough idea of what is needed can be gained from Table 10.5, an outline of the year-round training of Victor Saneyev, three-time Olympic champion with a PR of 57'2 3/4". At first glance, it does not seem a hardship. Note that during the second competitive period (June-July) he works hard only two days per week, and that during his toughest training period, he takes three days of rest. However, Saneyev was 31 when this was written, had years of training behind him, and so may not have needed the usual tough Russian work schedule.

In terms of workload, that of Vitold Kreyer (USSR, 54'1¼", 1956 & 1960 Olympic bronze medallist) was much heavier, certainly more than the average college jumper could sustain.[1] Note that this is a seven-day schedule during the month of January. The Russian competitive indoor season begins in February.

January 9. Morning. General exercises; jumping up and down on both feet 100 times, from foot to foot 100 times, on one foot 20 times.

Afternoon. In stadium. (1) Five exercises with the shot, repeated four times, (2) 500 m. running and general exercises, (3) 2 × 60 m. with short but fast strides, (4) 2 × 60 m. relaxed running with fast long strides, (5) 2 × 100 m. acceleration runs, (6) 4 × 75 m. of "hops," (7) 3 × 100 m. of "steps," (8) 260 m. with many successive jumps, (9) 50 m. "frog" jumping, (10) 260 m. of "steps," including 97 "steps," and finally (11) 500 m. running. (We can assume that these 500 m. are jogging runs—J. K. D.)

January 10. Rest in morning; General exercises in afternoon.

January 11. Morning. General exercises; jumping on two feet 100 times; jumping from foot to foot 100 times; jumping on one foot 20 times.

Afternoon. (1) 500 m. running; general exercises, (2) 6 × 50 m. acceleration runs, (3) standing hop, step, and jumping eight times (about 8.50 m.), (4) hop, step, and jumping on two feet four times, (5) hop, step, and jumping on one foot three times, (6) 400 m. covered with many successive jumps, (7) 2 × 10 sit ups, (8) strength exercises with a 32 kg. dumbbell, 2 × 10 repetitions, (9) hop, step, and jumping two times, (10) throwing 32 kg. dumbbells 3 × 4 series, (11) swinging dumbbell on the right side (like hammer throwing) eight times, (12) 400 m. covered with many successive jumps, (13) 250 m. running, (14) hop, step, and jumping with dumbbells in hands, two series.

January 12. Morning. General exercises; jumping on two feet 100 times; jumping on one foot 20 times; jumping from foot to foot 100 times.

Afternoon: (1) 1000 m. run, general exercises, (2) weight lifting with barbell. Two arm snatch, 60 kg., 2 × 3 repetitions. 65 kg. twice; 60 kg. once; 70 kg. two times; clean and jerk, 75 kg., three times, (3) jumps with 32 kg. dumbbell, 50 and then 40 times, (4) ten sit ups, (5) standing shot put, eight times, (6) throwing the shot overhead, backwards, six times.

January 13. Rest.

January 14. Morning: General exercises; jumping on two feet 100 times; jumping from foot to foot 100 times.

Afternoon. In stadium. (1) 1000 m. run. General exercises; 50 m. running with short but fast strides, (2) 3 × 100 m. acceleration runs, (3) six starts, (4) 5 × 80 m. performing "hops," (5) 5 × 100 m. performing "steps," (6) 200 m. covered with many successive jumps, (7) 800 m. run.

January 15. Morning: (1) General exercises, (2) weight lifting with barbells, two hand press using 60 kg. once; snatch, 60 kg. four times; snatch 65 kg. twice, 70 kg. once; clean and jerk, 70 kg. once, 75 kg. once, (3) jumps with 32 kg. dumbbell, 43 times and then 41 times, (4) throwing the dumbbell like the hammer 12 times, (5) shot putting nine times, (6) "sit ups," ten times and then eight times, (7) exercises for back muscles with dumbbells, ten times.

Though we might argue the relatedness of some of this training, we cannot question the zeal with which Kreyer prepared for competition.

---

[1]Ruddi Toomsalu, "Training and Technique of Soviet Triple Jumpers," *Track Technique*, Sept. 1960, 26.

PEAKING FOR THE TRIPLE JUMP

In his article, "Triple Jump Peaking," John Gillespie,[1] then coach at South Eugene High School, Oregon, gives a down-to-earth summary of year-round training:

This article will discuss methods of peaking triple jumpers for the big meets at the end of the season. It is possible to peak a triple jumper in five separate areas: speed, strength, spring, technique and mental attitude.

Speed is essential to a good triple jump. Basically, the faster the approach, the longer the jump. But speed kills. The beginner, or the veteran at the start of the season, should either run at less than full speed or else use a shorter approach. The jumper is not able to handle too much speed early in the year or his form will deteriorate. Besides, less speed means less force so it is easier to concentrate on jumping and correct technique. In this way the athlete has to improve by jumping farther in each phase rather than allowing improvement because of an increase in momentum. At the end of the season the athlete will be able to handle more speed and will naturally jump farther because of the longer, faster approach.

Sprinting speed itself can also be peaked by gradually shortening the length of interval runs and increasing the tempo. In this way the jumper should actually be faster at the end of the season.

Strength training is vital to triple jumping. The basic weight training principle for peaking is in three parts, plus. In the beginning we lift three days a week for endurance, or lots of repetitions with a medium weight in all exercises. During the preseason and early season we lift three days a week for strength by using only 1-4 repetitions with maximum poundage. Finally, during the middle of the season we change to lifting two days a week and then one day in the late season for quickness. A submaximum weight is used, increasing the repetitions slightly, but trying for quickness or speed. The plus in weight lifting peaking is achieved through rest or no lifting at all during the week of the final meet of the year.

Spring is really a combination of speed and strength. In jumping, however, we shall refer to bounce. One of the easiest ways of peaking a jumper is to control the amount of bounce in his legs. Some of the principles of "bounce control" are: (1) no days off before dual meets but give the athlete a day off prior to a big meet; (2) jumping takes a great deal of bounce out of the legs, so gradually give the jumper more rest between the last jumping practice day and the meet. You can usually jump the day prior to a meet in early season; run only on the day before a meet in the middle of the season, allow two days jumping rest near the end and have no jumping at all the week of the last meet of the season. Also, (3) depth jumping is great for the triple jumper, but it requires a lot of rest. Therefore, gradually give more rest so that there is no depth jumping during the last two weeks of the season.

The principle of technique peaking is to gradually teach the event concentrating on the fundamentals early and saving some ideas that can be picked up easily until later in the season. Stress an upright body position (no forward lean) and heel-ball-toe foot placement during the early season. This will not increase the length of a jump, only put the athlete in position to jump farther. Since most jumpers do not have a long enough step, work on that phase at the start of the season. Then work on the jump at the end. Finally, during the late season emphasize hopping as far as possible while staying low. (A good way of learning this is to practice hopping into the long jump pit with a towel at a specific distance, and gradually increase that distance.) Not only will the athlete hop farther, but he will create more momentum for the rest of the jump. Another late season clue is to have the jumper think about pushing off with the toes during each phase. This helps to create more forward speed.

The positive mental attitude, however, is the most important point in peaking. The athlete needs to pick a goal and believe that he can attain it. We use a system of goal and date pace with our jumpers (similar to distance running) to keep track of how well they are proceeding toward their goal. Auxiliary goals (in related events) give the athlete motivation for training and show progress toward the big goal. The quarter-mile and the long jump are good indicators for the triple jump. Note that it is quarter-mile speed plus the stamina which a triple jumper needs to survive the pounding of six jumps in a meet. Keep reminding the athlete that you are peaking him for the big meet and explain how bounce control and strength peaking work. The more he believes in the system the better it will work.

---

[1] John Gillespie, "Triple Jump Peaking," *Track Technique*, #73, Fall, 1978, p. 2313.

Parry O'Brien — "Mr. Shot Put."

Michael Carter, 1984 Olympic silver medalist and high school 12-lb. shot record holder./Photo by Bill Leung, Jr.

Chapter 11
THE SHOT PUT

The men who contrived the shot put must have sprung from a long line of Puritan gaolers who believed the stocks which secured both ankles and wrists were the best punishment for the sins of mankind. Of course, the event itself is no promoter of free movement. The shot has no wires by which to create far-flying centrifugal force, no flat surface to aid aerodynamics, no cord grip or long axis to assist being airborne. The shot is inherently a stodgy iron sphere which prefers above all else staying where it's at.

Any man with half a heart would have given such an event all possible freedom. But one of the first rules these masochists set up was that all its action must be restricted to a meager 7-foot circle. Not even a genius could be creative in devising better techniques within such a penned-in area. Oh, a few men have tried; some men just have to try. They tried throwing the ball. But a new rule decreed it must be put or pushed, not thrown. They tried holding the ball at arm's length at the back of the circle, then pulled it forward to its proper position on the neck as they glided toward the toeboard. But another restraining order stated that at no time could the shot drop behind or below the shoulder. As if the impounding circle were not enough, someone conceived a puny 40-degree enclosure within which the shot must land if the effort was to be legal. And then, to curb any remaining shreds of revolt, a new rule shackled the putter even after the shot had landed, and required him to leave the circle from its back half. In sheer unreasoning desperation, the human animal tried to free himself by rotating along a 580-degree arc (the discus style). One claimed a distance several feet beyond that ever achieved by the straight-line method. But problems of falling and fouling led more to failure and frustration than to fame and fortune.

Surely the joys of training for such an event will help compensate for its restrictions in competition. Surely--well, maybe; that is, if squatting down with a 600-pound barbell is your idea of enjoyment. Or perhaps you prefer the sibilant sound of dead-lifting 700 pounds. They are both listed as pre-requisites to even half-respectable shotputting.

If such masochistic exercises excite your interest, you'll be glad to read that the 1984 WR holder (Udo Beyer, EG, 72'10¼") felt that, along with six consecutive No. 1 world rankings and three world records, "the most important thing for me is that I gain so much pleasure from my sport." It is written that, after watching East German shotputters, Hoffman, Rothenberg and Gies sweep the European Championships, Beyer was "so excited he ran to his coach in his small hometown of Eisenhuttenstadt and said excitedly, 'I want to be a shotputter too!'" Little Udo was only 14 years of age! He already had a coach![1]

This tongue-in-cheek introduction may suggest that I have little respect and even less liking for the shot. On the contrary, when I had the honor of coaching WR holder Charles Fonville (1948 - 58'¼") we both worked at it and ate it and slept it with utmost enthusiasm. Humans are peculiar animals some of the--<u>most</u> of the time!

---

[1]"Udo Beyer: King of the Shot," *Track & Field News*, September 1982, p. 16.

TABLE 11.1
OUTSTANDING PERFORMANCES IN THE SHOT PUT

OLYMPIC CHAMPIONS -- MEN

Date	Record		Name	Affiliation	Age	Hgt.	Wgt.
1956	60'11''	18.57	Parry O'Brien	USA	24	6'3½''	230
1960	64'6½''	19.68	Bill Nieder	USA	26	6'3''	240
1964	66'8½''	20.33	Dallas Long	USA	24	6'4''	260
1968	67'4½''	20.54	Randy Matson	USA	23	6'6½''	265
1972	69'6''	21.18	Wladyslaw Komar	Poland	32	6'5¼''	276
1976	69'3/4''	21.05	Udo Beyer	E. Germany	20	6'5''	249
1980	70' ½''		V. Kiselyov	USSR	23	6'2½''	265
1984	69'9''	21.16	Alessandro Andrei	Italy	25	6'3½''	260

OLYMPIC CHAMPIONS -- WOMEN

Date	Record		Name	Affiliation
1972	69'0'' WR	21.03	N. Chizova	USSR
1976	69'5'' OR	21.16	I. Khristova	Bul
1980	73'6½''OR	22.41	Ilona Slupianek	E. Germany
1984	67'2¼''		Claudia Losch	W. Germany

WORLD RECORDS -- MEN

Date	Record		Name	Affiliation	Age	Hgt.	Wgt.
1948	58' ¼''	17.75	Charles Fonville	USA	20	6'2''	195
1950	58'10½''	17.96	James Fuchs	USA	22	6'1½''	224
1956	63'2''	19.26	Parry O'Brien	USA	24	6'3½''	230
1960	64'6½''	19.69	Dallas Long	USA	19	6'4''	265
1960	65'10''	20.07	William Nieder	USA	26	6'3''	240
1964	67'10''	20.68	Dallas Long	USA	23	6'4''	260
1967	71'5½''	21.80	Randy Matson	USA	22	6'6½''	265
1973	71'7''	21.84	Al Feuerbach	USA	25	6'4½''	262
1976	71'8½''	21.88	Terry Albritton	Hawaii	21	6'4½''	260
1976	72'2¼''	22.00	A. Barishnikov	USSR	28	6'6¼''	180
1983	72'10 3/4''	22.22	Udo Beyer	E. Germany	28	6'5''	288

WORLD RECORDS -- WOMEN

Date	Record		Name	Affiliation
1980	73'8''	22.45	Ilona Slupianek	E. Germany

OUTSTANDING PERFORMANCES -- UNITED STATES

1982	72'3''	22.02	Dave Laut (AW)	US record--men
1979	62'7 3/4''	19.09	Maren Seidler (Stars)	US record--women

HIGH SCHOOL--BOYS (12#)

1979	82'3½''	24.80	Mike Carter	Jefferson, Dallas	67'9'' (16#)
1984	74'10½''	22.60	Arnold Campbell	Air, BC, LA	
1984	68'4¼''	20.76	Brian Blutreich	CV, MV, CA	

HIGH SCHOOL -- GIRLS

1983	53'7 3/4''	16.35	Natalie Kaaiawahia	Fullerton, CA
1983	50'1½''	15.29	Carla Garrett	Santa Fe, NM
1983	48'2½''	14.70	Donna Williams	Ri, Ft. M., FL

A BRIEF HISTORY OF TECHNIQUE AND PERFORMANCE.

It is difficult to state in simple fashion what has been in fact a very haphazard, trial-and-error development, with few ways of knowing what had worked in the past or what methods others were trying. At the risk of confusing as much as clarifying, the development of shot-putting can be described as having five periods: (1) that of wide-open experimentation, (2) that of an exclusive emphasis on technique, (3) that of a 90 percent emphasis on weightlifting, (4) that of a science-related balance among strength, related power, velocity, mechanics of technique, and (5) that of slow-growing use of the discus technique. Needless to say, the details of how this development occurred never followed such a neat pattern.

SIZE PLUS TRIAL-ERROR AND LITTLE SUCCESS (1875-1934). Perhaps a personal story will best illustrate the haphazard efforts of this period. At 165#, wet-weight, I was hardly a prospect for the shot, even in the year 1924, but Coach Dave Holmes encouraged me to try. I doubt that he had seen anyone else put the shot but that was no deterrent. One year we stood on the right foot at the back of the circle facing the toeboard, then rotated clockwise as we hopped high, then down as low as we could before pushing the shot to--say, 40 or even 42 feet. Not bad! Considering the Big Ten record was 47 feet. The next year we tried hopping from both feet with no preliminary movements, while at the same time, driving the left arm clockwise to ensure full rotation of the shoulder. The point of this story is that we and everyone else began from point zero--no books or magazines or movies, no clinics, in fact, no big track meets where we could study the champions.

Few coaches and athletes were interested in the event. Naturally, those few tended to dominate it. For example, G. R. Gray, of Toronto and the NYAC, set his first world record in 1887 at 43' 11", raised it in 1893 to 47', and won his last U. S. title in 1902 at 46' 5". Similarly, Denis Horgan of Ireland continued to compete to the age of 43, winning his first English title in 1893, his last in 1912, and setting his world record at 48' 2" in 1900.

The greatest putter of this period was Ralph Rose, of California and the University of Michigan, whose 51 feet in 1909 stood for 19 years as as the world record; some said it would never be broken. His size, though common now, was rare then (6'4"--286#). His style--up and down and around and out. Templeton, Stanford's great weight coach, watched Rose perform many times. He said Rose began by facing about 45 degrees clockwise to the front of the circle. Action started with a high forward kick of the left leg and a high hop across the circle in which his right foot was perhaps six inches off the ground. Upon landing in the center of the circle, a clockwise hitch or rotation of the shoulders tried to ensure greater power. Momentum of the shot across the circle was actually negative as he stopped for the hitchback. Not until 1928 was Rose's record broken--by Emil Herschfeld of Germany (51'9½").

The greatest putter of this so-called "hop" period was Jack Torrance (6'4", 260#) who, in 1934 achieved 57'1", a distance so amazing that the astute Brutus Hamilton used it, in 1935, as a starting base on which to build a table of human-ultimate performances in all events in track and field. Torrance moved across the circle much faster than Rose, but he too depended mainly on size and natural strength.

TECHNIQUE 90% -- OTHER FACTORS 10% -- STRENGTH TRAINING 0% (1920-1948). During these decades, the more basic and sound techniques of shot putting were worked out. We have chosen 1920, quite arbitrarily, as beginning with Bud Houser, USC, who won the Olympic shot in 1924 (50'1") and the Olympic discus in 1924 and 1928. Bud was only 6 feet tall and 180#, so that he had to make up in the sound application of force what he lacked in size.

There were many fine technicians during these years--John Lyman, Stan Anderson, Wilbur Thompson--all of Stanford and Templeton-coached, and Hans Woellke of Germany, the 1936 Olympic winner. All these men devoted at least 90 percent of their energies to the virtues of sound technique. But the all-time Master in terms of body velocity and straight-line explosion across the circle was Charles Fonville, Michigan, who in 1948, though only 195#, 6'2", and 20 years of age, surpassed Torrance's 14-year old record with 58" 3/8". What were Fonville's special assets? First, an amazing degree of explosive power and quickness of muscle action. Second, a perfection of all the aspects of form then approved by the experts, not merely concerning foot-torso-arm positions but also in the velocity he gained across the circle and up into the shot. Even modern putters have not surpassed him in these aspects. Third, an ability to concentrate his energies in competitive performance that to me, his coach, is still beyond understanding.

One other man of this period earns mention because of his style of putting--Jum Fuchs, Yale, 58'10 3/4". Jim was not as fast across the circle as Fonville but at the toeboard he did achieve a backward lean so extreme that the line of his back was almost horizontal. This also is crucial in increasing the time-distance in which power is applied, and points a way to future improvement.

STRENGTH 60%--TECHNIQUE 30%--MENTAL PREPARATION 10% (1952-1967). Both the heading and the dates describe the career of Parry O'Brien, THE Mr. Shot Put of all time. He won two Olympic titles (1952, 1956) plus a silver medal in 1960, numerous world records outdoors and in, and a personal-best put of 65'7¼" in 1966 at the age of 35! We have mentioned his tremendous emphasis on emotional training and preparation for competition, which was as useful in shot development as was his invention of better mechanics. Also his use of a program of weight training in the same year (1951) that he adopted his new technique, so that we are inclined to conclude that greater strength was the secret of his tremendous success even more than was his unique style. In fact, he was once quoted as saying "the shot is 60 percent pure strength; 30 percent technique; 10 percent mental."

The crux of O'Brien's "new" style lay in his eye-focus toward the back of the circle that produced a 20 to 30-degree rotation of the right foot and right shoulder-hip at the back and center of the circle. But it was mainly weight-lifting that lay behind his improvement in performance.

Dallas Long, USC, (height--6'4"; weight--246-270) also belongs within this "O'Brien" period. Dallas was weight-trained in high school and college, but his O'Brien technique was superior even to that of the Master. He held his shoulder position steady and his center of weight low as he came across the circle; all with excellent momentum. His first world record (1960, 64' 6½") came at age 20; his final record (1964, 67' 10") at age 24. Though weight training was primary, he did not neglect practice of sound technique.

THE WEIGHT-LIFTERS (1946-present day). Though the dates of this period dovetail with those of the preceding period, the 95 percent concentration on strength training of its champions warrants a separate listing. Most agree that it began with Otis Chandler, now publisher of the *Los Angeles Times*, who in 1946 started lifting weights and putting the shot along with Norman Nourse at Andover Academy. His improvement in distance was immediate but, as happens so often, it required some four or five years before others could accept his radical and "mad" approach. Not even the perceptive coach Templeton gave approval until Chandler's senior year at Stanford.[1]

But then, again as happens so often, some men swallowed strength whole. They argued that muscle-fiber speed is innate; therefore greater speed of movement can come only through greater strength; that is, through greater basic strength regardless of its direct relatedness. Dave Davis achieved 63' 10½" when Dallas Long's world record was 64' 6½", almost exclusively, he said, on a program of heavy-weight lifting. Gary Gubner (6'2", 270#) did 64' 11", and was an active member of the U. S. international weight-lifting team. One of the better articles on the subject is by Joe Henderson[2],

Today's bigger, more powerful shot putters owe their amazing progress to weight training more than anything else. The world record is 13 feet beyond the 1950 figure, and last year (1968) 50 men topped 60 feet....The means--weightlifting for shotputting success-- almost seems to be an end in itself, lifting for its own sake. They love it..... (The following) statistics apply to the time the athlete was doing his best putting:

	Long	Gubner	Matson	Steinhauer	Woods
Best Put	67'10½"	64'11½"	71'5½"	68'11¼"	72'2 3/4"
Body Weight	270	280	265	270	295
Bench Press	550	500	425	440	480
Squat	500	630	505	600	635
Incline Press	475	440	325	---	445
Dead Lift	---	700	---	715	600

---

[1] As confirmed by a personal letter to me dated 4/14/70.

[2] Joe Henderson, "Weight Training Yields Power," *Track & Field News*, 11 March 1969, 20.

BALANCE AMONG THE ESSENTIALS (1973--). The year, 1973, was selected as that in which Al Feuerbach put it all together with his world-record put of 71'7". But we would be fairer to include Fonville, Long and Matson as important contributors to this balanced approach.

Randy Matson (Texas A & M, 6'7" 265#, 1967 -- 71' 5½") put 3'7½" beyond any previous shot-putter--over 14 feet beyond Jack Torrance's 1934 "human ultimate" of 57'1". Even today, the sources of his great achievement are somewhat of an enigma. He wasn't strong, as compared with the weightlifters of shotputting. He wasn't fast across the circle, as compared with O'Brien or certainly with Fonville. But he did evidence tremendous power at the front half of the circle--power in the sense of velocity x distance x force. His coach, Charlie Thomas, wrote me in October 1965,

On the push off or glide Randy keeps his shoulders well back and shifts only the weight of his left leg and hips; consequently the toes of the right foot leave the ground at the back of the circle last, not the heel as does O'Brien. With Matson's size and power (fast, explosive power) he does not have to rely on speed to the center of the circle from the push off. We think the position in the center of the circle is more important than speed up to it....If you study films on the good boys I think you will find that Matson is much faster than Long and O'Brien from the upward motion in the center of the circle through to the release--here is where he applies speed and power. He is slower than others from the push off to the center.

Fig. 11.1[1] The technique of Randy Matson (1967--71'5½"). His height, 6'7", forced a wide stance (not shown) at the toeboard and so a long time-distance through which to apply force. This led to an East German emphasis, climaxed by Udo Beyer's WR 72'10 3/4", 1984.

Actually, neither Matson nor his coach had much concern for perfecting technique, as compared with Parry O'Brien, Dallas Long and a 50-year tradition in shotputting. Coach Thomas wrote that in his senior year, twice-a-week practices on skill, "if he can immediately throw 64-65-66 feet, he will only throw 5-6-7 times. I think that most coaches will agree that technique reaches a leveling-off period kind of early."

Most coaches do not agree with that statement; mastery of skill in any complex human movement does become increasingly difficult at the upper levels, but only adamant practice (with plenty of intervening active-rest periods) can produce maximal performance.

One part of Matson's success lay in his height (6'7"), his short glide (.83m--2'8 3/4"), his wide stance at the toeboard with weight far back on the right leg, and so, the greater distance through which to accelerate the shot. This method became an important phase of East German shotputting, as evidenced by Briesenick, Gies, and most important, Udo Beyer.

Al Feuerbach. In my judgment, the most perfect achievement of the so-called O'Brien method up to 1984 was by Al Feuerbach (Emporia State, 6'1", 250#) whose style is featured in the section on "Essentials of Technique." Bob Daugherty wrote,[2]

Feuerbach trains almost the same--year-round, doing both weight and technique training. However, perhaps more than any other world-class performer, Feuerbach stresses technique

---

[1]These sequence drawings adapted from Jess Jarver, THE THROWS, Los Altos, CA: Tafnews Press, 1981, p. 69.
[2]Bob Daugherty, "Al Feuerbach," Track Technique, #58, Dec. 1974, p. 1852.

and actual throwing in practice. (He says,) "In this country, there's too much emphasis on strength development and not enough on technique development. You have to train your nervous system to throw with more speed and explosiveness. Throw, throw, throw."

To which I of course add my loudest-possible "Bravo"! Maximum performance in any human skill--shotputting, high jumping, flag-pole sitting or thumb-twiddling--requires balanced, year-round practice over many years; the greater the number of years, the more the emphasis on the perfection of skill, on what only the real Masters comprehend--the artless art of highest-level performance. Feuerbach says "The key is the mind. It takes ingenuity and a type of creativity to utilize all the things that are already known about the nervous system, muscular system, and so forth. You need an intelligent plan of attack."

Udo Beyer. From 1978 to 1984, Udo Beyer (Age 29--1984, 6'4¼", 287#), dominated the shot world performancewise. In 1976 he won the Olympic title with an OR 69' 3/4". According to *Track & Field News*[1] he ranked number one in the world a record six times. In June 1983, at the US vs EG dual meet, Berkeley, CA, he achieved a WR 72'10 3/4". A great career.

Beyer combined all the essentials of performance cited here--great size, longtime heavy-weightlifting, related power and velocity training, excellent mastery of technique that included a German emphasis on a short glide, a wide spread of the feet, and so a greater distance through which to apply force behind the shot. Considering his 287 pounds, Beyer's 11.2 100m, 6'4¼" high jump and 22'5½" long jump are remarkable.

Fig. 11.2. The Whole Action, Discus Style. The expression, "whole action," connotes a unified flow of action that gathers power but delays its explosion of energy until touchdown of the left foot at the toeboard. We have deliberately selected the discus-style technique to balance the major emphasis given in the following pages to the O'Brien method. This style does give greater momentum of the shot at center circle (position 4). But it is very difficult to achieve a maximal, straight-line power drive from positions 4 to 6. A circular drive is suicidal.

THE DISCUS TECHNIQUE IN SHOTPUTTING. Fuller description of the technique and its history will be given later in this chapter. It first received world attention in 1975 when two men (Barishnikov, USSR, WR 72'2¼", and Oldfield, USA, 75'!) used it. (As a professional, Oldfield's performance was not approved.)

At the 1984 Olympic Games, two of the three United States shotputters (Dave Laut, 6'4", 255# and August Wolf, 6'6½", 280#) used the discus technique. The silver medallist, Mike Carter, and the gold medallist, Andrei, Italy, used the glide.

---

[1] "Udo Beyer: King of the Shot," *Track & Field News*, Sept. 1982, p. 36.

ESSENTIALS OF TECHNIQUE

HOW TO HOLD THE SHOT

The shot should rest on the base of the fingers and high on the thumb.

Some, for greater strength, hold the fingers closer together, and the little finger behind the shot; ──────→

Others widen the fingers with the little finger on the side for better control.

Fig. 11.3. At back of circle, eyes and right foot are 180 degrees away from toeboard.

Fig. 11.4. Note shot is high on base of fingers, not in palm of hand.

PUTTING FROM A STAND

The eyes are focussed six to ten feet back of the circle.

Put the shot at 40-45 degrees.

The shot should land just to the right of the center-line of the circle.

Extend the hand and body fully in the direction of the put; do not reverse the feet.

The eyes and head should lift at about 70 degrees to the horizontal. ──────

The left hand is relaxed.

First drive up with the right leg, then rotate up and over the left leg.

Drop down to this low crouch while gathering your power for the explosive put.

The left toe is in line with the right heel. ──────

Fig. 11.5. From a stand, sideview.

Fig. 11.6. - From a stand, front view.

The recommended Feuerbach style plants this right foot parallel with the circle center-line.

PRELIMINARY MOVEMENTS

When using the full circle, shotputters usually make certain preliminary movements that establish the rhythm of action across the circle. Feuerbach's movements are best understood by studying carefully Figure 11.7 (1-3).   But however they are made--with what speed or pattern--they must be repeated until they are always the same, until balance and relaxation and rhythm become automatic.

THE SHIFT

The shift of the weight of the body and the shot across the circle, while holding the head and shoulders back in a powerful putting position, requires great power (strength and speed) in the related leg muscles. Although the right foot is last to leave the back of the circle, it must be pulled very rapidly under the body's center of weight before the upward drive can be started. If this action is slow, the foot will not shift far enough, and both momentum and power will be lost. A pre-season program of related strength exercises, especially of the push-off and pull-under, will aid greatly. During early season, try shifting as far as possible, with a 40-50# sandbag on the left shoulder, or with a heavily-weighted vest.

During the shift, the upper body (shoulders, head, eyes) must be held steady. There is a strong tendency (1) to let the shoulders fall forward across the circle with the hips, (2) to anticipate the forward rotation by swinging the eyes around, and (3) to straighten the body so as to lose the low powerful putting position. Such actions do aid momentum across the circle. But they lose much more in force for the up-over-and-out drive of the shot than they gain in momentum.

Various methods have been used to maintain both body torque and a low shot position. O'Brien fixed his eyes about ten feet directly back of the circle; others held this line of vision but rotated it to the left 15 degrees or so. This helped, but eye focus did not fix body position; torque was decreased; the shoulders did lift.

Fig. 11.7. Al Feuerbach's preliminary movements and glide across the circle. Feuerbach made an effort to keep his center of gravity and the line of his torso low during the glide. He was only 6'1" tall, so took a long glide and a shorter stance at the toeboard than Matson or the East German putters.

Feuerbach took this method a step further by focussing his eyes down vertically at the back of the circle (Figure 11.7 -6). By fixing a point on the rim about 10 degrees clockwise to the right of the centerline, he was much more likely to hold torso torque and angle.

A second method is to concentrate on holding unchanged (1) the position of the shoulders during the shift, or (2) of the right forearm and shot, or (3) of the left arm. Any one of these may be effective and should be tried. It is extremely difficult to flex-extend-flex the right leg in minimal time with no rise in torso angle or lift of the c.g. It is extremely difficult to avoid the gross error of anticipating the upward thrust against the shot during the shift. But it must be done. The power drive at the front of the circle provides some 90 percent of shot distance. Any loss of time-distance through which such power is exerted will more than negate what might be gained from full-circle momentum.

Note in Figure 11.7 that the line of Feuerbach's right foot in the center of the circle is about parallel with the circle diameter. Since his left foot is placed properly and quickly, this right-foot position speeds the explosive drive up-and-out.

210

MOMENTUM ACROSS THE CIRCLE

The final velocity of the shot at the last whip-cracking flick of the fingers starts with the first movement of the body at the back of the circle. Other factors such as balance and position being equal, the greater the acceleration of movement throughout the shift, the greater will be the shot's final velocity. Momentum is started by shifting the weight of the body off its base (the right foot) in the direction of the put. The heavy hips "fall" toward the toe-board (Figure 11.7), aided by the throw or backward kick of the left leg, and later, the powerful extension of the right leg.

Momentum across the circle is gained primarily by shifting the great weight of the hips across the circle. How far should they be shifted? Most shot putters have followed O'Brien's example, have shifted the hips so far and so fast as to cause the right heel to be the last to leave the back of the circle (Figs. 11.8 and 11.9). Explosive extension of the right leg increases momentum.

In general, a coach should avoid a direct emphasis on momentum across the circle. In general, a man will shift naturally at the natural speed of his muscles or in terms of the acquired strength and skill he now possesses. On the other hand, technique affects momentum. No putter could move fast with the methods taught 30 years ago. The method that is taught by which the putter moves across the circle will establish the limits within which the natural speed of the putter can be effective. The less time in the air during the shift, the greater the momentum across the circle.

HIP ROTATION AND STRETCH-REFLEX

Placement of the right foot parallel with the circle center-line (Fig. 11.7) puts the right hip in a relatively open position from which it rotates explosively to the left, producing a counter-rotation of the right shoulder to the right. The torso muscles are now "on stretch"-- at greatest contractile and time-distance power. This is a great advantage of the Feuerbach over the O'Brien style.

Fig. 11.8. The glide by Al Feuerbach is more straight-line than is that of O'Brien. The c.g. remains lower; the angle of the torso to the ground is less; the left foot, low to ground, will land sooner.

Fig. 11.9 -- The shift or glide across the circle. From a photo of O'Brien. In contrast to Matson, O'Brien's try for quickness across the circle caused him to shift his weight so that the heel was last to leave the back of the circle. Note the eye-focus on the spot six feet directly back of the center of the circle.

THE LEFT FOOT AND LEG

Correct placement and action of the left foot is a major factor in the powerful action of up-over-around-and-out. Figure 11.10 indicates the range of probable placement at the toe-board. Position "1" provides a closed stance and a solid brace or fulcrum which would force an upward drive, but rotation would be hindered. The shot would tend to land too far to the right. Action would be slowed and less powerful.

Position "4" would be "in the bucket." Rotation would be free but there could be little bracing action or upward drive of the left leg. The body would rotate and tend to fall off to the left. Usually, the shot would land to the left and at a lesser distance. There could be little follow-through up-and-out behind the shot.

This "in the bucket" position occurs (1) when the left leg is thrown too high or too far to the left across the circle and makes a late landing at the toe-board *after* body rotation has started; (2) when the eyes lose their focus upon the spot at the back of the circle and swing around too soon, rather than up-and-around; and (3) when, in summary, the "J" rotating action occurs too soon.

Position "2" is best of all. The toes of the left foot are about in line with the heel of the right. The left foot can now serve momentarily as a fulcrum, then as an aid to the upward drive. At the same time, it gives the hips full freedom to rotate upward (Figures 11.9 , 11.10).

It must be added that shot putters who attain great momentum across the circle make crucial use of the toe-board. The left foot slams hard against it at exactly the right moment and the right placement. A really great shot-putter should feel without measuring that a circle is one inch too wide.

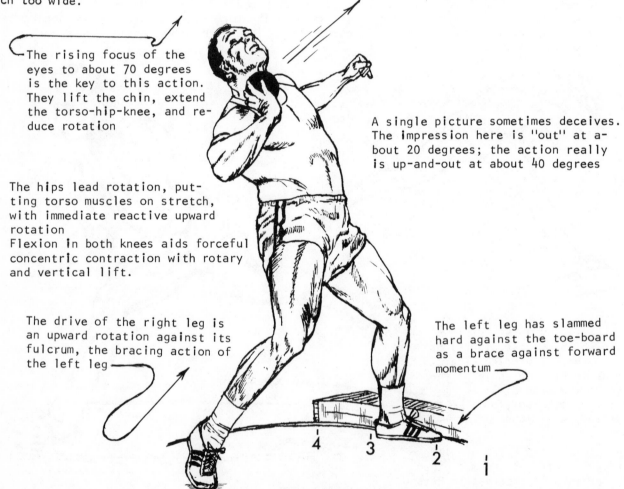

The rising focus of the eyes to about 70 degrees is the key to this action. They lift the chin, extend the torso-hip-knee, and reduce rotation

A single picture sometimes deceives. The impression here is "out" at about 20 degrees; the action really is up-and-out at about 40 degrees

The hips lead rotation, putting torso muscles on stretch, with immediate reactive upward rotation
Flexion in both knees aids forceful concentric contraction with rotary and vertical lift.

The drive of the right leg is an upward rotation against its fulcrum, the bracing action of the left leg

The left leg has slammed hard against the toe-board as a brace against forward momentum

Fig. 11.10. - The power (strength x velocity) drive at about 40 degrees upward. In particular note placement of left foot, the fulcrum that makes right leg power effective.

UP-OVER-AROUND-OUT-EXPLOSIVELY

By far the most powerful (strength x velocity) action of putting the shot lies in the explosive upward extension of the massive back and leg muscles, the same muscles that are strengthened by the squat, dead lift and pull-up and press.

Note that to be able to drive up, one must first be down; to be able to apply force counter-clockwise in rotation, one must first be rotated clockwise. *That is, it is no advantage at all to assume an "O'Brien" position at the back of the circle, if the shoulders are allowed to come up and rotate forward during the shift across the circle.*

THE FOLLOW-THROUGH

The follow-through is just that, no more--an extension of the entire person from toe-tip to finger-tip behind the shot, a continuation of the straight-line drive across the circle and up-out action at the toeboard. In itself, it has no positive effect on the put; but its effect on the mind of the putter as he or she seeks that all-important straight-line drive is critical.

The full follow-through produces a reversal of the feet (See Fig. 11.11) that helps maintain control and prevent fouling.

Fig. 11.11. The follow-through. The in-line position of the left foot forms a fulcrum for power and prevents fouling.

FOULING

Some may ask whether such a follow-through will cause fouling? On the contrary, a proper follow-through will prevent fouling. Since the forces of the body are directly in line with the flight of the shot, an opposite and equal reaction will tend to drive the body back into the circle. Fouling is much more the effect of imbalance and non-alignment than of over-extension of the body.

However, none are perfect, and a tendency to foul haunts many. Preventive steps include: (1) establish non-fouling habits in practice just as in meets, never foul through carelessness; (2) at the moment the shot leaves the fingers, drop the eyes down to the toe-board; (3) lower the center of gravity by flexing and relaxing the right knee and hip; (4) keep the left leg in line with the direction of the put.

CONTROLLED RECKLESSNESS

In shot-putting, as in all great competitive efforts, there must be a degree of recklessness, of setting aside all caution, of ignoring all the rules of proper technique, of blanking-out all doubts and distractions. The great shot-putter, in practice as in competition, so masters the details of technique that he can concentrate completely on the wholeness of the putting action. All his physical-mental-emotional powers are channeled in terms of putting the shot, much as a hypnotized subject centers all his energies on some directed goal, or as a madman performs feats of strength far beyond his normal powers.

Such reckless competitiveness is inborn; some have it more than others; but all have it within a wide range of possible action. An athlete reaches the upper level of his own range by the usual methods of learning, not by some mysterious inner magic, by related practice, every day and in competition.

This book has emphasized the techniques of putting the shot. In general, proper technique aids performance. But no over-serious concern for technique should be allowed to distract from concentration on all-out performance. The distance the shot travels is your real goal, not merely perfection of the mechanics of technique.

THE DISCUS-STYLE SHOT PUT

The discus-style shot put has now been used in competition for a score or more of years, time enough in which to establish its potential and useable value. The first is certain. Using this style, at least two men (Barishnikov and Oldfield) surpassed the then-existing world record. The second--its widespread use, its time required for mastery, its consistency in competitive performance, its actual gain as compared with the O'Brien style--all these are still to be established.

Barishnikov and Oldfield both did better with the discus style than they had ever done with the O'Brien style. But it took some seven years of inconsistent performance before Barishnikov attained his best distance of 72'2¼". No one can know how far he might have put if the same time-effort had been used in mastering the O'Brien style. Oldfield had a similar history.

The point of view taken here is admittedly conservative. The main questions are: To what extent is the discus style easier or more difficult to master? What are the best methods for ensuring balance-control and gradual acceleration during the back half of the circle, without diminishing power during the front half?

HISTORY OF STYLE DEVELOPMENT. Claims for discovery of the discus style come from many sources, including at least four nations. I remember, for example, that in the 1940s, Fred Tootell, world-record hammer thrower and coach at Rhode Island, told me of his own experiments with a hammer-style put of the shot--for fun. He thought it had potential. In the early 1960s, without knowledge of any other similar efforts, Bob Ward, coach at Fullerton College, encouraged various shot putters to try the rotation method. One, John McGrath, after graduation from Occidental, won the 1963 AAU title at 63 feet, using the discus style.

Tom Ecker[1] credits Toni Nett, West German author-coach with articles on the discus style in *Die Lehre Der Leichtathletik*, written in the early 1950s. Similarly, Fred Wilt[2] cites a 1957 article by Kerssenbrock, West Germany, in which he used a photo-sequence of a Czechoslovakian hammer champion, Josef Malek, to illustrate a rotation style. The *Yessis Review of Soviet Sports*[3] credits Coach Viktor Alexeyev with teaching "two young shot putters the circular swing in the 1950s. Certainly he coached Alexander Barishnikov who brought world-wide attention to the style with his 1976 Olympic bronze medal and world record of 72'2¼".

But the most shocking of all shot-put performances, regardless of style, was that by Brian Oldfield of 75 feet even, in a professional meet on May 10, 1975. Oldfield (30, 6'5", 275#) had put the shot, O'Brien style, for some ten years or more,

> I started using the rotation style about three years ago (1972), just playing with it, although I had seen John McGrath use it in the 1968 AAU. I tried it then but just fell down. But I soon discovered that I was getting better throws this way--and I didn't even know what I was doing...Having made a study, I now know what shot putting truly is...This is THE style, although it's taken me three years to learn how to do it.[4]

Having occurred in professional meets, Oldfield's performances have received no official recognition. But a put of 72'6½" was measured and his shot weighed as being 3½ ounces heavy by none other than Bert Nelson of *Track & Field News*. We have no such authentication of the 75-foot effort.

Sequence photos of Oldfield's style indicate a more upright body throughout the turn. In contrast to Barishnikov, his eyes focus horizontally and the line of his back is upright at

---

[1] Tom Ecker, "The Whirl Just Might be Better," *Track & Field News*, June 1975, p. 49.

[2] Fred Wilt, "Oldfield Revolutionizes the Shot," *Scholastic Coach*, Sept., 1975.

[3] Viktor Alexeev, "Alexander Barishnikov in the Shot Put," *Yessis Review of Soviet Sports*, Vol. 8 #2, June 1973.

[4] Brian Oldfield, "As The Whirl Turns," *Track & Field News*, May 1975, p. 49. Note: This was written after his put of 72'6½" but before his 75-foot put on May 10.

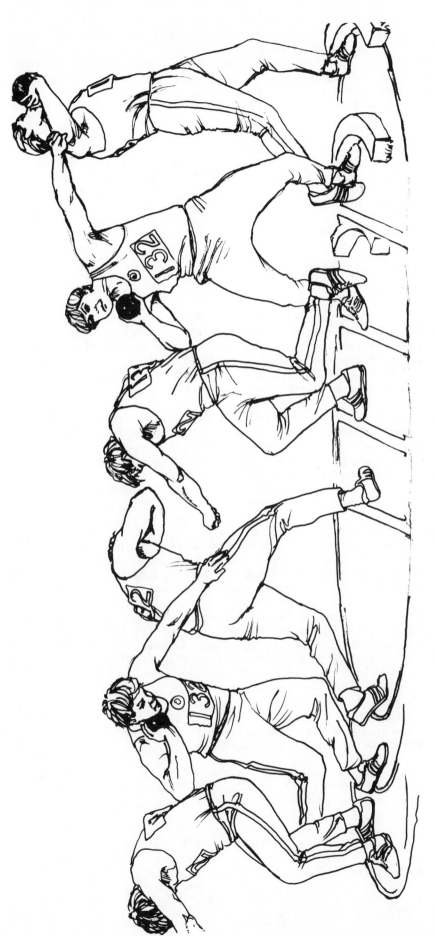

Fig. 11.12--Alexander Barishnikov (USSR, 28, 6'6¼", 280#). Study of a 33-frame sequence-photo (taken 1975) of Barishnikov suggests torso-legs whirling around a head held steady along the circle diameter. At the back of the circle, his eyes focus straight down at his feet. He crouches low until the line of his back is horizontal, knees bent at about 120 degrees. Keeping his eyes down vertically so that his head stays close to the circle diameter that bisects the toeboard, he leads the "whirl" with his right knee. The shift of weight from left foot to right foot at center circle is very rapid; actually the left toe leaves the ground at the instant that the ball of the right foot touches ground. During this action, the right knee angle increases to about 140 degrees and the line of the back lifts to about 60 degrees to the horizontal.

In this photo series, his left leg swings high and wide to an in-the-bucket position to the left of the toeboard. This fault, inherent in the rotation style, must have been corrected in his world-record put of 72'2¼". To help maintain body torque to the right, Barishnikov held his left arm both down and to the right, but such torque was lost through the delayed plant of the left foot.

In summary, though Barishnikov used a discus style, he followed to an amazing degree the basic tenets of O'Brien's straight-line drive within the back half of the circle.

215

about 80 degrees. At the back of the circle, his right leg swings well outside the circle, but his center of weight does move close along the diameter that bisects the toeboard. At the front of the circle, the overall action is the same as that in the O'Brien style. But overall rotation greatly aids the crucial left transverse rotation of the hips that, in reaction, puts the torso muscles on stretch. (This may be the primary advantage of the discus style.) This sequence shows at the toeboard that Oldfield's center of weight is higher than would be that of Feuerbach. On his best puts, he must have started his power drive from a lower position.

Commenting on his 75-foot series, Oldfield[1] said,

On my fourth put I had a foul at about 74 feet, and I just knew I could do better, so on the next put I just tried a nice smooth one with good technique and went 73'1/4". Then I knew if I just tightened my turn and stayed a little lower I could really get a big one--and I did.

In my judgment, to "tighten my turn" means to start the turn slowly, to maintain body torque, to hold the right knee in close, and, in summary, to follow a relatively "straight-line" curve along the circle diameter. "To stay a little lower" puts emphasis on increasing the distance-time through which power can be applied.

GUIDELINES TO THE DISCUS STYLE

1. The discus style requires years of exacting effort before mastery is attained. But it can be argued that to master the O'Brien style as did Feuerbach--to keep low in the glide, to plant the left foot immediately after the right, to minimize the slowing of linear momentum at center-circle--also requires years of exacting effort. Which style is more effective or more easily learned is open to argument--probably more a matter of individual differences and preferences than of biomechanical advantage either way.

2. Parry O'Brien's repeated improvements over prior world records came primarily as an effect of weight training, not of his unique style. However, his style did increase the distance/time and so the power that could be applied behind the shot. Feuerbach's improvements increased such distance/time. The primary objectives of the discus-style shot put are (1) to maintain all the values of the Feuerbach style, and (2) to increase angular momentum just prior to the Feuerbach power drive by utilizing the stretch-reflex contractions of torso muscles that are inherent in the discus-like turn.

3. In both the Feuerbach and the discus style, the great proportion of force--90 percent or more--is derived from the power drive at the toeboard. Dyson[2] estimates that, in the O'Brien style, about seven percent of a 60-foot put is derived from horizontal speed at the end of the glide. It is unlikely that even a most effective discus style could derive more than about ten percent from the turn; that is, a potential gain over the O'Brien style of about three percent.

4. The term, "discus style," is misleading in several ways. It was chosen here over such names as "rotation style" or "whirl style" because the movements of the discus are well known, and so provides a basis for understanding. However, learning the discus style will occur most effectively if we think of it as a modified O'Brien or straight-line style with minimal circular motion of the body's center of weight and the shot. The movements in the back half of the circle should form a flat oval, not a wide leg-hip-shoulder swing, as done by some discus throwers. The latter produces a three-foot sweep of the discus at the start of the turn, away from the vertical axis of the body. In contrast, the length of the "sweep" of the shot in the discus-style is only one foot or so, since the rules require that the shot shall be put from on or near the neck and not behind the line of the shoulders.

It may help the beginner if he makes the shift of weight, first to the left foot, then the right, as two pivoting steps during which the time when both feet are off the ground is

---

[1]"The Unreal Becomes Fact: Oldfield 75 Feet Even," *Track & Field News,* June 1975, p. 23.

[2]Geoffrey Dyson, *THE MECHANICS OF ATHLETICS,* London: University of London Press, Ltd., 7th edition, 1978, p. 212.

minimal. Such champion discus throwers as Bud Houser and Hugh Cannon proved years ago that such steps can be made just as rapidly as in a whirl. In fact, modern discus-thrower, John Powell (1974-227'11") stated,[1] "Basically, I try to develop linear, instead of circular, motion across the circle. I want to develop slow-to-fast across the ring." That's the key to the discus-style shot put.

5. The critical phase of the discus-style lies within the first 60 degrees or so of the pivot at the start--in technique, in relaxation, in balance-control, in gradual acceleration. A sound start tends to ensure a powerful drive at the toeboard. For most men, a fast start disrupts control and slows later action just when it should be accelerating.

6. In both styles, the shot must be put from a position close to the chin and in front of the line of the shoulders. In the discus style, force must be exerted to counter the centrifugal force of the shot during the turn. In the flat-curve style recommended here, centrifugal force is minor so that control and consistency are increased. The greater the radius and velocity of the whirl, the greater the forces that tend to fly away from center, and so, the tendency to lose balance and power.

7. In both the discus and O'Brien styles, effective use of body momentum at center circle can occur only through the hard bracing or fulcrum action of the left leg as it slams against the toeboard. This fulcrum stops the linear momentum of the left leg-hip so that the power-levers can accelerate the upper-body and shot velocity. Shift thinking for a moment to the high jump. Consider how much the modern emphasis on run velocity and the sudden bracing action of the takeoff leg has contributed to increased vertical velocity and heights cleared. In a similar way, both shotput styles achieve greater distances as compared with the zero momentum of putting from a stand. But in the discus style, body movements are rotational so that the left foot tends to swing high and to the left of the toeboard, beyond the right heel ("in the bucket"). Such a position nullifies all the potential benefits of the discus style.

8. Experts in biomechanics, such as Fred Wilt[2], believe that the special value of this style, the value that makes it superior to even Feuerbach's style, lies in an increase in potential power an instant before the power drive at the toeboard. As the right foot pivots at center circle to 90 degrees to the circle diameter, the left foot is braced against forward motion but implements a counterclockwise rotation of the left hip. In reaction, a clockwise rotation of the upper torso-head-shot·produces a stretching of the powerful torso muscles that greatly increases their reactive power. The angular momentum resulting from these stretch-reflex contractions is potentially greater than can be produced using the Feuerbach style.[3]

9. Men with prior experience with the discus may adjust to this discus-style shot put more quickly. But such men will also be handicapped by the need to unlearn certain phases of discus technique. The discus, weighing only 4.4 pounds, is carried "like a sling" well out from the center of body weight. In contrast, in the discus-style shot put, the rules require the shot to be held firmly against the neck, close to the axis line of the body. In the discus throw, the c.g. may sweep with a wide radius; with some throwers, such as Fitch and Silvester, this was quite wide. In the shot, such wide-radius rotation is likely to diminish power more than it gains in momentum.

10. In both the linear and discus styles, the line on which the shot moves, as related to the horizontal, rises from the back to the center of the circle. At what angle? How low should the shot be at center-circle? Individuals vary of course, both in potential and actual performance. Barishnikov sometimes started his turn from a very low position--the line of his torso was horizontal--but then he straightened as he moved across, more than did Feuerbach, for example. When a man puts the shot from a stand for maximal distance, he always squats very low, lower than is ever attained in a full drive across the circle. This suggests that, regardless

---

[1] Jon Hendershott, "Interview with John Powell," *Track & Field News*, Nov. 1974, p. 16.

[2] Fred Wilt, "Oldfield Revolutionizes the Shot," *Scholastic Coach*, September 1975.

[3] Tom Tellez, "Shot Put--Emphasis on Rotation," *Track & Field Quarterly Review*, Vol. 79, #4, Winter 1979, p. 22.

of the style used in getting across, the closer one can get to such a squat from-a-stand, the greater the potential power at the toeboard. This is a very important guideline--for this discus style, as for all others.

11.   Consensus seems to be that the discus style is most easily and effectively learned when physiques are shorter--though powerful--with great quickness and agility. A circle only seven feet wide greatly handicaps the tall and heavily muscled, especially in the upper torso. For these reasons, J. B. Durant[1] argues that "the rotation technique actually favors the female:" (1) a lower center of gravity "should make spinning easier and generate much less centrifugal force requiring resistance," and (2) angular velocity helps to overcome a woman's natural deficiency in power.

DETAILS OF TECHNIQUE--DISCUS STYLE

<u>At the Back of the Circle.</u>   Stand with the feet shoulder-width apart. the left foot just to the left of the circle centerline (Fig. 11.13). If the shot were dropped, it would land 6-8 inches to the right of the centerline. The eyes focus down at about 30 degrees to the horizontal--now and throughout the turn. The line of the head-torso is only slightly forward, to aid relaxation and control.

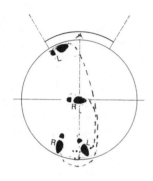

Fig. 11.13--Foot positions and flat-curve movements, discus style.

After a few preliminary short-range swings of the shot-shoulders, squat as low as leg power and the mechanics of the turn make feasible--a slight forward lean, head up. Lead the turn by pivoting on the ball of the left foot. This tends to produce an open left hip and a counteracting torque to the right of the right shoulder-arm-shot. The eye focus should aid torque by following the turn, not by preceding it. (Note: At first, this "unnatural" turn of the eyes-head to the right disorients. But many repetitions will overcome this and ensure a proper tail of the right shoulder.) Consistent with this, the left arm--elbow at about 70 degrees--should be held to the right during the turn.

As weight shifts to the left foot at the back of the circle, the right knee swings close within a short-radius curve (Fig. 11.13). To do this most effectively, individuals should try different positions of the left foot in the preliminary stance. Try moving it a few inches toward the toeboard, or closer to the right foot. This eases the pivot on the left foot. Some argue that it cuts the circle-size when it's already much too small. But since we're starting slowly, not seeking momentum at this phase, whatever works for smoothness and balance is worth trying.

<u>At Center-Circle.</u>   As the right foot swings around the left, it stays close to the ground to ensure a very quick "placement" at center-circle at right angles to the circle diameter (Fig. 11.13). Important: Actually there is no fixed placement of the right foot. The foot "placement" drawn in Fig. 11.13 is that from which the linear power drive begins. To have drawn that foot at a 45 degree angle to the centerline would tend to impede the explosive angular rotation of the hips to the left and countering torque of the shoulders to the right--an essential aspect of the discus style.

As with the right foot, the left swings close--to the ground and to the left leg--along a flat curve to its position hard against the toeboard, toe in line with the right heel, *as quickly as possible after placement of the right foot at center circle.* This is essential if the linear momentum of the shot is to be maintained, then accelerated during the power drive.

<u>Important:</u>   None of this description is intended to establish precisely fixed actions or positions. It all assumes a non-existent average person. All statements are subject to

---

[1]J. B. Durant, "Women and the Spin Shot Technique," *Track Technique*, #70, Dec. 1977, p. 2229.

individual variations in body size, levers, power, mastery of technique--all the factors that make each putter's style unique.

But four basic tenets are sound for everyone: (1) As with the discus throw, the effectiveness of the discus-style shot put relates first to the degree of relaxation-balance-control during the start. Start slowly; accelerate gradually; emphasize a pivot on the left foot, not a sweep of the right; feel weight on that left foot. To suggest two pivoting steps--on the left, then the right--may be extreme but it's close to what is intended. (2) All turning occurs within a short radius; the shot should move quite straight-line (flat curve) along the circle diameter. (3) During the turn, assume a partial squat with the line of the torso-head only slightly forward to aid relaxation-balance-control; this will keep the feet close to the ground throughout. The degree of squat at the start is related to balance-control; that at center circle is of first importance as contributing directly to both velocity and strength in the power drive. (4) The power drive in the discus style is identical to that in the Feuerbach style.

DAVE LAUT--ON LEARNING THE DISCUS STYLE

Dave Laut (1984, 6'4", 255#, PR--72'3") injured his knees in 1979 so that he could no longer use the glide. He found that he could use the spin style without pain, and was amazed he could put over 69 feet after only a few weeks of practice. Jon Hendershott reported an interview with Laut in *Track & Field News*,[1]

But at the TAC meet and Olympic Trials it backfired on me. It was that consistency thing. I started thinking too much about the style, complicating things unnecessarily....but I now felt I didn't have a choice...So I stuck with it, although there were times it was terribly frustrating. But Sam Adams, who has helped me a great deal, said to hang in there, that it would all come together. He told me I could put 72 feet weighing 250 pounds. I thought that sounded impossible. But I did it. I weighed 251 when I threw 72-3. That really opened my eyes....

The hardest thing (to master in the style) is to learn to harness the momentum you gain. I used to come out of the back of the circle very fast, but then missed positions. I have to come out...under control and land in a position where I can feel my legs under me and my hips moving into the put....

The biggest thing for my consistency this year was letting the style flow. (When I set the American record, 72'3", at Koblenz) I think the real big thing was speed and quickness from lack of weightlifting. You still have to train, but focussed toward throwing instead of lifting....

Dang, it was just an amazing feeling....It kind of shocked me, but everything just seemed to come together there.

Two-arm clean and press.

---

[1]Jon Hendershott, "Dave Laut," *Track & Field News*, October 1982, pp. 56-58.

I regret to add that in 1984, five years after first use of the discus technique, Dave Laut could achieve only 68'9 3/4" in taking the bronze at the 1984 Olympics--about what he put one month after first trying the discus style.

RELATED POWER EXERCISES

THE ORGANIZATION OF PRACTICE
Five essentials should guide the organization of practice:

1. The first, the last, and all the in-betweens must be concerned with the many aspects of the problem of motivation. Motivation can never be taken for granted. Without proper motivation, even the most perfect presentation of the mechanics of technique will go down the drain. Whatever goals, whatever rewards or incentives, whatever encouragements or kicks in the gluteus maximus, whatever competitions in practice or in meets, whatever coaching methods will lead to increased personal commitment to shot-putting as a challenging and exciting activity in itself or as a means to achievement or superiority should all be thoughtfully considered and used.

2. An adequate period of strength and power training should precede all shot-putting. To put the shot before one is strong is as unwise from a motivational standpoint as to enter competition with no practice in the skills of putting. Assuming at least ten months of work related to shot putting, the first two or even more should be devoted to strength exercises that are basic for all sports events. Most putters today continue these throughout the year and their entire career, though, to maintain strength, the number of days per week need not exceed one, (Steinhaus, 1963, 323). As the season moves along, power exercises that are more related both in movement and in velocity are introduced. The organization of training sessions in strength and related power is given in Chapters 6 and 16.

3. Maximum performance demands both strength and skill at maximum levels. Once mastered at a high level, skill diminishes rather slowly as compared with strength. But as I look back over some 50 years of great shot putters, only a dozen or so have really mastered the skill of putting. After about 20 years of practicing for greater skill, Parry O'Brien was still trying to improve. Even if skill is but 30 percent of performance, as O'Brien once said (but the validity of which I question seriously), that 30 percent is still crucial. Skill requires regular practice.

4. Sports on an avocational basis provide all too little time in which to perfect the many aspects of training for shot-putting. Careful planning must seek to make the most of this time. Should one work alone or with others? With competition in practice or with concentration on the details of one's own technique? What percentage of time should the coach be present: analyzing, encouraging, criticizing? The answers to these and other such questions will be found in Chapter 16, "A Field-Event Training System," and Appendix A, "The Dynamics of Skill."

5. The organization of any given day's practice of technique will depend on the personal, the seasonal, and the weekly goal for that particular day. The following pattern suggests what might be done during the competitive season:

a. The warm-up (At least 15 minutes). Warm up the legs first by jogging, striding, sprinting. Do calisthenic exercises consistent with shot put action (jumping jack, squat thrust, push-up) as warm-up movements, not as stretching exercises. Such "stretching" will occur more naturally and less dangerously through the full-extensions of strength training and putting the shot.

b. Put the shot from a stand without a reverse (Figure 11..5). From a standing position, the putter simply drops down into a low crouch such as he should attain in the middle of the circle when using the full action. He then drives up-over-and-out into the put, following through in the direction of the put as far as possible but delaying the rotation of the right hip and not reversing the feet. Such an action emphasizes the upward drive of the right leg-hip, the 70-degree upward movement of the eyes which aids the single-plane action of the put, and the crucial value of the left leg, first, as a fulcrum against which the levers of the right leg-hip can brace, and then, when the right foot has left the ground, as a power unit behind the shot. When done properly, the putter will end up high on the toes of the left foot with the right hand-arm, and the eyes-head extending as far as possible, without fouling in the direction of the put.

c. Use lighter-weight shots. In recent years, shotputters, here and especially abroad, have made increased use of lighter-weight shots. Prior to 1980, Terry Albritton (US, 69') reported that "I've also been putting 75 feet with the 14-pound shot just about every time I go out." Palamarchuck, USSR coach of 1980 Olympic champion, Vladimir Kiselyov (70'½").

reported[1] these ratios in the use of different weight shots (precise weights not specified): During the four years, 1977-1980, heavy shots--26%, 16# shots--26%, light shots--48%. During the five months in 1980 prior to the Games:

	March	April	May	June	July
Heavy shots	19%	25%	31.5%	37%	27.5%
16# shots	17%	42%	24.5%	26%	43%
Light shots	54%	43%	44%	37%	29.8%

During the last five microcycles prior to the Games:

	May 25-31	June 1-7	June 8-14	June 15-21	June 22-28
Heavy shots	47%	41%	38%	41%	31%
16# shots	6%	23%	40%	18%	27%
Light shots	47%	36%	22%	41%	42%

An even more extreme use of light implements was made by 1983 World Champion, Edward Sarul, Poland, 70'2¼", who "used only light implements (9#, 11#, 13#) during his entire preparation (1983) until the first competition, where he first used the regulation shot (Distance-- 66'7¼")".[2]

These experiences are of great interest. They are consistent with a gradual shift over the past 30 years in emphasis in power training from an 80% emphasis on strength toward a balance of strength-power-velocity. Once a base of strength is established, attention gradually moves toward quickness of movement.

d. <u>Achieving competitive skill</u>. Emphasize "competitive-skill" as a two-phased unity. A man may learn competitive attitudes but lack the mechanical skill to make them effective. Another may have mastered the mechanical skills of shot-putting but lack the know-how of mobilizing and controlling the tremendous power that is potentially his. Such a man should experience repeated competition in practice, even when working on technique. The degree of competitive climate will be low, of course, as compared with that in a meet, but much can be learned.

During this period, with or without competition, all efforts should be at near-maximum levels. Skill is specific, not only to the mechanics of the action but to its velocity and its degree of effort. To learn mechanics at 3/4th velocity and effort is to learn exactly that. For a 50-foot shotputter, any put under about 48 feet tends to be of lesser value in learning competitive performance.

Gradually increase the number of "good-form" puts that can be taken in one day's practice. Working with at least two shots that are being returned to the circle, a man in condition can profitably take 30 or more puts per hour. Such a man has no time for general conversation or "horsing around." He's working at a challenge that demands his best; he's trying to accomplish more in less time.

Obviously, a practice situation where three or four putters are working at one circle, or with one or two shots will frustrate such a dedicated athlete. To achieve his goals, Parry O'Brien sought out his own practice area where he could concentrate on his work. As he walked out after each shot, he analyzed the last put and practiced mentally the next. This phase of the practice session should be ended when fatigue disrupts skill.

e. <u>Achieving endurance-strength-speed-skill</u>. The emphasis now is upon endurance and developing the ability to make more puts each day. Work in spurts of about ten puts, with short rest periods between. Make as many puts in as short a time as good form will permit. Explode on every put. Shots must be rolled back immediately to the putter. PUT! PUT! PUT! Many worthwhile learnings result: how to concentrate when tired, how to relax when tired, to move with quickness and to do one's best when tired. On many occasions a putter will be amazed that his best puts of the entire practice session will come during this "gut" workout. It gives him a competitive toughness and confidence not achievable by other more comfortable methods.

---

[1] Peter Tschiene, translated from Legkaya Atletika, Moscow, 1980 #7. This valuable information passed to me by George Dunn, Jr., Oak Lawn High School, Oak Lawn, Illinois.
[2] Jean-Paul Baert, "IAAF Shot-Discus Conference," *Track Technique*, Vol. 84, p. 2811.

TRAINING FOR RELATED POWER.

George Dunn, Jr., Oak Lawn High School, Oak Lawn, Illinois, published the following article[1] based on many personal contacts with European coaches and some 28 years of coaching high school weight men--all in all, the most sound presentation on related-power training I have ever read. If followed, his methods will help to restore United States shotputting and, even more important, will develop high school putting toward maximal levels.

I have found that the athletes who follow this program make substantial gains in their strength and power and *never* plateau. Power is the most important aspect of a successful shot putter. If an athlete has great strength, but lacks explosive, ballistic power, his success in the shot put will be limited. The theories of my weight program were gathered from experience and from correspondence with Peter Tschiene of West Germany, and Jimmy Pedemonte of Italy. These men have had contact with the East Germans and Russians, who because of their state systems are able to do substantial research. The only problem has been that when we get this information, it is often outdated or incomplete. Thus we must stumble around experimenting to find the right combinations, systems, sets, weights, repetitions, etc.

Our program is geared so that the athletes will "peak" for the conference, district, and state meets at the end of May. I strive to have these top level throwers in a state of condition where they will be their strongest, most explosive, fastest, technique sound and *fresh*. They must be mentally alert and hungry, not tired, bored and burnt out. During the outdoor season, we have three track meets a week, but to reach the level we want to obtain, we must train "through" these meets, actually training before or after the dual meets on week days.

The program extends over eleven months. August is vacation month from the weight room. Training for each season starts on the first day of school in September. The following is our strength training program for each month. You will note an undulating progression in intensity as the program nears the state meet, and you will note that there is an alternation of the extensive and intensive levels to give variety.

The Vladimir Mihailovic Zaciorskiy table (Table #1) shows the percentages given to the number of repetitions used in each exercise. Research by Zaciorskiy indicates that if one were to do only three reps at 75%, there is no physiological change in the muscle to enhance neuro-muscular stimulation. In other words, one would be wasting one's time.

Table 1.			
1	—	100%	Maximal
2-3	—	95%	Sub-maximal
4	—	90%	
5	—	85%	High
6	—	80%	
7	—	75%	
8	—	70%	
9	—	65%	Medium
10	—	60%	

September (60%)

Back Squats	3 x 10
Front Squats	3 x 10
Supine Single Leg Press	3 x 10
Bench Press	3 x 10
Shoulder Press	3 x 10
Power Cleans	3 x 10
Shot Put Sit-Ups	3 x 10

October (75+80+85+90+95%)

Back Squats	5 x 7+6+5+4+3
Lunges	4 x 6-8 (80-70%)
Incline Bench	5 x 7+6+5+4+3
Bench Press	5 x 7+6+5+4+3
Power Cleans	5 x 7+6+5+4+3
Shot Put Sit-Ups	4 x 10

November (70%)

Back Squats	3 x 8
Front Squats	3 x 8
Supine Single Leg Press	3 x 8
Bench Press	3 x 8
Push Press	3 x 8
Power Cleans/Snatch	3 x 8
Shot Put Sit-Ups	5 x 10

Two-arm clean and jerk (squat).

[1]George Dunn, Jr., "Championship Shot Putting," *TRACK TECHNIQUE ANNUAL,* 1983, pp. 11-15.

December (85%)

Back Squats	4 x 5
Front Squats	4 x 5
Supine Single Leg Press	4 x 5
Bench Press	4 x 5
Incline Bench	4 x 5
Power Cleans/Snatch	4 x 5
Shot Put Sit-Ups	5 x 10

January (75%)

Back Squats	5 x 7
Front Squats	5 x 7
Supine Single Leg Press	5 x 7
Bench Press	5 x 7
Push Press	5 x 7
Power Cleans/Snatch	5 x 7
Shot Put Sit-Ups	5 x 10

February (95%)

Back Squats	5 x 3
Power Cleans	5 x 3
Push Press/Incline Bench	5 x 3
Shot Put Sit-Ups	5 x 10

March (60+75+85+85+75%)

Back Squats	5 x 10+7+5+5+7
Supine Single Leg Press	5 x 10+7+5+5+7
Push Press	5 x 10+7+5+5+7
Incline Bench	5 x 10+7+5+5+7
Power Cleans/Snatch	5 x 10+7+5+5+7
Shot Put Sit-Ups	5 x 10

April (85+90+92+95+100)
(Twice a week only)

Back Squats	5 x 5+4+3+2+1
Supine Single Leg Press	5 x 4 (90%)
Push Press	5 x 5+4+3+2+1
Incline Press	5 x 5+4+3+2+1
Shot Put Sit-Ups	5 x 10

May (85+92+95+100+92%)
(First Week)

Back Squats	5 x 5+3+2+1+3
Incline Bench	5 x 5+3+2+1+3
Power Cleans	5 x 5+3+2+1+3

May (85+92+95+100%)
(Second Week)

Back Squats	4 x 5+3+2+1
Incline Bench	4 x 5+3+2+1
Power Cleans	4 x 5+3+2+1

May (85+92+95%) (Third Week)

Back Squats	3 x 5+3+2
Incline Bench	3 x 5+3+2
Power Cleans	3 x 5+3+2

May (Fourth Week)

Tuesday:	Back Squats	1 x 3 (95%)
	Incline Bench	1 x 3 (95%)
Thursday:	Back Squats	1 x 2 (95%)
	Incline Bench	1 x 2 (95%)

June and July

"Body building time!" When the athletes begin to mature, there are some great gains in muscle definition and bulk. They have a good base to start with, so there is no harm in them going directly into such programs. They use a Pause Rest Routine, Pre-Fatigue, Training to Failure, Forced Reps, Negative Reps, Super Sets, etc. This is not easy, but it fires their imaginations and motivation.

During the month of August, I want them to get away from it all, to get out of the weight room and relax. But, there are always those who are highly motivated and continue lifting even through the month of August.

The "new" trend in Europe and Russia for alternating extensive and intensive workouts is now to use shorter micro-cycles. Peter Tschiene considers my system too "static." He states Kreyer of Russia says the changes must be every one to three weeks. You can change the program I have outlined into shorter micro-cycles. Remember, you want to "shock" the neuromuscular system out of plateauing.

As you look at the program I have outlined, you will note that there is an undulating type of progress that gradually gets more intense. The "old" one or two peak systems do not exist anymore in top level training; it is okay for the youngsters, however.

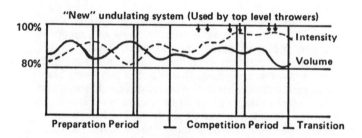

There are several other programs or modifications I insert for two-to-four week blocks. The first of these is the "Auxtonic Training Routine." 50% of maximum, 3 to 5 sets with 10 reps; the barbell is moved 5 seconds up and 5 seconds down. You can use this method for bench press, half squats, press behind the neck, etc. The psychological stress with this method is very high and requires high motivation.

The other method for weight training comes from Bulgaria. The basis of this method is that the throwers carry out sets of special jump exercises along with their great quantity of weight exercises. The training consists of so-called "weight units." One unit equals 2 reps=95%, 4=90%, 6=80%, 8=75%, 10=70%, and 12=60%. After every 5th set of each exercise, the thrower carries out 3 sets of jumps with varying quantities according to the period. After this first week, the following schedule is used:

2nd Week: 3 sets of jumps after the 3rd and 5th set.
3rd Week: 1 set of jumps after each set.
4th Week: Active recovery with tests.
(The basic exercises are the bench press, half or full squat, power cleans and snatch.)

A favorite modification is what Peter Tschiene calls "load leaping." Bondarchuk, the Russian hammer coach, devised the method and calls it the "three week cycle training program." He used it when he, Syedikh, and Tamm swept the hammer in the 1976 Olympics.

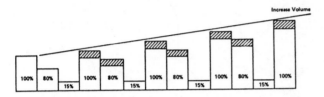

The first week is 100%, which means the volume of work, in tons lifted, number of throws, number of jumps, etc. is at a high intensity. There should be fatigue at the end of the week. An athlete will not be able to go at the same pace the following week, so we lower it to 80%. Again, this means the volume. The intensity is the same as the 100%. Physiologically, the organism is fatigued due to the intensity of the work and so we give him an opportunity to rest during the third week. This 15% volume is in the form of jogging, basketball, volleyball, even some swimming. There are no special exercises. In our case, because the throwing starts late January, we do throw during the rest week.

The fourth week or new cycle is a little bit more in volume than the last cycles 100%. This is an example of a one-to-three week change in the program. What is important after the week of rest is that there is this sudden jolt of hard work that sends a new stimulus to the neuro-muscular system.

Remember, athletes should have a solid background of hard work. I might mention that it does not matter if there is a meet during a 100% week. There can or cannot be meets scheduled during this time. An example of what the weight program might look like:

1st Week (100%) 5 x 3 (95%)   6 x 3 (95%) · 7 x 3 (95%)
2nd Week (80%) 4 x 3 (95%)   5 x 3 (95%) 6 x 3 (95%)
3rd Week (15%)   Active Rest . . . jogging . . . volleyball . . . basketball . . . swimming . . .

Even a pyramid routine can be used, as long as it is in the upper levels: 5 x 5(85) + 4(90) + 3(92) + 2(95) +1 (100).

Another program I will sometimes insert is called the "Mixed or Combined Routine." The examples below are from Peter Tschiene and Jimmy Pedemonte. The program from Peter was used by Bondarchuk to train a couple of 70m hammer throwers at a hammer clinic in Germany. Peter observed them doing this two days in a row. It is a high intensity training program.

Monday
High Pulls 7 x 30 (30kg).
Heavy hammer 1 x 10 (12kg).
Power Cleans 7 x 20.
Dead Lifts 6 x 16.
Throw weight 1 x 10 (20kg).
Squats 4 x 16 (for active recovery).

Tuesday
Weight throws 1 x 15 (20kg).
Dumbbell exercises, like body builders: 4 x 10 (circles in front of body) 3 x 120 (extended side curls).
Heavy hammer 1 x 15.
Dumbbells 5 x 15 (back circles).
Flat Bench 6 x 30.

Examples of Jimmy Pedemonte's Mixed Routines:
(I)
15 throws with light shot (10 lbs).
3 x 3 Push Press (95%).
10 Standing throws with 16lb shot.
3 x 3 Power Cleans (95%).
10 Throws backward with 35lb barbell plate.

(II)
Snatch (6 x 10 + 7 + 5 + 5 + 7 + 10).
20 throws with variable method (2 + 1 + 1).
Power Cleans (4 x 5 + 3 + 2 + 1 + 2 + 3).
20 Throws with variable method (2 + 1 + 1).

JUMP PROGRAM

Peter Tschiene said, "The engine for the long throw apparatus . . . are the legs." We feel so strongly about this, that besides the squats in the strength program, we include a high volume of various kinds of jumps. There has been much positive research by the Russians and East Germans in this regard that all their top level training includes an extensive jump program.

Jumps are necessary for the development of maximum neuro-muscular reflex. There is a high correlation betweel leg *power* and success in the shot put.

There are many different kinds of jumps, from depth jumping to triple jumping drills. What we are trying to do is develop the "stretch reflex" of the legs. Jumps should be performed only two times a week. A few of the jumps we use every Tuesday and Thursday are as follows:
1. Double leg hops over hurdles.
2. Hopping over low, then high hurdles.
3. Double and single leg hops up and down stadium stairs.
4. Progressive squat jumps.
5. Squat jumps over mini-hurdles.
6. Hopping back and forth the length of benches placed end to end.
7. Rapid leg splits or frog kicks.
8. Rapid jump tucks (knees to the chest).
9. Hopping backwards on one leg for 30 to 50m.
10. Bounding.

11. Jump combinations:

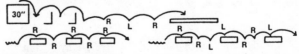

12. Triple jump boxes:

13. Depth jumping: We have 40", 30" and 18" boxes. These are the heights that are recommended by the Russian researchers. The most important aspect which must be stressed by the coach is that when the athlete makes contact with the mat after jumping from the box, he *cannot, must not* allow his legs to "give" before rebounding to the next box. The rebound or "explosive reflex" must be immediate from legs that are in a flexed position.

1. 30" to 18"
2. 18" to 30"
3. 40" to 18"

    Brian and Andrew Miller in *Circle* magazine (1) have come up with a new "twist" in box jumping. Shot putting is a rotational or twisting event. Why not put rotation or twists into the box jump drills? Examples:

(1)

½-twist jump after the jump down-land facing opposite direction.

(2)

½-twist off box so athlete faces box he just jumped from. Immediately bound backward onto box.

(3)

Jump backwards off box. Upon landing, ½-twist and jump onto box.

(1) *Bounding and Depth-Jumping: A Review* by Brian and Andrew Miller, CIRCLE, March 1981.

PENDULUM SHOT AND SHOT BOX

    The pendulum shot and shot box are plyometric drills developed by Sergio Zanon of Italy. These are used to develop the "ballistic reflex" of the throwing arm and power leg of the shot putter.

    For the arm, we use the pendulum shot. It is a 10kg weight, hanging on a suspended *rigid* pole 5 to 6m in length. The weight is pushed out by the left hand (a), the pendulum is stopped by the right hand, placed in the throwing position (b), and followed by a normal shot put action (c) after the amortization phase.

    The Shot Box is an exercise to develop the supporting and driving leg in the shot. This is performed by executing the start of a glide from an elevated position about 30 to 40m high. The athlete lands on level surface to perform a normal delivery.

    Zanon recommends that 5 to 8 repetitions and 6 to 10 sets of the exercises be performed in a training unit with 10 to 15 minutes rest between sets. Each repetition is performed flat out to develop maximum neuro-muscular effort. When the pendulum is used, it is advisable to progress by increasing the pendulum (drop) instead of increasing the weight of resistance. The breaking or amortization phase should be as short as possible and performed without changing the basic pattern of the movement. This allows for maximum strength to be developed in the second part of the acceleration phase.

    All plyometric exercises should be discontinued ten days before important competitions. The intensity must follow an undulatory course, with a frequency of about 20 days.

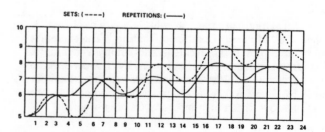

RUNNING PROGRAM

The running program is very simple. I do not believe in endurance running. The bulk of our running consists of sprints from the blocks of no more than 8 to 10m. Each sprint must be all out and as explosive as possible.

Starting in October, during our Tuesday-Thursday workouts, we do a form of agility sprints of 8 to 10m. We start at four sprints and gradually work up to 20 sprints. These, along with all the jumping drills which are increasing in number, result in a very exhausting workout. Example of agility sprints:

1. Squat jump sprints
2. Forward roll sprints
3.
4.
5.

6.
7.
8.
9.
10.

(→→→) Direction of sprint. On whistle, they get up as fast as they can and sprint.

We do other agility/mobility drills such as: forward and backward rolls, cartwheels, flip-flops, round-offs, etc. We will also do 360 degree turn-jumps over a hurdle, 360 degree turn runs, 360 degree-stretch leap followed by a forward roll (do a series of these), etc. Shot putters are usually big men and those who possess good body control have the most success in developing good technique through body awareness.

VARIABLE WEIGHT SHOT PROGRAM

The use of different or variable weight shots is as necessary as changing the weight program. The neuro-muscular system must be shocked if there is to be any progress. The purpose is to develop maximum ballistic power of the arm.

There are three different phases to the variable program. One phase is called "Analytical." Within this phase, there is the power component, where a heavy or overweight shot is used at maximum speed at 80% of maximum during all periods. The other component is speed, using a light weight shot at maximum speed. In the early part of the season, a large volume of this phase is called for. Do not use the analytical speed component during the competitive season.

The second phase of the variable training is called the "Variable Phase." This uses a combination of light, regular and overweight shots. What combination you will use depends upon the athlete's need:

Light	Regular	Overweight	Need
2	1	1	Speed
1	2	1	Regular
1	1	2	Power

The third or "Synthetic Phase" is used in conjunction with the analytical block during the competitive season. Only the twelve pound shot is used during this phase.

One final note concerning preparation for the big meet. There are many misconceptions about what to do during the last few days. What you do as a coach can have some beneficial or disastrous results for that potential champion. One rule to keep in mind is that there is no rest for the champions. Research has shown that a weight lifting session the day before the big meet is essential if the "tonus" of the neuro-muscular system is to "stay up." The Russians have shown that nerve excitation actually rises despite an intense workout the day before competition. It must be a short work program of specialized training for that specific event. □

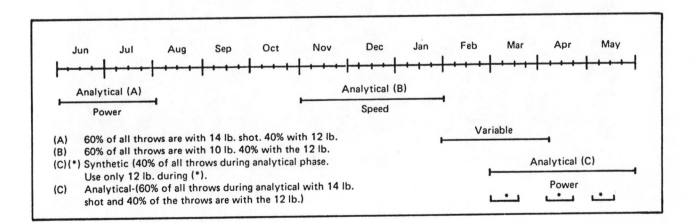

Jun Jul Aug Sep Oct Nov Dec Jan Feb Mar Apr May

Analytical (A)
Power

Analytical (B)
Speed

Variable

Analytical (C)

Power

(A) 60% of all throws are with 14 lb. shot. 40% with 12 lb.
(B) 60% of all throws are with 10 lb. 40% with the 12 lb.
(C)(*) Synthetic (40% of all throws during analytical phase. Use only 12 lb. during (*).
(C) Analytical-(60% of all throws during analytical with 14 lb. shot and 40% of the throws are with the 12 lb.)

Al Oerter, four-time Olympic discus champion./Photo by Don Gosney.

Cahpter 12
THE DISCUS THROW

To throw any disk-like object is inherently fascinating. Its aerodynamic qualities make it sail far beyond what its size and weight would seem to allow. Remember the fun of skipping stones far out over the lake? Who doesn't enjoy seeing and throwing the modern Frisbee? Or reading in science fiction of the Flying Saucers that now threaten the earth?

Apparently this same fascination was felt by the Ancient Greeks, for despite the warnings of their leaders that the inaccuracy of the discus made it useless for war, it continued to be one of the regular competitive events even in Games that occurred during their wars. This was true in their Olympic Games as in such games as marked the death of Patroclus at Troy.

Both the size and weight of the Ancient Greek discus varied greatly. Some weighed nearly 50 pounds; a metal ingot now in the museum at Cagliari weighs almost exactly the same as our modern discus.[1] But we can be quite sure that the method of throw was not basically different from our own. The Greek vases and sculptures tell us very little; a pose, such as that of Myron's "discobolus," that can be held for long intervals was more important to the artist than one more athletically valid. But Homer, among other poets, stated that Epeius "whirled and threw it." The Greeks threw the discus, not for a mere 75 years as have we moderns, but for centuries, and we can be sure their inventive minds would have created much sounder techniques than the stilted throw from a raised platform, without a turn, that was required in the Modern Olympic Games until 1908, and was known as the "Greek style." The style of the Ancients probably varied with the diameter and weight of the implement but one can assume a rather vertically-held discus with an up-and-down hop in the "whirl", not even an Al Oerter could maintain a highheld flat turn with a 25-pound metal ingot whose diameter was as much as 15 inches.

A SUMMARY HISTORY OF THE DEVELOPMENT OF TECHNIQUE AND PERFORMANCE
Modern discus throwing in America began with Robert Garrett's (Princeton) victory at Athens, 1896, despite his never having seen the event prior to his arrival. But the real champion of this earliest period was Martin J. Sheridan, a powerful Irish-American of the New York City Police Department. (Along with such other "whales" as Pat McDonald, Matt McGrath and Pat Ryan, who dominated world weight-throwing for decades.) Sheridan broke the unofficial world record seven times, was national champion four times, Olympic champion three times (1904, 1906, 1908), and made his best distance in his last year, 1911, -- 141'4½" from a tiny 7-foot circle.

The constant difficulty in avoiding fouls when working in this small circle finally produced an increase to 8'2½" (1½ meters) and a new world's record by James H. Duncan in 1912 of 156' 1 3/8". Duncan's style began with the discus high above and behind the head. From there it followed a down, up, down, up and out motion. A single turn of 360 degrees was used, a so-called spin in which at least one foot was on the ground at all times.

---

[1] For a fuller discussion of all these points, see H. A. Harris, GREEK ATHLETES AND ATHLETICS, London: Hutchinson & Co., Ltd., 1964, 85-92.

TABLE 12.1

OUTSTANDING PERFORMANCES -- DISCUS THROW

OLYMPIC CHAMPIONS

Date	Record		Name	Affiliation	Hgt.	Wgt.	Age
1928	155-3	47.32	Bud Houser	USA	6'1"	187	26
1932	162-5	49.48	John Anderson	Cornell	6'3"	215	25
1936	165-7½	50.48	Ken Carpenter	S. Calif.	6'3"	225	22
1948	173-2	52.78	A. Consolini	Italy	6'5"	120	24
1952	180-6½	55.02	Sim Iness	S. Calif.	6'6"	240	26
1956	184-10½	56.36	Al Oerter	Kansas	6'3"	230	20
1960	194-1½	59.18	Al Oerter	USA	6'3"	240	24
1964	200-1½	61.00	Al Oerter	USA	6'3½"	255	28
1968	212-6½	64.78	Al Oerter	USA	6'4"	270	32
1972	211-3½	64.40	Ludvik Danek	Czech.	6'4"	260	35
1976	221-5.4	67.50	Mac Wilkins	USA	6'4"	255	26
1980	218-7	66.62	V. Rashchupkin	USSR			
1984	218-6	66.55	Rolf Danneberg	W. Germany			

WORLD RECORDS OF SPECIAL INTEREST

Date	Record		Name	Affiliation	Hgt.	Wgt.	Age
1946	180-2 3/4	54.97	Robert Fitch	Minnesota	6'2"	220	24
1953	194-6	59.32	Fortune Gordien	Minnesota	6'2"	224	27
1961	198-4½	60.50	E. Piatkowski	Poland	5'11½"	195	25
1963	205-5½	62.66	Al Oerter	USA	6'3½"	245	26
1965	213-11½	65.25	Ludvik Danek	CSR	6'4"	231	28
1968	224-5	68.36	Jay Silvester	USA	6'3"	230	32
1972	224-5	68.45	Ricky Bruch	Sweden	6'6¼"	298	26
1975	226-8	69.13	John Powell	USA	6'2"	235	28
1976	232-6	70.86	Mac Wilkins	USA	6'4"	245	26
1978	233-5	71.16	Wolfgang Schmidt	E. Ger.	6'5½"	243	24
1983	235-9	71.86	Yuriy Dumchev	USSR	6'6"	282	25

OUTSTANDING PERFORMANCES -- HIGH SCHOOL BOYS

4.6# Discus

Date	Record		Name	Affiliation		
1971	201-7	61.49	Jim Howard	Scottsdale, Ariz.		
1976	202-9	61.84	Greg Martin	Pascagoula, Miss.		
1977	205-8	62.72	Dock Luckie	Ft. Pierce, Fla.		
1978	209-6	63.86	Dave Porath	Atwater, Cal.		
1979	207-4	63.23	Clint Johnson	Overland Park, Ks.	177-7	

OUTSTANDING PERFORMANCES -- WOMEN

Date	Record		Name	Affiliation	Hgt.	Wgt.	Age
1972	218-7[1]	66.62	Faina Myelnik	USSR			
1976	226-4[1]	69.00	Evelin Schlaak	E. Germany			
1978	232-0[2]	70.72	Evelin Jahl	E. Germany	6'0"	198	22
1980	177-7[3]	54.16	Leslie Deniz	Gridley, CA			
1980	207-5[4]	63.22	Lorna Griffin	Modesto, CA			
1980	229-6[1]	69.96	Evelin Jahl	E. Germany	6'0"	198	24
1981	221-5[4]	67.48	Meg Ritchie	Arizona			
1983	240-4[2]	73.26	Galina Savinkova	USSR			
1984	214-5[1]		Ria Stalman	Netherlands			

[1]Olympic champion   [2]World record   [3]High School record   [4]American record

Duncan's 1912 record was not broken until 1925--by Glenn Hartranft, Stanford, and a year later, by Bud Houser, USC, and 1924 Olympic Champion. Cromwell states that Houser made two separate steps (left then right) in completing 1½ turns. Houser was 6'1", 197#, and extremely quick. He could step around as fast and as smoothly as later throwers could whirl. To the best of my own knowledge, the last and best "stepper" was Hugh Cannon, Utah, whose no-hop style achieved 174' 10" in winning the national title, 1943.

THE HOP STYLE. The modern hop style began as an upward hop in which both feet were as much as 10 inches off the ground. In 1929, Eric Krenz, Stanford, dropped very low at the back of the circle, hopped high, then down and up for the final pull. But beginning with Phil Fox, Stanford, 1939, an attempt to gain greater momentum in the whirl, kept the feet close to the ground so that it became a horizontal hop around, not up and down. From a technique standpoint, very little improvement has been made over the methods advanced by Fox in his talk, 1941, before the National College Track Coaches Association,

From this initial position, you lead with your back and gain momentum with an off-balance drive. . . . The more centrifugal force you build up, the more you travel in an arc, rather than the old straight-line drive across the diameter of the circle. Instead of eight feet, you have about 10 feet to travel, measuring the line that the feet follow across the circle.

Instead of moving from the right foot straight across, you move almost backwards, letting your back lead the action. In this manner you shift the drive off your right leg onto the left, and around to the right so that you land in the throwing position in the proper place, with the left foot about one foot behind the diameter line, and the right toe on the straight diameter line. To do this you have to cut down somewhat on the drive--if you want to do it right. . . . I don't care how fast you whirl. You have to be in good throwing position before you can make a good throw. That is the important thing, landing in a good throwing position, and at the same time utilizing . . . the centrifugal force principle.

My follow-through action, rather than being a straight line action like Harris (Indiana) and Carpenter (U.S.C.) use, is a whirl, and the natural follow-through is a reverse. . . . When I get a good whirl, the momentum is so fast that, if I don't change my feet, they will wind up on me like a couple of pieces of rope. I have to change my feet into the reverse position. If I get a good whirl, I may turn several times after the reverse. My weight against the discus, in the proper way, will tend to throw me back into the circle, rather than throwing me out.

BODY MOMENTUM IN THE WHIRL. Both the speed of the whirl and the clockwise torque of the torso during the whirl have been improved since Phil Fox. But only one significant modification of his style has been used by an outstanding discus thrower-Bob Fitch (Minnesota, 1946, 180' 2 3/4"), whose style was carried to a somewhat extreme but remarkably successful degree by Fortune Gordien (Minnesota, 1953, 195'6"). Fitch's style (Fig. 12.1) emphasized momentum and centrifugal drive through an extreme leading of the turn with the left shoulder and entire upper body. He permitted the great weight of the upper body to "fall" around the circle, with the feet trying desperately to catch up and only succeeding after the reverse and after the

Fig.12 .1 -- Robert Fitch, Minnesota, 1946 world-record holder - 180' 2 3/4".

right foot had landed at the front of the circle.

All other successful throwers have used the left leg as a firm brace against which they could stop the momentum of the lower body, accelerate momentum in the upper body and especially in the right arm and hand, and still remain in the circle without fouling. Fitch did brace against the left leg, yet he carried his upper body momentum right on over the left foot with no hesitation for bracing, and drove his right shoulder into a very quick reverse which was an actual part of the throw rather than a consequence of it.

Al Oerter. Our interest here is in the evolution of technique more than in the history of performance, but Al Oerter, the only man ever to win four consecutive Olympic titles in a single field event, deserves special mention. Beginning as a 19-year old sophomore at Kansas U., Al not only won but set new Olympic records four times in succession--in 1956 (184' 10½''), in 1960 (194' 1½''), in 1964 (200' 1½'') and in 1968, at the age of 31, threw a personal best (212' 6½'').

The key to this unparalleled performance lay primarily in meticulous preparation--preparation ahead of time for all the difficulties (rain, wind velocity and direction, circle surface, early fouls or mis-throws, long delays between throws) that might arise. For example, major power in the discus is derived from the time-distance in which power is applied at the front of the circle. Body torque is essential. But in high-tension competition, men have a tendency to whirl too fast, to uncoil the hips and put the left foot in the bucket. The bracing function of the left leg is lost and force dissipated. Oerter is reported[1] to have planned ahead to offset this tendency at both Tokyo and Mexico City by deliberately slowing down his whirl and accentuating his body torque. It worked!

One other important contribution of Oerter deserves mention, though it has to do with preparation rather than technique. For 16 years he maintained his world ranking in the discus with a minimum of competition, of practice of technique, and of strength training. That is, each of these factors had been developed during the course of years near to Oerter's potential. His problem became one of organizing his training time and energies within the requirements of his full-time vocation and family (three daughters) responsibilities. There were periods of heavy training, of course, both as to strength and technique, but by and large, he found that "technique and strength can be maintained over prolonged periods of time with minimum effort."[2] Just what "minimum effort" means for most experts has still to be determined.

THE POWER TRAINERS

But modern improvement in distance thrown is primarily the effect of strength and related power training. For example, Jay Silvester threw the discus 181'8'' and the shot, 57'½'' in 1958, without a weight-training program. In 1961, after three years of heavy-weight training, but no noticeable change in technique, he achieved 198'8'' in the discus and 61'5¼'' in the shot, for the greatest double in history. In 1968, he upped this to a world-record 224'5'' and 64'4½''. His weight during this same period increased from 220 to 245. We shall write of his weight-training program under "Practice Organization."

Silvester's technique was marked by several inter-related features. First, his beginning stance was to the left of the centerline of the circle, so that his left foot was on the centerline. This tended to increase the number of degrees in his 1 3/4 turns. Second, as he started, he swung his right foot in a wide arc outside the circumference of the circle. This builds up the angular momentum of his leg so that when it is pulled in closer, body momentum is increased along with torque as between the hips and shoulders (Dyson, 1967, 207). However, this wide swing had a tendency to place the right foot in the front half of the circle, to give him a short throwing stance, a less effective bracing of the left leg (not unlike the technique of Bob Fitch), and all too many "lost" throws and even fouls. When all went well, the result was tremendous--a world record 224'5''. In 1976, at the age of 40, Silvester was still competing and hoping for that Olympic gold, following the example of Ludvik Danek.

Danek was first world-ranked in 1963 at age 26. He set world records in 1964 and 1965 (213' 11½''), took the Olympic silver in 1964, and bronze in 1968, then finally won that much-

---

[1] Jeff Johnson, "Al Oerter: Olympic Spirit," *Track & Field News*, December 1968, 10.

[2] Cordner Nelson, "Three Discus Stalwarts," *Track & Field News*, October 1966, 16.

desired Olympic title in 1972 at age 35. Danek (6'3", 230#) was a fine stylist, with a sound balance between time-distance power during the throw and velocity in the whirl, as well as between power training and technique practice.

In 1972, the irrepressible egoist, Ricky Bruch (Sweden, 6'6½", 298#) finally achieved his first goal by tieing Silvester's 224' 5". Bruch was--well, Ricky Bruch, an individualist of the first order who at 23 was predicting a personal record for 1970 of 73 meters (239'6"), and an ultimate of 80 meters (262').[1] By weight training, and tremendous food intake, he raised his weight from 199# to 298#.

His typical training day includes two periods of about two hours each. In the morning he generally concentrates on running a 1.5 mile course. In the evening he works with weights. His target under both accounts is the same--a steady increase of tempo and weight. "On the way to greatness in throwing," he says, "there are no short cuts. only hard work will pay."

The Master Technicians -- John Powell.

The next world-record holder, John Powell (1975, 226'8") felt that his "small" size (6'2", 235#) forced him to emphasize technique even more than power.[2] Silvester oriented his style toward that of Bob Fitch (Fig. 12.1) and Fortune Gordien, by leading with the torso at the back of the circle and swinging the right leg wide (Figure 12.15). Powell patterned his style along the lines of Oerter and Danek. He agreed with Silvester's tenet of keeping the first circle big and controlled; the second circle small and explosive. But he felt this could be achieved by actively turning the left foot at the back of the circle while swinging the right leg at short radius, holding the upper body and discus arm in full torque, and the left arm fully extended. Whereas Silvester's c.g. shifted toward the circle circumference, Powell's tended to follow the more linear diameter of the circle. By this means, less time would be wasted in the hop-around with both feet off the ground; more time used in driving with the foot on the ground (left foot in the first 360-degree turn; right foot in the second). At the front of the circle, Silvester's left leg, swinging minutely wider and higher, required an instant longer in getting to the ground, and often landed "in the bucket." Powell wanted the right-left feet to land almost simultaneously--snap-snap--so the left leg could be used immediately as the fulcrum for the powerful drive of the right and uncurling of the torso. The difference is not easily seen, one of degree, of 60-40 so to speak, but it is nevertheless significant in its effects. Which style is superior depends on the individual thrower's mastery of his own technique.

Powell's record was short-lived, as we can be sure will be those that follow it. In his first meet of the 1976 season, Mac Wilkins (6'4", 238#) reached 226' 11"; in his second, three consecutive world-record throws of 229' 0", 230' 5" and 232' 6". He was competing with Powell and the wind was perfect--"nice, steady 5-10mph wind drifting in across the right quarter, occasionally gusting to 15-20....Wilkins still wasn't happy with his technique. 'It just isn't there yet,' he ventured, 'I made some terrible mistakes out there today. Not one of my throws was really technically excellent. I've still got that big one inside me.'"[3]

But three years later, 1978, it was Wilkins' friend, Wolfgang Schmidt (E.G., 24, 6-5½, 243#) who held the record. Using excellent technique, great velocity in the turn, and a favorable quartering breeze, he added almost a foot--233-5 (71.16m)--to Wilkins' best mark. In addition to his silver medal at Montreal, Schmidt was selected by *Track & Field News* as number 1 in the world for 1975, 1977 and 1979, and also achieved a best-ever shot-discus double on a single day of 67-2 3/4 and 226-1; all-in-all, one of the greatest throwing talents ever.

Nothing new in technique became evident during the next four years, 1980-84. V. Rashchupkin, USSR, won the Olympics in 1980; Rolf Danneberg, West Germany, in 1984. The 1984 WR 235'9" was by "the mystery man," Yuriy Dumchev, USSR, who went unplaced in meets outside the Soviet Union.

[1]R. L. Quercetani, "Bruch Swedish Discus Talk," *Track & Field News*, November 1969, 6.

[2]"John Powell on the Discus," *TRACK TECHNIQUE*, #59, March 1975, p. 1875.

[3]Garry Hill, "Not Once, Not Twice, But Thrice," *Track & Field News*, May 1976, 18.

ESSENTIALS OF TECHNIQUE

As with all throwing events, the discus throw is a unified flow of action from first movement to last, a flow that starts slowly to ensure balance and control but, as the right-left feet drive at the front of the circle, accelerates explosively through the discus. That statement implies three factors essential to competence in the discus--balance and control, velocity in the spin, and power (strength x velocity) in driving the discus; all of which will improve and take on new meanings with each year of throwing, as well as with each new decade of throwers.

In terms of action, there can be no separation into "wind-up," "spin," left-leg plant," or "reverse." But putting action into words requires such separate names--in a book only, never on the field.

At the back of the circle, a position should be taken that best ensures good balance and control during the spin--shoulders level; eyes looking horizontally. The feet are somewhat spread with, assuming a right-handed thrower, the left foot close to the circle centerline.

Fig. 12.2--Preliminary actions in the discus--the wind-up.

Preliminary movements swing the discus to the left (steadied by the left hand), then full-stretch torque to the right with the discus held flat to the ground, not turned over to avoid dropping it. Keep the center of weight near the centerline, certainly between the feet. That is, though the hips swing, they do not shift left or right. (Figs. 12.2, 12.3.)

Fig. 12.3--The start of the spin.

On starting the spin, keep the weight over the left foot (Fig. 12.3). Lead only slightly with the left shoulder--in the direction of the throw, not in an off-line arc to the left for this diminishes control. In general, think of the center of weight as going straightline across the circle. Both the wind-up and the start of the spin should occur slowly. Mac

Wilkins said, "The better the thrower, the slower the wind-up and entry."[1] Gain velocity in the spin, not by an off-balance "falling," but by an on-balance pushing by the leg-foot muscles (Fig. 12.4).

The right leg should swing wide, knees wide apart (Figs. 12.3, 12.4). This is done by almost all better throwers; John Powell--perhaps because of his relative shortness (6'2")--was one of the few exceptions. Such a wide swing slows the start of the spin, helps maintain torque, and speeds up the final actions of the throw.

With most throwers, the focus of the eyes tends to precede the turning action (Fig. 12.4). But again balance will be better served if the eyes focus straight back at 90 degrees to the body centerline or even to the right of it. This is not a natural method of turning, but it is of great help in maintaining body torque during the spin, and so ensuring greater power as the final pull on the discus is made. Special practice, using the strapped discus (Fig. 12.5) will be helpful.

Fig. 12.4. Mac Wilkins at the start of the spin--knees and feet wide apart; eyes focussed horizontally at 90 degrees.

The less time spent in the air during the spin, the better. That is, while maintaining, then increasing body torque, the quicker the right foot and left foot are on the throwing surface, the more effective the throw. (Fig. 12.7ab). The heel of the right foot does not touch down at any time at center-circle; or, for that matter, at front-circle (Fig. 12.7). To do so, blocks rotation and throws body weight off-balance on the heels--a poor throw.

Final movements of the throw are initiated by the hips, certainly not by the left arm as some novices do (Figs. 12.7, 12.8). A firm, though active, plant of the right foot is vital to this forward hip thrust. However, Mac Wilkins wrote, "The right leg is not as important as the left. When I was throwing 210 feet, I could feel the right foot push; a year later, when throwing 220 feet plus, I was smoother and not stopping and throwing, and the left leg was contributing more in the way of power behind the throw."

This left leg at the front of the circle forms the fulcrum--the brace against which momentum of the legs is stopped suddenly and power is transmitted upward to the shoulder girdle, throwing arm and discus. (Fig. 12.6b). A left foot "in the bucket" has no such bracing effect, allows the line of the body to move to the left away from the line of the throw (Fig. 12.6a).

Fig.12.5. The left foot aids power when in a slightly open stance in line with the throw.

During the final movements of the throw, the bent left arm is held close, though not rigid, so as to block any tendency to open up the shoulders and pull the body off to the left. Both feet remain on the ground as long as possible to increase the time-distance of power application. Do not reverse the feet until the discus has left the hand. In practice, throw sometimes without reversing at all.

[1]Mac Wilkins, "On the Discus," *Track Technique*, Vol. 80, Summer, 1980, p. 2547.

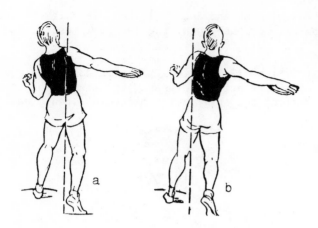

Fig. 12.6. Body inclination at the front of the circle; a, out-of-line to the left, pulling away from the discus; b, in-line, driving with force behind the discus.

A crucial problem--a paradox. The effort to maintain torque during the spin creates tension in certain muscles of the torso. At the same time, the major throwing muscles of the torso must be let go, held loosely, waiting for that powerful acceleration of force during the final effort.

Fig. 12.7. The final forceful movements of the throw. Many of special interest: eyes at horizontal; weight on ball of right foot; left foot in line with right heel and braced hard at front of circle; discus out at about 30 degrees; delayed reverse.

An optimal throwing angle and discus inclination, assuming no wind, has been determined by wind-tunnel research to be 35 degrees for the former and about 25 degrees for the latter. (Fig. 12.8). But winds are seldom lacking, and only studied trial-and-error can determine what works best today in this unique situation. A steady, fairly strong wind counter to the throw is helpful and requires a small reduction of angles.

Fig. 12.8. Flight angle, 35 degrees; discus inclination 25 degrees. Plant left foot quickly, in line, and braced firmly.

HOW TO BEGIN

How to begin is primarily a problem in arousing and maintaining enthusiasm for discus throwing. The first day's practice should be considered a success only if the prospect leaves with a sense of excitement and anticipation: "That discus sure does sail and I think I can throw that thing!" In the case of the shot, we emphasized the crucial importance of developing strength BEFORE trying to put. The difference between 40 to 50 feet for the experienced and strong putter and the 30 to 35 feet of the weak beginner is so noticeable as to embarrass and discourage the latter.

Related strength is important for the discus also, but not to the same degree. Its weight is only 4.6 pounds; even a weak prospect can handle that. Further, the difference between 150 feet and 100 feet is not quite so noticeable. The crucial factor with the discus is skill in throwing and lack of skill is not nearly so embarrassing as an exposure of muscular weakness. The straight-armed, lateral pull of the discus out away from the body is not duplicated by any other sports event. This, added to the unique platter-like shape of the discus, means that a new prospect has had no background of related skill such as is the case with the javelin or, to a lesser extent, the shot.

If then the beginner is to feel encouraged after his first day's practice, it will be because he has gotten the feel of it, more than because of brute strength. Since self-consciousness is so disrupting to skill, a wise coach would do well to emphasize encouragement rather than coaching. Give the man time and freedom to throw it thoughtlessly, or almost so. Let his eyes pick up hints, rather than his ears. If he wishes to turn, let him do so naturally with just a hint of the rhythm involved and the footwork. Let him feel the rhythm of a prolonged "tur-r-n-n-n-n and throw" with almost no concern for the direction the discus goes. You'd better mention that the discus rolls clockwise around the first finger (Figure 12.9), and that it will sail flatter if held out away from the hips (Figure 12.8). But beyond that, let him have fun doing it his way. Out of some 25 to 30 throws he's sure to get one that sails out--and out--and out, and that's all he needs to ensure he'll be back tomorrow.

But now that you've given him a chance to get his bearings, and before he establishes any bad habits, you'll wish to emphasize a few fundamentals. Most coaches try to teach a throw from a stand first, (Figure 12.7), or a simple one step forward and pivot on the right foot into a throwing position. Emphasize at the beginning that power in the discus is derived primarily in terms of centrifugal or "twisting" force, what in mechanics is called body "torque." But neither a throw from a stand or full turn is merely rotational. To the forces of rotation are added a powerful upward extension of the right leg-hip combined with a bracing and extensional force of the left leg. That is, the power of the whirl is enhanced by a very powerful upward-forward drive as the body weight moves from the right foot to the left. Usually, the left foot remains in contact with the ground until the discus leaves the hand, though in expert and high-velocity throwers, this may not be true.

Emphasize that the arm and discus during the forward pull should travel along the same plane as does the discus in its flight; there should be no down-and-up dip. This means the discus will be about six inches below shoulder height when the arm is at right angles to the direction of the throw. Similarly, the eyes should move along this same plane.

As he gets the feel of things, encourage him to twist clockwise as far as he can go: with his hips, his shoulders, his arm and hand, and importantly, with his eyes and head as well. If he can catch a sense of power from such a long time-distance pull on the discus, it'll be of great help to him later. When throwing from a stand, do not reverse the feet. The reverse should be merely a follow-through as a result of the momentum of a full turn. To reverse from a standing throw is to leave the base of force, the ground, too soon.

Keep a close check on his use of the left leg and foot when turning. The habit of bending the left knee too much, then dropping the foot too far to the left "in the bucket," is a tough one to break. Get him to keep the knee in close and the left foot low to the ground.

In summary, how to begin will depend upon each man and his year's time-table for practice. If he's likely to be a discus specialist and has a place and good conditions for throwing throughout the year, he had better concentrate first on developing related power. But keep in mind that, with the discus, the skill to make full use of that power comes slowly. Maximum performance requires both perfected skill and full power.

237

LEARNING TO THROW

Fig. 12.9 -- Grip for greater control of the discus. The discus rotates clockwise around the first finger -- not the second!

Fig.12 .10 - Grip for greater finger strength. Position of finger does not change from that in Fig. 12.5; the second finger moves to it.

Fig.12.11 - Throw from a stand. Beginners make low throws with a flatly angled discus. Start the throw by pulling on the discus, not by rotating the eyes-face, nor the left arm-shoulder. The left foot should be in line with the right heel.

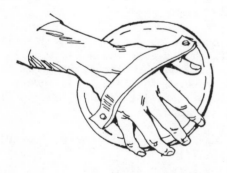

Fig. 12.12 - A strapped discus; not for throwing; for spinning only.

Fig.12.13 - Chin up, back arched, discus almost shoulder height.

Learning to Spin. The expression, "to spin" implies considerable velocity. But for beginners--in fact, for all but the rare expert technicians--the spin should start slowly, emphasizing full control and minimal off-balance. Start by shifting the buttocks to the left and toward center-circle; weight low on the ball of the left foot. For learners, the spin should not start as demonstrated by Mac Wilkins in Fig. 12.15; that is, should not start by throwing the left arm-shoulders-head to the left and across the circle. That method is only for the Masters, and as was demonstrated in the 1984 Olympic Games discus, even the Masters can lose control and distance when tensions are high.

Fig. 12.14. Optimal foot placement in the discus.

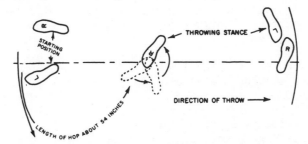

Instead of high velocity in the start, concentrate on a clockwise torque of the torso by holding the eyes horizontal and straight out or even a little to the right. Thereby body weight will shift more gradually, be an instant longer over the left foot. The right leg, knees separated, does swing in a relatively wide arc, but not so far as to shift weight beyond the left foot.

There should be no feeling of the discus pulling the body around. On the contrary the right shoulder, arm, and discus drag well back behind the body. They hang back, relaxed and waiting, waiting as might a sling for throwing stones, or as might the head of a golf club, waiting for the final explosive centrifugal pull around-up-and-out.

Fig. 12.15. Mac Wilkins, 1976 Olympic Champion, 1984 Silver Medallist (1984, age 33, 6'4", 260#). Wilkins sprinted with great velocity into the first turn, right foot wide, discus arm back, loose and away from the hip. This produces torque within the hip-torso that is maintained until the left foot touches down at the front of the circle.

Fig. 12.16. Turning with strapped discus. Eyes focus on discus. By twisting face to right, arm-shoulder are held well back.

Try a strapped discus as shown in Fig. 12.16; try making three or four continuous turns away from the circle, without stopping. Soon you'll get the feel of the discus hanging back behind the arm, waiting for the throw. Yes, you'll get dizzy, but stick to it. (Note: This use of the strapped discus with many continuous turns could be helpful throughout a man's career; each year he would learn to turn faster and with greater control, with no loss of power in the final sling of the discus.) Turn at the speed that seems natural; don't slow down to find balance or better foot position; keep the speed natural, then gradually acquire balance. An expert discus thrower must make thousands of turns. Be patient; have faith; it'll take time, but speed in the turn with balance will come.

COMMON FAULTS IN THE DISCUS

1. To allow awareness of momentum to become a problem before a degree of skill and a good sense of balance have been established. Ignore momentum in the turn during the early learning. Coach a style in which high momentum is inherent, but let action be as slow, or fast, as seems natural to the athlete.

2. To allow the eyes to focus above or below the line of the plane in which the discus is moving. Eye focus determines balance; if upward, the weight will tend to be on the heels; if down, too far forward on the toes. Horizontal focus keeps the body erect, the head up, and the shoulders horizontal.

3. To allow the eyes to lead the turning action. To focus them at right angles to the shoulders will aid good balance. Let the hips lead.

4. To lead with the discus in starting the turn. The discus should be held well back during the turn, until the final explosive pull. Start the turn by leading with the buttocks and by twisting on the left foot.

5. To throw the shoulders around and forward at the start of the turn. This creates too long a hop, makes balance precarious, application of power difficult, and fouling likely. Those champions that have used this method have found its potential excellent but have experienced years of inconsistent throwing.

6. To hop up rather than to hop around. A hop in which both feet are off the ground is an accepted part of discus form today. However, such a hop should lift the body upward as little as possible. The drive off each foot which creates the hop should push the falling body even faster in its whirl.

7. If left foot is in-the-bucket, or if head-shoulders lead the turn, hip rotation to place upper torso muscles on stretch will be ineffective. To be effective, torque must be maintained and left foot placed properly and quickly. It then serves as a brace to aid hip rotation; later, as a power unit in left-leg extension.

8. Explosive acceleration of discus momentum occurs at the instant the left foot touches down. Momentum begins slowly at the back of the circle, accelerates slowly during the turn, then explosively and powerfully. This explosive hip rotation to the left does not cause a counter-rotation that slows discus momentum; only a stretch-reaction that increases power in the upper torso muscles.

Fig.12.17 - The follow-through in the direction of discus flight; chin up, eyes on discus first, then to left.

9. To permit the discus to wobble in flight or to slide off to the right. Usually this fault results from failure to maintain the pressure of the first finger so that the discus rolls around the second finger instead. Sometimes the cause can be found in the tendency to pull the discus around in a low arc close to the hip. This brings the discus up on a concave curve with its front edge too high.

10. To over-emphasize the rotation of the head and eyes during the final action of the throw. If they pull hard to the left, force will be applied to the left rather than up-and-into the throw. In practice try holding the chin and eyes to the right of the circle center-line, or emphasize the pull on the discus rather than the head rotation.

11. To allow the upper torso to control the turning and lead the throwing. Throughout the 1 3/4 turns, Powell emphasized the pivot of the foot on the ground to lead the turning. This pulled the other foot-leg within a shorter radius circle, placed it on the ground sooner, increased upper-body torque throughout, and ensured a firm base at the front of the circle from which to apply maximal power up-and-out at the earliest possible moment.

POSSIBLE IMPROVEMENTS IN DISCUS TECHNIQUE

Considering the rotational technique of the discus, as contrasted with the more restrictive straight-line action of the shot within a 7-foot circle, it is somewhat surprising that no major changes in discus style have occurred in the past 30-40 years, since Phil Fox and Al Fitch.

Improvements related to two aspects of technique seem mechanically sound and feasible: (1) that related to a greater time-distance in which power is applied as the final pull is made, and (2) that related to greater rotational momentum in the early movements.

GREATER POWER + TIME-DISTANCE. Consensus is that the turn adds only about 10 to 20 percent to the distance made with a throw from a stand. The inexpert thrower derives only 10 percent or less, mainly because he uncoils (loses torso torque) as he starts his turn or during it; so that, as the left foot touches down at the front of the circle, the discus--along with the hips--has already moved to position 4 in Fig. 12.18. The hips are now "open;" little additional rotation is possible; whatever stretch-reflex occurs is too late and too little. Loss in both power and time-distance of power application is major.

In contrast, the expert discus thrower maintains torque during the turn. As the left foot lands, the hips rotate explosively to the left. A reaction of the upper torso occurs that places related muscles on stretch, increasing their power. But since torque has been maintained, little or no reactive rotation of the upper torso to the right occurs; the counter-clockwise momentum of the arm-discus is not slowed. Now stretch-reflex increases power; pull on the discus can begin from positions 1 or 2, Fig. 12.18; time-distance of power application is maximal.

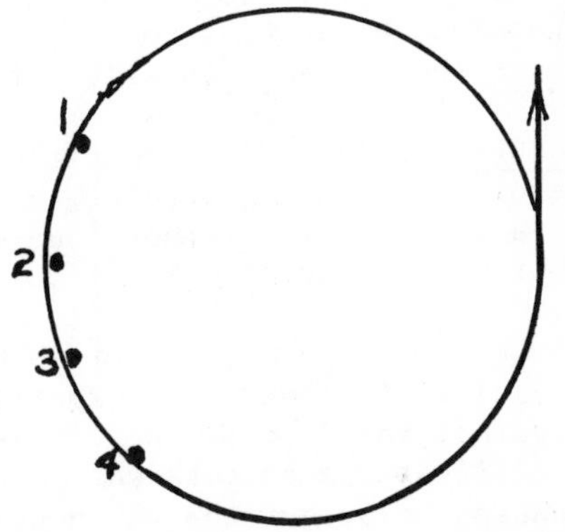

Fig. 12.18--Time-distance of pull on the discus.

To maintain body torque is extremely difficult. Most throwers, inexpert and expert, lead the turn with eyes-head. That's the "natural" way. But this tends to uncoil the upper body; that is, to anticipate counter-clockwise rotation. To prevent this, some throwers hold the left arm in an awkward position clockwise; others hold the torso rigid.

Based on my own long-time experience, the focus of the eyes during the turn is a far more effective way of staying relaxed while maintaining torque. Think of an eye focus at right angles to the line of the shoulders as being at 12 o'clock. During the turn, the eyes should never focus beyond this line; for example to 11 or 10 o'clock. The more they focus behind this line--to one, two, even three o'clock--the greater torque is maintained, and the greater the time-distance through which power can be applied at the front of the circle. Since torque is already maximal, the effect of the explosive hip rotation to the left is to put upper-torso muscles on stretch immediately, with no loss of discus momentum through a counter-rotation of the shoulders to the right.

This eye focus causes one to lose orientation while turning, and balance is precarious. But this is only temporary--hundreds of whirls, in and out of the circle, with multiple rotations, will restore orientation and balance. The time-distance of power application is greatly increased; one feels the weight of the discus and can really work on it to increase momentum. Admitted that body power implemented by clockwise torque affords more than 80 percent of distance; body rotation, less than 20 percent. It still remains that, if torque can be maintained (perhaps by some method as suggested above), any increase in speed of rotation means an increase in distance.

Apparently the most serious modern attempt at two turns was made by Bob Humphreys (USC, 1958-65, 202' 4½"). Lockwood[1] reports that:

The starting position at the back of the circle is identical with that used in the orthodox back-to-the-direction-of-throw technique. Having swung back the discus, the thrower "sets" the left foot in the same way as if he were starting a normal turn, but instead of driving forward off that foot, he continues to pivot on the ball, taking care to keep the body-weight over the feet. He then snatches up the right foot, which has been kept in contact with the ground as long as possible, and lifting the knee close in to the left leg, snaps the right foot down again in the place where it came from, having now reached the backward-facing position again. For a split second the body-weight is taken mainly on the right foot as the left continues to pivot into the "set" position once again. The thrower then drives across the circle from the left foot and completes the throw in the orthodox fashion.

Lockwood goes on to emphasize the importance of a powerful throwing position at the front of the circle, and the greatly decreased time that a faster whirl provides in which that power can be applied. The feet must move with great speed and the upward drive of the right leg against the fulcrum of the left leg must be instantaneous. But this is the same kind of problem faced by those who, over the years, have attempted greater momentum in any of the other field events--javelin, shot, hammer, high jump.

Humphrey's precise method may not be the way, but some such way will be developed, and new records gained. Of course, all such speculation is primarily for the more expert. The beginner should learn to walk before he tries to run.

A DISCUS WIND. The importance of just the right combination of discus angle of projection, angle of inclination (attack), wind velocity, and wind direction has been recognized for 40 years and more. I remember that when Bud Houser made his winning toss at the 1928 Olympics, he shifted his starting position some 90 degrees so as to throw into the wind.

Such knowledge was supported by research. For example, as early as 1932, Taylor[2] presented the results of wind tunnel experiments as to the effects of various wind velocities both with and against the discus. He concluded (1) that any following wind was progressively detrimental, (2) that "up to between 7 and 8 miles an hour, the elevating effects of a head wind is an increasing help, but that when greater than 7 to 8 m/hr. such help decreases steadily up to 14.5 miles per hour, when the head wind becomes a detriment, and (3) that an angle of 35 degrees is optimum for both the initial path of projection and the inclination of the discus.

But some 27 years later, Ganslen[3] found that there are too many variables in discus throwing to state the precise values of any given wind. The velocity with which the discus is thrown, and its angles of projection and inclination will affect wind values. He also made clear that the latter two angles should not be the same. That of projection should be at about 35 degrees; that of discus inclination at 10 to 15 degrees less. The discus is not a flat platter as were those of the Ancient Greeks. Its surface inclines upward toward its center, and this makes a difference in aerodynamic effects. Ganslen also emphasized that a greater angle of projection should not be the result of a flat arc in the forward swing of the discus. Rather it comes from an explosive extension of the right leg and a lift of the right shoulder which has the effect of flattening the discus inclination.[4]

---

[1] Bert Lockwood, "The Double-Turn Throw," *Track Technique*, 35, March 1969, 1110.

[2] James A. Taylor, "Behavior of the Discus in Flight," *ICAAAA Bulletin*, February 27, 1932.

[3] Richard V. Ganslen, "Aerodynamic Forces in Discus Flight," *Scholastic Coach*,

[4] For a much more complete discussion of aerodynamic factors in the discus throw, see Geoffrey Dyson, *The Mechanics of Athletics*, London: University of London Press Ltd., 7th edition. 1978.

DEVELOPMENT OF DISCUS POWER.

Discus power is the goal; power (S^4V^8) to throw the discus farther. Not basic strength, not basic power, not even power-velocity related to the discus. But all these combined and focussed specifically behind the discus provide the means by which the goal can be gained.

The pattern of such progression is described fully in Chapters 6 and 16, a pattern that includes basic strength work, related power exercises, plyometrics, circuit training and, of increasing use in recent years, throws with full spin-and-throw with lighter-than-standard implements. This last to acquire greater velocity in all phases of the throw.

All agree that basic strength is the foundation of discus power. Gary Schwarz[1] of Penn State University, recommends these exercises for discus throwers:

Legs--leg press with universal machine and/or vertical.
Legs-Back-Shoulders--squat clean, clean & jerk, power cleans, high pulls, power snatch, and squat snatch.
Shoulder Girdle--Lateral raises.
Lower back and abdominals--Roman chair sit-ups, incline sit-ups, rotators (twisting).
Legs and Lower Back--Full squats (front and back), split squats, dead lift.
Upper body--triceps and shoulder girdle--Military press (standing--front or back), seated (front or back); bench press--wide and narrow grip, incline press, dumbell press, one or two hands.
Anterior deltoids & pectoral muscles--Dumbell flys--one or two arms, straight or bent arm.
Note: Stretching and flexibility work is of the utmost importance to the discus thrower.

But in 1984, there is at least equal agreement that related power with increasing emphasis on velocity by using lightweight devices is also essential. The discus throw involves rotation of the trunk--the obliques and quadratus lumborum, as well as the leg extensors--the gluteus maximus, quadriceps, gastrocnemius and soleus. All these need development in specifically-related discus movements with gradually reduced resistances and increased velocities. Plyometrics for the legs using boxes but also for the torso-arm using objects of varying weights suspended from the ceiling, that produce a yield-reactive effect are of special value. Also, throws from a stand or with a spin using a lightweight discus or balls (some throwers use plastic highway cones) will have a positive effect on power-velocity (S^1V^9).

RELATED POWER EXERCISES

---

[1]Gary Schwarz, "Fundamentals of Discus Throwing," *Track & Field Quarterly Review*, Vol. 82 #1, 1982, p. 15.

RELATED POWER EXERCISES

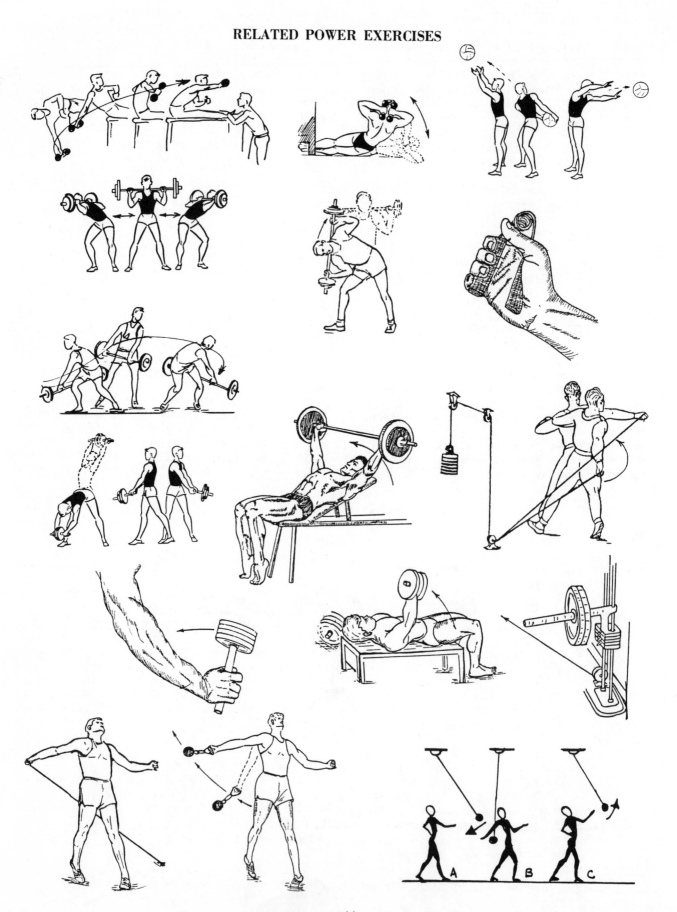

244

THE ORGANIZATION OF PRACTICE

The time, energy, interest, and opportunity for practice of different discus throwers vary so much as to make any one program of work of doubtful value. Many discus throwers are primarily shot putters in interest; some are primarily football players or basketball players with only a few weeks for discus practice. Some have year-round outdoor-indoor facilities; others, no indoor facilities and a late spring.

1. Whatever the length of time available, careful planning of the many aspects of training and competition is essential to good performance. This has always been true. But we never realized the real significance of such planning until the all-out concern for sports as an instrument of government policy was evidenced by the USSR and East Germany. Their term for year-round planning of both training and competition is "periodization";[1] in brief, identification of various periods of time in which gradual changes in emphasis are made in both training and competition. The key to periodization lies in analysis--identifying essentials--and re-synthesis of those essentials into a more complete and better way.

2. A first step in such planning relates to the balance in emphasis on strength-related power, on the one hand, and on technique, on the other. Both are essential to excellent performance. Usually basic-strength training comes first. But in our American school program, the first months of school provide such excellent outdoor weather that first priority should be given to technique. Weather, not theoretical planning, will determine when, and how, and how much the emphasis should be shifted toward strength and power.

3. If working for basic strength and related power, follow the approach provided in Chapters 6 and 16, but also your own preference. Some champions have chosen to do strength training three times a week; discus throwing for technique five or six times. When the two coincide, either may be done first but must be modified in both length and intensity. All champions set aside some days for lifting only; others for throwing only.

4. When throwing the discus, awareness of the specific purpose of each throw is essential. When skill in the full turn-and-throw is no longer a problem, practice throws can be at 80-100 percent effort. That is, throw habitually at maximum distances, but keep awareness on some phase of technique. After each throw, review mentally what was done, how it felt, how it could have been done better. Throw for distance but rarely measure distance in practice. Keep awareness on "how," not on "how far."

To make more throws in less time, someone should return the discus; if working alone, use three or four discuses. More than two throwers working from a single circle upsets concentration, and tends toward frustration more than improvement.

5. Establish your own practice routine; one that meets your needs and with which you feel comfortable. Some men have found this routine of value:

a. After a little running, and related warm-up exercises, start the session by throwing the discus from a stand. A dozen or so throws are enough.

b. Use your major time and energies throwing with a full turn from the circle. Emphasize the over-all balance and rhythm of the whole action. Put off attention to parts of action until a later period. Within the restraints of good form, throw again and again as though you were in competition. Your primary purpose is to develop a set pattern of movement such as you will use in competition. As you step into the circle, do everything the same way every time. Such unvarying routine will develop balance, skill, and especially, confidence, better than any other way.

c. As long as you are throwing well, continue the above method. As you begin to lose your coordination, or whenever judgment suggests, shift to throwing with a full turn from the circle, but with greater attention for the details of good form. Even here, maintain the routine of throwing, but become aware of whatever phase seems to be causing difficulty. Try the various suggestions for overcoming faults in the discus. Throw both with and against the wind. Shift your starting position in the circle so that you can throw into any sector of the landing area.

---

[1]Frank Dick, "Periodization: An Approach to the Training Year," *Track Technique*,#62,Dec. 1975.

d. If much difficulty is had in maintaining balance during the turn, practice with the strapped discus (see Fig. 12.5) in the circle, or take multiple turns on concrete away from the circle. Initiate the turn with the hips; hold the head, shoulders, and discus back during the turn. Relax! The main reason men do not turn with good balance is that they do not practice the turn often enough. A hundred turns in one workout is not enough!

e. Finish the workout by throwing from a stand. Have three or four discuses and a manager to return them. Experiment with wind velocities and directions. Try for high throws by emphasizing the upward drive of the right leg and hip. Try for low throws into a strong wind. Keep the discus off the hip as it is pulled through. Be sure the discus rotates around the first finger, not the second finger, of the discus hand. This ensures greater power and better control.

f. Patience! Persistence! It takes years, even as much as ten years, to make a skilled discus thrower.

Tom Petranoff, American javelin record holder./Photo by Diane Johnson.

England's Tessa Sanderson, 1984 Olympic champion./Photo by Maxine Clarke.

Chapter 13
THE JAVELIN THROW

Because of its uses for both hunting and war, the javelin has been included in the athletic competitions and legends of most peoples. We are all familiar with its use among the Ancient Greeks as a part of the pentathlon in the Olympic Games as well as a single event in other competitions. Also in the German legend of Siegfried, we read that as a precondition for King Gunther's suit for her hand, Queen Brunnhilde included the javelin throw as a trial of strength and skill. King Henry VIII of England is reported to have been adept in its use, and in the 16th century, Rabelais cited its values for the education of the young Gargantua.

A SUMMARY HISTORY OF THE DEVELOPMENT OF TECHNIQUE AND DISTANCE
Vase paintings and various brief hints from writers indicate that the Greeks used a thong in throwing the javelin. According to Harris[1] this thong was probably not fixed to the javelin but fell away from it in flight. His personal experiments indicated that when the thong was wrapped around the javelin to produce spin and steadiness in flight, distances tended to diminish. Many vases show the thrower using his left hand to press the javelin back to keep the thong taut just prior to the throw. However,

> Apart from these details consequent upon the use of the thong, Greek javelin throwing appears to have been identical with our own. The thrower ran up to the mark carrying the javelin on a level with his ear, took it back for the throw, at the same time extending his left arm to help his balance, and threw without overstepping the line. . . .
>
> Of Greek standards of performance with the javelin we know even less than of their achievements in the jump and discus throwing.

Evidence indicates that their javelins were about eight feet long of lightweight elder wood, and since the use of the thong increased distances considerably, Harris concludes that they probably could achieve some 300 feet or more in distance. The Greeks had no devices for accurate measurement.

EARLY AMERICAN TECHNIQUES. Acceptance of the javelin throw as a regular part of the United States track and field program was both late and uncertain. The first National AAU winner was the world-record shot putter, Ralph Rose, at 141 feet--"through brute force and beastly ignorance," as one writer commented. The ICAAAA, started in 1876, did not include the javelin until 1922. The NCAA threw the javelin in its first championships, 1921, but only a relatively few schools included it in their dual-meet program. For alleged reasons of "danger to others" and "lack of throwing areas," the Big Ten Conference discarded the event in 1943 and, up to 1984, has not restored it, even though it is now included in the women's program. At the high school level, only a few states (Oregon, Louisiana, New Jersey, etc.) have fully promoted the javelin.

Quite naturally, such uncertain acceptance was reflected in American javelin techniques--more related to throwing baseballs than to the unique skill of throwing an 8½-foot spear.

---

[1]H. A. Harris, GREEK ATHLETES AND ATHLETICS, London: Hutchinson & Co., Ltd., 1964, 92-97.

TABLE 13.1

OUTSTANDING PERFORMANCES -- JAVELIN THROW

OLYMPIC CHAMPIONS -- MEN

Date	Record		Name	Affiliation	Age	Hgt.	Wgt.
1968	295'7''	90.10	Janis Lusis	USSR	29	6' ½''	196
1972	296'10''	90.48	Klaus Wolfermann	W. Germany	26	5'10''	187
1976	310'4''	94.58	Miklos Nemeth	Hungary	30	6'0''	194
1980	299'2-3/8''	91.29	Dainis Kula	USSR			
1984	284'8''	86.77	Arto Harkonen	Finland	25	6'2¼''	196

OLYMPIC CHAMPIONS -- WOMEN

1968	198'0''	60.36	Angela Nemeth	Hungary			
1972	209'7''	63.88	Ruth Fuchs	E. Germany	26	5'6½''	138
1976	216'4''	65.94	Ruth Fuchs	E. Germany	30	5'6½''	141
1980	224'5''	68.45	Maria Colon	Cuba	22	5'9''	154
1984	228'2''	69.55	Tessa Sanderson	Gr.Britain	28	5'6''	152

WORLD RECORDS -- MEN

1955	268'2½''	81.80	Bud Held	USA	27	6'	170
1959	282'3½''	86.10	Al Cantello	USA	28	5'7½''	163
1964	300'11''	91.78	Terje Pedersen	Norway	22	6'3¼''	181
1969	304'1½''	92.76	Jorma Kinnunen	Finland	28	5'9''	165
1972	307'9''	93.86	Janis Lusis	USSR	33	6' ½''	196
1973	308'8''	94.14	Klaus Wolfermann	W. Germany	27	5'10''	187
1976	310'4''	94.58	Miklos Nemeth	Hungary	30	6'0''	194
1980	317'4''	96.78	Ferenc Paragi	Hungary	26	5'10½''	215
1983	327'2''	99.72	Tom Petranoff	USA	25	6'1½''	216

WORLD RECORDS -- WOMEN

1976	226'9''	69.12	Ruth Fuchs	E. Germany			
1977	227'5''	69.32	Kate Schmidt	USA	24	6'1''	175
1980	229'6''	69.96	Ruth Fuchs	E. Germany	34	5'6½''	158
1983	245'3''	74.76	Tiina Lillak	Finland			

OUTSTANDING PERFORMANCES -- UNITED STATES

1983	322'8''	99.72	Tom Petranoff	SCS, Westwood, CA (US & WR)
1977	227'5''	69.32	Kate Schmidt	PCC, Furth, WG (US record)

HIGH SCHOOL -- BOYS

1971	259'9''	79.18	Russ Francis	Pleasant Hill, Or (HS record)
1984	224'6''	68.50	Timm Rosenbach	Pullman, WA
1984	217'8''	66.20	Jeff Glass	Lancaster, PA

HIGH SCHOOL -- GIRLS

1967	198'8''	60.56	Barbara Friedrich	Manasquan, NJ (HS record)
1983	175'4''	53.51	Michelle Olivera	BD, SB, CA.
1983	163'9''	49.74	Karen Szarkowski	SM, Bis, ND

Until about 1940, most Americans used a "back cross-step," not unlike the natural skip with which every schoolboy tosses a stone or ball. At the 1952 Olympic Games, Helsinki, the United States gained its greatest javelin success, with Cy Young (242' -- Olympic record) and Bill Miller (237'9") taking 1-2, using a variation of the back cross.

The Hop Style. Even as late as 1961, Bill Miller[1] argued that a "hop-shift" method provided a most powerful throwing position without loss of momentum, if practiced perseveringly. No world-level throwers use such a style today, but it is easily learned. When motivations are low, or time for practice limited, acceptable distances can be achieved.

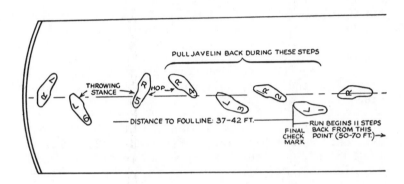

Fig. 13.1 -- Foot pattern in the now little-used American hop style.

In brief, the run-up and checkmarks are similar to those in the Finnish style. During the six-count transition phase, as shown in Fig. 13.1, the 2nd, 3rd, and 4th footsteps turn gradually more clockwise so that the 4th-count right foot is at about 60 degrees to the line of the run. Then, during the hop, that same foot makes a long, fast, and low rotation to a position that is at or beyond 90 degrees to the direction of the run. On this hop, Bill Miller travelled 8'6" and recommended as much as 11 feet during which the foot would be only a few inches off the ground. Note that the right foot (R5), as advocated by Miller, will produce a closed-hip position that delays the explosive hip rotation and stretch reflex so essential to modern throwing. But the foot angle (R5) can be modified to meet modern requirements.

United States Performance. Other than the 1952 Olympic 1-2 placement, United States achievement in the javelin world has been sparse. In 1953 (263'10") and 1955 (268'2½"), Bud Held (California, Berkeley) set two world records by emphasizing rotation of the right hip-shoulder and javelin to the right, while trying to increase time-distance in the pull. In 1959, Al Cantello (5'7½", 163#) of LaSalle College, Phila., threw 282'3½", also a world record. Cantello's forte lay primarily in a gradually accelerated and fast approach, maintained until the last possible moment, suddenly checked by a perfect left leg, then exploded into a full follow-through into the javelin that ended in a full-length sprawl at the toe-board. Cantello had been praised for several years as having a style that made maximum use of his power but had not thrown over 250 feet in 1958. He attributed the improvement to a more perfect use of the new Held javelin but even more to regular strength training which had boosted his weight of 153 by ten important pounds, as well as the power of his throwing muscles. But in early 1959, he also gave much time-energy to perfecting his technique in all phases of the run-gather-throw.

But America's greatest contribution to the event was through the genius of Bud Held and his brother Dick in developing the modern aerodynamic "Held" javelin. This javelin had a surface area that was 27 percent greater than the then-accepted Swedish Olympic model, which improved its "sailing" qualities. During the next five years, world distances increased by an average of about ten feet, as witness, Al Cantello. There were no IAAF rules as to javelin diameters, and controversy, world-wide, was heated. Later, Held made hollow and wider javelins that floated

[1]Bill Miller, "The Transitory Hop Shift Method of Javelin Throwing," *Track Technique*, December 1961, 174.

farther and farther, until precise specifications by the IAAF (1959) settled the issue.

Finnish Javelin Throwing. Finland has dominated Olympic javelin throwing since its inception in 1908. This, despite a population of only about four and one-half million, and a climate more conducive to winter sports such as endurance skiing than to thinly-clad javelin throwing. The Finns make much of the word "sisu," that relates to hardiness, toughness and indomitable will. Add to their climate the long-time threat of the Russian Bear and it's small wonder that "sisu" is so deep an aspect of the Finnish character.

At the 1920 Antwerp Olympics, Finland won the first four places; in 1932, the first three. Of a possible 45 medals (1908-1976), she won 17; of a possible 90 places, 31--leaving less than two-thirds for all the other Olympic nations. A most amazing record.

Perhaps the most important reason for such success lay in Finland's early adoption of a throwing technique that held a potential for maximal distances. At the 1920 Games at Antwerp, American Olympic Coach, Dean Cromwell observed Jonni Myyra use what he called a "front-cross style." But not until 1939 did any American champion (Bob Peoples, 234'2") adopt such a style. In describing the fundamentals of the Finnish front-cross, Cromwell stated, "Speed for the toss comes from the run, with the legs transferring momentum to the upper body, but one of the principle effects...comes from the mighty pull on the left side of the body."[1] Even modern biomechanics would accept such a description.

Perhaps the most famous of all Finnish champions, other than Paavo Nurmi of course, was Mr. Javelin, Matti Jarvinen. He set his first world record (234' 9 3/4") in 1930, age 21; won the 1932 Olympic title (238' 6", OR); set his 8th world record (253'4½") at age 27, and was still throwing over 220' in 1950, age 41.

In 1976, *Track & Field News* rated Finnish throwers 1st, 2nd, and 4th among the top ten in the world; in 1980, Finns were ranked 7-8-9 with 10 men over 275 feet. Prior to the 1984 Olympic Games, following withdrawal of Soviet-bloc countries, the Finns were placed 3-5-6-8 among the leading performers. But in actual competition, it was a Finn, Arto Harkonen, that came through with the winning toss. This, despite a pre-meet analysis by Track & Field News that he had been "having problems with inconsistency in the major meets." Finnish "sisu" had come through again.

Tom Petranoff, USA. On May 15, 1983, Tom Petranoff amazed the entire javelin world--and himself--by a stupendous throw of 327 feet 2 inches, a throw that bettered the world record by almost 10 feet and his personal best of 297 feet 2 inches by 30 feet. How was this possible? Could he ever better the throw, or even approach it again? Petranoff in 1983 was 25 years old, 6'1½", 215#, with only six years of throwing behind him, only two of which involved serious training. His overall records: 1980--280-4, 1981--249-6, 1982--290-0, 1983--327-2, 1984--293-8. He had six subsequent meets of 300 feet or better in 1983, proving his world record throw was no fluke. He reached only second place at Helsinki, however (280-10), and in the meet he most wanted to win, Tom could bring off only a puny 257-3 for 10th place at the Olympics in 1984.

In an October 1983 interview with Jon Hendershott of T&FN, Petranoff admitted "His WR achievement still boggles his mind" but was sure "it wasn't my best by any means."

That's (relaxing) the hardest thing about javelin throwing, but I think it's the most important part. Guys tend to try to kill it. They feel like they just have to kick the hell out of the thing instead of just letting it happen. You just have to let your technique catch up with your aggressiveness, instead of letting aggressiveness take over....
But my world-record throw was like it was on a string. There was no vibration; it was like it was still sitting in my hand. And that's the key to throwing far--just waiting a bit longer for the connection to be made by your arm to your lower body....And it takes a long time to learn to slow down and wait."

Apparently Tom didn't wait long enough at the '84 Games, but he's young, and '88 is only four years away, just long enough to master the javelin and himself.

---

[1]Dean B. Cromwell, CHAMPIONSHIP TECHNIQUE IN TRACK AND FIELD, New York: Whittlesey House, 1941, p. 299.

Fig.13.2. The Whole Action. Ignoring details, the sharp focus of all actions of the run-transition-throw of the javelin is on maximal force through the length of the javelin at a flight angle of 30 degrees (25-35 as related to wind) so as to create maximal velocity of the javelin at the moment of release. Optimal methods include a smooth, gradually accelerated run, a straight-line pull-back of the javelin during a five-stride surge of gathering power--all concentrated to produce maximal force behind and "through the point" of the javelin. To consistently achieve such a goal has defied even the Masters after a decade or more of related training and competition.

This sequence drawing is from L.S.Khomenkova, A TEXTBOOK FOR THE TRACK & FIELD COACH, Moscow: USSR Government Publishing Office, 1982.

HOW TO BEGIN

In my own coaching experience, how to begin has been more a problem of selecting the real throwers and rejecting those who merely enjoy throwing, than one of increasing motivation. Everyone wants to pick up that spear and try to sock it out of the stadium. Begin then with safety measures so that no skulls are pierced or javelins broken. A special section on this problem has been included in this chapter.

One worthwhile rule for both safety and performance is that NO ONE throws the javelin without the permission of the coach; another, that all javelin prospects must first put in a period of power training before throwing. This alone will discourage the playboys.

Begin training in the Fall, the best time for basic conditioning. Start slowly; develop gradually to ensure continuous improvement in overall cardiovascular endurance, related power and javelin technique. The actual work schedule depends on the local climate and the individual's school schedule. If climate permits an uninterrupted straight-line training schedule, as in the Southern and Southwestern States, begin with overall endurance, gradually introduce related weight-lifting and related power exercises, then move on to acquiring technique.

Fig. 13.3. Begin with short throws from a stand.

If in more northerly climates, technique needs emphasis during the good weather of the Fall, then shift to strength-power work, then back to technique in late Winter and early Spring. A small amount of related work can be done indoors, as in practicing the approach run and transition strides without actual throwing; or perhaps in throwing whatever implements are available into a large net as is sometimes used for a baseball batting cage. The value of this is doubtful, for it may lead to faults not easily corrected later.

When good weather prevails, practice the approach run and approach strides over the length of the infield, pulling the javelin into proper position 3 or 4 times during each long run, without throwing. Actual throwing of the javelin should begin with short throws from a stand, or from a few back-cross steps as would any baseballer, with or without a short hop. Later, progress to a 3-5 stride approach until the overall "feel" of throwing this 8-foot spear becomes more natural. Or, to vary the action, make approach runs that more closely imitate throwing technique, though without actually throwing. Count 10-11 strides, the last five of which drive more powerfully as the javelin is drawn back into throwing position--again, without actually throwing. Much can be learned from such exercises: how to remain relaxed throughout, how to increase momentum during the transition phase. Boring? Not if the javelin is your event and you intend to be good at it.

ESSENTIALS OF SOUND TECHNIQUE

THE GRIP. Two acceptable ways of holding the javelin are shown in Figs. 13.4 and 13.5. (1) The grip must be firm to prevent any slipping in the throw. (2) However, the hand-arm-shoulder must be relaxed during the run and especially during the power reach. (3) the javelin should lie within the hollow of the "heel" of the palm so that it is in line with the direction of run and throw. (4) The grip in Fig. 13.5 is preferred, as it tends to impart a more rotary javelin action during the throw, and so ensure a more steady flight.

Fig. 13.4. Acceptable method of holding the javelin.

Fig. 13.5. Preferred hand-hold. The first finger aids javelin rotation and also gives a lift to the tail which helps keep the javelin in line of flight.

THE CARRY. Before the start of the run, the javelin thrower faces straight ahead, with no rotation of the shoulder girdle. The javelin is carried approximately horizontal and over the shoulder, so that the hand is even with the ear. (Note that in Fig. 13.6 that the javelin is carried pointing down at about 30 degrees. This makes it more difficult to pull it straight back to throwing position and so is not recommended. Fig. 13.2 shows the approved method.)

LENGTH OF THE RUN. The run should be long enough to produce high but less-than-maximal velocity with complete relaxation throughout, just prior to the transition or pull-back checkmark. The total number of strides varies among champion throwers from about 14 to 17. A checkmark locates placement of the left foot five strides back from the foul line (left-right-right-right-left-throw and follow-through to the right). To use a seven-count pull-back tends to slow body velocity when it is most essential.

VELOCITY OF THE RUN. Velocity of the run relates to optimal use. A beginner must run slowly. If throwing distance is important this week or even this month, perhaps for team reasons, then obviously a learner must run slowly enough to apply full power during the throw. Perhaps one-fourth of javelin velocity is gained from a maximal-velocity run. Prior to Ferenc Paragi's world-record throw (1980, 317'4"), he warmed up with throws over 80m (262 feet) using only three steps[1]--a difference of only 18 percent. But at championship levels this 18 percent difference makes all the difference, making maximal, relaxed velocity the ultimate goal.

THE POWER REACH. What we have called here "the power reach" is also called "transition," "pull-back," or "delivery action." It is the most critical phase of the entire run-and-throw. During the last four strides (left-right-left-right) the javelin hand reaches back in a straight line, pulling the shoulder girdle around in line with the throw (90 degrees to the foul line), and the hips to a 45-degree angle. If full extension occurs at the last instant, a yield-reactive or stretch-reflex action provides increased potential power for the throw.

---

[1]*Track & Field News*, May 1980, p. 24.

Fig. 13.6. The Power Reach. Throughout the four strides of the power reach, body velocity is maintained by quick, low-to-the-ground strides. The reaching action, with its shoulder-hip rotation, causes the right foot to rotate clockwise as shown in the second figure, but the left foot tends to remain in line.

Fig. 13.7. The final and crucial phase of the power reach. As a natural but also practiced effect of the full extension of the right arm, the prior stride on to the right foot is long but low and quick, well ahead of the body's center of weight. This landing will be on the outer edge of the right foot, placing great strain on the ankle. But placement of the left foot as shown here must be "instantaneous"--as quickly as possible after the right if maximal power is to be gained. As shown in this Figure, the left foot-leg drives hard against the throwing surface--a brace or fulcrum on which torso velocity-power depends.

THE THROW. As the throw begins (Fig. 13.7) the left foot-leg is the fulcrum; the right foot-leg initiates and sustains the power drive. Once that phase is completed and body-weight moves forward over the left foot, the power drive shifts to the left foot-leg. Such a drive requires only an instant but it is crucial. In fact, Kevin McGill, in an important analysis (1982) of the techniques of a dozen or so world-level javelin throwers, goes so far as to conclude,

> *Through careful study...I have concluded that the right leg is a non-contributor just shortly after the left foot hits, and certainly well before arm strike."*

But the driving power of each foot and leg is keyed to velocity, to explosive power that must be maximal for each if maximal javelin velocity is to be attained. The question as to when each occurs in relation to the other is moot.

Fig. 13.8. The Throw. As shown here, hip rotation to a forward-facing position has already occurred; the forward drive of the shoulders and pull on the javelin have already started. The hard-planted left foot, in line with the preceding right heel, combined with the delayed left arm, is preventing any tendency to pull to the left, and so ensures a straight-line throw. As the hips rotate to the front, all the power generated by the run-gather-lower-body-drive culminates in an explosive whip-like arm-javelin action.

Note in Fig. 13.2 (4th and 5th from last figures) that the right elbow comes through first, well above the shoulder and right hand, forming a very acute angle with the forearm. That is, no attempt is made to use a straight-arm throw to gain a greater flight angle. As drawn here, the hand-javelin is relatively close to the ear and only slightly out from the vertical. Such a "vertical position" is not easily achieved. In fact, a pull-through that is out from the right foot produces a pull across the javelin and a loss in power and distance--the most common weakness in throwing, even among the Masters. A left foot "in the bucket" is its most likely cause. An early pull of the left arm to the left that opens up the shoulders-hips is also a contributing factor.

FOLLOW-THROUGH
The follow-through is just that, no more, an effect of a straight-line pull along the length of the shaft, so powerful and fast that the arm and torso must follow up and out in the direction of flight.

COMMON FAULTS IN THE JAVELIN

1. <u>Failure to align the javelin along the line of throw</u>, and therefore to pull straight along the javelin shaft. This applies both horizontally and laterally. If the javelin point drifts out or up as it is drawn back into throwing position, force will be applied <u>across</u> the shaft. Possible causes are too numerous to fully list here. The grip may be too loose. The right arm may be coming around to the rear; the left foot may be "in the bucket"; the eyes-face may be too high.

2. <u>To become overly concerned with the action of the feet and legs</u> in the so-called cross-over during the transition. If the shoulders (90 degrees) and hips (45 degrees) are brought around into optimal alignment, proper placement of the feet will follow naturally (Fig. 13.6 and 13.7). Primary attention during this action should be on placing the throwing muscles of the torso-shoulder-arm on stretch and so gain maximal power from them, with no loss of body momentum. These last strides (left-right-left) must be the fastest of the entire run-gather, with a shocking halt of forward movement of the feet as the final left foot is braced. Taken together, that is a very complex action, requiring years of persistent practice before mastery is complete.

3. <u>Throwing primarily with the arm</u> rather than through the momentum and force of the body in motion. The thrower can be compared with a whip whose explosive "crack!" of the tip would depend on flexibility, of course, but also on the forward velocity and the suddenness of the braking action of the handle. That is, force begins within the handle for the whip; within the legs-body, for the javelin. In the javelin the full momentum of the legs is suddenly stopped by the bracing, or braking action of the right-left legs; force then travels upward through the torso toward the tip (the wrist, hand, and javelin). Keep in mind that this fault must be balanced with that of #6, "failure to explode during the throw."

4. <u>Improper placement of the left leg</u>. This leg placement is crucial. If too far to the left: (a) the body will follow, and the line of force will be down and <u>across</u> the line of intended flight; (b) its bracing action will be lost; and (c) the final powerful extension of the left foot will not coincide with the final whip of the hand as it explodes the javelin on its way. This last point is very important.

If the left leg is extended too far in front, it may brake too much against the forward pull of the javelin; if not extended far enough, it will fail to provide the bracing action by which force is accumulated upward. For beginners the tendency is to cut the leg down too soon and too short, so that the body is above or ahead of it.

5. <u>Too much momentum in the early run; too little during the last three steps before the throw</u>. Only good judgment on the part of the coach can say which portion of this fault should be corrected. To cut down the momentum of the run may aid performance today and this week, but to do so permanently will limit ultimate distance. If time permits, a sounder policy is to maintain momentum of the run by ignoring it, then concentrating attention on the means of utilizing that momentum to the full: on perfection of the cross-over, on a full swing-back or pull-back of the javelin, etc.

6. <u>Failure to explode during the throw</u>. The term we have used in "controlled recklessness." An over-concern for the technical details of javelin throwing may cause the thrower to unlearn his natural tendency to "sock it out there," to forget everything except an uninhibited, all-out explosion of energy. After all, skill is merely a method of accumulating, controlling, and <u>releasing</u> energy. Any sense of caution or concern for style which limits this release of energy is a drawback. A sound style should aid good throwing, but they don't give medals for style; only for distance. EXPLODE!

7. <u>Failure to realize</u> that mastery of the javelin throw requires years of assiduous practice on technique and on training for optimal, related power. A glance at Table 13.1 will find that 68 percent of the outstanding performers are over 25 years of age, with 9 of 30 over 28. We can assume they average about ten years of training before reaching their peak.

8. <u>Failure to achieve</u> the optimal position just prior to the throw with the shoulders in line with the run at 90 degrees to the foul line, and the hips at 45 degrees. The left-foot should be in line with the right-foot heel.

SAFETY IN THE JAVELIN

1. <u>Injury to the thrower</u>. "Muscles that have been properly tuned up and made 100% supple never tear. . . no matter how strenuous the exercise may be." Though this may be an extreme statement, the modern approach to injury prevention is based upon it essential correctness. Traditionally in America, the almost universal prevalence of injury to javelin throwers caused coaches to shy away from the event, to cut fast running and hard throwing to a minimum, and, in general, to avoid injury by doing as little as possible. Today, the reverse is true.

Every link in the javelin thrower's chain of toughness must be gradually forged to withstand every test. Such links are numerous. "Javelin elbow" was so common as to become a by-word in sports. The back muscles are under tremendous strain as the javelin is pulled explosively forward. Tendons in the groin have often weakened as the fast run is suddenly stopped during the last two strides. In fact there are few muscle groups in the body that have not been injured at some time by javelin throwers.

The solution to this aspect of the problem lies in the year-round gradual toughening program outlined in this book. If a muscle or tendon is injured, the fault lies in improper or insufficient preparation, not in the event.

2. <u>Injury to others</u>. On the first rule, the coach must be a tough dictator who enforces without favor: No one throws a javelin unless he has the specific permission of the coach. Second, no one gets such permission until he has undergone a period of power training. Enforcement of just those two rules will avoid the greatest danger, that from casual passersby who want to give it a fling, then fling it into somebody's flesh.

Javelin throwers, that is, men who know something of how to throw, can control the direction of flight to a reasonable degree. The problem then is one of preventing others from approaching the landing area. A separate field for the javelin is one obvious solution. Though even then, the throwers must be taught to be constantly aware of danger, to follow a warning system of calls and arm signals. Lacking such a field, ropes should set off the landing area.

Most importantly, the coach must accept full responsibility for this danger; he cannot ignore it; he cannot leave it to the throwers, then blame them for what may happen. If he is constantly aware of danger; his men will be likewise. Certainly the answer does not lie in eliminating the event from our school program as has been done by some States at the high school level, and by the Big Ten College Conference. The javelin is an essential part of the track and field program. When they eliminate football or ice-hockey because of their numerous injuries, then let us consider eliminating the javelin; not before.

Where throwing conditions are limited, as is usually the case indoors, the cost of large nets is fully justified for both safety and gains in performance. Implements thrown vary. Stubby shafts with weighted rubber tips at both ends help to maintain body alignments. Or use bamboo poles, eight feet long, with partitions knocked out and filled with sand or any heavy material. Balls (3-4#) of solid rubber or other materials, as in the figure shown below, develop related power but tend toward carelessness in body alignments and proper javelin techniques in general.

RELATED POWER EXERCISES

Note - The black-shirted figures are excerpted from V. Mazzalitis, *Throwing the Javelin*, USSR Sports Publishing Office, 1970.

ORGANIZATION OF TRAINING

The great success of Hungary's javelin throwers, as evidenced by Nemeth (1976-310'4") and Paragi (1980--317'4") makes a summary[1] of their training program by Hungary coach, Jiri Simon, of special interest. The following is my own more concise restatement:

Four aspects of developmental training are emphasized: (1) Work on technique occurs year-round, even indoors when outdoor conditions are unfavorable. Primary emphasis on technique occurs in the spring. (2) Basic strength training follows the pyramid system. For example, during five of six series of squats, resistances are increased, repetitions are decreased, length of recovery periods are increased; during the 6th series, resistances decrease, reps increase, recovery periods increase. (3) Related power training parallels strength training and consists of (a) heavy-resistance movements that simulate javelin patterns of action, and (b) throwing overweight implements--iron rods, weightlifting discs, shots--weighing 1-4kg (2-9#). Gradually progressive overloading, as to both weights and number of throws, is carefully monitored to ensure against injury and for development. (4) Lightweight implements, including underweight javelins, are used for velocity training that closely simulates javelin movements.

Related power training for arm-shoulder development: (1) From throwing stance (left leg forward), lift upward 6 x 25 kg, 6 x 30 kg, 6 x 35 kg, 4 x 40 kg, 6 x 20 kg. (2) Inclined board with dumbbell behind the head, elbows in front. Repeated arm-extension lifts--10 x 5 kg, 3 x 10 kg, 10 x 5 kg. Use a barbell for two-arm extensions.

Related power development of legs: Repeated hops on one leg (R & L) with barbell or sandbags on shoulders--6 x 45 kg, 6 x 50 kg, 6 x 45 kg. For each leg, simulate javelin movements that place greatest stress or require greatest power.

The training year is divided into four phases: (1) September-January, transition periods I & II, (2) January-March, winter periods I & II, (3) March-July, pre-season I & II, (4) July-September, competitive season. Each phase merges smoothly into the next, with careful planning and testing of development throughout. Winter training is extremely intensive and time consuming. All phases include work on technique, on basic strength, and on related power, but the emphasis is constantly changing. For example, the relative emphasis on basic strength and related power (throwing heavy implements) varies for each phase: transition I--1/1, transition II--2/1, winter --3/4, pre-season I--2/3, pre-season II--1/2, competitive period--1/0.

Finnish Training Program.[2] The Finns use a similar year-round, progressive-overload schedule that gradually shifts to technique and velocity training. Velocity training uses implements including stubby shafts weighing less than the 800g javelin weight. Flexibility of related muscles and tendons is considered essential also and receives great emphasis, especially in areas where injury is most likely to occur.

Fig. 13.9 . A Stubby javelin.

Finnish summers are warm and pleasant--great for javelin throwing. But Finnish winters are cold-d-d and long-g-g with few daylight hours from October to March--not at all conducive to outdoor training. What we'd consider throwing weather comes in late May and ends in late August. But through Finnish pride in "sisu" and careful organization of year-round training, the Finns have dominated world javelin throwing over the past 75 years. The 1984 Olympic javelin competition was won by Harkonen of Finland, though experts doubted he would even place. It can be done when dedication and hard work and "sisu" are present.

---

[1]Juri Simon, "Hungary's World-record Javelin Program," *Track Technique*, #69, September 1977, p. 2194.

[2]Matti Salmenkyla, Finland, "Javelin Throwing in Finland," *Track & Field Quarterly Review*, Vol. 84, #1, 1984, pp. 27-28.

<u>An American School-College Program</u>. Many training programs, 1-5, for American high school and college throwers have appeared in *Track Technique* and *Track & Field Quarterly Review*. That by Harmon Brown, M.D.[6] of California State-Hayward, is carefully planned and easily adaptable to any section of the country.

<u>Basic Endurance-Strength Phase</u> (10-12 weeks).

A base of endurance, strength, flexibility, and general conditioning should be emphasized for 10-12 weeks, depending upon the maturity and fitness level of the athlete. This includes running, strength training, power development, and basic skills training.

   <u>Strength</u>
   a. General. 3 days per week, alternate days. Volume: 4-6 sets x 8-10 repetitions. Intensity. 60-65½ of the single repetition maximum. Exercises, dead left, squat, power clean, snatch, inverted sit-up, bench press, pullover, lat. pulldown.
   b. Specific. Begin after 6 weeks of general training. 1) Medicine ball throws for trunk and shoulder girdle. 2) Overweight implements or weights: for specific throwing muscles and throwing action. Use stubby javelins, rods, balls, of 1.5 to 2.0kg.
   <u>Running</u>. Jog 2-3 miles 4-5 times a week. Stride-accelerations 5-8 x 60-150m. Hill running and bounding. Stride and pullback with spear or stick. Run 600-800m timed every two weeks.
   <u>Ballistic training</u>. Horizontal bounding: (a) double leg hops 25-40m x 5-10. (b) alternate-leg bounding 30-50m. Do twice weekly. (c) stadium step or hill bounding once weekly.
   <u>Technique</u>. Throw stubby into net, or throw spear with short approach once or twice a week x 30-40x.
   <u>Flexibility</u>. Spend 15-20 minutes daily on gradual (Yoga) stretching of shoulder girdle, trunk, hips, legs.
<u>Power Training Phase</u> (12-14 weeks)

   <u>Strength</u>
   a. General. Every other day. Volume. 5 x 5 at 80%, or pyramid from 70-90%. Exercises. Snatch or power clean, squats, incline pullovers with bar or dumbbell, bench press, inverted situps, horizontal trunk twists on bench, lat. pulls, quarter-squat "pops."
   b. Specific. Throw balls, rods or stubbies in ratio, 2 heavy (1.5-2.0kg), 1 standard weight (600 or 800g), 1 light (500g). Do 75-100 throws twice weekly.
   c. Medicine ball drills x 20 min.
   <u>Running</u>. Jog 1-1.5 miles warm-up each day. Cariocas 5 x 100m. Sprint 60-100m x 5 twice weekly. Pull-back accelerations with stick 10-15 x 30-40m.

---

[1]Ed Tucker, "Javelin Training Program," *Track Technique*, #60, June 1975, p. 1904.

[2]Bill Webb, "The Javelin," *Track & Field Quarterly Review*, Vol. 80, #1, 1980, pp. 3-7.

[3]Glen DeGeorgio, "Introduction to Javelin Throwing," *Track & Field Quarterly Review*, Vol. 81, #1, 1981, pp. 29-32.

[4]Bob Myers, Arizona, "A Year-round Training Program for Javelin Throwers," *Track & Field Quarterly Review*, Vol. 81, #1, 1981, pp. 35-38.

[5]Sherry Calvert, USOC Development Camp, "Throwing the Javelin," *Track & Field Quarterly Review*, Vol. 82, #1, 1982, pp. 23-26.

[6]Harmon Brown, M.D., California State-Hayward, "The Javelin Throw," *Track & Field Quarterly Review*, Vol. 82, #1, 1982, pp. 18-20.

Ballistic activities. Twice weekly. Horizontal bounding 5 x 30-40 m single and double legged. Boxes, cones, or hurdles-double and single leg hops 5 x 10 reps once weekly.

Technique. Focus on various technical points--relaxation, hips and trunk drive, leg speed and acceleration into throws. Throw 3-4 x a week. Throw rocks on week-end.

Competition Readiness (6-8 weeks)

Strength
a. General. Circuit training x 1 week at 40-50%. Then resume 5 x 5 at 80% three times weekly for 4-6 weeks. Taper to twice weekly, reduce to 4 x 4 and 3 x 3 at 90-99% prior to major meets.
b. Specific. Throw rods, balls or stubbies in ratio, 2 light, 1 standard, 1 heavy.

Running. Sprints 30-80m x 5-6 at full effort. Approach runs on runway with spear x 10-15. Controlled speed and acceleration. Cariocas 3-4 x 100m.

Ballistic. Horizontal bounding 4-5 x ten once weekly. Jump cones or hurdles 5 x 10 once weekly. Omit jump training for 2-3 weeks before major meets.

Technique. Focus on refining skills, concentrating on the whole movement pattern. Upper body relaxation. Throw under-weight implements relaxed, explosive effort. (Men can use women's spear). Throw 15-20 throws at full effort with recovery between once weekly. Use smaller meets to rehearse for major competitions.

Post-Season "Active Rest."

Maintain fitness. Try to retain a base conditioning, but relax with other sports activities. Maintain a base of strength by training every 3-4 days using sets of 3-4 repetitions x 4-5 at 75-80%.

West Germany's Karl-Hans Riehm, 1984 Olympic silver medalist and former world record holder./Theo Van de Rakt Photo.

Chapter 14
THE HAMMER THROW

Throwing the hammer is a very ancient event, having been traced as far back as about 2000 B.C., when the Tailteann Games were held at Tara, Ireland. Folklore still tells of the amazing exploits of Cuchulain, the Irish Hercules, who in one instance performed what was called the "Roth Cleas" (wheel feat) in which, as one teller has it, he threw a single spoke of a chariot wheel to which the hub was still attached. While spinning with it at incredible speed, Cuchulain and the weight parted company and, much to the delight of the onlookers the weight (or was it Cuchulain?) would fly through the air far beyond the marks of ordinary men.

According to the English historian, Joseph Strutt,[1]

Casting of the barre is frequently mentioned by the romance writers as one part of a hero's education, and a poet of the 16th century thinks it highly commendable for kings and princes, by way of exercise, to throw "the stone, the barre, or the plummet" . . . The sledge hammer was also used for the same purpose . . . and, among the rustics, if Barclay is correct, an axletree.

An axletree! Perhaps the tale of Cuchulain had some truth in it, though that would be odd for a brawny Irish hero!

A SUMMARY HISTORY OF TECHNIQUE
Moving ahead a few centuries, Shearman[2] informs us that at a championship meeting, 1886, at the London Athletic Club grounds at Stamford Bridge,

a gigantic Irishman, J. S. Mitchell . . . has won the hammer throwing (a 16# hammer, four feet long, thrown from a 7-foot circle) with a throw of 110'4". . . . The original rules allowed the hammer-thrower to use a hammer [wooden handle--J.K.D.] of any length, to take as much run as he liked, and throw from any place he liked, the judge marking the place where the thrower had his front foot at the moment the hammer left his hands. . . . In 1887 the circle was enlarged from 7 to 9 feet, and in 1896 a handle of flexible metal was legalised.

When the size of the circle was finally standardized in 1907 at a diameter of seven feet, most of the throwers were using one or two turns (not until the 1920s did three turns become accepted.) In part, this was because of the method of turning on the ball of the left foot (often called a "toe turn"), which required a jump around with both feet momentarily in the

---

[1] Joseph Strutt, SPORTS AND PASTIMES OF THE PEOPLE OF ENGLAND, London: William Tegg and Co., 1855, 75.

[2] Montague Shearman, ATHLETICS, London: Longmans, Green & Co., 1904, 61.

TABLE 14.1

OUTSTANDING PERFORMANCES -- HAMMER THROW

OLYMPIC CHAMPIONS

Date	Record	Name	Affiliation	Age	Hgt.	Wgt.
1908	170'4¼''	John Flanagan	USA	35	6'2''	270
1912	179'7''	Matt McGrath	USA	34	5'11 3/4''	248
1920	173'5¼''	Pat Ryan	USA	33	6'2''	250
1924	174'10''	Fred Tootell	USA	24	6'2''	215
1928	168'7¼''	Pat O'Callaghan	Eire	23	6'1''	215
1932	176'11''	Pat O'Callaghan	Eire	27	6'1''	215
1936	185'4¼''	Karl Hein	Germany	28	6'	210
1948	183'11½''	Imre Nemeth	Hungary	31	6'	195
1952	197'11''WR	Jozsef Csermak	Hungary	20	5'11''	204
1956	207'3½''	Harold Connolly	USA	25	6'	235
1960	220'1½''	Vasily Rudenkov	USSR	29	6'1½''	215
1964	228'9½''	Romuald Klim	USSR	31	6'1''	240
1968	240'8''	Gyula Zsivotsky	Hungary	31	6'3''	205
1972	247'8½''	Anatoliy Bondarchuk	USSR	32	6'	245
1976	254'4''	Yuriy Syedikh	USSR	21	6'3/4''	220
1980	268'4''WR	Yuriy Syedikh	USSR	25	6'3/4''	243
1984	256'2''	Juha Tiainen	Finland	28	5'11½''	236

RECORDS OF SPECIAL INTEREST

Date	Record	Name	Affiliation	Age	Hgt.	Wgt.
1913	189'6½''	Pat Ryan	USA	26	6'2''	250
1938	193'7''	Erwin Blask	Germany	28	6'	210
1956	220'10½''	Mikhail Krivonosov	USSR	27	6'2½''	198
1962	231'10''	Harold Connolly	USA	31	6'	235
1967	235'11''AR	Ed Burke	USA	27	6'1¼''	220
1968	242'	Gyula Zsivotsky	Hungary	31	6'1''	205
1969	247'7½''	Anatoli Bondarchuk	USSR	29	6'	240
1975	260'2''	Walter Schmidt	W. Germany	27	6'3½''	253
1978	263'6''	Karl-Hans Riehm	W. Germany	27	6'1 3/4''	234
1983	276'	Sergey Litvinov	USSR	25	5'11''	216
1984	283'3''	Yuriy Syedikh	USSR	29	6'3/4''	243
1984	251' AR	Bill Green	USA	24	6'2''	227

OUTSTANDING PERFORMANCES -- 35 lb. WEIGHT

Date	Record	Name	Affiliation	Age	Hgt.	Wgt.
1984	78'6½''WR	Tore Johnsen	Norway	22	6'7''	265
1984	75'3½''AR	Jud Logan	USA	24	6'4''	272

BEST PERFORMANCES -- HIGH SCHOOLS --12 lb.

Date	Record	Name	Affiliation
1972	227'8''	Alvin Jackson	Classical, Providence, RI
1972	219'	Phil Bartlett	Classical, Providence, RI
1974	213'1''	Ed Ajootian	Classical, Providence, RI
1974	209'8''	Emmitt Berry	Hope, Providence, RI
1976	231'11''	Manny Silverio	North Bergen, NJ
1979	222'3''	Keith Bateson	East Greenwich, RI
1982	251'9''	S. Dorozhev	USSR (with a 16 lb. ball, age 18)
1984	226'8''	Alan Lareau	Cumberland, RI

air. This loss of contact with the ground made balance and straight-line progress across the circle very uncertain. Even with but two turns, fouling was very common and throws flew off in almost any direction.

In consequence, the danger to nearby athletes and spectators was very great, and the event was barred from all high school and most college programs. Only in recent years has the prod of Olympic needs produced an increase in college participation. A few Eastern preparatory schools have maintained hammer competition through the years, primarily through the enthusiastic dedication of a few coaches and ex-throwers

THE IRISH WERE FIRST. In the early years, the Irish were clearly the chief movers in the event. At least in America, from about 1890 into the 1920s, it was dominated by such good Irish-Americans as John J. Flanagan, Matt McGrath, and Pat Ryan, known as the "whales" of the New York City police force. Between the three of them, they won every Olympic Games from 1900 through 1920. Flanagan won the first three and moved the world record to a very respectable 184'4" in 1909. McGrath won in 1912 and extended the record to 187' 6½". Pat Ryan won in 1920 after having achieved 189'6½", a record that stood for 25 years. Each of these men turned on the ball of the foot in a low-hop style, but were able to maintain balance and control through their great body-weight which averaged about 270 pounds. By the way, in defense of the Irish--as if they ever needed it!--they also won the 1928 and 1932 Games through the throwing of Pat O'Callaghan.

Another great hammer thrower, Fred Tootell, appeared during the twenties. Fast and extremely powerful, Tootell perfected the "toe turns" method and added the concept of letting the hammer "hang" during a portion of each turn. He would permit the hammer to lead him for an instant at its highest point, then, with a burst of speed, turn his body so it was ahead of the hammer as it approached its low point. In this manner, Tootell was able to pick up a tremendous amount of speed and still secure a strong finish position. The record books credit him with a best throw of 185', but after leaving amateur ranks, he officially whipped the hammer some 212', truly remarkable when compared to Ryan's world record of 189'6½". By the way, Tootell was a native of Rhode Island, the only State in the Union to sponsor hammer throwing in its high school program.

In the early 1930s, the upsurge of interest in sports in Germany led to the work of Sepp Christmann who carefully analyzed the hammer throw in terms of its mechanical principles and their application to human powers and movements. He concluded: (1) For good balance and control the left foot must maintain firm contact with the ground throughout all turns. This was done by starting the turn on the outside of the heel of the left foot, rolling on the outside of the foot to the ball-toe, and around to the heel again. The pattern of the foot now moved in a straight line toward the front of the circle. This method is still valid today. (2) The hammer must hang from passive arms directly in front of the thrower's chest so that it neither leads the turns nor retards their movement. The net effect was a smooth, seemingly effortless progression across the circle, with constant acceleration of the ball of the hammer.

Using these two methods, Karl Hein and Erwin Blask of Germany placed one-two in the 1936 Olympics, and moved the world record to 193'7" where it remained for 12 years.

MODERN TECHNIQUES. In the 1950s, three new approaches radically changed hammer methods and performance. Between 1911 and 1951 (40 years) hammer world records improved approximately 20 feet; in the next decade they improved about 30 feet (201-231'). Primary among these new approaches was basic strength training. Second, the extension of training greatly increased--in hours per week and number of weeks until the latter became year-round. Third, hammer-throwing techniques were improved to provide greater velocities in the turn and greater power in the final pull on the hammer. These three concepts are interdependent; certainly the last could not have been achieved without the first two as a foundation.

In the Olympic Games, the Hungarians first led the assault with Imre Nemeth winning in 1948, and Jozsef Csermak in 1952 with a world-record 197'11". In 1956 Hal Connolly (US) set an Olympic record at 207'3".[1]

[1]The remainder of this Chapter on hammer throwing--comments, Figures, charts and all--is the work of Kevin McGill, assistant track coach at Columbia University, N.Y. He is editor of *Hammer Throwing Notes*, the only magazine in the world devoted exclusively to hammer throwing. He has published numerous articles in *Track Technique* and *Track & Field Quarterly Review* in recent issues. At the August 1984 Congress of the International Track & Field Coaches Association, he gave the lecture on the hammer. Harold Connolly, 1956 Olympic Champion in the hammer, helped in editing the Chapter.

But, since that time, the U.S. position has eroded and the Soviets, West and East Germany, Hungary, along with other countries, have dominated the scene. In the Olympic Games, 1960-1980, the USSR won 11 places including four golds; Hungary, seven places; West Germany, four; East Germany, two, leaving six lower places for all others. Americans had no places in that period.

In the decade 1951-61, the WR improved about 30' (201' to 231'); between 1961-71 about 20' (231' to 251'); between 1971-1980 about 17' (251' to 268'). The most remarkable improvement of all occurred on July 3, 1984 in Cork, Ireland, when Yuri Syedikh moved the record to the fantastic 283'3", a 7'3" increase over Sergei Litvinov's 1983 mark of 276'.

Such great distances are obviously dangerous to others on and off the field so that it seems quite likely that appropriate changes in the event, at least at Olympic and world levels, will be made.

Russian Techniques. It is very important to keep the "s" in "Techniques" when speaking about the Russian throwers. No one else throws like Syedikh, although his teammate Yuri Tamm has some similar characteristics. Since 1976, Syedikh has demonstrated his technique all over the world and his success has influenced many. Nikulin's technique is vastly different and his 274'1" gives an indication that in Russia the technique fits the athlete, not the athlete adapting to a specific exact model. Tamm's PR of 273'4" rates him 4th in Russia.

How have the Russians produced such an array of throwers? They have paid attention to the basics, and in general, do the following:

(1) Catch the ball very early by planting the feet off to the side, and keeping the hips on the ball, or facing it.

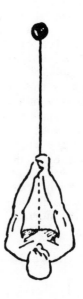

Fig. 14.1[1]. A wide radius   Fig. 14.2[2]. Hips on the ball.

(2) Maintain a very wide radius throughout the throw. Most Russians keep the ball in front of the chest in the turns, eliminating the "dragging" technique used a few years ago. This is not a new idea, as Sepp Christmann[2] described this over thirty years ago. Fig. 14.2 is his drawing from a 1951 book.

(3) Keep the legs tight to enable them to turn faster. Although the Russians are superb athletes, film analysis will show how it isn't just speed, strength, or athletic ability that gives them the edge.

[1]Michel Thieurmel, *Amicale Des Entraineurs Francais D'Athletisme*, #75, Dec. 1981, p. 57.

[2]Sepp Christmann, *Speer und Hammer*, West Germany, Leichtathletik, 1951, p. 64.

The Technique of Yuriy Syedikh. In various publications since 1977, Anatoliy Bondarchuk, head coach USSR hammer throwing, has detailed the following points of Syedikh's technique:

(1) Yuri moves his center of gravity up and down very little in the throw, about 10cm/4 inches. This is the major difference between Syedikh and Nikulin, as Nikulin comes up a great deal at the low point, necessitating a big drop by the high point.

(2) He makes good use of the hammer's inertia in single support. He lets the hammer turn him.

(3) He does not move ahead of the hammer when the right foot touches the ground, but rather drives the whole body to accelerate the hammer.

(4) He has a definite rhythm to the throw.

Further information about Syedikh was gleaned from a biomechanics film shot during the 1982 USSR/USA meet in Indianapolis by Jesus Dapena. This study differed somewhat from Bondarchuk's statements on the liftoff of the right leg. At the speeds he is travelling, the right leg could never get around at the proper time if he stayed until 90 degrees. At the same meet, Litvinov lifted a bit later, but he also landed later. He lifted his right foot at about 75 degrees. If the goal of the thrower is to extend the active phase, not just double support, then the right foot must come off the ground before 90 degrees is reached with the hammer, and be placed down quickly before the ball reaches 240, if possible. Slower athletes will have to lift earlier and try to plant before the hammer gets past 260 or so.

Another factor in Syedikh's technique may be the unique position with the left foot when his right foot lands. His left foot just about faces the right foot, thus giving him a twisting moment with the body over a greater range than perhaps any thrower in history. He has disciplined himself to look at the ball, and even behind the ball to insure that the right arm does not bend, nor the left drag the ball.

There will be those who cannot believe that the Russians have succeeded without some dark secret. Some have noticed slight changes in Syedikh since 1976, but the basic technique follows the three ideas above: (1) early right foot landing, (2) wide radius; (3) tight, fast turns. If there is a secret, it is this--the Russians have a lot of throwers! They have studied the proper way to prepare for competitions, recuperate from workouts, maximize throwing workouts, etc. Young Russian throwers are culled out early for the top coaches. A 70 meter throw with a light hammer is expected after three years of throwing. Heavy weight training for the teenagers is held off until the technique starts to develop. Igor Nikulin's results are interesting:

Year	Age	3KG	4KG	5KG	6KG	7.2KG
1974	14	66.52	58.40	52.50	-	-
1975	15	75.20	67.60	58.00	54.35	49.92
1976	16	-	77.80	69.70	60.50	57.52
1977	17	-	84.40	78.48	73.46	62.18
1978	18	-	-	88.70	79.60	71.70
1979	19	-	-	95.32	82.86	75.20
1980	20	-	-	-	-	80.34
1982	22	-	-	-	-	83.54

We can safely say that no American has ever trained with such precision, at the age of 14. It is very helpful to achieve a speed pattern prior to weight training. Our throwers learn at 18 and must throw the 16 lb. hammer immediately, eliminating the speed period. Many Eastern colleges compete in the 35 lb. weight, thereby slowing the beginning throwers even more. Our common 180' thrower has a counterpart in the USSR throwing 230' with the same weight implement. The Russians have hundreds of young kids throwing all kinds of hammers; in the US we have perhaps 20 youngsters involved, almost all in Rhode Island high schools.

Other Europeans. Briefly, while no other country has had the success the Russians have had since 1976, a few are knocking on the door. Karl Riehm, coached by Ernst Klement, is a master technician using a slightly different approach. Karl tends to straighten his legs more than Syedikh, causing a drop at the high point, and he works toward a "Charlie Chaplin" position with the left foot pointing away from the right when the right foot lands. The Polish star Kwasny made a remarkable improvement to 263'1" using an older technique involving overturning (opposite to the Russian underturning--right foot spends more time in the air and lands past the line of the left), a steep hammer, hips off the ball--but, he has the needed ingredient of rhythm. Tiainen and Huhtala of Finland have also impressed hammer observers.

Americans. 1984 marked a revolution in the recent American hammer scene. The old guard of McKenzie, McArdle, and Bessette were surprised by two youngsters, Jud Logan and Bill Green. Jud Logan (6'4", 255) had a PR of 244'7", while Green (6'2", 227) was the first American over 250', reaching 251'.

Ed Burke, ex-AR holder, is right behind these two 24 year olds. At the age of 44, he finished third in the Trials and led the Americans into the Coliseum for the Olympics. He retired in his prime in the late 1960's. After seeing Litvinov on the TV, he returned to throwing. "They call your name to throw, your heart jumps in your throat, you're frozen, like a rabbit in the headlights. Maybe your body secretes a kind of joy juice. It feels good. There's nothing like it..."[1]

BASIC MECHANICS OF THE HAMMER

While certain aspects of hammer technique have changed during recent decades, the basic mechanics are the same.

A. A Long Hammer Radius. In the 1960s, Sam Felton[2] and Gabor Simonyi emphasized the importance of a long hammer radius as measured from the axis of rotation to the center of the hammer head.

Turning speed (rev/s) at instant of release	Distance thrown[a] based on effective hammer radius		
	6'0"	5'9"	5'6"
2.0	180'	166'	151'
2.1	200	186	168
2.2	220	203	185
2.3	240	221	203

(a) Based on 44° angle of release.

If the thrower does not have the ball "out", or away from the body, the radius will suffer and distance will drop. Felton also mentioned that it is not the speed of the thrower that counts, but the speed of the ball. With a short radius, it is possible for a beginner to turn rapidly and achieve a distance which will win a dual meet. In order to achieve a greater radius, the Russians collapse the chest and let the upper body get pulled forward.

B. Velocity. Toni Nett drew this graph in the 1960's. It shows that a mere 10% increase in linear velocity at release can produce up to 40' or more, providing the release angle is between 42-44 degrees.

In attempting to utilize this information, remember that the radius is critical! Do not bend the right arm, nor let the left arm drag across the chest.

A different perspective is given by the drawing (Fig. 14.4) and comments by V. Petrov[3], Nikulin's coach.

---

[1] "World Scene," *Track and Field News*, Nov. 1983, p. 19.

[2] Sam Felton, Jr., and Gabor Simonyi, *Modern Hammer Techniques*, Rosemont PA, 1968/69 Edition p.3.

[3] V. Petrov, "Hammer Throw Technique and Drills," *Hammer Notes #6*, edited by Kevin McGill, p. 25.

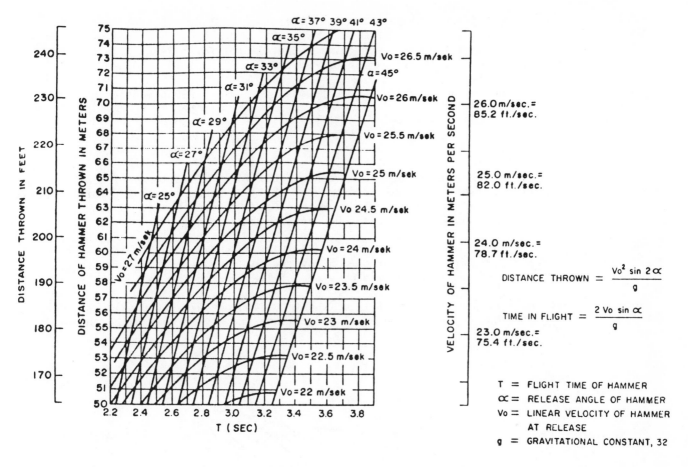

Fig. 14.3. Relationship between Distance Thrown, Release Velocity, Angle of Release and Flight Time of Hammer.

"The hammer path is lengthened by increasing the turning radius through bending of the hip joint and an inclination of the trunk. This allows to increase the radius by 10¼" and the total acceleration path up to 21'4". For example, a 4'5½" turning radius is responsible for a 28' hammer path in one turn, and a 112'1" in four turns. By increasing the radius to 5'3 3/4" the hammer path lengthens to 33'4" in a single and 133'5" in four turns. This represents a difference of 21'4" and naturally allows the thrower to increase the release speed."

On viewing Fig. 14.4, Harold Connolly warned that to drop the chin down so as to achieve a wider radius lessens balance and power. Keep the head up! Similarly, Coach Petrov warned that increasing the forward inclination of the torso would interfere with the delivery angle.

C. Forces affecting the hammer throw. The forces affecting distance when throwing the hammer are complex--vertical, horizontal, tangential and even such exotic force as the coriolis effect (turning of the earth). But centrifugal force is known and most studied. Table 14.2 by Sam Felton[1] shows the effect on distance thrown of different

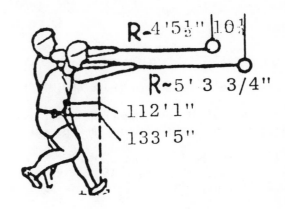

Fig. 14.4. Torso inclination.

[1]Felton and Simonyi, op. cit., p. 2.

271

release velocities and two hammer radii of six feet and 5.75 feet.

Table 14.2. EFFECTS OF RADIUS AND CENTRIFUGAL FORCE ON DISTANCE

Distance Thrown	Linear Velocity at Release (45°)	Approximate Centrifugal Force Required with--	
		6.0' radius	5.75' radius
180'	75'/second	460 pounds	490 pounds
200	79	520	540
220	83	575	600
240	87	630	660
260	91	690	715

From this Figure, one might conclude that a centrifugal force of well over 700 pounds would be needed to produce Syedikh's record distance of 283'3". Readers desiring more information should check works by Howard Payne, Bernard Hopper, and Geoffrey Dyson. Up-to-date studies on forces have been published by Jesus Dapena in *Hammer Notes*.

D. <u>Trajectory and Path</u>. The Toni Nett chart (Fig. 14.3) shows proper release angles. Exact placement of the low point, a matter of controversy for many years, varies with each athlete, including those Soviet throwers who have been filmed during the past eight years.

Fig. 14.5[1] (Syedikh's winning throw of 77.52m (254-4 OR) in the 1976 Olympics), shows the constant changes of the hammer path--steeper with each turn and moving toward the thrower's left.

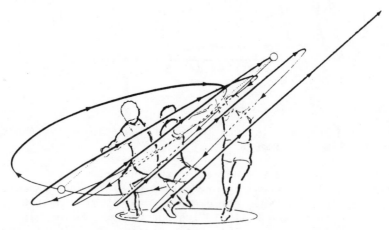

The changing tilt of the hammer plane during Yuriy Syedikh's winning throw in the 1976 Olympic Games.

Fig. 14.5. The changing tilt of the hammer plane.

<u>MODERN HAMMER TECHNIQUE</u>

A. <u>The Winds</u>.

1. Offset the feet to the right, left foot near the center, right foot back a few inches.

2. The ball is off the right rear, weight mostly on the right leg. Pull the arms to the front and twist the shoulders back parallel with the hips.

3. As the ball goes past the left foot, begin to bend the arms, left arm first, and bring arms in close to the face. At this time, the shoulders will rotate clockwise and reach back, arms still bent, with the left arm wrapped across the upper body. Weight is on both legs.

---

[1]Howard Payne, *THE SCIENCE OF TRACK AND FIELD ATHLETICS*, Pelham Books, London, 1981, p. 353.

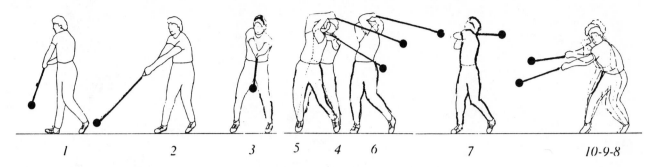

Fig. 14.6.[1] First Preliminary Swing.

4.   The first wind for three turn throwers has a low point off the right side at about 300; for four turners, 210-250. The second wind low point will be around 0 for both styles.

5.   As the ball hits 180, three turners will just have the shoulders turned, with hips only slightly turned; four turners will turn the hips and shoulders back to keep contact with the ball on the right side.

6.   The legs do not pump as in earlier techniques, but rather absorb the changes in the center of gravity shifts. Three turners will not shift much at all; four turners must try to keep pressure on the right side as the low point for the first wind is behind them. The difference here is caused by the flat trajectory of the four turn entry vs. the steeper entry used by three turners.

7.   As the ball goes left at the end of the first wind, some throwers will shift the right foot out a few inches to increase the stability of the base. All of this depends on the thrower's aptitude and the ball's velocity. The second wind must be faster than the first. Countering is easier with the increased resistance.

8.   The second wind is different. Three turners keep hips to the front, some four turners shift the right foot and try to get a flatter ball. While the three turn thrower has to have steeper winds, the four turner must shift from a somewhat steep first wind to a flat wind as the ball is taken from the high point at 180 and swept in front with the left hand on top of the right--a scything motion. This "steering" allows the four turner to bring the ball to the front correctly. The speed of the wind should be the maximum that the thrower can handle. You'll know that you wind too fast when the ball isn't where it is supposed to be in the turns!

9.   As the ball comes off the high point, the three turner will be winding with a bit more velocity. Both throwers must now lower the center of gravity to prepare for the entry. As the ball comes through 270, both will initially put more weight on the left side. This will be necessary to prevent "falling away" on entry. When the ball comes past 0, the three turner may counter with the hips set way back (Syedikh), with a fairly straight left leg. As the left is straighter, the advanced thrower like Syedikh can "cook" on the winds and let the ball carry him into the first turn. Most throwers will keep the left leg bent.

10.   Throwers with good speed can let the ball go by the 0 point and concentrate on controlling the entry with the right arm.

11.   The pendulum motion doesn't apply to the first two turns with a four turn throw. As the three turner has a steeper ball, he should really feel the ball accelerate downward to the low point. The four turner should only be 5-10% slower going into the first turn. His advantage will be starting the second turn faster than the three turner's first. Theoretically,

---

[1]Michel Thieurmel, op. cit., p. 36-37.

Fig. 14.7.[1] Sweep to the entry.

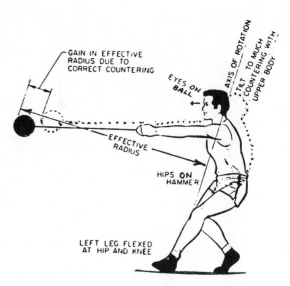

Fig. 14.8.[2] As the hammer rises, relax the arms and shoulders and let them be pulled forward in the direction of the hammer. Keep your left knee flexed as you do this. Keep chin up.

the four turn thrower should have a longer throw if he can accelerate throughout the turns.

12. The trajectory is very different for three and four turners. The three turner cannot enter with a flat ball as he will surely be incapable of reaching the proper release angle of about 43 degrees or so.

B. The Turns.

1. Three turners will start the turn with the left foot by lifting the toe and twisting to the left. The right foot is not very active, but keeps pressure behind the ball after the ball passes it in front. The four turner leans forward more to get a wide radius with the toe turn. Sedykh in recent years has worked at increasing his radius going into the turn. In a 1982 film, it appeared that Litvinov and Nikulin had a wider radius on the entry than Syedikh, but the ball was moving slower due to the difference between the toe turn and the regular heel/toe turn.

2. Slower throwers cannot keep the foot on the ground and expect to pick up the ball early. Syedikh has used the following angles on a 264' throw, winning the 1982 USSR/USA meet; 74 degrees for the first right foot pickup; 61 for the second; 55 for the third. He landed at the following degrees: 220; 218; and 231 for the final turn. If the thrower appears to have good right leg action, but lands late, he must work on getting his foot off the ground earlier and keep it tight. From this information, we can generalize: (1) leave before 90 on the first turn, (2) leave earlier on subsequent turns. The objective is to have a long active phase, not just a long double support.

3. Syedikh has used a technique of tracking across the circle which can aid in placing the right foot down and behind the left. As the left foot turns toward 130-160, he shifts onto the ball off the side of his foot. This causes him to curve slightly down the circle as in Fig. 14.9-- a 264-foot throw.

If the thrower works on twisting the left foot all the way around prior to grounding the right, he will achieve a bowed leg effect, similar to many of the German stylists. This is

[1]Michel Thieurmel, op. cit., p. 55.

[2]Felton and Simonyi, op. cit., drawing #12.

different technique which can be successful, but may require more body strength as the hips are usually off the ball when the athlete attempts to accelerate the hammer. If the thrower can keep the knees off to the right when the right foot lands, he will be able to use his entire body in the active phase of the throw.

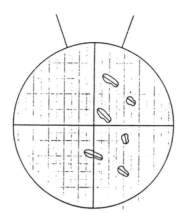

Fig. 14.9.[1] Syedikh's tracking method.

4. Ernst Klement, coach of Karl Riehm, described another key phase of the throw: "Blocking is a term used to describe holding the body rigid. In each turn there are two stages when the thrower should block. The first block occurs at the entry into each turn as the hammer passes through the 60 degree position. Hold the arms and body rigid as the body turns to the left and the hammer rises to its high point. Block again when the right foot is placed at the completion of each turn."[2]

This action will prevent the thrower from separating the hips and shoulders and will enable the ball to help turn the thrower, and then the athlete to accelerate the ball.

5. The right leg must move quickly to step over the left ankle causing the thighs to either touch, or get very close.

6. Many throwers try to stand up a bit at the low point to get more on the ball. This causes a marked raising and lowering of the center of gravity. Bondarchuk believes that the up and down movement should be kept to a minimum. However, Nikulin has had great success going up and down like a yo-yo! The switch from heel to toe can give the impression of a great drop on the left leg, even if there is little center of gravity movement. This must be worked out by each athlete as there are so many variables. Bondarchuk's theory is simpler: stay low! What does happen at each low point is a sitting back against the ball's pull. This helps to accelerate the ball and gets you back on your left heel so that you can turn down the circle, not in one spot. The excellent drawing (Fig. 14.10)[3] shows clearly that, to maintain his balance, the thrower must "sit back" against the hammer as the centrifugal force it exerts on him during each turn gets progressively larger.

The two smaller pictures illustrate how bent over the athlete is in the first turn compared to a later turn. The back becomes more vertical. Regardless of how much the athlete may come up at the low point, the one fact remains: you must be lower at each high point. While this sounds complicated, it really isn't once you are out at the circle.

While the radius in the first turn (Fig. 14.10--1) is longer, by actively straightening the back on entering the second turn, the speed of the ball will increase.

---

[1]Dapena, op. cit., p. 26.

[2]Ernst Klement, "Thoughts on the Hammer Throw," by Merv Kemp, *Modern Athlete and Coach*, Australian Track Coaches Assoc., Vol. 21, #4, Oct. 1983, p. 42.
[3]Jim Hay, *The Biomechanics of Sports Techniques*, Prentice Hall, NJ, 1978, p. 493.

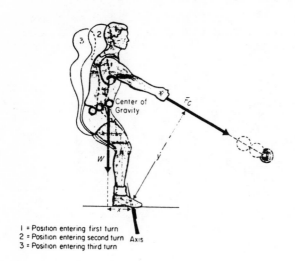

I = Position entering first turn
2 = Position entering second turn   Axis
3 = Position entering third turn

Fig. 14.10. "Sitting back."

Fig. 14.11. Increased force changes the body's position in subsequent turns.

7. In each turn, the thrower will have to counter more by: (1) bending the left more each turn, (2) leaning more to the center of the axis. Fig. 14.8 showed how it is important to

Fig. 14.12[1]. Sequence of a hammer throw. The initial trajectory of the hammer after release (position v) is up and to the right in this drawing. The black and white horizontal bars indicate time intervals when both feet, and the left foot alone, respectively, are in contact with the ground. Each white-plus-black section indicates one turn.

---

[1]Jesus Dapena, "Factors Affecting the Fluctuations of Hammer Speed in the Throw," *Hammer Notes*, #8, 1984, p. 57.

maintain what Sam Felton called the "hip angle." If you go into the turn with a straight left leg, you will have to counter with your shoulders, as few have been able to use the hip counter employed by Syedikh in the first turn. Nikulin's left leg is almost straight going into his first turn. His ball is very flat and his turn is not that fast. There are no exact angles to work for as each athlete has different skills. Litvinov has to counter with his shoulders in the final turns because he is light. Even then, his arms and shoulders are pulled forward to keep the radius loss at the minimum.

8. Fig. 14.12 gives a view of a total throw. You can see many of the previous points: (1) increased sitback, (2) lower each turn, (3) straight arms, (4) hips on the ball, etc.

C. Delivery.

1. The final phase of the throw is the delivery. Proper mechanics here add a great deal to the throw. Here is what Jesus Dapena wrote about Jorg Schaefer's delivery in the 1982 West Germany/USA dual meet:

All the throwers except Schaefer had their knees pointing more or less toward the left. This reflected various degrees of compliance with the modern "270 degree landing" technique. Schaefer, on the other hand, had his knees and feet pointing more or less toward the reader, with a great degree of twist of his shoulders relative to his hips, very similar to Klim's older "0 landing" technique. Schaefer's sequence shows a very strong pulling position in the third image, and very violent knee and hip extension between the third and sixth images. Perhaps this was the key to his great acceleration of the hammer...It is left to the reader to speculate on how he did it![1]

SCH

SYE

Fig. 14.13.[2] The delivery. On this throw, Schaefer (SCH) achieved 248'3"; Syedikh (SYE), 264'.

Dr. Dapena went on to say that, based on normal increase in hammer speed in the release, he thought Schaefer would have thrown around 220' on this throw. However, this release (Fig. 14.13--SCH) yielded a 248'3" throw!

---

[1]Jesus Dapena, op. cit., 1981, p. 56.

[2]Jesus Dapena, op. cit., 1981, p. 54.

Keeping in mind that these two men have PR's 35' apart, we can learn something from both throwers. Syedikh has some advantages, as shown in Fig. 14.13 SYE: (1) the ball is moving much faster at the start of the sequence, (2) he has a longer radius combined with a longer double support, (3) he keeps his weight in the center and drives up with little falling away, which would reduce the radius. Schaefer does the most in a short time: (1) keeps his legs down longer which gives him more force as the ball rises, (2) employs great explosive strength at the right time.

Both throwers must do the following: (1) drive the ball down to the low point without straightening the legs, (2) keep the arms out and use the large muscles of the body, (3) sit back hard against the pull of the ball when it is near the low point, (4) lift the legs and lean back only enough to keep balance as the ball hits the low point.

Litvinov told American thrower, Andy Bessette, during a training session that the release is like a car hitting a wall and the passenger (the hammer) keeps going through the wind-shield. This concept was popularized by Syedikh during the 1976 Olympics. The left foot stops turning which stops the pelvis from rotating, creating a whip-like action. Of course, the right foot must also be in the right position, behind the left, to accomplish this hip stop. Litvinov used this delivery action to win the 1979 World Cup and any observer would have to say the above description is correct.

After all this technique talk, it is imperative to repeat the old coaching law: KEEP IT SIMPLE. Some hammer throwers work on the most obscure point of the throw that they can find. You'll hear things like: "Whip that left heel," etc. Be polite but stick to the basics.

HOW TO BEGIN

First, refer to Fig. 14.14 to get yourself oriented. The direction you are throwing is called "180 degrees," while the general direction of the low point is around "0 or 360 degrees." In the remainder of this chapter, there will be many references to degrees.

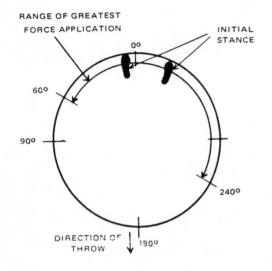

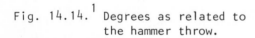

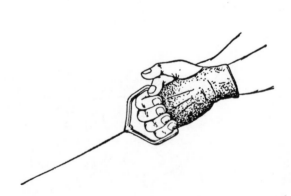

Fig. 14.14.[1] Degrees as related to the hammer throw.

Fig. 14.15. The grip.

The Teaching Progression.

Start with light hammers, medicine balls in a sling, sandbags on a rope, etc. High school athletes should use a 4 kilo ball for boys, 2 or 3 kilo for girls, if you have hammers.

---

[1]Mike Cairns, "The Hammer Throw," *Track Technique*, Vol. 8, Spring, 1981, p. 21.

These weights should be lowered depending on the strength of the athlete, not raised. Do not reach the hammer with a 25 or 35 lb. weight!

1. Grip the hammer as in Fig. 14.15. The gloved left hand is placed in the handle so the middle phalanges of the fingers are against the handle. Place the right hand over the left and

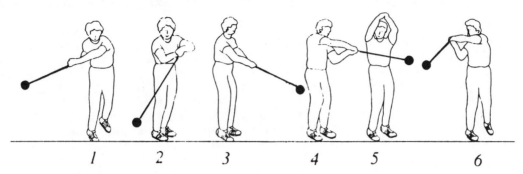

Fig. 14.16.[1] The wind.

cross the thumbs as shown, left thumb over right. The ball is behind the thrower's right side. The feet are more than shoulder width apart; weight more on the right leg at the start. Pull the hammer and begin to wind it concentrating on the left arms and shoulders. As the ball passes the left side of the body curl the left arm back-- right arm just follows--and twist the shoulders to the right as the ball goes behind. Lean to the front, then SNAP--pressure all the time. Do this until the left arm and shoulders are co- ordinated, taking a few winds at a time. SWEEP-CURL-TWIST.

The wind used to be marked by big weight shifts, pumping legs, and a low point way to the right. Syedikh winds very fast; but stays more upright than he did when he was throwing 30' less.

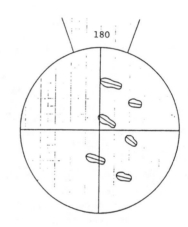

Fig. 14.17.[2] The footwork of Yuriy Syedikh.

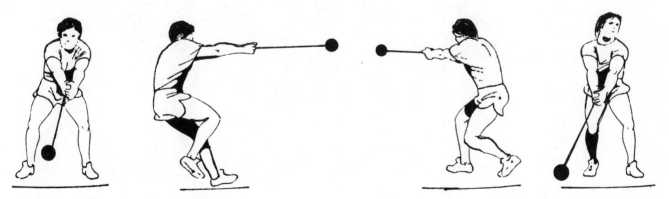

Fig. 14.18.[3] The basic turn.

[1]Michel Thieurmel, op. cit., p. 36-37.
[2]Jesus Dapena, *Biomechanical Analysis of Hammer Throw*, #1, USOC/TAC, July, 1982, p. 26.
[3]Michel Thieurmel, op. cit., p. 57.

2. Try using the left hand with a light hammer or sandbag, then the right. Sweep, curl, past the face, cast it out--repeat. It's quite an exercise and will loosen tight shoulders.

3. Next, try the turns. Show a 90 degree pivot on the left heel and right ball. In the beginning, you can turn 180 degrees on the left to get the feel while the right foot is down. As soon as the turn can be done with some reasonable skill, abandon that practice except as a drill.

4. We are at the stage of a 180 degree turn. Next is to feel the weight transfer to the left ball. While rotating on the left ball, place the right foot down a bit less than 270. The right foot and left foot are pointing in almost the same direction--off to the right. Not many throwers have developed the footwork shown in this diagram of Syedikh (Fig. 14.17).No one can "copy" this exactly, and many have tried. The goal is just to get the feet off to the side, and not to the front. In earlier techniques, the feet did point to the front, eliminating the early work on the hammer in double support. Now, your weight is on the balls of both feet. Twist both feet to 0 degrees, or the original position. Practice this footwork, and keep the hips and shoulders together--don't try to twist the hips further around than the shoulders. Your arms should be in the proper position, after you've worked on the footwork for a few minutes. Keep them out in front of your body as in Fig. 14.16 #2. When you get a hammer in your hands and learn to turn faster, you will learn about the necessity of "sitting back" against the hammer pull at the low point so that your body weight will shift back to allow you to make the heel turn. Fig. 14.18 summarizes the motion.

5. Now, pick up the hammer again and place it directly in front of the chest with straight arms. Keep the arms straight! Turn slowly to 90, then 180, then about 260, then back to 0. Correct balance. Once you can do one turn reasonably well, try two. Right now, since the athlete is holding an implement, the path will widen more each turn and a low/high point pattern emerges. A very talented athlete will be able to keep the low point in front, with others, work on the turns with the feet and don't distract from this major task. Try three, even four turns emphasizing balance, continuous rotation, and neat, tight turns. The Russians do this same drill up to 50 turns!

6. Go back to the wind and have the athlete practice the final segment of the throw--the release. Many coaches will do this at the start so that the athlete will be excited about throwing. It is preferred to wait so that the athlete has handled the implement a bit. A 30' throw might not have the desired effect. Do two winds, but as the ball descends from 180 on the last one, have him bend only his legs as if he had a weight on his back. As the ball gets to 0, he will be squatting. Keeping the arms straight, the athlete will turn to the left 90 degrees and lift his legs to deliver the ball. A weighted medicine ball is even better for this drill. Use the legs! Fig. 14.19 by Jesus Dapena shows the basic delivery action. It's not that hard.

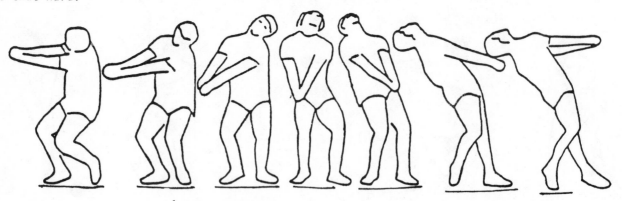

Fig. 14.19.[1] Klaus Ploghaus.

7. Now, put it all together. For 10-15 minutes, work on two winds, one turn, and a release. In about 45 minutes, a good athlete can do two winds, two turns, and a release. The

[1]Jesus Dapena, *Biomechanical Analysis of Hammer Throw #2*, USOC/TAC, June 1983, p. 100.

"hook" will be in deep then and few athletes have resisted the hammer once they get the basic feeling.

TRAINING FOR THE HAMMER

Hammer Notes #1-8[1] contains many examples of training outlines. The following general principles are followed by most of the world's top throwers. Keep in mind that what works for a full time European thrower will not apply to a typical college thrower in the US who has less time to work out.

Heavier hammers and the regulation hammer are generally thrown early in the year, while the lighter hammers and the regulation hammer are thrown in the competitive period.

Current hammer throwers include gymnastics, bounding, sprinting in the program all year. The gymnastics and bounding are tapered down in the competitive period.

For basic strength, hammer throwers stick to a few weight exercises: power cleans, squats-- front and back, and the snatch. Weaker throwers may have to include some deadlifts, rowing, pulls--at the discretion of the coach. Upper body exercises such as curls and bench presses are rarely done.

Beginning throwers should use hammers lighter than the regulation hammer. It is wise to build in speed early in the career. Nikulin is a perfect example of this philosophy.

Running, stretching, and easy drills are included in the warm up.

As with any form of exercise, the volume should be decreased as the competitions approach. A short, intense workout, followed by a proper rest period is far better than a long, tiring workout before a meet.

Every thrower is different and will have to work on the weak spots in his throw, and not aim to "throw far" on every throw.

The modern hammer thrower is no longer a large, slow, ex-shotputter, but is more likely to be a 220-240 pound, fast athlete who could excel in a number of different events or sports. During the off-season, many of the Russian throwers get so proficient at their play in other sports such as volleyball and basketball that you would hardly guess that throwing was the number one priority. In the past, American throwers spent too much time in the weight room. This has changed while the level of throwing has risen.

Double Periodized Year. The following chart[2], adapted from Frank Dick, presents the situation for most of our throwers in the US:

MONTHS	Aug	Sep	Oct	Nov	Dec	Jan	Feb	Mar	Apr	May	Jun	Jul
PHASES	1_1			2_1		3_1		2_2	2_2	3_2	4	5
PERIODS	Preparation (1)				Competition (1)			Prep (2)		Comp (2)		Tran-sition

This chart is not meant as an absolute, but merely a general guide. The NCAA has the 35 lb. weight as an official event, therefore hammer throwers have a competition period from the beginning of December to mid-March. A few high schools and college women are throwing the 25 lb. weight during this period. International level throwers would adjust this chart to extend the competition into August. If the hammer thrower does not throw the 35 lb. weight the first competition period is eliminated.

---

[1] For further information about back issues of *Hammer Notes*, write to Kevin McGill, Columbia University, Dodge Fitness Center, NYC, NY 10027.

[2] Frank Dick, *Training Theory*, BAAB, London, 1978, p. 56.

Assuming that a proper warm up is included, the following is an example of the 7 day microcycles used in the two periods, Preparation and Competition:

Preparation

Day 1   Circuit training: hurdle hops, crunch situps, squat thrusts, pullups, 30 yd. sprints, etc. 15 minutes.
30-50 throws with 20, 18 and 16 pound hammers 75 minutes.
Sprints--10 x 40 yds - 10-15 minutes
Weights--Heavy day 60-90 minutes.
Total time: will vary from about 2 to $3\frac{1}{2}$ hours. Emphasis on throwing and conditioning.

Day 2   30-50 throws. Drills with a "pud," or 35 lb. ball with handle welded on; release work with a rubber medicine ball about 11 lbs; finish with 18 and 16 lb. hammers. 75 minutes.
Jump training--various bounding drills 20 minutes.
Sprints--starts from blocks 10 minutes.
Stomach work--10 minutes.
Total time: varies from 2 to $2\frac{1}{2}$ hours.

Day 3   Same as Day #1 except weights medium or light. This means in comparison to the hard weight workout Monday, not "light" weights!

Day 4   Basketball, soccer, volleyball, etc. 30 minutes.
Medicine ball work--release drills and regular medicine ball drills--20 minutes.
20-40 throws with 14 and 16 pound hammers 60 minutes
Jumps and sprints 20 minutes.
Total time: $2\frac{1}{2}$ to 3 hours.

Day 5   Circuit training 10 minutes.
30-50 throws with 20, 18, and 16 lb. hammers 75 minutes.
Weights--light or medium, alternate with Day #3 60 minutes
Sprints--starts and 40 yds. 15 minutes.
Total time: varies from $2\frac{1}{2}$ to $3\frac{1}{2}$ hours.

Day 6   Throw in a development meet or simulated competition.

Day 7   Basketball, soccer, or a racquet sport 60 minutes.

Competition

Follow the same general plan as for Preparation with these modifications:

1. Weights are reduced gradually in volume as the big meets approach.
2. Jump drills are cut back drastically.
3. Circuit training is dropped.
4. Emphasis is on hammer technique and specific drills.
5. Workout time is reduced significantly, but the intensity is kept high. This is no time for slow throwing in practice!
6. Use more of the 13 and 14 pound hammers and knock off the 18 and 20.

Developing greater speed in the turns. After a basic technique has been mastered, the question arises as to how best to increase the speed of the turns. Coaches have tried sprinting, multiple jumps, games, explosive lifting. All of these play a key role in the power program. But one area remains relatively unexplored in the U.S.: different weighted hammers. Bondarchuk[1] has tried to construct programs varying one of the following--months, weeks, even days. Early in the season, you would throw heavy hammers only when you adjust monthly. Weekly, you use either light, normal, or heavy hammers for a whole week. Daily, use the same procedure as for weeks. Let's look at the final choice, the one most critical in developing speed in the hammer: the daily workout.

Here are a few alternatives using 30 total throws as a norm:
a.   heavy + standard + light (10 sets of 3 hammers)
b.   10 light + 10 standard + 10 heavy (Complete each set before going on.)
c.   light + standard (10 sets of 2 hammers) + 10 heavy
d.   light + standard + heavy (10 sets of 3 hammers)
e.   5 heavy + 1 standard (5 sets)
f.   9 light + 1 standard (3 sets)

Training for Related Power in the Hammer. There are as many cycles as there are coaches writing them. No one particular cycle has emerged as the "secret." Heavy weight training year round has given way to the cycle. One coach uses 3 sets of 5 reps, another a pyramid, a third coach only does doubles. It can get confusing for the athlete. To summarize the massive amount of literature on the subject, we will list the following principles:

1-- Use variety in your training, especially with weights. Doing the same thing--3 x 10, or 3 x 5, etc. will slow progress.
2-- While the 35 lb. weight has been criticized in the U.S., intermediate range throwers can benefit by using heavy hammers, such as the 35 in the early stage of training. The Russians take thousands of throws each year with heavy weights, a bit longer than the normal length for our 35.
3-- Use less intensity, higher volume weight training, 3 to 5 sets of 10 in the early stage of the preparation period to establish a base.
4-- Use pyramids, 3 sets of 5, etc. after the base is established.
5-- To develop power, the use of jumping drills and depth jumps may be more specific to the hammer than repeated heavy squats. As the hammer is a rotational sprint, a quick reflex is needed to turn fast.
6-- Jumping with weights, sprinting, throwing, and jump drills can be combined in the same workout for a challenging power workout.

In training for power, it may be wise to avoid the following:

1-- Dropping down during the Olympic lifts. A deep position is nice for the lifters, but does nothing for hammer throwers. Bill Green, AR holder in the hammer, is one of our top throwers who avoids the deep positions in the clean and the snatch.
2-- Training only in the frontal plane. Remember that the hammer is a rotational event and involves the muscles in the back and the sides. Do twisting exercises!
3-- Not tapering for competitions. The easiest weeks of the year are those before the big meets. Train short and fast in everything you do.
4-- Copying the workout of a champion. The last thing you need as a younger thrower is to follow the workout of someone older, stronger, and more experienced. When you read that so and so does 15 sets of deadlifts with 500 lbs., you might try to key in on that exercise with disastrous results.

---

[1]Anatoli Bondarchuk, "Improvement of Speed Through the Use of Different Weighted Implements," trans. by Jimmy Pedemonte, Hammer Notes, #7, p. 25.

RELATED POWER EXERCISES

V. Petrov

Decathlon great Rafer Johnson.

Daley Thompson, Olympic decathlon champion, 1980 and 1984./Photo by Theo Van de Rakt.

Chapter 15
THE DECATHLON

Of all Modern Olympic contests, the decathlon most clearly reflects the Ancient Greek Games ideal of all-round, balanced excellence in sports. A full track meet in miniature, it provides the most demanding test of the five "s" words: speed, stamina, strength, skill and self-discipline--ever devised in any sports competition.[1]

The decathlon includes ten events: four track events--100m dash, 110m high hurdles, 400m dash, 1500m run; three jumping events--running high jump, pole vault, running long jump; three throwing events--16# shot, discus, javelin. Performance in these ten events is scored, not by comparison with those of other competitors, but by reference to a scoring table. Examples: on the 1962 tables, six feet (1.83m) in the high jump scores 743 points; 50 feet (15.26m) in the shot 804 points; 50 seconds in the 400m dash, 805 points. The man gaining the greatest number of points for ten events is the decathlon winner.

Five events are held during each of two days; the 400m dash completes the first; the 1500m run, the second. An impression is held generally, eagerly nourished by the media, that such a schedule is cruelly exhausting or grueling. But we need only to watch such Olympic champions as Bruce Jenner or Bill Toomey as they scamper joyously around the track immediately after finishing the last event, the 1500, to know they are far from utter exhaustion. Year-round, effective training has prepared them for such a high level of energy output; such words as "grueling" are valid only when preparation is inadequate for attempted performance.

Personally,[2] the decathlon--in competition and for the most part in training--was an exciting joy. It was fun to move from one event to another, not once or twice, but ten times--ten phases of a single competition. Of course, in the 1920s, the high tension that exists in today's attitude of win-or-nothing was absent. Few cared--nationally or locally, even in an Olympic year--if we won or lost.

Secondly, and most important, I have always rejected sport as a violent struggle against antagonistic opponents. In the decathlon, the struggle is against time, distance, fatigue, and one's inner fears of weakness or failure. Other decathletes are fellow-competitors, helpful motivators to doing one's best, often ignored, often good friends, never hostile. Each concentrates on doing his utmost, without concern for diminishing the efforts of others. Whoever scores the most points on the Tables is the victor.

In my years of decathlon competition--Olympic and National--I cannot remember a single incident of hostility--no attempts to intimidate or even belittle, no unsettling jibes at the start of a sprint or hurdle, no "hogging" of implements during warm-ups. But I do remember a

---

[1] In writing this Decathlon Chapter--its facts, its scoring tables, its enthusiasm for the decathlon--I am heavily indebted to Dr. Frank Zarmowski for numerous letters and his excellent publications: THE DECATHLON GUIDE (published annually by The Athletics Congress, P.O. Box 120, Indianapolis, Ind., 46206; his 1984 OLYMPIC GAMES HANDBOOK FOR THE DECATHLON, and especially his DECA NEWSLETTER (published 8 times a year), both of which are obtainable from the author, Dean of Graduate Program of Business, Mt. St. Mary's College, Emmitsburg, MD 21727.
[2] The author was U.S. Decathlon Champion, 1928 and 1929, and bronze medallist, 1928 Olympic Games, Amsterdam.

TABLE 15.1

OUTSTANDING PERFORMANCES -- DECATHLON

OLYMPIC CHAMPIONS

Date	Record[1]	Name	Affiliation	Age	Hgt.	Wgt.	Y[2]	D[3]
1912	6649	Jim Thorpe	USA	24	6'0''	190	(Note: Thorpe, 1912, disqualified but in 1984 was reinstated.)	
1912	6044	Hugo Weislander	Swe					
1920	5882	Helge Lövland	Nor					
1924	6562	Harold Osborn	USA	22	5'11½''	170	6	6
1928	6667	Paavo Yrjölä	Fin	26	6'	185	11	14
1932	6814	James Bausch	USA	26	6'2''	210	2	5
1936	7341	Glenn Morris	USA	24	6'2''	185	1	3
1948	6713	Robert Mathias	USA	17	6'2½''	190		
1952	7668	Robert Mathias	USA	22	6'3''	199	5	10
1956	7657	Milton Campbell	USA	23	6'3''	208	3	5
1960	7990	Rafer Johnson	USA	25	6'4''	200	7	11
1964	7816	Willi Holdorf	W.Germ	24	5'11½''	198	6	10
1968	8158	William Toomey	USA	29	6'1½''	195	11	38
1972	8467	Nikolay Avilov	USSR	24	6'3''	192	5	17
1976	8634	Bruce Jenner	USA	26	6'2''	198	7	29
1980	8522	Daley Thompson	G.B.	21	6'	195	6	14
1984	8846	Daley Thompson	G.B.	25	6'1''	190	10	25

WORLD-RECORD PERFORMANCES OF SPECIAL INTEREST

1912	6649	Jim Thorpe	USA
	11.2	6.79	12.89	1.87	51.2	15.6	36.98	3.25	45.70	4:40.1

1952 7668 Robert Mathias USA 7887 by 1920 T
10.9 22-11 50-2½ 6-3 50.2 14.7 153-10 13-1½ 194-3 4:50.8

1960 7990 Rafer Johnson USA At Final Olympic Trials
10.6 24-9½ 52-0 5-10 48.6 14.5 170-6½ 13-¼ 233-3 5:09.9

1969 8158 Bill Toomey USA Won 5 AAU titles (1965-69)--most ever
10.3 25-5½ 47-2¼ 6-4 47.1 14.3 152-6½ 14-¼ 215-8 4:39.4

1976 8638 Bruce Jenner USA 26 6'2'' 198 Set in winning Montreal OG

10.94 23-8½ 50-4¼ 6-8 47.5 14.8 164-2 15-9 224-10 4:12.6

1980 8649 Guido Kratschmer W. Ger. 25 6'1½'' 200
10.58 25-7 50-9 6-6 3/4 48.04 13.92 149-4 15-1¼ 218-2½ 4:24.15

1983 8831 Jurgen Hingsen W. Ger. 25 6'6 3/4'' 214
10.70 7.76 16.42 2.07 48.05 14.07 49.36 4.90 59.84 4:19.7

1984 8846 Daley Thompson G.B. 25 6'1'' 190
10.44 8.01 15.72 2.03 46.97 14.34 46.56 5.00 65.24 4:35

U.S. COLLEGIATE RECORD

8278 William Motti Mount St. Mary's College
11.28 7.76 16.42 2.07 48.05 14.07 49.36 4.90 59.84 4:19.7

Important

[1]All scores converted to new 1985 Tables.   [2]Number of years of decathlon competition. [3]Total number of career competitions in the decathlon.

number of helpful acts--sharing a blanket in the cold or poncho in the rain, or loaning tape, a pair of spikes, even a vaulting pole. In fact, most decathlons bring forth such acts of helping each other, and may the best man win. More so, I think, than in single-events. Perhaps the long and varied competition tends to avoid concentrations of tensions and emotions that spill over into aggression against others. Perhaps it's the scoring Tables that intervene between potential adversaries and become the real enemy. But whatever the reason, the decathlon is great fun, and fair play is the very essence of its attitudes.

Sam Adams, decathlete, UCSB track coach and U. S. National Decathlon Coach, strongly supports these views,[1]

(The decathlon) is an event that gives you, not one, but ten chances. It is an event that takes all your skills, and all your strength, and all your heart if you are to excel. There are no short cuts. There are no tricks. There are no easy ways to achieve your potential in this event. There is intelligent, progressive training for achievable goals. When goals are grasped, higher goals are always there to be reached for.

Take up the challenge. You will find a close knit group of decathletes with a common goal, and an understanding of what you are experiencing. You will find challenge, frustration and satisfaction, disappointment and achievement, woe and joy. But most of all, you will find the Decathlon is the best of Track and Field, and Sport itself.

The Ancient Greeks Had No Decathlon. Though the word, "decathlon," is Greek in origin-- *deka* (ten) + *athlos* (contests)--its use is modern. The Ancient Greek Games included only a five-event all-around: a running long jump with weights ($2\frac{1}{2}$-10#); a javelin throw using a thong looped over one or two fingers and twisted several times around the javelin shaft; a discus throw of varying weight from three to as much as 49 pounds; a stade race (sprinting one length of the stadium); and, most admired by all, wrestling. As soon as any man won three events, as with sets in modern tennis, he became pentathlon champion.[2]

The Ancient Greek Olympics occurred during a thousand years (776 B.C.-384 A.D.), with an almost unchanged schedule of events. Surprisingly, the first three events listed above were never held as single events, only as related to the pentathlon. This gives us some awareness of the high regard the Greeks has for well-rounded development as contrasted with one-event specialization. A man could be the greatest long jumper, discus thrower or javelin thrower of his time but never win an Olympic victory other than in the pentathlon with its emphasis on a harmony of speed, power and beauty of style.

HISTORY OF DECATHLON DEVELOPMENT

The first scoring tables for a ten-event all-around were constructed in 1883 by W. B. Curtis, sometimes called "the father of United States track and field" because of his early and vigorous efforts in organization. As with all later systems, scoring occurred without reference to others' performances, only by reference to some arithmetical standard. Curtis allowed 1000 points for equalling the 1883 AAU record, then scaled points down with little beyond good judgment to guide him, and with almost no basis for balanced scoring among the events.

Since then, at least a dozen versions of the decathlon have been proposed; some with other events; most with a "new and better" method of scoring; almost all by one of the Scandinavian countries: Sweden (1902, 1906, 1909, 1912, 1952, 1962); Finland (1909, 1934); Denmark (1901, 1910); Norway (1909). The only other proposals were by Germany (1911) and that by the United States (1920) used in the Antwerp, Paris and Amsterdam Olympics. Sweden's 1962 Tables (modified, 1971, by conversion to 100ths) remained in use through the 1984 Los Angeles Olympic Games. In 1984 new Tables were officially accepted to become effective April 1985. Throughout this Chapter, all scores are from the 1985 Tables.

[1]Sam Adams, "Reflections on Decathlon," *Track & Field Quarterly Review*, Vol. 79 #2, Summer 1979, p. 5.

[2]The most authoritative and fascinating source for these statements is H. A. Harris, *GREEK ATHLETES AND ATHLETICS*, Hutchinson & Co., London, 1964, 242 pps.

1985 Scoring Tables. In August 1984, the Technical Committee of the IAAF established new Tables for the Decathlon to become effective April 1985. In general, the intent of these Tables was to form a better balance in scoring (1) consistent with recent improvements in equipment, techniques or training, and (2) to improve the obvious imbalances present in the old 1962 Tables. The most serious of these were apparent in the pole vault and 1500 meters. In the pole vault average scores by great decathletes was over 700 points (Thompson, 1984 WR, vaulted 5 meters for 1052 points). In contrast, that for the 1500-meters run on the 1962 Tables was less than 600 points (Thompson, 1984 WR, ran 4:35 for 556 points). Under the new 1985 Tables for these same performances, Thompson would have scored 910 points for the pole vault: 712 points for the 1500--quite obviously a better balanced scoring.

On the other hand, Frank Zarnowski, an astute critic of the old Tables, finds such "improvements" inadequate in that the slope of scoring (increments increase for higher performances) has been changed. For example, "though the pole vault has been devalued in actual scoring, its slope of scoring has been increased so that it now pays decathletes to work on improving their vaulting. In contrast, even though the 1500 will give more absolute points on the new Tables, they will give 15.7 percent fewer points for every increment of improvement, and so, will discourage emphasis on that event and defeat the very purpose the 1985 Tables were intended to achieve. Conclusion: even newer Tables within the decade."

GREAT OLYMPIC DECATHLETES

The first decathlon in the Olympic Games was in 1912 at Stockholm, Sweden. Events were scheduled during two days in the same order as today's competitions. New scoring tables gave fairer, better-balanced scoring. As today, only three attempts were allowed in the three throws and the long jump.

Jim Thorpe, 1912 Olympic "Champion." This first Olympic decathlon was actually won by the Carlisle Indian, Jim Thorpe, generally considered America's greatest all-time, all-sport athlete. It was his first and only decathlon! But his total of 8412 points (1912 Tables) surpassed by almost 700 points that of the official winner (Hugo Weislander, Sweden, 7724 points), a point difference exceeded only once in Olympic history (Mathias, 1952, 912 points).

Today, with our perfect conditions for performance, we find it hard to appreciate the amazing quality of his achievement (6756, 1962 Tables). In 1912, facilities, equipment, training were all at lowest levels. Jumping pits were of turned-over earth; high jump and pole vault standards were but eight feet apart; the pole vault runways were "as long as possible--say 50 feet;" poles were of spruce that, for a big man, weighed about eight pounds; hurdles were heavy and, when hit, rose on their inverted-T-shaped bases; throwing surfaces were of dirt; running tracks were soft. Even more astonishing, Thorpe also won the pentathlon (winning four of five events by wide margins); and was among the finalists in three individual events--high jump, long jump, shot.

But in 1913, a newspaper disclosed, and Thorpe naively confirmed in writing, that he had accepted money (small even for those days) for playing semi-pro baseball during summer vacations prior to the Olympics. If we weight 1912 Olympic attitudes and rules of amateurism plus Thorpe's written acknowledgement of payments, the U.S. Olympic Committee (the I.O.C. was not involved) had no choice but to ask that Thorpe's name be erased from the official books and his prizes returned. For a half century Thorpe's pre-eminence as an amateur athlete was unrecognized. But amateurism gradually acquired a more relaxed code; by present-day Olympic rules and practice, Thorpe's misconduct would be ignored. In 1976, he was inducted into the National Track and Field Hall of Fame which recognizes only amateur performances.

Jim Thorpe's great achievement through natural, untrained talent set the pattern for decathletes in the United States for the next half-century, until about 1960. It was generally considered a noteworthy but freakish event for which interest of spectators, media and competitors was almost nil for three years of each Olympiad, and rose but little during the Olympic year. The National AAU Outdoor Championships was the only regular competition. For this meet, open to all with no qualifying standards, a paltry score of men might enter and a dozen or so actually compete. In addition, the Relay Meets at Pennsylvania, Drake and Kansas variably did and did not hold the event. With such minimal competition, no one trained seriously for the decathlon as a separate event; a few weeks usually sufficed.

Harold Osborn, 1924 Olympic Champion. Harold Osborn is the only man in Olympic Games history to win the decathlon (6668 pts., 1962 tables, a world record) and an individual event (high jump, 6'6", Olympic record). Unlike other decathletes, Osborn entered the decathlon very gradually and late in his career--just after graduation from the University of Illinois, 1922. As a freshman, he first signed up as a distance runner, but, discovering on his own initiative that he could outdo all others in the high jump, he shifted to that event.

During my sophomore year in the fall, I started to enlarge my field a little. I tried hurdling and also took up my old event, the broad jump. In addition I generally managed to put in a little time with the weight men [he weighed about 160# at the time---JKD] and shortly afterward I took up cross-country work and made the squad.[1]

Osborn's coach at Illinois was Harry Gill, former Canadian All-Around Champion, so we can assume he was encouraged in such experiments. In his junior year, he "put in too much time training for the Pennsylvania Relays pentathlon. It finally proved to my satisfaction that running and jumping do not mix." In his senior year, he tried the septathlon in the Illinois Indoor Relays. But he did not compete in any decathlon until after graduation--1922, National AAU, second place. He won the National AAU titles in 1923, 1925 and 1926, as well as the Olympic title in 1924.

In 1924, Osborn established a world-record 6'8¼" in the high jump with a self-created, controversial style that resulted in changes in both high jump rules and construction of the standards. Also, Osborn undoubtedly had the longest multi-event career at high-quality levels in all track and field history. During 20 years (1923-1943), he won 18 National AAU outdoor and indoor titles in six events (35 medals in nine events), including the standing high jump and triple jump; and at age 37, in an informal competition, cleared 6'8½" in the high jump, a personal record.

Paavo Yrjöla, Finland, 1928 Olympic Champion. Paavo Yrjöla fully deserved selection to the DECA Hall of Fame for Decathletes. He competed in three Olympics during ten years (1922-1932) with a total of 14 decathlons--the most ever until Toomey's 38 in 11 years (1959-1969). He set four world records, climaxed by his 8053 (1920T) at the Amsterdam Olympics, but he also took 6th place at Los Angeles, 1932, at age 30.

Perhaps most remarkable, Yrjöla was a farmer, living some distance away from a track and field, and even further from a coach. In a 1976 TV interview he told how he constructed his own throwing and jumping facilities and ran over his own fields and through his own woods. (I was the U.S. champion and third at Amsterdam, 347 points behind. I had often wondered if a better effort here or there--. But as I listened to Yrjöla on TV, I bowed low to a superior decathlete who had overcome more handicaps than any of us.)

Jim Bausch, 1932 Olympic Champion. As with Osborn, Jim Bausch had no decathlon competition while in college; in fact, showed almost no potential. Bausch was known primarily as "Jarring Jim," a football fullback and basketball star at Kansas University. His best in track was a sixth place in the 1930 NCAA shot put championships at about 48 feet. But in his first decathlon, he won the 1931 Kansas Relays with an American record 7847 points (6529, 1962 tables). In total he competed in but five decathlons in a two-year career, climaxed by his world-record 8462 points (6896, 1962 tables) in winning the 1932 Olympics.

Glenn Morris, 1936 Olympic Champion. Equally remarkable in terms of natural, untrained talent was Glenn Morris, 1936 Olympic champion--7900 points (7421, 1962 tables). Glenn was an outstanding three-sport athlete at Colorado Agricultural College but in college track and field he showed no potential for the decathlon: 24.7--220y low hurdles, 15.4s--120y highs, 54s-- 440y hurdles. Amazingly, two years later, in his first decathlon, he won the Kansas Relays

---

[1]R. L. Templeton, *THE HIGH JUMP*, New York: American Sports Publishing Co., 1926, p. 157.

with an American record 7576 points (7192, 1962 tables). He then set successive world records at the American trials and Olympic finals. That was his entire decathlon career, all in one year--three attempts--one American record, two world records, one Olympic gold. Morris worked in Denver, hardly a decathlete's paradise. How much and what quality decathlon training could he have gotten in Denver with limited indoor facilities and coaching?

Keep in mind that during these years endurance training was considered to have negative effects for decathlon performance. What it might gain for the low-scoring 1500 was more than lost through its disastrous effects on muscle quickness and skill. Also that strength training was not merely ignored but actually abhorred for similar reasons. It's not surprising that, when setting his world record of 8462 points, Bausch did poorly in the endurance events (400m--54.2s, 1500m--5:17); and all the more credit to him that he did so well in the throwing events (shot--50'3", discus--146'3", javelin--203'1"), each of which surpassed the performances of all previous world-record decathletes. Even more amazing, Morris ran his Olympic 1500 in 4:33.2, not surpassed until 1972 when Avilov ran 4:22.8. Could his living and training, however limited, at Denver's 5000-feet altitude have been a contributing factor? Incidentally, his 4:33.2 was 25 seconds faster than he had ever run before, and was essential to his victory. Apparently his will-to-win was also a factor.

Bob Mathias, 1948, 1952 Olympic Champion. In contrast to late-blooming Bausch and Morris, the next two Olympic champions and world-record holders, Bob Mathias and Milt Campbell, began their track careers as decathletes while still in high school. Mathias' first attempt was at age 17 on June 10-11, 1948, at the end of his senior year. He won with 6790 points (1962 tables).[1] On June 26-27, he won the Olympic Trials--6902 points; on August 5-6, the London Olympic Finals--6826 points under the handicaps of heavy rain, soft takeoffs and track, and long delays in competition. During the next two years (Kiski Prep and Stanford--freshmen not eligible), Mathias won four decathlons, including two National AAU championships and a world record of 7452 points. That totalled seven decathlons during three pre-college years. He did not compete again for two years, winning the 1952 Olympic Trials with a world-record 7690 points, and the Olympic Finals with his third career world record of 7731 points.

But once into his college career of varsity track and football, Mathias insisted that his contribution to the Stanford team was primary. By competing in 4-5-6 events "wherever I could score a point or more," he somehow achieved a more balanced all-round performance, as evidenced by his amazing attainment of eight personal records in winning the 1952 Helsinki Olympics. But during these two college track seasons, "he works out on the track from three to five or six o'clock,"[2] hardly an adequate time for a ten-event specialist.

As with all previous decathletes, endurance training was ignored, even shunned. His biographer[2] states that his endurance training consisted of "jogging a couple of laps," or more rarely "running for ten minutes on the Stanford golf course." During his years of competition (1948-1952), power training was just beginning. Weightmen such as Parry O'Brien, USC, and Otis Chandler, at Bob's own University, both praised and practiced its values but weight lifting is not even mentioned in Mathias' biography. That, at Helsinki, he achieved 50'2" in the shot and 153'10" in the discus is all the more noteworthy.

Milt Campbell, 1956 Olympic Champion. Before entering Indiana University in 1954, Campbell competed in three decathlons: (1) At the end of his high school junior year (age 18), he qualified for the American Olympic team by taking second to Mathias, defeating Floyd Simmons, the 1948 bronze medallist. His total points (7176) are were the highest ever recorded for a first decathlon. (2) He took the 1952 Olympic silver medal (7132 points). (3) In 1953, after high school graduation, he won the National AAU title (7253 points).

Add that at Plainfield, N.J. High school he was an all-state football fullback, a letter

---

[1]Throughout the remainder of this section, all points, unless stated otherwise, will be scored on the 1962 tables.

[2]Jim Scott, *BOB MATHIAS, CHAMPION OF CHAMPIONS*, Englewood Cliffs, N.J.: Prentice-Hall, Inc., 1952, pp. 189, 191.

winner in wrestling, and an All-American high school free-style swimmer. (In 1953, black swimmers were rarely welcomed in swimming pools.) All in all, perhaps the most remarkable high school career in all of sport.

But then, strangest of all, during two years at Indiana, Campbell specialized in one event, the 120y high hurdles. In 1955 he won the National AAU championships in the fast time of 13.9s, but won no important college competitions. Though in the 1956 Olympics, he put the shot 48-5, high jumped 6-2½, ran the 400m in 48.8, and threw the javelin 187-3, he placed in none of these events while in college. One explanation of this is that he went to Indiana on a football scholarship, and was required to take part in spring football training. Lacking proper training for track, his interest in dual and conference meets would undoubtedly be low. In football he was outstanding; in 1956 he was drafted and played briefly for the Chicago Bears.

But, however he perfected his skills or gained power and endurance, his performance in the 1956 Melbourne Games was superb--seven personal bests out of ten events, totalling 7708 points for a new Olympic record, only 48 points behind Rafer Johnson's world record. In summary, one more example of tremendous natural, all-round talent, supported by minimal conditions for development.

Rafer Johnson, 1960 Olympic Champion. If anyone has surpassed Milt Campbell's record as an all-sports performer while still in high school, it was Rafer Johnson. In fact, if injuries had not handicapped him, he might have been the greatest all-time all-arounder at any level. A four-sport star at Kingsburg (CA) High School, Rafer, in June 1954, first won two prep decathlons, using the high school shot, discus and hurdles; then, on July 2-3, took third in the AAU championships with 6329 points. As a freshman at UCLA, he won three decathlons: 7055 in the Pan-Am Qualifying Meet in February, 7144 in the Pan-Am Finals in March, and 7758 for a new world record in the Central California AAU meet in June. All this at age 19. But, in his sophomore year, 1956, he competed and trained only for regular varsity meets. In dual meets he would compete in five or six events, winning some and scoring in most. On June 15, in the NCAA championships, he took two seconds to two future Olympic champions: Lee Calhoun in the high hurdles (13.8s), and Greg Bell in the long jump (25'4"). A month later he won the U.S. Olympic decathlon trials (7591 points), but in December at Melbourne, handicapped by an injured knee, he took second (7568 points) to Campbell's Olympic Record 7708 points. Injuries continued to plague Johnson during the next three years. Throughout 1957, he competed once in the javelin and in but three events in a hometown decathlon. In 1959, leg injuries and a serious auto collision with back injuries kept him out of all activity until he started jogging in February, 1960. In 1958, his college senior year, a serious thigh pull eliminated all sprinting, hurdling, and jumping, but somehow he achieved a great triple in the weight events--54' 11½", 170' 9½", 237' 10". After graduation (June 1958) he recovered enough to win three decathlons, including (July 3-4) an AAU title and (July 27-28) a world record 7896 points against his repeated rival, Kuznyetsov of the USSR.

In 1960, Johnson took no sprint starts until April, nor long jumps until June, but July 8-9, in the U.S. Olympic Final Trials, he was able to gain his third world record (8063 points), the first-ever over 8000 points. Then, Sept. 5-6, Rome, he gained that all-important goal, the Olympic championships with 8001 points. With only the final event (1500m) remaining, Johnson held a lead of but 56 points (a ten-second differential). With a previous best time of 4:54.2, made four years earlier at Melbourne, this was Johnson's weakest event in both points and confidence. Yang had trained at UCLA under Johnson's coaches Ducky Drake and Jack Davis, so Johnson was well aware of his best time of 4:36.9. But by clinging adamantly to C. K.'s shoulder, he finished within one second of Yang's time with a P.R. of 4:49.7, a great victory over a most worthy opponent.

It must be added that Rafer Johnson was an all-round person as well as decathlete. He trained for government service and acting as a future career. He lettered in basketball (UCLA was a basketball power!), spoke often before Los Angeles youth groups, and in his senior year, 1958, was elected president of the student body. In the decathlon, he won two Olympic medals--one gold, one silver. During seven years (1954-1960), he broke the world record three times while winning nine of 11 competitions. In regular college meets, he recorded: 100m--10.3, HH--13.8, long jump--25' 5 3/4", shot--54' 11½", discus--172' 3", javelin--251' 9½". But during his college years, Johnson was a team competitor. Only after the team season was over (1956 and 1958) did he train specially for the decathlon. At the 1984 Olympic Games, Rafer Johnson was honored at the highest level of his sport by his selection as torch-bearer to ascend the "101" steps and light the flame. Naturally, though now 44, he did it perfectly.

<u>Bill Toomey, 1968 Olympic Champion</u>. Bill Toomey was the first world-level decathlete that, on the crucial balance between natural talent and proper training, weighed heavily on the side of training. At the University of Colorado, Bill's range of events was less than promising--24'8½" in the long jump, 51.7 for 400m hurdles, and good times in the 440-600 indoors--far from a firm foundation for the decathlon. His physique (6'1", 172#, 1962) was ordinary. His first decathlon score (1959, age 20) was 5349, as compared with 6790 (Mathias, age 17) or 7176 (Campbell, age 18). His first official world record (8417, Dec. 1969) was not achieved until age 31, after 34 decathlon competitions and ten years of year-round training specifically pointed toward improving his score in the decathlon.

Not until he was 24 (1963, 7066 points) did he take the decathlon seriously. But once committed, it became a matter of supreme importance, for which he allowed no hindrances and few distractions. He sought competition everywhere, in the United States and in Europe, even urging new meets so that he might have one more try at the record or merely at improvement--against the world's best performers or whatever local talent was available. He moved to California to earn an M.A. in Education at Stanford, 1963, and ensure better year-round training conditions and coaching. At Santa Barbara he worked with Coach Sam Adams, a former decathlete (1956--7106 points) and generally considered America's foremost coach of this event. There he found a group of dedicated decathletes, including such champions as Russ Hodge, and John Warkentin. This provided an excellent situation for mutual help and development.

But, seeking perfection, he also spent six months (1965) in West Germany where he discovered the decathlon to be an event of long-time national interest. Its advocates argued that the nature of the decathlon and its training was inherent in the character and tradition of the German people--a disciplined approach to life, a belief in versatility and balance as opposed to narrow specialization, and in the unity of mind-body.

Of more direct value, Toomey sought the help of Friedel Schirmer, National Decathlon Coach. Schirmer had competed with high scores in the decathlon, had coached many decathletes including Holdorf, Walde and Beyer who had taken first, third and sixth in the 1964 Tokyo Olympics, and had studied thoroughly the requirements of decathlon development. He organized a decathlon training camp in a suburb of Cologne where all prospects could come for help. He systematized all aspects of training. He organized decathlon teams of six and eight men that had regular dual meets with other teams--club, area, national in scope--so that there was no need for competition in individual events. He followed a sequence of training consistent with the order of events in the decathlon. Above all, he planned development years ahead--in terms of a career as well as of this year, month or week.

It was too late in Bill Toomey's career to make such radical changes in techniques and methods. That would risk complete failure. But the experience was most encouraging; he was more convinced of his potential, and even more determined to gain both the Olympic championship and a world record. From July 1965--when his world-record 8234 points in winning the National AAU championships was disallowed for meet management errors--until December 1969, he competed in 23 decathlons (ten in 1969 alone) in an all-out drive for the record. He won five consecutive NAAU titles (1965-1969). He won the 1968 Olympic title with a new Olympic record of 8193 points. He scored over 8000 in 11 meets; over 8200 in four; but time and time again fell short in some small but crucial way, leaving the field frustrated, even disgusted, but also determined to try again. Finally, on Dec. 10-11, 1969, some three months after the track season is usually over, in a specially organized competition against three other decathletes (all over 7000 points), Toomey gained his goal--a world-record 8417 points, 98 points over Kurt Bendlin's (West Germany) record.

In summary, probably no decathlete ever achieved so much from such an unpromising beginning. With full commitment throughout an 11-year career, he depended primarily on himself, with only temporary help from coaches. Needing power and weight, he followed a power-training program and related diet, gaining a powerful body and 195# in weight. Needing endurance, he took basic mileage running during the early months of each year. Needing even greater speed, he took related speed-power exercises. From a beginning of 23'2" in his one high-school event, the long jump, he finally achieved: 1500m--4:12.7; 100m--10.3, 400m--45.6, 110m hurdles--14.2, long jump--26'¼", and most amazingly, discus--154'2" and javelin--225'8". During 11 years, he competed in 38 decathlons; his last was his best.

Bruce Jenner, 1976 Olympic Champion. Bruce Jenner was the first United States champion decathlete to combine great all-round talent with all-out training. He started pole vaulting in the 7th grade. While still in high school, he played football, was an expert competitive water skier, and in track, high jumped 6'2", vaulted 13', triple jumped and threw the javelin 180 feet.

At Graceland College, Iowa, Jenner's track coach was L. D. Weldon, a fine javelin thrower in college, a decathlon enthusiast and, most important, coach of Jack Parker, third in the 1936 Berlin Olympic decathlon. Weldon saw the great potential in Bruce and made sure that first impressions were positive. In his first decathlon (sophomore year, age 20), Bruce scored 6991 points and found "it was so much fun, such a challenge...something I wanted to do. I decided right then to run cross-country next fall."[1]

As for dedicated training, for three years (April 1973 to July 30, 1976 when he won the Olympic title at Montreal with a world-record 8618 points), Bruce and his wife Chrystie lived in an apartment across the street from the San Jose City College track and field. "I couldn't get away from my training if I wanted to. If I had trouble getting started in the morning, I just looked out of my bedroom window at the running track. There it was out there--my destiny."

At San Jose he made the shocking discovery that he was not really strong, nor had basic endurance, nor speed, nor even much skill. At Graceland college he had been the best in everything. Here everybody was bigger, faster, stronger, more skilled, and even more dedicated. In power training he worked with such experts as shot-putter Al Feuerbach and discus throwers Mac Wilkins and John Powell. They also coached him in their specialties on the field. He sprinted with Olympian John Carlos. In fact, in every event, he could work out with men superior in performance and knowledge. "With that atmosphere, training all the time, with all those specialists to help me, I just had to get better." In the fall of 1975 he undertook basic endurance training. "He ran 10 miles a day beginning in October." Somedays he went to the 11th green on the Stanford University golf course. "That long fairway is 300 yards long, and steep. Twenty times he sprints up the hill, then jogs down to the bottom."

His wife, Chrystie, was a strong help-mate in many ways. Her earnings as an airline stewardess was, at first, their only income. When things went wrong and Bruce was discouraged, she was strongly supportive. After the 1976 Olympic triumph, his first words were, "We did it; you and I did it together." And he repeatedly said he could never have achieved so much without her help. In 1975, Bruce sold life insurance with $700 a month guaranteed if he could sell a certain quota every three months. This he found he could do within a week or two, so the remaining weeks were free for full-time training.

During the six months prior to Montreal he did just that--on a 24-hour-a-day basis. In their apartment he had a hurdle, a vaulting pole, a shot, discus, javelin. Often he spent hours thinking-feeling in a muscle-nerve sense, just how it should be done, unknowingly consistent with the methods now advanced by psycho-cybernetics.

I might run through a whole decathlon in my mind, over and over again every day. I think about each event and the things I have to do to score high. Then, when I'm actually in competition, I find myself doing those things naturally. That's why I have a hurdle here in the living room. Just walking through the motions here, looking at the hurdle and knowing what it feels like, all helps me run the hurdles better in a race....What I see in my mind changes as I progress in the event....Over the years I've watched my mind and my body grow closer together.

In another interview[2] Chrystie added to this,

He even visualizes the events in his dreams. He runs in his sleep. He falls

---

[1]Bruce Jenner & Peter Finch, DECATHLON CHALLENGE--BRUCE JENNER'S STORY, Englewood Cliffs, N.J.: Prentice-Hall, Inc., 1977. Quotes from pps. 42, 72, 73, 94, 93.

[2]Frank Zarnowski, THE DECATHLON GUIDE, "Interview with the Jenners" by Jeannette & Bert Nelson, Emmitsburg, Md: DECA, 1976, pps. 37-41.

asleep in 20 to 30 seconds and then I can see his legs moving...for about ten seconds. I know he's doing the 100. Or he'll give a big grunt and move his arm and shoulder. He's putting the shot.

In his seven year career (1970-1976), Bruce Jenner completed 27 decathlons with 16 victories including 10 over 8000 points, seven over 8200 points, and a final 1976 Olympic win with 8618 points, a world record. His best-ever performances, metric system, were 10.7, 7.32, 15.35, 2.03, 47.5-14.3, 51.70, 4.80, 69.48, 4:12.6.[1]

In summary, Jenner's career evidenced most of the essentials for great performance in the decathlon. True, at age 20, he had not performed at such high levels as had Milt Campbell or Rafer Johnson. But on the training-development-competition side of performance, he surpassed them all. Only two essentials of highest achievement were lower level--a Master Coach and time for development. For example, consider that in West and East Germany, National Coaches give full-time attention to one event, such as the decathlon, and that those showing talent and interest are placed under their care at an early age. Great as were Jenner's achievements, even greater decathlon scores lay in the future.

Daley Thompson, Great Britain, two-time Olympic Decathlon Champion: (1980--8522WR) (1984--8846WR). Up to 1984, during ten years of decathlon competitions, about two dozen in number, Daley Thompson has shown remarkably consistent improvement. Today it is obvious he has great talent. However, on his first try in 1975, age 17, he scored 6685 as compared with the first efforts of Bruce Jenner (6991) or Milt Campbell (7176). But on his third try (1976, age 18) he set a World Junior Record (7905); on his 11th try (1978, age 20), he won the British Commonwealth Games (8467); on about his 15th try (1980, age 22) he won the Moscow Olympics (8522WR); and at the 1984 Los Angeles Games, he won the gold with a WR 8846 points. (Note--All points shown based on 1985 Tables.)

That may not seem like much improvement--941 points gained during 8 years of year-round training and competition (1976-1984). But keep in mind that the decathlon comprises ten events, each of which can consume the full concentration of, say, a pole vaulter such as Earl Bell, a high jumper such as Dwight Stones or a shotputter such as Brian Oldfield, But let Thompson speak for himself:

It's fascinating to me. It isn't a one-off thing like a sprint or something like that. There are so many different facets you have to try to master. Plus there are so many different combinations of how things can go. Obviously, with 10 things you have 10 times the chances of things going wrong. Once you get to a high level, it's difficult to get back into it if something does go wrong. So it can be very complicated--or very simple. But you never know how it will be until you are in the middle of it. It's like a chess game. It's not that there are tactics in it, but there are variations. It's not going to be done the same way every time.

Yes, you have to get geared up 10 times and that's the difficult thing. The actual competition isn't that physically demanding. The thing is to try to get the mental push to get 10 personal bests; you aren't going to manage it--but you don't tell yourself that. You just get on with it and try to do your best regardless. That's really the hardest thing about decathlon; trying to do 10 things better than you have ever done them before.

According to a New York Times article, Thompson was able to train full time for the decathlon (9/9/1979):

He receives about $11,000 a year for training expenses through Olympic-sanctioned broken-time payments. And because the decathlon is such a grueling event.... Thompson trains 'from 10 or 10:30 in the morning until 7 or 8 at night, seven days a week'...Each week, Thompson works on at least seven of his 10 events, and three days a week he competes against British decathletes and track specialists in practice meets.

---

[1] Frank Zarnowski, ibid., p. 4.

POTENTIAL TALENTS FOR THE DECATHLON

Whether or not an athlete, now scoring more than ten points in various dual-meet events, should concentrate all his efforts on one event, the decathlon, depends on several factors--individual attitudes, his obligations to the team and institution, and, of special import, his potential for success as a decathlete.

Up to 1970, the decathlon was an extramural event for college men. Only off-and-on did the Relay Carnivals include it in their schedule. During the team season, potential decathletes competed in a number of single events. Even high school Olympians such as Bob Mathias or Milt Campbell competed as regular members of their college teams. Fifty years ago, in the entire U.S., there were only three weekends in the year when decathlon competitions were held.

Today, all that is changed. For 1984, Frank Zarnowski listed 81 decathlon competitions open to college men--most in April-May, but extending from Feb. 1 to Dec. 4. Prospective decathletes and their coaches now face a serious dilemma. Is it worthwhile to give up sure points in a number of single events? Even more fundamental, is it worthwhile to give full time-energy to this demanding ten-eventer despite its probable conflict with high-level academic work; not to mention, normal college life.

An Exciting Challenge. The first question in assessing an athlete's potential for the decathlon should be whether or not it appeals to him as an exciting challenge. He may be dismayed by its awesome heights but should be assured by Bill Toomey's slow climb from two mediocre performances (long jump and 400m) to a world record score in ten events. He may be turned away by the all-too-common description of the event as "grueling," "agonizing," "a man-killer." But decathletes know these are the judgments of the untrained and untried, those who lack a valid basis for judgment.

Experienced decathletes become inured to the pains of fatigue and effort just as they do to the physical effects of oxygen debt or lactic acid. Sure they are aware of pain and exhaustion, but not as problems or fears. In short, if a man can accept the pain (often called loosely "agony" or "torture") of his first six-minute try at 1500m, he'll find no greater pain at five minutes or even four. Inurement to pain parallels performance.

Physique. Next to personal interest in the event, physique might be considered a basic approach to talent. In Table 15.1 the 14 Olympic Champions averaged 6'1.8" in height and 195# in weight. But in his 1984 U.S. DECATHLON HANDBOOK, Frank Zarnowski listed 117 decathletes in the U.S. who had scored 7000 points or more. They averaged about 6'2" and 180# but more revealing was their wide-range in physique from 150# to 218#, and in height from 5'8" to 6'4".

These figures are supported by Zarnowski's report[2] of the opinions of national decathlon coaches as to optimal size. They averaged 1.88cm (6'2"), with a range from 1.85 to 1.95. But Zarnowski emphasizes that this is just an average. "Today's decathlete comes in all shapes and sizes...Any size will do!"

At one extreme, he cites the 1974 Soviet champion, Rudolph Zigert, 6'6", 235#, but able to high jump 6'10"; and Rick Wanamaker, 1971 AAU champion, 6'9", 210#, but able to pole vault 15'1"! At the other extreme was Jeff Bennett, "by far the smallest top-grade decathlete in history," two-time AAU champion, who was only 5'8" tall and weighed but 152#. With this physique, he scored 8121 points and had best performances of: high jump--6'4 3/4", pole vault--16'7 3/4", long jump--25'3½", 100m--10.3, 400m--46.3, 1500m--4:08.9, and remarkably, shot put--42'6".

All of this discussion is based on scores drawn from the 1962 Scoring Tables. Change the Tables, and physique requirements will change to correspond.

---

[1] Tom McNab, DECATHLON, London: British Amateur Athletic Board, 1971, paperback, 68 pps., p. 21.

[2] Frank Zarnowski, op. cit., p. 19.

Basic Talents. A third approach to potentials for the decathlon focuses on basic qualities: speed, spring power, endurance, facility in motor learning, and most important, basic stick-to-itiveness and competitiveness. The last three of these underlie performance in all events.

Such basic qualities can be judged by two criteria--decathlon events and decathlon scoring tables. The events selected by Curtis for the 1884 all-around placed great emphasis on power (shot, hammer, 56# weight throw) and endurance (880 walk and mile run), with lesser emphasis on speed (100, high hurdles, long jump).

I doubt that the makers of the modern decathlon approached the problem of selecting events in this formal way but, clearly, the full range of sports talent was planned. At least four events were chosen in which leg speed is essential: (100, high hurdles, long jump, 400); three events for power (shot, discus, javelin); two or more events for spring (high jump, pole vault, long jump); and but one for endurance (1500), plus of course the 400.

Talent as determined by the scoring tables will be analyzed in detail in the next section, but in summary, Table 15.2 makes clear that the 1962 Tables provided highest scoring for Olympic champions (1912-1972) for the speed events--long jump, high hurdles, 400 and 100, in that order of points scored; lowest scoring for endurance (1500-10th in scoring) and power (javelin, shot, discus--9th, 8th, and 7th in scoring); with spring in the middle (high jump and pole vault, 5th and 6th in scoring). Table 15.3, based on 1962 Tables, shows a different rank of events for scoring in the 1976 Olympic Decathlon, produced by modern improvements in implements and training methods. Surprisingly, such upgrading lowered scoring in the 100m dash from 4th down to 8th. Greatest increases occurred with the pole vault (6th to 1st) and javelin (9th to 5th).

The IAAF 1985 Tables were designed to reduce such imbalances, with increases in 1500m scoring and decreases in pole vault scoring, but all events are modified somewhat.

A Talent for Competitiveness. Highest scores in the decathlon demand great talent for competitiveness of a unique kind. First it is an inner struggle to do one's best, not against a human opponent as in such sports as football or boxing, but against such abstractions as time, distance, inertia, gravity; or such "mental" deterrents as fatigue, pain, impatience, tension, stress. All-out efforts are essential but always within the limitations of relaxation and control, what might be called controlled recklessness or cold fury.

More than this, such drives must be repeated not merely ten times, but a score or more-- if we count the attempts within such events as the weights and jumps. Further, there are long delays between events and single efforts. I sometimes think that the old ten-events-in-one-day method was more an advantage than a handicap; one moved quickly to the next event without the long cooling of muscles and competitive fire. It takes a special person to do his best, sometimes under conditions of rain and wind and cold, again and again and again, in events of such varied requirements in body and mind.

To me, it is truly fantastic that such Greats as Jim Thorpe, Bob Mathias, Milt Campbell or Rafer Johnson, in their first try at the decathlon, should have reached some 7000 points of a "perfect" 10,000; or that Bruce Jenner could score 8618 points in ten separate and varied events. Just think, if, on decathlon tables, we score the performances of the 10 relevant single-event champions of the 1976 Olympics, they would average roughly 1097 points. That is, Jenner in ten events came within 79 percent of equalling the level achieved by ten champions competing in but one event each. Along with talent and training, that takes competitiveness.

BALANCE IN SCORING AND TRAINING

The concept of balanced scoring, so seemingly obvious, is actually defined and used in various ways. The simplest way is to assume equitable tables and equal potentials for scoring for all events. A 7000-point scorer would score 700 points in every event. A more realistic way uses the difference between highest and lowest event scores. Zarnowski[1] and Nelson used this method, but excluded the 1500 since scoring is so unduly low in this event. Their method gave best-balanced scores and lowest differences to Mathias (130) and Kuznyetsov (131), and poorly-

---

[1]Frank Zarnowski & Bert Nelson, *op. cit.*, p. 32.

TABLE 15.2

SCORING[4] AND BALANCE IN OLYMPIC CHAMPIONS

Name & Yr.	Ave.[1] Sco	100	LJ	Sh	HJ	400	HH	Dis	PV	Jav	1500	Ave.[2] Dev.	Dev.[3] Rank
Thorpe '12	676	756	776	658	743	712	787	623	601	574	524		
Deviation		+80	+100	-18	+67	+36	+111	-53	-75	-102	-152	79.4	5
Osborn '24	667	756	804	561	831	712	749	574	672	588	464		
Deviation		+89	+137	-106	+164	+45	+82	-93	+5	-79	-203	90.3	8
Yrjola '28	677	622	761	735	743	671	694	727	615	708	500		
Deviation		-55	+84	+58	+66	-6	+17	+50	-62	+31	-177	60.6	1
Bausch '32	690	643	810	808	588	633	730	774	807	785	321		
Deviation		-47	+120	+118	-102	-57	+40	-16	+117	+95	-369	108.1	11
Morris '36	742	780	814	734	725	833	859	744	672	692	568		
Deviation		+38	+72	-8	-17	+91	+117	+4	-70	-50	-180	63.9	2
Mathias '52	773	828	816	806	769	797	881	816	807	751	460		
Deviation		+55	+43	+33	-4	+24	+108	+43	+34	-22	-313	67.9	3
Campbell '56	771	853	887	774	760	860	963	781	644	713	461		
Deviation		+82	+116	+3	-11	+89	+192	+10	-127	-58	-310	99.9	10
Johnson '60	800	828	891	837	725	854	817	845	832	877	466		
Deviation		+28	+91	+37	-75	+54	+17	+45	+32	+77	-334	82.0	6
Holdorf '64	788	879	820	786	716	889	848	801	859	729	561		
Deviation		+91	+32	-2	-72	+101	+60	+13	+71	-59	-228	72.9	4
Toomey '68	842	986	972	751	796	943	926	809	876	830	528		
Deviation		+144	+130	-91	-54	+101	+84	-33	+34	-12	-314	99.7	9
Avilov '72	845	804	957	750	959	875	926	818	945	781	639		
Deviation		-41	+112	-95	+114	+30	+81	-27	+100	-64	-206	87.0	7
Total Score		8735	9308	8200	8355	8779	9180	8312	8330	8028	5492		
Score Rank		4	1	8	5	3	2	7	6	9	10		

[1] Average score for all ten events.
[2] Average deviation of each event from average score.
[3] Decathlete rank compared with 10 others in average deviation.
[4] 1962 Scoring Tables were used throughout.

TABLE 15.3

SCORING AND BALANCE IN SIX PLACE-WINNERS--1976 OLYMPICS

	Ave.[1] Sco.	100	LJ	Sh	HJ	400	HH	Dis	PV	Jav	1500	Ave.[2] Dev.	Dev.[3] Rank
1.Jenner	USA	819	865	810	882	923	866	882	1005	863	715		
	862	-43	+3	-52	+20	+61	+4	+20	+143	+1	-147	49.4	1
2.Kratschmer	WG	890	901	774	882	889	895	795	957	837	595		
	841	+49	+60	-67	+41	+48	+54	-46	+116	-4	-246	93.4	5
3.Avilov	SU	749	925	778	1017	891	939	793	920	798	614		
	837	-88	+88	-59	+180	+54	+102	-44	+83	-39	-223	96.0	6
4.Pihl	SW	822	820	825	857	900	767	769	909	961	597		
	822	0	-2	+3	+35	+78	-55	-53	+87	+139	-225	67.7	3
5.Skowronck	Pol	799	873	726	779	903	876	789	1005	789	590		
	811	-12	+62	-85	-32	+92	+65	-22	+194	-22	-221	80.7	4
6.Stark	EG	721	816	794	779	844	782	751	969	927	625		
	805	-84	+11	-11	-26	+39	-23	-13	+164	+122	-180	67.3	2
Total Score		4800	5200	4707	5196	5350	5125	4819	5765	5175	3736		
Score Rank		8	3	9	4	2	6	7	1	5	10		

balanced scores with highest differences to Yang (335) and Johnson (269). Zarnowski and Nelson also studied balances: (1) between group scores in the three throws, the three jumps and the three runs, again excluding the 1500; and (2) between total scores on the first day and the second.

In my judgment the most useful way to define balance in scoring is to compare an individual's score for each event with his average score for all events. Such deviations are not between the extremes of performance as when contrasting high and low scores. They do not exclude any event. Their sum provides a total deviation for all ten events. In Table 15.2 Jim Thorpe, for example, had a total deviation of 794 from his average score of 676 points (1962 Tables.)

In his 1979 analysis of elite decathlon performances, William H. Freeman[1] concluded that,

> *To develop the elite decathlete, attention must be paid to a balanced develop-*
> *ment of the athlete's abilities across all ten events until they reach an*
> *optimal level, after which the specialty events can be emphasized. This obser-*
> *vation agrees with the so-called West German School of decathlon training, led*
> *by Friedel Schirmer, which prefers not to permit the decathlete to develop*
> *specialty events until he can achieve a balanced effort at the 7000 point level.*

Such may have been the plan and even the training. Actual performances, however, did not support either. Defining balance as the deviation of each event score from the average score for all ten events, we find that Holdorf had a deviation total of 729; Walde, of 934; and Bendlin, of 1581. Surprisingly, these are not an improvement over American college products: Morris--639, Mathias--679, Johnson--320, Toomey--997, Campbell--999, Bausch--1081, or even Thorpe--794.

The question arises as to what extent such deviations are produced by the natural inconsistencies in competitive performance found, not only in the decathlon, but in all single-events. The answer would require considerable study but a hint can be gained from Jenner's best decathlon scores in each of five years, 1972-1976, climaxed by his Olympic Games 8618 record. Not only did Bruce improve his total score each time, his total deviation decreased quite consistently--894, 593, 600, 487, 494.

Scoring by Events--1976 versus 1912-72. Tables 15.2 and 15.3 show there has been a gradual increase in total scores and average scores from 1912 to 1976 for all ten events. But Table 15.4 indicates a change in relative scoring by events. Scoring for the pole vault moved from a 6th place ranking to 1st place; that for the javelin, from 9th to 5th. Improvements in implements, facilities and techniques are probable causes. Relative scoring lowered for the hurdles (2nd to 6th) and 100 (4th to 8th). Speed has a lower range of possible improvement as compared with power or endurance or skill; as they improve, speed will tend to hold even.

TABLE 15.4
RELATIVE SCORING BY EVENTS--1976 versus 1912-1972

	PV	400	LJ	HJ	Jav	HH	Dis	100	Sh	1500
1976 Event Ranking	1	2	3	4	5	6	7	8	9	10
1912-1972 Event Ranking	6	3	1	5	9	2	7	4	8	10

Balance in the Basic Elements. Performance totals of the 17 decathletes listed in Tables 15.2 and 15.3 show decisively that the 1500 is by far the most difficult event in which to score points. In Table 15.2 the 11 decathletes scored a total of only 5492 points, as compared with the next lowest total 8028 in the shot. From such facts Bert Nelson[2] concludes

---

[1]William H. Freeman, "An Analysis of Elite Decathlon Performances," *Track and Field Quarterly Review*, Vol. 79, #2, 1979, p. 49.

[2]Frank Zarnowski and Bert Nelson, *op. cit.*, p. 8.

that scoring for the 1500 should be upgraded, that is, should be based on a different standard from that used for the other nine events.

In my judgment, such views ignore certain underlying principles of the decathlon. No scoring tables can provide equal opportunities for scoring for all individuals. All tables arbitrarily assume a certain kind of decathlete--somewhere between a distance runner and a shot putter or sprinter, between a high jumper and discus thrower. All tables must be based on compromise, and cannot provide allowances that equalize individual differences.

The originators of the decathlon gave a first priority to speed. The four highest-scoring events among these Olympic champions (long jump-9308, hurdles-9180, 400-8779, 100-8735) have a high-level requirement in speed. Second priority was given to power. Three events involving big-muscle power achieved closely grouped scoring: discus-8312, shot-8200, javelin-8028. We should note that scores in Table 15.3, made by place-winners in the 1976 Games, do not coincide with these figures. Recent improvements in discus technique and both technique and construction of the javelin account for such differences. As pointed out previously, shot performances in the decathlon over the past 50 years have held relatively steady because of decathlon size limitations. Scores for 1976 athletes averaged 784 points; for earlier athletes 745. Improvement has come primarily through basic strength training. For example, Jeff Bennett, only 5'8", 152# in size was still able to put the shot 42'6".

That leaves but one event, the 1500, as a test of what might be called slower-paced endurance. (The 400 has an important endurance factor, but it's what can be called speed-endurance in which scoring is much more closely correlated with speed in the 100 than with endurance in the 1500.) But this concentration of testing within a single event simply multiplies the importance of that event, and does not imply a lesser role for endurance. As a fundamental principle, the basis for scoring should be the same for all ten events. That principle forces decathletes to compromise, to make-do as between body-size and excellence in such other events as the 1500, pole vault, hurdles or high jump. We are unlikely to ever see a 1000-point (61'5½") scorer in the shot that will do well in those four events, especially in the 1500. The opposite is equally true. In 1971, Brian Oldfield (6'5", 275#) set a record 60'1½" for the shot within a decathlon, but scored less than 7000 points total. In contrast, in 1972, Jeff Bennett (5'8", 152#) ran the 1500 in 4:08.9 (744 points), and in 1973 scored 8121 points total, but his shot was usually under 42 feet.

It is clear that decathlon tables are not pointed toward achieving 10,000 points, with adjustment of scoring criteria for each event to ensure that possibility. Rather, they seek to ensure equality of opportunity for every decathlete to do what he can within both the positives and the negatives of the scoring system.

Summary. (1) To define balance in performance as the deviation of each event score from the average score for all ten events provides a useful and valid basis for analyzing and comparing point scores. (2) Even though the facts disclosed here are inconclusive, we are still justified in assuming that balanced performance, and so balance in training for the ten events, is an ideal to be carefully planned and diligently sought. (3) the inconsistency of performance inherent in any competition might outweigh the low deviations from the average score gained from balanced training. Bruce Jenner's scores during five years were remarkably low in such inconsistency. (4) Balanced training requires long-time and continuous planning by well-trained experts. For example, within the ten-event format, highest-level endurance (1500m) and power (shot) oppose each other, cannot occur together. To be world's best in either is to rule out balance in the decathlon. Balanced training must seek a compromise between the two, and that requires expert planning. (5) Balanced training can be achieved in the United States only when men specialize as decathletes throughout their sports careers-- post-college, college and high school.

Scoring, not balance, is the goal. The concept of balance, like that of technique in single events, may contribute to performance but actually wins no competitions. Perfect balance, like perfect technique, may end up last. In Table 15.3, Jenner was first in total scoring and in balanced scoring. But Kratschmer was second in scoring though 5th in balance; Avilov third in scoring, sixth in balance; Stark sixth in scoring, second in balance. In summary, the correlation between total scoring and balance is not high.

College decathletes will tend to plan in terms of short-time goals--this year or, at most, four years. Though working toward better balance, first time-energy will be given to those events in which progress will come quickest. Example: A beginner can now vault 3.60m (11'9 3/4" --700 points) and put the shot 10.55m (32'9 3/4"--500 points). The West German approach would advocate basic strength training and work on shot technique. But for various reasons of size and aptitude, an equal mount of time given to the pole vault might easily add some 15 inches (100 points) as compared with almost five feet (100 points) in the shot, for this man a more slowly gained improvement.

As a second example in which balance is secondary, a beginner can be weak in technique and confidence, though not necessarily in performance, in those three critical events--pole vault, hurdles and discus. Time and again, talented competitors slip the discus outside the sector three times (no points), fall down and out in the hurdles (no points), or fail to clear the first height in the pole vault (no points). A first priority should be practice for consistency and sureness in these events, even though other events might be weaker.

This argument is not at all against the concept of balance; in the final tests at highest levels, the decathlete with even one weak event in which he scores 300 points under his average for the other nine, is certainly handicapped and not likely to win. But it does argue that the main goal is highest scoring for ten events in whatever competition, late or soon, is considered important for this individual. First priorities in time-energy should be on whatever procedures best further that goal.

TABLE 15.5
SAMPLE DECATHLON SCORES
1985 Decathlon Tables
(effective April 1985)

	100	LJ	SP	HJ	400	110H	Disc	PV	Jav	1500
5000	12.81	5.59	10.24	1.65	57.57	18.25	31.78	3.57	43.96	5:10.73
5500	12.53	5.83	11.07	1.71	56.25	17.73	34.30	3.76	47.36	5:01.78
6000	12.26	6.06	11.89	1.77	54.98	17.23	36.80	3.94	50.74	4:53.20
6500	12.00	6.29	12.71	1.83	53.76	16.76	39.26	4.12	54.12	4:44.94
7000	11.75	6.51	13.53	1.88	52.58	16.29	41.72	4.30	57.46	4:36.96
7500	11.51	6.73	14.35	1.94	51.43	15.85	44.16	4.47	60.78	4:29.25
8000	11.27	6.94	15.16	2.00	50.32	15.41	46.60	4.63	64.10	4:21.77
8500	11.05	7.15	15.98	2.05	49.24	15.00	49.00	4.80	67.40	4:14.50
9000	10.82	7.36	16.79	2.10	48.19	14.59	51.40	4.97	70.68	4:07.42

THE DECATHLON COACH

Traditionally, the American track and field coach is just that--a multi-event coach whose primary responsibility is to the team and the team schedule. Until about 1950, the Olympic Games were relatively unimportant. College and high school events were selected and organized exclusively in terms of their own interests. Distances were not metric. Such events as the 400m hurdles, steeplechase, three-mile, six-mile, 440 relay and decathlon were not held.

But with the development of the two wars--the Cold War between the USSR and the USA, and that between the NCAA and AAU--all this changed. To substantiate its claim to international recognition, the NCAA pointed its program toward Olympic events and the development of Olympic competitors. The responsibility of the college coach became divided between local success in dual meets and Conference championships on the one hand, and making a direct contribution to United States success in the Olympics on the other.

This evolution is reflected clearly in the changing attitudes of college coaches toward the decathlon. In 1948, Tulare High School coach, Virgil Jackson, stimulated Bob Mathias to try the decathlon. Bob was Olympic decathlon champion (1948) before he enrolled at Stanford, and (1952) after graduation. But during his three varsity years, he concentrated in both training and competition on University team events, including a year of football.

From 1956 to 1964, Ducky Drake of UCLA, gave much time and personal concern to the development of Rafer Johnson and C. K. Yang, the great Taiwan athlete who came to this country primarily to develop as a decathlete. But even for them, University competitions came first. Decathlon preparation came indirectly and after the school year was over.

In 1968, Coach L. D. Weldon of Graceland College, Iowa, recruited Bruce Jenner, primarily as a decathlon prospect. Weldon was a decathlon enthusiast who, in 1936 had coached Jack Parker to an Olympic bronze medal in the decathlon. While in college, Bruce competed in nine decathlons during the college track season, with the direct help of Coach Weldon. But Graceland, Iowa, provided limited opportunities and insights as to what was possible. After graduation Jenner moved to San Jose where he found no coach, but all the other essentials for development--unlimited time, good climate, training facilities, and most important, expertise among such single-event champions as shot-putter Al Feuerbach, and discus-thrower Mac Wilkins. On a questionnaire from THE DECATHLON GUIDE, Jenner listed as his coach, "Bertha Lou Jenner," that being the name of his constant companion, a Labrador retriever. Clearly the burden of overall planning was on his own shoulders.

Now that, as of 1970, the decathlon has become an official responsibility of the college coach, we can assume most coaches will regard it as just one more event in a track and field program of 21 wide-ranging events--far more than they, even with one or more assistants, can handle adequately. Most will argue that points scored in several single events will total more than those scored in one event, the decathlon, and so will ignore, if not discourage, the latter. Even if the decathlon is chosen, most coaches will assume that their prior experience with single events will provide adequate knowledge. And if scoring in Conference Championships is the criterion for success, they might get by.

But the decathlon, if taken as more than a mere "fun" event with minimal training, is not "just one more event," comparable to the addition of the steeplechase or 400m hurdles. A Dwight Stones can break the world record in the high jump without the help of a coach or even regular practice of technique. A Dave Roberts can do the same in the pole vault, even though a serious fulltime student in medical school. But the decathlon is far too all-encompassing and demanding of time-energy-commitment for such methods; assuming of course that highest personal levels are desired.

Bill Toomey did not become active in the decathlon until after graduation from the University of Colorado. Desperate for specialized coaching, he went for six months, 1965, to Cologne, Germany, to train under National Decathlon Coach, Friedel Schirmer. There he found large numbers of decathlon prospects from Olympic champions to beginners, but even more important, systematized training in all its aspects. Decathlon teams of five or more men each of similar scoring potential competed with those of other clubs or other nations. Training was focused on development for the decathlon as one's only event. An optimal number of competitions each year were scheduled for each individual. Though much of all this came too late for Toomey's effective use, he came home convinced of the great superiority of such a system for maximum development.

In Europe and the USSR, track and field has always been organized through clubs not connected with educational institutions, clubs that are organized, coached and financed by the National Governing Body for Sports. Primary goals relate to national achievement in the Olympic Games and other international meets. Both coaches and athletes are selected and trained accordingly. With team dual-meets at minimal levels, the need for all-event coaches is low. Usually, their coaches are certified to be expert in but one or only a few related events. If long experienced and well trained, both practically and scientifically, a man may be certified as a Master Coach, or even a National Coach for a single event such as the decathlon. He then concentrates his energies toward becoming a true Master of that event and its athletes. Small wonder that the most knowledgeable and respected decathlon coaches have developed, not in America, but abroad.

All this makes clear the wide range of decathlon attitudes and action by coaches--from that in the United States up to about 1960 to that in West Germany today. Even now, the American college system and coach are strongly oriented toward local dual-meets and Conference competition. If, as of 1984, the Big Ten Conference still refused to give field space and coaching time to such events as the hammer and javelin, what better treatment can be expected for the decathlon?

A few exceptions are notable. At the University of California (SB), Coach Sam Adams has been of great help for many years to both on-campus and off-campus decathletes. Adams was 5th in the 1956 Olympic decathlon trials, as well as a contestant in the 1974 Masters' decathlon. He coached a half-dozen on-campus decathletes, as well as many graduates from other colleges, including John Warkentin. Because of his wide reputation as a coach of decathletes, his own University created a special post as Director of UCSB's Outreach Track and Field Program with special responsibility for the decathlon. He is also Official National Coach for decathletes competing in international meets, here and abroad.

Another decathlon stalwart is Frank Zarnowski, Dean of the Graduate Program of Business at Mount St. Mary's College, Maryland, acknowledged here and abroad as "the most knowledgeable decathlon authority," perhaps in the world. Zarnowski has organized numerous competitions, announced, officiated, and even paid out of his own pocket for dozens of decathlon meets. In 1984, 12 decathletes, ranging in scoring from 6667 points to 8266, trained under his guidance. Even more, he writes and publishes a DECA Newsletter as well as compiling a DECATHLON GUIDE for TAC. All with the greatest of enthusiasm and urge to be helpful, as evidenced by his many contributions to this Chapter.

In summary, the United States decathlon situation is improving rapidly, despite our failure to even place in the 1984 Olympic event. Zarnowski's 1984 HANDBOOK listed 112 U.S-born decathletes who have scored 6900 points or more, along with some 81 competitions from February to December in a dozen or more States.

Even more important, we are discovering that the decathlon is fun, a challenging contest among friends--for the team or just for the excitement of such diverse competition.

HOW TO ORGANIZE YOUR OWN TRAINING SYSTEMS

In the discussion of "Potential Talents" the point was emphasized that the vaguely interested decathlete should try it or some portion of it simply because it's fun. But even at that level, he'll derive more satisfaction and encouragement if first efforts are preceded by a little preparation. No fun in trying to vault if one doesn't know how to hold the pole or make a takeoff. No fun in hurdling if such problems as which leg goes first, or how many strides between have not been worked out. No fun in running 400m or 1500 m if one drops exhausted at the finish. The decathlon is like the marathon--no matter how slow the pace, just covering the distance demands planned preparation.

Basic Needs. Because of the decathlon's all-inclusive demands, planning should first clear away the possible negatives--the basic needs of the athlete--food, shelter, sleep, vocation or studies, finances, and the like. Read the biography of any decathlon champion. You will find that he has found a solution for these basic life problems. In the early years, of course, such concentration is relatively low. A college decathlete, training-competing at low levels of time-energy, can be an excellent student and take part in most phases of college life. But as with any art, and certainly with one so total in its requirements, highest achievement in the decathlon demands that what must be done is done and, equally important, whatever prevents or detracts is nullified.

Up to about 1960, even Olympic champions could win on talent only. But the use of sports as an instrument of governmental or institutional prestige changed such a dilettante approach. Full-time concentration became a necessity; not even such essentials as earning a living or, for college men, high-level academic work could be permitted to interfere. Stick-to-itiveness became as necessary as physical talent. During his decathlon years, Toomey was given financial support by his father. Bruce Jenner had a selling job with brief time requirements and a major portion of wife Chrystie's income as airline stewardess. Daley Thompson was given Olympic-sanctioned "broken-time" payments ($11,000).

Without some such provision of basic needs and time-energy commitment, performance will be limited. Doubt as to whether such concentration and restriction is really worth the cost in human terms is certain to arise. For most, the answer will be negative; other interests and activities will be judged more worthwhile. It's a serious problem for both athletes and coaches.

Technique is Primary. Not all coaches or athletes agree that technique should be given first emphasis in training. Bob Hayes, an all-time Great in sprinting, almost ignored technique. Neither Dick Fosbury nor Dwight Stones spent much time on high-jump technique in practice. Bob Beamon was not the long jump's greatest technician. Many great shot-putters give power a 70-80 percent emphasis; technique only 20-30. Such natural decathletes as Jim Thorpe, Bob Mathias or Rafer Johnson scored over 700 points in their first attempts in the technique events within a decathlon. Why then should technique be a primary concern in decathlon training?

First, because for most athletes, acquiring a dependable and effective skill is a long-time undertaking. By 1976 Dave Roberts had practiced vaulting technique for some ten years. But in the Montreal Olympics he lost the title through defective technique in one miss at a lower height--17'6 3/4". Many a decathlete has eliminated himself by missing low heights in the pole vault or high jump, heights he would usually clear easily; or by falling from a hurdle, or by throwing the discus outside the throwing sector--all for lack of control in technique. It is important to add that the techniques acquired so early--junior high school is not too soon--should be biomechanically sound. To unlearn an unsound skill is time consuming, often ineffective and always disrupting. Innumerable instances suggest that no-learning is far better than established learning of poor technique.

BASIC-RELATED TRAINING. A first emphasis on sound technique has just been made. On the other hand, experts have long agreed that prior development of the basic qualities of speed, strength and endurance facilitates both technique and performance. Greater leg-speed helps technique in the hurdles and long jump. Greater basic strength gained from the Olympic lifts helps technique in the throwing events and jumps. Greater basic endurance helps performance in the 1500, as well as "technique" in a special meaning of the word.

Training for Speed. Velocity of muscle action underlies performance in at least nine of the events--critically in four (100, hurdles, 400, long jump), as shown by the high correlations among their scores. No need to repeat here the various ways of increasing basic speed described in Chapter 27.

Training for Power. Training for power in all its phases--basic, related and imitative--presents a difficult and even unsolvable problem for the decathlete. Event movement patterns vary greatly; to organize all three phases of power exercises for each of eight events is impossible within the same time frame that the single-eventer uses for his one event. The decathlete can only seek to understand his complex problem, plan his time-energy carefully, and accept compromise. Basic strength training, well-planned, becomes all the more essential. Related power training should not be neglected, especially for the six field events. Though all such training is less than the maximums of single-event athletes, it can be entirely adequate, capable of producing a 9000-point decathlete.

A 1976 study by M. Letzelter[1] and E. Schubert of West Germany, supports this approach. They conclude: (1) Individuals differ widely. (2) General strength development through weight-training exercises is sufficient for the decathlon. (3) Using average values, an athlete whose decathlon score is about 7500 points can snatch 85 kg, clean and jerk 110 kg, bench press 120 kg, clean 115 kg and squat 140 kg. (4) Better decathletes have a higher maximum basic strength level. In summary, "the decathlete has to economize his strength development and therefore finds that a general all-round development is for him more valuable than a specific approach for each event."

Such conclusions are supported by those of Schirmer[2], based on his actual experiences with decathletes. "Training to increase muscle strength ensured the basic conditions that enabled an athlete to learn the technique of a particular event better and faster. On the other hand, I learned that too much training to increase muscle strength could impair the sense of movement in a specific event."

Training for Endurance. The new 1985 scoring tables do upgrade scores for the 1500, but the need for basic endurance training for the decathlete will not change. Tables 15.2, 15.3 show

---

[1]M. Letzelter & E. Schubert, "Strength Level in the Decathlon," reported in *Track Technique*, # 70, Dec. 1977, p. 2244.

[2]Friedel Schirmer, "Decathlon Training, West German Style," in Frank Zarnowski, *The Decathlon Guide*, Emmitsburg, Md., DECA, 1975, p. 46.

that Olympic champions have averaged only 517 points (4:41.3) in the 1500, 244 points less than their average for all events. But such failures were not necessary, even for men over six feet in height and 180# in weight. They were primarily the effects of a long-time misunderstanding, even a phobia against long-distance running, not unlike that against strength training prior to 1950. Some "authorities" argue that such running, even at the start of each year, slows the muscles; others that the time consumed is not warranted by the 300 or so points that can be gained in only one event.

With such attitudes, the very thought of that last "grueling" race exhausts many decathletes even before the gun is fired. Their complex fears of the pain-agony-failure syndrome dinimish performance more than does actual impairment from physical exhaustion. In contrast, those with a solid background of basic endurance training have no such handicapping fears. In the Fall of each year they'll run 5-10 miles away from the track, including some hill work. Most of this will be aerobic (pulse rates under 150). As Bill Bowerman used to say, "If you can't tell a few jokes while running, you're going too fast." But a change of pace, as of terrain, is refreshing. Include some anaerobic fast-slow running (pulse rates up to 180, then down to 110 or so during recovery jogs). Gradually, it becomes fun.

Finch[1] provides details of Bruce Jenner's workouts in October, 1975. Each morning, every day, rain or shine, he ran 10 miles, sometimes all-out as though he was actually in Olympic competition. Perhaps because of its location across the street from his apartment, such runs were on the track. Then twice a week, in the afternoon, he motored to the Stanford University golf course. "The 11th fairway is 300 yards long, and steep. Twenty times he sprints up that hill, jogging down to the bottom each time." On other afternoons he worked on field events and hurdles, primarily for technique.

How long should such basic running be continued? Lydiard's Marathon Training System advocates mileage work to within a few weeks of competition, with only a relatively brief period of sharpening speed work. This would be unwise for the decathlete, especially since endurance adds points in but one event, the 1500. Decathletes, properly trained, should be even more confident of their ability to run 1500 meters than for any other event, for that is the last and, often, the crucial event. Great championships have been won and lost there. In June 1980, after nine events, Daley Thompson knew he had to run 4:26 or better if he was to gain his first world record. His previous best was 4:20.3, giving very little margin for confidence. He ran 4:25.5. With maximal endurance training, both his confidence and his time would have improved.

At the 1976 Olympics, Bruce Jenner (6'2", 198#) ran 4:12.6 (715 points). In 1972, Horst Beyer, West Germany (6'5", 212#) ran 4:14.8; Leonid Litvinyenko, USSR (6'1", 192#), an excellent 4:05.9. The accepted world's best for the 1500 within a decathlon is 3:54.2 by Simo Salorana, Finland, 1965. We can be certain that, in the future, world-class decathletes will regularly go under four minutes (816 points). Not until then will their claim as "world's greatest all-round athletes," balancing speed-power-endurance-skill, be truly valid.

<u>Training for Spring</u>. I have intentionally left out "spring" as a basic quality for which specific training should be done. "Spring" is a less definable quality, related to muscle velocity or explosiveness, skeletal leverage, coordination, but always specific to a particular action. For example, we might assume that the vertical jump-and-reach is a valid test of spring, and that great high jumpers would score well. But in tests given at the 1975 Olympic Development Camp at Indiana University, Donald Chu found low correlations. Shot-putters had a higher average jump-and-reach than did high jumpers. (Al Feuerbach, 260# shot-putter, easily surpassed Dwight Stones, 7'7" high jumper.) Chu concluded that ability in the high jump is specific to the particular actions and demands of that event, including the run-conversion-spring-clearance, and that the Sargent Jump was of little value in diagnosing talent for the high jump.

If such specificity holds for the high jump, how much more so for the long jump, in which velocity is so much a factor, or for the pole vault in which velocity-technique plays a primary role. In summary, basic work in terms of "spring" seeks related power in the specific muscle groups and movements of each event.

---

[1]Bruce Jenner & Phillip Finch, *op. cit.* pp. 91-94.

Training by Event Relatedness. Decathletes usually practice two, three or even more events during a single workout. In what order of events should such practice occur? East German coaches have emphasized the values of sequence training--practicing events in the same order they occur within a decathlon. They argue that a major problem in decathlon competition lies in performing maximally while transferring from one event to another of a quite different character and challenge; example--from the long jump to the shot. After being totally concentrated in a 130-foot run-and-jump, the decathlete must relax briefly, then re-orient and re-focus his energies within a seven-foot circle and behind a 16# iron ball, with only three trials in which to do his best without fouling. It's a physical-mental problem that the German coaches think is best solved by sequence training.

While not denying the potential values of any training that simulates competitive conditions, it seems clear that other considerations (basic training, weakness in one or more events, a need for greater balance and consistency, training time) must also be given their share of emphasis. Take the last--training time. A full training session for three or four events in sequence requires up to three hours. But many times, a day's work is divided into two sessions: mileage running in the morning and a shorter workout (1-1½ hours) on technique in the afternoon.

Sequence training would seem most helpful when preparing for competitions with only a dozen or so decathletes. Each day's events are completed within five hours or less, so that there is little time between events. NCAA rules state, "Whenever advisable, at least a half hour's rest between events shall be allowed each competitor." But actually, it is not always advisable; groups in running events are drawn by lot, so that the last to high jump may be the first to run the 400. Knowing that one has practiced that sequence on many occasions could help mind and body. But even for such small meets, the assumption of carry-over from practice to competition seems very doubtful. Practice is one thing; competition is quite another. Of course, if you think it helps, it helps.

But in large competitions, ten or more hours are needed for each day, with long waits between trials within an event, as well as between different events. In such competitions there is plenty of time for adjustments and related energy build-up. Actually, the tensions of waiting are often more of a problem than are event sequences. In fact, careful thought suggests that the crux of the problem lies within multiple competitions rather than in event sequences. One learns to compete by competing, more than by practicing certain simulated aspects of competition. Bruce Jenner competed in 27 decathlons; Bill Toomey in 38; John Warkentin in 49. They undoubtedly felt each decathlon to be important for itself, but equally as training in the many ways and means of competition. How marvellous that Jenner in winning his 27th decathlon at the 1976 Olympics, should have brought forth five personal records: pole vault, 1500, and three that occurred in sequence at the end of the first day--shot, high jump, 400. Call it what you will--concentration, confidence, relaxation, snowball effect, will-to-excel--such a performance requires a specific talent developed to its ultimate by both related training and many competitions.

In keeping with such thinking, some decathletes have tried to score as many points as possible in ten events, all within the shortest possible total time. In 1978, Warkentin held an unofficial USA record of 6747 points for ten events within a total of 30 minutes! A miracle of concentration--ten times within 30 minutes in widely varied events.

A different approach to training by event relatedness is derived from the 100-year experience of multiple-event athletes in non-decathlon competition and training. Doublers in the shot-discus have always practiced the shot first. "It just feels better that way." Men high jump before they pole vault; take sprint starts before hurdling or long jumping. As a rule of thumb, technique events are practiced first, though often preceded by sprint starts for reasons of technique and warm-up. If three or more activities involving high speed, power and endurance occur in a single session, they are practiced in that order. Saying that differently, events requiring quickness and little fatigue are practiced first; events requiring great effort and strain, or overall exhaustion, are done last. (Often, special time is set aside for heavy basic work in strength or endurance--in the morning, on a weekend, on a change-of-pace day.) There's no set pattern or requirement in all this; each decathlete should follow his own judgment, unique time allotments, and preference. But such long-time experience should not be ignored.

These over-all views are in agreement with those of Fred Kudu, USSR Chief Decathlon Coach, in his 1975 book, *DECATHLON*,[1]

> *Each training session has to solve several different problems and usually includes development of technique in one or two events. As the decathlon has a competitive order of events, it is advisable to follow this order in training.*
> *However, it is not necessary to be strict about it. Far more important is to perform technique training and speed exercises at the start, strength and jumping exercises in the middle, and endurance development at the end of a training session.*

The Beginner. "Beginners" in the decathlon vary greatly in age and related experience. Contrast the problems of a 16-year old high school junior with those of a 22-year college graduate in his first decathlon but with seven years of track and field competition and training behind him. But the basic goal is the same: to complete all ten events with a sense of satisfaction and encouragement for future decathlons.

Obviously, careful planning and preparation must be made.

(1) Since skill is the most difficult and gradual of all basics to acquire, first emphasis should be on adequate skill in all eight events. Of special concern are the danger events (pole vault, hurdles, discus, long jump) in which skill consistency will ensure against no-points performances.

(2) Related power is basic to at least five events and enhances performance quite apart from skill. Safest and best when acquired gradually and so, when started early.

(3) Practice events in decathlon order (e.g., 100-SHOT-LJ).

(4) A few trial runs in the 400 and 1500 may prevent too fast a pace in the first competition, and so avoid the "agony" of exhaustion no one cares to repeat.

(5) Various triathlons can be attempted in which any three events are competed in the same sequence as in the decathlon: LJ-SHOT-HJ, or PV-JAV-1500. Later, add a fourth event in decathlon sequence: 100-LJ-SHOT-HJ, or HH-PV-JAV-1500.

(6) Some authorities suggest prior competition in the pentathlon (LJ-JT-200-DT-1500), using regular decathlon scoring tables. This has an undoubted value of open competition in a sequence of events, with little or no stigma of failure in terms of one's own event, the decathlon. Another device is to organize a competition using the five events of the first day. Then, some days or weeks later, after proper preparation, compete in the second day's events.

A 1976 study by R. Kuptschinov,[2] USSR, reported that 78% of 64 decathlon coaches recommended that decathlon training be started at the ages of 13-14. First year: four two-hour sessions with a 50-50 balance between technique (no throwing events), and general conditioning in endurance, flexibility, sprints, easy long runs. Second year: four three-hour sessions with a 70-30 distribution between technique (including shot, javelin, no discus), and general conditioning with emphasis on developing power and more intensive endurance training (including interval runs at 150-300m). Third year: five three-hour sessions with a 75-25 balance between technique (all events) and general conditioning work in which strength training, mileage running, and gradually more intensive anaerobic endurance are added to the work load. In this third year, an eight-event competition using a decathlon sequence of events is introduced—the first competition mentioned in the study.

---

[1]Quoted as a footnote in *TRACK AND FIELD QUARTERLY REVIEW*, Vol. 79, #2, 1979, p. 19.

[2]R. Kuptschinov, "Training of Young Decathletes," reported in *TRACK AND FIELD QUARTERLY REVIEW*, Vol. 79, #2, 1979, p. 18.

TRAINING FROM BEGINNER TO MASTER. By Vern Gambetta and Gord Stewart.[1]

The very nature of the decathlon suggests that training should be a slow, methodical process. Training can be likened to putting together a large mosaic. Each piece (event) must be carefully prepared for. After much effort the pieces come together in a good score.

A proper foundation must be carefully laid in the first years of training. Progress should not be hurried. One must not think in terms of days or months, but in years. Few decathletes have risen to national class in less than three years.

Generally, the development of the decathlete can be divided into two distinct stages: the *learning stage* and the *specificity stage*. The main objective in the learning stage is to balance performance by working on the weaker events. During this stage the decathlete should concentrate on good all-around physical training aimed at developing speed, general strength, and endurance. During this stage, the athlete should compete often in those events in which he has reached a reasonable level of proficiency. He should also try to compete as often as possible in the "key events": 100m, 400m, 110H, and PV. During this learning stage, it would be advisable to compete each season in the number of decathlons that allows adequate time to recover and train between each one. For most decathletes this learning stage lasts for three or four years until the weak events are brought up to a standard of good all-around performance.

The specificity stage of training should begin when the athlete achieves a certain amount of parity between the three groups of events, (i.e. when there are no apparent weaknesses). The emphasis in this stage of training is on giving reasonably equal attention to each event.

TRAINING COMPONENTS
A sound decathlon training program should include the following components:

1) Speed--The development of sprinting speed is an integral and important part of training from the very beginning. At least five events are directly related to speed. Speed training should be carried out year round, not just as pre-season and in-season activities. Methods used should be sprint form drills, starts, and sprinting over 30m, 60m, 100m, and 150m.

2) Speed Endurance--Essentially this is 400 meter training. The emphasis here is on carrying the speed developed in the speed component over longer distances. Training would consist of running 200m, 300m, 400m, 500 and 600m at various speeds and combinations.

3) Technique--The goal in technique training is...not to develop a flawless technique, but to find one that is simple, mechanically sound and suited to the individual athlete....The greatest emphasis on technique should be during the learning stage--a time when the fundamental concepts and sound motor patterns are developed...

4) Strength Training--This can be divided into two kinds. *General strength training* consists of the traditional weight training exercises including squats, snatch, clean and jerk and bench press. These exercises emphasize the development of total overall body strength. The younger or beginning decathlete may initially confine his general strength training to a circuit on a Universal Gym...

Specific strength training encompasses the more dynamic exercises to develop power for running, jumping and throwing. This includes bounding, hopping, jumping over hurdles, depth jumping and medicine ball exercises.

General strength training dominates the learning stage. Once the decathlete becomes more proficient and enters the specificity stage of training, strength training is divided almost equally between general and specific strength.

It is important that strength training parallels technique work (not taking precedence over it.

---

[1]Vern Gambetta and Gord Stewart, "Decathlon Training: From Beginner to Master," *Track Technique* #70, Dec. 1977, p. 2219. Gambetta and Stewart (7438 pts--Canadian record) were both decathletes. Gambetta is editor of *Track Technique* and Director of Coaches Certification Program, TAC, 90 - 120th St., Indianapolis, IN 46206.

5) <u>Endurance Training</u>--The purpose of endurance training is to develop the aerobic base to run a good 1500m and to provide the general endurance necessary to handle the long hours of competition. This running should be based on the need for general endurance while keeping in mind that the 1500m has a 50%-50% aerobic anaerobic split. This can be accomplished by an off-season 20-30 minute steady run every other morning and a 20-30 minute fartlek session once a week. During the season, several paced 800m or 1200m would be advisable.

6) <u>Mobility (flexibility) Training</u>--This area is often neglected or played down as an important component of training. However, it is important since it assists in injury prevention as well as aiding technique (by allowing larger range of movement and faster movement through a given range). A daily fifteen minute pre-workout stretching session will pay large dividends.

TRAINING ORGANIZATION

On any given training day one should do sprint and technique work before any speed endurance training. Endurance and strength or power training should be at the end of the session.

In a sequence of training days the same principle holds. Technique work should follow a rest or light training day. Speed and speed endurance should be in the middle part of a training cycle with endurance and strength work towards the end of the cycle.

Because of the sheer demands of the decathlon, the training load will be heavy. Workload should be evenly distributed over a period of time interspersed with an adequate number of rest days. Planned rest periods during a training cycle should help minimize on overuse injuries and ensure that a large buildup of fatigue does not occur.

TRAINING CYCLES

An early, training cycle could be broken down into four phases. (1) Total rest and active rest take up the month of October. (2) Off-season training (strength, speed endurance, endurance emphasis) occupy the months November through January. (3) The four-month February to May period takes in indoor and pre-season activities. Speed endurance and technique work dominate this phase. The work load should not be sacrificed for indoor competitive results. (4) The in-season activities June through September ensures sharpening of speed and speed endurance and refining of technique. These are obviously crucial during the competitive phase of the yearly cycle.

There are a variety of short-term cycles which can be split into the three longer training phases of each year's activity. The crucial element is the number of training days before a planned rest day is taken. Experience will dictate the right combination.

To provide more specific guidelines, three short-term training cycles are outlined: A preparation period (off-season or pre-season) 21-day cycle; an in-season, competitive, 14-day cycle and a 3-day competitive season cycle.

The <u>21-day cycle</u> is designed for a younger decathlete in his first two or three years of training. The emphasis is on weak events and development of the fitness component.

The <u>14-day cycle</u> is for the young or seasoned decathlete alike. Both athletes could pursue the same general plan with the seasoned athlete emphasizing a lighter but more intense work load.

The <u>3-day cycle</u> is meant for the mature athlete preparing for important competitions.

Off-Season or Pre-Season Preparation Period
21-day Cycle for the Younger Decathlete

Day 1--1st day events: Sprint, LJ, SP, strength training
Day 2--A.M. 20 min. steady run. P.M. 2nd day events:HH, Dis, (PV), 400m training
Day 3--Weak events, strength training
Day 4--A.M. 30 min. fartlek. P.M. 1st day: SP, HJ, 400m training
Day 5--2nd day: PV, Jav, 1500 training
Day 6--A.M. 20 min. steady run. P.M. Warm-up, strength training

Day 7--Rest
Day 8--Sprinting, SP, HJ, strength training
Day 9--A.M. 20 min. steady run. P.M. HH, (PV)
    Jav, 400m training
Day 10--Weak events, strength training
Day 11--A.M. 30 min. fartlek, P.M. LJ, SP
    400m training

Day 12--HH, Dis, PV
Day 13--Warmup, strength training. P.M.
    A.M. 20 min. steady run
Day 14--Rest
Day 15-21--Same as Day 1-7

In-Season Competitive Cycle
14-day Cycle for the Younger or Seasoned Decathlete

Day 1--Sprinting, LJ, SP. P.M. Special
    strength training
Day 2--HH, Dis, (PV), 400m training
Day 3--Weak events. P.M. strength training
Day 4--Sprinting (starts), SP, HJ. P.M.
    400m training
Day 5--HH, PV, Jav, 400m training
Day 6--General strength training
Day 7--Rest

Day 8--Sprinting, SP, HJ, P.M. Special
    strength training
Day 9--HH, (PV), Jav, 400m training
Day 10--LJ, SP, 1500m training, strength
    training
Day 11--HH, PV, 400m training
Day 12--Warmup--General strength training
Day 13--Competition, 4 or 5 events
Day 14--Rest

Note: in preparation for a decathlon on the 13th or 14th day of the 14-day cycle, the overall volume of work is reduced on days 8 through 12. Technique work should be minimal. On day 8, a fast 300m; on day 10, 2 x 60m and 2 x 150m fast; day 11 should be off and day 12 should include warmup activities only.

3-day Competitive Season Cycle
for the Mature Decathlete

Day 1--A.M. SP, Dis. P.M. HJ, 6 x 50m 4 x 150m
Day 2--A.M. HH, Jav. P.M. PV, 400m training
    (e.g., 150m, 300m, 200m--fast with full
    recovery)

Day 3--A.M. LJ, 1500m training (e.g., 800,
    300, 200 at race pace). P.M. General
    strength training
Day 4--Rest

Note: Events not done or not emphasized in the cycle can be done in the next cycle. Sprint technique, suppleness, "light" special strength training and easy 1500m work can be incorporated into each day's warmup.

Chapter 16
A MODERN SYSTEM FOR COACHING FIELD EVENTS

Not so many decades ago, it was a relatively simple problem to propose a program of field event training that would have relevance at all levels from junior high school through college and in the various areas of the country. Training was largely a six-months affair beginning after the Christmas holidays and ending in May or early June; in some areas, a single outdoor season about two months long; in other areas an indoor season of four to six weeks that shifted outdoors in late April.

Most important, the needs of the team were pre-eminent; those of the individual, secondary. If an athlete could gain six points by taking two second places in a dual meet, he was contributing more than if he gained five points in one event, even if at record levels. That is, the dual and conference team meets had precedence over the few invitational meets, and the individual trained accordingly. Planning for such a limited program was relatively simple and so, much neglected. The influence of the Olympic Games on the program of events, or on length and intensity of training, was non-existent; and on continuance of training beyond the college years, limited to a very few.

About 1950, weightlifting and then related power training became part of the training routine, and training for both throwing and jumping events was extended in time as well as in complexity. How soon, how often, how long, and how much stimulated long clinic discussions.

In addition, the late 1970s saw the start of college women's programs in track and field. Primarily this came about through the growing emphasis on equality of the sexes, including Title IX legislation. But in recent decades, this expansion has been swollen almost beyond control, by the world-wide use of sports as instruments of government policy, as political weapons even, by way of the Olympic Games. Up to 1950 the USA was supreme in the Olympics, primarily because we were the only nation with a well-organized school-college sports program, with paid and to some extent trained coaches. In general our program and our coaches were the best in the world. For us, the Olympics were a mere adjunct; planning was a not-to-be-accepted Communist word; scientifically-planned training was unthinkable, especially if related to the training of young boys and girls, for whom having fun and enjoying life was primary.

Now, all such simple-minded attitudes are changed, jerked out of the old routine and complacency; especially when we realize how Eastern bloc planning, research and control of all aspects of sports was leading to Olympic supremacy and international prestige. The June 10, 1984 issue of *Sports Illustrated* carried a story of Bulgaria's rise to world-supremacy in weight-lifting, even above the Russians. Twelve-year-old boys with special related talent are admitted into Sports Schools that feature sports training classes five days a week with two sessions a day of two hours each, plus a special Saturday two-hour session--all related directly to weight lifting. Their most famous pupil, Suleimanov, "pound for pound the greatest weight lifter in history," is 16 years old, 5 feet tall and weighs 125 pounds. At age 8, though officially "discouraged," he helped weight lifters in their training sessions by putting weights on bars and the like; at age 12 he was admitted to the Sports Training School.

In Russia and East Germany, sports clubs, separate from the school system were formed, serving both boys and girls. Youngsters of 10-12 were encouraged to participate. Those of outstanding potential were moved to new locations, sometimes hundreds of miles from home, to train under National coaches, specialists in one or two events to which they devoted full time planning and research. The individual athlete, not the team, became the focus of attention, and planning could be done in terms of a full career over twelve months of each year. That is to say, a system of coaching and training was created that was almost the opposite in every way from what had been developed in the United States.

We should be clear, however, that the Communist countries were aware of the importance of the number of participants in sports. Prestige and rewards to successful athletes were considerable; millions of youngsters admired and sought to emulate them. Great Spartakiades were organized with thousands of participants and many tens of thousands of spectators. When I was in Moscow in 1961 I watched hundreds of youngsters--boys and girls about 12 in age, together under one coach--playing at running and jumping and throwing on the same field, though not in the same area of course, with Olympic prospects. But as soon as special aptitude became evident, the individual was often separated and given special attention. In contrast to the United States system, National interests were primary; those of the local team were not important.

Obviously, planning was inherent, even inevitable within such a sports system--planning for each year's training as well as for the entire career of the athlete. Experts gave full time to the construction of such plans, experts who were knowledgeable of basic training for power and endurance as well as of techniques, but equally essential, knowledgeable of the human needs related to training: recovery, relaxation, variety, motivation, competitive zest. When, in 1959, the Russian team came on Franklin Field, Philadelphia, prior to their first-ever dual meet in the USA, I was amazed, even shocked, to see them having fun with a soccer ball up and down the infield! All part of careful planning.

In 1962 L. P. Matveyev, USSR, published his work on "Periodization," a method of dividing each year into periods or cycles of varying lengths, and so making clear to both the coach and the individual athlete the precise goals, methods and loadings that ensured optimal outcomes. It featured planning, carefully thought out and clearly stated.

Matveyev assumed year-round training, including a single competitive period leading up to one all-important competition. The year consisted of three main periods: preparation, competitive, and an active-rest period. These three periods were divided into macrocycles, what we shall call "phases", cycles in which each athlete seeks certain specific objectives; for example a certain strength or power level, or volume of work, or competitive performance.

Figure 6.1
Matveyev's Plan for Single Periodization

Month	Oct-Jan	Feb-Apr	May-June	Jul-Aug	Sept
Period	Preparation		Competition		Active Rest
Phase	I	II	III	IV V	VI

With a double competitive season with both indoor and outdoor meets, the number of phases would increase to eight or even more. Note that the first preparation period requires four months, allowing a gradual approach to its two-phased objective of "training to train." This is a period in which the athlete gradually increases his overall capacity for great loadings and intensities of training. Its focus is primarily basic--heavy-weight lifting-- but consistent with the important principle that all phases intermesh with each other, training in power and techniques related to the athlete's event are also introduced and gradually emphasized.

Phase II, described as "training for competition," is the hardest working phase of the entire year. It continues the increase in loadings, but also leads into Phase III, the competitive phase.

Phase III opens the competitive period. Work loadings are reduced, gradually but considerably. Workouts will be shortened with an emphasis on intensity of work. Peaking for high-level performance is carefully planned. Personal-best records may occur during this phase.

Phase IV is a recovery and restorative phase, preparatory to the major competitions of Phase V. Intensity of competition is reduced, volumes and loadings or work are increased.

Phase V is assumed to include the major competitions of the year when winning is paramount and highest performances are hoped for, though not at all certain. Work of all kinds is lightened, though not discontinued, patterned to the competitive build-up. Precise methods of peaking (see Pat Reid's approach as described in Chapter 17) become crucial.

Phase VI, called a transition period leading toward the following year's training, is described as a period of active-rest. Training does not stop suddenly; rather loadings are gradually reduced, with an emphasis on physical and emotional relaxation and related play. Even this period is considered to be an essential part of year-round development.

Matveyev, in his meticulous planning of all aspects of training, broke down his phases (macrocycles) into microcycles: weekly cycles of work that varied, wavelike, between work and recovery, among successive days of work and also within each day's workout. If within Phases I and II, loadings in terms of strength and power would vary rhythmically; if within the competitive phases, technique and high-performance work would be alternated with days of active-recovery work.

And finally, the Matveyev system followed a similar approach in planning each day's work-out, what he called "units." Work is pinpointed to a specific objective, whether of general strength or of a specific aspect of technique. Once again, work is alternated with recovery. A single workout may have several units of work, with rest between; or but one, with active recovery--jogging, relaxation exercises--at the end.

To make even clearer the careful planning of Matveyev's system, we should be aware that each of these concepts--periods, macrocycles, microcyles and units--were considered in relation to the essentials of training: basic strength, power that combines strength and velocity, velocity both basic as in sprinting and specific as related to each event and movement of that event, as well as to suppleness and flexibility, technique or skill training, the mental-emotional aspects of both training and competition, and through it all, of critical importance, recovery and rest in both its physical and mental aspects.

Actually, this summary of Matveyev's system of periodization is far too brief and fails to give the reader a working understanding of its potential. An excellent and fuller discussion can be found in the writings of Frank Dick,[1] and each year brings an increasing number of published papers that clarify doubtful points, and adapt both the jargon and the schedule of training and competition to the United States program.

One of the best of these is by Robert Thayer,[2] of Canada but consistent with the United States school schedule. It relates most directly to our high-school program but is readily adapted to any level of performance.

Overload, Adaptation and Training Effect. As an athlete is exposed to a training stimulus, his coach hopes his performance will improve. Continued exposure to the same stimulus over a prolonged period, however, may result in a plateau or even a decrease in performance.

Therefore the volume or intensity of training must be progressively increased, resulting in an overload. The athlete adapts to each new training load. This adaptive process, where the athlete adjusts physiologically to the work load, is termed the training effect. The above relationship may be represented by the following scheme (Figure 1).

Super Compensation Cycle. The entire process, of Stimulus, Overload, Adaptation and Training Effect, has been referred to as the super compensation, or super adaption, cycle. In order to take full advantage of this cycle the coach must plan for the correct alternation between effort and rest. The overall cycle may be represented by **Figure 2**.

Figure 2 is based on the rationale that training results in fatigue, which may cause a

[1]Frank Dick, "Periodization: An Approach to the Training Year," *Track Technique*, #62, Dec.1975, p. 1968, #63, March 1976, p. 2005; #64, June 1976, p. 2030; #65, Sept. 1976, p. 2068.

[2]Robert Thayer, "Planning a Training Program," *Track Technique Annual '83*, pp. 4-7; and also in *Coaching Review*, Vol. 3, No. 17, Sept/Oct, 1980.

decrease in an athlete's performance over a weekly practice schedule. If the coach fails to plan for recovery, during the week and between weeks, eventually he may have a group of fatigued athletes on his hands, who cannot respond favorably to a training stimulus.

An adequate degree of rest, or compensation, following an exhaustive 2 to 3 weeks of practice may allow the athlete to recover to the point where he or she is ready for a greater training stimulus, or super compensation. One method of determining the proper timing of rest and overload is to use the morning pulse rate and practice session pulse rates.

A RESTED ATHLETE IS
A TRAINABLE ATHLETE

In figure 2 we have athletes participating in three different programs. It is obvious in the one case that the coach is pushing the athletes too hard and is not providing for adequate rest intervals in the training program.

So the coach provides a training stimulus, but the fatigued athlete fails to respond (see

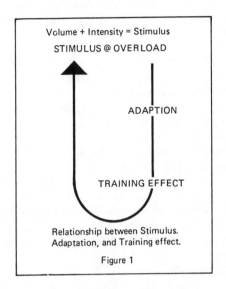

Volume + Intensity = Stimulus
STIMULUS @ OVERLOAD

ADAPTION

TRAINING EFFECT

Relationship between Stimulus.
Adaptation, and Training effect.
Figure 1

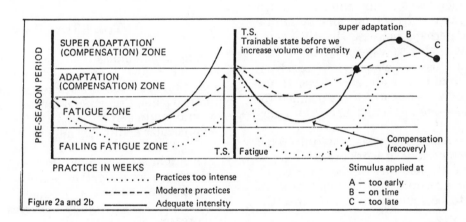

Figure 2a and 2b

SUPER ADAPTATION (COMPENSATION) ZONE

ADAPTATION (COMPENSATION) ZONE

FATIGUE ZONE

FAILING FATIGUE ZONE

PRACTICE IN WEEKS

PRE-SEASON PERIOD

T.S.

T.S.
Trainable state before we increase volume or intensity

super adaptation

A   B   C

Fatigue

Compensation (recovery)

Stimulus applied at
A — too early
B — on time
C — too late

.... Practices too intense
- - - - - Moderate practices
————— Adequate intensity

figure 1). In fact, the athlete's performance may decrease.

In contrast, the coach who provides adequate recovery intervals, supplies the proper stimulus and the athlete responds with improved performance. Weight training is a prime example. An athlete works hard in the weight room, attempts a maximum lift, fails and then takes a week off. After the rest period walks into the weight room and makes the lift. The possible explanation, the super adaptation zone.

THE READINESS FACTOR

The Readiness Factor determines the appropriate time to overload the athlete.

Increasing the intensity of practice at a time when the athlete has not fully recovered from previous sessions, when he is still in the failing adaptation zone, may be frustrating for both coach and athlete since no improvement in performance will occur.

However the stimulus appropriately applied will result in a maximum training effect *(see Figure 2b)*.

COACHING TIPS—REST

Too Little Rest
1. Excessively high heart rates between work intervals in spite of the appropriate rest periods.

315

2. Performance times in quality work are very poor or skill level appears to drop.

3. Competitive results are below expectations. Athlete displays signs of physical

fatigue.

4. The morning pulse rate (normal resting heart rate) experiences a dramatic rise which persists for several days.

5. A marked change in attitude, i.e., complains in practice

reluctant to work

constant focus on injuries

begins to miss practice

6. The sudden appearance of small nagging injuries which appear to be legitimate.

7. Repeated failure to complete required number of sets or reps if interval training.

8. Failure to respond when challenged in practice.

Too Much Rest

1. Athlete will complete interval work out without too much effort. Check heart rate immediately following a specific drill to see if the drill is demanding enough. May have to shorten rest interval.

2. If there is too much rest between work intervals or practices are not intense enough (suspected by the coach) the morning pulse rate will plateau or perhaps increase slightly over a period of time. This is especially important during the pre-season where the coach is attempting to build an endurance base. If the practices are not intense enough the planned for bradycardia (decrease in resting heart rate) may not occur.

3. If a coach suspects that the relief intervals between periods of work are too long to substantiate the suspicion he or she must check pulse rate. For example a work-relief ratio of 4:1 may have to be reduced to 2:1 to stress the athlete sufficiently.

4. Communication with the athletes may support the coach's feelings that the practices are not intense enough.

5. Poor competitive result may also be an indication of insufficient work.

PLANNING THE TRAINING PROGRAM

With the above concepts in mind the coach must not only plan the weekly practice schedule but also the annual training plan. The various stages of training are represented by **Figure 3.**

The overall training program must take into consideration the maximal development of the following areas:

1. physical preparation

2. technical preparation

3. tactical preparation

4. psychological preparation.

Furthermore in order for the coach to attack the four above areas in a logical fashion he or she must divide the season into the following:

1. pre-season

2. competitive season

3. off season

THE PRE—SEASON

General guidelines

Physical preparation emphasis in the early portion of the pre-season should be on the improvement of general motor fitness.

—maximum aerobic capacity

—muscular endurance and strength flexibility.

The volume of exercises for their development is high but intensity is low. However, as we get into the late stages of the pre-season, exercises become more specific to the sport and volume decreases as intensity increases.

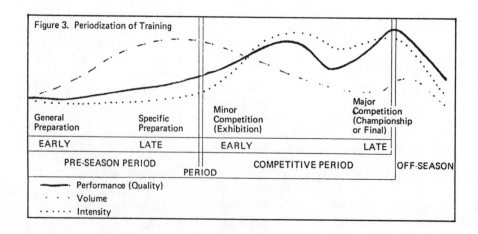

Figure 3. Periodization of Training

General Preparation | Specific Preparation | Minor Competition (Exhibition) | Major Competition (Championship or Final)

EARLY | LATE | EARLY | LATE

PRE-SEASON PERIOD | PERIOD | COMPETITIVE PERIOD | OFF-SEASON

——— Performance (Quality)
· · · Volume
· · · · · · Intensity

Proper physical preparation in the pre-season is essential in order to insure the maximum learning of technical skills. For example, a coach who allows his athletes to neglect aerobic fitness in the pre-season, may retard the athlete's skill learning because of their premature fatigue.

Technical Preparation

To introduce new and fundamental techniques of the sport. In the latter portion of the pre-season drilling the techniques are more intense with a greater emphasis on refinement of skill.

Psychological Preparation

In this early phase the coach should primarily concentrate on the motivational area. However, towards the end of this phase the coach should work on the psychological preparation for competition. This may be done by the simulation of competitive situations during practice.

Tactical Preparation

Introduction of tactical elements necessary to competition.

THE COMPETITIVE SEASON

General guidelines

Physical Preparation

The coach should concentrate on maximum development of motor fitness components specific to the sport. Intensity is high and volume low. Late in the competitive season where major competitions are planned the coach must insure adequate recovery as practices are specific and intense in nature. Training is highly specific.

Technical Preparation

The emphasis here is a stabilization of technique and quality performance of technique. The technique drills should be related to the competitive situation. In the latter stages of the competitive season technical preparation should be performed under competition conditions. High intensity drills, scrimmages and competitions are the major component of this period.

Psychological and Tactical Preparation

Work in this area is confined to preparation for specific competitions.

THE OFF-SEASON

General guidelines

The major emphasis in this period is threefold:

1. the athlete's psychological and physiological recovery

2. to evaluate the past year's performance and plan for the new season

3. to provide a period of active rest in order to prevent a significant decrease in motor fitness. Athlete may be involved in other sporting activites to maintain fairly high fitness level. Volume may be quite high but intensity is low.

THE WEEKLY PRACTICE PLAN

Planning the weekly practice schedule is a complex process demanding a high degree of organization on the part of the coach. The weekly plan should be based on scientific principles, a few of which are outlined at the beginning of the article.

As well the weekly practice schedule must reflect a specific phase of the overall seasonal plan. For example the weekly plan in the competitive season will have to be geared to the competitive schedule. The weekly practice plan must also reflect the delicate balance of the following:
a) the volume—intensity relationship
b) the stimulus—adaptation—training effect relationship
c) the overload principle of training
d) the specificity of training principle.

The coach should employ the above principles when planning for one super adaptation cycle. What does this mean? Perhaps the best way to illustrate is to use a specific example. In the pre-season the coach is concerned with the enhancement of cardio-vascular fitness.

There is evidence to show that the super adaptation cycle for endurance fitness is three to four weeks. In other words the coach provides a stimulus over a three to four week period with a variety of drills and exercises designed to improve endurance fitness.

However, prolonged exposure to these exercises without planned rest may lead to a fatigued athlete. Therefore the coach plans for a rest interval after three to four weeks which allows the athlete to recover. Hopefully this will coincide with the super adaptation zone.

CONCLUSION

Planning the yearly training program is a complex and demanding task for both the coach and athlete. With the development of the yearly training plan both coach and athlete leave nothing to chance. Therefore the competitive results attained by the athlete should reflect this diligent preparation by the coach. □

Chapter 17
HINTS FOR COMPETITION IN FIELD EVENTS

HINTS FOR COMPETITION IN FIELD EVENTS

Competitiveness is a word. Like all such words, it has a dictionary or average meaning--ability to attain a desired response in a competitive situation. But such a definition has real meaning only as it relates to this unique individual in this particular situation in this competitive action--here and now.

Each athlete and coach approaches the problem of competitiveness in his own way. For some it seems to come naturally, along with a natural physical aptitude for sports; for others it requires gradual development through longtime practice, much the same as for developing skill or relaxation (See Chapters 18-19). Therefore I emphasize the word "hints" as providing ideas--no more than that--to be discarded if they fail to fit.

A Climate of Competitiveness. A man's competitiveness can be derived from his surround as well as from within himself. A team tradition, a coach's charisma, or even a firm friend can ensure a quiet expectation of maximal performance that can be unbeatable.

At certain schools (Southern Cal, Michigan, Oregon), during certain decades, the simple act of donning a track suit added feet and subtracted seconds. By various means, such institutions developed a tradition or climate of success that enhanced competitiveness.

Outstanding qualities of leadership by coaches can have a similar effect. Dean Cromwell, USC's longtime Master Coach, had a habit of greeting a new prospect with an enthusiastic "Hi Champ." A small thing. He did it with everyone. But the prospect was pleased and, strangely, believed. Cromwell--"Call a man a champion and he'll be the more likely to prove you a prophet." Over a 40-year career, Jumbo Elliott, Villanova, acquired a similar reputation for coaching competence and success. His athletes dressed the part, talked the part, felt the part, acted the part. It almost seemed they could do no other than perform well when the going was toughest--22 Olympic team members and over 225 IC4A individual champions. He recruited great talent of course, but also he created a climate of success that strengthened even the weakest competitor on his squad.

Of course, the competitive surround can have much smaller dimensions. Some Catholics place themselves at a higher level of confidence simply by making the sign of the cross before stepping into the circle or starting a run-up. I had the great privilege of coaching the Hume twins who held hands at the NCAA mile finish line to make certain they won together. Running separately they had less confidence; together they "knew" they would win.

Competitiveness has a thousand roots; the art of good coaching lies in creating a healthful soil and climate by which each root can thrive and bear fruit. Brutus Hamilton, a Master at developing young men, once wrote, "For the most part I coach by indirection. I like to coach men without their realizing they are being coached. A coach can only point the way; inspired performances must come from deep within the boy himself." Perhaps so, but by such attitudes Hamilton created a climate of mutual supportiveness within which individual inspiration was most likely to grow.

Planning for Competitiveness. Al Oerter was the only man ever to win four Olympic golds in a single event, a great record of competitiveness at the most crucial moment. But that record didn't happen by mere inspiration or chance. Oerter told Jeff Johnson,[1]

In the weeks before an Olympic competition, I mentally simulate every conceivable situation for each throw. For example, I imagine I'm in 8th place. It's my fifth throw and it's pouring rain. What do I do? An inexperienced thrower might panic, or be thinking, "Gees, I hope I don't fall down." I know ahead of time what I will do under every condition. In Tokyo I won on my 5th throw. I passed the 6th because of the pain in my ribs and because my position in the order was such that it was clear that I had won. But I know to this day that if I had had to take my final throw that it would have been further than the 5th. I'm not saying it would have been good enough to win. I can't control how far the others are going to throw. Only that it would have been further. I knew just how I was going to throw it.

Clearly, such planning worked for Oerter. Parry O'Brien's methods were somewhat more esoteric, derived from a college course in yoga, the Indian mental discipline aimed at concentrating the self into "that special world."

Alongside the practical physics belongs Parry's fierce concentration. He spends as much time just thinking about his shot as fondling it in the putting circle. Parry spent many of his nights alone in his ascetic bedroom, the lights dim, his weighty frame slack on the bed. From his tape recorder trickled the soothing sound of his own voice: "Keep low, keep back, keep your movement fast across the circle. Fast now! Fast! Fast! And beat them! Beat them all!" Parry is convinced that this nocturnal rite adds inches to his toss.[2]

Dwight Stones' inability to jump well at the Montreal Olympic Games under rainy conditions led to the only double flop in Olympic history. As early as March 1976, he had spoken of his lack of confidence when a wet runway forced him to slow his approach run. But apparently he did nothing in the way of preparation. In contrast, Rolf Beilschmidt, after clearing 7-6½ in the rain,

I remember my coach coming out sometimes with a watering can and saying, "Now we'll try such-and-such a height; it's raining cats and dogs." Then he'd cover the approach with water until it was nice and slippery.[3]

Practicing Maximal Efforts. Whether or not to attempt maximal efforts in practice depends on the event and, certainly, on the individual athlete. Some do and some don't. Dave Roberts, former world-record pole vaulter, often vaulted for height in practice, explaining, "Vaulting is a 100 percent event; it takes 100 percent to even make it to the pit." In my judgment, he was saying that a vault at 18 feet or so is simply a different event from one at 15-16, requiring different velocity-timing-spring-power. Practice should be specific to the effort that highest heights require.

High jumpers such as Fosbury and Stones never jumped at highest heights in practice. For them, the excitements of competition were required to produce the adrenalin necessary for such attempts. However, there is a great difference between jumping for and jumping at highest heights. In the latter case, awareness is centered on "how," not on "how high." Technique determines success or failure, not clearance. In fact, clearance of maximal heights will almost never occur in practice, but practice of the effort is the best way to ensure clearance in competition.

One solution to this problem in all field events is to fix meet priorities. Now one can use meets of lesser importance as "practice" meets which prepare for the BIG meets. Each athlete and coach will need to analyze just what is needed in the way of preparation, and "practice" accordingly.

---

[1] Jeff Johnson, "Al Oerter: Olympic Spirit," *Track & Field News*, December 1968, 10.

[2] *Time Magazine*, December 3, 1956.

[3] *Track & Field News*, September 1979, p. 34.

Hu Hongfei, coach of 1984 world-record (7'10") jumper, Zhu Jianhua, wrote[1] that "After he jumped over 2.13m in 1979....I drew on the wall two long lines, one indicating the bar at 2.29m, the Asian record; the other at 2.36m, the world record at that time. Every day before training, I would tell him to (concentrate on those lines), to feel himself clearing them. Through this 'visual aid,' he not only gained confidence but also became more energetic in training than ever before."

Hu also wrote that in competition, "the aim...should be to raise your personal record, even more than to win the competition....To be obsessed by the idea of winning, tends toward nervousness during competition." Sound advice, but Zhu did less than his best at the World Championships, 1983, and at the 1984 Olympics. Competitive experience develops competitiveness.

Develop a Pre-Competition Routine. Each event calls for a different approach, and each man will develop his own unique methods, but these procedures are basic:

1. Before dressing, check the general lay-out for competition. What about the weather? Number of competitors? Probable length of the competition? Opportunities for warm-up? Where and how can I get myself ready for each competitive effort? What is the condition of the run-up and take-off surfaces? In the shot put, is the toe-board firmly fastened? Is the concrete at the back of the throwing circle rough or slippery? In the discus what is the direction and velocity of the wind? There are many other details to check, any one of which may decide the winning.

2. Before dressing, check in your implements, if so required; or better, have someone dependable do it for you. The process of weighing and measuring can be long and irritating to nerves already edgy.

3. Before dressing, check your equipment--shoes and shoelaces, spikes, competitor's number, sun lotion, towel, letters from Henrietta--whatever ensures confidence and relaxation. Need I add--*leave your valuables at home or in the hotel safe.*

4. Be ready for competition ON TIME--certainly not too late when things get hectic; and better, not too soon when delay wears away the competitive edge. Allow plenty of time in which to follow a routine of warm-up. On the other hand, disruptions of such routine occur frequently in competitions, and should not be mentally upsetting.

The Power of Positive Thinking. The concept of positive thinking has had popular acceptance, especially in the areas of religion (Norman Vincent Peale) and public relations (Dale Carnegie). Certainly it has great usefulness in sports competition if based on more than mere faith in good luck or intervention "on my side" by Providence. Such faith may work, but it's weak-minded, to speak softly.

But positive thinking that evolves out of careful preparation and competence is unbeatable. Now things happen, not by thinking so much as by assumption and certainty. Yashchenko had these reactions to his world-record 7-8 high jump in June, 1978:

While I was jumping, I wasn't thinking of records, only of jumping. When I cleared the world record, I was thinking a bit to myself, "Be surprised." But I wasn't surprised; it was too familiar. It really was...What I did think was, I could have gone higher....And later-- It was not really a test as such. For me the height did not exist as a barrier, or as a limit.

That may not be positive thinking, nor even thinking at all, but it's a sense of certainty in one's own competence that's hard to beat.

Controlled Recklessness. Research has shown that inexperienced athletes have inhibitions

---

[1]Hu Hongfei, "Zhu Jianhua's Psycho-Training", *China Sports*, Beijing, China, Vol.16, #3, 1984.

[2]Jon Hendershott, "Vladimir Yashchenko," *Track & Field News*, Sept. 1978, p. 12.

or "fears" that prevent all-out effort. But experienced athletes learn to disinhibit, to set aside or go with such fears. Blowing up the flames of competitiveness has a strong element of recklessness in it, of letting oneself go--all-out, for broke, nothing held back. Though made 30 years ago, O'Brien's comments are still valid: "You've got to get keyed up to a point where everything about you is so taut it might break. You've got to be mentally ready to make the toss. You've got to be nervous, get your blood flowing, your metabolism working faster and faster. Your heart has got to beat like a trip hammer. When I'm ready for a toss I'm all wrapped up in myself. I'm in a different world."

To veer away from sports a moment, I enjoyed Cyril Ritchard's remark on the TV recently that, even after a thousand or more performances, "I always keep a bucket handy to be sick in just before I go on stage." That's the attitude of a real champion. Not that being sick is a requirement, but having butterflies is.

But recklessness must be controlled. When extreme emotional stress is present without the means for its control, its effects are dissipated, tend to discoordinate action, even block action. Somehow the nerve impulses must be insulated within those positively related to the desired action. Somehow the energies must be channeled within those muscle groups which contribute to the action and withheld from those which inhibit it. Here, as with skill and power, there's no short cut for practice-practice-practice, combined with competitive experience.

<u>Self-Detachment</u>. There's a converse approach, that of losing all self-awareness in the competitive situation and action. Yashchenko implied this in his remarks. But recently I read[1] the comments of the great golfer Tom Watson, on the eve of the U.S. Open, 1980, that there had been a handful of occasions when he found himself in the twilight zone, when he just knew he would win:

"There have been five times when I've felt I could beat anybody," he said. Four of those times, he added, he won.

But he also understands that you do not climb to this lofty plateau; rather, you just are deposited there. In fact, if you try to hypnotize yourself into that frame of mind, you'll probably miss the cut instead. It is something that cannot be made to happen. Like the appearance of the leaves on trees every spring, you awake one day and it is just there.

"You can't control it," Watson agreed. "It just comes when it wants to, I guess."

In 1982, *Track & Field News*[2] interviewed Debbie Brill (high jump, 6'6¼").

T&FN: Do you ever feel that the instincts take over when you're competing?
Brill: Oh yes, that's when it's best. You can let go of all the thoughts, 'I gotta do this right, I gotta do that right.' When I can let go of that and just look at the bar and say, 'I can jump that,' then I feel great. I can't always do that though.

T&FN: High jumpers have their own little reverie. It's obvious, as you stand way out there staring at the bar and your eyes glaze over. Where do you go?
Brill: It's a fine kind of concentration, kind of like meditation. You're thinking of the jumping, but you're not really thinking. It's like a trance.

T&FN: 'Unthinking?'
Brill: That's best. That's it. You want to feel like you could get over that bar if it was a mile high. Indoors you have people running around, people walking in front of you. You can barely see the bar, but all of that stuff doesn't bother you. When you're at your best nothing gets in. The only thing I'm aware of is the bar and that I'm going to jump over it.

---

[1]Bill Lyon, *The Philadelphia Inquirer*, June 17, 1980, p. C-1.

[2]Garry Hill, *Track & Field News*, March 1982, p. 11.

PART 3
Coaching Endurance Running

In this 1968 race Australian distance great Ron Clarke
leads Americans George Young and Pat Traynor.

Chapter 18
WHY MEN RUN

Why do men run? The wisest answer would undoubtedly be given by a child, or by a runner, or by a Zen Master; without saying a word, they each would start running. Men do run, and that is the most penetrating reason of all as to why they run. It tells us, beyond all words and abstractions, that men are made *for* running, and have been made as they are by running.

Unfortunately I am not so wise, and so must use mere words. Why do men run? If I were a physiologist I would answer that they run because they have running bodies: running hearts, running lungs, running muscles, running bones. Without a long racial history of running, these would not be what they are. Man is a land animal. His use of other land animals for transportation has been limited and part-time. His use of machines is a last-minute innovation. Throughout a long racial history, he has had to depend upon himself whenever he wanted to go, and sometimes he wanted to go in a hurry. He had to run and by running he became a man-that-runs. Had he stuck to walking, he would now be quite different physically. The maximum stroke volume of his heart would never have reached the 200cc of blood, nor the number of beats --180 or so per minute--that a trained runner's heart can put forth. His muscles would contain only a fraction of the 317 billion blood capillaries that are now present. Of course there have been other developmental activities, such as fighting or making love, but even in these a little running ability was helpful.

Why do men run? If one were a cardiologist with a strong bent toward religious philosophy, as is George Sheehan, M.D., one would seek spiritual reasons as he tends to do. Though well into his 40s, George still ran in the Boston Marathon but, in a strange way, for the fun of it quite apart from any hope of recognitions or even first-50 placements. His answer:[1]

For the runner, less is better. The life that is his work of art is understated. His needs and wants are few, he can be captured in a few strokes. One friend, a few clothes, a meal now and then, some change in his pocket, and for enjoyment, his thoughts and the elements....

I see this simplicity as my perfection. In the eyes of others, however, it appears completely different. My success in removing myself from things and people, from ordinary ambition and desires, is seen as lack of caring, proof of uninvolvement, and failure to contribute.

So be it. A larger view of the world might include the possibility that such people are necessary, that the runner burning with a tiny flame on some lonely road does somehow contribute.

Now if I were a historian, I would explain that men run because running is deep in our social history. We are all familiar with the glorious run of Pheidippides from the battle ground of Marathon to cry, "Victory!" in the market-place in Athens. But all peoples have such tales of great running. Students of the ancient Inca civilization have become aware that the

---

[1]George Sheehan, M.D., "On the Run But Not in a Hurry," *The Daily Register*, Red Bank, N.J., April 1975.

323

very extensive system of roads throughout the widespread Inca territory was entirely for foot travel, and more specifically, running. They had no horses or other animals for rapid transportation. Messages were sent by relay runners, each of whom ran about a mile in distance, carrying knotted ropes by which to refresh their memories of the details they were to transmit by word of mouth. Much of this running was done at 9000 feet or more over the Andes mountains, so that development through stress must have been to highest potentials.

Why do men run? If I were a sociologist I would try to explain man's running by way of society's basic need for self-fulfillment through the self-discipline of striving and struggle whatever its forms--in the arts, in exploration of the earth, of outer space, and the great inner space within the individual self, in meaningful work of all kinds. Every sound society must have a foundation of what can be called moral energy, of courage and will to begin and maintain the development of energies and talents toward their highest potentials, despite all fear of danger, exhaustion, ridicule and ultimate failure. Inconsequential as running may seem in our society, what more available, more healthful, more developmental, more satisfying activity do we have to meet this universal need for self-affirmation? Small wonder that endurance running is the foremost activity in the Modern Olympic Games. It attracts more spectators, more world-wide attention, and more representatives from more nations than any other. The rising new nations of the world are keenly aware of this showcase and of society's tendency to accept the victory of even one man as proof of the virility of an entire nation. It has not been by chance that the 1960 Olympic marathon was won by an unknown from Ethiopia, or that recent Olympic medals have been won by men from Morocco, Kenya, and Tanzania, as well as Ethiopia.

To understand why men run, a sociologist might well turn to Finland where, between 1912 and 1980, a mere four millions of people produced more Olympic champions in running than any other nation. There he would find a great social need and readiness, born out of Finland's struggle for independence from the heavy hand of Russia, but he would also find that it was individual achievement which turned this social readiness into widespread action. The victories of Kohlemainen and Stenroos over the 1912 Olympic world excited the Finnish people tremendously; they made heroes of their runners, and villages a 100 miles north of the Arctic Circle built excellent running tracks and organized long-distance-running clubs. The astounding victories of Vasala and Viren in the Munich Olympic 1500, 5000 and 10,000, individual triumphs as they were, should also be judged as the outcome of Finnish "sisu," of social hardihood and courage.

Why do men run? If I were a psychologist, I might answer that to run is satisfying, that it is a natural activity which provides a sense of achievement for its own sake. I would quote a great runner like Roger Bannister, "I find in running - win or lose - a deep satisfaction that I cannot express in any other way....I sometimes think that running has given me a glimpse of the greatest freedom that a man can ever know, because it results in the simultaneous liberation of both body and mind."[2] Or I might quote a great coach of runners, Arthur Lydiard of New Zealand, "It is a simple unalloyed joy to tackle yourself on the battlefield of your own physical well-being and come out the victor."[3]

A psychologist would find great resources for study in the small-group dynamics of running. England's former mile champion, Bill Nankeville, has written of the closely-knit group of non-school running enthusiasts who nourished each other toward international levels of performance. Such great Irish runners as E. M. N. Tisdall, Ron Delany, Noel Carroll and Eamonn Coghlan developed out of small running clubs and the energies of individuals such as Billy Morton of Dublin. The great Gunder Haegg of Sweden probably never would have run competitively if his own father and his friends had not had an enthusiasm for running. Eugene, Oregon, with its 10,000 run-for-fun enthusiasts, is widely known as "the running capitol of the world." But who would know of Eugene without Bill Bowerman, his jogging medics and his champions?

In summary, it is impractical, if not impossible, to try to comprehend the innumerable cross-currents of racial inheritance, social customs, institutional incentives, family expectations, friendly encouragements and personal aggressions, impulsions, insecurities, and frustrations that can and do motivate a boy to run. Actually, there is never a single motive that

---

[2]Roger Bannister, THE FOUR MINUTE MILE, New York: Dodd, Mead & Co., 1955, p. 229.

[3]Arthur Lydiard and Garth Gilmour, RUN TO THE TOP, London: Herbert Jenkins, Ltd.,1962, p. 46.

can be isolated as exclusively responsible. As with other basic activities, men run for a great complex of reasons, limited only by one's discernment in abstracting them.

One of the most discerning stories of long distance running is by Alan Sillitoe, "The Loneliness of the Long Distance Runner."[4] When the big race is about two-thirds over, the "hero's" impulsion to prove his worth forced him to pour it on - "so by the haystack I decided to leave it all behind and put on such a spurt, in spite of the nails in my guts, that before long I'd left both Gunthorpe and the birds a good way off." Yet his sense of what he called honesty and realness would not let him win; or rather, would not let his dishonest trainer-jailer win through his efforts. In full sight of the finish line and the crowd, he deliberately slowed down, waited for his opponent to break the tape, then finished with his back straight and his eyes looking disdainfully into those of his trainer.

Few readers will suffer the twisted life that produced such a twisted motivation, but many will run with a similar tangle of likes and dislikes, tenacity and weakness, of which they are quite unaware and certainly could never put into words.

When a boy first starts to run competitively, his motives tend to be of as low an order as are his performances: to win a medal or a varsity letter, to make the team, to be one of the gang, to get one's picture in the school paper or year-book. Such a boy is likely to understand verbal motives that are only a short step beyond what he has already experienced. The coach who emphasizes the deeply hidden satisfactions that lie in hard work and self-discipline will find his words wasted. Even such a sensitive person as Roger Bannister admitted that, as a boy, he took up running as an escape from the gibes of his school-mates so that he would be free to do what really interested him: to be active as a student, a musician, and an actor.

In each instance, some obstacle becomes a challenge to overcome, some disinterest becomes a hobby, some inspiration cries out, "Begin!" But inspiration produces only the first few steps. During early stages, the runner may need a sort of baby's walker to hold him erect, and a fatherly voice to give encouragement. Until he was sure Gunder could go it alone, Haegg's father devised endless ways, even falsifying times on one occasion, to develop his son's confidence and belief in his running future.

Later, running may become an inescapable way of life. In 1957, at the age of 68, Clarence DeMar competed in a 10-mile race, notwithstanding the presence of a surgical colostomy. In 1978, at age 58, George Sheehan, M.D., published RUNNING & BEING,[5] a record of his total experience--spiritual, mental, physical--during some 15 years, including about 50 marathons.

Of course, some men by body structure, energy, and chemistry are better made for running than others. For these men, distance running is a challenge even when it is a hardship; play even when they slave at it; fun, even when they hate it. Cerutty wrote, "Running at its best is an outpouring, a release from tensions....An hour, two hours of hard training slips away as so many minutes. We become tired, exhaustingly tired, but never unhappy. It is work but it seems only fun. Exhilarating, satisfying fun."

We understand this when we realize that such attitudes were developed at Camp Portsea, Australia, where men ran along the beautiful seacoast, up great sand dunes, across open country --sometimes nude--then back, following Cerutty's uninhibited methods, to plunge into the cold sea. It is much harder to understand the motivations of the Englishman, W. R. Loader, who described his early training experiences through the sooty brick and stone deserts of Clyneside, Tyneside, and Merseyside, with their coke ovens, foundries, ship yards, blast furnaces, and machine shops. In one instance he had to run through a certain tough district of his town where the handicaps of terrain were as nothing compared with the derisive jeers of the onlookers, especially of the girls,

"Yah, look at the runner coming!...Mary Ann, look, it's a runner! He's got nae claes

---

[4]Alan Sillitoe, THE LONELINESS OF THE LONG-DISTANCE RUNNER, New York: New American Library of World Literature, 1959, p. 34.

[5]Dr. George Sheehan, RUNNING & BEING, New York: Simon & Schuster, 1978, 256 pps.

on!" Faces rose up all around, derisive, jeering, insulting. A scabby mongrel dog snapped at the heels, delighted for once to discover that someone else's life was being made a misery. Urchins sprinted alongside, mocking the runner's strides with their own exaggerated movements. It was a torment of the soul far more bitter than any torture of the body. And through it all one had to run with measured step, eyes fixed ahead as if unaware of the tumult, trying to abolish it by ignoring it....But it is a hard thing for youth to set itself alone against spite and hostility. I did that run a number of times and never faced it without a premonitory chill of the spine. Having stood the jeers to the point where I could persuade myself I wasn't giving up through cowardice, I quietly abandoned the practice.[6]

Though Loader's experiences and his way of relating them are unusual, the hindrances and distractions of social environment are common deterrents to why men run, or better, why men continue to run. Lasse Viren: "Sometimes...I realize I am running because I want to know how good I can become...That is still the main motivation, but gradually running has also become a narcotic for me. It is a lure I can't resist."

Viren was 31 when he ran at the Moscow Games, about right for maximal performance. But the eight years between Munich and Moscow had been long and arduous--training, training and more training--enough miles between 1971 and 1980 to run twice around the world. Maintaining enthusiasm was a serious problem. Especially since his wife and child must not be neglected. Viren: "We have been discussing this problem. Paivi won't put me in chains. A marriage shouldn't be a prison. And, as Paivi says, four years is just a twinkle in a human life." Maybe so, but twinkles sometimes become frowns, and frowns diminish enthusiasm for training.

So also with George Young, the first American distance runner to compete in four Olympic Games. The Olympic gold was never his, but during some 15 years he defeated Olympic champions and set American records.   George once said, "If I didn't have to work and I didn't have a family to support and if I didn't have to worry about anything else than running, maybe I could work twice as hard. And if I could work out twice as hard, what kind of runner could I be? That's always in the back of my mind." But George failed to understand the value of such limitations. Amateur running is avocational; studies or some vocation other than sport has first priority on one's time-energy-devotion. Both training and competition for running must occur within what's left over. To ensure fair competition, rules and regulations as to conduct off the field must be established, rules that can be only partially enforced. Others will break the rules, gain some real or imagined advantage. And therein lies the great burden but also the means to deep self-respect, if not glory, of the long-distance runner. One of the better ways of judging any man--in or out of sports--is by the degree of his adherence to social agreements that are not fully enforceable. Integrity and personal honor are words of high value, whatever their import in today's society.

Today's society. No way can we avoid it. After all, today's society is the only one we can live and run in. What are our motivations for running in a society that has taken on many of the connotations of George Orwell's 1984. Actually, the inherent racial reasons are still here with us, as they always will be as long as men are human. But our Machine Society has added a new dimension--the grease that lubricates its wheels--money, Big Money.

Not that our Machine Society is the first to use money as a motivator. The Greek Olympics were rife with paid performers. As early as 1860 English gentlemen bet fortunes on the running abilities of their "coachmen" who were often paid primarily because of their speed-endurance in racing. Then there were the illegal but popular races among the professional "peds", notorious for their "roping" and "squaring" tactics.[7] I knew Steve Farrell, highly respected coach at the University of Michigan in the 20s. Steve was great at telling stories, such as his winning the English Sheffield Handicap, 1892, and his travels in America to various county fairs where he, under an assumed name, and such cohorts as Tom Keane (later, coach

---

[6]W. R. Loader, *TESTAMENT OF A RUNNER*, London: William Heinemann Ltd., 1960.

[7]Montague Shearman, *ATHLETICS IN ENGLAND*, London: Longmans, Green & Co., 1889.

at Syracuse) and Keene Fitzpatrick (later of Princeton) contrived to fleece the local yokels of their silver dollars; in fact, even a measly two-bits was accepted into the pot.

No, we clearly are not unique in our use of money in answering, why men run. But we do appear to be rapidly becoming foremost in doing so openly, with large sums. "He's the best: he worked hard to get to the top; why shouldn't he be paid?"

With a dateline of July 15, 1984, Frank Dolson[8] wrote in the *Philadelphia Inquirer*,

In Europe it's another story: sellout crowds at $25 a ticket, gross gates of half a million dollars or more....No wonder James Robinson, the veteran U.S. half-miler who was upset in his bid to make the Olympic team, had set his sights on winning a gold medal in L.A., then cashing it in the next year before retiring.
'I hope I can make a million dollars off of it,' Robinson said....'so I will run through '85. I'm planning to make me some money.'

I began this chapter by saying that men, even modern men, are men-that-run; that their vital organs and systems and chemistry are as they are because of the eons of running. Just as the salt content of our blood is that of the sea because of eons of sea-living. To say that running is socially recognized or personally satisfying cheapens the argument, makes running an artificial action that waits upon cultural whims. Running is not so much a tool of the "New Emerging Nations" as an inherent part of a man-society-nature interaction. Not to run is as unthinkable as not to eat, or not to sleep, or not to make love.

But try as I may, I shall never say it as well as did Brutus Hamilton, head coach of the University of California and the 1948 U. S. Olympic track team,

People may wonder why young men like to run distance races. What fun is it? Why all that hard, exhausting work? Where is the good of it? It is one of the strange ironies of this strange life that those who work the hardest, who subject themselves to the strictest discipline, who give up certain pleasureable things in order to achieve a goal, are the happiest of men. When you see 20 or 30 young men line up for a distance race in some meet, don't pity them, don't feel sorry for them. Better envy them instead. You are probably looking at the 20 or 30 best "bon vivants" in the world. They are completely and joyously happy in their simple tastes, their strong and well- conditioned bodies, and with the thrill of wholesome competition before them. These are the days of their youth, when they can run without weariness; these are their buoyant, golden days; and they are running because they love it. Their lives are fuller because of this competition and their memories will be far richer. That's why men love to run. That's why men do run. There is something clean and noble about it.

---

[8]Frank Dolson, "A Track Promoter's Life is Simpler: Now You Just Write Checks," *Philadelphia Inquirer*, July 15, 1984.

Sebastian Coe./Photo by Theo Van de Rakt.

Chapter 19
TRAINING SYSTEMS FOR ENDURANCE RUNNING

Modern training systems tend to be eclectic, selecting and adapting from past systems what best seems to fit local conditions and this individual's abilities and needs. Haikkola, coach of Lasse Viren, is frank in stating his indebtedness, "My coaching system is a mixture of Arthur Lydiard, Mihaly Igloi, Percy Cerutty, and Paavo Nurmi." But after telling the particulars of each man's contribution, he adds his own variations of their systems as they apply to the Finnish surround and Viren's unique needs.

To be truly eclectic in constructing one's own method, a coach must know and understand past training systems--fartlek, interval training, marathon training and the rest. Out of such understanding, he must be able to digest the essentials of training--those activities basic to every system, however peculiar it may be to a particular place and time and person.

This and the following two Chapters seek to provide a summary of such knowledge--the systems, their essentials, and how one might best set up one's own system. But they do not; in fact there's no way they can do the job for you. That's your responsibility, and no book, no other person can shoulder it for you. Just as you, Coach, can never do the running for your athletes. In your coaching you must undergo the hurt of being uncertain, the pain of doing less than your best, and the agony of doubt that you'll ever become a genuine, respected coach.

True, Kenny Moore saw little of such eclectic uses by Sebastian Coe's coach, his father. Peter Coe was an engineer, without personal experience or special training in distance running. He studied everything he could find on endurance running, then "got rid, he says, of 95% of what he learned." Sebastian explained, "Essentially it has been 100% quality, not quantity. It is speed endurance, that is, seeing how long you can endure speed. In the winters I very seldom have run more than 50 miles per week, less in the spring."

The direction of the Coe experiment thus far has been to train Sebastian as a sprinter, and, that done, turn his speed loose over longer and longer distances. "What we do are ranging shots, as I call them, running under and over distance races to bracket the target," says Peter. "In 1978, when Seb was aiming for the 800, we raced at 400 speed and 1500 for endurance. Last year the bracket was 400 and 3000 meters, and he got the records for three of the distances in between (800, 1500, mile--KD). This year the overdistance will be up to 5000 meters."[1]

Does such a system that ignores 95% of other's ideas, also ignore the essentials? Of course not. It can't. Careful analysis of the year's total program would disclose them, no matter how disguised or modified. For example, Moore tells of a workout at 14.4 miles ("a hard effort, a 5:30 pace in wet track suits and slickers--with wind and rain"); also a seven-mile race on the Sunday before Christmas ("It was cold, perhaps 36 degrees, and uphill into a headwind until the turnaround at halfway.")

The system may not emphasize mileage or long-slow-aerobic running, but clearly the essentials of endurance are there--must be there if maximal performances are to result.

---

[1]Kenny Moore, "A Hard and Supple Man," *Sports Illustrated*, June 20, 1980, p. 80.

FARTLEK

Fartlek is a system of endurance training for running which alternates strenuous and easy running over varied and interesting terrains. Both work distances and recovery times have been unmeasured. Interest in the terrain tends to pull attention away from the pains of fatigue; attitudes tend to reflect the zest of self-directed play.

Fartlek, in English, means "speed-play," which in itself is a happy contrast to our American term "workout." Play is activity for its own sake, activity in which awareness of exertion and even of oneself is lost in the action. The activity of play can be as exhausting as that of any work but the fun of playing absorbs the feelings of fatigue, if not its physical effects.

As Major Raoul Mollett (Wilt, 1959, 97) points out,

Fartlek was perhaps the most alluring discovery since the beginning of the century in the realm of training. . . . A window was opened on the forest, and at the same time an idea of training emerged which one would classify as "happy." Fartlek, with its walks, its runs at slow pace through the woods, its short sprints, was able to revolutionize the training of the track world. . . . There is without doubt not a single irreconcilable sedentary person who would not feel a twinge of nostalgia when faced with the thought of a man running barefoot on springy moss, in a setting of forests and lakes reflecting the sky. Faced with this picture, the track world felt an irresistible rise in spirits.

Fartlek is not merely an outworn training system of the past, suited only for Scandinavians. It can be made a sound modern system within which the essentials of endurance training can be effectively organized. Were this not so, fartlek would not be worth explanation here. True, its main tenet is get tired without feeling tired, or doing more work in less time without suffering the aversions of work.

HARDFARTLEK. But don't underestimate fartlek's total work output. In its own way, fartlek demands as much developmental work-rest as does any system; it must if it is to be effective. I've often thought that a better name would result by adding Gunder Haegg's concept of *hardfart*, which means hard fast running. It would then be *hardfartlek*, to make hardy with speed-play. As in interval training, fartlek increases the total amount of relatively fast running that is done by alternating recovery jogging with hardfartlek. The research of Åstrand (1970, 286) and others concludes that this permits faster-pace running with lower heart rates and related fatigue effects despite a much greater total work output. Fartlek could be defined as unsystemized interval training off the track. This opens up exciting possibilities to be discussed under "Modern Uses of Fartlek."

THE USES OF FARTLEK. Fartlek is a flexible and wide-ranging system which lends itself to a variety of needs and methods of organization. But we should be clear that fartlek requires specific purposes and precise organization as much as any system, including interval training. Fartlek is not a carefree "go-as-you-please" system as some have described it. Certainly it is not an escape from hard work. From a physical standpoint there is no more value in easy running on pine-needled paths than in easy running on a cinder track. To serve its goals, fartlek must be as physically demanding in both mileage and intensity as any system. There is no other way to development and great performance. To misunderstand this is to deny the system and follow a fool's path. Keeping all this in mind, we shall consider the various uses that past champions have made of fartlek.

GUNDER HAEGG. Though the word "fartlek" does not appear in Gunder Haegg's training diary, his methods were clearly a forerunner of the system. In the 5000-meter training course he laid out at Volodalen there were three places where he ran with bursts of energy ("Ryck"), four hills ("Uppfor") including one steep hill, two bogs or marshy areas ("Mry") in which the footing was heavy, and at least one area of hard fast running (Hürdfart"). On this course and others of similar merit, Haegg trained for five years, 1940-1945. One need only read his carefully maintained training diary to understand the careful thought that went into planning the exact details of his program and the inexorable insistence upon doing what must be done whether one feels like doing it or not.

HERB ELLIOTT AND PERCY CERUTTY. Undoubtedly Cerutty's training methods were self-created out of his personal training experiences and his personal attitudes toward life. It was natural that his craving for self-sufficiency should have denied any indebtedness to others or being bound by others' systems. Actually, however, Cerutty's creed of stotanism (a union of sto-ic and spar-tan), with its insistence on hardihood and simple living was a variation of primitive camping at Volodalen, his sand dunes and surf-running a heightening of Haegg's steep hills and deep snow, his demands for repeated wild surges an outgrowth of the varying pace in competition and training by Zatopek and Kuts (Track & Field News, December, 1956, 10-12). This in no way belittles Cerutty's very important contribution to training for endurance running. It does emphasize that fartlek is inherent in his methods and attitudes. For example, this excerpt (Cerutty, 1959, 17) sounds much like the writings of Gosta Holmer,

In his ordinary life he [man] has little chance to escape from the humdrum, the routine. Why then . . . add his exercise . . . to the list of compulsions? Athletics should be, and with me is, a prime means to escape from these imprisoning conditions to exult in our liberty, free movement, capacity to choose. Our training should be a thing of . . . enthusiasm . . . not a daily grind upon a grinding track, artificially hard. . . . How much better to run with joy, sheer beauty and strength, to race down some declivity, to battle manfully to the top of another.

Or better, here is a rather typical day for Herb Elliott at Cerutty's Camp Portsea, as described by the Australian track writer, Joe Galli,[1]

Arrived Saturday afternoon. Elliott and two friends had just returned from a 30-mile hike over the rugged terrain, sleeping under the stars at night. A day previously Herb had run a mile in four minutes. We dived into bunks at Cerutty's headquarters and slept nine hours. At 5:00 A.M. we were up. We jogged half a mile to the beach, spent 30 minutes running along the hard sand and plunging into the surf, then back for breakfast. Soon we were off again, running over a sandy, bush track course of just over a mile with two killing climbs. I was proud to break ten minutes for the course. Herb ran it five times, never in more than 6:10. Next--weight lifting. Elliott lifted 200 pounds in the ordinary dead lift, and 125 in the press. Lunch was followed by a discussion of training. Then we tackled a giant 80-foot sandhill. One run up the hill finished me. I found it even hard to walk through its deep loose sand. Elliott scampers up as though it were a moderate grass slope.

Note that the word "fartlek" is not used here; nor is it used in any of Cerutty's writings. But the basic idea of fartlek (making hardy with speed-play) is definitely here.

TERRAINS. The essence of fartlek lies in distraction from awareness of fatigue. Part of such distraction comes from ever-changing speeds, but the major factor lies in ever-changing terrains. Choose fartlek as the core of your training program only if your locale affords at least one and preferably a number of challenging terrains. Train at racing altitude, but also at altitudes higher by a 1000 feet or more. Train in the cool woods and around cool lakes, but also under the hot sun and at high humidity. Train on the golf course or in the park. A hiking trail through the mountains or along a river might be ideal. Run under whatever conditions present a challenge: sand, mud, snow, rain, cold; what may seem a handicap can be a stimulus for developing what the Finns call "sisu," a hardiness of spirit and body that accepts no barriers.

EVALUATION OF FARTLEK
ADVANTAGES. 1. It develops self-dependent and resourceful runners. No coach is present; no measured distances exact effort; no watch forces the pace. For a mature runner, it affords freedom of self-development. He alone decides how far and fast he shall run, and when and where he shall run again.

2. It is mentally refreshing and invigorating. Its varied challenge makes work seem like play. Time-effort tend to slip away so that only after the workout is finished will the total

---

[1]Joe Galli, "Australian Report," *Track & Field News*, Box 296, Los Altos, Calif. 94022, February 1959, 13.

work output be realized. Runners cover more miles at greater and changing speeds; blood lactates and heart rates are lower; awareness of fatigue is less.

3. It provides a foundation of endurance for all running events from the marathon down to the 440. As Lydiard claims, rightly, for marathon training it provides the stamina by which to do more speed work when the training program calls for speed.

4. The daily training session tends to be run on a total time basis. This reduces the mental tension created by repetitions of measured distances, measured times, measured heart rates, measured recovery periods.

5. The softer running surfaces of field and woods paths result in greater relaxation of muscles and less muscle soreness.

6. The uncertain footing of open running tends to develop a shorter and more efficient stride, especially helpful in longer distance running.

7. Fartlek reduces track caretaking and the need for ever-open locker rooms. A man can roll out of bed at 6 AM, into his running togs, and out on whatever running area is near. Sometimes men spend more time travelling to a track than is spent running on it.

8. Fartlek encourages group running. That makes for more work and more fun.

WEAKNESSES. 1. The greatest strength of fartlek--free running in a low-tension situation-- is also its greatest weakness. Training must be relevant to the conditions of competition: measured distances, continuous and relatively steady pace, enurement to increasing discomfort and tension.

2. Free running means unmeasured work loads and work effects. One's training diary tends to show time and perhaps mileage of training, not much more. Comparison of performances-- today's with that of last month or year--is not measurably exact. Proof of progress is an important factor in any training system.

3. The advocates of fartlek tend to extol the glories of nature: soft pine-needled paths, sea-beaches, and the challenge of a wooded hill. But most of the runners of the world do not have such natural glories at hand. Rather, they have paved streets, reeking with exhaust fumes, concrete walks with strait-laced pedestrians who, as the Englishman Loader writes, are likely to jeer, "Mary Ann, look, it's a runner! He's got nae claes on!" But even the worst cities have cemeteries and river banks and zoos and golf courses which the determined will seek out, even though forced to do so at hours when decent folk--and the police--are indoors.

4. Group running has disadvantages as well as advantages. Beginners and those of lesser talent tend to be neglected and mis-used. They tend to do both too much and too little.

INTERVAL TRAINING

Interval training, as organized by Reindell, Roskamm and Gerschler (1962), is a training system for endurance running which alternates measured runs on a flat track at a measured pace with easy recovery jogs for a measured length of time. Precise measurement of all phases of work is essential to interval training; without it, the system becomes fartlek or some other form of fast-slow running.

Reindell and his associates centered their research on heart development. They chose the name "interval training" because the greatest stimulus for heart development occurs during the first ten seconds or so of the recovery interval. That is, the run provides the developmental challenge while the interval provides the developmental response. Immediately after completion of a run, the heart cavity is filled up suddenly, strongly, rhythmically to exert a very strong expansion stimulus on the walls of the heart.

Each run should not exceed 90 seconds and should produce a heart rate of 170-180 during the first ten seconds of the recovery period. This should drop to about 130 within 30 seconds-- and in all cases not more than 90 seconds--of the recovery period. Should the pulse at the end of 90 seconds be above 140, the pace should be slowed or the distance shortened.

It is commonly stated that there are four factors in interval training: (1) a measured distance to be run, (2) a pace that will produce a developmental heart stimulus, (3) an interval of easy jogging, and (4) the number of times the run is repeated. Depending on the precise purpose of a series of workouts, any three of these factors can be held constant while the fourth is gradually increased. Actually this is an oversimplification. In a single workout, the distance can be varied, as in one of Igloi's favorite methods (100y-200y-300y-400y-300y-200y-100y). Or the recovery interval can be varied: allow 30 seconds between efforts but 90 seconds between each set of efforts. The pace can be varied: slow the pace during the early and late efforts; increase the pace during the middle efforts when the body is most efficient. Or, other factors can be abstracted as our understanding of training becomes more clear. For example, to perform a given workout once is not enough; it should be repeated until mastery is certain. Mastery can be equated with degree of ease. A workout is truly mastered when it can be done free of physical and mental strain.

INTERMITTENT WORK. Interval training and intermittent-work training are basically the same in their repeated alternation of work and recovery. But they differ in that interval training emphasizes the number of recovery intervals--therefore many brief workloads--with their positive effects on heart development; whereas intermittent work emphasizes the stressful work period that tends to be longer--"60 seconds to five minutes" (Costill, 1979, 83). Both are anaerobic. Original researchers for interval training--Reindell, Gerschler, Roskamm--dealt primarily with heart effects; those for intermittent work--Scandinavians Christensen, Bøje, Anderson, Åstrand--centered on oxygen uptakes out of which came the terms aerobic and anaerobic. A later section will explain intermittent work more completely.

MODERN INTERVAL TRAINING. Interval training is not a year-round, total-development program. Nor was it ever considered to be such by its originators. The training of Harbig, its first great champion, was preceded by several months of cross-country running, and during the racing season, included runs off the track. The research by Reindell and his associates was basically sound. However, it did occur within the limits of the heart-centered viewpoints these men held which had a tendency to ignore other considerations and thus to exaggerate anaerobic training, both in months of its use and the degree of its stresses.

As happens so often with every new idea or system, interval training was overused and misused by many coaches and runners who failed to understand its limitations. All too many prospective champions showed signs of overtraining, with limited energy reserves and enthusiasm for the Big Race. Most of these neglected to build a firm foundation of longer, less stressful work away from the track. Perhaps they lacked a suitable terrain. As a result, some coaches and runners today tend to reject both interval training and intermittent work.

This is a mistake. Such repeated-stress work is of great value. For example, Lasse Viren, in training for his great races at Montreal, used fartlek throughout the year with its unmeasured fast-slow alternations; intermittent work as early as February with 400-800m bursts; and interval training from June on--example, July 14, 20 x 200m average 28.8, pulse 172; after 2 minutes, 96. That is, he used his own versions of all systems--LSD work, (call it a Nurmi or Lydiard workout, as you prefer), fartlek, intermittent work and interval training. Note that the interval-training workout gave an excellent test of running condition, in some ways more informative than a trial race. The work load in distance-time was precisely measured, but also heart effects could be monitored.

THE FACTORS OF INTERVAL TRAINING
The following detailed discussion of the four factors of interval training assumes a separation of intermittent work from interval training, as explained above. The original research related to heart rates, not to oxygen uptakes. For example, for sound though arbitrary reasons, the greatest distance used--on rare occasions 500 or even 600m--is 400 meters; that is, a distance that can be covered within 90 seconds.

Important: each of these four factors has its own unique value for endurance. Full use of interval training will hold three factors constant, while using the fourth as a developmental variable that provides increments of stress.

THE DISTANCE OF EACH RUN. The word "distance" is used here as though it were a separate entity; actually, in running, such a factor is never separate from pace--is always a way of looking at distance-pace as one aspect of the workload.

The first researchers of the interval-training idea, with their focus on repeated heart effects, assumed distances of 400m or less--300m, 200m, 100m--distances that were long enough to push heart rates to near maximums (170-200 b/p/m), but short enough to allow many recovery intervals within a single workout--intervals in which heart rates dropped rapidly in the first ten seconds, then more slowly back to 120 or even lower.

As research shifts to maximal oxygen uptakes, distances tend to lengthen beyond 400 meters. But, as previously explained, the training system is now called "intermittent-work training"-- an arbitrary distinction but useful. Sebastian Coe called it "speed-endurance work"--increasing the distance over which you can run with speed, or in which you can endure speed. It's a different approach with special values and weaknesses.

The most commonly-used distance today, certainly for beginners, is 200 meters. There's no special developmental virtue in that exact distance, but as a half-lap or an eighth of a mile it is convenient. Indoors a single lap of about 160 yards, or two laps of 320 yards, would be both convenient and sound in their effects. All these distances satisfy the requirements of number of repetitions and cardiovascular development in general.

Another commonly-used distance is 400 meters. Such a distance is long enough to provide the benefits of more sustained running, with its steady rhythm and pace. If individual development is high enough, it permits many repetitions. Zatopek ran as many as 40 x 400 at about 65 seconds each. It is interesting that, at the age of 21, when Zatopek was training for the 1500 meters, he ran shorter distances. For example, 10 x 200m with 100m jog, or 2 x 100, 2 x 200, 1 x 300, 2 x 200, 2 x 100, with similar jogging distances--what has been called the funnel system.

Such a practice of increasing-decreasing the distance is consistent with Nocker's (1960, 81) conclusion that early and late efforts should be less stressful. Others argue that practice should simulate racing conditions in which stress is greatest at the end of the race. It was for this reason that Zatopek, and others, often reduced the recovery interval near the end of a day's practice, even though the pulse did not drop to the theoretically optimum 130 beats.

THE PACE OF EACH EFFORT. There are at least five criteria for judging the pace at which each effort should be run:

1. The distance of each run. As previously stated, pace cannot be separated from distance. But assuming equal pace, the greater the distance of each run, the greater the stress produced (Åstrand, 1970, 382), even though the rest intervals are increased correspondingly: 3 x 400 @ 60s with 60s rest produces greater stress than 3 x 200 @ 30s with 30s rest. Ordinarily, the shorter the distance, the faster the pace, or the greater the number of repetitions.

2. Recovery heart rates. According to Reindell (1962) the intensity (distance x pace) of each effort should allow the pulse to drop to about 130 within not more than 90 seconds of the recovery interval. If the pulse is higher, the running pace should be reduced. However, he and his associates were working with older, more experienced runners. Most authorities today accept 120 b/p/m as an optimal figure.

Some workers make heart rate the criterion by which the length of the recovery interval is determined, prolonging it until the heart rate drops to 120. To count pulse rates, the athlete places his finger tips on the opposite wrist or on the carotid artery in the neck. When the count for ten seconds reaches 20, the next run can be started. Or to put it the other way, at the end of an optimal recovery interval, the heart rate should have dropped to 120.

3. Innate sprinting speed. A man with greater natural speed for sprinting can carry a given pace for a short distance with a relatively lower level of stress. Interval pace should be adjusted accordingly.

4. Competitive racing pace. Interval-training pace can be related to racing pace. A pace that is several seconds faster than racing pace not only achieves a developmental heart stress, it also develops a fast-twitch function in leg muscles so necessary for a sustained sprint at the finish.

On August 12, 1975, John Walker (NZ) set the world mile record at 3:49.4, an average 400 pace of 57.5s. Six weeks earlier, after running 8 miles steady in the morning, he completed an interval workout (PM)--8 x 300m @ 40.5 average, with a 300m jog between; fastest 300--39.8.[1] An equivalent 400m time would be 54s, 3.5s faster than racing pace. In various workouts during the preceding two months, Walker used these runs in his interval workouts--400, 300, 200, 150; on one occasion he ran 8 laps @ 69-70s, with four 50/60 yard dashes in each lap (50y sprint--60y float).

To use another example, British correspondent, Dave Cocksedge, gave this information to Track & Field News,[2] in a discussion of Steve Ovett's training,

"Coach Harry Wilson gives him a killer session of 12 x 200m @ an average 26s, with 15-second rest intervals. This is done in three sets of four, with three minutes between each set. When he can manage this session comfortably, he knows he's ready."

The 200m average pace would be roughly three seconds under racing pace.

5. General feelings of fatigue. In interval training, the amount of work done, that is, the number of repetitions, is crucial in developing the cardiovascular and related systems (Åstrand, 1970, 382). Using this as your guide, set a pace-distance that produces relatively high feelings of fatigue at the end of the run, and relatively low feelings after a recovery interval of from 90 to 30 seconds--and which allows you to run at least six and up to about 20 repetitions. Equally important, you should no longer feel tired after about one hour following the total workout. This method may not be technically precise, and may not be scientifically measureable in its effects, but it is both practical and sound. As training and maturity move upward, your feelings will become more objective and reliable.

THE RECOVERY INTERVAL. Though we use the adjective "recovery" to describe the time period between runs, Reindell (1962) emphasizes that, from a heart standpoint, the interval is as much a developmental period as a recovery period. During the first 30 seconds immediately following each run, the heart undergoes its greatest stress, and therefore its greatest stimulus for expansion and development. Heart development can be judged in part by the greater volumes of blood delivered to the working muscles. Since maximum heart rates do not increase with training, such greater blood volumes are achieved by heart hypertrophy through more complete filling and emptying of the heart cavities. Such hypertrophy is entirely normal and healthful, certainly not harmful as was once implied by the term "athlete's heart."

Physical activity during intervals. Both research and practice have concluded that relaxed jogging, or at least fast walking, is most beneficial during recovery intervals. Such rhythmic movement of the large muscles has a massaging or pumping effect which ensures a full venous return of the blood to the heart. The heart can eject out to the lungs and muscle capillaries only as much blood as it receives. The full suffusion of blood to the heart cavities subsides rapidly (10-30 seconds) when the running stops. Mild activity helps to maintain it and its beneficial effects within the muscles.

For purposes of research, Gerschler asked his trainees to lie on a horizontal table immediately after running, with both the head and feet elevated. He found that their pulse rates

---

[1] "How They Train--John Walker," Track Technique, #64, June 1976, p. 2040.

[2] "Ovett: Changing Speeds," Track & Field News, November 1979, p. 47.

returned to normal by this method just about as quickly as they did when jogging. Gerschler followed this method while working with Gordon Pirie in June 1960, when the latter was training for the 5000-10,000-meter runs at the Rome Olympics. He found that 100 meters at three-quarters speed raised Pirie's heart rate (normal resting rate--38) to about 170, and that about 15 seconds of horizontal rest with feet and head raised brought the rate down to about 120; then, he would run again. But when Pirie was working away from Gerschler, he did the usual jogging between runs.

Length of recovery interval. From a cardio-vascular standpoint, the research of Reindell and his associates suggests an interval of less than 90 seconds. But later research (Astrand and others), based on oxygen uptakes, recommends a more flexible approach which tends to allow at least as much time for recovery as was needed for the run. For example, for the training of anaerobic power, Åstrand (1970, 388) recommends alternating periods of maximal effort for 1 minute with rest periods of 4 to 5 minutes. Shorter rest periods would result in quick exhaustion and a decrease in the total work load. Even for the training of aerobic power, Astrand (1970, 391) suggests equal work and rest periods of from 3 to 5 minutes each.

On the other hand, the research of both Reindell and Åstrand (1970, 386) agrees that maximal oxygen uptakes and heart output can be attained by repeated work and rest periods of 10 to 15 seconds. Such a method can place great stress on both the muscles and the oxygen-transport systems without involving the anaerobic processes or producing high blood lactates.

The sport of swimming has adopted short-interval training as one of its most basic methods. For example, Counsilman[1] reports,

There has been a definite trend toward a shorter rest period between repeat swims when swimmers use interval training. Mike Burton, 1968 Olympic Champion for 400 and 1500-meter freestyle events, reports that one of his favorite workouts is 15 x 100 meters with 3 to 5 seconds rest between each 100. This would permit very little drop in pulse rate.

Counsilman then reports a workout by Fred Southward, National Four-Mile Champion, of 15 x 50-meter swims with 10 seconds rest, in which the mean heart rate after exertion was 185.9 and that before exertion, 180.1, an average drop of only 5.8 beats. When Fred took this same workout but with 50 seconds rest between, the work rate was 186.9; the rest rate was 149.8; difference--37.1. When emphasizing endurance, Fred kept the interval short; when speed was primary, the interval was lengthened. (Pulse rates were taken with a Gulton EKG telemeter.)

This points up the important suggestion that track coaches should keep in touch with modern trends in training for swimming. The problems are basically the same and we can learn much from them as they have learned from us. Counsilman's textbook, *THE SCIENCE OF SWIMMING*, contains much of value for training for running.

In summary, the length of the rest interval depends on the precise purpose of a workout. Interval training focusses on the number of times the heart is subjected to stress-recovery--any number from 6 to 60 (remember Zatopek's 60 x 400m?). Therefore, as a rule of thumb, the length of the recovery interval should be one that increases the number of repetitions within the total workout time. As another guideline, fit the time of the interval to that of the run--10s run, 10s rest; 60s run, 60s rest. Or let the heart rate be your guide--when the pulse drops to about 120, you are ready to run again.

It follows that modern interval training requires understanding of the many physiological effects of work stresses and intervals. Early users of interval training tended to follow certain very restrictive rules without understanding their special purposes. Today the rules are more permissive but, thereby, are more difficult to use properly. That is to say, modern research provides more and better information for making judgments, but this has the dual effect of making the art of good coaching more complex.

---

[1] James E. Counsilman, "Conditioning in Competitive Swimming." Paper presented at Symposium on Sports of the American Association for the Advancement of Science, Dallas, December 17, 1968.

THE NUMBER OF REPETITIONS. As a rule of thumb, the interval-training method emphasizes many repetitions; as said before, any number from 6 to 60, with 20 as a valid average figure.

The assumption here is that a sound foundation of endurance running has been laid, and that interval training is inserted into the schedule for some special purpose--speed-endurance training, speed under stress, repetitions at faster than racing pace, near-maximal sprint work; or even, as in Viren's example, to serve as a test of racing condition.

Rick Wohlhuter (1974, 880-1:44.1WR; mile-3:54.4) used intervals 3 or 4 times a week indoors, but limited pace to no-faster-than racing pace because of the danger of muscle injury on an un-banked 220 track. Since he took long runs in the morning, the number of these intervals was six or under, sometimes only two or three. When he moved outdoors, the number sometimes moved to 20 x 220 @ 29-30s with 60s rest; or 4 x 440 @ 60s with 60s rest, plus 4 x 330 @ 39s with 110 jogs, plus 4 x 220 @ 29s with 110 jogs between. The rest between sets was kept under 60s.[1]

In summary, the number of repetitions relates to workout purpose within the total context of training.

Working in sets. One way of maintaining a large number of repetitions along with a highly stressful pace is to work in sets. For example: 5 sets x (3 x 200 yards @ 7/8 speed) with 30 seconds between each 220 but 3 to 5 minutes between the sets.

MASTERY. Progressions in interval training can and should be based on the degree to which a given work load is mastered, that is, handled with full confidence and relative ease. All too often, coaches and runners feel they are ready for the next progression when they have achieved an interval workout once on the stop watch. This practice leads to a feeling of hurry and uncertainty, as well as to over-intensity of training.

Once a certain goal is achieved--say, 10 x 440 @ 70 with 90 sec rest between--it should be repeated several times during succeeding weeks, each time with greater relaxation and certainty of control. Now you have a fixed base of accomplishment from which you can move surely and safely upward to the next level. Each new level imposes more severe demands; a more gradual approach ensures that you are ready for those demands.

THE PROPER USE OF PROGRESSIONS

Traditionally, interval training has been organized by different progressions of stress factors (distance, pace, interval, etc.) within each of which there are gradual increments of stress. Study of Table 19.1 should make this clear. However, there is no necessary or even desirable

TABLE 19.1

CONSTANTS AND VARIABLES IN INTERVAL TRAINING

Method	Constant	Constant	Constant	Constant	Constant	Variable
A	Distance	Pace		Interval	Mastery	Repetitions
B	Distance	Pace	Repetitions		Mastery	Interval
C	Distance		Repetitions	Interval	Mastery	Pace
D	Distance	Pace	Repetitions	Interval		Mastery
E		Pace	Repetitions	Interval	Mastery	Distance

progression from Method A to B-C-D-E. So much depends on the inter-relationships between distance, pace, and rest interval. For example, in a study of Christensen (reported in Astrand, 1970, 383), when a subject alternated 10 sec of high-speed running with 5-sec rest intervals, he could do 120 repetitions without exhaustion and with a low blood lactate. If the rest pause was increased to 10 sec, the peak O_2 uptake was reduced from his maximum of 5.6 liters/min to 4.7 1/m. If the periods of rest and work were increased to 15 sec, the O_2 uptake was 5.3 liters/min, less than his maximum. Such knowledge is crucial in organizing progressions.

---

[1]"How They Train--Rick Wohlhuter," *Track Technique*, #58, December 1974, p. 1851.

PROGRESSION BY NUMBER OF REPETITIONS. Having selected a fixed distance-pace-interval that meets the specific purpose of the workout--and the ability-condition of the runner--the number of repetitions is gradually increased from one workout to a later workout during the next week or so.

Examples:

Distance	Speed	Interval	Repetitions
400m	3/4th	90s	4 and progressively up to perhaps 10
300m	3/4th	60s	5 and progressively up to perhaps 10
200m	3/4th	30s	6 and progressively up to 10 or even 20
100m	3/4th	15s	10 and progressively up to perhaps 20

When the projected number of reps is reached, either the speed is increased or the interval time is decreased; reps drop back, and the cycle is repeated. The examples given can also be organized in sets. Example: 2 x (3 x 200m @ 30s) with 30s rest; allow 2-3 minutes between sets.

PROGRESSION BY INCREASING THE PACE. The overall pattern follows that for number of repetitions, only now increasing stress is produced by gradually increasing the pace. This progression is perhaps the most developmental of all interval-training methods, for doing more work at faster-than-racing pace is a primary purpose of interval training. The number of reps is fixed arbitrarily to fit runner, distance and purpose.

As a muscle-safety factor, do not increase pace more than 1-2 seconds faster than racing pace, but a later-season need to increase sprinting speeds (fast-twitch muscle fibers) may warrant 7/8th maximal pace.

In an eclectic training system that emphasizes aerobic, steady paced LSD, along with an ample portion of playing at relaxed speeds (fartlek), this progression normally occurs late season, within the 4-6 week period before the Big Race. Since muscle stress is great, several days of full-recovery work should follow.

PROGRESSION BY SHORTENING THE REST INTERVAL. Holding the other three factors constant, gradually decrease the length of the recovery interval. This is perhaps the most stressful way of developing anaerobic power. It should be used cautiously by even the more mature runners, with special emphasis on the principle of mastery discussed earlier. Move to the next level of work only when the present level can be done easily. Do not confuse this progression with the fully approved practice of using short work periods (10-15 seconds) of very fast running with rest periods of similar duration. See the discussion on short-interval training in swimming and also Åstrand (1970, 386).

PROGRESSION BY LENGTHENING THE DISTANCE. The development of one's ability to run at slightly faster than racing pace over longer and longer distances could become the main focus of a training system, especially for shorter distances--400 to 1500 meters. Increasing distances by 50m increments from 200 to 300m would serve the needs of 400m; from 200 to 600m, the 800m; from 400 to 1000m, the 1500. As distances increase, it will be found necessary to increase the recovery interval.

INTERVAL TRAINING INTENSITIES

Lydiard very wisely warned against over-intensity of training, and devoted much time to organizing Tables of Effort by which runners could adjust their exertions to the needs of that particular day. Endurance energy is to be conserved, not merely burned up, by training.

Interval training is inherently high-intensity training. But the principle of developmental load-rest applies here just as much, and even more than it does to marathon training. Reindell concluded that heart development occurred primarily during the recovery interval, hence the name of the system. That is, the rest period is crucial; without adequate rest, the endurance systems break down. This applies just as much to alternating days of work and rest as it does to alternating periods of work and rest in a single workout. Increments of intensity should be added gradually; that's why we train the year-round to gain time for the gradual approach.

WAYS OF USING INTERVAL TRAINING. One of the important assets of interval training lies in the great variety of workouts that can be devised. When I visited him at his home in Freiburg, Germany, Woldemar Gerschler made a strong point of this, and indicated how it had been carried out in the training of Harbig. He then suggested this basic approach as a guide:

1. Warm-up by jogging and repeated wind sprints to raise the heart rate to about 120.

2. Run a series of repetitions--for example, 6 x 220--at such a pace as brings the heart rate to about 170-180/min, that is, 10-15 beats below maximum rate.

3. During the recovery interval, walk or jog until the heart rate drops to 130-140. This length of time should not exceed 90 seconds; if it does, decrease the pace.

4. As physical condition improves, the number of repetitions can be increased to what is judged to be optimum, depending on the runner's maturity and condition, and on his racing distance.

5. When the number of repetitions is adequate, the time needed for recovery will gradually decrease. When this time drops down to that considered best for a given running distance-- in this example, about 30 seconds--the pace is increased to one that again requires a recovery period not exceeding 90 seconds. This sequence can be repeated several times this year and throughout the runner's years of training.

It hardly needs to be added that this approach is merely suggestive, and that Gerschler's actual methods were much more complex than this. We have related his schedule for Pirie of repeated 100-meter runs at 7/8 speed with only about 10 seconds recovery. For greater detail, see the training of Harbig in Wilt (1962, 5).

TABLE 19.2

Examples of Development in Interval Training

About two months of conditioning in cross-country and fartlek are assumed. Most sessions are preceded by 20-30 minutes of warm-up.

Weeks of Training

	1st	3rd	5th	7th
Mon.	Fartlek	3 x 3/4 @ 3:30	8 x 440 @ 70s	Fartlek
Tues.	3 x 880 @ 2:20	Fartlek	Fartlek	12 x 440 @ 70s
Wed.	Fartlek	6 x 440 @ 70s	10 x 440 @ 70s	Fartlek
Thurs.	6 x 440 @ 70s	4 x 880 @ 2:20	4 x 880 @ 2:20	6 x 880 @ 2:20
Fri.	2 x 3/4 @ 3:30	Fartlek	3 x 3/4 @ 3:30	8 x 440 @ 70s
Sat.	6-8x440 @ 70s	8 x 440 @ 70s	Fartlek	4 x 3/4 @ 3:30
Sun.	Rest	Easy Fartlek	Rest	Fartlek

	9th	13th	17th
Mon.	12x440 @ 68s	12x440 @ 66	12x440 @ 64
Tues.	4 x 880 @ 2:20	4 x 880 @ 2:15	4 x 880 @ 2:12
Wed.	12x440 @ 68s	3 x 4/4 @ 4:40	3 x 4/4 @ 4:35
Thurs.	Fartlek	Easy Fartlek	12x440 @ 64
Fri.	4 x 3/4 @ 3:28	12x440 @ 66	Fartlek
Sat.	Rest	6 x 330 @ 45s	6 x 330 @ 42s
Sun.	Fartlek	Fartlek	Fartlek

-Table 19.2 outlines a basic, one-a-day schedule for beginners. This schedule assumes sufficient mileage is to be found in 12 x 440 @ 70s. Beginning with the 9th week, pace is increased by 2-second increments. This schedule suggests trends, not actual workouts.

LONGER VERSUS SHORTER PERIODS OF WORK-REST.   Tradition tends to advocate shorter and
more intense work periods in late-season training. However, a strong case can be made for long
intermittent-work periods closer to the event distance, so as to simulate the continuous running of competition. In such case, the interval should be long enough to ensure full recovery
(Åstrand, 1970, 387). Sebastian Coe's training made use of this method.

THE VALUES OF INTERVAL TRAINING
Any sound evaluation of interval training must keep clearly in mind its intended use, not merely its misuse by those who have never taken time to study it. Certainly its creators, Gerschler and Reindell, never intended it to serve as a year-round, total program of running (Wilt,
1964, 229). Their greatest champions always engaged in several months of off-the-track running prior to the interval-training period. Again and again they have spoken out against the
fanatic zeal toward ever-greater intensities of work. Such goals tend to destroy both physical
and mental energies, not develop them.

In summary, the following values can be claimed for interval training when used intelligently:

1. By reason of the endless variety of its increasing challenges, interval training is
interesting, satisfying, even enjoyable at times. Motivation is a built-in essential; ignore
motivation and the system deteriorates.

2. It repeats measured dosages of stress-recovery many times in a single workout. In
developing endurance, the number of times of stress is important, as well as the kind and degree
of stress. In steady running, the condition of stress-recovery occurs but once.

3. Each stress-recovery period is a strong stimulus for development of the heart stroke-
volume and allied effects. (Stroke volume = heart output ÷ heart beats).

4. At each stage of a workout, the heart effects of the work load can be quickly   recorded, and the work adjusted accordingly. Heart rates can be taken by "feeling," by manual-
ly touching the wrist or carotid artery, by modern telemetering devices, or by the heart-rate
meters that are certain to be developed in the near future.

5. More high-quality work can be done. When the running pace is faster, the total work
done is greater if periods of work and rest are alternated (Åstrand, 1970, 382).

6. More work is done with less awareness of fatigue (Åstrand, 1970, 287). Lower heart
rates and related fatigue effects, the distraction of repeated changes in work-rest, awareness
that this run-effort will soon be over, attention on the stopwatch--all combine to take awareness away from the discomforts of fatigue. Discomfort-pain-agony may still be there, but at a
lesser level of awareness.

7. Interval training, properly used, tends to increase aerobic power and heart stroke-
volume in a shorter training time than can other methods. Precise dosages of work provide an
optimal stimulus for this particular runner. Other systems tend to use shotgun methods; interval training uses a scope rifle.

8. It is goal oriented. Each year, each season, each phase of training, each workout,
each work effort--all have goals that can be clearly stated and measured.

9. Its methods are so varied and flexible that each coach and each runner can have a personal approach to training. Apart from the physiological advantages, this gives a feeling of
special personal meaning; I'm training my way. This adds zest to what might otherwise be only
zeal.

THE WEAKNESSES OF INTERVAL TRAINING.

1.   The main weakness of interval training lies in its greatest strength--in the fact that its work is necessarily discontinuous, in contrast to the relatively steady-pace, continuous stress of competitive racing. Mastery of discontinuous work does not ensure mastery of continuous work.

2.   Interval training enthusiasts tend to concentrate on intensities of anaerobic running, before laying a firm foundation of aerobic running. Astrand's statement (1977, 389) is of crucial importance, "There is no evidence to support the assumption that it is of importance to engage the anaerobic processes to any extreme degree in order to train the aerobic power." Note: this weakness has a lesser application to training for the short-fast races from 220 yards to the mile.

3.   Interval training, by its lowered fatigue, both physical and mental, deceives men into attempting too much, too fast, too soon. Even if we ignore possible dangers to the vital organs, muscles and tendons are strained and careers interrupted. Major Raoul Mollet (see Wilt, 1959, 97), in an excellent summary of endurance training systems, praised interval training highly, but also warned,

> *No doubt there will be more and more victims of the method, socially as well as physiologically, for such a way of life has great risks. For every experienced athlete, carefully observed and examined, aided in his training by blood analyses, electrocardiograms, etc., how many other athletes are there, dazzled by the thought of emulation and the spirit of imitation, but deprived of medical advantages and other paraphernalia of champions, who will suffer grave damage to their health?*

4.   Interval training is heart-centered. That is, its creators and users assume that the heart, as the most vital organ, is a sufficient criterion of training effects. But it is a person-situation that runs; the more a training program is founded in and simulates the whole person and the whole competitive situation, the more valid it becomes. No matter how vital the part, it is never a full substitute for the whole.

5.   Interval training is monotonous in its terrain--a flat track. As practiced traditionally, it allows none of the varied and fatigue-distracting terrains so essential to fartlek, marathon training, and the like.

6.   Interval training emphasizes analysis, and thereby awareness of all aspects of training. The runner is aware of each short run, its effort and possible failure in time; of the beating of his heart while running and during the interval; of the number of efforts still to be made; of the ever-present demanding coach; all of which taken day after day after day, tends to multiply tensions and fatigue. Fatigue lies in feeling as much as in physical impairment; there are few ways of avoiding the adamant demands of interval training.

DANGERS IN INTERVAL TRAINING

The basic assumption of this discussion is that the normal, healthy heart is immune to impairment from the stresses of cardiovascular training, but there are two reservations. First, we can never have absolute assurance that any given heart is completely normal and healthy. Weaknesses can be minutely specific and present in an otherwise highly functional organ. Also, infection or disease may produce weaknesses not previously present. Physiologist Herbert A. de Vries states, "the extreme fluctuations of the pH of normal blood lie within pH values of 7.30 to 7.50. The extreme values in illness have been known to go as low as 6.95 and as high as 7.80."

Second, excessive intensities of training without concern for immaturity or lack of condition have caused both scientists and coaches to withhold full approval. One hardly needs the research of Hans Selye to prove that adaptation energy is limited. In every field of human exertion: mountain climbing, starvation, cold, heat-humidity, fear of danger, there are limits of tolerance. Endurance running is no exception. Reckless efforts to do more and more high-intensity work can cause retrogression, and certainly will not produce highest-level performance.

THE LYDIARD SYSTEM OF ENDURANCE TRAINING

A careful analysis of the Arthur Lydiard[1] system of training for endurance running discloses a thoughtful and shrewd selection and balance of most of the essentials of training we have listed in this book. Among these important points of emphasis are the following:

1. Marathon training, the core of Lydiard's system, includes at least five basic endurance procedures: time running, cross-country, marathon training, road running, and speed-hill training. All but the last is at less than maximal steady state, but it is never slow running.

2. Zest in training should balance zeal.

3. On a year-round work schedule, aerobic/anaerobic training should be in a ratio of about 9/2. Usually sharpening for a Big Race can occur within about four weeks.

4. The development of steady-state endurance over long distances best ensures a solid foundation for sustained speed over shorter racing distances.

5. Planning of training and competitive schedules should be in terms of a runner's entire career--ten years or even more--not for just this one year, or for 3-4 school years.

6. Training stress as between work-rest should rise and fall from day to day, period to period, month to month. That development occurs during active-rest as during stressful work is as valid for marathon as for interval training.

7. Variety in all phases of training and competition is essential--variety of terains, of kinds of running, of kinds of running stress, and so much more.

8. A year's program should be pointed toward a few Big Races, for which all others are developmental.

9. Racing, especially over shorter distances, puts a premium on sustained maximal speed at the finish. The developmental of such sustained speed requires related speed-endurance training.

10. Prior to the Big Race, the conservation of endurance energy is a primary concern.

---

[1]This entire discussion is paraphrased from three sources:

Arthur Lydiard and Garth Gilmour, *RUN TO THE TOP*, London: Herbert Jenkins Ltd., 1962, 182 pages, hard cover.

Arthur Lydiard, "Arthur Lydiard's Running Training Schedules," *Track and Field News*, Box 296, Los Altos, California, 94022, 25 pages, 1970, paperback.

Arthur Lydiard, "Marathon Training," *USTCA Quarterly Review*, Vol. 70, No. 4, Feb. 1971, 9-29.

THE YEAR'S TRAINING SCHEDULE

Lydiard considered variety to be a crucial consideration in all aspects of training and competition: variety of terrains, of speeds, of challenges, of degrees of stress. He therefore developed, not two or three kinds of experience, as in our American system, but nine or ten kinds of running.

TIME RUNNING (For beginning runners). Begin by running steadily for a length of time that can be handled easily. Neither mileage nor pace are important. Gradually increase this time until you can run steadily and without severe stress for two hours.

CROSS-COUNTRY. Lydiard divides cross-country into two six-week periods. The first period includes time running and, later, mileage running up to 100 miles per week. The second period includes faster (what Lydiard calls "sharpening") running and time trials of various distances, paces and efforts. Competition should be delayed until needed as a developmental and motivational device. If a man is well prepared, competition is both fun and an aid to development; if not, it can be deadly.

THE GIST OF LYDIARD'S TRAINING SYSTEM

	New Zealand Time Schedule		Adapted to American Time Schedule	
Weeks	Date	Program	Date	Program
0	Mar. 26	Training-off period (3-4 weeks)	June 2	Training-off period (3-4 weeks)
4	Apr. 24	Cross-country (12-14 weeks) Time running Mileage running	June 30	Time running
			July 20	Mileage running
			Aug. 15	Marathon training
		Marathon training	Sept. 10	Cross-country training
16	July 17	Cross-country BIG RACE	Nov. 15	Cross-country BIG RACE
17	July 19	Road-racing Road relay-racing (6-8 weeks)	Nov. 17	Marathon training
			Dec. 15	Speed hill-training
24	Sept. 15	Marathon training (8-10 weeks)	Feb. 1	Indoor track season
32	Nov. 10	Speed hill-training	Mar. 10	Indoor BIG RACE
40	Jan. 1	Track season (10-12 weeks) Repetition training	Mar. 12	Marathon training
			Apr. 1	Speed hill-training
		Interval training Trials: over-and under-distance	Apr. 20	Outdoor track season Interval training Repetition training Development races
		Development races		
52	Mar. 25	Outdoor BIG RACE	June 1	Outdoor BIG RACE

Note: Actual dates vary greatly; those given are merely suggestive.
The various types of training actually blend into one another and cannot be separated sharply as this Table seems to imply.

For explanation of the terms in this Table, see related article headings.

CROSS-COUNTRY RACING SCHEDULE (12 weeks). Train and compete on all kinds of surfaces and under all weather conditions. Alternate steady-pace running one day with repeated speed work at shorter distances the next, with the tempo of each gradually increased throughout the 12 weeks. As examples:

First Week		Eighth Week	
Mon:	15 miles ($\frac{1}{4}$ effort)	Mon:	12 x 220 ($\frac{1}{2}$ effort)
Tues:	880 ($\frac{1}{4}$ effort)	Tues:	Six-mile time trial
	mile ($\frac{1}{4}$ effort)	Wed:	Three miles of 50-yard dashes
	880 ($\frac{1}{4}$ effort)		

	First Week		Eighth Week
Wed:	10 miles (½ effort)	Thur:	Three-mile time trial
Thur:	Mile (¼ effort)	Fri:	3 x 220 (full effort)
	Mile (3/4 effort)	Sat:	Three-mile race
	3 x 100 (3/4 effort)	Sun:	Jog 20 miles
Fri:	6 x 220 (½ effort)		
Sat:	Competition		
Sun:	Jog 20 miles		

During the eighth week of this 12-week training schedule, Lydiard has placed two time-trials and one competition--a large number. But he interprets trials, as well as races, in terms of degree of effort, self-control, and improvement, NOT of all-out performance. In fact, he strongly holds back the latter until the few BIG RACES on which the entire year's program is based. On all other occasions, the man runs well within himself. He does his "best," but within the limits of control and of doing even better next week and next month.

MARATHON TRAINING. Lydiard states that 100 miles a week of marathon running is the key to his training system. On a basis of seven days each week, this averages 14 miles per day--or better, provides three days of 20 miles each, and four days of 10 miles each. If the 20-mile run is exhausting, an easier and shorter run the next day or even for two days, allows complete recovery before another strenuous run. In addition, for both physical and mental reasons, Lydiard varies his terrains and varies the degree of effort that goes into each run. Lydiard states that this marathon training is continued until 18 weeks before the first important track race, but in actual practice, the interval is sometimes less than this. On one occasion, Peter Snell broke the world-record for the half-mile less than six weeks after competing in a marathon race! Lydiard suggests this marathon schedule as having the necessary balance of essentials:

Monday: 10 miles (½ effort)--hilly course.
Tuesday: 15 miles (¼ effort)--easy undulating course.
Wednesday: 12 miles fartlek.
Thursday: 18 miles (¼effort)--easy course.
Friday: 10 miles fast (3/4 effort)--flat course.
Saturday:23-30 miles (¼ effort)--easy course.
Sunday: 15 miles (¼ effort)--easy course.

In his talk before the United States Track Coaches Association, January 1970, Lydiard stated that "my distance runners were actually running from up to 200-250 miles a week," counting all jogging and other easy running. He emphasized that the 100-miles-a-week was all "running just under the maximum steady state. It was hard, strong running. The pressure was always on; it was never slow running." He was referring to such men as Halberg, Snell and Magee whose ages were 26, 22, and 25 respectively, and who had a gradual build-up in stamina.

ROAD RACING. Lydiard undoubtedly adopted road running and racing because it was already well established in New Zealand. But he also argues its values as being a logical extension of the fence-climbing, changing terrain, and changing pace of cross-country. Road racing requires steady-pace running on firm surfaces. The races are strenuous, so that training is light and pleasant. Training should still be over all kinds of surfaces in order to maintain the flexible toughness of muscle and tendons gained in cross-country. But since Lydiard recommends the same training during this period that is followed for a two-mile track schedule, we can assume that the lack of this kind of program in our American system is not a critical loss.

SPEED-HILL TRAINING. This is the most strenuous part of Lydiard's entire year's program of training. He assigns about six weeks to it as compared with about ten weeks for marathon training and about 12 weeks for cross-country. A fairly steep hill (a one-in-three gradient is considered best) is found that is about one-half mile long. After a two-mile warm-up jog, the runner springs up this hill on his toes, exaggerating his knee lift. Lydiard emphasizes the springing action rather than speed of running. After about one-half mile of jogging, the man now sprints down hill, with full but relaxed strides. At the bottom he does repeated fast work: perhaps 3 x 220, then 6 x 50 on alternating runs. These are gradually increased in number and speed as condition improves. Each of these efforts totals about two miles of running; the four repetitions that Lydiard recommends, plus the preliminary jogging and warming-down afterwards, would total more than ten miles each day.

Lydiard cautions that this work must be done carefully and with just the right amount of emphasis on each phase, as this will affect later stages of the training program. He found that about one hour of this kind of springing up hill is enough. His experiments with longer periods brought diminishing and even negative returns.

TRACK TRAINING. Lydiard believes strongly in planning both competition and training. The relative importance of races must be clearly and adamantly established, and all phases of train-ing, mental and physical, must build precisely toward the BIG RACES. He is highly critical of shot-gun systems that hope to be in shape for the BIG race by being in shape for all the races, as well as of the "peaking" systems that work at minimum levels, then by intensive work, bring the runner quickly and briefly to a peak performance--as was done so well by Roger Bannister. He therefore divides his track training into two periods of six weeks each.

First track-training period. The first period includes speed work but it is geared down to what the runner can handle easily and thus reserves the more-sharpening, faster runs for the later and more important period. Typical of these workouts are:

(a) over-distance at a steady, easy pace,
(b) under-distance at a faster but controlled pace,
(c) the actual racing distance but at a deliberately slower-than-racing pace,
(d) steady runs at from two to six miles,
(e) repetition running over distances between 220 yards to 880 yards,
(f) 15 or 20 x 440 yards,
(g) Two or three miles of alternating 50 yard dashes with 60 yards of recovery striding.

Second track-training period. The second six-week period continues the balance between repeated speed running and steady-pace running. Speed work is now "all-out" although even here Lydiard pushes or restrains according to how the boy seems to react. To the over-and under-distance work of the first six weeks, he adds time-trials. These trials do not attempt to see how fast the runner can cover a certain distance; rather they build on the experience of the first six weeks and provide a certainty of future improvement in time as well as of control over tension and fatigue. Improvement is planned so as to continue evenly from trial to trial. Lydiard thinks it is necessary to race twice a week during this last period, but these are mostly under- and over-distance races, so that effort and attitude is focussed strongly upon the BIG RACE coming later. One becomes racing fit by running races, not just by running.

THE BIG RACE. Before each crucial race--the one that has been planned for a full year ahead--Lydiard uses a full ten days for conserving energy. His men run every day, of course, but within easy effort. Steady-pace work, rather than repeated fast work, is best. If the year's schedule has been well planned not even psychological conditioning should be a con-cern, though of course with some men it always is.

TRAINING-OFF PERIOD. Lydiard's "training-off" period is comparable to the "active-rest" of the Russian programs. The running continues but at an easier and more enjoyable level. He suggests, for example, 45 to 60 minutes each day of light jogging over varied surfaces and also once a week a long run

Fig. 19.1. Peter Snell, 1960 Olympic 800-meter champion - 1:46.3, and 1964 Olympic champion in the 1500-meters - 3:38.1 and the 800-meters - 1:45.1.

345

of 20 miles easy. Certainly, for Lydiard, running is a Way of life with a capital "W". There is no other way to running supremacy!

SAMPLE 880 SCHEDULE

	First Week	Tenth Week
Mon:	Mile (½ effort) 6 starts at 30 yards	660 (3/4)
Tues:	6 x 880 (¼ effort) 2 x 100 (3/4 effort)	880 time trials (improve without strain) 4 starts at 50 yards
Wed:	Competitive sprint 2 or 3 x 300 yards	4 x 440 at 880 racing speed 2 x 440 (full effort)
Thurs:	½ mile of repeated 50's 6 x 300 striding 1 x 200 (7/8 effort)	2 miles of repeated 50-yd. dashes 3 starts at 50 yards
Fri:	2 miles (½ effort)	
Sat:	6 starts at 50 yards 6 x 300 striding 1 x 300 full effort	6 x 220 (½ effort) Compete 880 yards
Sun:	Jog 10-14 miles	Long jog

SAMPLE MILE SCHEDULE

	First Week	Tenth Week
Mon:	Two miles (¼ effort)	Mile of rep. 50's: 3 x 100 (full effort)
Tues:	4 x 880 (¼ effort)	Mile time trial (improvement only)
Wed:	12 x 300 striding 1 x 880 (½ effort)	6 miles, sprint 100 yds. in each 440
Thur:	6 miles (¼ effort)	Mile time trial (improve)
Fri:	6 x 440 (¼ effort)	3 x 220 (full effort)
Sat:	One mile (¼ effort) One mile (½ effort)	Mile competition
Sun:	Jog 15-20 miles	Jog over 20 miles

SAMPLE TWO-MILE SCHEDULE

	First Week	Tenth Week
Mon:	Two miles (¼ effort)	15 x 200 (¼ effort)
Tues:	10 x 300 (¼ effort) 2 x 100 (3/4 effort)	2 mile time trial (improve)
Wed:	One mile (½ effort) 6 starts at 50	880-yard competition
Thur:	One mile (¼ effort) 2 x 880 (½ effort)	2 miles of rep. 50-yd dashes
Fri:	6 x 200 (¼ effort)	3 x 220 (full effort)
Sat:	3/4 mile (½ effort)	Jog 20 miles or more
Sun:	Jog 15-20 miles	

SAMPLE SIX-MILE SCHEDULE

	First Week	Tenth Week
Mon:	Two miles (¼ effort)	One mile of 50-yd. dashes 3 x 100 (full effort) 3-mile time-trial (improve)
Tues:	4 x 880 (¼ effort)	
Wed:	12 x 300 striding 1 x 880 (½ effort)	6 miles, 100-yd sprint in each 440
Thur:	6 miles (¼ effort)	6-mile time trial
Fri:	6 x 440 (¼ effort)	6 x 220 (3/4 effort)
Sat:	One mile (¼ effort) One mile (½ effort)	Jog 20 or more miles
Sun:	Jog 15-20 miles	

Note: first week schedule for one mile and six miles is the same.

346

TABLES OF EFFORT

Graded effort, from the standpoint of both mental and physical stress, is a crucial part of the Lydiard system; another example of his studied attempt to achieve the freedom from tension which is so vital a part of Swedish "fartlek." In his book (1962, 87ff), he presents full tables of effort for each event from 220 yards to six miles. For the mile run, for example, he gives equivalent times for all best average times from 3 minutes 55 seconds to 5 minutes 30 seconds. The following incomplete tables indicate the method:

880					One Mile			
Average Best Time	Effort 3/4	1/2	1/4		Average Best Time	Effort 3/4	1/2	1/4
1:52	1:58	2:03	2:08		4:15	4:21	4:28	4:38
1:55	2:01	2:06	2:11		4:20	4:26	4:33	4:44
1:58	2:04	2:09	2:14		4:25	4:31	4:38	4:50
2:01	2:07	2:12	2:17		4:30	4:36	4:43	4:56
2:04	2:10	2:15	2:20		4:35	4:41	4:48	5:02
2:07	2:13	2:18	2:23		4:40	4:46	4:53	5:08
2:10	2:16	2:21	2:26		4:45	4:51	4:58	5:14

TIME TRIALS

By "time trial" Lydiard does not mean to run a certain distance for best possible time. Rather he means a preparatory trial or rehearsal by which (1) the athlete can assess his weaknesses and so plan his future training, (2) he can accustom the body-mind to steady, hard running at an overload pace, which may be less than the projected racing pace, and (3) he can develop his courage and self-confidence. Successive trials should produce progressively better performance in which the time is but one factor.

OTHER IMPORTANT PROCEDURES

WEIGHT TRAINING. "I never allow my runners to use weights." (1971[1], 20)

AEROBIC-ANAEROBIC TRAINING. Develop aerobic power first and completely. "I never went on to another stage of training until I had developed the (aerobic) cardiac system first. . . . I never mix aerobic and anaerobic training." (1971[1], 10)

WEAKNESSES. "I was very careful to try to find the weaknesses of each athlete and through exercise evaluation, I would try to strengthen these weaknesses." (1971[1], 10)

STAMINA TO SUSTAIN SPEED OVER THE DISTANCE. "I used to try to get my athletes running a little slower in training rather than a little faster. . . . We would encourage him . . . to run aerobically as far as he could, not as fast as he could." (1971[1], 15). Running faster means a lesser total workload.

A HIGHER MAXIMUM STEADY STATE. Lydiard tried to increase maximum oxygen uptakes; that is, he gradually tried to raise the pace level at which a steady state could be maintained. (1971[1], 14).

ONE-A-DAY TRAINING. "We gained better results if an athlete ran two hours continuously than if he ran an hour in the morning and an hour in the evening." (1971[1], 13)

SPECIFICITY OF TRAINING. The athlete (body-mind) learns both basically and specifically what he does (1971[1], 24)

DEVELOPING SPRINTING ABILITY. Power for sprinting is developed by sprinting against resistance, either the resistance inherent in maximal speed work on the flat, or in such work as springing up hills. In doing the first, we use "typical American sprint training workouts."

---

[1]Arthur Lydiard, "Marathon Training," USTCA *Quarterly Review*, Vol. 70, No. 4, February 1971, 9-28.

The second has been explained under the head, "Speed-hill Training."

SHARPENING. Lydiard interprets the word "sharpening" as final preparation for important competition. The crucial question is "what does he need for this particular race." It does not necessarily mean either speed work or anaerobic work. Building absolute confidence is essential. Under-distance races may help the man who lags at the start of a race; over-distance races, the man who feels he lacks staying power. In summary, analyze weaknesses and strengthen them.

PEAK FITNESS. "Once you get a man to peak fitness, there is no more need for hard training. . . . It is hard racing that we want and very, very light training." (1971[1], 27)

SHOES. "I was a shoemaker and I got the shoes in good condition. I realized that the half inch or so of rubber under their feet was very, very important. . . . The skin underneath my foot is very soft because I always used well fitted shoes." (1971[1], 18)

EVALUATION: STRENGTHS

We have already emphasized the great strength of Lydiard's system that lies in its precisely balanced emphasis upon such related but contrasting factors as stamina and speed, and need not repeat it here. He claims that marathon training is the key to his system, in the sense that such "marathon" stamina provides a sound foundation for an even greater emphasis on speed than other systems can provide.

A second great strength of the Lydiard system lies in its variety. For example, it insists upon a variety of terrains--and by terrains we mean not only hills and woods paths and running tracks, but also deliberately selected mud and slush, soft sand, fences and stone walls, paved roads, uneven bush country--all for the purpose of establishing a wide and firm foundation of running fitness. On these varied running surfaces, Lydiard planned a variety of training methods: cross-country, road racing, marathon running, speed hill-training, and when he finally got on the flat running track, many of the devices of modern interval training and even of the old American over-and-under-distance training with its repeated time trials. I have often criticized the latter because of its over-emphasis upon all-out performance in each trial. Lydiard answers this by insisting upon planned increments of improvement: run what you can today, while being certain that you'll be able to improve upon it next week and six weeks from now. He even has gone so far as to provide detailed tables of effort on a time basis, as we have already described.

Another great advantage held by Lydiard does not lie so much within his system as in his location in New Zealand where he has almost complete freedom to fix his competitive schedule so as to further the development of the individual runner. He can decide what races a boy should enter so as to best prepare him for his BIG races of the year, regardless of the team situation. Competition, which we tend to rate as all-important, can be considered a motivator for training. In New Zealand, Lydiard can organize about eight months of training in which competition is secondary. In contrast, in the United States school program, there are about seven months in which team competition is crucial; individual development through daily training must often be a lesser concern.

This relative freedom meant that Lydiard could start beginning runners from where they were. They could then progress *gradually*--what a sound word that is!--*gradually* through the various steps of Lydiard's plan: through time training, mileage training, cross-country, road racing, and all the rest. Each new level could be attempted when the preceding level had been, not merely tried, but mastered to the point of certainty of control and ease of action.

This freedom from the burden of winning-them-all, which I have attributed to New Zealand, should also be credited to Lydiard's insistence upon first things first, then second things, then third--and so on. He is adamant in looking ahead twelve and fifteen months to THE BIG RACES and in planning the year's program in terms of them. Even more, he insists upon planning an entire career. For example, he wrote (1962, 29),

---

[1]*Ibid.*

So in 1953 I started these two nineteen-year-olds (Halberg and Magee) off together, although I still eased back on the work I gave Halberg because I still did not consider him strong enough for the full treatment. It was in the 1953 cross-country season--late in the year--before I finally got to work on him. In July that year I predicted publicly that Halberg would be the greatest middle-distance runner New Zealand had known and that he would start cracking world records at twenty-seven-- the year he actually won his Olympic title. . . .

EVALUATION: WEAKNESSES

As it is used in New Zealand, it is difficult to suggest important weaknesses in the Lydiard system. Unfortunately, it does present difficulties in its application to the American school-college program. Coaches are under pressure to win team victories, and such an emphasis is often opposed to individual development. School boys tend to judge their coach and his system-- as well as their personal success--on the basis of immediate results this year, this month, and even this week, rather than on gradual development toward some greater but doubtful goal far over the horizon and some ten years away.

Lydiard's system uses about six months of training with only minor competition prior to the track season; we now use only a few weeks. His system requires 52 weeks of some kind of running each year; our American school program, only about 40. His system calls for at least six different kinds of terrain and methods of running; ours, only two or three--and in most cities, only one! The relative disinterest of the New Zealand public allows Lydiard to evaluate the win-loss record of his team as his judgment may decide; ours tends to encourage individual development, of course, *but only as long as the team wins.*

But despite these and other difficulties, Lydiard's system can be of great help in our efforts to improve American running. Adopting its basic tenets will not require us to begin over again. We shall not need to abandon either fartlek or interval training. Actually, Lydiard uses his own versions of both, though he seldom uses the terms as such. But the clarity with which Lydiard has presented the major goals for training and the step-by-step methods by which those goals can be achieved provides us with a fresh and better way than we have ever had before.

A classic example of the problems and the benefits of attempting to transpose a coach-training system (no matter how effective in the home situation) to another different situation occurred when, between 1967-1969, Finland employed Arthur Lydiard as its chief national coach of distance running. Finland had a proud tradition, knowledgeable coaches who in their day had been champions, outstanding running talent. But Finnish distance running was in the doldrums; international success, certainty of training methods, confidence in coaches were all missing. With a sense of shame, Finland had to ask for help from outside.

Lydiard brought that help. His book, *RUN TO THE TOP*, was published in Finnish; for some runners and coaches it became a Bible to be followed precisely as done in New Zealand. A new national enthusiasm arose--not just for competitive running but equally for jogging for fun and fitness. But some coaches of high repute resented the outsider, and expressed their resentment publicly. Several national champions refused his coaching and system entirely. When Lydiard left Finland after only two years of trying, many considered him a complete failure. Matti Hannus wrote,[1]

Before leaving, Arthur wrote an article in which he said, 'Finnish runners are very talented--maybe the best in the world--but they are difficult to handle. It is hard to get them out to train. Results were expected too soon from me. I am sorry to notice I was given very little help but was needlessly criticized.'

But Lydiard had been both the stimulus to new efforts and the means to better training methods. His book became a guide that de-emphasized the earlier interval-training approach, and restored a more gradual and varied system that assimilated Lydiard within the Finnish tradition, climate and terrain, and time schedule. In 1972-1976 Finland enjoyed its greatest Olympic success in distance running since the 1920s, with five gold medals and one bronze. A Finnish triumph. I am reminded of Laotse's definition of the truly great departed leader of whom people say, "We did this thing ourselves."

---

[1] Matti Hannus, *FINNISH RUNNING SECRETS*, Mountain View, Cal.: *World Publications*, 1973, p. 31.

TODAY'S ECLECTIC SYSTEMS.
The dictionary definition of the word "eclectic" is "not following any one system...but selecting and using what are considered the best elements of all systems." This is an apt description of most training systems today throughout the world. The essence of fartlek, interval training, marathon training are carefully analyzed, then synthesized to form an intelligent method based on the local environment, schedule of competition and the unique qualities of the individual runner.

THE SOVIET SYSTEM. As an example of this eclectic approach, A. Yakimov[1] of the Soviet Union describes their methods of training middle and long distance runners by first analyzing certain systems of the past--long continuous running, fartlek, interval training,--but ignores Lydiard's marathon training. He then advocates a method of Repetition Training similar to Interval Training but one that emphasizes running somewhat longer distances, even longer than racing distance. Pace is necessarily slower than racing pace but longer repetitions develop both the confidence and the ability to sustain racing distance-pace.

But even this method fails to reproduce racing reactions. In their endeavors to do precisely this, Soviet researchers and coaches have conceived a "Modelling Method." The word "modelling" was chosen carefully as suggesting work in practice that challenges the runner's energies but also most closely models the conditions of actual racing. The Modelling Method is introduced into the year's program only after long basic training and just before the most important race of the year.

The Modelling Method.

The previous methods do not bring on physical reactions which correspond precisely to those encountered in competition. This is most easily achieved by running the race distance at full effort. However, running the race distance at full effort cannot be done too often in training without a bad effect on the athlete's spirits.

Working from the above problems, we theoretically worked out (and later confirmed it in practice) the following idea. If in the course of a workout the heartrate begins to rise to the level achieved in racing, and if the runner is given at that moment a little rest, sufficient for a partial repayment of the oxygen debt and a slight recovery of the heartrate (for example from 185 to 170), and then returns to the workout, the athlete is not worn down as much by this method as by time trials or races.

An example of this method, an 800m runner (1:50, say) would do the following: 400m at race pace (55sec.), then rest 20sec.; then do 200m in 26sec., rest 10 sec. and then 200m in 28 sec. The total running time is 1:49, and the total time is 2:19.

The basic principles necessary for using the modeling method: 1. The rest should be fairly short--the heartrate should drop at most 15 beats/minute. 2. The work intervals should decrease in length. 3. The first interval should be equal to or (for distance runners) slightly shorter than half the racing distance. 4. The total running time should be close to (or better) than the athlete's best time over the distance.

This workout should be used most carefully, like intervals run at full effort. It should be included in a workout only after special training. Hence, more than anything it belongs in the period of intense training or as leading to the most important race of the season.

Time-Trials and Races.

A major part of the training plan for any runner trying to reach peak form will be the use of time-trials or outright participation in races. One should be extra careful in using runs at full effort, as in the time-trials. The frequent use of such work in a program can have a negative effect on the runner. Racing has the same effects physiologically and helps develop the will. While the use of races must never be a universal method of training, it has an important role in the winter and summer competitive seasons.

---

[1]A. Yakimov, "Middle and Long Distance Training Methods," *Track Technique* #83, Spring 1981, pp. 2633-36.

A further look at the Soviet System is provided by Michael Yessis,[1]

This author believes that the key to Soviet success lies in a comprehensive training system of a longterm program divided into yearly, monthly and even weekly cycles. Their system is based on strong scientific data derived from their extensive applied research programs. The research encompasses many areas critical to world-class performances: technique analysis, race analysis, physiologically based conditioning programs, tactical training, psychological training, medical control, injury prevention and rehabilitation, ergogenic aids and sophisticated means of recuperation (restoration)....

The greatest advances in Soviet training, however, clearly lie in the actual training programs. The actual training is monitored either through heart rate, blood analysis, ventilatory rates or a combination of these and other factors. For example, the Soviets can obtain constant heart rate in runners and they telemeter this information to the laboratory where the exercise physiologist or coach can monitor the workout and then radio back specific instructions. In some of their more sophisticated research, the Soviets record up to six physiological functions, giving even more precise information on what is happening within the athlete.

Contrary to popular Western belief, their research on ergogenic aids is directed more at effective means of restoration than stimulation of physiological changes, so the athlete can run faster or longer in his next race. Soviet athletes use many different supplementary drinks, and usually add vitamins and minerals to the daily diet.

FINLAND'S TRAINING SYSTEM. Kari Sinkkonen,[2] coach of the 1972 Olympic 1500-meter gold medallist, Pekka Vasala, summarized Finnish training methods for middle distances this way:

The main problem in the preparation of long distance runners is to reach peak form at the time of the most important races. It is necessary to organize the annual training plan to meet this demand by dividing the year into four periods:

1. *The period of aerobic endurance.*
2. *The period of muscular strengthening and development of elastic qualities of the muscles (special period).*
3. *The pre-competition period.*
4. *The competition period.*

The yearly program for each athlete should be based on the number of miles to be covered, the percentage of aerobic work and the percentage of anaerobic and special work for each week. Both the coach and athlete must know exactly what type of training in what quantity is required for the monthly and weekly cycles in each period.

Development of Aerobic Capacity.
The development of aerobic capacity lasts 26 weeks and incorporates an active rest during the first four weeks. The aim during this period is to improve the level of steady-state performance, essential to develop basic endurance....
It is a known fact that running speed corresponds to differences in maximum oxygen uptake, making it necessary to establish a running rhythm that corresponds to the athlete's steady-state. Based on this theory, three types of endurance runs can be distinguished:

a) *High uniform speed (HS)*
b) *Medium uniform speed (MS)*
c) *Prolonged low speed (LS)*

Assuming that the steady-state of an athlete corresponds to 4 min. ± 10 sec. a kilometer speed, his:

---

[1]Michael Yessis, "The Soviet System," *Track Technique*, #87, Winter 1984, p. 2787.

[2]Kari Sinkkonen, "Distance Training the Finnish Way," *Track Technique*, #80, Summer 1980, pp. 2541-43.

a) *High uniform speed (HS) is: 4:00 ± 10 sec. (steady-state)*
b) *Medium uniform speed is: HS + 30 sec. (4:30)*
c) *Prolonged low speed is: HS + 60 sec. (5.00).*

The differences between the high and prolonged low speeds (HS and LS) is usually 40 to 60 seconds. Naturally, when a high uniform speed workout is planned the distance is shorter than in a prolonged low speed workout.

The development of aerobic capacity is performed in a pattern of three to four weeks of intensive training, followed by a less intensive recovery week, that corresponds to about 70% of the previous week's load. This pattern allows the organism to "absorb" the work accomplished and prepares it for the work that follows. Progress is achieved by beginning a year's training with the mileage attained during the 26th week of the previous year.

What is the correct work load for different athletes? Between 12 and 14 years--aerobic work only.
At 14 years--daily aerobic work.
At 15 years--40 to 60 miles a week at speeds suitable to individual capacity.
From 20 years on--2-3 training sessions can be accomplished daily. The weekly load is generally around 120M or more.

A typical week during the aerobic endurance development period for an athlete, who intends to cover 60M during this week, could be made up of the following:

Sunday:	*12 miles,*	*prolonged (LS)*
Monday:	*6 miles,*	*high (HS)*
Tuesday:	*9 miles,*	*medium (MS)*
Wednesday:	*6 miles,*	*fartlek*
Thursday:	*6 miles,*	*high (HS)*
Friday:	*6 miles,*	*high (HS)*
Saturday:	*9 miles,*	*medium (MS)*

The annual increase in the quantity of work must be around 25%. An athlete who has done 1200M in 25 weeks of aerobic training in one year, must lift it to 1500M the following year. Progress of the athlete's steady-state capacity is during this period evaluated every 3-4 weeks by a uniform speed test run. Every 6-7 weeks the athlete is subjected to a blood test.

Development of Muscular Strength.
A more exact definition for this training phase would be "muscular strengthening and development of elastic qualities of the muscles." This period extends 6 to 8 weeks and aims, besides power development, to improve muscle elasticity to make up losses in speed that occurred during the preceding period. The amount of aerobic work is reduced and anaerobic work is increased.

The improvement of muscular elasticity allows a much more economical exploitation of power reserves with consequent better performances. The best way to develop muscular elasticity is uphill bounding. It can be made up in a training session of the following procedures:

After a 2-3M warm-up, the athlete bounces up a not too-steep hill, about 200 to 800m in length. The upper body is relaxed, the knees are lifted high and the hips well forward. The bounding strides are from 3-0 to 5-0 long. At the top of the slope the athlete runs relaxed on a flat terrain before descending in long strides. Back at the departure point he performs 2 to 3 repetitions at average pace over distances ranging from 100 to 400m (e.g., 2 x 200 or 3 x 100 or 3 x 300m). The procedure is repeated up to five times (only one for beginners), according to the performance standard of the athlete.

The distance the athlete covers in uphill bounding depends on his ability to perform the exercise correctly. The exercise loses its value when the athlete fails to raise his knees at the height of the hips. The uphill bounding is usually in the program every second day (four times a week), gradually increased to 6 times a week. The bounding action is not absolutely necessary and can be replaced by skipping up the slope. It should be kept in mind that the athlete should during this training phase have massage 2-3 times a week.

Pre-Competition Period.

The pre-competition period lasts eight weeks and aims to add speed progressively to the aerobic base. Aerobic work, already reduced in the second training period, is reduced further during this phase as anaerobic work is increased.

The pre-competition period requires careful and meticulous planning of the training program. It includes training to improve rhythm, speed endurance and speed--each performed once a week. For variety it is advisable not to use the same distances but have a choice of at least three.

Rhythm training is performed in the first weeks, speed endurance training starts from the third or fifth week, according to the competitive distance of the athlete. Speed training should start from the first week.

Competitive Period.

The reduction of the work load is characteristic of the competitive period when anaerobic training diminishes notably.

West Germany's expert in techniques, Peter Tschiene,[1] was intrigued by Sinkkonen's emphasis on developing the elastic qualities of the running muscles and wondered if this was a key element in Finnish successes in distance running.

Sinkkonen has his athletes do a bounding run up a 5-15° hill over a circuit; length 400m. Before and after the hill, the athlete does easy running (jogging/striding). The foot should not land with a jerky action; it should give way (bounce), so that the athletes obviously "jumps with a delay." There should be a "bouncing effect."

Furthermore it is important to Sinkkonen that the runners pay attention to a high lift of the thigh of the swinging leg. (Here we have a typical form of training for the improvement of local strength-endurance). By means of pictures of the men's 1500m final at Munich in 1972 the Finnish coach proves Vasala's better preparation in comparison with his opponents: Even in finish-situations he runs with a high knee lift; the advantage is obvious.

This route is performed all year round by the Finnish middle distance runners; however, with varying quantity according to the tasks of the training periods.

Tschiene suggests that this form of training is most suitable for the 800m and 1500m runner, but adds that elasticity running should be only one phase of year-round training that includes all other well-known methods. He also warns against the danger of over-emphasis, that is, doing too much too soon. Such bounding does place added stress on leg tendons and muscles that are already heavily taxed.

HARRY WILSON'S TRAINING SYSTEM.[2]

It is evident that there are several ways of preparing middle-distance runners and the approach I use is only one way. It seems to work, which is the only criterion to use (at present I coach 6 men below 3m 45s) but it relates to the British climate, facilities and racing programme and may not suit other countries. Of course there are coaches in Britain who have also produced excellent results with other methods.

I believe that each athlete is an individual with his or her strengths and weaknesses, likes and dislikes, etc., and therefore any training programme should reflect these individualities.

---

[1] Peter Tschiene, West Germany, "Finnish Middle Distance 'Elasticity' Training," *Track Technique*, #58, Dec. 1974, p. 1850.

[2] Harry Wilson, "Preparation of 1500m Runners," *Track & Field Quarterly Review*, Vol. 83, #3, Fall, 1983.

 Note - This paper by Harry Wilson, English coach of Steve Ovett, 1980 Olympic 800m champion and a dozen or more mature runners assumes years of gradual development and racing experience. Harry Wilson, *RUNNING DIALOGUE: A COACH'S STORY*, London: Stanley Paul & Co.,231pp.

I try to:
1. *Analyse the needs (physical and psychological) of an event.*
2. *Analyse the present condition and future potential of an athlete.*
3. *Devise a programme of training that will gradually narrow the gap between the requirements of an event and what the athlete has to offer.*

I use the word gradually as the full development of an endurance athlete takes a long time and it may take as long as 12-14 years before full potential is achieved. I am aware at all times that the results achieved by any particular approach are closely related to the talent of the athlete who adopts the approach. You cannot make a diamond from a piece of granite, so my aim is to try to have each athlete achieving his or her full potential--to have an athlete say "I'm satisfied with what I've achieved."

Time is a vital factor and you cannot legislate to produce results in a certain time for each athlete. We each have our physiological peculiarities and the natural laws which govern the body's adaptation and over-compensation procedures are not made by coaches. The athletes I coach all follow the same broad programme, i.e.,

1. *An Autumn/Winter period of mainly endurance work.*
2. *A Spring/Early Summer pre-competition period of varied training--endurance, speed-endurance, pure speed, race-practice, technique, strength.*
3. *A competition period in which the training is used to hold the fitness level while the races bring out the best in an athlete.*

The first phase is very much the same for all the athletes--the difference being in the quantity of the training. The quantity is related to each athlete's training age, physical and psychological capabilities and prevailing personal circumstances. It is in the 2nd and 3rd phases that the programmes vary to meet the needs of each individual athlete, i.e., the emphasis that is placed on the various training ingredients.

The whole programme has a large endurance base and obviously does not accept the often quoted premise that the 1500m event is 50% anaerobic. I believe in a large amount of aerobic training that will increase oxygen intake, thus delaying the accumulation of lactic acid. Several physiologists now agree that in the past they have placed too much emphasis on the anaerobic side of the event. You may use the analogy of a car driver setting out to make a journey knowing that he has insufficient petrol to last the distance. One can merely tell him what to do when he eventually runs out of petrol. I'd prefer to advise him first of all how to drive economically so as to make the petrol last out as long as possible, then advise the steps to take when the petrol is finally used up. I'm constantly trying to raise an athlete's "cruising-pace": Example: when Steve Ovett was 18 he could cruise at 61 seconds per lap then finish fast--he can now cruise at 58 seconds per lap then finish fast.

When building up oxygen uptake it's important to remember that this should be related to an athlete's cruising pace. I can see no point in a maximum oxygen uptake at 9 minute mile pace when an athlete races at 4 minute mile pace. This means the need for plenty of high quality aerobic work--and in addition to steady state runs the athletes use repetition sessions where the pace of the fast section is only steady but the recovery is short, e.g.

    6 x 1000m--30 seconds recovery
    2 sets of 6 x 300m

            30 seconds recovery
            2 mins. between sets

Another point I stress, particularly for experienced athletes is the use of short intensive oxygen debt sessions rather than prolonged less intensive sessions, i.e. small sets of very fast repetitions with a very short recovery between, e.g. for a 3m 42s 1500 runner

    2 sets of 2 x 400 (55 secs.)
    30 secs. recovery between each
    3 mins. recovery between sets

The athletes tell me they don't really look forward to this type of session, but feel it has a better effect than, say 10 x 400 in 58 secs. with 1½ mins. recovery between. I'll now go through the 3 phases of training in more detail.

354

Autumn/Winter Phase.   Usually commencing Mid October.

After a rest period of 2-4 weeks, athletes start off with one steady state run each day of about 4-6 miles for 3-4 weeks. This gives a rough average of 40 miles per week. After this the athletes (according to experience and other factors) start running a second session each day so that by the end of December an experienced runner will be up to approximately 80 miles per week done in 12-14 sessions. In addition to steady state runs varying from short fast over 4 miles to long steady over 12 miles the athletes start to include 2 sessions each week of long repetitions interspersed with very short recoveries, e.g.

4-5 x 1500m or 6-8 x 1000m usually over a hilly road or grass circuit with just 30 seconds recovery.

Also included each week is a session of sprint drills:
high knee lifts
heel pick-ups
acceleration runs
stride changers
flat out efforts.
A fairly low key cross-country race (about 10 km) is often included once every 3 weeks.

This programme is maintained at the 80 mile per week level for 2-3 weeks then is followed by a period of higher mileage of 4 weeks at about 100 miles per week for the experienced runner. During this period one of the aerobic repetition sessions is dropped each week in favor of a session of hill-runs--usually 6-8 repetitions lasting from 75-90 seconds up a fairly shallow hill with a quick jog back down in about 90 seconds as a recovery. This period is followed by reduction in mileage (about 80 miles per week) and an increase in the pace of the shorter steady state runs to allow the athletes to peak up to the major cross-country races which are a vital part of the British running scene.

A very easy week of relaxed running follows the end of the cross-country season. Two similar weeks will have been included at approximately 5 week intervals during the Winter programme. I feel it is better to deliberately plan to continue these easy weeks rather than to have to bring them in because the athlete feels he is in need of a break. The coach of this Winter period is emphasizing the idea of the phase being one of quantity rather than quality and the success of the period is the sum of all the sessions. I don't put a great deal of pressure on athletes during this period to run fast times but to have them concentrate on the week after week of regular running.

Spring/Early Summer Pre-Competition Period.

This period commences with a transition phase of 2-3 weeks during which time more anaerobic work is gradually introduced so that by the middle of April the weekly programme is usually:
1 steady pace run of 5-7 miles each morning
1 hill session--2 types used
   A--400/500 shallow
   B--100/150 steep
1 session of longish repetition (fast with medium recovery)
2 sessions short intensive speed endurance work
2 farther, long, steady state runs
1 session pure speed work (150-300m)
2 sessions sprint drills

This programme is maintained until the start of the competition season (usually beginning of June) and although the pattern remains the same, in practice, a 2 week cycle is usually followed during which the athlete places the emphasis on certain sessions during the first week, then emphasis on other sessions during the second week. Individual variations are made by varying the number of repetitions carried out, carefully choosing the distances of the repetitions and by carefully setting the recovery time.

Progression is the key-note during this period and again the emphasis varies according to the individual
One athlete may progress by concentrating on increasing the speed of his repetitions;
another athlete may have commenced the period doing quite fast repetition and then
   concentrate on increasing the distance of the reps or increasing their number;
another athlete may place the emphasis on reducing the recovery time, whilst maintaining
   speed;

another athlete may concentrate on developing a more powerful stride on the uphill runs.

Three or four low-key races would be included in this period--probably 2 at 3000m, 1 at 800m, and 1 at 1500m. Here is a typical week during this period (an actual week by one athlete, not a magazine invention):

Monday to Friday
    5-7 miles each morning--pace dependent on the athlete's feelings each day.
            Evening Sessions Monday to Friday
Monday: *8 runs uphill--fairly shallow hill--60/70 secs. each. Run, quick jog back between*
Tuesday: *8 mile steady run.*
Wednesday: *5 sets 3 x 200m (25/26 secs.) 30 seconds rest between each run, 3 mins. rest between sets. 30 minutes sprint drills.*
Thursday: *4 x 500m (65/66 secs.) 2½-3 minutes recovery between each*
Friday: *5 miles fairly fast run*
Saturday: *AM--8 miles run*
        PM--4 x 1000m round hilly circuit, 1½-2 minutes recovery between each. 30 mins. sprint drills.
Sunday: *AM--10 miles steady run*
        PM--9 x 200 fast relaxed runs--200 jog between each.

We also usually spend two weekends training on the sand dunes and beaches in South Wales during March and April. During this period the coach's role has changed considerably from that adopted in the Winter period. I put the pressure on the athlete to be constantly trying to improve the quality of the training sessions. "The steel is now being tempered." I also feel it useful to have one easy week in the middle of the period and another just before the major races commence.

Competition Period
    Training during this period is built around the racing programme and once again there is a change in my role. During this period I am not pressing for better and better training performances but I emphasize the point of achieving good sessions in a relaxed way, i.e. 6 x 600 in 54 secs. done in a relaxed way with the runner knowing he has something in reserve seems better than 6 x 53 secs. done in a tense struggling manner. There is enough pressure on the athlete during races without the coach demanding high intensity training as well. The fitness should be there--the races bring out the best in an athlete--he doesn't need to be constantly proving his fitness in training sessions.

    It is difficult to quote a normal training pattern during this period as so much depends on each individual athlete--one athlete may enjoy racing regularly once or twice a week while another athlete may alternate short periods of training with periods of racing. Also much depends on the athlete's physical and mental recovery from the hard races or the pressure an athlete places on himself prior to a race--both of these factors influence the intensity of the training load.

Strengths-Weakness to Improve in 1500m
Needed:

Max O_2 Uptake	6 x 1000m with 30 seconds rest
Improve Quality Performances	6 sets 2 x 300 or 2 x 400
	Better quality hill training. Weight training. Mobility exercises.
	Sprint drills--longer strides
Better Performance in Heats	Good Tactics
	Several sessions back-to-back runs
Self Image--Survival Ability	Learn to adjust to bumping
Acceleration Ability	Basic speed 800's-600's race pace, accelerate last 100's.

Modern Trends in Middle Distance.
1. *Move away from belief in one correct system. Away from Coach as a cult figure--"Do it because I say so!" Adapting basic principles towards individual needs. Still not very scientific. Greater need for observation and understanding.*

2. Shift towards bigger endurance base. Building up oxygen uptake will delay onset of lactic acid production.
   O_2 uptake related to cruising speed needed. Need to have quality in place of steady state runs.
   France, Holland, Sweden are examples of L.S.D. hooked countries.

3. Aerobic work not necessarily all steady state.
   6 x 1000 steady--30 secs. recovery.
   15 x 3000 steady--100 metres recovery jog.

4. Move away from huge number of interval reps.--using sets of more intensive reps.

5. Need to sprint: Practice speedwork and technique. Strength development if necessary.

6. Realization that 30 is still young.

7. Acceptance of need for rest periods. Not afraid to be unfit.

8. Little support for statement "800m will be taken over by 400m runners." Suitability for improvement related to innate physiological and psychological characteristics.

9. At top level must be much fitter for longer periods. No easy years. Few easy races. Promoters need high level performances. Athletes may need to be full time for periods-- Income? High plateau of performance series of races--period of heavy training. Athletes used to paced races can be inexperienced tactically. Need for athletes to be self contained.

10. Risk of injury higher. Coaches watch and listen. Medical back-up. Correct footwear.

11. Young athletes need skilled coaches. Bad techniques and faulty beliefs are difficult to alter later. Coaches to deal with smaller groups. Need more coaches and opportunities to develop.

COSTILL'S SCIENTIFIC APPROACH TO DISTANCE RUNNING[1]

David Costill is a scientist, not a coach. In this booklet he makes no attempt to develop a well-rounded system of training for distance running. Rather, he attempts to digest the great wealth of related scientific research, to present his findings in clear, concise language the coach or runner can understand, and in the final 20 pages, to suggest both guidelines and specific details of training that are consistent with such a scientific approach.

To attempt to summarize here what is itself a summary is beyond the skill of this OMNIBOOK. The interested reader will gain valuable insights by studying the book itself. But we can out-line its approach. It has four chapters: 1, Profile of the Distance Runner; 2, Physiological Response During Distance Running; 3, Adaptations to Endurance Training, and 4, Training and Preparation for Competition.

Chapter 1 reviews the wide range of differences among runners in anatomical, physiological and psychological qualities. Previous workers have emphasized the values of a well-developed cardiovascular system for endurance running. Costill concludes that of equal importance are the contractile characteristics and oxidative potential of the running musculature. Recent microscopic analysis of human skeletal muscle has disclosed two muscle fiber types--slow twitch (ST) fibers and fast twitch (FT) fibers. Successful endurance athletes have relatively more ST than FT fibers in their muscles. Certain high-level U.S. distance runners were found to have greater than 90 percent ST fibers in their gastrocnemius muscle. However, muscle fiber compo-sition alone is a poor predictor of success in endurance running. A reference list includes 55 related research studies.

Chapter 2 summarizes the wide range of demands placed on the body during competition, notably energy expenditure, circulatory demands, respiratory demands, demands on muscle meta-bolism, and others. Wide-ranging variations of individual responses to these demands create difficult problems for both the coach and athlete. Seventy-seven related research studies are provided at the end of the Chapter.

Chapter 3 states briefly the various adaptations made by the body to endurance running, and, of special value, "what science has to offer the coach who might' wish to use the laboratory in furthering his runners' performances."

Cycles of Work-Rest. For example, Costill points out (1979, 113) that "most physiological systems require three to four weeks to show a response to a given training stress." It therefore seems good judgment to plan workouts in terms of four-week cycles--in terms of total mileage (preparatory season) or in terms of total intensity of work (winter and early compe-titive season). Figure 19.2 shows two four-week cycles in which total mileage gradually in-creases but with alternating weeks of heavier and lighter stress. In this way, the basic principle of work-rest=more vital to success than work alone--operates from month to month, from week to week, and from day to day. For example, the first week in Cycle A should alternate its days of heavy load and light load, thus ensuring both optimal work and adequate recovery.

I repeat, such cyclical time-segments relate to stress of all kinds--mileage, pace of inter-mittent work, length of recovery periods in interval work, but also to mental stress as occurs in competition or time trials--whatever challenges the adaptation energies. A chart similar to Figure 19.2 could be drawn for a single week in which days of heavy mileage (intensity-stress) are alternated with days of lighter work in which full recovery is gained.

The overall intention of such planning of year-round time-energy would be developmental--gradual increments of workloads and related rest, and from that, gradual improvements in performance.

Intermittent Work. As a second example of body adaptations to various training programs, Costill discusses the concept of "intermittent work" as developed by Scandinavian researchers and explains its special values as distinguished from the Reindell-Gerschler forms of interval training. (1) Intermittent work-recovery focuses on maximal oxygen uptakes (VO_2 max) and

---

[1]David L. Costill, PhD., A SCIENTIFIC APPROACH TO DISTANCE RUNNING, Los Altos: CA, Track & Field News, 1979, 128 pp.

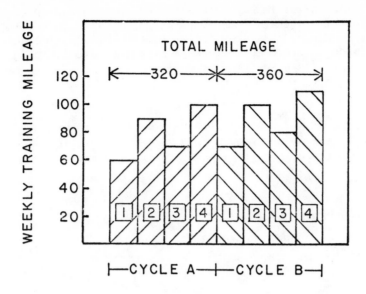

Fig. 19.2. Two 4-week cycles of work-rest based only on total mileage by a mature runner. In general: (1) weeks of long mileage alternate with weeks of shorter mileage; (2) total mileage in any given week in Cycle B tends to be greater than that for the corresponding week in Cycle A; (3) within each week, days of high stress will be balanced by days of low stress-recovery.

transport, and so requires work periods of a few minutes duration. Its runs tend to be 600 meters or more, and varies its recovery periods to fit the specific goals of the workout. (2) Intermittent work-recovery is done at relatively fast pace, usually faster--though sometimes slower--than race pace. It tends to develop fast-twitch (FT) muscle fibers over a time-distance period closer to that of the race, though without the intensity of interval training. (3) Intermittent work-recovery simulates the special mechanics-rhythms-stresses of the projected competition in a holistic way so that the runner is perfectly adapted to all aspects of racing.

For example, Costill recommends that each week should include days of LSD work of various kinds, but also "intermittent bouts of running at speeds equal to or faster than racing pace." During early preparatory phases, these would be limited to one day per week. During later preparatory phases or the early competitive period, they might well be increased to two days per week, or even three, though of course with varying distances-paces-recovery intervals. During competitive periods, such a faster-than-racing pace serves the dual role of increased developmental stress and of so-called sharpening--developing muscle speed-power through recruitment of the fast-twitch function in muscle fibers.

The final chapter of Costill's study focuses on training and preparation for competition. Despite the many gaps in our understanding, research does give us a more valid basis for constructing a training program for this unique individual. Many of the guidelines used by successful runners can be applied to the novice, provided they are scaled down and even restructured to meet his lesser abilities in both performance and restoration.

Costill begins by emphasizing a gradual approach: only after months of training can we test innate capacity to adapt to running.

While VO₂ max seems to reach its full potential within a few months after the start of training, reducing the cost of submaximal running may take years to develop fully....

Table 19.3 provides an example of the type of training that will establish a strong endurance base (non-competitive training) and the necessary sharpening for optimal race performance (competitive training). However, this training format illustrates only the relative emphasis on distance running and speed running. Begin-ning runners may be able to cover only 30-40 miles per week, while the experienced runner may be able to manage more than 100 miles per week....Similarly, the emphasis on speed training should relate to the runner's physiological capacity, which improves gradually with training.

Table 19.3

AN EXAMPLE OF DEVELOPMENTAL WORK SCHEDULES WITH INCREASING
WORK-REST CYCLES OF BOTH LSD AND INTERMITTENT WORK

NON-COMPETITIVE PHASE

Day of Week	WEEK 1	WEEK 2	WEEK 3	WEEK 4
1	10 miles	15 miles	15 miles	20 miles
2	5 "	5 "	5 "	5 "
3 a.m.	4 "	8 "	6 "	8 "
p.m.	4 x 800 m	4 x 1 mile	4 x 800 m	6 x 1 mile
4	10 miles	12 miles	10 miles	12 miles
5	8 "	10 "	8 "	10 "
6	10 "	12 "	10 "	15 "
7	6 "	10 "	6 "	8 "

Total Weekly Mileage

	55 miles	76 miles	62 miles	84 miles

COMPETITIVE PHASE

Day of Week	WEEK 1	WEEK 2	WEEK 3	WEEK 4
1	10 miles	10 miles	10 miles	10 miles
2 a.m.	8 miles	6 x 1 mile x 100%	8 miles	7 x 1 mile x 100%
p.m.	15 x 400m x 125%	8 miles	15 x 400m x 125%	8 miles
3	8 miles	10 miles	8 miles	10 miles
4 a.m.	6 miles	4 x 1.5 miles x 100%	6 miles	5 x 1.5 miles x 100%
p.m.	10 x 800m x 100%	6 miles	10 x 800m x 100%	6 miles
5	8 miles	6 miles	8 miles	6 miles
6	6 miles	4 miles	6 miles	4 miles
7	TIME TRIAL*	RACE	TIME TRIAL**	RACE

Total Weekly Mileage

	55-60 miles	55-60 miles	55-60 miles	55-60 miles

*Time Trial = 75% of racing distance
**Time Trial = 1.0-1.25 times racing distance

Note: During the non-competitive phase, all LSD running is performed at 60-70% of the runner's oxygen uptake capacity (% VO_2 max); all intermittent work at 85-90% VO_2 max, with rest inter-vals equal to the exercise periods. During the competitive phase, LSD is at 70-80% VO_2 max; in intermittent work, rest intervals should be 1.5 to 2.0 times the duration of the run.

BOWERMAN'S ECLECTIC SYSTEM IN AN OREGON SETTING.

During a 38 year career as track coach (12 at Medford High; 26 at the University of Oregon), Bill Bowerman gradually developed into one of America's most successful coaches in both team and individual championships won, as well as in numbers of men on United States Olympic teams. This is remarkable in light of Bowerman's insistence that men seek his guidance, rather than his seeking their talents. Recruiting to Oregon's track program did occur but without Bill's blessing.

Throughout his career, Bowerman thought of himself as a teacher--"teaching is the root of all good coaching." In his judgment, college coaching in the United States was increasingly corrupted by recruiters and salesmen more interested in winning than in developing, more interested in personal gain than in the values of a sound college education for their boys.

These strong views are at the base of Bowerman's system of training--moderation; studies first, running second, no third activity that required major time-energy-devotion; running that must be fun if maximal development is to occur.

To understand that base and the system derived from it, one must first understand the "surround" out of which it emerged. Bill, very properly, preferred to call it "The Oregon System," in part through his respect for his own Oregon coach, Bill Hayward, but much more, because it was indigenous to Oregon, indigenous to Oregon's woods and rivers and hills, but also indigenous to Oregon's simple, unstructured, "small-town" environment.

Perhaps the significance of that statement can be better understood if we contrast Oregon's orientation in the 1950-70s with that among Eastern schools and colleges. Think of the large-city surroundings of such successful track schools as Manhattan, Fordham, Pennsylvania, Yale, Villanova. Where would they do Swedish fartlek in which the pains of fatigue are assuaged by the beauty and quiet of one's surroundings. On the sidewalks of New York or Philadelphia?

In contrast, Medford's population was about 3000, Eugene's 5000. A TV special of the 1984 Prefontaine Track Classic showed woods and hills just above the stadium. One could be on soft pine-needled paths within minutes of leaving the dressing room. No wonder Bowerman adopted Sweden's fartlek system of training. Bill was a fine woodsman; hunting and fishing were great enjoyments. The woods and streams were home to him and to his runners. Under such a set-up, training really could be fun, refreshing to body and spirit.

Second, Bill was able to plan his training and competitive program along a single straight line of gradual development from November to June without interference from non-college pre-established programs. Contrast this with the clutter of big-time meets--LA Times, Millrose, Penn Relays--that required peak performances during three separate periods of the running season--four if you count cross-country.

The Oregon System had everything its own way. Many would call that a minus, not a plus. But it did allow Bowerman to construct his own eclectic system drawn from Holmer's fartlek, Gerschler's interval training, Igloi's meticulously documented repeat-running, and later, Lydiard's marathon training.

In 1983, Chris Walsh[1] authored a 72-page outline of THE BOWERMAN SYSTEM including a summary of Bowerman's career, the gist of his methods, Bowerman-devised Training Tables, and of special interest, Walsh's selection of Ten Principles that guided Bowerman throughout his long career. Lack of space forces my own condensation of those principles, hopefully, without lessening their full significance.

Principle #1--Regularity. Planned regularity in all aspects of the training process is of first importance--regularity in daily running, in adequate rest, proper diet; regularity in following a longtime training plan fitted to the needs and temperament of the individual athlete and to his gradual maturation as a runner and a person; regularity that seeks enjoyment

---

[1]Chris Walsh, *THE BOWERMAN SYSTEM*, Los Altos, CA: *Tafnews Press*, 1983, 72 pp.

Note: Students of training for running will gain valuable insights as to The Middle Way in coaching by studying this book as well as that of Bill Bowerman, *COACHING TRACK AND FIELD*, Boston: Houghton Mifflin Co., 1974.

and maintains an appetite for running. To accomplish this, written plans prepared well ahead of time--weeks and even months in advance--are crucial.

Principle #2--Workload. "Many of the coaches work their runners too hard," said Bowerman. As an observer of the Bowerman program over the past 30 years, it seems clear that his principle of modified workloads and enjoyable running--"if you can't carry on a conversation when doing LSD training, you're running too fast"--is truly basic to Bowerman's system and almost unique among today's world coaches. It is inherent in Oregon's beautiful terrain and soft footpaths and reminiscent of Mollett's description of fartlek--"A window was opened on the forest, and a concept of training emerged that can truly be described as 'happy'."

Principle #3--Goal Orientation. Bowerman's goals for his athletes were what I call holistic--whole-life oriented. "Be a student first, then a runner." But that's enough for one man; to attempt a third action area detracts from all areas. Second, goals assume gradual development, an improvement of perhaps 10-15 percent every year. Third, progressive training during each year should enable each runner to reach his peak in the school-college championship meets at the end of each year.

All such goal-centered training requires studied planning and record keeping. Where and how far we are going depends on where we have been. Bill therefore devised detailed record charts and insisted they be maintained by all runners. Samples of such charts are provided on later pages of this Chapter (Fig. 19.5).

Principle #4--Hard/Easy Training. A hard training session should be followed by an easy one. Individuals vary greatly as to the meaning of "hard." When in doubt, choose the easier way. Only a few thrive on repeated hard workouts. Bill Dellinger, one of Bowerman's greatest, attempted at age 29 two weeks of successive hard workouts, but then had had enough and went back to the work/rest regime.

Principle #5--Moderation. This principle relates closely to numbers 2 and 4 but emphasizes the total work load in terms of mileage and pace. Bowerman's long experience with runners, mostly of college age, led him to conclude that optimal conditioning could be ensured on a relatively low total mileage of 25 miles a week. Fifty miles is achievable by some. "One hundred miles a week is ridiculous. It will only give the guy sore legs. And he probably won't be able to study either." Bowerman inquired carefully into the training of Sebastian Coe during the year 1979, that of Coe's greatest performances. He found that Coe's highest mileage in one week was about 50 miles and that he used both fartlek and fast intervals, as did Bowerman.

Principle #6--Rest. And the sixth principle, as they say, is like unto the fifth--rest is as necessary as work. Bowerman even goes so far as to reduce workouts if an athlete has missed his sleep the previous night--for whatever reason. "There's no reason for TWO persons to be fools. If the athlete doesn't have enough sense to go to bed early, there's no reason for a coach to risk injury or illness by overworking him." There are coaches I've known who would pour it on to make sure the athlete got the message and didn't repeat the error.

Principle #7--Diet. A balanced diet of meat, fish, fruits, and vegetables will provide all the needed nutrients. Vitamins? "They're as magical as sawdust....Usually all an athlete will get out of them is expensive urine."

Principle #8--Enjoyment. Running should be fun; training should not be forced. Fun requires variety--variety in running schedules and, especially variety in terrain. For both reasons, fartlek is mentally and physically refreshing.

Principle #9--Mechanics. Bowerman had an uncommon interest in the mechanics of running--an erect body posture, proper foot placement, and overall care of the feet. He even hand-fashioned running shoes for his best runners, and, on retirement, acquired a most profitable interest in the sale of running shoes by a foremost foreign shoe company.

Correct body posture--head up, chest raised, arms 60-90 degrees at the elbows and swinging slightly across the chest--is shown here in Fig. 19.3. Proper placement of the feet is shown in Fig. 19.4. On the other hand, Bowerman warned, "If something works, don't try to fix it."

362

Fig. 19.3. An Erect Posture in Distance Running.

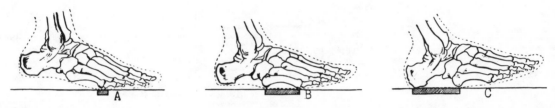

Fig. 19.4. Placement of the foot in running. Figure A suggests the placement of a sprinter-440 man; B, that of an 880-man or miler; C, that used for long distances. In actual running, no such clear-cut difference exists. In C there is a cushioned roll of the foot as the body moves lightly over it. In B, the heel drops buoyantly to the ground and cushions placement.

Principle #10--Pace. Bowerman considered pace judgment and an unyielding will to maintain it to be as essential as endurance and speed in the training of a runner.

Maximal economy of energy in running is achieved by running the first half of a race at a pace slightly slower than even pace, then holding or gradually increasing pace until the final finishing sprint during the final 200 meters. A runner who lacks speed in the finish must increase pace sooner, even as much as 600m from the finish. A well-trained and mature runner can sometimes increase pace during the third quarter and so gain a lead that is never overcome.

Bowerman developed pace judgment and the will to maintain it by use of his Date-Pace/ Goal-Pace Charts. Goal-pace is that pace projected for best performance during the coming year--for a 4:20 mile, 65 seconds. Date-pace is a 3/4th effort pace in a 3/4th distance time trial. Early pace in the trial should allow increased "finishing" pace during the final 200m or more, without undue exhaustion.

Progression in performance throughout the year, in theory, should follow a projected straight line drawn from the first Date-Pace test in November to the last Date-Pace test in June. For example a straight line from, say, 4:40 (70s) in November, to 4:28 (67s) in March, to 4:20 (65s) in June.

In my judgment [Doherty] these ten principles form a valid summary of Bowerman's approach to training. But I would add at least one more--simple, even spartan-like living, with an adamant requirement to do what needs to be done when it needs to be done, even when it hurts. Read the thumb-nail sketch in this OMNIBOOK of Bowerman's career. He was and is a tough guy-- soft-spoken, often smiling, sometimes slow to make his views known, but basically a Spartan-- sternly disciplined, rigorously simple, authoritarian even though benevolent. Somehow, how he looked and what he had done spoke so loud one heard every quiet word he said, and carried it out even when it hurt. No wonder he felt at home at Sweden's Volodalen, Finland's Vierumachi and would have at Cerutty's primitive shack at Australia's Portsea.

363

880 TRAINING SCHEDULE: 6

880-Yard Run	NAME	DATE *March*

1. A. Jog 1 to 3 miles
   B. Weights & jog
2. Fartlek A. Varied (1) 30 min. (2) *60 min.*
   B. Steady (1) 2-4 mi. (2) 4-6 mi. (3) 7-10 mi.
   (4) *45 min.*
3. Weights *and jog*
4. High knee and power run
5. Intervals
   A. 110 (1) 18-16-14 (2) 17-15-13 (3) *12.5* (4) *12.0*
   B. 165 (1) 25 (2) *19*
   C. 220 (1) 35 (2) *25-27* (3) *27*
   D. 330 (1) 52 (2) 48 (3) 45 (4)
   E. 440 (1) 70-73 (2) *65-70* (3) *63*
   F. 660 (1) 1:45 (2)
   G. 880 (1) 70 (2)
   H. 3/4 (1) 70 (2)
   I. Mile (1) 72 (2) 68-70 (3) 64-67 (4)
   J.
   K.
   L.
6. Sets A. 660-440-330-220-110
   (1) 1:45-68-49-32-15 (2) *1:42-66-46-30-14*
   B. 440-660-440-220 (1) 63 (2)
   C. 550-165-165 (1) 55 pace (2)
   D. *220-440-220*
7. Squad meeting
8. Special A. Sauna B. Swim C.
9. Drills A. Sprint-float-sprint (165)
   B. 1-step acceleration (165)
   C. 40-30 drill (1) 4 laps (2)
   D. 70-90 drill (1) 1-1 (2) 2-1
   (3) 3-1 (4)
   E. Cut-downs (1) 110 (2) 165 (3) 220
   (4) 330 (5) 440 (6) 880 (7)
   F. Simulate race drills (1) 1st 220-last 220
   (2) 2½-1½ (3) 10 miles-3/4 drill (4)
   G. 2-4 miles at (1) 80 (2) 75 (3)
10. A. Test B. Trial C. Compete
    (1) 3/4 date pace (2) Over (3) Under
11. Hill interval A. 110 B. 220 C.
12. With coach (A) Bill B. (B) Bill D. (C)
14. A. Wind sprint B. Hurdle drill
    C. Spring and bound D.
15. Finish work
16. Acrobatics or apparatus
17. 3/4 effort
18.
19.
20. Secondary event
21. A. Pictures B. Film

M /A	9E(3)(33-30-27)—2A(1)—5A(2) [3x ... 2x]
T 2A(2)	1A—5A(3)—5C(2)—6A(1)—2A(2) [4x 4x]
W /A	2A(1)—3—5A(1) [2x]
T 2A(1)	1A—5B(⅞₀)—2B(4)—9E(4)(47-45-42) [2x]
F	1A—3—9E(3)(36-33-30-27) [4x]
S /A	1A—6C—2A(2)—5C(1) [2-3x]
S	Runner's choice
M 5A(1) [2x]	3
T /A	10A(330 at pace, 220 jog, 330 at pace)—6A(3)—5A(1) [2x 3-5x]
W 5A(1) [2x]	1A—3—8A
T /A	5B(2)—2A(2)—9F(4)(51-48-45) [6x 2-3x]
F 5A(1) [3x]	5B—2A—5A(3) [4x]
S 2A	10A(880 at date pace)—2A(2)
S	Runner's choice
M /A	1A—5E(2)—5C(2)—2A(2)—9E(4)(47-45-42) [4x 2x]
T 2B	5A(4)—2A—5A(1) [4x 3x]
W /A	1A—5E(2)—5D(⅞₀ effort)—2A
T 2A	2A or 2B—5A(1) [2x]
F /A	5A—3—5A [3x 2x]
S	10C or 10A
S	Travel for spring trip
M 2A	1A—2A or 2B—5A(1) [2x]
T 2B(1)	1A—5E(2)—6D—2A(1)—5A [4x 4x]
W 2A	2A or 2B—5A(1) [2x]
T 5A(1) [2x]	5C(1)—2A [4x]
F 5A(1) [2x]	Jog
S	10C
S	Home and re-register (spring term)

MILE TRAINING SCHEDULE: 6

One-Mile Run	NAME	DATE *March*

1. A. Jog 1 to 3 miles
   B. Weights & jog
2. Fartlek A. Varied (1) 30 min. (2)
   B. Steady (1) 2-4 mi. (2) 4-6 mi. (3) 7-10 mi.
   (4)
3. Weights
4. High knee and power run
5. Intervals
   A. 110 (1) 18-16-14 (2) 17-15-13
   B. 165 (1) 25 (2)
   C. 220 (1) 35 (2)
   D. 330 (1) 52 (2) 48 (3) 45 (4) *42*
   E. 440 (1) 70-73 (2) *66* (3) *60*
   F. 660 (1) 1:45 (2)
   G. 880 (1) 70 (2) *63*
   H. 3/4 (1) 70 (2)
   I. Mile (1) 72 (2) 68-70 (3) 64-67 (4)
   J.
   K.
   L.
6. Sets A. 660-440-330-220-110
   (1) 1:45-68-49-32-15 (2) *1:42-66-46-30-14*
   B. 440-660-440-220 (1) 63 (2)
   C. 550-165-165 (1) 55 pace (2)
   D.
7. Squad meeting
8. Special A. Sauna B. Swim C.
9. Drills A. Sprint-float-sprint (165)
   B. 1-step acceleration (165)
   C. 40-30 drill (1) 4 laps (2)
   D. 70-90 drill (1) 1-1 (2) 2-1
   (3) 3-1 (4)
   E. Cut-downs (1) 110 (2) 165 (3) 220
   (4) 330 (5) 440 (6) 880 (7)
   F. Simulate race drills (1) 1st 220-last 220
   (2) 2½-1½ (3) 10 miles-3/4 drill (4)
   G. 2-4 miles at (1) 80 (2) 75 (3)
10. A. Test B. Trial C. Compete
    (1) 3/4 date pace (2) Over (3) Under
11. Hill interval A. 110 B. 220 C.
12. With coach (A) Bill B. (B) Bill D. (C)
14. A. Wind sprint B. Hurdle drill
    C. Spring and bound D.
15. Finish work
16. Acrobatics or apparatus
17. 3/4 effort *A. Mile*
18. *Steeplechase A. Hurdle drill B. Water jump*
19. *Park run A. Around B. Short hill*
20. Secondary event
21. A. Pictures B. Film

M A.M. /A	P.M. 1A—4—2B(1)
T /A	1B—19B—19A—5A(1) [2-6x 4-6x 2x]
W /A	1A—1B
T /A	18A—18B—9A(1320)—2B(1) [4x 4x]
F	Light
S	10B(17A)—2
S	2
M /A	1B—4
T /A	2
W /A	1B—4
T /A	6B—18AB—6A(2)—2A [2-4x]
F	1B—4—2B
S	Light
S	2
M	Exam week—2A(1)
T	5G(3)—5A—5F(1)—5A—5E(2)—5D—2A [2x 2x 3-4x 4-6x 6x]
W	1B—2B(1)
T	2B
F	Gear ready—14A
S Travel	10C—Dual meet
	Travel—Spring trip
M /A-14A	5E(3)—2A(1)—6A(1)—2A(1) [4x 3x]
T 1B-14B	5D(4)—5A(⅞₀ effort)—2 [3x 4x]
W /A	Light
T /A-14A	2 (Hills)
F	1B
S	10C—Triangular meet
S	Travel home—registration

DISTANCE TRAINING SCHEDULE: 5

Distances	NAME	DATE *March*

1. A. Jog 1 to 3 miles
   B. Weights & jog
2. Fartlek A. Varied (1) 30 min. (2) *45 min.*
   B. Steady (1) 2-4 mi. (2) 4-6 mi. (3) 7-10 mi.
   (4) *12-14 mi. easy* (5) *8-12 mi.*
3. Weights
4. High knee and power run
5. Intervals
   A. 110 (1) 18-16-14 (2) 17-*16-15-14*
   B. 165 (1) 25 (2)
   C. 220 (1) 35 (2) *32-34* (3) *27*
   D. 330 (1) 52 (2) 48 (3) 45 (4) *46-47*
   E. 440 (1) 70-73 (2) *68*
   F. 660 (1) 1:45 (2)
   G. 880 (1) 70 (2)
   H. 3/4 (1) 70 (2)
   I. Mile (1) 72 (2) 68-70 (3) 64-67 (4)
   J.
   K.
   L.
6. Sets A. 660-440-330-220-110
   (1) 1:45-68-49-32-15 (2)
   B. 440-660-440-220 (1) 63
   C. 550-165-165 (1) 55 pace (2)
   D.
7. Squad meeting
8. Special A. Sauna B. Swim C.
9. Drills A. Sprint-float-sprint (165)
   B. 1 step acceleration (165)
   C. 40-30 drill (1) laps (2)
   D. 70-90 drill (1) 1-1 (2) 2-1
   (3) 3-1 (4) *2-2*
   E. Cut-downs (1) 110 (2) 165 (3) 220
   (4) 330 (5) 440 (6) 880 (7)
   F. Simulate race drills (1) 1st 220-last 220
   (2) 2½-1½ (3) 10 miles-3/4 drill (4)
   G. 2-4 miles at (1) 80 (2) 75 (3)
10. A. Test B. Trial C. Compete
    (1) 3/4 date pace (2) Over (3) Under
11. Hill interval A. 110 B. 220 C.
12. With coach (A) Bill B. (B) Bill D. (C)
14. A. Wind sprint B. Hurdle drill
    C. Spring and bound D.
15. Finish work
16. Acrobatics or apparatus
17. 3/4 effort
18.
19.
20. Secondary event
21. A. Pictures B. Film

M A.M. /A	P.M. 2A(2)
T 2B(2)	5E(2)—9G(1)—5A(2) [6x]
W 2B(2)	2B(2)
T 2B(2)	5H(1)—2B(1)
F /A	2B(1)
S	5C(2) [12-20x]
S	2B(4)
M 2B(1)	2A(2)
T 2B(2)	5D(4)—2B(2)—9E(4) [6x 6x]
W 2B(2)	2B(2)
T 2B(2)	9D(4)
F /A	1A
S	10A(880)—2B(3)—9E(4) [6x]
S	2B(4)
M 2B(1)	2A(1-2)—5A(2)
T 2B(1)	9E(4)—2B(1)—9E(2x32-30-28) [6x 6x]
W 2B(1)	2B(2)—5A(2)
T /A	5C(3)—9G(1)(2 mi.)—5A(2) [2x]
F /A	1A
S	10C—Fresno meet
S	2B(5)
M 2B(1)	2A(2)—5A(2)
T 2B(1)	5D(4)—2B(1)—9E(4) [6x]
W 2B(1)	2B(2)
T 2B(1)	5C(3)—9G(1)—5A(2) [2x]
F /A	1A
S	10C
S	2B(4)

Fig. 19.5. Training record samples, reproduced from *THE BOWERMAN SYSTEM*, by Chris Walsh, *op. cit.*, pp. 50, 59, 67.

Chapter 20
ESSENTIALS OF TRAINING FOR ENDURANCE RUNNING

The essentials of training for endurance running underlie and support all sound training programs. If they are truly essential, no sound system can ignore them. But what is an essential? Forty years ago we might have answered, "over-distance, under-distance and time trials, not much else." Today, we are much more aware of the multiplicity of forces that influence development. A great deal of trial-and-error experience, stimulated and supported by scientific research, has ennabled us to differentiate the various aspects of endurance, to work in terms of each, and then to achieve just the right balance in our final preparations for competition.

In fact the scope of what we call essential is limited only by our powers of analysis and discrimination of meanings. We have listed some 28 essentials; the number could easily be doubled. But even more important than analysis is our ability to synthesize and balance these essentials. Keep in mind that some of these essentials have been emphasized by some coaches following certain systems, to the underestimation and even exclusion of other essentials. Fartlek was misused as merely enjoyment of running in the woods. Interval training was misused as intensive anaerobic training without a long background of cross-country running.

Obviously some of these essentials are more crucial than are others; some are important only at certain stages of training. The art of sound coaching lies in weighing and selecting, lies in the wise choice of precisely what, precisely how much, and precisely when is best for this uniquely different runner at this stage of his career.

It's somewhat like the art of good cooking. My wife now has a 24-volume ENCYCLOPEDIA OF COOKING, a bewildering wealth of possible recipes. But her high reputation in the dining room has grown out of her good judgment in selecting just the right items in the right combination for these special guests.

ENDURANCE TRAINING IS ORGANICALLY BENEFICIAL AND MENTALLY WHOLESOME
In a valid sense, endurance training is the development of our capacities into the higher levels of health and energy. For too long, we have thought of health in the medical sense as being freedom from disease and impairments. Actually the truly healthy man is free from such obstacles but also free to function at his highest potentials of energy. Our organs and systems have evolved for use within the entire range of action--for restful inaction, for slow, easy movements, but equally for the utmost demands of work and play. As between hard but reasonable training, on the one hand, and low level or complete inactivity, as in bed rest on the other, hard training is far the more healthful. When it comes to the furtherance of positive health, we in track coaching need make no apology to any profession.

This assumes of course that our training programs are sound, gradually developed, individualized. Such programs seek the conservation of energy. We spend energy today in order to build more energy for tomorrow. We undergo the arduousness of work today in order that tomorrow we can do that same work more easily and enjoyably or at a higher level. By wise use of our powers, both physical and mental, our nature rebuilds them in ever greater abundance.

Energy is present in each of us, not fixed at one level or another, but within a range of possible use and development. This range is both broad and flexible. Its upper limits are far beyond what seems humanly possible and healthful if one considers the limited demands for human energy made by our machine culture. Further, those who reach the upper levels of that range of energy can be active day after day, year after year with no ill effects to their health or longevity. Their organisms develop not only resistance to fatigue but also increase their rate of recovery. Few of these individuals need more sleep than the average; many need less. They have learned to increase their supply of energy, not by saving it, but by using it wisely--gradually building up their demands on it.

ENJOYMENT OF RUNNING IS ESSENTIAL

The word "essential" means absolutely necessary, and that is its use here as we speak of enjoyment of training. True, awareness of enjoyment is not always present but, if long neglected, what is essential exacts its measure of retribution. Without enjoyment, running becomes a task, even a drudgery, and development less certain. Of course enjoyment has a range of meaning. Hopefully, it has a connotation of fun, laughter, even joy in running--joy in the effort and pain of running. But its lesser meanings are also valid: satisfaction, the sense of being wholly absorbed in action, cleaness after a hot shower following a long run.

In our culture, professional attitudes tend to predominate. Professionals emphasize winning and extrinsic rewards. "Fun in sports is for children. It's a job; get it done right and you will get paid for it." But the fact is that in every undertaking that requires long time and hard effort, human beings demand a portion of play in their effort, of doing it because it's fun. The reward may shift the degree of demand; it never erases it. Modern coaching has emphasized goal-insight methods. The goal motivates the action. But absorbing action needs no goal other than itself. Every champion works hard, sometimes to the point of drudgery, but how often they say simply, "I enjoy running; when I no longer enjoy it, I'll quit."

A growing emphasis in endurance training--in swimming as well as running--is what Joe Henderson used to call the "PTA school of running: pain-torture-agony." Certainly a gradual development in courage toward pain is necessary to great performance in running. But this must be balanced by the fun of running, not merely because boys tend to make fun out of everything they do, but because fun and enjoyment are planned, are a built-in approach to both training and racing.

No wonder Brutus Hamilton described distance runners as "the best bon vivants in the world." No wonder Arthur Lydiard, that hardened "slave driver," emphasized,

All my search for the perfect training system convinced me of something else: The essence of athletics is the pleasure you can get out of it. . . . I actually came to enjoy knocking myself about because I came to grips with myself so frequently and at such a challenging physical and mental level. . . . It is a simple unalloyed joy to tackle yourself on the battlefield of your own physical wellbeing and come out the victor. . . .

Run for fun and from the fun will come the will to excel. From the will to excel could come an Olympic champion. Once you have found the fun there is in running, the task of training to the limits I prescribe will be much easier for you. . . .

There are jokes and laughter in training with these boys [Halberg, Snell, Magee], not a grim, grasping grind with an eye on the watch and the mind concentrating on forcing the body to do the mind's bidding.

A MEDICAL EXAMINATION MUST PRECEDE EACH YEAR'S TRAINING

Training for endurance running should be preceded by a thorough medical examination of the related organs and systems. Findings should be interpreted by a medical doctor with special training in sports medicine. As Roger J. Williams has demonstrated beyond all doubt, normal men often have structures and functions that are outside the range of normality. To be sure, a weakness of a lung, a kidney, or even the heart can be compensated in various ways. Examinations of successful marathon runners have disclosed organ deficiencies that would normally rule out competitive running.

However, in addition to using good judgment as related to the physical and emotional stresses of both training and competition, the track coach should do all he can to ensure healthy and normal systems. By requiring a medical examination, he reduces the chances of such weaknesses, he puts such responsibility where it belongs--on the medical profession, and very importantly, he removes from the minds of his runners all doubt as to their own health status for running.

MORE RUNNING = BETTER RUNNING

The most crucial principle in training for endurance running is that development is primarily the effect of more running: more miles per day that include both steady-state and quality running, more days per year, more years per running career. Underlying all the training systems of the past century, with their special emphases on this or that alluring secret of development is an increasing emphasis on mileage and pace. In 1904 Alfred Shrubb (2-mile W.R. - 9:09.6) trained exclusively on steady running twice a day, five days a week. But his week's total mileage was only about 35 miles. In the 1930s-40s, the American system of alternating days of over- and under-distance usually totalled even fewer miles per week, and certainly fewer miles per year.

Swedish fartlek was sold on a slogan of "get tired but don't feel tired." Actually, since men didn't feel so tired, they worked longer--and more intensely. When we first heard of interval training, we were excited by the prospect that our school runners could spend less time and do more quality work. Only later did we realize that the real emphasis was on more work, not on less time, and that Harbig's interval training was based on months of cross-country running. Similarly, Cerutty intrigued us with: "We train as we feel....Our training should be a thing of enthusiasm...to run with joy, sheer beauty and strength, to race down some declivity, to battle manfully to the top of another." We often failed to read his next sentence that "Elliott has run up to 30 miles before exhaustion set in. This was in the heat of our summer."

Though done about 15 years ago, a study by *Track & Field News* of the training of 30 world-level runners is still valid: it can be summarized as requiring more years, more days per year, and more miles per day.

MORE YEARS. The average number of years of serious training was 11.8. The average age of first competitive running was 14.5; that of best competitive performance, 25.2. The number of years of training between first and best competitive performance ranged from 4 years for Jim Ryun (assuming he did not improve on his 1966 world records) to 19 for George Young, America's greatest steeplechaser. Bolotnikov, USSR, and Young did their best running at age 31, while Jim Ryun, up to 1970, made his world records at age 19.

MORE DAYS PER YEAR. These same 30 champions averaged 6.2 days per week and 10.6 months per year during their years of best running. It should be added that such daily training undoubtedly developed as a guarantee that enough work of the right kind was being done. Research supports this. For example, Åstrand[1] emphasizes that year-round training is especially important in development of the oxygen-transporting system. Such training also fixes the habit of training and thereby avoids the danger of other interests and activities which might detract.

Apparently a few great runners have been exceptions to this rule. Kip Keino (Noronha, 1970, 55) reported that, with the exception of a few high-stress training periods, he trained only three times a week throughout the three years (1965-1968) of his best running. True, he usually worked out three times a day (6AM, 12N, 5PM), and was vigorously active on three other days, carrying out his duties as a physical instructor of the Kenya police. But he claims he averaged only about 50 miles a week in this program.

But David Costill[2] concluded from available schedules "that only with 5 or 6 training day per week can a runner...achieve maximal benefits."

MORE MILES PER DAY. The most striking conclusion to be drawn from Greg Brock's survey[3] of the training of 67 high school runners is of the wide range of mileage within which they all do well. In speaking of his high school training, the 1972 Olympic marathon champion, Frank Shorter, emphasized that his coaches' first concern was that they enjoy their running. In the early spring he averaged about 25 miles per week, with 5 miles on Tuesday and Thursday,

[1]Per-Olof Åstrand, *TEXTBOOK OF WORK PHYSIOLOGY*, 2nd edition, New York: McGraw-Hill Book Co., 1977, p. 395.

[2]David L. Costill, *A SCIENTIFIC APPROACH TO DISTANCE RUNNING*, Los Altos: *Track & Field News*, 1979, p. 85.

[3]Greg Brock, *HOW HIGH SCHOOL RUNNERS TRAIN*, Los Altos, CA, Tafnews Press, 1976, paper, 95 pps.

and 10 miles on Sunday (4m-AM, 6m-PM). In contrast the diary that coach Bob Timmons kept on Jim Ryun showed that, during his junior year, he totalled 4380 miles. Assuming 330 days of running, that averages over 13 miles per day, 90 miles per week.

For all runners, there is a level of diminishing returns at which increased mileage will not produce comparable improvement in performance; in fact, may even have a negative effect. General stress may produce specific illnesses or injuries--from stomach ailments including ulcers to Achilles tendonitis, shin splints or stress fractures; perhaps from too much; more likely, from too much too soon.

Training Twice a Day. A second training run, usually in the early morning when it's cool and traffic is minimal, is now generally accepted as a part of modern training, even at the high school level. For many the discipline of early rising is mentally stimulating, even toughening. Total mileage tends to increase. However, many variables make research on its values for performance very difficult and of doubtful significance.

Costill found no greater improvement among the 2-a-day runners (4.5-5 miles jogging each morning) than in those practicing once a day. His criteria included heart rates during and after a standard treadmill run, and time in both the mile and ½ mile run. However, he did observe that the supplemental training did seem to benefit certain individuals. Whether this was the effect of individuality or of differences in degree of fitness was not indicated.

MORE RUNNING = BETTER RUNNING BUT ONLY WITHIN ITS STRESS LIMITS

We have emphasized the important values of mileage training, but these values are limited by the degree of stress produced during that mileage. Christensen studied the effects of contin- uous running on heart rates. He found that regular training at a fixed pace gradually lowered the heart rate for that load; for example, from 180 to 160 beats/min., but that eventually a sticking point was reached. *Continued training at that same intensity of work produced no further improvement.* After training with a more demanding load, the heart rate during the ori- ginal work load gradually lowered again, perhaps to 150. Each intensity produced its own level of development, no more.

Two reservations must be made. First, that "intensity" should be interpreted in terms of stress, not merely running pace. True, most training systems increase intensity by increasing pace. But it is also increased by such methods as speed-hill training, driving runs up 80- foot sand dunes, or varied and hilly terrains during fartlek. Such actions increase stress and so lower heart rates and allied effects below those of fixed-pace continuous running.

Second, we should keep in mind that Christensen's "continued training at that intensity of work" was probably not maintained nearly as long as do modern marathon and mileage trainers. Some time after the body has reached a steady state for a certain running pace, a secondary increase in heart rate and general sense of fatigue can be observed, and at later intervals, further changes in awareness of stress. De Vries (1966, 74) explains this "in terms of fatigue of the skeletal musculature, which results in the recruitment of larger numbers of motor units, which results in a greater metabolic demand for the same level of work load--and thus an in- crease in the heart rate." That is, continuous steady-pace running creates a series of step- ups in intensity as general fatigue develops. To this degree, greater mileage produces greater intensities.

TRAINING AEROBIC POWER

The distinction between aerobic and anaerobic training is a crucial one in modern distance running. In brief, aerobic running is at a pace that can be maintained indefinitely, with an ample O_2 supply to oxidize the carbohydrate sources of energy completely to CO_2 and H_2O, and therefore with no accumulation of lactic acid. Such a balanced aerobic condition is often called a "steady state." Pulse rates may range between 130-160 b/p/m.

In contrast, anaerobic running is at a faster pace than can be maintained in a steady state. It requires more oxygen than can be supplied, an "oxygen debt" is incurred, and a high lactic acid condition is built up in the muscle tissues and blood stream which, eventually, ends in exhaustion. Pulse rates may rise to sub-maximal (180-190 b/p/m).

In everyday distance running terminology, we tend to equate aerobic running with long-slow continuous running, though, as we shall see, a slower-paced interval training can also be aerobic. Anaerobic running tends to be related in both research and actual practice to repetitions of faster-paced distances, as in interval training or intermittent work, as the Scandinavian researchers call it.

We should be clear that, to be continuously developmental, aerobic training must progressively overload the endurance systems. When an optimum distance has been achieved, pace must be increased so that higher levels of stress will stimulate development to higher levels of energy. This will cut mileage temporarily while the organism adapts to the new challenge.

RAISING THE LEVEL OF ONE'S STEADY STATE.
One of the goals of every training program is to increase the pace at which the athlete can run without an increase in lactic acid in the blood, one of the limiting factors in running. In other words, to increase the level of one's steady state. A steady state denotes a condition while running in which oxygen uptake equals the oxygen requirement so that such functions as breathing, heart rate and stroke/volume attain fairly constant levels.

Powers and Steben[1] suggest that early training should set up a "target heart rate" that will produce such an improvement. *This is calculated by multiplying .85-.90 times the maximal heart rate (220 - age) ...Use .85 for less fit; .90 for the more highly trained. The target heart rate must be reached and maintained for at least 20-30 minutes during a training session, and must be repeated at least three times a week....This could substantially improve performance...a faster pace without accumulating lactic acid."*

Related research in physiology tends to focus on such measures as maximum oxygen uptakes (VO_2 max) or the anaerobic threshold, "the greatest VO_2 max beyond which lactic acid begins to build up rapidly in the athlete's blood." One of the conclusions from such research is that a steady state can occur within a range of stress, not merely at a single point of stress. That is, there is a lowest pace that will produce maximal oxygen uptake and the allied phenomena, and also a highest pace that still will not produce oxygen debt. Aerobic training can proceed in progressive step-ups of pace, somewhat as occurs in the maximums for a given pace are reached, the pace is increased slightly even though distance be reduced temporarily. Then a gradual process of adjustment ennables the runner to maintain that pace at a lower level of stress, though still within the range of maximum oxygen uptake. Once again a step-up occurs.

TRAINING ANAEROBIC POWER.
For a relatively short period of time, the energy needs of high-intensity running can be met through physiological processes for which oxygen is lacking (anaerobic training.) All racing distances from the marathon down to 400m make some demand on anaerobic power--if not during the major portion of the race (400-800), then during the final drive for the finish line; or more rarely, during the increased-pace laps by which men try to break away from the field during later portions of longer races.

It follows that anaerobic training will comprise some portion of training for all distances, including the marathon. In brief, such training will be either continuous running at close to racing pace or intermittent (interval) running with repetitions of work-rest at faster than racing pace. Training effects relate to the ability to consume, transport, and utilize large volumes of oxygen (as with aerobic training), but also to the development of muscle power and effectiveness to sustain the faster pace of shorter races or of the finish in longer races (Costill, 1979, 26-27). Aerobic training alone fails to serve this latter need.

HEART RATES AS A MEASURE OF RUNNING FITNESS. The use of pulse rates to monitor bodily responses to endurance running is of value primarily for interval (intermittent) training, in its active phase but even more important, in its recovery phase.

In fact, it was an essential part of research in interval training by Reindell and Gerschler in the 1950s, and so is described more fully under that heading in this book. In summary,

---

[1] Scotty Powers, Ph.D. and Ralph E. Steben, Ph.D., "Shifting the Anaerobic Threshold in Distance Runners, *Track Technique Annual*, 1983, pp. 10708. A clearly-stated summary of the problem.

heart rate is the most valid measurement of bodily response; the major problem is to ensure its reliability.

ACHIEVING AN OPTIMUM RATIO OF AEROBIC/ANAEROBIC TRAINING

Scientists and modern coaches are in general agreement (1) that a sound endurance-training program should include both mileage training (aerobic) and speed-endurance training (anaerobic), and (2) that first emphasis during one-half to three-fourths of the training year should be on aerobic training. Disagreements occur as to the time at which anaerobic training should be introduced, and as to the degree to which the two types of training should be inter-mixed.

In general, the proponents of interval training have used about two or more months for aerobic fartlek; the remaining nine months, for anaerobic interval work. In contrast, Lydiard[1], the chief advocate of aerobic training, more than reverses the ratio. He suggests that about four weeks is sufficient to bring about the benefits of anaerobic work. This is borne out by his training of Snell who ran a marathon just 55 days before setting his world record of 3:54.4 in the mile and two weeks later in the 880 in 1:45.1, and who had only a few weeks of intensive anaerobic and speed work just prior to these races.

In his discussion at the USTCA clinic at Washington, 1970, he suggested an 8-week "sharpening" period prior to the Big Race. The first four of these are "hard anaerobic work" consisting of repeated intervals at 400, 800, and 200 meters:

In this period, I had the athletes in good condition. They had a high steady state, had their speed back, and the capacity to run anaerobically.

During the second 4-week period, Lydiard tried to achieve several things along with the anaerobic interval work: (1) wind sprints for greater sprinting speed, (2) progressively faster trial runs at or near his racing distance, (3) under-distance competition, and (4) a conservation of energy by easier training.

GRADUALISM IN RATE OF DEVELOPMENT. We have mentioned how Lydiard placed great emphasis on a gradual approach to development, and how he predicted when Halberg was 17 that he would be world's champion, not in three or four years, but in ten years' time. Lydiard knew by experience that he could increase the intensity of training and thus advance performance this year, but he patiently refrained.

But very few United States runners are trained by one coach throughout their running careers. And each coach tends strongly to limit his vision and judgment to his own period of influence. In junior high school, in high school, in college, everyone involved to even a minor degree-- the boy himself, his girl friend, parents, the school principal and janitor, the local postman, and the coach--all recognize achievement now, not at some far-off and uncertain future. Not to mention the demands of the track team and of the adamant school competitive schedule.

Some State high school rules limit the date of first organized track practice, hoping thereby to lessen the pressures on high school boys. The intention of such rules is good; the effect, a loss of the gradual approach, a great increase in intensity of training, and a strong tendency to do too much too soon.

In Europe and the USSR, when asked how long he intends to continue training and competing, a runner tends to answer, "As long as I enjoy it and can see some worthwhile goal ahead of me." He knows the wherewithal will be provided. Under such a program, a more gradual approach can be made. Coaches and runners can plan ahead over a span of 20 years instead of four (for high school), then four more (for college), with little certainty of a program or coach or proper facilities beyond. Costill (1979, 13) says there is little doubt that the distance runner is at his best between 27 and 32 years of age, with many doing well at 35 and even beyond.

THE USES OF VARIETY. Today, in 1984, many respected coaches, here and abroad, are so impressed with the critical need for variety and freshness in all distance training that they deny they

---

[1]Lydiard, op. cit., p. 26.

follow any given system of training. "I analyze all systems so as to understand their essentials, then dispense them in such variety that the individual runner is unaware he's following a carefully laid-out plan."

Other than the physical act of running per se, the need for interest, enthusiasm, excitement--all enhanced by variety--is the most potent essential of all training.

VARIETY IN TERRAINS. Every training system must include varied terrains in its year-round program. It is the heart of fartlek. Olander's Swedish training center, Volodalen, provided Gunder Haegg with curving paths through woods and around lakes, up-hill and down-dale, with sometimes marshy footing. Percy Cerutty's Australian topography included high sand dunes, long sea beaches, dirt roads, and runs over the plains "in any direction our whim took us, followed by a dip in the ocean." Oregon's excellent training program, as first organized by Bill Bowerman, used four terrains--the running track, a golf course, the seashore and nearby mountain paths. Even interval training, as invented by Germany's Woldemar Gerschler, included cross-country and road running in its total schedule of training. Lydiard (1962, 62) placed strong emphasis on variety of terrains.

The time training we have outlined includes running over country roads, hills, flats, everything, to accustom our learner to all conditions and running surfaces. He is not going to be a fair-weather, fine-track athlete. He runs on turf as much as possible and deliberately seeks out mud and slush as well as fast, hard surfaces. . . . He doesn't mind whether there is a blazing sun overhead or it is pouring rain--out he goes.

True, Lydiard is emphasizing toughness, but he makes it clear that variety helps to make the toughening process easier, without boredom.

VARIETY IN PRACTICE RUNNING. It's very difficult for today's coaches to realize the great increase in the kind of things that can be done in training for running today as compared with early years. It's almost shocking to me to remember that in 1948 I tried to help Herb Barten on his way to a third place in the London Olympic 800 meters with only four or five workouts in my coaching bag: Monday--1½ x distance; Tuesday--time trials, 3/4 distance; Wednesday--2 x ½ distance; Thursday--4 x ¼ distance; Friday--rest. A few short-relay events, a little sprinting, that was about it. All on a cinder 440-yard track.

In contrast to such wearisome sameness, look through Frank Calore's HOW HIGH SCHOOL RUNNERS TRAIN.[1] Each man will have a dozen or more running patterns. A list of all the patterns might number a hundred or so. Another excellent example of variety is to be found in Coach Timmons'[2] account of Jim Ryun's workouts during the 12 weeks preceding his world-record mile and 880. The hard or easy workouts occur either AM or PM. Off-the track running is cross-country, steady-pace, fartlek, or even road running. No two interval workouts are the same. Any one workout is likely to contain 3 or more interval distances, with varying paces. Within each workout there are intervals requiring 9/10 effort; others, very relaxed, easy effort. Such variety helped greatly to hide the very demanding exertions of the training schedule.

It should be added that variety can become confusing and defeat its purpose if it fails to follow a sound plan of progression.

VARIETY IN COMPANIONSHIP. Most men like to vary their running mates. First, it is important, even essential, to do some running alone, especially when the conditions are difficult and discouraging. There's no better way to develop self-dependence and stick-to-it-iveness. But also, there's value in running with men you enjoy. There's value in running with men of greater competitive experience--as also, occasionally, with those of lesser experience. There is value in training with men of superior endurance, or of superior sprinting speed at the finish. Many a champion has progressed by working out with four or five groups in a single workout.

---

[1] 1982 edition available from *Track & Field News*, P.O. Box 296, Los Altos, CA, 94022.

[2] Bob Timmons, "Jim Ryun--How He Trains," *Track Technique*, 31 March, 1968, 963.

VARIETY IN ALTITUDE. Costill (1979, 99) concluded from related research that "sea-level performance is not improved by altitude (2300m) training in men who are already well trained." However, the psychological uses of varied altitudes make them a worthwhile adjunct to every training system.

VARIETY IN TEMPERATURE-HUMIDITY. For many years, Scandinavian runners have claimed that their custom of regular sauna baths has been beneficial in their adjustment to the variety of weather conditions they meet in competition. Certainly it has been proved time and time again that those who have acclimated themselves to high temperatures have a great advantage when such conditions prevail.

VARIETY IN DEGREE OF STRESS. The concept of work-rest has many implications. It contrasts the training season with the active-rest season, the periods of major competition with those of developmental competition, weeks of high-stress training with weeks of free running with enjoyment, and of course, days of maximum effort with days of conservation of energy. It should be clear that variety in degree of stress should be a constant goal in every phase of the developmental process. In his excellent chapter on "Physical Training," Åstrand (1977, 375-430) strongly recommends the values of submaximal aerobic training as compared with maximal anaerobic training, but to ensure maximum training effects he feels that both are necessary, and suggests that training programs should provide a variation in intensities which covers the full range of running from long-slow to short-fast, with both continuous and intermittent run-rest. Just how much variation should depend on individual differences in both attitudes and physical reaction, not merely on the coach's planned program or on group preferences.

VARIETY IN COMPETITIONS. Obviously the men against whom the team members compete will provide variety in pace, in length and speed of finish, in racing tactics generally, and in competitive challenge. But there must also be variety in degree of emphasis on competitions from week to week. There is agreement among the world's master coaches of running that the year's competitions must be classified into at least three groups: (1) Crucial, (2) Important, (3) Developmental. The words don't matter. Lydiard called the first, "Big Races;" Timmons, high-goal races. But for pacing one's energies and attitudes, such variety is necessary.

TRAINING SYSTEMS MUST ADAPT TO THE UNIQUE INDIVIDUALITY OF EACH RUNNER.
This principle does not suggest that there should be as many training systems as there are individual athletes. That would be chaos. Despite wide variability, men are more similar than they are different. But training systems, as set down on paper, necessarily relate to groups or to the non-existent "average" individual. Somehow, someway, within every training system, both the amount and the kind of training must be individualized.

Chapter 19 reviewed "Training Systems for Endurance Running"--the long-established systems but also the Russian, German, Finnish approaches as well. They all insist upon individualization of their systems; they all tend to prefer one-on-one coaching, or at least one coach for a small group of runners. Harry Wilson, respected coach of England's world-record miler, Steve Ovett, writes,[1]

If I had a method--which I don't--in the tradition of the great coaching theorists, the Harry Wilson method would be to treat each athlete individually. You see, training for running is fairly easy; anybody can become a runner. ...The individuals are the unknown variable; they are different both physically and psychologically. The difficult part of ...coaching is making sure that technique and training are adapted to the individual....One theory that has definitely gone out of vogue is the notion that there is one right way to do it.

Wilson exaggerates of course; he does have a system, a basic approach that applies to everyone. Every effective coach has a system. Runners, male and female, are more alike than they are unique; they're all human. But they are also all different. As with food, we all must eat, but just what food, how often, how much applies to wide-ranging individual needs.

---

[1] Harry Wilson, *Running Dialogue*, London: Stanley Paul, 1982, p. 20.

How can the American school-college coach individualize training when he is responsible for perhaps a half-hundred youngsters, male and female, training for more than a dozen events? How individualize each of them? Obviously, he or she can't, at least not adequately. But the effort must be made.

INEXORABLE TRAINING

The word "inexorable" was chosen carefully as implying "relentless," "implacable," "unyielding." Such terms relate both to regular training according to plan regardless of weather conditions or personal convenience, and to an unflinching attitude toward arduous effort. Old-time distance buffs tend to think immediately of two persons--Emil Zatopek and coach Percy Cerutty. Zatopek was one of the first (1946-1956) to extend both mileage and intensity of training. His 40 x 400 that gradually increased to 60 x 400 were considered superhuman, especially since they occurred in the snow and cold, and with army boots on his feet. He wrote, "Is it raining? It doesn't matter. Am I tired? That doesn't matter either...I practiced regardless, until will power was no longer a problem."

Percy Cerutty, Australian coach of Herb Elliott, preached a creed of Stotanism--"seek suffering."

Confidence grows if we overcome our tired bodies, running harder when we want to slow down. With confidence comes character and strength of body, will, and soul. No man becomes a champion without training hard; one of the reasons there are so few champions is that when the going is tough the weaker men drop out.

Haikkola, in training Lasse Viren, felt that schedules were made to be followed:

The schedule is cut into months, then weeks, and finally days. This kind of farsightedness makes sense. It eliminates drastic changes in the schedules. "This is too hard; this is too easy"--that is something Lasse has never had to tell me. And best of all, Lasse always carries out the plans. It is not his habit to change his mind...The amount and load of training must not be compromised. It is essential to follow the plans exactly. Changes make an athlete uncertain.

In Jim Ryun's story, (Nelson, 1967, 72) coach Timmons recalled:

Jim worked for six weeks to do one thing--to learn to sprint when he was tired. The poor guy had a mean old coach who would get him out and work him until he was exhausted, and then say, "Okay, Jim, we're going to do a little work now. You're going to sprint... I've a surprise for you. Im going to open the gates and let you run a little outside." He pointed up Campanile Hill, rising at a 25 degree angle for 230 yards from the stadium. "Run up there and back four times." Wearily, Jim looked up the hill, then back at Timmons. "You'd better call your wife," he said, "and tell her we'll be home for dinner at 8:30 instead of 7:30 as you told her."

The meaning of hard work is always relative. It is just as hard work for Joe Public to jog one mile as for Jim Ryun to jog ten. As long as the increments of hard work and denial are gained gradually, there is relatively little awareness of pain or self-sacrifice. J. W. Alford explained this very well in his comments on the training of Zatopek:

I am reminded of the early rather inaccurate accounts of Zatopek's training, and the awe that was felt for the gruelling work we were led to believe he undertook. Zatopek did, of course, train very hard, and nobody is going to become a champion at the distance runs without a great deal of hard work. But his training was not so 'inhuman' and 'man-killing' as many still believe. It was a build-up, and the intensity of the training increased only as he felt himself ready for it.

Ron Clarke worked "hard." At least, over a period of 15 years he averaged 100 miles or more per week for 52 weeks a year, along with his duties as a family man with three children, and as a successful accountant. Still, he wrote (1966, 22)

There is no sacrifice in it. I lead what I regard as a normal life. . . . In my family physical fitness has always been regarded as important. . . . In my case I thoroughly enjoy running 100-odd miles a week. If I didn't I wouldn't do it.

HURT-PAIN-AGONY

In recent years there has been growing acceptance of the hurt-pain-agony approach to training and competitive efforts. Unless you're willing to pay the price at the highest levels of discomfort from fatigue and all-out effort, you're not likely to reach the top in sports. Swimming seems to have adopted this as an essential tenet. For example, Counsilman (1968, 337) states

We try to build pride in the ability of the swimmers to push themselves hard in this manner (the agony phase of exertion) when it is requested of them....Social pressure is thus imposed on him to produce in practice or be ostracized.

By making it an everyday experience, shared by all members of the team, the aversion to suffering tends to subside. Sure it hurts; it hurts all of us, but so what? The more men talk about agony in an unemotional way, the more it takes on the connotation of acceptable discomfort. Men develop mental as well as physical callouses to pain.

Murray Halberg relates that when he first started training with Lydiard, he would always feel sick after a few miles. So he'd throw up and keep on running. As matter of fact as that. Similarly, Snell (1965, 31) writes that at his first workout at Rome where he won his first Olympic championship, Lydiard had scheduled six 300s. After the fifth,

I tottered to Arthur and said, 'Arthur, if I do another, I'll vomit.' I was rather staggered when Arthur replied crisply that I should still do it and that I would probably be all the better if I did vomit....Obediently, I did as he said--and just made it to the dressing room in time to heave out the contents of my stomach.

The late Professor Bykov reported to the Montreal Physiological Congress that the skin can be made to react to hot water (62C) as it normally does to warm water (42 C) if, after a period of conditioning to the feeling of "warm," the subject is told the water is warm when it is really hot. Words and the meanings that are given to them can change body chemistry, circulation of the blood, modify reactions to physical or mental stress. We have reason to believe that the psychological limits which often keep performance below physiological limits are due to inhibitions implanted by endless cultural influences--the printed and spoken word, warnings and attitudes given by parents, teachers, peers--often early in life. One of the major goals of coaching is to remove those inhibitions.

There is an all-important reservation to these views: that of individual differences in sensitivity to such hurt-pain-agony. For example, as related to skin pain receptors, Roger J. Williams[1] examined the hands of 21 "normal" persons. On one hand, a given area evidenced 25 spots that the subject described as "insensitive to pain," and none, "highly sensitive to pain." In contrast, another subject responded that in this same area only one spot was "insensitive to pain," whereas 19 spots were "highly sensitive to pain." Obviously the results of such a test would be influenced by psychic as well as physical differences. But other observations led Williams to the conclusion that pain spots on people's bodies "are widely unequal in number and are distributed differently in individual people."

True, the pain of a pin-prick is not at all the same as the pain of anaerobic effort in running. But such research leads us to assume that the general pattern of individual differences would be similar. We coaches should be aware that Stotanism is a two-edged sword. One edge can cut away the inhibitions against pain. But the other can cut through the very tenuous threads by which beginners and more sensitive athletes are attached to running. It could cause them to quit running altogether, or even to avoid turning out for it at all. Great prospects for running are sometimes very sensitive--sensitive to pain and stress. A dozen world-level runners come to mind who were far from being Stotans. A tough coach would have lost them before they had a chance to get started. Without gradual adaptation to its meaning, agony is something to shudder over and certainly to avoid. The "joy of suffering" may be sought by ascetic saints or masochists, but not by the average boy. The coach who promotes it as a basic tenet of his training is likely to be held suspect.

SUSTAINED FINISHING SPEED. Up to this point, the problem of training for anaerobic endurance has been discussed as if it were related only to the processes of circulation and

---

[1]Roger J. Williams, *BIOCHEMICAL INDIVIDUALITY*, New York: John Wiley & Sons, Inc. 1956, p. 38.

respiration. But read the biographies of great distance racers and you will be made aware of how closely anaerobic endurance is intertwined with the power to run fast near the end of a long race. Keino, who always considered himself a 5000-meter runner because of his inability to match the speeds of men like Jim Ryun or Michel Jazy, ended up as Olympic champion, 1968, at 1500 meters by means of his sustained finishing speed.

I emphasize the phrase, "sustained finishing speed." Races are won by taking the lead at the right instant and being able to sustain that lead to the finish line. That may involve a desperate gamble of ten yards. But few men can wait so long; most try for the lead over a longer, surer distance--200-400-800--even 1200 meters.

In the Olympic 1500 at Montreal, John Walker (NZ) took the lead with 300m to go. He sprinted the backstretch 100 in 12.5; the curve in an incredible 12.2; the final 100 in 13.2. The sustained finishing drive was at least 300 meters, but it was his speed on the last curve that ensured his victory.

In the Munich 1500, the crucial kick came later. Keino (Kenya) had run a fast third lap (55.3 as compared with 61.3 for the second lap). Vasala (Fin) stayed on his shoulder with Boit (Kenya) and Dixon (NZ) close behind. Only on the homestretch was Vasala able to sprint past Keino to the finish line. In the Rome 5000m, Murray Halberg (NZ) broke contact with three laps (1200m) to go by sprinting a shocking 61.1 lap.

In summary, each race is different, depending on the relative finishing drives of oneself and one's competitors. A "sustained finishing drive" can be defined two ways: (1) begin the final drive as early as possible without losing the lead at the finish, or (2) begin the finish drive as late as one can be certain of reaching the finish line first. Training should be specific to each individual and to each race.

ENDURANCE TRAINING AND MUSCLE-FIBER TYPES

Experiments by Costill (1979, 16) suggest that slower-paced endurance running impairs leg speed and power. This follows the basic principle underlying all training that muscle development corresponds to the kind and amount of stress the muscles incur. But in recent years research has disclosed just how such speed impairment takes place.

Muscles are composed of fibers, the number of which remains relatively unchanged throughout life regardless of training. Such fibers can be classified into two types--fast twitch (FT) fibers that relate to speed and power, and slow twitch (ST) fibers that relate to endurance. The number of fibers of each kind also remains relatively unchanged throughout life regardless of training--a fact that leads Costill to believe "it may be possible to identify individuals with endurance potential early in life. Fast-twitch fibers possess fast, more powerful contractile properties; slow-twitch are slower, more prolonged, and less susceptible to fatigue.

The muscles of individuals differ in the percentage of FT as compared with ST fibers. "Recent studies of top-flight U.S. distance runners revealed that some had greater than 90 percent of their gastrocnemius muscle composed of ST fibers (Costill, 1979, 27). In contrast the leg muscles of world-class sprinters are mainly of FT fibers.

Though the number of fibers of each type remain relatively unchanged, "It is well known that FT fibers begin to take on the endurance characteristics of ST fibers" (Costill, 1979, 28). Consensus is that hypertrophy of ST fibers is one important effect of endurance training.

WEIGHT TRAINING FOR ENDURANCE RUNNING

The tremendous effectiveness of weight training in modern sports has quite naturally led to its use in all phases of sport, even when such phases are largely irrelevant to the uses of strength, that is, to strength as the ability to move a few times against a heavy resistance.

Coaches and others often speak of "strong" runners. For example, even such an astute and experienced worker as Woldemar Gerschler has stated, "The maximum development of strength must favor running performance...running demands strength and therefore a runner needs strength training." Today, for whatever reasons, coaches and runners tend to praise the values of strength training, even to the point of using weightlifting as a way to strength in running.

For example, Robin Sykes[1] of Dublin states that "the importance of sheer all-round physical strength in middle-distance running can never be overemphasized....other things being equal, the stronger man or woman will always win. In that final home stretch of the 800 and 1500 the legs have long since 'gone' and the athlete 'runs' on his arms and shoulders."

What is the real meaning-in-action of such statements. Strength, as developed by weight training, ennables a muscle group to move against heavy resistance once, or not more than a few times. Such increased strength activates muscle fibers not previously functional; it does not increase the capillary bed so essential to endurance. Such strength increases are specific to the actions of their training, to the actions of the clean and jerk, or of the press. These are not at all running actions, neither in the structures involved nor in their function.

Greater sprinting speed, both in the 440 and in the final half-lap or so of a long distance race, can be improved by strengthening the muscle motor units involved in sprinting, but this is done best by sprinting against progressive increments of resistance: by repetitions at faster than racing pace, by gradual increases in sprint speed on straightaways, by endurance runs on varied terrains against resistances--sand beaches, sand dunes, long hill work.

Physiologist De Vries suggests that repeated isotonic contractions, as occur in running, require several groups of motor units for maximum endurance. As one group of muscle-fiber units fatigues, another group takes over the action. As general fatigue increases, each motor unit contributes less force, so that more and more units must be recruited to maintain pace. We can conclude validly that some kind of power-endurance training is indicated. But again, such training should be specific to the desired action, training that develops the capillary beds along with the muscle fibers.

Many champion runners, such as Sebastian Coe, do many repetitions with light weights during the off and early season, but Coe has indicated that this related more to self-preservation during races than to enhanced endurance; unfortunately, elbows in big-time racing are becoming an essential tool to ensure victory.

In summary, we agree with Åstrand's (1979, 81) statement, "When striving for muscle strength for a particular activity, the best training is that activity itself." However, as we have said so many times, it is a man that runs, not a mere body. Whatever raises running morale, whatever helps the runner feel more capable, more fit, more competent to do the job, is of value and, other things being equal, should be done. Thus, some form and degree of power training (not weightlifting) is justified, training that involves light weights and many reps such as often occurs in circuit training. A developing but skinny runner can acquire confidence and greater competitiveness along with larger arm muscles and shirt size.

DEVELOPMENTAL REST PERIODS.

For the purpose of great emphasis, this essential is placed last. There really are only two essentials of all endurance training--work and rest; the second is just as important as the first. Rest is a total-person concept. The athlete must be restored wholly if he is to continue on to higher levels of work.

This principle applies equally to the alternations of stress-days with rest-days, of stress periods with rest periods; and certainly it applies to mental-emotional stress as to physical stress.

The optimal ratio of work to rest is an individual problem solved only by trial-error-success. As running maturity increases, so does one's tolerance of work--within a single workout or in repeated days of high stress. Most non-beginners tolerate two days of hard work followed by a day of active rest. Some work best under alternate days of high stress and rest.

But for all--Olympic champion or beginner--an optimal ratio of stress/recovery is at the core of every sound training program.

---

[1] Robin Sykes, "Strength in Middle-Distance Running," *Track & Field Quarterly Review*, Vol. 83, #3, Fall 1983, p. 35.

Chapter 21
HOW TO ORGANIZE YOUR OWN SYSTEM

In the light of all that has been said here up to this point, how would I proceed if I were given responsibility for a program of distance running in a school or college or club?

START RUNNING
First, beyond all question, I'd begin with myself. Unless I have the feeling and spirit of running, the enthusiasm for running, the personal involvement in running, how could I be a sound coach of others? How would I acquire this? In three ways. First, I'd start jogging twice a week for five minutes - ten - twenty - thirty: then three times a week, then daily. I'd do it on a time and fun basis with no concern for the miles or the training effects. I'd try to find my first fun in the terrain. Wherever I could get away from people, from noise, from cars and trucks; wherever there was good footing, a hill or two, a few trees, a turn of path, there I'd run. If no such terrain was nearby, I'd run on the track week-days: change my pace, mark my distances, find my fun in measuring my progress; then run in the country on week-ends. In other words, I'd prefer a fartlek method, if the terrain made it possible; if not, I'd choose interval training.

A MAN RUNS WITH HIS HEART.   But just to run wouldn't give me enough foundation for sound coaching. I'd want to know more and feel more about distance runners and running. I'd sub-scribe to *Track & Field News*[1] that tells of competition and "how they train," throughout the world and at home--amateur, college, high school. Then, to get the inside story of distance running champions, I'd send to *Track & Field News* for one, then three, then all the biograph-ies listed at the end of this book. These are wonderful stories: true stories of challenge, toughness, heart-break, blisters, but, since they were world-champions, triump and self-realization.

START THE BOYS RUNNING
Distance runners develop primarily by a very simple process--progressive increments of enjoy-able running. They don't need theories and systems and scientifically based essentials of training. Basically, more running = better running. So, before all else, start the boys running.

Where would I get the boys and how should they begin? First, I'd make my cornerstone the fact that all men--some more, some less--are made for running. Throughout a long history of racial development man has had to depend on his own body when he had to get somewhere in a hurry. He had to run, and by running, he acquired a running heart, running muscles, running bones. Running is doing what comes natural; though of course some, by excess weight, may have to find this out very gradually. Running is fun, as long as one runs within one's own capacity today.

For team members I'd start by organizing a time-running group. On a prominent bulletin board, I'd place the names of all those who can jog without walking for a given length of time: 20-minute joggers; 30- or 40- or even 60-minute joggers. I'd appoint leaders who would en-courage beginners and laggards.

---
[1] *Track & Field News*, P.O. Box 296, Los Altos, CA 94022, published monthly.

STUDY TRAINING SYSTEMS

Of course, I'd want to understand all I could about the various training systems. As a starter, this book provides the gist of such systems, but I'd want to go also to the original sources. I'd try to acquire Fred Wilt's book, *RUN RUN RUN*, which summarizes the viewpoints and experiences of coaches and runners from all over the world (unfortunately the book is now out of print). I'd study *A SCIENTIFIC APPROACH TO DISTANCE RUNNING* by David Costill, a simplified but authoritative explanation of the physiology of running, including "training and preparation for competition." But much good material is not in books. I'd subscribe to the various track journals, especially *Track Technique* and the USTCA *Quarterly Review*. Now I'd have a background for making judgments, and a reference for every problem.

ANALYZE AND ORGANIZE THE ESSENTIALS OF TRAINING

It's not enough to know the various training systems. I'd want to understand them. This would come about by analyzing their essentials. What are the key ideas and actions that underlie all systems. The section on essentials in this book is the gist of some 20 years or more of study. Though far from being final or complete, it is a sound starting point. By re-reading and understanding, not their words, but the actions they demand, you can build the skeleton of your own training system. But to that skeleton you must add the flesh and blood of your own unique situation. Flesh and blood don't come cheaply; they demand effort--and time, years of time. You expect your runners to train year-round, five, six, even seven days a week. Do they deserve any less from you?

THE ACTION IS CRUCIAL-- NOT THE NAME OF THE TRAINING SYSTEM. A man develops in running by what he does, not by the potency of the name that is given to what he does. Much as the name may impress the mind, and perhaps give a sense of assurance to the coach, it has absolutely no direct physical influence on the development of the body. Ron Clarke (1966, 158) makes a strong point of this in his chapter "The Secret of Training,"

> *The athlete who thinks for himself and works out his own methods is going to enjoy his sport all the more, as well as being a better athlete.*

> *It follows that no individual type of training for distance racing, be it branded as interval, repetition or fartlek training, has any overwhelming advantage over another. The main essentials are that attention be paid to the athlete's weaknesses; that the training is not so intense that it unnecessarily exhausts; nor so easy as to be of no use; and, above all, that the training is consistent.*

We repeat--don't allow another coach's winning record, or his winning personality, or his winning words to sell you on the merits of his system, then try to adapt your local situation to it. That's like buying a hat because of its appearance or low cost, then trying to re-shape your head to fit its size.

DEVELOP YOUR OWN ECLECTIC TRAINING SYSTEM

An eclectic system is one that analyzes the various training systems and selects from them the best, or the gist of their values, and then adapts those values to the unique situation (terrain, climate, training time available, age level, competitive schedule, and all the rest) that this coach and these boys find themselves in.

Yes, in the next few pages, we could outline what we believe is a sound training system. We do have certain viewpoints on the relative values of the systems and the so-called essentials. But for you to use our viewpoints is comparable to an expectation by your boys that you will do their training for them.

Instead, we suggest that you find your own answers. As a beginning, try answering the following questions in the light of your reading in this book and, hopefully, in the many references we have provided.

1. What is the broad spectrum of motivation that will support my system? Have I included the right proportions of community-institution-team enthusiasm, of work-play, of reward-intrinsic satisfaction, of self-dependence with followership, of hurt-pain-agony with the joy of running, of training-competition, of developmental races-BIG races?

2. Is my system based on the gradual approach to development? Gradual as related to this

year? to 3-4 years at this school? to the athlete's running career?

3. What terrains are available in our situation? How will they determine our training system? Is fartlek feasible?

4. What is meant by an eclectic training system? What are the criteria by which we can select our system? How distinguish between a "quantity" and a "quality" approach to training?

5. What is meant by "periodization of training"? By gradations of cycles? How do they affect outputs of energy?

6. Distinguish between LSD, marathon training, fartlek, interval training and intermittent work.

7. Consider Costill's remark, "We can only judge from current training methods which suggest that only with 5 or 6 training days per week can a runner perform sufficient work to enable him/her to achieve maximal benefits."

8. What is meant by developmental work-rest as two phases of one process? What is a developmental training stimulus? for heart development? for developing aerobic power? for developing anaerobic power? What is meant by "aerobic training is a process of gradually raising the pace at which a steady state can be maintained"?

9. What are the relative demands of the various racing distances for aerobic as compared with anaerobic power?

10. What are the implications of variety for the various aspects of distance running?

11. Discuss: individual variations--physical, biochemical, mental-emotional--make it *impossible* to design a single training system for everyone. Are training systems therefore invalid?

12. How does one peak for major competition?

13. What is the difference between a strong runner and a strong shotputter? Will strength training help develop a distance runner?

14. Why maintain a training diary? for the coach? for the individual runner?

OVERTRAINING. As a final and most important essential in constructing my own system of training, I'd consider CAREFULLY the implications of overtraining in both its physical health aspects and its whole person aspects. Near the end of his important book on a more scientific approach to the problems of endurance running, David Costill (1979, 116) emphasizes the dangers of excessive work--too much too soon:

> *"Overtraining" probably constitutes the greatest single error made in the management of the beginning runner. In light of the high rate of injury, emotional staleness and physical exhaustion which often accompany overtraining, the first principle to remember is to begin training at a very low level, estimated to be well within the runner's capacity. If after the first training sessions the runner develops muscle soreness, the work is too difficult. Should the runner find it impossible to complete the training distance or to maintain the training pace, the total training effort should be reduced. Symptons of overtraining generally include restless sleep, loss of appetite, reduced performance, and elevated resting heart rate. These responses are applicable to runners with varied levels of experience, and generally demand several days to a week of reduced work or complete rest.*

For all runners there is a level of diminishing returns at which increased volume will not produce comparable improvement in performance; in fact, may even have a negative effect. This raises the specter of Hans Selye's research on the limited adaptation energies of animals and men--as a General Stress Syndrome but also as a specific maladjustment of muscles-tendons to overwork.

Most important, a sound training system worthy of its place in an educational institution holds a clear commitment as coach-teacher of these young men and women to running as only one part of their lives--now and in the future, and almost never the most important part.

I am reminded of the implications of Head Olympic Coach Bill Bowerman's refusal to respond to the label, "Coach." In his experience its connotation of using athletes for personal gain, of winning-at-all-costs is unworthy of what he considered to be primarily an opportunity to teach and develop young men and women. That's a distinction that is crucial--crucial in the dictionary meaning of "a final and supreme decision."

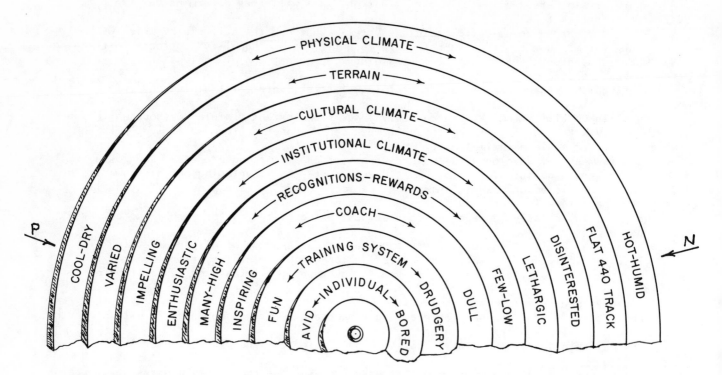

Fig. 21.1--A whole-part-whole approach to training for endurance running. Begin by seeing the chart as a whole; only as the overall system is supportive--point P on chart--can training be judged theoretically maximal. Now analyze the chart as though the disks could be rotated separately. Leave seven disks at point P, but rotate one--for example, terrain--so that the negative or non-supportive portion is at point P. With only a flat 400m track to run on, the entire training system is changed, along with each of the other six factors.

Or to take a different problem, leave the four outer disks at point N (Negative)--a difficult surround in which to train--but rotate the four inner disks--coach, training system, recognitions, individual--to activate their most positive aspects (now drawn at point P). Amazing what those four factors can accomplish, even though the other factors be non-supportive or even detrimental.

Note that the disk marked "individual" is analyzed in terms of only one factor: avid-bored. Actually, individuals differ in many ways--innate speed or endurance, time available for training, reaction to various stress factors, and a hundred more. That's what is meant when we say, "for 20 runners, there must be 20 training systems."

A wise coach will understand and use the fact that his real training system is not merely the running schedule, not merely what the runners' legs and bodies do, but rather is the sum-total of all related factors. This sum-total must be strongly positive if his system is to succeed. Such a wise coach will give as much thoughtful attention to these factors as a whole as is now commonly done for the running alone.

Take ten minutes to review this distance-training section of the OMNIBOOK, especially the Chapter on Training Systems. You will find that all systems seem to require year-round, increasingly stressful running. All systems seem to assume that the WAY to better running is by more running, faster-longer, even twice a day. When first presented in 1968, Mateyev's "Periodization" was largely ignored as being too controlled, too rigorous in its time-demands, a system well-fitted to Communism and State-control of all citizens; not at all a valid method in a non-structured democracy. But this OMNIBOOK 4th edition seems to approve fully such a system.

True, it does approve, but not fully, not without reservations. Whatever statements here and there in the text may be extreme, the overall view of this OMNIBOOK is the Golden Mean, nothing to excess, everything within the restraints of a well-rounded life. Such a Golden Mean is the restraining rule that must guide every sports program in both its competitive and its training aspects.

Periodization? Yes, but as a better method of organizing one's time-energy so as to train optimally for running and also do much more in other even-more-important areas of life--all with no more overall stress and no more need for sleep and rest. Frankly, throughout a 30-year career as coach I was torn many times by self-made and social pressures to coach maximums, all-out, go-for-broke. "If it's worth doing at all, it's worth doing to your utmost." I never succeeded fully in finding a Middle Way, but I tried, even to the point of being fired. It isn't an easy way; much easier to coach as though winning were the only thing--that is, if your skin is calloused and your intelligence is warped.

Puzzled? Welcome! Join the company. Suggestion--turn to Chapter 4 and read again the story of Brutus Hamilton. Then turn to the Dedication of this OMNIBOOK: read again its tribute to those
>   WHO honor the agreements of amateur sportsmen that other life commitments--
>   vocation, studies, service--have first priority; that sports are and should
>   be avocational, and act within the restraints of material rewards, time for
>   preparation and competition, and self-commitment that it requires; but

>   WHO, within those restraints, strive to their utmost to raise performance
>   higher, faster, farther to the highest levels of their potential.

Chapter 22
HINTS FOR COMPETITION IN ENDURANCE RUNNING

Winning a race is usually a problem of stamina and speed, but often, it is also one of careful planning ahead of time and of skillful tactics. The dozen or more biographies of great runners are filled with stories of the hardly perceptible maneuvers by which important races are won or lost. A moment's hesitancy here, a single step to the inside there, a slight miscalculation of the pace or of the degree of acceleration with which the final kick is started--any one of these can nullify all the months of inexorable training.

PLAN AND PREPARE AHEAD OF TIME

The tactical possibilities in endurance running are numerous. As in a game of checkers, for every move there is a countermove; for every attack there is a defense. But as in checkers, such counteractions are as much the product of prior study and careful preparation as they are of inspiration and skill. Weeks and possibly months before a BIG race, a number of questions need to be answered. What men will be in the race? How will each of them run in terms of position? Who will set pace and how fast? How even will the pace be? How and when will the various competitors try to break contact with the field? Finally, what should be my tactics?

The answers to such questions might well affect a runner's training for some weeks or even months prior to the BIG race. For example, Bannister (1955, 225) relates how, three weeks before meeting Landy at Vancouver, he tried to impress Landy with his great finishing speed by deliberately holding back in the British championship mile and then sprinting an amazing :53.8 last quarter, "almost as fast as I can run a flat 440 yards!" Apparently this bit of tactical showmanship reached Landy; at least he ran the first half at Vancouver in 1:57.2--too fast for either runner. At this point Bannister had lost the advantage of contact, but he had planned that this would happen and psychologically he was still "connected." He felt he had forced Landy to run too fast and in the last half held the upper hand. In races, a feeling such as this often makes the whole difference.

In 1984, prior to the final U.S. Olympic trials in the 800, the favorites were James Robinson, a two-time Olympian and seven-time National Champion, and Don Paige, Villanova. Both men were assumed to be on the team by way of their driving finish on the final straightaway.

But their rivals used those facts--the finishing kick and the self-confidence--in their final preparations and planning for the race. Earl Jones, 19, a sophomore at Eastern Michigan University, planned to counter their finishing speed by going all-out all the way. He ran the first 400 in a suicidal 50.2, just ahead of Stanley Redwine and John Gray. Down the backstretch, when everyone expected him to tie up, he kept on driving. First Redwine, then Gray tried to pass.

At 350m, John Marshall of Villanova was fourth, with his "coach," Don Paige a yard back and wide, waiting to take over. Robinson, the sure-thing, was moving up easily. In the stretch, Jones led by two yards with Gray at his elbow. Redwine faded; Paige started to go but the fast pace was too much for him. That left the final Olympic team spot to Marshall and the fast-charging Robinson who had been seven yards back with 100m to go. "I kept expecting them to come back to me," he said afterwards. They never did. Jones broke Rick Wohlhuter's 10-year American record in 1:43.74. Robinson seemed to have squeezed in. The review board took several long minutes reaching their decision. But finally, they placed Marshall on the team; Robinson and Paige were off, largely through Jones' planned tactic and his guts in carrying it out.

Our real point here is not so much the tactic as the well-thought-out planning and pre-

TABLE 22.1

OUTSTANDING PERFORMANCES -- 800m RUN

OLYMPIC CHAMPIONS -- MEN

Date	Record	Name	Affiliation	Time at 400m	Age	Best 440 Time
1932	1:49.8	Tom Hampson	Gt. Britain	55		
1936	1:52.9	John Woodruff	Pittsburgh	57	20	47
1948	1:49.2	Mal Whitfield	Ohio State	54	24	46.2
1952	1:49.2	Mal Whitfield	USA	54.2	28	
1956	1:47.7	Tom Courtney	Fordham	53	23	46.0
1960	1:46.3	Peter Snell	N. Zealand	52	21	
1964	1:45.1	Peter Snell	N. Zealand	52.4	25	
1968	1:44.3	Ralph Doubell	Australia	51.3	23	
1972	1:45.9	Dave Wottle	Bowling Green	53.3	22	
1976	1:43.50	A. Juantorena	Cuba	51.0	25	44.26
1980	1:45.4	Steve Ovett	Gt. Britain	54.5	24	
1984	1:43.0	Joaquim Cruz	Brazil	51.2	21	

OLYMPIC CHAMPIONS -- WOMEN

Date	Record	Name	Affiliation
1960	2:04.3WR	Lyudmila Shevtsova	USSR
1964	2:01.1WR	Ann Packer	Gt. Britain
1968	2:00.9OR	Madeline Manning	U.S.
1972	1:58.6OR	Hildegard Falck	E. Germany
1976	1:54.9WR	T. Kazankina	USSR
1980	1:53.5WR	N. Olizaryenko	USSR
1984	1:57.5	Doina Melinte	Romania

WORLD RECORDS OF SPECIAL INTEREST -- MEN

Date	Record	Name	Affiliation	Time at 400m	Age	Best 440 Time
1932	1:50.0	Ben Eastman	Stanford	52.0		46.4
1936	1:49.7	Glenn Cunningham	Kansas	54.0	27	
1938	1:48.4	Sidney Wooderson	England	52.7	24	
1939	1:46.6	Rudi Harbig	Germany	52.2	26	46.0
1957	1:45.8	Tom Courtney	Fordham	52.2	24	46.0
1962	1:44.3	Peter Snell	N. Zealand	51.0	23	
1966	1:44.8	Jim Ryun	Kansas	53.3	19	
1972	1:44.3	Dave Wottle	Bowling Green	52.8	22	
1973	1:43.7	M. Fiasconaro	Italy	51.2	24	45.5
1974	1:43.9	Rick Wohlhuter	U.Chgo.T.C.	51.0	26	
1977	1:43.4	A. Juantorena	Cuba			
1979	1:42.4	Sebastian Coe	Gt. Britain	24.6-26.0-24.8-27		46.8
1981	1:41.73	Sebastian Coe	Gt. Britain			

RECORDS OF SPECIAL INTEREST -- WOMEN

Date	Record	Name	Affiliation	
1983	1:53.28	J. Kratochvilova	CZE	(World record)
1983	1:57.1	Mary Decker	USA	(American record)

HIGH SCHOOL PERFORMANCES -- BOYS

Date	Record	Name	Affiliation	
1981	1:47.31	Pete Richardson	Berkeley, CA	(HS record)
1984	1:51.3	Ted King	Westbury, NY	
1984	1:51.49	Rodney Clarke	Auto, Brooklyn	
1984	1:51.5	Mike Huber	St. Igna., Cleveland	
1984	1:51.5	Mark Sullivan	Scarsdale, NY	

HIGH SCHOOL PERFORMANCES -- WOMEN

Date	Record	Name	Affiliation	
1974	2:02.3	Mary Decker	Orange, CA	
1982	2:00.7	Kim Gallagher	Ft. Wash., PA	(HS record)
1984	2:06.99	Kerri Zaleski	Mill. Long Beach, CA	
1984	2:07.09	Trena Hull	Compton, CA	
1984	2:07.9	Shelly McBride	CM, Crete, Ill.	

paration that was made for it. In the 1960 Olympic Games, Herb Elliott won the 1500 meters. Perhaps he was the best man in the field and would have won whatever the tactic. But the fact is he won by an astonishing 20 yards in world record time by use of this tactic as told by Cordner Nelson (1970, 137),

> At 800 meters he was a close fourth behind Bernard's 1:57.8. He had wanted to make his break here, but now he felt too tired. Only his long practice at punishing himself enabled him to try. They had been averaging 14.7 seconds for each 100 meters. Suddenly he ran the next 100 in 13.2 seconds and he was ahead of a long line of discouraged runners.

Examples of the crucial importance of planning for tactics in the BIG races are countless. Every championship meeting affords new ones. Just one more--that of Kipchoge Keino against the field and especially Jim Ryun in the Mexico City Olympics, 1968.   Handicapped by a gall bladder infection that caused him to collapse in the 10,000 on Monday of that week, Kipchoge was not at all sure he could complete the 1500 final. As told to us by Noronha (1970, 148), the medical doctor recommended that he not compete,

> Before we could say anything else on the matter, he began to discuss tactics for the big race. We realised that in his present condition he had not the slightest hope of outkicking Jim Ryun at the end of a slow race and we would have to plan for a fast race. . . .

> From the gun, Ben Jipcho (Keino's fellow-countryman) shot away as if his life depended on it. . . . Ben Jipcho continued with unabated pace to reach the half-way mark in 1:53.3. At this point, Kip sprinted wide and took over the lead while Ryun started moving up from last place, obviously preparing for his dramatic final lap sprint. Suddenly, however, the American realized that the gap between him and Keino was widening. Kip was sprinting. He was now 40 yards in the lead and increasing speed. Ryun broke into his famous sprint, . . . but he had left it too late; Kip was far ahead, still going strongly at the tape. . . .

> Keino shared the credit for his convincing and glorious victory with Ben Jipcho, without whose invaluable pace-setting early in the race, it might have been quite a different story.

We have given four examples. In each, the crucial element was not so much that the tactic was clever or shrewd, as that these men had the toughness of spirit to make the tactic work under conditions of high stress. Such toughness isn't inborn; it arises out of repeated practice of just such toughness. Herb Elliott (1961, 169) tells of a practice just prior to the Olympics,

> I then started off from the 1500m. mark and ran the race I wanted to run in the final-- only at half-pace. My concentration was as though I really were in the final. I cruised around for two laps and, with about 700 yards to go, I increased the pace, pretending that I was running at full gait as I wanted to in the race. I practiced passing a couple of blokes and imagined myself swooping to the front. From there I imagined the physical tiredness that would come in the last lap and how I would overcome it. With one lap to go I increased the effort a little more as I hoped to in the race.

We have already read how well he carried out this rehearsal in the Olympic final. But here we are emphasizing the importance of inuring oneself to the agony of effort. Again Elliott (1961, 160) writes, in his diary,

> I ran out at a reasonable pace, and set off back . . . determined to finish really tired and satisfied. I squibbed on it without realizing it and finished too fresh. It annoyed me. I began to think I had lost my capacity to hurt myself. I must be careful and see that I cultivate this capacity again. I mustn't become a sub-conscious squib. I was so annoyed that I did three laps of the Shrine hill to finish off.

Strategic moves are likely to be successful only after everyone, including yourself, is undergoing the pains of fatigue. The difference is that you know what you are doing, have learned how to come to terms with such pains , and thus are able to drive on when the physical energy seems gone. It's as much a mental as a physical effort.

TABLE 22.2
OUTSTANDING PERFORMANCES -- MILE AND 1500m RUNS

OLYMPIC CHAMPIONS -- MEN

Date	Record Mile	1500m	Name	Affiliation	Age	Quarter Times
1936		3:47.8	Jack Lovelock	N. Zealand	26	61.4-64.1-62.0-40.3
1948		3:49.8	H. Eriksson	Sweden		
1952		3:45.2	Josy Barthel	Luxembourg	25	58.2-63.6-61.7-41.7
1956		3:41.2	Ron Delany	Eire	21	60.0-61.4-61.0-38.8
1960		3:35.6	Herb Elliott	Australia	22	58.5-59.5-56.0-41.6
1964		3:38.1	Peter Snell	N. Zealand	24	58.3-61.5-58.7-38.6
1968		3:34.8	Kip Keino	Kenya	28	57.0-58.3-58.0-41.6
1972		3:36.3	Pekka Vasala	Finland	24	61.6-60.0-54.8-39.9
1976		3:39.17	John Walker	N. Zealand	24	
1980		3:38.4	Sebastian Coe	Gr. Britain	24	
1984		3:32.53OR	Sebastian Coe	Gr. Britain	28	59.0-58.0-56.3-39.3

OLYMPIC CHAMPIONS -- WOMEN

1972		4:01.4WR	L. Bragina	USSR	(First time contested in OG)	
1976		4:05.5	T. Kazankina	USSR		
1980		3:56.60R	T. Kazankina	USSR		
1984		4:03.25	Gabriella Dorio	Italy	27	66.5-68.3-62.3-46.3

WORLD RECORDS OF SPECIAL INTEREST -- MEN

1933	4:08.7	3:48.8	William Bonthron	Princeton	22	61.2-62.3-65.1-40.2
1934	4:06.8		Glenn Cunningham	Kansas	25	61.8-64.0-61.8-59.2
1937	4:06.4		Sidney Wooderson	England	31	58.6-64.0-64.6-59.4
1944		3:43.0	Gunder Hagg	Sweden		56.7-59.8-61.5-45.0
1945	4:01.4		Gunder Hagg	Sweden	27	56.5-62.7-62.2-60.0
1954	3:59.4		Roger Bannister	Oxford	21	57.5-60.7-62.3-58.9
1954	3:58.0	3:41.8	John Landy	Australia	25	58.5-60.2-58.5-60.8
1958	3:54.5		Herb Elliott	Australia	20	58.2-59.9-60.9-55.5
1964	3:54.1		Peter Snell	N. Zealand	24	56.2-57.8-60.0-60.1
1967	3:51.1	3:33.1	Jim Ryun	Kansas	20	59.0-59.9-58.5-53.7
1974		3:32.2	Filbert Bayi	Tanzania	21	54.9-57.3-58.0-41.4
1975	3:49.4		John Walker	N. Zealand	23	55.9-59.2-57.0-57.3
1979		3:32.1	Sebastian Coe	Gt. Britain	22	
1979	3:49.0		Sebastian Coe	Gt. Britain	22	57.5-57.0-57.5-57.0
1980	3:48.8		Steve Ovett	Gr. Britain	25	56.0-57.5-57.5-57.8
1983		3:30.77	Steve Ovett	Gt. Britain	28	54.3-57.5-57.4-41.6

RECORDS OF SPECIAL INTEREST -- WOMEN

1980		3:52.47	T. Kazankina	USSR	(World record, 1984)
1983		3:57.12	Mary Decker	USA	(American record, 1984)
1982		4:05.88	Leann Warren	Oregon	(Collegiate record, 1984)

HIGH SCHOOL PERFORMANCES -- BOYS

1964		3:39.0	Jim Ryun	East, Wichita	(HS record, 1984)
1984		3:53.2	Roman Gomez	Belmont, LA	
1984		3:53.4	Steve Schadler	Bergenfield, NJ	
1984		3:54.1	Tracy Garrison	Klam F, OR	

HIGH PERFORMANCES -- GIRLS

1982		4:16.6	Kim Gallagher	Ft. Wash., PA	(HS record, 1984)
1984		4:26.0	Kelly Madden	SC, Roslind, MD	
1984		4:28.6	Chris Curtin	Mep, Belim, NY	
1984		4:29.9	Shola Lynch	Hunter, NYC	

TACTICS CAN BE SELF-DEFEATING. We must distinguish between the strategy that develops out of a calm and reasoned assessment of the situation, and that which grows out of desperation and uncertainty. Hamlet would have made a poor distance runner. In contrast, a great one, Herb Elliott, (1961, 52) writes,

[Fleming] was trying to anticipate everything that was going to happen in the mile, so that he could devise a counter. I told him that it was no wonder he vomited before most of his races; he was wasting all his nervous energy thinking about them. . . . Your mind is in such a jumble that it won't give your body a chance.

As to his own attitude toward tactics, Elliott (1961, 145) adds,

I rarely go into a race with any preconceived tactics. If I do, it means I'm not parti- cularly hopeful of my chances. Athletes who resort to tactics have no real confidence in themselves and lose as many races as they win. Dr. Roger Bannister apparently didn't train too well and needed tactics, as did Chris Chataway. If tactics are going to be used, they are best determined after the race starts, because no one can be sure how a race will be run. . . . The only tactics I admire are those of do-or-die.

Well, that's one side of the story, though it would not be difficult to refute Elliott's contention, even from among his own races. His point of a decisive determination to win in any event is well taken, however.

BE OPTIMISTIC BUT REALISTIC IN PLANNING. Of the six or more men in any race, only one can win. You know that's true. Come to terms with it as a fact. You can't always win. Planning always to win is unintelligent, blind, foolish. Plan to do even a little better than you and others think you can but plan in terms of the realities of the situation. Then execute that plan with fortitude. A win-or-nothing attitude often ends up with very, very little, and breaks a man's spirit for future races.

KEEP YOUR OPTIONS OPEN. One hardly needs to quote Robert Burns to remind you that the best laid plans of men, as of mice, often go awry. So--make your plans carefully and harden your- self to them, BUT keep your mind and your options open. Thus Bruce Tulloh (1968, 110) tells of his planning for the 1962 European Championship 5000 meters, with 11 outstanding runners including Bolotnikov of Russia, Zimny of Poland, and Bernard of France,

My plans were therefore as follows: (1) If Bolotnikov set a fast pace I would just try to hang on. (2) If Bolotnikov did not get away I would have to watch the others for a break. (3) If no one did anything decisive, then I would go myself in the last 800 meters, as I did not want to risk all in a last lap sprint.

As it turned out, the third plan worked without the front running expected of Bolotnikov, and nobody else seemed to have much idea as to what to do. I took off on the back straight of the 11th lap and . . . won easily from Zimny and Bolotnikov.

WHEN SHALL I TAKE THE LEAD? Often it is said that there are two kinds of runners--pace setters and those that sprint from behind at the finish. But this avoids the question as to just when the latter sprint from behind--during the last 100 yards? 300 yards? 600 yards? 1000 yards? In general, with certain exceptions, once a man has taken the lead, he should maintain that lead to the finish. The question then becomes "what is the least distance at which I can take the lead and hold it?" For Ron Delany in the Melbourne 1500 meters, the last 150 meters was the crucial distance. For Herb Elliott in the Rome 1500, he felt he could hold the lead for the last 600 meters, and did so. For Kipchoge Keino in the Mexico City 1500, if we except his pace-setting teammate, Ben Jipcho, he held the lead all the way. Any lesser dis- tance would have given Jim Ryun the encouragement he needed. In this sense, there is but one basic question, "when shall I take the lead?"

STRATEGY SHOULD BE RELATIVE. The chosen tactics for any given race must depend on your own capabilities in stamina, toughness of will, and sprinting speed as related to these same quali- ties in your opponents. You might well be a front runner in this race, a sprinter from behind in the next. This of course means that "knowing your opponents" is almost as important as "knowing yourself."

TABLE 22.3

LONG DISTANCE RUNNING

OLYMPIC CHAMPIONS -- 5000m -- 10,000m RUNS -- MEN

Date	4000m	10,000m	Name	Affiliation	Age
1920		31:45.8	Paavo Nurmi	Finland	26
1924	14:31.2		Paavo Nurmi	Finland	30
1924		30:23.2	V. J. Ritola	Finland	
1928	14:38.0		V. J. Ritola	Finland	
1928		30:18.8	Paavo Nurmi	Finland	34
1932	14:30.0		L. A. Lehtinen	Finland	
1932		30:11.4	J. Kusocinski	Poland	
1936	14:22.2		G. Hockert	Finland	
1936		30:15.4	I. Salminen	Finland	
1948	14:17.6		Gaston Reiff	Belgium	27
1948		29:59.6	Emil Zatopek	CSSR	26
1952	14:06.6	29:17.0	Emil Zatopek	CSSR	30
1956	13:39.6	28:45.6	Vladimir Kuts	USSR	29
1960	13:43.4		Murray Halberg	N. Zealand	27
1960		28:32.2	V. Bolotnikov	USSR	30
1964	13:48.8		Bob Schul	USA	27
1964		28:24.4	Billy Mills	USA	26
1968	14:05.0		M. Gammoudi	Tunisia	30
1968		29:27.4	Naftali Temu	Kenya	23
1972	13:26.4	27:38.4	Lasse Viren	Finland	23
1976	13:24.76	27.40.38	Lasse Viren	Finland	27
1980	13:21.0	27:42.7	Miruts Yifter	Ethiopia	33
1984	13:05.59		Said Aouita	Morocco	24
1984		27.47.54	Alberto Cova	Italy	26

OLYMPIC CHAMPIONS -- WOMEN   (3000m)

1984	8:35.96	Maricica Puica	Romania (First time run OG)

WORLD RECORDS OF SPECIAL INTEREST -- MEN

Date	5000m	10,000m	Name	Affiliation
1966	13.16.6		Ron Clarke	Australia
1972	13:13.0		Emile Puttemans	Belgium
1972		27:38.4	Lasse Viren	Finland
1973		27:30.8	Dave Bedford	Gt. Britain
1978	8:13.6		Steve Ovett	Gt. Britain
1978	13:08.4	27:22.4	Henry Rono	Kenya
1982	13:00.42		Dave Moorcroft	Gt. Britain
1982	13:11.93	27:25.61	Alberto Salazar (AW)	(American record, 1984)

RECORDS OF SPECIAL INTEREST -- WOMEN

1982	15:08.26	31:57.58	Mary Decker	USA	(World record, 1984)
1983	15:33.43		Betty Springs,NC St.		(Collegiate record)
1979		32:52.7	Joan Benoit	Bowdoin (Collegiate record)	

HIGH SCHOOL PERFORMANCES -- BOYS

1964	13:44.0		Gerry Lindgren	Rogers, Spokane (HS record, 1984)
1976		28:32.7	Rudy Chapa	Hammond, In. (HS record, 1984)
1969	8:08.0 (3000m)		Steve Prefontaine	Marsh, C Bay, OR (HS record, 1984)

HIGH SCHOOL PERFORMANCES -- GIRLS

1975	9:08.6 (3000m)	Lynn Bjorklund	Los Alamos, NM (HS record, 1984)
1979	16:13.7 (5000m)	Mary Shea	Gibbons, Raleigh, NC, (HS record, 1984)

SELF-ASSURANCE. Once plans are made and supported by related experience in training or competition, there must be belief in their workability. Many a man has fussed and fumed over the possibility of a better plan, and so drained his nervous energy and will-to-win that an effective performance was impossible.

TACTICS WHEN SETTING PACE

EVEN PACE. Physiologically, even pace is considered most economical. On July 7, 1982, Dave Moorcroft of England set an amazing world record for the 5000 of 13:00.42. Later he told of his plans and how they were carried out:

"Four days before the race, I figured out the laps needed to break the World Record and the British Record. 63s all the way for the World so I scrubbed that and worked out 64s for the British. That looked a little more realistic to me.

Approaching the race, I felt my usual before races; panic-stricken, wobbly knees. I was nervous because this was, in effect, my trial for the European Championships.

I expected Henry Rono to run even faster than he had the day before. But the early pace was very slow and I thought, 'This is going to be stupid,' so I went to the front to keep the pace going; really.

I ran what I thought was a steady 63--and it turned out to be a 61. I started to break away on the third lap and I just kept going. In for a penny, in for a pound.

When I got to the bell and it had just turned 12:01, I knew I had the World Record. For the whole of that last lap, although I was shattered, I was savoring the fact I was going to be World Record holder...

[Running from the front] was so totally out of character for me. If anybody thought I would break a record, I would be No. 1 on the list for needing helpers. But I felt good, I felt strong and I enjoyed it. I guess it's an added satisfaction knowing I did it all on my own..... "

Coach John Anderson told writer Neil Allen, "I feel we now have the complete 5000 runner, for the first time in history. David can break away in front, kick off a fast pace or take you from the back. At 29, he is only just approaching his peak with some great years ahead."[1]

However, there is sound research backing for the view that in middle-distance races the pace should be slower than even during the first portion of the race. Sid Robinson explains

From the data on hand we are able to make some very interesting deductions regarding the purely physical aspects of running middle distance races. It is obvious that the runner should pace himself so as to delay until near the end of the race the sudden increase in energy cost of running associated with great fatigue and high lactic acid concentration. If the first part of the race is run too fast the runner may acquire most of his oxygen debt and be forced to run the remainder of the race with a high lactic acid, with his efficiency greatly reduced, and at a much slower pace...

PROGRESSIVE EFFORT. Ordinarily a front runner tries to maintain even pace. But mentally, this should be interpreted, not as shown on a watch, but as indicated by one's muscle and organ sense, by one's feelings of effort. Maintaining even pace is not at all to maintain an even effort. On the contrary, even pace requires a progressive increase of effort, certainly as the stage of steady state is passed and that of anaerobic running is reached.

FASTER THAN EVEN PACE. If the early pace of a race is faster than even pace, the steady state condition of all competitors will have been lost too early, oxygen debts will have built up, and awareness of the discomforts of fatigue will be sharp. Assuming all men are of equal stamina, it will not now be the fastest man that wins the race, but the man who slows down the least. That is, the man who has so inured himself to fatigue, physically and mentally, that he can drive himself forward despite the dragging weights in his muscles and chest.

---

[1]*Track & Field News,* August 1982, p. 7.

BREAKING CONTACT.   The runner who tends to set pace assumes that he cannot match the finishing speed of one or more of his competitors. Therefore, at some point in the race, he must break contact with them. The crucial questions are how and when. The gist of "how" lies in "getting the jump" on the field, either by suddenly sprinting from in front as did Herb Elliott at Rome, or by gradually pouring it on faster and faster until your opponents finally acknowledge your superior stamina and toughness and allow themselves to lose contact (Kipchoge at Mexico City).

Neither method will work unless accompanied by an inexorable determination, a bulldog tenacity to KEEP the lead. It's rather easy to pick up a few yards' lead; it's agonizingly hard to hold and increase that lead. We repeat with emphasis--a lead is something to be tenaciously maintained; that's the reason for taking it. If you don't intend to make the hard struggle to keep the lead, you're better off not taking it at all, assuming of course you plan to win. Sure you're tired, painfully tired. But everyone's at least equally tired; otherwise your tactic of breaking contact would never work at all. The success of your tactic lies in making them believe they are even more tired than they actually are, AND THAT YOU ARE MUCH LESS SO.

We are saying that awareness of fatigue is a prerequisite to success in this tactic, and therefore, as a rule of thumb, the effort should be made at a point least distant from the finish line. The more tired they AND YOU are, the better your chances. From the standpoint of preparation, it follows that it's not your sprinting ability that will assure success so much as your ability to speed up when utterly exhausted. Murray Halberg (1963, 105) had a 12-yard lead in the 5000 at the Rome Olympics,

One lap to go. I looked back. They seemed to be gaining. Already I felt as if I was at the end of my run. My whole body screamed to stop, to lie down. But only for an instant. It was this race or none. The hours and hours I had put into my training flashed through my mind. IT WAS MY DESTINY TO WIN, NOT TO QUIT.

Only 300 metres to go. From somewhere the strength returned to my aching body. Two hundred to go, and I knew I could not be caught. I threw in that last reserve of energy that always seemed to be there. . . . I reached the tape, relaxed completely--and hit the deck.

I am reminded of Herb Elliott's concern that "I had lost the capacity to hurt myself," and so at the end of a dispiriting workout, he forced himself to take three rounds of the heartbreaking Shrine hill to finish off, and so prove his mastery over his body.

THE SIZE OF THE FIELD.   In a large field of runners, the man leading at the end of the first lap has usually gone faster than even pace, and may have paid a high price in energy for his position. Outdoors, such a position has little value, for the long straights allow a man to move up when he wishes. Usually, mature runners stay back for several laps, move up gradually and easily around the middle of the race, then pour it on for the later laps.

Indoors, this latter tactic does not work so well. Crowded conditions and the short straights often require a considerable expenditure of energy and even more frustration as the attempt to move up and into the lead is made. All runners tend to be worried and incautious; in one straight a hard-gained improvement of position may end up in last place again. Under such conditions, having and keeping the lead has definite advantages.

CHANGE OF PACE.   To convince your opponent of your own stamina and determination to win, it is often wise to raise the pace when your lead is challenged. The challenger may feel he is at the end of his rope and must make one last effort; your pickup of pace will ensure his rope's end.

THE STRESS OF LEADING. Many coaches and runners feel that it is more fatiguing to lead than to follow. Certainly breaking the wind requires more physical energy. But the well-trained and mature runner who feels certain he is both physically and mentally more enduring than his opponents, relaxes in front. After all, that's his place; he belongs there. Why run behind men of less stamina than himself. Ron Clarke usually ran that way, won that way, set world's records that way. But sometimes, especially at the shorter distances, the result was less than his intent.

Running in front tends to increase self-awareness, especially of one's feelings of lethargy, and all too often, of the rising tide of doubt. To avoid this, a runner should try to maintain awareness of his rivals, not out of worry, but to know where they are and thus keep one's mind off oneself. Murray Halberg (1963, 105) wrote that after taking the lead at Rome, "I kept looking back. As in Cardiff, I had to know where the others were. I wasn't going to be taken by surprise."

In the 1984 Olympic 800 meters, despite a strong field including Olympic champions and world-record holders, Sebastian Coe and Steve Ovett, and strong finishers Earl Jones and Johnny Gray, the ultimate gold medallist, Joaquim Cruz, Brazil, adopted the suicide tactic of leading or near-leading throughout the three qualifying races and the final, with a new Olympic record of 1:43.0, 3rd fastest time in history. This, after running three races within 3 days of 1:45.7, 1:44.8 and 1:43.8. R. L. Quercetani of Track & Field News, (Sept., 1984, p. 16) wrote, "Intermediate times (in the final) aptly tell the story of Cruz's greatness, as he covered the first half in 51.16 and the second in 51.84, just about as close to even-pace wisdom as you can get in this type of super-race." Fellow-competitor Coe said, "The guy is a supreme champion worthy of an Olympic crown. He doesn't think too much or worry about the speed he runs at, which is the sign of a great runner." For such a runner, even in such competition, setting pace is safer and surer.

Fig. 22.1. The 800-meter final at the 1960 Rome Olympic Games--about 150 meters from the tape. Peter Snell, 3rd from left here, was boxed in by Schmidt, but when Waegli, the leader here, moved out on the final straight, Snell came through fast to win in Olympic-record time--1:46.3.

TACTICS WHEN FOLLOWING PACE

As we have written, the key question for the follower, assuming his superior speed-stamina at the finish, is "What is the minimum distance within which I can take the lead and maintain it to the finish?" There is a second question, "How much of a lead can I get?"

Assuming more or less equal abilities, the answer lies in surprising ones' rivals. The sprint should come when they least expect it, they're absorbed in their own fatigue, or perhaps at some point in the curve "Where one should never attempt to pass," or immediately after dropping back from a fake attempt to pass. To move up, drop back, then surge suddenly forward has often gained the yard or two margin of victory.

Another tactic is to lay back, not in second, but in third or fourth position where the leader is not aware of your actions. Keep a half-lane to the outside. Then a fast acceleration will build up speed so that you're well past the leader before he knows what's happening.

BEING BOXED. Every coach and coaching book warns against being boxed in, and yet almost every championship race produces just such a situation, even with very experienced runners. In the Rome 800-meter final, had Waegli of Switzerland, the leader as they came into the final stretch, remained on the pole, Snell, boxed on the inside lane by Schmidt of Germany, would have undoubtedly finished up second or worse (See Figure 20.1). Some times, a man must allow the entire field to go by before he can break to the outside and make his try for the tape. Usually such an effort is too late.

When following, the more flexible position is a half-lane wide from the runner immediately in front of you. As you feel the challenge of a man on your right shoulder, you can now move up ahead of him, or by moving a few inches outward, discourage him from trying; this of course, without interfering with his progress.

EXPLODE INTO THE LEAD. When you have decided to take the lead all the way to the finish line, do it all-out, with as much shock to your opponent as possible. Thus Snell (1965, 53) tells the story of a race against the great West Indies 440 and 880 runner, George Kerr,

> But in Napier, George taught me a sharp lesson in tactics which cost me the race. He used a stratagem which I promptly added to my repertoire and used successfully several times.
>
> I was leading confidently along the back straight, second time around, when George (Kerr) unexpectedly sprinted past with an electrifying burst. He went past with such acceleration that I was partly demoralized. . . . This kind of lightning burst completely, if only momentarily, deflates the runner who is caught by it. Psychologically he is trapped into a feeling of hopelessness by the impression of sheer speed which his opponent's surge gives.

MAINTAINING CONTACT. Contact is as much a mental as a physical concept. A man must be adamant in his determination to never allow his rival(s) to achieve a lead that he cannot overcome. For the inexperienced, contact can be said to be present only when you can reach out and touch your opponent.

Once that distance widens to even four or five feet, it easily increases to four or five yards. Stay close so you can hear his labored breathing, so you can see his worried glances. It helps to keep your mind on him and off yourself; even more, it tends to keep him in doubt.

Actually, contact is a flexible thing that is measured by the toughness and self-control of the man maintaining it. In the 1954 Vancouver Mile, Bannister was 15 yards behind Landy at the half-mile mark. Landy was the world-record holder. Surely one would say that effective contact had been lost. But Bannister had planned it that way. He was prepared for the tough third quarter in which closer contact would have to be gained. As Bannister (1955, 235) tells it,

> I quickened my stride, trying at the same time to keep relaxed. I won back the first yard, then each succeeding yard, until his lead was halved by the time we reached the back straight on the third lap. How I wished I had never allowed him to establish such a lead!
>
> I had now "connected" myself to Landy again, though he was still five yards ahead. . . . I tried to imagine myself attached to him by some invisible cord. With each stride I drew the cord tighter and reduced his lead. . . . I fixed myself to Landy like a shadow.

This was truly an instance in which contact, and victory as well, were affairs of the mind as much as of the body.

PART 4
Coaching Sprints, Hurdles, Relays

In this famous 1967 race, Tommie Smith (right), later to become Olympic 200-meter champion and world record holder, defeated San Jose State teammate Lee Evans, later to become Olympic 400-meter champion and world record holder, at 440 yards in a WR 44.8.

Chapter 23
THE 400-METER DASH

A SUMMARY HISTORY OF METHOD OF RUNNING

When track and field competition began in England in the early 1800s, men were not well trained either in terms of months of training or of intensity. It was obvious to such men that no one could sprint all-out for 440 yards, and that it was therefore a grueling endurance race which should be run with a good deal of speed held in reserve for the finish.

There were very few specialists in running. For example, in 1868, E. J. Colbeck won the English championships in 50.4, after having first taken a second place in the 100-yard dash and a first in the 880 in 2:02, for a new English record. A much more startling example was Lawrence "Lon" Myers, one of the all-time greats of track athletics. Myers held every American record, from the 50-yard dash to the mile. In 1880, he competed in seven races in a single afternoon and won four American championships in the 100, 220, 440 and 880. In 1881, he won the English 440 championship in a best time of 48.6. Unquestionably, Myers was capable of better time than this. He had been timed at 05.5 for 50 yards, 10.0 for 100 yards, and 20.2 for 200 yards, as well as 1:55.5 for the half mile. No times are available for the first 220 of his 48.6 race, a fact which in itself indicates that coaches and athletes were not then conscious of the importance of this knowledge.

However, we do know that in 1886, Wendell Baker, Harvard, set a 440-straightaway record of 47.6 on a track whose "loose upper surface was scraped" specially for the one-man race against time. His 220 was 23.2; the 350, 37.0; the 400, 42.9. That is, he "floated" the third 130 yards in 13.8, and the last 90 yards in a dying 10.6. By the way, he had torn a shoe in an attempt a half-hour earlier to break the 100-yard world record, lost it at 285 yards of the 440, but still "flashed a burst of speed to snap the tape in 47.6."[1]

The first official world's record for the 440 (47.4, 1916) was set by Ted Meredith, Pennsylvania, whose primary association with the 880 (he was the 1912 Olympic 800-meter champion), strongly influenced methods of training and competing in the 440 for several decades. All coaching books printed during this time include the 440 under middle-distance events and training.

However, between about 1920 and 1950, the exclusively American custom of running the first 220 on the straight gradually changed the event to an endurance sprint. There were no lanes and, since it was a distinct advantage to have the pole position around the curve and lead into the final straight, there was intense competition to be first at the 220 mark. This led to faster and faster times for the first 220, an increasing handicap for the half-miler type. I remember so well in 1940 how we shifted a fine junior 440 man, Breidenbach (47.0), to the 880 simply because he couldn't stay with the sprinters in National Championship competition. The great victory of Eric Liddell, of Scotland, in the 1924 Olympic 400-meter championships provided a clear example of the trend toward sprinters. Liddell was best known as a 100 and 220 sprinter, having best times of 09.7 and 21.4, but when religious scruples led him to refuse to

---

[1]"Wendell Baker--Record Breaker," *The Amateur Athlete*, July 1935, 7.

TABLE 23.1
OUTSTANDING PERFORMANCES -- 400m DASH

OLYMPIC CHAMPIONS -- MEN

Date	Record	Name	Affiliation	Age	Best 220 Time	1st 220 Time	2nd 220 Time
1932	46.2	William Carr	Penna.	23	21.5	21.5	24.7
1936	46.5	Archie Williams	Calif.			21.6	24.5
1948	46.2	Arthur Wint	Jamaica	28	21.9	22.2	24.0
1952	45.9	George Rhoden	Jamaica	25	20.6	22.2	23.7
1956	46.7	Chas. Jenkins	Villanova	22	21.2	22.2	24.5
1960	44.9	Otis Davis	Oregon	28	21.1	21.8	23.1
1964	45.1	Mike Larrabee	Okla.	31	21.0	22.2	22.9
1968	43.86	Lee Evans	San Jose		20.7	21.4	22.4
1972	44.66	Vince Matthews	USA	25			
1976	44.26	A. Juantorena	Cuba	25		21.8	22.5
1980	44.60	Victor Markin	USSR				
1984	44.27	Alonzo Babers	USA	22		21.7	22.6

OLYMPIC CHAMPIONS -- WOMEN

Date	Record	Name	Affiliation	Age	Best 220 Time	1st 220 Time	2nd 220 Time
1964	52.0	Betty Cuthbert	Austria				
1968	52.0	Colette Besson	France				
1972	51.08	M. Zehrt	E. Germany				
1976	49.29WR	Irena Szewinska	Poland				
1980	48.88	Marita Koch	E. Germany				
1984	48.83	Valerie Briscoe-Hooks	USA			23.5	25.4

RECORDS OF SPECIAL INTEREST -- MEN

Date	Record	Name	Affiliation	Age	Best 220 Time	1st 220 Time	2nd 220 Time
1948	45.9	Herb McKenley	Jamaica	26	20.4	21.0	24.9
1950	45.8	George Rhoden	Jamaica	23	20.6	20.9	24.9
1956	45.2	Lou Jones	Manhattan	25	20.9	21.3	23.9
1960	44.9	Carl Kaufmann	Germany	24	20.9	21.8	23.1
1967	44.5	Tommie Smith	San Jose	23	20.0	21.7	22.8
1968	43.8	Lee Evans	San Jose	21	20.7	21.4	22.4

RECORDS OF SPECIAL INTEREST -- WOMEN

Date	Record	Name	Affiliation				
1983	47.99	J. Kratochvilova	CZE	(World record)			
1982	48.16	Marita Koch	E. Germany				
1983	48.59	Tatiana Kocembova	CZE				
1984	48.83	Valerie Briscoe-Hooks	USA	(American record)			

HIGH SCHOOL PERFORMANCES -- BOYS

Date	Record	Name	Affiliation				
1982	44.69	Darrell Robinson	Wilson, Tacoma	(HS record)			
1984	45.66	Roddie Haley	Texarkana, TX				
1984	45.82	Henry Thomas	Hawthorne, CA				
1984	45.94	Kevin Robinzine	Everman, TX				

HIGH SCHOOL PERFORMANCES -- GIRLS

Date	Record	Name	Affiliation
1982	50.87	Denean Howard	Kenn, G. Hills, CA
1984	52.32	Chewuakii Knighten	Locke, LA
1984	53.20	Paulette Blalock	Compton, CA
1984	53.78	Linetta Wilson	Muir, Pasadena, CA

run the 100 trials on Sunday, he shifted his efforts to the 400. With almost no experience in the event, he sprinted all-out to a clear lead at the 200 post in 22.2, and ripped through the tape in 47.6 for a new Olympic record.

So two schools of coaching engaged in many an argument--the middle-distance group versus the sprint group. But it was often a confused argument. It was the sprinters that had speeded up times for the first 220, and yet logically, the 880 men should set a fast pace and run the sprint out of the less-well-trained dashmen.

The issue was well joined in 1932 through a series of duals in the ICAAAA and the Olympic Championships between Ben Eastman, Stanford, who had recently set a world-record 1:50.9 for the 880, and Bill Carr, Pennsylvania, a place-winner in the sprints and anchor man on Penn's sprint and mile relays. In a special record attempt at Palo Alto, Eastman had recently cut the world 440 record (two turns) down to 46.4.

Most American coaches, including Templeton, Eastman's tough-minded coach, believed that the half-miler should set a pace fast enough to kill off the sprinter. Apparently this was Eastman's plan for, though his best unofficial time for the 200m was 21.6, he ran 21.4 in the Olympic race, a "mad" pace for 1932 racing. (As a matter of interest, Lee Evans ran 21.4 on his way to a world-record 43.8 in 1968.) But Carr stayed right on Eastman's heels, was able to run faster down the finish stretch, and so to win. Perhaps the 440 was a race for sprinters, after all. Though a few die-hards argued that Templeton had used bad judgment in coaching his boy to set a 21.4-24.9 pace. If the pace had been slower, the half-miler would have won.

Both this judgment and the close relationship between the 440 and 880 was strongly supported some seven years later when Rudi Harbig of Germany shocked everyone by setting new world's records for the 400 meters (46.0) and 800 meters (1:46.6) within a period of three weeks. His splits for the 400m were 22.1--23.9, with a time difference of only 1.8 seconds as compared with Carr's 3.2 seconds. Harbig's best recorded time for the 200m curve was 21.6, so that he was running within 5/10th second of his best effort.

One of the greatest trios of all time, Herb McKenley, Arthur Wint, and George Rhoden, were all natives of the little island of Jamaica with a population of only 1 1/3 million people. McKenley first attracted world attention by running 46.2 for the 440 in May, 1946, a new world's record. The race started on the 220 straightaway and I, clocking the 220 times very carefully, was amazed to see 20.9 on my watch. Two weeks earlier, McKenley had made his best personal record for the 220 of 20.6, so that, like Harbig, he had run within 3/10th second of his maximum speed. Two years later, 1948, McKenley again ran 20.9 on the way to a new world record-- 46.0.

The 1952 Olympic final between Rhoden, McKenley, Wint, Whitfield, Matson of San Francisco, and Haas of Germany showed a different pattern. Following the general background as here related, one would have expected a blistering pace during the early stages of the race. However, Rhoden (22.2), McKenley (22.7), and Whitfield (22.9) were content to let 31-year old Wint set the pace at 21.7. This was the slowest pace ever run by either McKenley or Rhoden. But Rhoden, by pouring it on during the third 110 yards, and McKenley by a tremendous spurt in the final straight, were able to come within 1/10 second of the best ever recorded, each with 45.9. Wint, the 1948 winner at London, was 5th in 47 flat. He said later that his 21.7 was 2/10 faster than he had ever run for 200 meters, and that he had made a great mistake in going out so fast.

The 1956 Olympic 400-meter final at Melbourne included Lou Jones of Manhattan, who had run 21.3 when he established his world record of 45.2 early that year, Karl Haas of Germany (best 400m--46.5, best 200m--20.7), A. Ignatyev of the USSR (best 400m--46.5, best 200m--20.7), Mal Spence of South Africa (best 400m--46.6), Voitto Hellsten of Finland (best 400m--46.5, best 200m--21.1) and Villanova junior, Charles Jenkins (best 400m--46.1 in winning the final Olympic tryout). The experts picked Lou Jones as a clear favorite; Jenkins as a possible place-winner.

In August, 1956, D. H. Potts,[1] an astute observer, wrote the following:

---

[1] D. H. Potts, *Track and Field News*, August 1956, 7.

I disagree with those who claim that Lou Jones has re-established the McKenley theory (1948) of how to run the 440. The secret of Jones' success is not running that first furlong at practically top speed as did Hustlin' Herb in the late 40s. What Lou has done is solve the problem of running his own race; that is to say, how to dole out his reserves so as to deplete them at the precise instant of finishing.

But in the Olympic final, Jones led by two meters at 200 meters in 21.8, with Spence and Ignatyev two meters back, held his lead by one meter at 300 meters (33.4), then slowed down rapidly to an inglorious fifth place (48.1). Ignatyev held the lead for a few meters, but Jenkins, strong and relaxed, soon took over and went on to win by a full meter in 46.7 (22.2--24.5, time difference--2.3 seconds).

Potts wrote in the December, 1956, issue of *Track and Field News,*

Afterwards Jones said he had no excuses. He felt he was physically in condition. . . . He said his defeat was due to the unexpected psychological shock of coming off the turn with Ignatyev practically even with him. He had run the first 300 meters hard and expected to emerge with at least a three or four meter lead. He was so unprepared for the possible failure of this strategy that he actually froze mentally. . . . Jenkins attributed his somewhat unexpected win to his coach's last letter, admonishing him to run relaxed, and to his Olympic roommate, Andy Stanfield, who kept him from getting nervous. Jenkins said he followed instructions and ran the first 300 relaxed. . . . I felt very strong after my semi-final, and I was confident I had a chance.

The 400-meter final at Rome, 1960, produced a photo-finish between Otis Davis, U.S.A. and Oregon, and Karl Kauffmann of Germany. Both men were credited with "a fantastic world record of 44.9!" Both men had identical 200-meter splits (21.8--23.1). The difference between them, and the key to success in the race, lay in their 300 meter time. Usually Davis started his finish as he came out of the final curve, but on this occasion he started earlier than ever before and thus picked up a full three meters at 300 meters (32.9) over Kauffmann (33.3). Kauffmann was gaining on Davis all the way to the tape but failed by two inches to catch him. Davis (lane 3) had men ahead of him at 200 meters and therefore a guide for his efforts. He was in front from about 290 meters to the finish. Kauffmann (lane 1) had Davis ahead of him all the way.

Four years later, at Tokyo, the 200 meters was 2/10th faster (21.6), and the race was won in quite different fashion. Syd DeRoner,[1] of *Track & Field News,* tells it this way:

Larrabee (the winner--45.1) had three of his top opponents on his outside with only Badenski of the contenders for the gold medal behind him in lane 2. Larrabee was off slowly and at the 200 meter mark was 6th. . . . Mottley, in 21.6 had a slight lead over Badenski, Williams, and Brightwell in that order. Larrabee started to move going into the turn but he caught only one man, Skinner, in the turn. Coming off the turn at the head of the straightaway it was Mottley, Badenski, Brightwell, Williams and Larrabee. Larrabee . . . was about 4 meters behind the leader, Mottley, as they started the final 100 meters. . . . Finally about 10 meters from the tape he caught Mottley and won going away in 45.1.

Cordner Nelson[2] tells the story of tactics at Mexico City, 1968:

Before 1968, 15 men had run under 45.5; at Mexico City it happened 18 times. . . . Personal records fell to at least 25 men. . . .

Evans ran hard from the start. He usually follows and comes from behind in the homestretch, but he was in lane six with nobody to follow and he knew he would have to hurry

---

[1]Syd DeRoner, "Larrabee Wins in Stretch," *Track & Field News,* October/November 1964, 7.

[2]Cordner Nelson, "Evans 43.8 Stops James," *Track & Field News,* October/November 1968, 10.

to beat James. He made up the stagger on both Badenski and Omolo before the final turn.

"Art Simburg and Bud Winter helped me with my strategy," Lee said later. "The most important aspect was to run the first 100 hard, which I've never done before. In the back stretch I did my 'Winnipeg tip,'" which he explained was a tactic he learned from Vince Matthews at last year's Pan-Am Games. "Vince runs a great backstretch effortlessly, but faster than anyone. I tried to run as fast as possible while staying relaxed."

His third 100-meters was the key, Evans said, "I took out my aggressions against the US Olympic Committee with a hard turn." Around the turn he tried to relax by picturing Tommie Smith's smooth stride, a sharp contrast with his own struggling lunges. Into the stretch he led by three yards and he seemed to have it won. "Anyone who has seen me run knows I can usually muster a kick after almost any pace," Lee said. But James in lane two ran beautifully down the long stretch. . . . But the tape appeared too soon and Larry's 43.9 was a yard short of winning.

At the 1984 Olympic Games, Bert Cameron, Jamaica, was the favorite in the 400m. He was 1983 World Champion in 45.05 (21.8-23.3). Howard Willman of T&FN described Cameron's Olympic semi-final, 45.10 (22.6-22.5). "At 130m the UTEP grad shot up in the air--a cramp in his left hamstring. He hopped along for some 40m, losing ground, but the cramp miraculously worked its way out....Last at 200m, he blazed the third 100m in 10.8 to be 7th with 100m to go....But Cameron showed a helluva lot of courage. Just 15m from the finish he secured 4th and his place in the final." Cameron said "I didn't even think about stopping. I don't think that way. In the final I will be there; if I have to walk on one leg, I will be there." The final was won by Alonzo Babers, USA in 44.27 (21.7-22.6). Cameron could not run.

HOW TO RUN THE 440
This summary history of the various tactics used in running the 440 suggests at least two approaches to the problem--that of the physiology of efficient running at near-maximum pace, and that of know-how based on actual experience. The latter has many aspects, for each athlete-competition-situation is unique in certain details and each runner must handle a race in his own unique way. In summary, however, (1) a man must have a mental-muscle sense of knowing-feeling pace when running in lanes all the way and there's no one in the outside lanes by which to guide, (2) he must be able on the backstretch to go "faster-looser" even though already sprinting "all-out," and (3) he must be able to maintain control-tenacity-drive down the finishing stretch when there's nothing left to control nor energy with which to drive.

We shall discuss these two approaches in turn.

PHYSIOLOGICAL EFFICIENCY. From a related research standpoint, the work of Franklin Henry,[1] done in 1952, is still valid. Among his many conclusions, the following are relevant:

1. That men generally reached their top speed about 6 seconds after leaving the starting blocks.

2. That "it is physiologically impossible for the runner, after he has reached his peak velocity, to maintain it for more than about 15 or 20 yards."

3. That an earlier study by Sargent showed "that the energy cost of running increases as the 3.8th mathematical power of the speed."

4. That "it can be said with confidence that insofar as the physiological limit is involved in setting records, a steady pace will result in faster time for the 220 and 440 as well as the half, the mile, and the two-mile."

---

[1] Franklin M. Henry, "Research on Sprint Running," *The Athletic Journal*, February 1952, 30.

In 1960, Henry Taylor[1] reviewed related research on "The Oxygen Cost of Maximal Work," and concluded, "These data make it clear that athletes should conserve their anaerobic reserves until late in the contest." The answer to the question of how this can be done most effectively is--consider speed-endurance as a unity; each contributing its part to the whole. The greater one's sprinting speed, the easier one can run at a high-level speed; and the greater one's endurance, the easier and longer one can sustain speed at high levels.

This view is supported by an Estonian study[2] on 400-meter limits,

400 METER LIMITS, by J. Razumovski

Analyses of more than 1500 world-class quarter-milers indicate that basic speed is the most important single factor in 400 meters performances. There is a close correlation between 100 and 400 meter times, showing that a 56.6 second 400 meter clocking requires a 100 meter time not slower than 11.6 seconds. To reach 46.0 seconds one needs a minimum 100-meter speed of 10.6 seconds, while 10.3 seconds is the basic requirement for clocking 45.0 seconds.

Another important component for the 400 meter is a specific endurance. Research has shown that the relationship between aerobic and anaerobic processes in a 50.0 seconds performance is 1:6 and in a 46.0 seconds performance 1:8. In other words, a fast 400 meters is covered by using roughly 90 percent anaerobic energy production and 10 percent aerobic. From the anaerobic energy production 80 percent is made up from lactate processes. The lactate processes, which act unfavorably to fast and powerful muscle contractions, can be delayed when sufficient basic speed reserves are available. Consequently, the correct approach to 400 meter training is to develop muscular power and speed before attention shifts to specific endurance.

EXPERIENTIAL KNOW-HOW. A study of Table 23.1 discloses that in no instance of a world record or Olympic championship in the 440 has the time for the first 220 been slower than or equal to that for the second 220. That is, all such record runs have been in defiance of the findings of research as to economy of pace. The runs that came closest to even time were those by Larrabee (45.1) and Juantorena (44.26) with .7s time difference; Babers (44.27), .9s difference; and Evans (43.86WR), 1.0s difference. Cameron's amazing semi-final 45.10 (22.6-22.5) doesn't count--muscle cramp.

Near-maximum pace. Study of the right-hand column of Table 23.1 shows that all great 440s have been run at a near-maximum pace. Our figures are not entirely valid, for quartermilers do not train for or compete often enough in the 220 to disclose their true maximum for this distance. Note that Arthur Wint ran his 1952 Helsinki race at a faster pace by 2/10th second than he had ever run for the 200-meters alone. But for our purposes, they are acceptably valid.

When Tommie Smith ran 21.7 on the way to a 44.5 440, he was 1.7 seconds over his best time for the 220 of 20 seconds around one curve. This was the slowest relative time for any of the great 440s. In contrast, Lee Evans ran within 6 and 7/10ths of his maximum pace in his greatest 440s, as did Curtis Mills in running 44.7. Smith was primarily a 220 man. Had he trained fully for the 440, and run about 20.9, he might well have hung on for a 22.4 second 220 (a la Evans) and have achieved a 43.3 final time.

In summary, experience in competition suggests that a man can run the first 220 within less than one second of his 220 maximum without slowing down more than about one second in the second 220.

Minimum deceleration. This brings up the problem of sustaining minimum deceleration during the last 220 when lactic acid in the muscles is extremely high and the anaerobic mechanisms are

---

[1] Henry Longstreet Taylor, "Exercise and Metabolism" in *Science and Medicine of Exercise and Sports*, edited by Warren R. Johnson, New York: Harper and Brothers, 1960, 155.

[2] J. Razumovski, "400-Meter Limits," *Track Technique*, #72, June 1978, p. 2308.

much less efficient. It seems that record performers have ignored Taylor's warning that anaerobic reserves should be conserved until late in the race.

The interview between Cordner Nelson and Lee Evans after his 43.8 race at Mexico City is of special significance. (1) Evans had to run the first 110 "hard, which I've never done before." (2) On the backstretch "I tried to run as fast as possible while staying relaxed." (3) Around the turn, he tried to relax, though without slowing down. (4) At the finish, he hung on, again with minimum slow-down. Of course, words are only a simulation of action, but Evans' words suggest a principle of very-close-to-maximum pace throughout with minimum deceleration at the finish.

Such a principle, based on actual experience but somewhat contrary to a sound body of related research, suggests that, if we ignore the competitive phase of racing, pace for the 440 should be based (1) on one's best time for the 220, (2) on sound and solid training for the 440, and (3) on extensive competitive experience by which a man learns how to sustain an all-out relaxed pace (what Winter called "faster-looser") for the full distance. Needless to say, without the latter two factors, pace would have to be much slower.

I am reminded of Dean Cromwell's response to the statement of his outstanding quartermiler, Cliff Bourland, that during his "float" on the backstretch, he dropped his arms and settled down in his striding. "In fact, Mr. Champion, you merely drop your tensions and everything else remains the same." To carry that thought farther, the whole problem of relaxation during maximum effort is one of the most fascinating in all of sport. It's what Alan Watts calls a double-bind action, an artless art in which true relaxation nullifies the very idea of effort or that a problem exists. The most interesting book I know on the subject is Herrigel's *Zen in the Art of Archery*.[1] It may not be track and field but it points the way to greater self-control and greater performance.

SCIENCE AND EXPERIENCE. After decades of disagreement, the conclusions of science and experience are finally being resolved. On the one hand, the maximal sprinting speeds of 400-meter runners is increasing, making it easier to run faster. That is to say, though the first 200m in today's 400m races are faster, they are also slower--relative to the runners' maximal sprinting speeds. On the other hand, as science directs, anaerobic reserves are being conserved by more effective training, specifically related to the demands of the 400-meter distance. When science and experience coincide, human ultimates are being approached.

ORGANIZATION OF PRACTICE FOR THE 440
In terms of pace, the 440-yard race is certainly a sprint event. Training for it must therefore include the usual sprint work--starting practice, short sprints at 50 to 180 yards, and the like. We have therefore placed this chapter just before that on sprinting, and so provided easy access to the methods of practice described there.

But of at least equal import, the aerobic-anaerobic demands of the 440 are just as stressful as for any endurance event. Therefore this chapter follows immediately after those on training for endurance running. Chapter 21 on "How to Organize Your Own Training System" has direct application. Certainly training the year-round has as much validity for the 440 as for the 880 or mile. A modified Lydiard or Fartlek program would be entirely sound during the early months of each year. Variety of terrain, distance, and pace is just as essential for quartermilers as for any distance men.

But the most related of all systems for 440 training is interval training that emphasizes repeated distances of 350 yards and under. The discussions in Chapter 20 on short-distance interval work should be of value.

Over the past 20 years, there has been a tremendous increase in the amount and intensity of

---

[1] Eugen Herrigel, *ZEN IN THE ART OF ARCHERY*, New York: Pantheon Books, Inc., 1953.

work done by quarter-milers. Formerly, they worked out with sprinters, and then finished with a few 220s or several 350s. Today they continue to work with sprinters about two days a week but on the other days they challenge the 880 men as to who can work the hardest. James Elliott, coach of Olympic champion Charlie Jenkins and many other excellent quarter-milers, stated this point very concisely:

> *You have to sell quarter-milers on a program of hard work. The only way they can become great runners is by living track 12 months a year, 24 hours a day. How they live and what they do during that time determines the degree of greatness they achieve....They must be convinced that there is no shortcut to success....During the fall our quarter-milers jog a mile before practice and a mile after. We often run repeat 220s, concentrating on relaxation not speed, hitting them in about 28 seconds....At first they can only do five or six 220s but they build up to where they are able to run 13 or 14 of them.*

During the competitive season, Elliott's men emphasized hard work during the early days of each week. They often ran repeat 660s on Mondays and repeat 300s on Tuesday.

TRAINING FOR THE 400m DASH

A thorough search among related articles and texts ended with the following article by Tim Rademaker[1] as being the most scientifically based and down-to-earth. It assumes the usual college-school schedule of both an indoor and outdoor period of competition. For full understanding it requires a certain knowledge of physiology, but it's more than worth the effort. A few paragraphs have been deleted but, hopefully, without loss of substance.

"The first step in setting up a cardiovascular training program for any athlete is determining and identifying the physiological capabilities that must be developed within the athlete. The most important of these capabilities deals with the appropriate energy systems that provide the runner with ATP (Adenosine Triphosphate), the high energy compound that is necessary for any muscular movement of physical activity. While all three energy systems (the phosphagen system, the lactic acid system and the oxygen system) are continually working to some extent in any activity, for the 400m sprinter it is the phosphagen system and especially the lactic acid system that are the most important.

"The phosphagen system is the chief supplier of ATP during the first 30 seconds of intense exercise. From 30 seconds to approximately two or three minutes, it is the lactic acid system that becomes the primary energy system being used. Therefore, for a 400 sprinter who will take approximately 47.0 to complete the race, both energy systems come into play. Neither system by itself is capable of supplying the total amount of ATP necessary for entire 400 meters.

"However, when the approximately 0.6 mole of ATP that the phosphagen system is capable of supplying is combined with the approximately 1.2 moles of ATP that the lactic acid system is capable of supplying, the total amount equals the 1.8 moles necessary for the performance of a 400m run. Although these figures are close estimates based upon world-class performances, they do point out the fact that both energy systems are necessary and that the lactic acid system is the predominant energy system.

"Not only is the total amount of ATP supplied by the runner important, but so is the rate at which that ATP is supplied. While the phosphagen system is important in meeting the total amount of ATP required by the runner, the oxygen system is important in meeting the necessary rate at which that ATP must be supplied. The result is that both systems combined can supply approximately 2.5 moles of ATP a minute. Since it is estimated that about 2.3 moles of ATP are required per minute in a 400, it becomes obvious that the only way to meet this requirement is by combining the lactic acid and oxygen energy systems. Again, although all of the above figures are estimates based upon world-class runners and performances, it can be assumed that the basic concepts would hold true for a runner capable of running 47.0(2).

"Thus it can be seen that in a 400, all three energy systems are needed. The phosphagen and lactic acid systems provide the necessary total amount of ATP, and the lactic acid and oxygen

---

[1]Tim Rademaker, "Training for the 400 meters," in Jess Jarver, *SPRINTS AND RELAYS*, Los Altos, CA: Tafnews Press, 1983, p. 79-83.

systems provide ATP at the necessary rate. It can also be seen that the lactic acid system is the predominant energy system for the 400 sprinter.

"While energy system specificity is important, there are also other types of training specificities that must be taken into consideration. One of these is exercise-skill specificity. That is, to produce maximum training benefit, the mode of exercise engaged in during training must be similar to the skill that is going to be executed in competition. In other words, while the 400 runner may experience improvements in VO_2 max. and heart rate from such exercises as swimming, cycling or racketball, those gains most likely would not equal the gains that he would accomplish through a running program. The running program is exercise that is specific to his skill (3)....

THE TRAINING PLAN

"With a knowledge of which energy systems, muscle groups and motor patterns must be developed and which exercise skills must be engaged in, one may begin to put together the training plan. Basically, the training plan takes the entire year, divides it up into various "seasons," and proposes specific training workouts for those seasons. Naturally, the training workouts for each portion of the year must be flexible....The training program can be broken down into six separate but not totally distinct seasons. Those seasons are: the early pre-season, the late pre-season, the early competition season, the mid-season, the late competition season and the championship season.

The Early Pre-Season.
"The early pre-season lasts from approximately mid-September to mid-October. This period is devoted to a general conditioning program to improve the over-all fitness of the individual athlete. To accomplish this objective, not only must the athlete lift weights three times a week, but he must also be given a program of aerobic running for five days during the week. Although the oxygen system is not greatly involved in the 400 it is vitally necessary, as pointed out earlier, that it be combined with the lactic acid system for the supplying of ATP at the appropriate rate. In addition to this function, training the oxygen system through aerobic running will also aid in increasing capillary beds throughout the muscle, increasing and strengthening connective tissue in and around the joints, increasing the size and strength of the tendons and increasing the size and strength of the bone.

"As a result, the program for the early pre-season period might be constructed as follows:
Mon.--5km run in 20:00, weight training.
Tues:--sprint drills, 4 x 5 sets of 100m striders with 100m jog recoveries.
Wed:--5km run, weight training.
Thurs:--sprint drills, 4 x 5 sets of 100m striders.
Fri:--5km fartlek, weight training.

The Late Pre-Season.
"Training during this particular season, which lasts from mid-October until early December, must begin to prepare the athlete for the early competition season. As a result, the training will begin to shift more toward the lactic acid system once it is felt that the oxygen system has been sufficiently developed.

"Thus, the training program for the late pre-season would be constructed as follows:
Mon:--5km fartlek in 18:00, weight training.
Tues:--sprint drills, 500 in 70.0 (50.0 recovery), 400 in 56.0 (50.0), 300 in 42.00 (45.0),
      200 in 28.0 (40.0), 100 in 14.0.
Wed:--6 x 150-200 hill sprints up a slight grade.
Thurs:--2 x 220 in 27.0 (60.0), 2 x 220 in 26.0 (60.0), 2 x 220 in 25.0 (60.0), 1 x 220
      in 24.0.
Fri:--5km fartlek in 18min.

"As can be seen, the lactic acid system is being brought more into play at this stage with additional fartlek work as well as some slow repetition work on Tuesday and faster repetition work on Thursday. The oxygen system has not been totally abandoned, since fartlet work, and especially slow interval work, actually stresses the oxygen system more than the lactic acid system. Of course, for the fartlek training this largely depends upon how the sprint portions are attacked.

"Although the pace for specific bouts of work done during these workouts is still well below that needed to run a 47s 400, the pace is quickening compared to the work done in the early pre-season where no specific pace was set other than that for the long aerobic runs. Thus, the lactic acid system is being slightly stressed. The total distance for interval workouts on Tuesday and Thursday is at least three times the competition distance of 400m, while the recovery period is twice the competition distance.

The Early Competition Season.

"The early competition season signifies the start of the indoor track season that begins in mid-January and progresses through early March. By now the training program has, in many areas, been moved inside to a 220-yard track. Therefore, all of the times discussed in workouts on this track are calibrated from 50.0 440 which would be a good performance and probably close to 48.0 or less for 400 on an outdoor track.

"As can be seen in the following workouts, the lactic acid system is coming under increasing stress:
Mon:--sprint drills, 8 x 100y in 11.5 (60.0), weight training.
Tues:--sprint drills, 300m with the last 100 in 12.5 (2:30), 300m with the last 200 in 25.0 (2:30), 300m with the last 100 in 12.5.
Wed:--6 x 30m starts, 5km easy run.
Thurs:--sprint drills, 200 in 27.0 (81.0), 200 in 26.0 (78.0), 200 in 25.0 (85.0), 200 in 24.0 (72.0), 200 in 24.0.
Fri:--warm-up, easy jog.

"All of the training times for workouts in this season are very near race pace for a limited size track at this time of the year. The phosphagen system comes into increased stress during the early competition season with the 100 yard sprints on Monday. As can be seen in the form of negative split training done on Tuesday, the entire competitive distance is not carried out as would normally be the case. This is due to the possible injury from running too many tight curves.

The Mid-Season.

"During mid-season, competition and training again shift to the outdoor track. This season lasts from early March until late April. It is characterized by intense training of the phosphagen and lactic acid systems. All workouts are close to the race pace goal of 47.0, or slightly better.

Mon:--sprint drills, 8 x 150y in 17.7 (60.0), weight training.
Tues:--sprint drills, 400m with the last 100 in 11.8 (2:30), 400 with the last 200 in 23.6 (2:30), 400 with the last 300 in 35.4 (2:30), 400 with the first 300 in 35.4 and last 100 in 14.6.
Wed:--sprint drills, 6 x 400m starts, 3km run.
Thurs:--2 x 200 in 24.0 (2:00), 2 x 200 in 23.5 (4:00), 2 x 200 in 23.0 (6:00).
Fri:--warm-up, easy jog.
Sat:--race.
Sun:--weight training.

"It can be seen that the training program for the mid-season incorporates fast interval training on Monday, negative split training on Tuesday, and repetition training on Thursday. Note that with the negative split training the athlete is still not permitted to complete the full 400 at the race pace goal. The author would rather have the runner ease to the finish line during the last 100 after running an outstanding 300. This would leave the athlete feeling confident that he could have finished the 400 in his desired time if he had tried.

The Late Competition Season.

"This season covers the final few weeks of the regular competition year. Normally this would extend from the last week in April until the middle of May when the conference is held. The goal of training during this time is to provide very intense work of short duration in order to increase the speed of the runner as much as possible.

"Repetition training and sprint training form the basis of the late competition season. These are designed to stress the anaerobic energy systems and to develop speed. It should be pointed out here that the "hard-easy" theory of training is employed, as it is throughout the year, by having an easy sprint day on Monday and an easy distance running day on Wednesday.

"Therefore, a week's workout may be arranged as follows:
Mon:--8 x 100m striders in 11.5 (60.01), easy jog, weight training.
Tues: 6 x 200 in 22.5-23.0 with at least 6:00 recoveries, easy jog.
Wed:--6 x 40m from blocks, 3km run in 13:00.
Thurs:--10 x 100 in 11.6 with full recoveries.
Fri:--warm-up.
Sat:--race.

The Championship Season.

"This particular season concerns those athletes who qualify for national championships. These meets are normally held from the last week in May through mid-June. Thus, the athlete will have approximately three weeks of training before the next important competition. The author feels that once late-season competition ends with the conference championship, the athlete should be run through a mini-phase which incorporates all of the above seasons into that three-week period. Basically, therefore, the first week is mainly aerobic work designed to let the athlete relax mentally and still maintain his conditioning. The second week includes the oxygen system again, but mainly stresses the lactic acid system. The final week, of course, must stress the lactic acid and phosphagen systems. For example:

Mon:--5km run in 20:00, weight training.
Tues:--400 with the last 100 in 11.8 (2:30), 400 with the last 200 in 23.6 (2:30), 400 with
       the last 300 in 35.4 (2:30), 400 with the first 300 in 35.4 and the last 100 in
       14.6 easy jog.
Wed:--sprint drills, 6 x 40m from blocks, 3km run.
Thurs:--sprint drills, 3 x 200 in 23.0 (6:00), easy jog.
Fri:--warm-up.
Sat:--race.

RECOVERIES

"Five areas need to be considered in proper recovery: the phosphagens, O_2-myoglobin stores, muscle glycogen stores, lactic acid removal and activity during rest.

"After short, intense maximal exercise, both the phosphagens needed to resynthesize ATP and O_2-myoglobin must be restored. Myoglobin is a protein in the muscle cell that transports oxygen into the cell and stores it. It is this oxygen that is then used during the first few seconds of exercise to break down ATP for energy. The phosphagens, which are themselves resynthesized through the release of energy during the breakdown of ATP, need 22 seconds to be restored half way to the level at which they are prior to exercise. The half-time for O_2-myoglobin is as fast or faster than the phosphagens because there is no resynthesis necessary. The oxygen taken in during the alactacid debt merely unites with the myoglobin (6).

"However, the restoration of muscle glycogen after short, intense exercise is a different matter. More rest is necessary to significantly replenish the glycogen stores in the muscle cells than was needed in replenishing the phosphagens and the O_2-myoglobin. While significant amounts can be restored within two hours of exercise, it normally takes much longer to completely restore the muscle glycogen. This time, of course, would increase if the exercise were of a prolonged endurance nature.

"One of the reasons for a shorter replenishment time during recovery from intermittent exercise is that the blood glucose levels are not depleted as they are in endurance exercises. Also the muscle glycogen levels themselves are not depleted nearly as much in short duration intense exercise. Muscle glycogen, of course, is the fuel used in the lactic acid and oxygen energy system (7).

"One of the by-products of energy supplied by the lactic acid system is lactic acid itself. If allowed to accumulate to a great degree, it will lead to an increase in the acidity of the blood and eventually cause fatigue. Thus, it must be removed. The half-time for the removal of lactic acid is approximately 15 minutes. This is naturally longer than rest periods allowed during anaerobic training.

"However, during the recovery period between exercise some lactic acid can be removed. This is aided by light exercise during recovery, such as walking. Therefore, light activity should always be engaged during the recovery period. That not all the lactic acid is removed is good from a training standpoint; the body can adjust over a period of time to lowered pH in the blood dur to larger and larger accumulation of lactic acid.

"Thus, the recovery periods used in this cardiovascular endurance program are normally between one and three minutes. This allows the phosphagens and the O_2 myoglobin to be significantly replenished and the heart rate to return near 120 beats per minute. Only during slow interval training is the recovery period less than one minute. This forces the athlete to work aerobically, which is a goal of slow interval training. Only during repeat and sprint interval training is the recovery period extended beyond three minutes. This is done to allow complete recovery, since these training methods emphasize anaerobic endurance and speed respectively.

"The pattern of "hard-easy" workouts also has a purpose. Since 24 hours are needed to restore muscle glycogen, the athlete's body is given this chance when an easy day follows a hard day."

REFERENCES

1. Edward L. Fox, "Sports and the Energy Continuum," *SPORTS PHYSIOLOGY*, Philadelphia: W. B. Saunders Co., 1979, pp. 21-23.
2. Ibid.
3. Ibid, p. 195.
4. Ibid., pp. 195-196.
5. Ibid., p. 197.
6. Edward L. Fox, "The Recovery Process," *SPORT PHYSIOLOGY*, Philadelphia: W. B. Saunders Co., 1979, pp. 55-64.
7. Ibid., pp. 64-70.

1984 Olympic 400 champion Valerie Brisco-Hooks (left) and high school record holder Denean Howard at the 1984 TAC Championships./Photo by Don Gosney.

Villanova's John Marshall edges David Patrick of Tennessee in the 1982 Penn Relays sprint medley relay./Photo by Victor Sailer.

Chapter 24
THE RELAYS

HISTORY OF DEVELOPMENT

Relay racing as a form of sports competition originated entirely in the United States. There were several background activities that might have germinated the idea. For example, there were the relays of horses by which stagecoaches went long distances and the Pony Express, by which news and mail were relayed to distant points in the country. Along more recreational lines, there were the old holiday competitions between firemen's cart-and-hose teams in which the fastest men "raised the alarm" by sprinting to and touching the cart so their teammates could start pulling it. The *Encyclopaedia Britannica*[1] credits the Massachusetts Firemen's "bean-pot" race as having been the model for relay racing:

> *The old method was for the men running the second quarter of the race each to take over a small flag from the first relay men as they arrived, before departing on their own stage of the race, at the end of which they, in turn, handed on their flags to the awaiting runners. The flags however were considered cumbersome, and for a time it was sufficient for the outgoing runner to touch or be touched by his predecessor.*

However, the origin of relay racing as a part of organized track and field athletics is clear, for no one questions that the University of Pennsylvania was the place, and Frank B. Ellis and H. L. Geyelin the "inventors" of the four-man race. Edward R. Bushnell, writing in the 50th- anniversary program of the Pennsylvania Relay Carnival, tells how these two men deliberately searched for something to make track sports draw more contestants and spectators. They conceived group effort as the solution:

> *The first experiment was made in 1893, with two teams of four men, each of whom ran a quarter mile. It worked so well in practice that it was decided to add the event to the spring track program and to invite Princeton to send a team. . . .*

> *The first race was such a success that it was repeated in 1894. . . . By this time the new event had aroused so much interest among coaches, athletes and the public that the Pennsylvania committee resolved to expand the idea and hold an invitation meet the following year with outside schools and colleges invited. Apparently the committee was not sure that a meet devoted entirely to relay racing would satisfy the track fans, because only nine races were scheduled for the first meet and they alternated with the events of the University's annual spring games. . . .*

> *In addition to Pennsylvania and Harvard, the other competing colleges in this first carnival were College of the City of New York vs. New York University, Rutgers vs. Swarthmore, Lafayette vs. Lehigh and Cornell vs. Columbia. The competing schools were Germantown Academy vs. Penn Charter, Cheltenham vs. Haverford, Episcopal vs. Delancey and Central High vs. Central Manual.*

---

[1]*Encyclopaedia Britannica*, 14th Edition, Vol. 19, p. 666.

406

It will be noted that this first carnival included races at all four levels: university, college, academy and preparatory school, and high school. The high schools were slow to organize and enter teams but soon they were sending the largest numbers of competitors. Estimates have been made that over 263,000 athletes competed in the Pennsylvania Relays during its first 91 years, with average numbers in the past ten years exceeding 6,000. In 1984 over 500 high schools entered teams in one or more races.

THE EXPANSION OF RELAYS

The original Penn Relays program was expanded in 1897 to include the 2-mile and 4-mile relays; in 1915, the sprint medley and distance medley relays; in 1922, the 440 and 880 relays, and in 1926, the shuttle-hurdle relay.

From these experiences the relay idea has expanded rapidly in all phases of track and field. In 1910, the Drake relays were instituted by Drake University and the Greater Des Moines, Iowa, Relay Committee. These relays have been a distinctively community venture and, in addition to the competitive program, have made the relay weekend a time of city-wide holiday, pageantry, and hospitality. The program has been similar to that at Pennsylvania with its emphasis on numbers of competitors and on all levels of competition.

EMPHASIS ON NUMBERS. This emphasis has made these two great relay meets entirely unique in the sports world in terms of the soundness and the broadness of their base of competition. In a single afternoon, thousands of athletes compete on the same field and track, although the youngest is still in fifth grade of grammar school and running for the first time in a competitive track meet and the most experienced is several years beyond college and may have one or more world's records to his credit. It is difficult to conceive of an annual event occurring at a single place and time that is a more complete answer to those who accuse modern sports of encouraging only the few and the talented.

Relay meets have increased in number and influence quite consistently during the past 30 years. In 1930, the *National Collegiate Athletic Association Track and Field Guide* listed only four such meets: Pennsylvania, Drake, Kansas, and Ohio State. In 1984, 35 meets were considered large enough to be listed in detail. In addition, about a dozen lesser meets and indoor meets were sponsored by colleges across the country.

SPECTATOR INTEREST. The relay meet with its group competition has also increased spectator interest in track and field. Time schedules have become tight and precisely followed. For example, at the Penn Relays in 1984, 45 relays (4 x 100m) were run during two periods totalling 3 hours (20 HS girls' races on Thurs.; 25 HS boys on Fri.), one race every four minutes. Consider that for each race, 32 competitors, often inexperienced, must be placed in their proper lanes, that eight leadoff men must be started together from staggered lanes, that all results must be recorded, violations reported--all within four minutes!

To add to all this, a so-called "Spectator Period" of three hours duration is scheduled at the end of the Carnival in which the Championship and Invitation events on the track and the field are presented. The spectators love it!

INDOOR RELAYS. During the indoor season, a large number of "Games" or "Invitation Meets" have been organized in large cities throughout the country under the sanction of the National governing body (TAC, The Athletics Congress). These meets are pointed toward spectator interest and feature invitation events in which six or eight champions compete. But they also include a number of relay events for colleges, for clubs, and occasionally for high schools. Often the mile relay for colleges will climax the evening.

RELAYS IN THE OLYMPIC GAMES. Relays have gradually taken a more important role in the track and field portion of the Olympic Games. They were first included in the 1908 London Games with a medley (220-220-400-800). This was dropped in the 1912 Games at Stockholm but two relays were added--a 4 x 100m and a 4 x 400m. Because of its great wealth of sprinters and 440 men, the United States has dominated these relay events. Of the 25 competitions that have been run since 1912, the United States has won 20. But in almost all instances, the competition has been extremely close and exciting. As a matter of interest, the use of relay batons originated in the 1912 Stockholm Games.

ESSENTIALS OF TECHNIQUE IN RELAY RACING

We shall consider two aspects of technique in relay racing--the passing of batons, and the use of personnel, especially as to order of running.

PASSING THE BATON--THE VISUAL PASS. In all relays longer than 4 x 220 the outgoing runner (the receiver) takes primary responsibility for getting the baton by focussing his eyes on it until it is firmly grasped in his hand. This is commonly called the "sight" or "visual" pass (Figure 24.1).

Fig. 24.1 -- An inside (left-handed) sight or visual pass. The receiver focuses his eyes on the baton while at the same time attending to the entire situation which may change at the last instant. As he takes the baton, usually near the center of the zone, he accelerates quickly.

It is assumed that the incoming man will be fatigued from his endurance running, and so not in complete control of his efforts to transfer the baton. He simply does his best to stick the baton up in the air where his teammate can see it and grasp it. The three most common methods of accomplishing this are shown clearly in Figure 24.2

In the visual pass, the skill of getting a sure and effective pass, in terms of gaining time-distance, depends on the judgment of the receiver. There are no set marks on the track as occurs when using the blind pass. The receiver must judge, first, the lane in which he will get the baton (and sometimes the lanes are crowded and crossovers do occur at the last instant). Second, he must judge the speed of the incoming runner, and move out just fast enough to gain as much ground as he can, without running away from his man. Experienced runners are sometimes very adept in this, and can so time their pickup of acceleration at the last instant as to burst away from the field. This is especially important in the mile relay or sprint-medley relay in which incoming speeds are high. Such skilled receivers will often pick up three to five yards on their opponents. Method C in Figure 24.2 is usually used in shorter-faster relays in which the incoming man has good control. It may then become a semi-blind pass in which the receiver can, at the last instant, lose sight of the baton, glance ahead, and so orient himself to the difficulties of making his way through the pack. It has its advantages and its dangers!

PASSING THE BATON--THE BLIND PASS. The blind pass is used in those short-distance relays (440, 880 and sprint medleys) in which victory often depends on maintaining continuous maximum velocity of the baton throughout the exchange. Any deceleration for even a tenth of a second will lose a yard or more, and that may make the crucial difference in the final result.

In the Olympic Games, despite our great success, the precision of U. S. baton passing in the short relays has usually been something short of perfection. Of course, the team members have not practiced together until a few weeks before the Games, but also we've had such confidence in our superior sprinting ability as not to be impressed with the crucial importance of precision in baton-passing technique. A 1970 survey of U. S. college teams in major relay

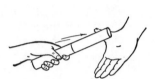

Fig. 24.2. Three accepted methods for the visual pass in longer relays.

meets indicated widely differing methods in all phases--an up-thrust (preferred) or a down-thrust of the baton into the receiving hand, taking the baton with the inside left hand or the outside right, switching the baton from one hand to the other while running, or starting position as related to the passing zone.

In contrast, a study by Dostal[1] of the 16 national teams that made the 1972 Olympic semi-finals showed a definite trend toward one overall method. Not being blessed with great sprinters as in the U. S., and so compelled to minimize time-loss in baton-passing, the national specialists of these countries have studied related techniques very carefully. Dostal's conclusions are therefore of special value. In summary, they were:

1. A strongly predominant use of the upward baton thrust (Figure 24.3).
2. No switching of the baton by a runner from one hand to the other.
3. Runners taking the baton on the curve receive with the inside left hand; those on the straight, with the outside right hand. That is, the baton is carried by successive runners in the right-left-right-left hands.
4. Baton exchange occurs in the last quarter or fifth of the passing zone (50-60 feet), the point of maximum speed for both runners (and the baton!). At the moment of exchange the torsos of the runners are about one meter apart.
5. The second and fourth runners started from a half-crouch position (sometimes called

---

[1]Emil Dostal, "400m Relay Exchange Techniques," *Track Technique*, #57, September 1974, p. 1802.

Fig. 24.3. Blind pass with upward thrust of the baton.

Fig. 24.4. Half-crouch starting position; better if left leg forward.

the Korobkov style after its originator, Gavriel Korobkov, former USSR National Coach), with one hand on the ground, and the inside left leg forward for better balance and support while waiting, and better arm-leg coordination on the first step (Figure 24.4). Some runners crouched with the right leg forward.

6. Some of the third runners also used the Korobkov method--head turned inwards--(and Dostal recommends it) though receiving on the straight and taking with the outside hand.

Practicing technique. As with any skill, perfect baton-exchange technique requires constant practice. The most obvious demonstration of this occurs every four years at the Olympic Games in which (1) the U.S. relay foursomes have only a half-dozen practice sessions prior to the Games--and show it; and (2) the relay teams of other countries are selected months ahead of time, practice baton exchanges thoroughly, with the same four men running in the same order--and show it by gaining ground on each exchange.

A second example occurred in the 1976 NCAA Championships on Franklin Field, Philadelphia, when Tennessee's superior passing brought them the title. Not only had these four men been together at Tennessee for four years, their coach Stan Huntsman had devised a warm-up and practice drill in which the four men, spaced within six feet of each other, circled the track at something less than a slow jog, while passing the baton forward, simulating race methods, then handing it overhead back to the first runner. The thrust-grasp of the baton was precise and crisp each time. Practice!

Fig. 24.5. When passing on a curve, the left-handed pass (outer land) has a definite advantage in visualizing the running situation.

The 20-meter + 10-meter zones. In 1962, the IAAF (International Amateur Athletic Federation) passed a rule which allows a man to take a position anywhere within a 10-meter zone and then run into the 20-meter passing zone as the baton is passed. Primarily this change cut down on the number of teams disqualified for passing outside the zone, but it has also produced faster baton velocities during the exchange.

Just where within the 10-meter zone an outgoing runner will start depends on several factors: (1) The degree of acceleration from the starting mark. Walker advocates a crouched-start

Fig. 24.6. Blind pass (20 meters plus 10 meters). Here the baton exchange is at 18 meters, a legal but unsafe area. Maximum baton speed can be attained and still pass at 12-15 meters.

position similar to that of "set" in sprint starting and urges an acceleration such as occurs in competitive sprinting.[1] (2) The spot at which the exchange of baton is to occur. If one man can maintain top momentum longer than the other, he should be asked to carry the baton a few yards further within the passing zone, and they will set up their method accordingly. Whitehead[2] made a careful study of movies of the excellent passing of the Russian team, 1964, and the British team (world record, 1963), and found that the first exchanged the baton at about six yards before the restraining line; the second, at about seven. These marks ensured high velocity of the baton and safety of passing within the zone.

Emplacement of Receiver's hand. It is crucial that the incoming runner have a clear and steady target, the hand, on which he can focus his actions. During the early acceleration period into the 20-meter zone, the receiver will drive both arms forcefully. But two strides (L-R-L or R-L-R) before the actual exchange point (C in Figure 24.6) is reached, the hand must be fixed at full though relaxed extension in receiving position. The shoulder girdle does not twist; eyes focus straight ahead; PMA (Positive Mental Attitude) is crucial; all-out velocity is not reduced as the critical last six yards are reached. *The baton will come when it is needed.*

Placement of the Baton. The incoming runner must grasp the baton near its lower end to expose a full six inches of its 11.81-inch length for a firm placement in the receiver's hand. The movement is not a hurried slapdash of the baton; rather, it is a careful press into the hand. Concentration is the key. *Keep your eye on that hand and see it grasp that baton.*

"Go!" Whatever the location of the starting point of the receiver within the 10-meter zone, he must have a marker by which to judge his "Go!" With the growing use of hard-surface tracks, a strip of tape is placed on the spot, its exact location being a matter of repeated trial in practice. Coach Walker[3], who has had many fine sprint relay teams, times his relay men to make certain they reach the 26-meter point in close to the same time they can achieve it in sprinting out of starting blocks.

Some coaches add sound to sight, and have the incoming runner call "Go!" or "Hike!" as he reaches a certain spot. In my judgment, it's better that a man depend on himself, and that his mind be pin-pointed in terms of the one sense, vision, rather than divided between eye and ear, especially when other disruptive sounds are certain to be present.

USE OF PERSONNEL--SPRINT RELAYS. In the sprint, blind-pass relays, the usual preference is to get a lead as soon as possible and keep it through the finish line. This would suggest that men run in order of 100-yard dash time. However, mental attitude is very important, and most coaches feel it helps confidence to have that best man running anchor. The others then rely on his ability to gain back what may have been lost. This then changes the order to 2-3-4-1 in order of merit. Some consideration should be given to fast and dependable starting out of the blocks, and most importantly, to the long-time pairing of men in perfecting the skill of passing. Some men have confidence in each other, practice a great deal together, take pride in their passing skill.

Fig. 24.7. One method of holding the baton at the starting line.

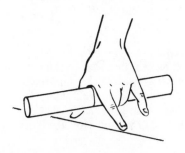

The all-important point is to make a decision as to the order of running early in the season, then have those combinations practice-practice-practice, until both their muscles and their minds know it will come off right! Such practice has its dangers. Men are going all-out (if the practice is to be effective); at times they may be off-balance in reaching forward; muscles may be contracting against resistance. Many a fine sprinter has lost weeks of competition through relay work. Precautions as to warming-up, overwork, or practice temperatures should be carefully taken.

[1]Leroy T. Walker, *CHAMPIONSHIP TECHNIQUES IN TRACK AND FIELD*, West Nyack, N.Y.: Parker Publishing Co., Inc., 1969, 56.
[2]See Nick Whitehead, *ibid.*, 5, for more detailed discussion.
[3]Leroy T. Walker, *ibid.*, 56.

<u>USE OF PERSONNEL---LONGER-DISTANCE RELAYS</u>. The use of personnel in longer-distance relays, including the mile relay, depends so much upon the competitive situation in a particular race, as well as on individual abilities and attitudes. How many teams in the race? What lane do you have and what chance of getting a sound position at the start? Even with a good start can and should the lead-off man spend his energies in holding that position? Some crazy running occurs during the first 200 yards or so, and a lead position can become a tail position within a distance of 20 yards, so that the job of passing has to be done all over again.

On the other hand, do the team members have the confidence and poise to take it easy at the start, then as the field thins out, move up with comparatively little interference to the position they want? In the meantime, what has happened to the leading contenders? Have they now built up such a lead that contact is lost and most difficult to regain? That is, your order of running depends somewhat on the order of running of your opponents.

When only two or three teams are competing, the main problems are first, to have the best anchor man, and second, to maintain contact. But when the field is crowded, the first leg is often the toughest. Some coaches decide in such a situation to run their strongest man first, then follow with numbers 3-4-2 in order of merit. The lead he may build up may hold through to the finish. But in many instances, the superiority of such a man is nullified in the frustrations of changing pace and place. It's a gamble!

No final conclusions can be reached here, other than the necessity of careful study by the coach of the competitive situation, of deciding as early as possible just what order to run, and then preparing the men, both physically and mentally for their task. Confidence and competence are two sides of one coin.

<u>Indoor Relay Running</u>. The usually crowded conditions of indoor running accentuate the problem of personnel use. Some coaches try to get a lead on the first legs so as to free the running of the later runners. Others use men of lesser ability first, wait for the field to spread out, then come from behind in the later stages. Each team and each situation has its own unique solutions.

In indoor relays there is a definite advantage in taking the baton with the inside left hand, especially when on the curve. Thereby the receiver can see the entire situation as it develops at the last instant, be aware of the lane line or curb, avoid fouling a competitor on an inner lane, and prevent both disqualification and injury.

HOW THEY TRAIN

Bill McClure has had great success for several decades with his relay teams at Abilene Christian and Louisiana State.[1] From his presentation at the 1978 U.S. Track Coaches Association Olympic Development Clinic, I have extracted only those portions that relate directly to exchanging the baton. In addition, McClure placed great emphasis on the importance of careful selection and use of personnel--relative sprinting speeds, endurance, curve-running abilities, etc.

The method we use at LSU is what I choose to call the "palm up" exchange. We have the lead-off man carry the baton in his right hand and exchange to the 2nd runner's left, and he retains the baton in his left hand exchanges to the 3rd runner's right, and he retains the baton in his right and exchanges to the 4th runner's left. We believe this gives us an advantage in allowing each runner to run the shortest distance to the exchange point...

In the lead-off position we would like to have our best man off the blocks and a good curve runner. He could be a high hurdler or the 2nd best sprinter. The second man is our best long-sprinter generally a quarter-miler or intermediate hurdler, someone who is big and strong and can fly on the straight-away. He will run, as will the anchor man, approximately 120 yards. The third man is generally either our second sprinter or a hurdler or quarter-miler who can really run the turn as

---

[1]Bill McClure, "Relays," USTCA *Track & Field Quarterly Review*, Vol. 78, #3, Fall 1978, p. 54.

his entire run is on the curve. The anchor man is our best sprint competitor-- the man who can reach down and get a little more when called on to perform. He (as the 2nd man) will run a bit farther than the 1st and 3rd men. Our 1st and 3rd men run the turns and the 2nd and 4th run the straights...

On the 1st and 3rd exchanges we want the outgoing runner to get the baton immediately after he crossed the near exchange zone mark. The 2nd exchange we want the outgoing runner to get the baton 15-17 yards into the exchange zone area. This enables us to run our strength on the straight and our weakness, the shorter distance, on the curve...

The responsibilities of the incoming and ougoing runner are specific and vital for the success of the team. For a successful exchange of the baton the incoming and outgoing runners need to make the pass while running an equal rate of speed, the rate being tops for each at the point of exchange.

1. Responsibility of the Incoming Runner.
    a. Finish strong thru the exchange-run only on your 2/3 part of the lane (not behind the outgoing runner)
    b. Identify your teammate-check lane inside and outside yours as well as your own (colors, similar, etc.)
    c. Know where the exchange is to take place in the zone (early, middle, late)
    d. Know the emergency command and when to give it.
    e. Be Positive the outgoing runner <u>takes</u> the baton from you.
    f. Look the baton into the exchange.
    g. Stay in your lane after the pass. (Be sure you are clear before leaving track)

2. Responsibility of the Outgoing Runner.
    a. Locate your station 15 minutes prior to race.
    b. Make your check mark(s) as soon as permissible (consider weather, wind, etc.)
    c. Identify the team inside and outside of your lane. (Uniform color, etc.)
    d. Do not anticipate--rely on your practice and marks.
    e. Stay in your 1/3 part of the lane.
    f. Expect a good exchange.

3. The Lead-off Runner Has Other Responsibilities Concerning the Race.
    a. The lead-off man is responsible for the baton.
    b. The grip on the baton for the start should be comfortable, legal and in the passing hand, with the grip being on the first 1/3 of the baton.

Believing practice makes for a better exchange we involve our relay units in baton work as part of their warm-up and warm-down, each man working with his partner(s) twice a week at their stations. As our exchange is from right to left, left to right, right to left, we do not have to worry about changing the baton from hand to hand. We work our alternates at all positions and if we have an injury we simply put the alternate in the injured man's position.

In the 4 x 200 relay we use the same personnel as our 4 x 100 unit. The only adjustment we make is in our marks. Each man divides his "go" mark in half and adds one foot, leaving the lean mark the same (if we have one). In the mile and other relays we use the visual exchange (right to left) or a combination of the sprint relay.

I do not look for "daylight" between the runners as criteria for a good exchange. I'm interested in the exchange being made at optimum speed. Once our athletes are settled on their distance for the "go" mark, most of our practice is done on the straight-away to prevent injuries. We also have a rule that a runner never tries to make an exchange if he has to stretch in a workout.

<u>Confidence is the key to success and drill is the route to confidence.</u>

Jesse Owens.

Chapter 25
THE SPRINTS

Racing short distances has been a part of the competitive play of every civilization and has been described in the literature of almost every people. We in Western civilization naturally turn to our own sources in Western literature. We refer to the foot races of the beautiful Atalanta whose love of the hunt and speed of foot were exceeded only by her love of beautiful apples or greed for gold, as you may prefer to look at it. Every schoolboy knows of Achilles, who held games as part of the funeral ceremonies for his friend Patroclus. One event of those games was a foot race, won by Ulysses, for which a great silver bowl, a huge ox, and half a talent of gold were offered as prizes.

But apart from legend, we have facts and artifacts to prove that sprinting was included in the ancient Greek Olympics. Excavations at Olympia, Delphi, Corinth, and other sites of the ancient games disclose well thought out devices for achieving a fair start--the toughest problem in sprinting. For example, at the Delphi stadium, 20 blocks of marble for starting are now in place. In each there are two grooves in which the racers set their feet, and adjacent to those grooves, a socket. Harris[1] explains both clearly and at length that a "husplex," that is, a post and arm, was set in this socket, that a string went from each arm through a groove (if rock surface) or a pipe (if earth surface) to the starter's pit. The few references to it in Greek literature indicate the husplex arm dropped, but it seems more effective to me if it lifted. By pulling all strings at once, the starter could lift the arms together and release the sprinters. (How Ben Ogden, of Temple University and Madison Square Garden starting-gate fame would take delight in these disclosures.)

Woe to him who sought a flying start. Not only would the rising arm catch him in the chin, the Greeks also had long forked sticks handy, and "Those who start too soon are beaten," said Andeimantus to Themistocles at the historic council before Salamis.

Incidentally, the threat of physical punishment is not entirely unknown in modern times. For instance, Webster[2] tells a story of how Arthur Duffey, the Georgetown champion, while touring England in 1902, had an even more threatening experience.

Duffey was a tremendously fast starter, and an amusing story is told of one experience with a North Country starter, who is said to have uttered a warning as he stood behind Duffey's curved end:

"Sitha, Duffey, lad," said the official, "Ah've brought shot gun for t'startin'. Ah've blank i't first barrel an't shot i't second. Tha canst guess where tha'l't get shot if tha tries any flyers."

---

[1] H. A. Harris, *GREEK ATHLETES AND ATHLETICS*, London: Hutchinson & Co., Ltd, 1964, 68. (Harris includes drawings of the husplex.)

[2] F. A. M. Webster, *ATHLETICS OF TO-DAY*. London: Frederick Warne & Co., Ltd., 1929, 46.

TABLE 25.1
OUTSTANDING PERFORMANCES -- SPRINTS

OLYMPIC CHAMPIONS -- MEN

Date	Record 100m	200m	Name	Affiliation	Age	Hgt.	Wgt.
1956	10.5	20.60R	Bobby Morrow	USA		6'1"	170
1960	10.20R		Armin Hary	Germany	23	6'	156
1960		20.5WR	Livio Berruti	Italy			
1964	10.0WR		Bob Hayes	USA	21	6'	189
1964		20.30R	Henry Carr	USA	22	6'3"	185
1968	9.95WR		Jim Hines	USA			
1968		19.8WR	Tommie Smith	USA	24	6'3"	173
1972	10.14	20.00	Valeriy Borzov	USSR	23	6'	174
1976	10.06		Hasely Crawford	Trinidad	26	6'1"	165
1976		20.23	Donald Quarrie	Jamaica	25	5'8"	155
1980	10.25		Allan Wells	Scotland	28	6'0"	168
1980		20.19	Pietro Mennea	Italy	28	5'10"	154
1984	9.99	19.80	Carl Lewis	USA	23	6'2"	175

OLYMPIC CHAMPIONS -- WOMEN

Date	Record 100m	200m	Name	Affiliation	Age	Hgt.	Wgt.
1960	11.0	24.0	Wilma Rudolph	USA			
1964	11.4		Wyomia Tyus	USA			
1968	11.08WR		Wyomia Tyus	USA			
1968		22.58WR	I. Szewinska	Poland			
1972	11.07WR	22.40WR	Renate Stecher	E. Germany	22	5'6½"	145
1976	11.08		Annegret Richter	W. Germany	26	5'6"	115
1976		22.370R	Barbel Eckert	E. Germany			
1980	11.06		L. Kondratyeva	USSR	22	5'6¼"	132
1980		22.03	Barbel Woeckel	E. Germany			
1984	10.97		Evelyn Ashford	USA	27	5'5"	115
1984		21.81	Valerie Brisco-Hooks	USA	24	5'6½"	130

WORLD RECORDS OF SPECIAL INTEREST -- MEN

Date	Record 100m	200m	Name	Affiliation	Age	Hgt.	Wgt.
1935	09.4y	20.3y	Jesse Owens	Ohio State	20	5'10"	156
1967	09.21		Charles Greene	Nebraska			
1968	09.95		Jim Hines	USA			
1971		19.81	Don Quarrie	Jamaica	20	5'8"	155
1974	09.0y		Ivory Crockett	USA	26	5'8"	145
1975	09.9		Houston McTear	Baker HS, Fla.	18	5'7"	155
1979	10.01	19.72	Pietro Mennea	Italy	27	5'10"	154

WORLD RECORDS OF SPECIAL INTEREST -- WOMEN

Date	Record 100m	200m	Name	Affiliation	Age	Hgt.	Wgt.
1984	10.76		Evelyn Ashford	USA	17	5'5"	115
1983	10.81		Marlies Gohr	E. Germany		5'5"	118
1979		21.71	Marita Koch	E. Germany			
1979		21.83	Evelyn Ashford	USA	23	5'5"	112

HIGH SCHOOL PERFORMANCES -- BOYS

Date	Record 100m	200m	Name	Affiliation			
1976	10.16		Houston McTear	Baker, Fl.	(HS record)		
1976		20.22	Dwayne Evans	S.Mtn, Phoenix	(HS record)		

HIGH SCHOOL PERFORMANCES -- GIRLS

Date	Record 100m	200m	Name	Affiliation			
1976	11.13	22.77	C. Cheeseborough	Rib, Jack. Fl.	(HS record)		
1984	11.55		Wendy Vereen	C. Trenton, NJ			
1984		23.54	Paulette Blalock	Compton, CA			

Modern organized sprint races had their origin in professional racing, which was very prevalent in England during the entire 19th century and in much less organized fashion in this country until about 1910. The story of methods, stratagems, and gambling in professional racing forms is one of the most fascinating pages in all sports history. From the standpoint of techniques, one of the best of the scattered writings is that by William Curtis, written in 1899,[1]

During the early years of American amateur athletic sport, all the methods of management were naturally copied from the professionals. Running was limited almost entirely to matches, as there were no open competitions which athletes could enter, and the distances were in nine cases out of ten one of the two extremes--one hundred yards or ten miles. As there were but two starters in these match races, the methods of getting away were more primitive than at present and had been cunningly devised by veteran professionals to give the expert an advantage over the novice.

Several styles were in common use, the oldest being what was called the "break start." The judge stood on the starting line, the men went back fifteen or twenty paces, stood side by side, joined fingers lightly and trotted up to the judge. As they passed on either side of him, his body broke the touch of their fingers and they dashed away at full speed. If the judge thought the start fair, he said nothing, but if he thought either man had an unfair advantage they were recalled. . . .

However, the cunning of professional runners had devised methods of outwitting inexperienced opponents. A few steps from the judge the expert would slacken his trot and the other almost invariably would do the same. Just as he reached the judge the expert would suddenly quicken. As it required some fraction of a second for the other to follow this example, the men would pass the judge almost exactly abreast, the expert more than likely a few inches in the rear, but he would be running, while the other was only trotting. The advantage thus gained would amount to two or three yards in the first twenty-five yards of the race.

A more complicated style was the "mutual consent" start. A line was drawn across the track, fifteen or twenty feet behind the starting scratch. The men were placed between these lines and told to start by mutual consent, and whenever both men touched the ground in front of the starting scratch at the same time with any part of their persons it was considered a start.

A race of this kind between two experts was amusing. The men stood between the lines facing each other, pranced up to the starting mark sideways, and the one who was ahead would put his foot down over the mark, hoping that the other would follow. If he did, it would be a start, with the first man a foot or two in front; but if the second man did not like the start, he held back, did not put his foot over the mark, and the first man was ordered back for a fresh trial.

Starts of this style frequently lasted over an hour, especially if one of the runners was not extremely anxious for a race, and eventually this system was modified by inserting in the articles of agreement a clause substantially as follows: "Start by mutual consent; if not off inside an hour [or some other specified time], then to start by pistol." Resort to the pistol was necessary in so many cases that it gradually supplanted the mutual consent system, and became the customary way of starting sprints. . . .

These professional wolves usually traveled and prowled in pairs, one going first to a town, securing some employment, exhibiting his proficiency as a runner to a select few, and finally making a match and beating the local champion. Then the winner would explain that he knew a man in a neighboring town who thought he could run, and whose friends would back him heavily, but who really was several yards slower than championship speed and could be easily beaten. Negotiations would be opened with the stranger and a match arranged. All the men who had won on the first race wished to double their gains, while those who lost were anxious for a chance to get even, so the betting was heavy. The stranger won, of course; the town was pretty thoroughly cleaned of money, and the partners changed their names and moved to fresh harvest fields.

If, after beating the local champions in races on even terms and under ordinary conditions, any money still remained in sight, the professionals tried to secure it by offering contests on novel terms, and with such conditions as seemed to the uninitiated, foolhardy and sure to lose. One of these was called the "lying down start." The novice stood in his usual position, while the professional would lie flat on his back, with his head at the scratch and his feet pointing away from the finish, and the race started by pistol shot. To men unacquainted with this trick, it seemed as if the novice must win, and elderly know-it-alls, standing about, shifted their quids and wisely drawled out: "Why, Jimmy will be down to the other end before that fellow gets started."

But it did not work that way. When the pistol sounded, the professional turned on his face, rose to his hands and feet, and found himself in the attitude now universally adopted by present day sprinters (the crouch start), and which is much better than the old-fashioned erect position. This preliminary movement cost the professional about half a second, or five yards, and as this was about half the handicap, he could beat the novice in 100 yards. He usually caught his man near the seventy-fifth yard mark.

MODERN DEVELOPMENT OF STARTING TECHNIQUES

Such experiments in professional starting would naturally lead to the use of a crouch start in sprinting. Mike Murphy[2] the remarkable Pennsylvania, Yale, and Chief Olympic track coach, took credit in his book for inventing it,

The crouching start was introduced by me. This was in 1887, at Yale, and Charles H. Sherrill was the athlete who first demonstrated its superiority. When he used it in his first race, he was laughed at, and the starter, thinking that Sherrill did not know how to start, held up the race to give him instructions. Finally he was made to under-

---

[1]William Curtis, quoted in Archie Hahn, *HOW TO SPRINT*, New York: American Sports Publishing Company, 1925, 189.

[2]Michael C. Murphy, *ATHLETIC TRAINING*. New York: Charles Scribner's Sons, 1914, 32.

stand that Sherrill was using a new start. Sherrill immediately demonstrated how superior it was to the old standing start, which it displaced, and now the crouching start is used the world over for sprinters, hurdlers, and even quarter and half-milers.

Apparently, sound techniques as to foot placement in the starting holes, a high support on the fingers, and an effective "set" position, were all worked out in the first decade. A picture of Arthur Duffey, Georgetown champion, 1900-1903, shows him in a crouched "set" position very similar to that used today (Figure 25.1).

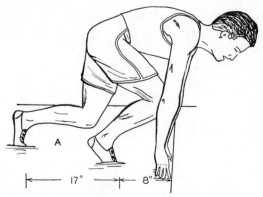

Fig. 25.1 -- Drawn from photo of Arthur Duffey (1902 - 09.6). For some 50 years or more (1880-1940) this was called the orthodox or regular block placement and set position.

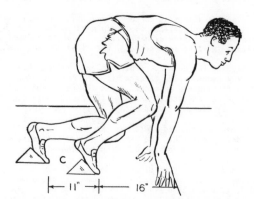

Fig. 25.2 -- For many years this block placement was called the Australian or kangaroo start as used by Australian professional sprinters. Drawn from Golliday (1955 - 09.3)

Duffey's ideas[1] on getting out of the holes are sound. For example, he emphasizes that "often the arms are not used to full advantage"; that the primary push comes from the front leg although "both legs must be called into action at one moment"; that "at the report of the pistol, the left arm is swung directly ahead, flexed at the elbow, the right arm swinging directly backwards"; and, lastly, that there is "the necessity for forward action, by lifting the knees in a straight line and jabbing directly downward, without any of the side deviation which is such a common fault with the novice sprinter."

Around 1935 when Larry Snyder was coaching Jesse Owens and other fine sprinters, he believed a position which "crowded" the starting line was best. When starting from holes, "if the boy's foot is within 8 inches to a foot away from the starting line, never more than a foot, I feel that boy is ahead of the one whose front foot is 18 inches back." When starting from blocks, "he will probably have the front foot 2 or 3 inches from the starting line."[2] Snyder did not follow these instructions through the years, but they illustrate the trends of thinking and of trial-and-error efforts that coaches were making.

Early in the 1920s, a "Kangaroo" start (now commonly called the "bunch" start because the feet are close together) placed the front foot 17 to 19 inches back of the starting line and the back foot 10 to 12 inches behind the front one. This elongated position did not gain rapid favor for it seemed to put the sprinter that much farther from the starting line. However, the research studies of A. D. Dickinson in 1934 proved that this position was faster than any other in producing clearance of the starting blocks. This conclusion influenced increased use of the "bunch" start until by the 1950's it had become probably the most common of all.

However, in 1952, two pieces of research pointed out that a man might clear his blocks in a short time and yet not have either the momentum or the good balance to get him into fast

[1] Quoted by Archie Hahn, *op. cit.*, 65.

[2] Larry Snyder, an unpublished talk before the National College Track Coaches Association, June 1939.

action down the track. Both studies concluded that the "bunch" start was actually the least efficient. Henry[1] states:

> It is clear that the 16 and 21 inch toe-to-toe distance is the best. . . . The 11 inch "bunch" start is definitely the poorest of the four. While it is true that this position gets the runner off the blocks quickest, he is going slower as he leaves them and never recovers from this disadvantage.

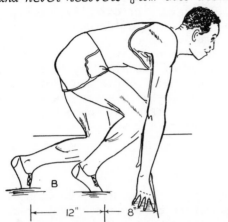

Fig. 25.3 -- Jesse Owens, 1935, "better than 09.4," crowded the starting line "to be nearer the finish line" - Coach Snyder.

Fig. 25.4 -- Bobby Morrow, 1956 Olympic champion. His block placement is close to Henry's "best possible".

DEVELOPMENT OF SPRINTING TECHNIQUES. A similar history of experimentation and development cannot be traced for the techniques of sprinting. After all, running, both fast and slow, is a part of man's evolution; its techniques grew with his bone structure and his way of living. The sprinting figures that circle the vases of ancient Greece give evidence of techniques of sprinting such as high knee action that would do credit to Jesse Owens or Tommie Smith.

DEVELOPMENT OF FINISH TECHNIQUES. Experimentation as to methods of finishing a race occurred early in modern sprinting. As far back as 1904, J. W. Morton[2] attempted a "throw" at the finish, which is still advocated by some good coaches today:

> At about twenty yards from the tape I take a long breath, quickly pulling myself together for a final effort. At this point a thrill seems to pass through my muscles; I travel much faster and, should it be a close finish, at about 8 feet from the tape I throw myself off the right leg, striking the tape with the left breast, and saving myself from collapsing by the left leg.

Charley Paddock, "world's fastest human" during the 1920's, made occasional and successful use (according to his coach, Dean Cromwell) of a full jump at the finish. Paddock frankly admitted that this leap "has been referred to as 'grand-stand play' and the 'freak finish of a freak performer,'" yet he firmly believed that "the jump has won so many more races for me than it lost that I can do no less than suggest it to the sprinter who runs high and has the patience to learn it, and the courage to use it."

Other methods of making the finish apparently also had an early origin. The lunge finish, which consisted of throwing the body well forward with the chest out and the arms far down and back, was originated by Arthur Duffey in 1900, according to Charley Paddock.[3]

(Cont. p. 421)

---

[1]Franklin M. Henry, "Research on Sprint Running," *The Athletic Journal*, February 1952, 30.

[2]J. W. Morton, quoted by Archie Hahn, *op. cit.*, 70.

[3]Charles W. Paddock, *TRACK AND FIELD*, New York: A. S. Barnes & Co., 1933, 25.

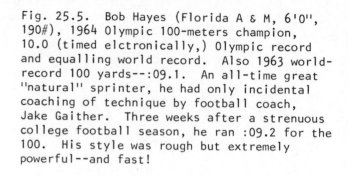

Fig. 25.5. Bob Hayes (Florida A & M, 6'0",
190#), 1964 Olympic 100-meters champion,
10.0 (timed elctronically,) Olympic record
and equalling world record. Also 1963 world-
record 100 yards--:09.1. An all-time great
"natural" sprinter, he had only incidental
coaching of technique by football coach,
Jake Gaither. Three weeks after a strenuous
college football season, he ran :09.2 for the
100. His style was rough but extremely
powerful--and fast!

Fig. 25.6. Armin Hary, Germany, 1960 Olympic
100 meters champion and world-record coholder
100 meters, "10. This drawing is from a
photo of the actual start of the Olympic
final. The line of Hary's torso is close to
the horizontal; yet he is gaining a full
first stride beyond the starting line.

Fig. 25.7. Valeriy Borzov, USSR, 1972
Olympic 100 meters (10.14) and 200 meters
(20.00) champion. Note: (1) The 90-degree
focus of the eyes downward at the start and
relatively low focus throughout. (2) The
close placement of the feet but long spread
between hands and front foot. Only great
speed-power can now bring the legs forward
for full strides without stumbling. In
summary, Borzov had great potential as a born
sprinter (at age 17 he ran 10.5 and 22.0 for
the metric sprints), but that potential was
developed by scientifically-planned training to its highest levels. Result--
Olympic gold.

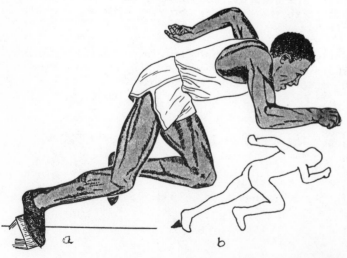

Fig. 25.8. Carl Lewis, USA, 1984 Olympic
4-gold-medal winner: 100m (9.99), 200m
(19.80), long jump (28'¼" OR), 400m relays
(37.83 WR). Fig. 25.8b is taken from film
of Lewis by Dorothy Doolittle, women's
coach, University of Houston. Fig. 25.8a
illustrates a lifelike Lewis start though
with feet reversed. These Figures suggest
maximal force against the blocks--body angle
45 degrees, eyes 90 degrees to line of body,
arms (elbows) stay close and lead leg action
on each stride.

a

b

Arthur Duffey was one of the first to scientifically use it. The Boston boy employed the lunge in a race against Bernie Wefers of the New York Athletic Club, who was American champion in 1895-96-97, and he won by the width of a hand. Wefers saw the advantage of the lunge, and at once set out to improve upon this method of finishing if possible. And his studies resulted in the introduction of a still better style.

This new finish was soon known as the "shrug," and it was accomplished by throwing the side of the body into the string with one hand held high, and the other held back behind the body. The forward lean of the "lunge" was maintained in the "shrug" but the tape could be broken 6 inches sooner, since the side of the body can be brought that much nearer the string than the chest....This "shrug" finish first perfected by Bernie Wefers had grown in popularity during the past thirty years until today it is in general use by a majority of the best sprinters throughout the world.

BASIC PROBLEMS IN SPRINTING

Sprinters--Born or Developed? Up to about 1960, consensus was that sprinters were born; you either had it or you didn't. Study the techniques and training of Jesse Owens (1934-1936) and one can only conclude he was a natural, largely unmade sprinter. He had fine coaches in high school and college, but their knowledge of sprinting was that of the 1930s--the less one sprints, the less the chance of injury; strength work and endurance work slow, even deaden, the muscles; "the closer one's blocks are to the starting line, the closer one is to the finish line;" during the start, focus the eyes on the finish line, and the like.

Beginning with Armin Hary (1960 OG Champion, 100m--10.0) and Valeriy Borzov, USSR (1972 OG Champion, 100m--10.14) realization gradually spread that even the most talented sprinter could be developed beyond what was previously accepted so as to reach true potentials when performance was most important. Carl Lewis is one of the greatest sprinting talents ever, but Carl Lewis at Los Angeles, 1984, was also a developed sprinter, as is indicated by discussions later in this Chapter. True, the time difference between Jesse Owens and Carl Lewis was a "mere" four-tenth second, but that mereness means at least four meters, a difference of being champion or going unplaced.

Strength-Power-Velocity in Sprinting. Understanding of this problem will be aided by a review of Chapter 6 with its clarification of the meanings in action of (power= strength x velocity). In brief, these never can be separate or isolated words; they are in action a continuum with maximal strength at one extreme and a theoretical velocity-without-resistance at the other. In sprinting velocity is the goal, velocity that requires only enough "strength" to overcome resistances such as internal movements and external air. It follows that weight-lifting, even with sprinting muscles, is a sound basic method but only to the extent that (1) such strength is related to sprinting and (2) an optimal balance between strength and velocity is gained, as might be suggested by the term (S^3V^{10}). That is, as in training for the javelin, a velocity event includes throwing with lighter-than-normal implements, so sprinting for greater velocity on a slightly downhill surface will prove helpful.

Maximal Power-Maximal Relaxation. How is it possible to exert all-out power in the sprinting muscles while remaining completely relaxed? As in the principle just stated, power and relaxation are words, words that tend to separate actions that are actually two aspects of one action. Limited space limits adequate explanation. For the physical aspects of the problem, look up "reciprocal innervation of antagonistic muscles" in your favorite physiology textbook. Such an alternation of contraction-relaxation is inherent, involuntary--that is in non-human animals. In a human animal it becomes discoordinated, unrhythmic, high-tensioned--all induced by mental-emotional factors. Much of the job of coaching and of learning to compete in the sprints relates to ways of reducing such tension, doubts, anxiety--at all competitive levels, especially the Olympic, as we have just witnessed at the Los Angeles Games.

TIME/ACTION IN SPRINTING

The Scope of the Problem. From the standpoint of time and action, any sprint begins in reaction to the sound of the starting gun and ends as the finish line on the ground is reached. This time-action period can be arbitrarily divided into five phases: (1) reaction time to the sound of the starting gun, (2) block-clearance time, (3) acceleration time, (4) velocity-maintenance time, and (5) the finish time.

1. Sprinter's Reaction Time (time lapse between sound of gun and first movement in response) is both inherited and improveable. The inborn tendency of some sprinters is to react to sound quickly; that of others, more slowly. Further, the consensus of related research is that reaction time is not correlated with speed, either out of the starting blocks or when sprinting. A great sprinter can have relatively slow reaction time; and an ordinary sprinter relatively fast reaction time. Further, Franklin Henry's research concluded that reaction time is uninfluenced by block spacing.

Ruddi Toomsalu[1] improved the average reaction time of 122 trainees from .139 seconds to .119 seconds. An insignificant improvement? In 1979, Pietro Mennea (Italy, 200m-19.72WR) won the European Cup 100-meters by only 1/100th of a second. But time-analysis found he reacted (0.13s) to the starting gun 2/100th faster than did 2nd-place winner Woronin (0.15s). Toomsalu does not state how he achieved this improvement in reaction time, but we can be certain that such improvements in sprinting would be specific to sprinting patterns of action.

It should be noted that these reaction times of over one-tenth second are consistent with those found by other investigators.[2] With such rare exceptions as Armin Hary, the 1960 100-meters Olympic winner, whose reaction time was reported to be .08 second, no man should be able to move a muscle until after one-tenth second has elapsed after the firing of the starting gun.

2. Block-Clearance Time requires a significant fraction of total sprint time. Dickinson[3] found that the average time required to get clear of the blocks (including reaction time) was 0.244 seconds for a 10.5-inch bunch start, 0.326 seconds for a 21-inch medium start and 0.387 seconds for a 26-inch elongated start. (Inches here refer to the distance between the two starting blocks.) But in later research, Franklin Henry[2] concluded that velocity out of the blocks is a greater concern than block-clearance time, and that in this respect, the longer 16- and 21-inch block placements were best. When the front block is moved forward, the front leg has a greater time in which to apply force against the block and thereby increase velocity. "Although the rear leg develops considerably more maximum force than the front, the latter contributes twice as much to block velocity because its impulse has a longer duration." Henry also reached another conclusion which I consider of even greater significance. "With block spacing held constant, speed in the sprint is significantly related to how close the individual approaches the ideal start." That is to say, is significantly related to the degree of perfection with which he has mastered the skills of starting.

3. Acceleration Time is the length of time-distance in which the sprinter accelerates his velocity. Earlier research had stated this length in terms of yards, but Franklin Henry found that time was a more valid measurement, and concluded that six seconds was the greatest time in which a man could continue to increase his velocity. We should keep in mind that Henry's subjects were experienced but not great sprinters, and should assume that highly skilled and talented sprinters can possibly shorten this time and certainly increase the number of yards covered.

4. Velocity-Maintenance Time is the length of time-distance in which a sprinter can

---

[1]Ruddi Toomsalu, "Sprint Start Speed Factors," *Track Technique*, No. 11, March, 1963, 325.

[2]Franklin M. Henry, "Force-Time Characteristics of the Sprint Start," *The Research Quarterly*, 23:3 (October, 1952).

[3]A. D. Dickinson, "The Effect of Foot-Spacing on the Starting Time and Speed in Sprinting," *The Research Quarterly*, 5:1 (February, 1934).

maintain maximum velocity. Though we may not accept at full value Franklin Henry's[1] conclusion that "it is physiologically impossible for the runner, after he has reached his peak velocity, to maintain it for more than about 15 or 20 yards," we should assume that he is not far wrong. Even in a 100-yard dash, the problem becomes one of minimum deceleration. Certainly, in the 220 and 440, other things being equal, the winner is the one that slows down the least.

5. The Finish Time is that small fraction of a second in which by some action such as forward lean or shoulder shrug, the sprinter can gain a difference in place in the eyes of the judges, and conceivably, a difference in time from the timers.

In summary of these five phases of the sprinting problem, it should be noted (1) that each phase requires learning and specific practice if mastery is to be attained, and (2) that the allocation of practice time should be in terms of all five phases, and not predominantly in terms of starting as has been so much the custom in the past.

ESSENTIALS OF SOUND TECHNIQUE
Sound technique in sprint starting and running has two aspects: (1) soundness from the standpoint of generalized biomechanics, and (2) soundness for this particular sprinter in his mastery of all the related factors. In theory, the two should be in harmony, if not actually the same; or better, should differ only as the individual differs from the average. In practice the individual sprinter's style may have significant "faults" even though his achievement is at world-record levels. Quick consideration of the world-record holders of the past thirty years will show that most had significant variances from what is generally considered to be sound technique.

Human beings are amazingly adept at adjusting to an imperfect method so as to produce an excellent result. This is the bane of so many research studies that assume "other things being equal"; they never are equal in human action. Whatever specific changes the researcher or the coach makes in technique are never performed in isolation. The athlete immediately balances these changes by making many small adjustments, largely undetectable to the coach. For

---

[1]Franklin M. Henry, "Research in Sprint Running," *The Athletic Journal*, February 1952, 30.

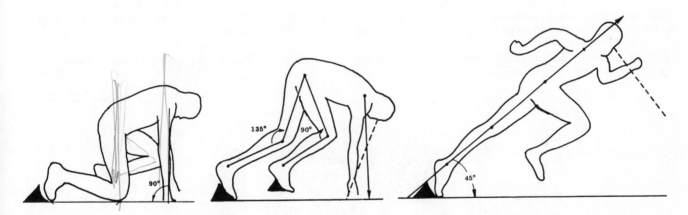

Fig. 25.9. Carl Lewis during the start. These figures from Tom Tellez and Dorothy Doolittle, University of Houston, "Sprinting--From Start to Finish," *Track Technique*, Vol. 88, Spring 1984, pp. 2802-05.

Fig. 1--"On your marks," places the toes on the blocks in contact with the track surface. Head-neck are in relaxed, natural alignment with torso; eyes down vertically. Fig. 2--"Set" raises the hips just high enough to fix a back-knee angle at an optimal 135 degrees; that at the back knee at about 90 degrees, depending on block placement and length of sprinter's legs. Fig. 3--"Gun" releases support by the hands-arms. A stretch-reflex action increases power in the foot-ankle that pulls the rear leg forward as shown for an optimally long stride. As the front foot leaves its block, body angle is at 45 degrees. Left arm in this figure drives forward until hand is at chin height, thus helping the low-angled drive forward.

example, take the mechanically unsound "set" position of Jesse Owens (Fig. 25.3)--his feet 8 and 20 inches from the starting line; his head up and eyes focussed on the finish line--a position well designed to drive him straight up in the air. But Jesse's urge to go forward, not up, caused him to make the best of a bad position by adjusting his arm-leg actions and torso angles so as to gain an excellent start, at least by the standards of 1935. His total pattern of response was sound, despite the initial errors in starting position.

All this suggests that it is important that a sprinter's style be mechanically correct in all respects, but it is crucial that he master his own style, whatever it may be.

RESEARCH ON STARTING BLOCK SPACING
Undoubtedly, in the United States since 1890, there have been more speeches, more arguments. more try-this-try-that, more research on the placement of starting blocks than on any other track or field problem. Up to 1930 there was a generally accepted "orthodox start" as shown in Fig. 25.1. Jesse Owens moved both feet up as shown in Fig. 25.3, on the theory of being closer to the finish line. In the 1920s, there was some use of a so-called "kangaroo" start with the front foot 17-19 inches from the starting line, and the back foot 10-12 inches further back (Fig. 25.2). Research by Dickinson (1934) and Henry (1952) indicated that there should be a greater spread between the feet:

It is clear that the 16 to 21 inch toe to toe distance is the best....The 11 inch "bunch" start is definitely the poorest of the four. While it is true that this position gets the runner off the blocks quickest, he is going slower as he leaves them and never recovers from this disadvantage.

This research assumed that first power came from the back foot; longer time of power application, from the front foot--an entirely sound assumption. But proof of the superiority of one placement over another is far from simple, for the many related factors can never be held constant. Change weight balance by changing block spacing and the sprinter naturally, without coaching, adapts his body balance, eye-focus, arm drive so as to compensate. In fact, the full merit of any block spacing can be judged only after long, thoughtful practice has enabled a sprinter to perfect that particular method. Henry's research assumed that the initial and most powerful drive came from the back leg, but that the front leg was more effective in providing power over a greater duration of time.

The first research based on angles of flexion in the related body joints--knees, hips, arms--was apparently done by USSR scientists in preparing Valeriy Borzov for the 1960 Olympic Games. On retirement, Borzov continued such research and concluded,[1]

Our study encompassed a group of the top Soviet sprinters of recent years. According

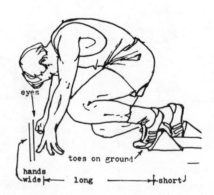

Fig. 25.9b. Valeriy Borzov's placement of starting blocks.

---

[1]Valeriy Borzov, "The Optimal Starting Position in Sprinting," *Soviet Sports Review*, Vol. 14, #4, December 1979.

to our data, in spite of the differing heights of the athletes in our group (165cm to 183cm), the angular values are of similar magnitudes in most cases. This suggests an optimal starting position based on angles at the various body joints, as shown in this Figure and Table.

In 1983, research by Tom Tellez and Dorothy Doolittle[1] with Carl Lewis as a major subject, reached similar conclusions. For Lewis, they found that, in the "set" position, angles of about 135 and 90 degrees at the knee joints of the back and front legs were most effective (Fig. 25.8).

Such methods of spacing starting blocks in terms of the relative lengths of lower leg-upper leg-torso-arms of each unique sprinter is so "obviously" sound one wonders why it took 50 years to discover. In fact, without benefit of research, early coaches and sprinters were vaguely aware of such positions when "set." I have pictures of Tolan, Morrow, Stanfield, Dillard, all Olympic sprint champions, that approximate such angles--"common sense" adjustments to whatever block spacings were popular at the time. But sound research is of great value in settling such issues and furthering precision. For example, Borzov advises this method,

When teaching starting technique to beginning runners, we recommend use of a straight-edge (ruler), positioned at the athlete's center of mass. Using a protractor, position the athlete's body in accord with optimal angles of flexion in the primary body segments, and then "place" the starting blocks "under" him. This provides the beginning sprinter with the prerequisites for the most effective and fastest start at the very beginning of his training.

An added suggestion to Borzov's method is to practice starting, using such a placement, for some time, perhaps weeks. At first you may stumble but you'll learn to bring the knees up-under faster and faster; reach out for additional inches on each stride; adjust arm action. Only after such longtime efforts prove ineffective should the blocks be re-adjusted.

You're still in doubt? Don't fret about it! A half-century of experimenting still leaves us all in doubt. *The most important concern is to master your own method and have complete confidence in it.*

Training for greater power for sprinting. The belt can be of any soft material: rubber, towel, or wide belt.

---

[1]Tom Tellez and Dorothy Doolittle, "Sprinting--From Start to Finish," *Track Technique,* Vol. 88, #2, 1984, pp. 2802-4.

ON YOUR MARKS

Using the block placement previously suggested, back into your blocks: (1) place the back foot against its block first, with the toe just touching the ground as required by the rules; (2) place the front foot in its block; then (3) place the fingers just behind the starting line (Figures 25.10,25.11). The weight is on the front knee and fingers, though there is pressure against the back block. The eyes are focussed on a spot three to five feet from the starting line; neck muscles are relaxed. The arms are straight down from the shoulders (Figure 25.10). Actually we are unsure of the value of being high on the finger tips, since today's starting direction is forward, not up, but custom has followed such a method for decades.

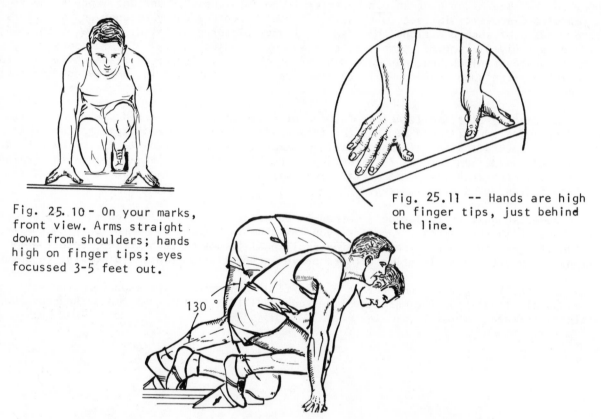

Fig. 25.10 - On your marks, front view. Arms straight down from shoulders; hands high on finger tips; eyes focussed 3-5 feet out.

Fig. 25.11 -- Hands are high on finger tips, just behind the line.

130°

Fig. 25.12 -- "On your marks" and "set". The angle at the knee joints when "set" are equally important with the distances between the hands and feet. That of about 130 degrees provides maximum initial drive.

SET

At the command "set," the hips are pushed upward and forward until the desired angle of 130 degrees at the back knee is reached. Since the weight when "on your marks" is primarily on the front knee, the weight must roll up and forward. With a proper hold by the starter of about two seconds between the two commands, "set" and "go," there is plenty of time in which to do this; no need to pop up into the "set" position, then be forced to wait an unfair length of time before the gun. But the rules are clear that the set position must be gained "at once and without delay." Now the weight will be on the hands and on the front foot, in that order.

In the "set" position, four inter-related points are critical--the height of the hips, the angles at the knees, the amount of forward lean and the contact of the back foot with its starting block. Only the last needs additional comment.

In the "set" position, the toes of the back foot are firmly against the block. In reaction to the firing of the gun, a stretch-reflex action occurs; the heel is forced back against the blocks putting related muscles on stretch, with instant and powerful reaction that initiates the drive forward.

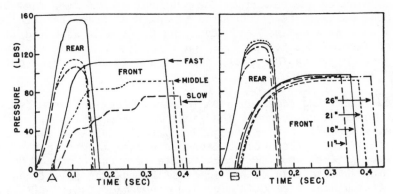

Fig. 25.13a. Pressures applied against the blocks by "fast," "middle" and "slow" sprinters. Note the quicker pressures, the higher pressures, and the more steady pressures applied by the faster sprinters. The back foot is off its block at about .17 seconds; the front, at about .37 seconds. Contrast the duration of force against the front block with that against the back block.

Fig. 25.13b. Comparison of average block pressures using four measurements between the blocks: 11, 16, 21, and 26 inches. On a basis of velocity out of the blocks, the 16- and 21- inch spacings were best *for these sprinters*. Both diagrams are from Franklin M. Henry, *op. cit.*

In the set position, the line of the back will be downward; that is, the hips will be above the shoulders. At first, this will cause stumbling. By lowering the hips, the stumbling may cease immediately, but this is a negative solution. Better to keep the hips high where maximum force can be applied; now practice, practice, PRACTICE! until you have learned to bring your knees and feet up, forward and out under the center of gravity, and so prevent stumbling this way, with no loss of force.

At "set" a full breath will usually be taken. This lifting and fixing of the chest is a normal and usually involuntary method of fixing attention and muscular readiness.

Fig. 25.14. Ira Murchison, 1958, 100 meters--:10.1. Murchison had an amazingly fast start. His starting style may well have been a function of his short, powerful legs. His height was 5'5". He emphasized a forward pull of the rear leg rather than the usual push against the back block. His coach, George Dales[1], wrote as follows:

[1]George G. Dales, "Coaching for the Sprint Start," *The Athletic Journal*, March, 1959, 24.

Murchison's powerful arms permit him to exaggerate the forward lean. . . .
With his controversial, straight, but relaxed back leg barely in contact with the
rear block, he has eliminated one motion in the movement of his leg, that of straighten-
ing a conventional bent back leg before bending it again as some sprinters do. Murchi-
son merely rests his back foot against the block and he is able to bring it up more
quickly to a bent position at the sound of the gun. He feels he can combine the
drive-off from the front block by the strong front leg with the running out of the
block by the relaxed back leg. . . .

(At "go") the relaxed (back) leg comes up from the rear block and drops just ahead
of the starting line where it now becomes the front and driving leg. . . . We found
no change in body angle at this point although Murchison's legs and arms have alter-
nated positions a full stride. The only observeable change is a slight rise in the
focus of his eyes a bit farther down the track toward the finish line. Murchison's
ability to maintain his forward lean in the early stages of the sprint and his abil-
ity to combine this with a high knee lift give him a powerful thrust with each stride.

Mind Set. Throughout the entire starting process--just before and during--an increasing
focus of attention occurs. That means a shutting-out of all extraneous sounds-sights-thoughts
and a concentration on the going: on the forward drive of the off-arm and a reactive thrust of
the rear foot. The mind is not "on the gun," or "on the sound of the gun," as so many say.
The mind set is like a compressed spring that is released by the gun-sound. To fix the "mind"
on the gun is to focus it "there," but the action is "here." That's not quibbling with words;
such words make a significant difference.

SPRINTING ACTION

The dynamics of sprint action can be considered roughly as those of the legs and arms. These in turn can be analyzed exceedingly fine. I have at hand a 120-page doctoral thesis concerned only with the mechanics of the leg-recovery phase. But our treatment here of the problem must be brief and over-simplified.

LEG ACTION---DRIVING PHASE. Other things being equal (which, in human sprinting, they never are), speed in sprinting is the resultant of three interdependent variables--cadence or rate of striding, length of strides, and power of forward thrust.

Cadence is often called leg-speed. Innate muscle-fiber speed of action cannot be improved and will always set the limits of potential leg-speed. But other factors are variable and do allow a rather wide range of possible improvement in leg-speed--and by progressive overloads of work which bring more fibers into action, by a more effective use of the forward thrust of the legs, or by relaxation of all unrelated and opposing muscle groups. That is to say, leg-speed can definitely be improved by sound practice.

Elbow above shoulder aids forward lean

Eye-focus

Straight alignment of head and torso

60 degrees

Hand well below shoulder aids forward lean

DRIVE! Drive off!

In this still picture it appears as though foot extension would place the foot too far ahead where it would brace against forward drive. But by the time it lands, the body will have moved forward.

Fig. 25.15.-- Maintaining maximum velocity beyond 60-70 yards.

Ozolin's[1] summary of how to improve speed in any sports action is of great value, especially since he recognizes the uses of both physical and mental approaches to the problem. He mentions, for example, the tendency to level off at a certain speed of action; plateaus of speed are reached, just as in other human learning, which are fixed by following a set pattern of training in all its aspects. I am reminded of the weight-lifters "sticking points." Ozolin says that it requires a new and stronger stimulus and proportionately increased

---

[1]Nikolai Ozolin, "How to Improve Speed," *Track Technique*, 44, June 1971, 1400.

conditioning to move to a higher level of speed. For example, speed running against the resistance of a sandy surface, followed immediately by sprinting on a hard track. Competition in practice may lead the sprinter to ignore his built-up inhibitions and sprint faster than he thinks he can. As a third method, Ozolin mentions the research of A. V. Korobkov who found that the gradually accelerated rhythm of a metronome increased stride frequency in running in place by five to eight percent. This reminds me of the work of Ben Ogden, coach of Eulace Peacock, a 26-foot long jumper and one of the very few men ever to beat Jesse Owens, who coached his men to maintain cadence with the rapping of his cane on a board floor. Many hours were spent bouncing the feet in time with his stick: slowly, then faster-faster-faster. To work the knees and ankles, he'd then require them on each stride to touch a string stretched 24, 30 and even 36 inches high. Or, as a second variation, he'd hold the cadence even, and require them to bring their knees higher and higher.

Ozolin also suggests improving leg-speed by setting up conditions which overload the speed of action, as contrasted with the force of action--sprinting while attached by elastic cable to a motorcycle, or by sprinting on a down-hill track. Soviet researchers concluded that the motorcycle run gave "a feeling for a higher speed." One man improved his 50-yard time by 0.3 seconds after such a run. Other researchers found that down-hill sprinting, using a 2-3 percent decline, gave an average increase of "about 13 percent due to greater stride frequency." In his overall conclusions, Ozolin warns that development by such methods should be on a gradual step-by-step basis, that it takes three to four months to establish a new speed-level firmly, and that such work should be but one phase of the regular sprint-training program.

LENGTH OF STRIDE. A second variable in sprinting speed is the length of strides. Given a certain cadence, force, relaxation and other related factors, the longer a man's stride, the sooner he will reach the finish line. Stride length, in both the early acceleration and full-speed phases of sprinting, is highly trainable. I remember clearly how Coach Hoyt emphasized it greatly in the training of 1932 100-200 Olympic Champion, Eddie Tolan, and how such lack of stride length was a major factor in the failure of Ralph Metcalfe to be rated along with Jesse Owens as an all-time great sprinter. I can see Hoyt adding increments of distance as he marked each stride in the cinder track and required Eddie to reach out during the first 30 yards to the new and greater distances. In contrast, Metcalfe was coached that leg-speed was the crucial factor in the start so that his feet pattered out of the blocks.

Dyson (1967, 111) notes that in efficient running, the leading foot never reaches out "grotesquely" for a longer stride, and that "stride length is the product of a driving forward of the entire body." But the length of time in which the "driving forward" occurs is also a factor, especially during the acceleration phase. In running, the foot does land slightly in front of the center of body weight, though this distance does decrease with increased speed of running. There is also general agreement that if force can be exerted at all by the backward "pawing" action of the extended foot, that force is very slight and is mainly related to getting the foot down on the ground more quickly. But there is an optimum time-distance in which forward push or thrust should occur. Especially during the start, this time-distance tends to be cut short, so that special related practice is needed.

POWER OF FORWARD THRUST. Successful coaches of sprinting agree that forward thrust, or drive, or bounce as it is called variously, is essential and can be improved by training. Bud Winter, San Jose State, who probably developed more sprinters than any other coach, including Hal Davis, Ray Norton, and the great Tommie Smith, required practice of the forward drive from all his men. Time and time again, they drove up and down the grass infield--pushing, pushing, pushing more forcefully with each foot. This was also emphasized in gaining greater acceleration during starting practice.

Bill Marlow, coach of Peter Radford, one-time world-record holder in the 220 on the curve, called it "greater forward drive from the rear." He believed that putting first emphasis on a longer stride by way of a high knee lift and foot extension was "putting cart before the horse," and concentrated on "driving every time a foot contacts the ground."

The word "bounce" also has its uses--"to leap or spring quickly." This suggests relaxation, resilience, quickness of force rather than hard effort. Coach Snyder used to speak of Jessie Owens as sprinting as though his feet were touching a hot stove. An exaggeration of course which denied Owens' full-stride action, but it does give a feeling of explosive ease of movement. As meet director, I watched Owens on that greatest-ever day in Ann Arbor, Michigan, and marvelled at his complete relaxation and seeming lack of effort. Many asked, "What will he do when he really tries to run?" But Charlie Hoyt, an astute observer, replied, "If he ever really tries, he'll never run as fast."

THE RECOVERY PHASE. Shortly after the toes of the driving foot leave the ground, the thigh begins an accelerating swing forward, then upward which Dyson (1967, 111) states "increases the forward force exerted by the ground, thus increasing the speed with which the Centre of Gravity is moved away from the supporting foot." Perhaps this is the source of the value which some coaches place on bringing the leg forward quickly and forcefully, with the thigh high and the foot reaching forward. Incidentally, still or sequence pictures which catch the forward foot off the ground and well ahead of the body are deceiving; in action, by the time the foot reaches the ground, the body has moved forward so that the center of body weight is above the foot and not behind it.

USE OF THE ARMS. Primarily, arm action achieves balance, offsets the twisting effect of the legs as they drive on each side of the body's centerline, and, according to some research, aids directly the straight-line thrust of the legs. Jokl[1] concluded from a study of the relative educability of the hands, arms and legs that "the complex flexion and extension pattern in hips, knees, feet, and toes, on which running and jumping are based, can be triggered off most effectively from the upper extremities." This is of great interest and possibly of real value to the mechanics of sprinting, but educability is not the same as actual use in action.

Dyson (1978, 117), however, supports Jokl's point,

. . .in sprinting, particularly, the arms may be used to spur on the legs, which speed up and consequently add to their horizontal component of drive; . . . Since both arms accelerate upwards and downwards simultaneously, . . . their upward movement adds to the vertical component of drive; and their downward acceleration coinciding with touch down, lessens the impact between the ground and front foot.

Moreover, by losing upward speed fractionally before the completion of leg drive, they ease the compression of the thrusting leg--and so permit more forceful and freer use of its foot and ankle.

In summary of the uses of the arms, they do aid greatly the steady straight-ahead position of the torso and shoulder girdle so important for balance, relaxation, and straight-line drive. They do, if properly used, help to ensure a sound body angle, especially during the start but also throughout the entire sprint. They do serve as a focal point for overall relaxation; if the hands are relaxed, the sprinter is more likely to be relaxed. And apparently, in the ways described by Jokl and Dyson, they can stimulate faster movements within the legs.

To best implement such uses, the angle at the elbows should remain the same throughout--about 90 degrees. Certainly there should be no increased flexion at the elbow and upthrust of the arm as it swings forward.

Fig. 25.16. Carl Lewis--driving reaction to the gun. From Tom Tellez, op.cit., p.2805.

[1]Ernst Jokl, M.C., "Some Physiological Components of Modern Track Training," *Clinic Notes, National College Track Coaches Association,* 1956, 226.

RELAXATION WHEN SPRINTING. Whatever one's degree of natural relaxation in sprinting, it can be improved by practice, both in competition and while training. In races, be aware of the looseness of your hands, of your arms, or of your neck and chin muscles. Always feel that you could have run just a little faster. A man's greatest races are "easy;" observers get an impression of "not trying," and wonder how much faster a man could do if his competition had forced him to go "all-out."

I hardly need repeat that relaxation is a whole-person concept--physical-mental-emotional. By-passing the book-length analysis of what might be meant by those three aspects, the sprinter experiences relaxation as an underloading of what we call "all-out" effort, or as a one percent reduction of tensions. Each athlete has a critical level of tension at which he performs best. If tension is lower, he is not properly "tuned up" for competition; if higher, he feels "tight," "lacking eagerness," "preoccupied as though in a trance."

In his research on weight-lifting, Arthur Steinhaus spoke of "disinhibiting the inhibitions," an awkward phrase, but it applies equally to relaxation in sprinting. The same impression of "taking it easy," of "sprinting as though on a red-hot stove" can be felt in the sprinting of Jesse Owens, Tommie Smith, Jim Hines, Valeriy Borzov or James Sanford. One is reminded of Coach Winter's admonition, "Think faster-looser, faster-looser; not harder but quicker." Anyone who questions that leg-speed is, in part, a function of the mind doesn't know sprinting.

Wysotschin's research[1] using a method of polimyography, concluded that, once beyond about 60 meters, relaxation plays an increasing role in sprint performances. Among a group of 50 sprinters, the relaxation factor had a value of 21.2% in improving 100-meter times; 48.32%, on 200-meter times. (No report was made of how relaxation was trained.)

In practice, run a series of 110-meter sprints, with full recovery between. From a running start, sprint at 98 percent speed for about 80 meters, preferably with a sprinter a meter or more ahead of you. Then sprint faster-looser; try to catch the man ahead over the last 20 meters. Impossible? But gradually you feel that you can run easier with no loss of velocity. Gradually you get a muscle-sense that to go faster, you let them flow--"faster-looser." You don't drop your arms; merely your tensions, or inhibitions. Of course you don't realize you have inhibitions until after you let them go. Gradually you learn to thrust more forcefully with each foot, not so much as an effort for power as a release of power. The power is there; you must, by repeated practice, get the knack of letting it go. It sounds like nonsense to make an effort not to make an effort, but great athletes learn to put into action what is non-sense in words.

Loader[2] puts all this into words that have the feel of action:

The sprinter knows when he (is running well). . . . .The ease, the apparent lack of effort with which he moves, inform him. Conscious thought plays little part in his effort, for thinking did its work in the past, when the long routine of training had to be endured. . . . Motion is light and fluid, trammeled by no barriers. Limbs thrust, press, recover, thrust, in a cycle of movement so smooth as to be almost mechanical. . . . His body is being carried forward with a swift-sure speed so easy that he is hardly conscious of speed. The track does not seem to be traversed by individual, separate steps deliberately taken by flesh and blood but rather by a surging flow of spirit. . . . At such a moment there is no need for anyone to tell you. You know you can run. I mean, really run.

---

[1]Juri Wysotschin, "Relaxation in Sprinting," *Track Technique*, #68, June 1977, 2180.

[2]W. R. Loader, *THE TESTAMENT OF A RUNNER*, London: William Heinemann Ltd., 1960, p. 170. (This is a great book for sprinters--fascinating and helpful.)

MAINTAINING VELOCITY

Even in such a short sprint as the 100-meter dash, the problem is one of <u>maintaining velocity</u> as much as of achieving it. Franklin Henry's 1952 research[1] on the force-time characteristics of sprinting concluded: (1) That men generally reached their top speed about six seconds after leaving the starting blocks," (2) "That it is physiologically impossible for the runner, after he has reached his peak velocity, to maintain it for more than about 15 or 20 yards." Henry's subjects were not talented or highly-trained sprinters, so we should not interpret these conclusions as the last word. But they do indicate the great significance of the problem.

In 1981, Dr. Dietrich Harre,[2] East Germany, reported that

Studies by Henry Shdanov, Ozolin and Khomenkov have shown that maximum speed in the 100m sprint is reached between the fifth and sixth second. Athletes of lower performance capacity reach maximum speed earlier. According to Gondlach, the distance covered in maximal or within 1% of the maximal speed ranges, according to performance level, between 20 and 45m.

The optimal length of the distance for development of speed depends therefore on individual performance capacity. It corresponds to a distance between 35 up to 80m (20 to 60m for Juniors) when the acceleration starts from a motionless position.

The obvious implication of such studies is that, assuming equal <u>acceleration and maximal-velocity</u>, the winning sprinter will be the one that slows down the least. The problem becomes one of maintaining closest-to-maximal velocity, even for the 100m dash and obviously for the 200m and 400m dashes.

Obviously, this is as much a mental-emotional problem as a physical one. In terms of action, what does it mean to maintain control? to hold your form? How does one run with "reckless abandon"? "controlled recklessness"? How does one "<u>stay loose</u>"? The important thing, of course is the meaning of these terms *in action*. Actually, as Franklin Henry states, it may be "physiologically impossible" to sprint "top speed" at 80 yards, and then pick-up speed at the finish. But in terms of how a sprinter feels, it CAN be done.

THE GATHER AND FINISH

"<u>Twenty yards from the finish you should gather for a burst to the tape; many races are won, or lost, here.</u>" Those are the words of Bud Winter, San Jose State College retired, coach of Tommie Smith, 1968 Olympic 200m champion (19.8 WR), and many other fine sprinters. Coach Winter conceded that his "gather" was primarily in the mind, but always added that the art of great sprinting was as much a matter of mental control (positive thinking) as of physical relaxation. As a matter of interest he headed up a program of relaxation dynamics when in the Navy in World War II.

Fig. 25.17. Evelyn Ashford, 1984 Olympic Champion, 100m (10.97 OR) sprinting through and beyond the finish line.

---

[1]Franklin Henry, "Force-Time Characteristics of the Sprint Start," *The Research Quarterly*, October 1952, 301-318.

[2]Dr. Dietrich Harre, "Development of Speed," translated from the author's book, *TRAINGSLEHRE, EG*, in Jess Jarver, *SPRINTS & RELAYS*, Los Altos: Tafnews Press, 1983, p. 71.

(1) At 20 yards from the finish line, take a breath and gather mentally for the finish.
(2) Get higher on your toes to lengthen your strides. (3) Say to yourself "Faster-looser," to ensure relaxation. If you say "Go" or "Try harder," you will tighten up and shorten your strides. (4) Reach with your arms about as high as your navel to lengthen strides. (5) Keep head down; eyes on finish line. (6) Fix attention on relaxing (letting-go) the hands and mouth. (7) In summary, run faster and looser. (8) Drive through the tape as though the finish line were five yards beyond. (9) Lean forward right at the tape and throw a shoulder into the tape; the added inches can make a crucial difference.

These are words at which the researchers may scoff. "It is physiologically impossible for a sprinter to maintain maximal velocity beyond five or six seconds." Yet Winter says, "Go faster--looser," even at 180 meters. As I judge it, it's the effect that counts, not the facts. Actually, Winter was certain that the facts proved mental control and relaxation could produce a physical increase in speed.[1] After Tommie Smith's record 220 on the straight in 19.5, they measured his stride-marks. From 120 to 200 yards, they measured 8'5"; in the next 12 yards, 8'7"; for the last three strides, 8'9". Was Smith "coasting" between 120 and 200 yards? Coasting on a 19.5 220! But how else can this increase be explained? One answer is that pick-up and increased stride length was an inexorable requirement in Winter's schedule of practice for all his sprinters. He had an "ankle bounce" exercise, a "leg reach" exercise, a "bound forward" exercise, a "knees-up" exercise; and they all had to be done every practice. Pick-up may be "physiologically impossible," but it does seem to help get you there first, and that's what puts you on the top Olympic stand.

---

[1]Lloyd C. "Bud" Winter, *SO YOU WANT TO BE A SPRINTER*, San Francisco: Fearon Publishers, 1956, 48 pages.

THE ORGANIZATION OF PRACTICE

Sprint training demands a year-round program of vigorous related activity which is just as carefully planned as for any other track or field event: a program of gradual development, first, in all-round endurance and physical condition; and later, toward specific sprinting skill and condition.

Modern training for sprinting emphasizes methods of gaining maximum velocity in the least possible time-distance, but equally important, emphasizes methods of maintaining maximum velocity through the finish line. In the past, such top speed began to diminish after about 80 yards. This is a serious problem in the 100; it is crucial in the 220. We tend to think of this maintenance of velocity as a problem in endurance, but it is equally a problem in relaxation, control, and skill. Call it what we may, the answer in terms of action lies in long-time related practice.

Perhaps toughness is the important word: toughness of muscle and tendon to withstand up-hill speed-training during the Fall of the year; toughness to practice day after day after day while following an interval-training schedule such as quarter-milers and half-milers might follow; toughness to work hard, but always within the limits of complete control and complete relaxation. Some call it will-power, and certainly that's part of the problem, but equally, it's a letting-go, a dropping of inhibitions against the pains of fatigue or against the dangers of all-out effort. We've used the term "controlled recklessness," as related to the field events, but it applies as well to sprinting.

By training the year-round, a man gradually learns to let himself go; he maintains control--in fact, his skill and control become automatic--but like the uninhibited madman, he throws away all restraint and releases his power. For the most part, a sprinter is unconscious of this release of power through daily practice. He may feel he's running faster and easier; that's about as far as his words will go. But release does come--through inexorable daily practice: tough, enjoyable, carefully planned, and reckless.

PRACTICE PROCEDURES

Each coach and each athlete must organize his own schedule, first on a year-round, then on a next-four-weeks basis. Judgment must consider ability, maturity, physical condition, season of competitive year, weather, interest, and personal problems. Thus to print a practice schedule here would be foolhardy.

Alternate days of hard work and easy work.

Injury and mental staleness do not result from too much work so much as doing too much work *too soon*. Use the gradual approach.

Light jogging for at least 20 minutes immediately following competition, or for an hour or more on the day after competition will ensure a better practice on the next day.

A proper workout requires about 90 minutes of continuous activity, divided into three equally important parts: (1) Twenty minutes of warm-up jogging and flexibility exercises; (2) Forty minutes of intensive work on endurance, speed, or skill; and (3) Twenty minutes of enjoyable relaxed jogging with other men regardless of their events. This last period is an excellent means of removing fatigue, preventing injury and muscle soreness, and building team morale.

WARM-UP AND PRE-SEASON PROCEDURES

1. Warm-up for 20 minutes with jogging, flexibility exercises, upper body strength exercises, and increasing-speed windsprints. Always finish up with easy jogging.

2. Fartlek. Get off the track to any varied terrain that is available. Enjoy getting tired while alternating repeated fast work (80% effort) with relaxed jogging.

3. If only a track is available, follow fartlek methods on the track. Devise methods that are enjoyable, that change speeds repeatedly, and that toughen.

AEROBIC SPEED-PLAY (Primarily Fall and early Spring running.) This should be thought of as a Run-for-Fun program to establish a base of general fitness for later training. Modern sprinters have banished the old fear that long running will slow muscle action. That's just not true! But such fartlek away from the track develops self-confidence if nothing else, and, lacking coercion from anyone, can be mighty satisfying.

TRAINING FOR GREATER SPEED-ENDURANCE

1. Repeated sprints with running start at from 60 to 120 yards, 80% speed, with short recovery jogging between. Build up gradually over several months to take three or more series of three or four sprints each. Get tired, rest by jogging, then get tired again. Do some curve sprinting.

2. Interval training on an organized basis. Use a fixed distance, 120 yards to 220 yards. (1) Use slower speed, set the rest interval at three minutes, then gradually increase the number of sprints up to six. When this workout is mastered, that is, when it can be done with no muscle soreness or stiffness the next day, then (2) use slower speed, run six sprints, but gradually decrease the rest interval until the heart rate is reduced to about 110 beats within 60 seconds. Continue to full mastery. Finally, (3) gradually increase the speed of the sprints.

3. As condition improves, spring, that is, bound up low-grade hills, following the methods of Arthur Lydiard. The goal here is power and endurance. Spring forward with long strides, not short ones as is normal on hills. <u>Warning</u>: This is tough on the Achilles tendon. Use gradually and carefully.

4. Sprint 330 yards all-out *relaxed*. The emphasis here is on relaxation when tired. Try to maintain maximum velocity, but maintain control and relaxation. Repeat this workout until the problem of control is just no longer a problem.

5. Repetition relays--220 yards each leg. Use an odd number of men each team. Each man runs many times, from three to a dozen or more legs. Anchor man passes baton back to lead-off man. A valuable procedure with which to complete a day's work. Be sure opposing runners are paired for endurance and speed. First few legs are pace work; last legs are competitive.

TRAINING FOR GREATER RUNNING POWER

1. Take bouncing or leaping strides over various distances on track or grass. Drive forcefully forward with maximum-length strides, thrusting the ground backward in a "pawing" action as the free foot first touches the ground. High knee action is important, not in itself, but to ensure a full-length stride. Accentuate a forceful arm action. Variation 1--Same general procedure but emphasize quickness of foot-placement even though this decreases stride length. Variation 2--Same general procedure but wear weighted vest or belt. This is strenuous and injury-prone work; use gradual approach as to number of strides, rest between runs, number of repetitions, use of weights. Though greater force is the objective, emphasize quickness, an easy flowing of movement, rhythm and balance throughout. Variation 3--Take starts out of blocks, emphasizing explosive forward thrust for longer strides.

2. Organize a program of power exercises specifically related to the sprint muscles--the front thigh (quads), rear thigh (hamstrings), extensors and flexors of the lower leg-ankle-foot. Keep in mind the formula (power = strength x velocity) in which either strength or velocity can be emphasized as is now done in training for javelin power. A heavy load with few repetitions develops strength^{5x} x velocity^x; a light load develops strength^x x velocity^{5x}. Both are essential, though as with the javelin, speed-power is prepotent over strength per se. Good judgment suggests that such power-exercise periods be followed by easy running and sprinting as fits within the schedule.

3. Wearing ankle weights between 1-2# each, gradually build up speed over about 50 yards--slowing down slowly. USSR research[1] found such resistances to be most effective; those above 2# changed the pattern of action and had a negative result. They also found that long jumpers gained more than sprinters by using such ankle weights, especially with those above 2#.

<u>TRAINING FOR GREATER RUNNING SPEED</u>. (Always run relaxed at 99 percent effort, especially when maximum speed is attempted.)

1. Starts at 20 yards. Take during middle of workout to ensure full warm-up and minimum fatigue. A dozen is not too many. Not merely quickness out of the blocks but quickness to 20

---

[1]N. Smirnov, "Ankle Weights in Training," *Track Technique*, #72, June 1978, p. 2308.

yards and beyond. On occasion, give team-mate one to three-foot handicap, then catch him before the tape--with a feeling fo being relaxed, of releasing power, not forcing it.

2. With a running start, take repeated sprints (all-out but feeling 99 percent effort) at from 50 to 80 yards. Full rest (jogging-walking) between.

3. Sprint on downhill grade of 5 percent or less. Soviet research found an increase of 17% in stride frequency on the flat immediately after downhill sprints on a 2 to 3-degree grade, but concluded the primary value of such work was to "give an extra little push that may dislodge the sprinter from his plateau." Consensus was that grades should not exceed 5 percent and such work should be light and increased carefully to avoid strains.

4. Run curves 95% effort-counter-clockwise and clockwise.

5. Competitive sprints at 3/4 competitive distance--75 or 180 yards. Variation--give team-mate of equal ability a one-yard handicap at start, maintain handicap for 50 yards, then catch him in the next 25.

UP-HILL AND DOWN-HILL TRAINING.
A study by Kunz and Kaufmann[1] measured the effects on sprinting mechanics of training on uphill and downhill slopes of 3 percent grade. All agree that changes in running mechanics do occur naturally in such running. But there has been little knowledge of the carry-over effects to later sprinting on the flat.

"The subjects were 10 male sprint candidates and 10 male decathlon candidates for the Swiss 1978 National Track Team. All subjects were trained for competition in the 100m dash...."

Results of this study included a detailed analysis of the changes in body mechanics while doing such slope running--changes in stride lengths, body angles, arm action, knee lifts and the like. Conclusions were that,

Sprinting up a positive grade (3%) and down a negative grade (3%) results in some dissimilarities in their technical aspects. Our data indicate that downhill sprint training will develop: (1) the stride push-off angle; (2) the trunk-thigh angle; (3) the knee-lift movement....

Sprint training uphill (1) increases the length of stride and (2) shortens contact time....We use both uphill and downhill training to develop both coordination and power in our sprinters. Specifically, we emphasize uphill training during pre-season to develop basic power in the legs. Then, we emphasize downhill training during the competitive season, (thus combining) basic power with improved technique so as to develop greater speed of movement."

SUMMARY OF THE ORGANIZATION OF TRAINING
Today, no self-respecting advocate of track and field training can advance a program without deferring to Matveyev's system called Periodization,[2,3] with its assumption of year-round training of all aspects of the athlete--mind, body and "soul" down to the tiniest details. Periodization is an organismic concept in which each phase, large or small, is essential to the whole; neglect one phase and the entire machine may break down. To construct this Control Plan, Matveyev conceived macrocycles, mesomycles, microcycles and a detailed analysis of the components of training--their number limited only by their creator's powers of analysis.

I've thought a lot about Periodization and its implications--specifically for sprinting but, more than that, for our United States school-college program in general. In our zeal to surpass the Communists in the Olympic Games, is it possible we have swallowed the duck whole--head and tail, bones and feathers--with little thought as to its actual nutritional values,

[1]Hansruedi Kunz and David A. Kaufmann, "Biomechanics of Hill Sprinting," *Track Technique*, Vol. 82, Winter 1981, p. 2603.

[2]Gary L. Winckler, "Training Program for the Sprints," *Track Technique Annual 1983*, Los Altos: Tafnews Press, pp. 46-52. A carefully prepared overview of sprint training, with an analysis of sprinting components and a year-round schedule--all based on Matveyev's concept of Periodization.

[3]Remi Korchemny, "Sprinting," *Track Technique*, Vol. 86, Fall 1983, pp. 2774-2778. Korchemny, now sprint coach at Stanford, formerly worked with Valeriy Borzov, 1972 Olympic gold medallist, 100-200 meters.

to say nothing of its effects on the digestive system.

I keep thinking back to little Eddie Tolan (1932 Olympic 100m Champion--10.3, made on the Los Angeles "clay" track), and comparing his performance with that of Carl Lewis (09.9) made on a perfect-traction plastic track, in the 1984 Games. That's a four-tenth second difference--in itself a significant difference--but about two-tenths of that should be subtracted because of marked differences in overall sprinting conditions. What produced that two-tenths of a second difference?--talent, training methods or training time?

No one could disagree that Lewis has a great talent for sprinting. His build, his way of moving, his times at an early age, all compare favorably with such talents as Ralph Metcalf, Bob Hayes, Jim Hines, or Tommie Smith. Lewis was trained, for the most part, by Tom Tellez, University of Houston, a man well versed in the scientific aspects of modern training and sprinting techniques. I've read nothing to suggest that Tellez or Lewis were followers of Periodization in their training. But Lewis did train "year-round," certainly with no hindrances to training time or his concentration on sprinting.

Now by way of contrast, consider Eddie Tolan. Eddie was no superman. At Cass Tech High School, Detroit, he won the City Championships in his senior year in 10 seconds flat. I knew him well. He was 5'7" tall, perhaps 150 pounds--track historian John Kieran called him "chunky" and "squat"--certainly not a body type that one would expect to display a surging finish as did Tolan during the last 20 yards of the 100m, let alone the 200m. But Eddie acquired just such a finish through carefully planned training within the limits of less than six months of the year.

His coach, Charlie Hoyt, was a nationally-ranked sprinter at Grinnell College. Hoyt learned his sprinting from Doc Huff, also a former sprinter, and from Steve Farrell, Head Coach at Michigan and winner of the professional English Sheffield Handicap in 1894. The words they used in coaching exuded from their own sprinting muscles. Don't shrug off that statement. I was assistant coach at Michigan and tried to learn everything that Hoyt knew, but somehow I ended up feeling he had forgotten more about sprinting than I could ever know.

Eddie Tolan, 1932 Olympic 100- and 200-meter champion.

438

Each year at Michigan, Eddie first reported for practice on December 1 in Yost Field House. Fall speed-endurance work? Nonsense! Who wants endurance for sprinters. It would slow you down. Practice couldn't be sooner, for Coach Hoyt served full time as Head Trainer for football. Such training was only for two weeks, climaxed by an intra-squad meet, but that was two weeks more than other Big-Ten track men had, including Ralph Metcalfe at Marquette. More was time wasted. "Why train all your speed away--in practice"?

Did we need time for power training? Up to about 1950, we never used--in fact, never heard the expression. Weightlifting? Coach Farrell would look sidewise, spit copiously and --"Phooey! Musclebound! Look at Hackenschmitt!"

Our entire outdoor season included four meets--three duals and the Big Ten--plus, perhaps, the Penn or Drake Relays and, for three or four men, the NCAA in mid-June. But everyone went home for half of a two-week Easter vacation in April. What right did we coaches have to keep a man away from family and friends? Sports just were not that big a deal. Somehow that reminds me of the Oxford professor's question after being told breathlessly of the earth-shaking feat of Roger Bannister when he finally broke the four-minute barrier in the mile run, "Just what earth-shaking use did Mr. Bannister make of the one second of time he saved"?

An interesting question, especially in light of the fact that Lewis "saved" a mere four-tenths second or less. Is that four-tenth of a second really worth the six months of additional training time, to say nothing of the millions of hours and ergs of energy spent in constructing modern tracks, starting blocks, electric timing devices, shoes, whatnots? Somehow it smacks to me of time-energy borrowed at usurious rates of interest.

Am I serious? Do I really think the extra six months of training time is wasted? Would I actually throw out the dish pan of Periodization with the dirty dishwater we've put into it? Frankly, with certain exceptions and limitations, the answer is "yes,"but also, in lesser degree, "no."

The gist of Periodization is a more effective and efficient use of training time, and a more careful analysis of the component essentials of training and performance. That is a completely sound approach--for all events in track and field. But that does not require that we accept--whole or nothing--Matveyev's bone-felt assumption of year-round training (a month or so of active rest) for all events. I wonder how he would organize training for tiddley-winks if it were included in the Olympic events. Obviously, sprinting makes vastly different demands on time-energy from, say, distance running. All agree the latter requires "year-round" training. It doesn't necessarily follow that sprinting requires the same.

Secondly, Periodization is based on the premise that Olympic success justifies everything. The Russians and East Germans take seriously the Marxian phrase, "from each according to his talents." True, they have discovered that enjoyment-rest-relaxation are essential and now make them a planned aspect of all their work. But essential for better performance, especially in the Olympics, not because they are essential to a well-rounded whole-person education, the very essence of our Founding Fathers' hopes for Democracy.

In my judgment, Periodization as now formulated is not our way--not for sprinting, not for shotputting, nor even for distance running. The concept of Periodization has important uses, but only within those limits of time-energy our school-college system believes valid. Fulltime training was justified for Carl Lewis and a few dozen others. They say he's now a millionaire. (Can't help wondering what social good will come of it.) But what about the tens of thousands of other school-college men and women who might come under the influence of Periodization and its year-round training?

I suggest we make a new beginning. Organize our time-energy by all means. It's essential to doing our best. But organize in ways consistent with our own values and our own school-college time schedule. Ignore the jargon of Matveyev's system. Invent our own terminology-- simpler, less abstruse. Make our own careful analysis of the components of training. Use Periodization, not as a guide, but as a checkup device. In summary, weigh the two-tenth difference in competitive time between Eddie Tolan, 1932, and Carl Lewis, 1984. Then weigh the six-month training time required of Tolan against the 10-12 months required of Lewis. Somewhere between lies a solution fitted to each unique individual and to the ambitions of his institution and coach, as well as to the demands of the Olympic gods.

RELATED POWER EXERCISES

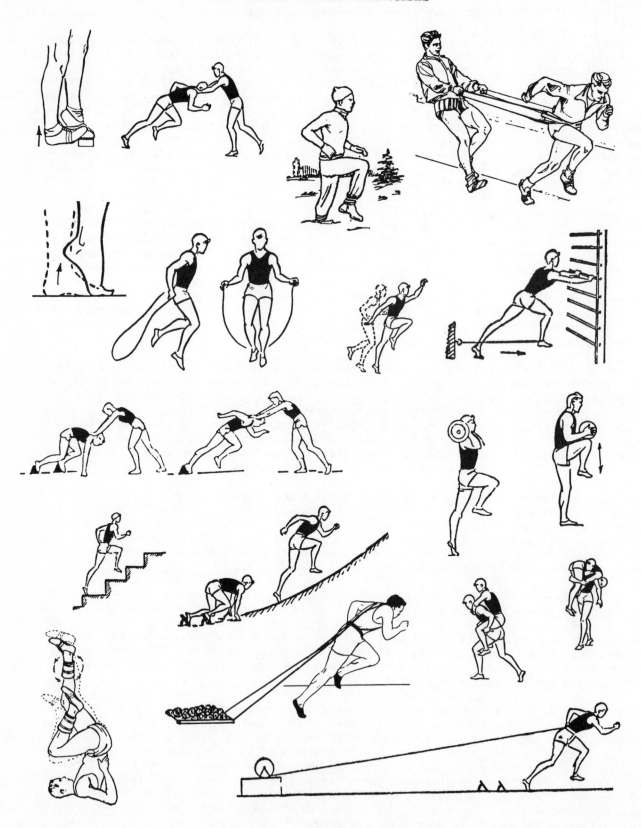

RELATED POWER EXERCISES

Chapter 26
COMPETITIVE HINTS FOR SPRINTS AND HURDLES

Competitive hints usually relate to the minutes and actions that immediately precede competition. These are crucial of course and must be carefully organized and carried out. But it would be fatal to think that they were the main part of developing a maximum competitive attitude and action. Actually, a competitive attitude in a mind-body sense is acquired primarily in the weeks and months and years before major competition. If a boy is careless in practice in the placement of his starting blocks; if he is discouraged by continually practicing against faster starters; if in practice or in minor competition, the starting gun is fired carelessly; if his track suit is sloppy or his spikes badly worn; if the institution he represents has little respect among track buffs; if any of these or a hundred other details are negative, or for that matter positive, in their effects, the athlete's competitive approach will be affected.

This holistic approach to competition is so crucial as to be explained in different ways. To a real degree, a man's total pattern of habitual response is sharply channeled or focussed within a single action. Because this action is so narrow in time and movement, we tend to isolate it, and minimize its backgrounds. But time and time again, I have watched great performers in competition, been amazed at their concentration and control, then later discovered a great breadth of preparation and thoughtful planning and wise counselling that lay behind their efforts. A man is born with a certain potential in terms of competitive spirit just as he is born with a certain potential for muscle velocity. But whether that potential is realized at maximum levels is determined by development through environment and experience and inspiration.

Since each athlete and his background are unique, it is difficult to prescribe specific measures that will ensure high competitive spirit as the man approaches the starting line. Some great champions tend to withdraw within themselves, to shut out the world, to concentrate their energies by eliminating the distractions of people and influences around them. Other equally great champions seem to expand under competition, seem to be unaware of the negatives, become talkative and cheerful and eager for the race to start. Only by knowing his man, can a coach give help that will be helpful.

However, a few suggestions may open possibilities. First, there should be a routine of action and attitude leading up to important competition. Whatever its details, they should develop confidence and a maximum of what we call nervous energy. The word, "routine" is crucial, a set pattern of action that one knows by past experience will lead to the single-mindedness needed at the start. Throughout the weeks before the BIG meet, a routine of practice, of eating and sleeping, of thinking and talking, should build the confidence and poise for this special competition and its special conditions.

I had the great privilege of coaching John Haines, National champion at 60 yards indoors for four straight years, 1953-1956. John was beaten occasionally in lesser meets. But during the week of the Championship, he was a different person. He spoke more confidently, laughed more, practiced with greater relaxation, started more sharply. Somehow, we all KNEW he was going to win. I repeat, WE ALL KNEW, and that's mighty important. The calm, undoubting attitude of high expectancy, whether created by the man himself, or his friends, or his coach and team-mates, is its own assurance of high performance.

The crucial time of course is during the last hour or so before the final race. During that brief period one's energies can build and build to the point of controlled but explosive tension. Or they can seep away, erg by erg, through distracted worry over one's opponents, through irritation with the starter and his uncertain way of handling men, through concern for one's shoe laces or spikes, or for the sudden awareness of an ache in the left knee, or--but the possible ways of escape are endless.

One of the best ways of finding concentration is to have a set pattern of things to do:

1. Report to the dressing room well ahead of time.

2. Dress steadily but leisurely.

3. Warm-up fully but gradually.

4. Go back to dressing room, towel off the sweat, check your shoes carefully: leather, spikes, laces, put on your number, etc., all ahead of time so that if something is wrong, there is plenty of time to fix it.

5. Back on the track, check the starter: his tone of voice in saying, "set," his steadiness and relaxation in holding men at "set," his gun reaction when several sprinters have false starts--whatever seems vital.

6. Ignore your opponents, or respond to them as you may prefer, but don't allow your contact with them to distract you or disrupt your concentration.

7. In all these actions, expect and welcome the nervousness, the dry mouth, the cold sweat, the stomach butterflies. They all signify the clearing of decks for action, for powerful action--just as long as you maintain control. This isn't self-hypotism, or if it is, it is of the common-sense kind by which men rise in so many emergencies to their highest achievements. Call it what you will: competitive spirit, positive mental attitude, courage, willed control; the words mean little. But it is a range of quality that we all possess, and only needs careful and patient training to attain its full use.

8. Begin the actions of "go to your marks" early, and therefore calmly. Do it the same way every time (in practice as in the meets). In a very important sense, you're not thinking of anything. At this point thinking would be a distraction. It all becomes automatic. You're not attending to anything consciously. The world doesn't exist. Only afterward to you realize that there was "awareness" of many details; just as at this moment, by setting aside this page, you realize that you "heard" the noises in the next room, without really being conscious of them.

A sprinter or hurdler goes through the motions of starting, in somewhat the same manner as a pianist goes through the hand-finger motions of playing. In a sense, his fingers do the playing; through much practice, they have become "aware" of when to hit softly or when to slow the tempo. True, the player is conscious of how the playing is occurring, but it's a holistic consciousness. If the player thinks about it in a divisive way, in a way that analyzes how, that takes his technique apart, his playing will flounder. Or let his mind wander, and the music will suffer even though it's something he has played "perfectly" for years. So with starting, or, for that matter, with any competitive situation in sports. "Get with it, man!" may be jazz slang but it's also a sound attitude in competition.

Perhaps the best description ever written of both high and low competitive attitudes in sprinting is given by W. R. Loader[1] in TESTAMENT OF A RUNNER. His first story is of his great victory as a schoolboy at the English championships in 1935:

> Excitement was now working in me like yeast. Gone were all lethargy and detachment. . . . Coming second in both heat and semi-final had not taken undue toll of nervous energy. I was anxious for the start, desperate to go, knowing I had it in me to mount a desperate effort. . . . Previous doubts and anxieties now seemed ridiculous. Confidence burned like a flame.

---

[1] W. R. Loader, TESTAMENT OF A RUNNER, London: William Heinemann Ltd., 1960, 125-144.

The second description is of a similar situation a year later, in which, after a year of college where he met coldness and discouragement, he failed to even qualify for the final:

Suddenly it became desperately important to get into that final. . . . But through excessive brooding on mere part-success, the nerve had failed. The prospect of the contest did not induce a feeling of excitement so much as a feeling of dread. Even the most wishful thinking could not convince that this last chance was more than the slenderest. The finality of the affair turned the bowels to liquid. There was no spearhead of resolution, sharp and shining, but only a dull obstinacy. A year ago the White City had been warm and bright in the sunshine. This time it was grey and chill. Influenced by weather, the blood ran even cooler than before. Instead of creating confidence, memories of the other, triumphant occasion, merely deepened the sense of inadequacy. . . .

Apathetically I dug my holes. The other runners were jigging around, taking deep breaths, high-stepping, obviously keyed up at the prospect of the race. Beside them I felt heavy and lackadaisical. When we got down to our marks, my mind wouldn't concentrate. It wandered, thinking of Berlin, thinking of the season's mediocre efforts, thinking of how the promise had not been fulfilled. The gun took me by surprise.

In these two situations, the same individual was involved, but the dynamics in his life-situation had changed. If anything, desire was greater in the second race, but it had been dulled by discouragement and repeated defeat.

1980 U.S. Olympic Trials 100 Final: L to R, Harvey Glance (2nd), Houston McTear (7th), Steve Williams (6th), Jerome Deal (8th), Willie Gault (5th), Stanley Floyd (1st), Mel Lattany (3rd), Carl Lewis (4th)./Photo by Don Chadez.

World record holder Renaldo Nehemiah./Photo by Gale Constable/Duomo.

Chapter 27
THE HIGH HURDLES

A BRIEF HISTORY OF THE DEVELOPMENT OF TECHNIQUE

As with throwing the javelin, long jumping, or for that matter with any field or track event, technique cannot be separated from speed of action. In the final analysis, the best technique is the one that gets a man to the finish line first. But you wouldn't think so, if you listened to the endless controversies of the past 90 years between the advocates of hurdling technique and the get-there-first boys. I remember so well how the admirers of Dick Attlesey's beautiful style looked down their noses when Harrison Dillard, the 1948 Olympic 100-meters champion, won the 1952 Olympic hurdles. What lousy form! Notice how he sails over the hurdle! That controversy hasn't quieted down entirely even today, though 13-second times require hurdlers that are tall, fast, and in complete control.

As a sports event, hurdling goes back no further than the early 19th century in England. No mention of any such competition over obstacles has been found in ancient Greek or early European or Irish literature. Webster[1] states,

> There were hurdle races at the tutors' and dames' houses at Eton College as long ago as 1837, and that is the earliest reference to competition in this kind of sport that I have been able to find, but in BELL'S LIFE of 1853 mention is made of a match between two amateurs, one of the events included being a race with jumps over 50 hurdles each 3 feet 6 inches high. . . . The first authentic records of a hurdles time are supplied by A. W. T. Daniel, CUAC. He won the first Oxford and Cambridge 120 high hurdles event, 1864, in 17 3/4 seconds.

Similarly, Ross and Norris McWhirter[2] write:

> Ten flights, ten yards apart, seemed to be the accepted test from the earliest mentions but the height was merely that of the accepted sheep hurdle of the day, about 3½ feet. In 1866 there was some attempt to standardize the height, for a rule in the first Oxford minute book states "the hurdles shall be 3 feet 6 inches in [above-- J.K.D.] the ground." It is not recorded how many of the early pioneers were maimed by these crude jagged barriers, which were rigidly staked into the meadow, but it is at least certain that if any of them could now see six rows of zebra striped slats, with their 8 pounds toppling moment, they would wonder if it were the same event.

Although no mention of "sheep hurdles" has been found in American track literature, Comstock[3] suggests a similarly diabolical device--a single rope or pole all the way across the track

---

[1] F. A. M. Webster, *ATHLETICS OF TO-DAY*. London: Frederick Warne & Co., Ltd., 1929, 132.

[2] Ross and Norris McWhirter, *GET TO YOUR MARKS*. London: Nicholas Kaye, 1951, 135.

[3] Boyd Comstock, *HOW TO HURDLE*. New York: American Sports Publishing Co., 1924, 90.

TABLE 27.1

OUTSTANDING PERFORMANCES--HIGH HURDLES

OLYMPIC CHAMPIONS -- MEN

Date	Record 110m	Name	Affiliation		Hgt.	Wgt.	Time 100y	Est.HC[1]
1952	13.7	Harrison Dillard	Baldwin-Wallace		5'10''		9.4	
1956	13.5	Lee Calhoun	No.Caro.Col		6'2''	165	9.7	
1960	13.8	Lee Calhoun	No.Caro.Col.					
1964	13.6	Hayes Jones	East.Mich.		5'10''	162	9.4	
1968	13.3	Willie Davenport	Southern U.		6'1''	175	9.4	
1972	13.24[2]	Rod Milburn	USA					
1976	13.30[2]	Guy Drut	France		6'2''	161		
1980	13.39	Thomas Munkelt	E. Germany		6'3/4''	172		
1984	13.20	Roger Kingdom	Pittsburgh		6'0''	185		

OLYMPIC CHAMPIONS -- WOMEN (100m--33'')

Date	Record	Name	Affiliation		Hgt.	Wgt.		
1964	10.5	Karen Balzer	E. Germany					
1968	10.3	Maureen Caird	Aus					
1972	12.59WR	Annelie Erhardt	E. Germany	26	5'5½''	128		
1976	12.77	Johanna Schaller	E. Germany	24	5'9''	143		
1980	12.56	Vera Komisova	USSR	27	5'6½''	132		
1984	12.84	Benita Fitzgerald	USA	23	5'10''	141		

WORLD RECORDS OF SPECIAL INTEREST -- MEN

Date	Record	Name	Affiliation	Hgt.	Wgt.	Time 100y	Est.HC[1]
1948	13.6y	Harrison Dillard	Baldwin-Wallace	5'10''	155	9.4	2.6
1951	13.5y	Dick Attlesey	So. Cal.	6'3½''	178	9.6	2.0
1956	13.4	Jack Davis	So. Cal.	6'3''	178	9.6	2.0
1958	13.4	Elias Gilbert	Winst.-Salem	5'11''	155	9.7	2.0
1959	13.2	Martin Lauer	Germany	6'1½''	165	9.4	2.1
1960	13.2	Lee Calhoun	No.Caro.Col.	6'2''	170	9.5	1.8
1981	12.93	Renaldo Nehemiah	Maryland U.	6'1½''	170	10.1m	1.90

WORLD RECORDS OF SPECIAL INTEREST -- WOMEN (100m - 33'')

Date	Record	Name	Affiliation
1979	12.63	Zofia Bielczsyk	Pol
1972	12.59	Annelie Ehrhart	E. Germany
1980	12.39	Vera Komisova	USSR
1980	12.36WR	Grazyna Rabsztyn	Pol

HIGH SCHOOL PERFORMANCES -- BOYS

Date	Record	Name	Affiliation	
1982	13.41	Steve Kerho	Mission Viejo, CA	(110m--39'')
1977	12.9	Renaldo Nehemiah	SP-F, SP, NJ	(120y--39'')
1977	13.89	Renaldo Nehemiah	SP-F, SP, NJ	(110m--42'')
1984	13.25	Arthur Blake	Haines City, FL	

HIGH SCHOOL PERFORMANCES -- GIRLS

Date	Record	Name	Affiliation
1979	12.95	Candy Young	Beaver Falls, PA
1983	13.63	LaVonna Martin	TM, Trot, Ohio
1983	13.83	Shirley Walker	Gar, Seattle, WA

[1]Estimated Hurdle-Clearance Time.

[2]Electronic timing.

which undoubtedly evolved from the cross-country stone and rail fence-hopping in vogue at the time.

This, however, was found to be impractical for general usage, as one runner would gain an advantage over another by reason of the general hurdle being knocked down by the leading man. The installation of the individual hurdle was the result. This hurdle, made after the style of a sawbuck, was of substantial construction and being a dangerous piece of furniture to strike, the hurdler made an effort to clear it by a good margin.

But a picture I have of F. G. Maloney, Chicago, winning the 1901 Big Ten Conference hurdles in 16.2, shows every hurdle sawbuck of the first two men flat on the ground. No blood-spattered leg bones are apparent but that might be for lack of color photography.

Shortly after 1900, increasing interest in the low hurdles (in America only) created one that swung down in the middle to provide a low hurdle 2'6" high. The base of this hurdle was 24 inches wide, with the uprights placed in the middle to form an inverted-T shape. A man was disqualified if he knocked down three hurdles.

Not that a man would try to knock them down. For as they fell, they first had to rise on the 12-inch extension of the base, and that made clearance problems for a man's thigh or trail leg. To avoid this, Harry Hillman, 1904 Olympic 400-meters hurdles champion and coach at Dartmouth, invented the present L-type hurdle which swings down immediately on being hit. This hurdle greatly increased the confidence, hair-breadth clearance, and so the speed of hurdling, a factor to be kept in mind when comparing hurdlers before and after.

Of the many excellent hurdlers prior to the L-type hurdle (1935), only two warrant special mention in this recital of techniques development--Alvin Kraenzlein and Earl Thomson. Though actually he was not the first to do so, Kraenzlein is generally credited with originating the straight-forward, though bent, lead leg, and with sprinting over the hurdles instead of jumping them. He was a fine athlete, holding world records in the high and low hurdles as well as in the long jump. The unique contribution of Earl Thomson (Canada, Dartmouth, and long-time coach at Annapolis; 1920 Olympic champion and world-record holder--14.4) was a two-arms-forward drive "through" the hurdle that ensured forward lean and balance beyond the hurdle.

Fig. 27.1. Evolution of the high hurdle--a carpenter's horse with high-hurdle attachment, a T-type hurdle (about 1912), and an L-type hurdle (about 1942).

Up to about 1940, hurdling technique and size requirements seemed well established. Every record holder (Simpson, 1916-14.6; Thomson, 1920-14.4; Anderson, 1930-14.4; Beard, 1931-14.2; Saling, 1932-14.6; Keller, 1932-14.4; Towns, 1937-13.7) was 6'3" or taller, and followed about the same pattern of action over the hurdle.

But with the coming of Fred Wolcott, 1941, and Harrison Dillard (1946-1954), the shift toward sprinting ability was on. Wolcott did attempt both arms forward as did Thomson, but failed to lean into the hurdle or to cut down the lead leg beyond it. His clearance was high and a hurried trail leg straightened the torso prior to the landing. Coaches began to speak of a new style for shorter men who could sprint. Get those feet down fast--both off the hurdle and in between hurdles, and leave aesthetics to the Greeks and the tall boys.

Fig. 27.2 -- Jack Davis, USC, 1956 - 13.4, showing excellent straight-ahead action. The lead leg is coming straight through; hips are square to the hurdle; though the left arm-shoulder are out of line as the trail leg is brought through.

Dillard's scant 5'10" and imperfect technique ruled out any chance of his becoming a great hurdler--they said! But after winning an NCAA hurdle trial (1947-13.9), he won 82 consecutive races, indoors and outdoors, and broke Towns' "human-ultimate" time of 13.7 by one-tenth second. Dillard's lead leg was locked at the knee, his torso somewhat twisted over the hurdle, his off-arm was wide and relatively uncontrolled, and his body lean upright on landing. But he ran 10.3 in winning the Olympic 100 meters in 1948, and that made the difference.

Then a new trend began--height, technique, AND speed. Dick Attlesey was 6'3½" tall. He used a modified two-arms-forward style, an excellent forward lean into and through the hurdle, a relaxed lead leg which snapped down quickly, and a delayed trail leg which drove forward with remarkable speed. Add to this that he had been timed in 10.5 for 100 meters in official competition. Small wonder he was the first to record 13.5.

Similarly, Jack Davis, the first (1956) to run 13.4, was 6'3" tall and had officially run 09.6 for the 100. On the other hand, Lee Calhoun won the 1956 Olympics in 13.5, despite a best time of only 09.9 for 100 yards and a height of 6'2". During the next four years, Calhoun concentrated on sprint work so that, prior to the 1960 Games, he had improved to 09.7. Undoubtedly this enabled him to win again at Rome, and, prior to the Games, to tie Martin Lauer's (Germany) world record of 13.2. Along with excellent technique over the hurdles, Calhoun had worked hard on perfecting a method of thrusting his head down and forward and so gaining an extreme forward lean at the tape. This gave him a number of important races, but especially that over his teammate, Willie May, in the 1960 Olympic final.

But over the past decade, the sprinters have dominated the high hurdles competition. First came Hayes Jones, Eastern Michigan, 5'10", 162#, with many a win in the open 60 indoors and 100 outdoors, a best 100-yard time of 09.4, and the 1964 Olympic championship, 13.6. Then Willie Davenport, Southern U., 6'1", 175#, an official 10.3 for the 100 meters, the 1968 Olympic gold medal (13.3), a tie for the world record in 13.2, and in 1969 alone, the winner of 21 races under 14 flat. As to his technique, Jon Hendershott[1] describes his style as "near-flawless" and quotes Berny Wagner, coach at Oregon State,

> Davenport's excellent balance is maintained throughout. His fine lean into the hurdle, his lead with the knee, the flat action of his trailing leg with the knee barely clearing the hurdle, all give quickness and power over the barrier.

---

[1]Jon Hendershott, "Davenport Rare Master," *Track & Field News*, May 1970, 3.

His lead foot lands well under his body so that he is in a running position when he hits the track after clearing the hurdle. He doesn't let his trail leg rise as high as most other hurdlers...and this saves time in getting his first stride down fast.

Rod Milburn (Southern U., 1972 Olympic champion--13.24 WR). The first approved 13s time (hand-timed) for 120-yard high hurdles was made in the 1971 National AAU semi-finals by Rod Milburn. Milburn combined at highest levels the twin essentials of sprinting speed and technique. His arm action (two arms forward) was forceful and well balanced both over and between hurdles. His lead leg cut down quickly; his forward lean enabled the rear leg to drive quickly to a full stride beyond. In 1971, he won 28 consecutive races; in 1972, his Olympic championship was preceded by 12 wins at 13.5 or faster, plus two windy 13.0s.

Hurdlers are Sprinters. By way of emphasizing the all-importance of sprinting speed for high-level hurdling, consider these facts: Harrison Dillard (HH-13.6y--100m-10.3); Hayes Jones (HH-13.6m--100y-09.4); Willie Davenport (HH-13.2y--100m-10.3); Rod Milburn (HH-13.0y--100y-09.3est). Dr. Dick Hill, coach of both Davenport and Milburn, stated that the latter was never timed for the 100 "but off the speed he showed in his 13-flat, I would equate it with 9.3 or better."

The next great hurdler was, apparently, even faster. Two weeks before setting a world hurdle record of 13 flat for 110 meters, Renaldo Nehemiah ran 100 meters in 10.1; 200 meters in 20.38--both in an Atlantic Coast Conference Championships.

Hurdle-Clearance Times. Judging the merits of hurdlers on the basis of the differences between their 120-yard sprint times (estimated from 100-yard times) and their 120-yard high-hurdle times is not a fully valid method. A hurdler's 100-yard speed is seldom tested and times given in papers and journals are as much hearsay as facts. Also a man's momentum over the 120-yard distance is continuous; his speed between the hurdles influences his speed over them. However, the attempt is interesting, if not of practical value.

Using this method, Table 27.1 discloses that, of earlier hurdlers, Lee Calhoun (1956-1960) was the most technically efficient with a time-difference of 1.8s. All others were estimated at two seconds flat, except for Milburn at 1.96s. In 1978, Nehemiah ran 13 flat which, off his 100-meter time of 10.1 gives him a 1.9s difference.

Fig. 27.3--Lee Calhoun, North Carolina State, 1956 and 1960 Olympic champion, 1960 world-record co-holder - 13.2, showing excellent forward lean into the hurdle. Note relaxed bent knee of lead leg. The lead foot has reached its greatest height in front of the hurdle and has now started to cut down to a quick landing. These men are sprinting "through" the hurdle.

Renaldo Nehemiah (Scotch Plains HS, N.J., U. of Maryland; 1978--110m HH-13s flat, WR, electronically timed.) "The greatest natural athlete ever to concentrate on hurdling." "Always in control--off as well as on the track." "At age 20, the greatest hurdler ever." "At 6'½", 170#, a 37-inch inseam, and with the sleek lines of a greyhound...". "Superb fluidity and grace, no strain, smooth and easy like--well, like Jesse Owens."

These reactions by such hurdling experts as Wilbur Ross, Russ Rogers and his capable high school coach, Jean Poquette, provide a glimpse of the early career (1976-1980) of Renaldo "Skeets" Nehemiah. World politics eliminated the Moscow Olympics as a showcase for his talents; otherwise, he might have gained the renown of even the great Owens. An exaggeration? Perhaps. But I watched Jesse in 1935 on his greatest day ever--3 world records and a tie--and, in Nehemiah, I saw and felt the same fluid power, graceful ease, and complete control. Jesse, of course, went on to Berlin and to his media-invented "confrontation" with Hitler. It takes such headlines to make heroes, along with an ability to maintain personal poise and control within a climate of world adulation.

Coach Frank Costello once claimed Skeets had the ability to hold world records in five events--high hurdles, 400m hurdles, 200 and 400m dashes, and long jump. Then, to support his claim, mentioned 18-year-old performances of 09.4 for the 100y, 24'11½" for the long jump-- "just lifting his legs"; a 44.3 anchor leg on a 1600m relay; and this in practice--550y in 62s, walk 440; 440y in 47.1s, walk 440; 330y in 33.5. Some claim! Not bad support! At age 18, just out of high school, Skeets ran the 42-inch hurdles in 13.23s and the 39-inch in 12.9, surpassing all previous records.

In a 1979 *Track & Field News* interview[1], Jon Hendershott elicited these insights into Nehemiah's approach to hurdling:

T&FN: Why is running the highs well so important to you?
Nehemiah: I've never wanted to be a contender, just one of the crowd. I want to be someone who turns the event around, who goes out and explores new territory. But it's more than that ,too. It's so much a part of me. I'm learning each day what I can do and what I have to do.
T&FN: What factors make you the best high hurdler in the world?
Nehemiah: My consistency. In the few short years I've been running, I've learned that it isn't one fast time that's important. Consistency at a high level will make you the victor, rather than having to depend on catching one fast one.

Basically, last year for me was one of learning how to be in control at all times-- regardless of the meet, who was running, the conditions, what happened in my previous meet. Just establishing that consistency, both physically and mentally.

My biggest hang-up last year was the idea that, "It's a learning year. You have nothing to lose and everything to gain." Deep down inside, I just couldn't accept that. Or people would say, "You lost the race but set a new Junior Record." That was great to them, but to me it was a putdown. I was in there running against the big guys and I wanted to be considered as one of them.
T&FN: You obviously take running very seriously. It must play a major role in your life.
Nehemiah: It's very major and very serious. I'm totally serious about doing everything I possibly can to improve and I'm tuned in to finding any way possible to do that. No meet is insignificant or unimportant. I can't go halfway. I have to make a total effort.

That's why my high school coach, Jean Poquette, and I are so close. He has taught me never to rely on my natural ability, to always look for ways to improve. I'm never at perfection. There is always something I can work on to better my technique.
T&FN: You have mentioned competitive consistency frequently, but what do you really want to achieve in the highs?
Nehemiah: To be the best, from the time I start until the time I end. To do whatever I have to do to become the best.

---

[1]Jon Hendershott, "Renaldo Nehemiah," *Track & Field News*, February 1979, p. 10.

Like running under 13.20, breaking the World Record as many times as I can. These are goals of mine. It's all part of bringing out the best in me. I don't know what is my best, so the only way to find out is to try. I'm just not comfortable laying back. I want to go further.

T&FN: Does Renaldo Nehemiah, the man, apply those same powers of determination to other things in his life as Renaldo Nehemiah, the athlete does to the hurdles?

Nehemiah: Yes, in terms of total dedication to what he is doing. His sole purpose is to please himself and not deprive himself of the very best he can achieve. In anything, I always want to do the very best I can.

After running 12.9 in high school, I know a lot of people expected me to break the World Record right away. But last year, for me, was a transition year from high school to college--and more in academic and total environment than the height of the hurdles. I used last year as a time to really find out about myself. To decide what I really wanted, to see how I cope with pressure and to find out what kind of athlete I am. I wanted to put things into their proper perspective.

T&FN: Were there any races last year which turned out to be particularly valuable learning experiences?

Nehemiah: The NCAA Indoor was probably the biggest lesson I ever learned indoors. I took that race totally for granted. In the heats and semis, I was running very well: 7.11 and 7.13, no pressure and I was running fast.

But at the third hurdle in the final, I realized, "Hey, you're not only behind, but you're losing," and there were only two more to go. I snapped out of it, or I probably would have lost it. It was just a matter of realizing it at the right time, in time, and really wanting it. Ever since that day, I've never underestimated the field, regardless of how fast or slow they are capable of running. The hardest defeat to live with is your own. You can always push the blame off on someone else, but the hardest one to accept is when you know you were the total cause of it.

T&FN: Was any one race last year particularly satisfying?

Nehemiah: AAU semi-finals, not so much the final. Beating Greg Foster there. It was a stacked heat with Greg and Charlie Foster. I was coming off that NCAA defeat and pretty much automatically assuming I wouldn't face him in the semis. I just assumed it would be the finals.

It was a do-or-die situation; it was there whether I was ready to accept it or not, so I had to do it. If I were to beat him and be superior at that time, it was then and there. And I rose to the occasion. When I had to dig down

Fig. 27.4--Renaldo Nehemiah, 110mHH--12.93 WR. He here demonstrates perfect balance and control, forward alignment, and great sprinting speed. /Photo by Janeart Ltd.

and get it, I got it. I couldn't shortchange myself, even though the second of those two
losses had been only a week before. I learned a lot from those losses. I was never convinced he could beat me. The thing that always kept me confident was that, at some point
in both of those races, I was winning. Then I made a technical error and lost to him. I
think if he had beaten me head up, no mistakes, then it might have been a different ball
game. But I knew I was winning and he had to come get me and that helped keep me stable.

T&FN: After the AAU, you said a winner doesn't make mistakes. Do you mean mental or physical?

Nehemiah: I would say a winner doesn't make physical mistakes. He knows what it takes to be in
top condition; he knows what he has to do in preparation of his body, the preparation for
each race.

The mental mistakes are something that you have control over, depending on the situation.
Of course, everyone is different; not everyone can endure pressure. That's where the fine
line comes. With me, I would have to blame an error on a physical mistake, because I'm
in control of my mind at all times when it comes to running. I know what I'm going to do
throughout the race.

Because of the long season I had last year and the number of races I ran, and because of my
lack of experience, I didn't know what to expect from myself in the big races. Then, too,
I was running a lot of other races and I couldn't give my full concentration to the hurdles,
which is what I obviously wanted to do. Now if anything is going to take away from my
hurdles, I won't do it. I don't want to meet anybody, whether American or foreigner, unless
I'm at full strength, so I must be.

T&FN: What former greats do you like?

Nehemiah: I base everything I've done, including my style, on Rod Milburn. Our forms are very
similar. His strength was his technical ability off the hurdle; once he was over, getting
on the ground as efficiently and quickly as possible.

I've compared our progressions at each age and what he did in certain meets: at the Junior
nationals, his record was 13.7. I ran 13.89. He ran 13.24 as a best and I'm at twenty-
three. I've used his progressions as a guide, not so much that I have to run better than
his times, but because I want to better his standards. Those are my goals. People say he
was one of the greatest, but I'm going to find out what I can do, too. I got a lot of
confidence from Milburn because he was a small guy compared to the others, and I'm small
compared to the others. There was something he had that the others didn't have, technically or physically. That's how I learned that size isn't the main thing; it's what you can
do with what you have.

It was phenomenal how he could start out even and almost at will take control of the race.
That's what I looked into the most. Not just to outlean someone at the tape or outsprint
somebody off the last hurdle, but how was it that he could surge like that. That's what
caused me to get into hurdling so deeply; I wanted to learn how to do it. The first race
I ever did it was in high school when I ran 13.2 to tie the national record. All my others
up to then I had just been stepping through, still running 13.5s, 13.6s. But this one was
different--and I've felt that way only two other times, my World Record indoors in '78 and
the 13.23 at Zurich.

T&FN: What was the feeling?

Nehemiah: An abnormal feeling, like I was running on the air. I almost had both feet on the
ground before they touched. That's when I know I'm really running the hurdles. It was
like a sprint; except for the long movement over the hurdle. I was sprinting. My legs had
the chance to be in the sprint form.

I know the feeling when I get it. I was seeking that feeling all through my first year of
college. But when I got it, I told my coach that something had been different in my
rhythm and he said, "You have finally learned to run the hurdles."

T&FN: Is that the closest to "ideal" you have come?

Nehemiah: Yes, it is. I was never satisfied all last year because I wanted to find that feeling. When I did, I got a whole different attitude. When it came down to one-on-one
hurdling, I had the right attitude. I was ready.

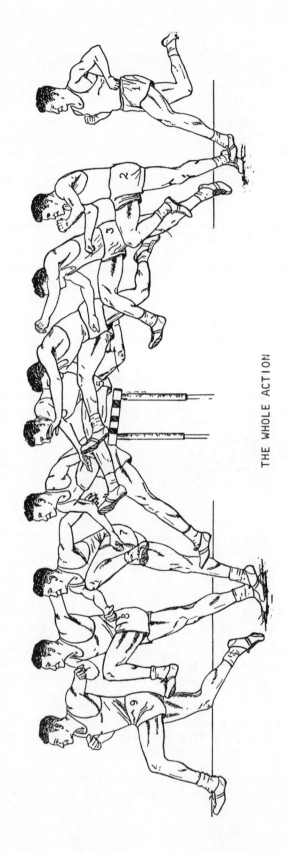

THE WHOLE ACTION

Fig. 27.5. Flowing "Through the Hurdle. The intended impression to be gained from this sequence drawing is that of a single sprint stride accentuated only by the need to clear a hurdle (men--42 inches high, women--33 inches). Such "Accentuations" should be minimal in both leg and arm movements; an expert hurdler requires less than two-tenths second more than sprinting time to clear the hurdle. Concentrate attention on the wholeness of this movement. Try to feel in your mind-muscles the action of the lead leg (Figs.2-8). Feel how it maintains a single plane of action as in regular sprinting. Feel the emphasis on knee drive with its shortened, and so faster pendulum drive than can be gained if emphasizing foot drive. Feel how it extends down beyond the hurdle quickly but naturally without attempting a shortened stride. Feel how it then drives forward (Figs. 8-9) into full stride beyond the hurdle. At the end of this Chapter read how Nehemiah concentrated much of his junior year in high school on just this one lead-leg action. Now, holding all this in your mind-muscles, concentrate on the trail leg, as did Nehemiah during the later portion of his junior year. Feel how it flows up-under the arm pit without raising the center of gravity beyond that required by the hurdle, and without straightening the overall forward body angle. Feel how the trail leg reaches out for a full stride (Figs. 7-9) toward the next hurdle. Feel how perfect balance throughout the whole action helps this full stride and also minimizes time lost in movements that tend to upset this balance. Feel how the curve of the center of gravity (hips) rises only slightly ("to minimal levels") while clearing the hurdle.
    Done with concentrated and sharp imagery, you'll feel, "I'm hurdling"! For as a matter of fact, you are. Feeling through an action in this way innervates the related nerves, though at such a low electrical potential that muscles are not activated.

454

ESSENTIALS OF HURDLE TECHNIQUE

Consistent with the discussion of Fig. 27.5, hurdle technique is mainly concerned with seven basic phases--(1) sprinting balance throughout, (2) the approach to the first hurdle, (3) action of the lead knee-leg, (4) action of the trail leg, (5) action of the torso-head, (6) actions of the arms and (7) the finish action through the tape. Note the word, "phases"; these actions, separate in words only, are but ways of speaking about hurdling technique; hurdling is really only one action from the reaction to the gun to reaching the finish line.

Sprinting balance in hurdling. By this expression is meant that all phases of balance--leg actions, torso-head angles, arm movements--should be the same as those used in sprinting with the same certain sense of sure balance that sprinters take for granted (Fig. 27.5). Balance is basic, fundamental, the underlying principle of technique in hurdling. A coach could go far by focussing on balance only with all other aspects of technique being learned as they relate to better balance. We shall of course shift our attention here to other aspects--approach, lead leg, trail leg, and the like--but always within the scope of good balance.

Approach to the first hurdle. The goal in learning the approach to the first hurdle is to gain optimal velocity as soon as one can "through" the hurdle without contact and with full control as in sprinting. "Optimal" in the expert means "maximal," but in the learner it means relaxed, controlled speed that achieves a last-foot takeoff between 6½ and 7 feet from the hurdle.

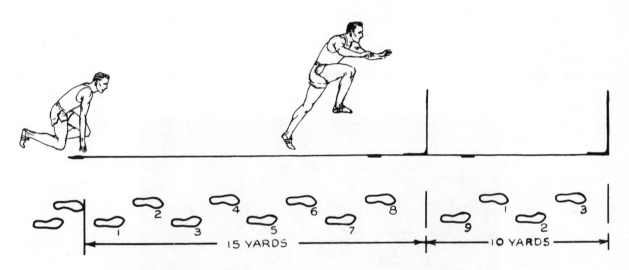

Fig. 27.6. Number of strides to the first, and between hurdles.

Normally there are eight strides as shown in Fig. 27.6, but a fast long-legged hurdler may feel cramped with eight and may achieve a more effective approach with but seven strides. Normally, the last stride before takeoff will be two to four inches shorter than the preceding stride.

Action of the lead knee-leg. All strides at each hurdle are led by the flexed knee of the lead leg as shown clearly in Fig. 27.7. This is usually a natural action, needing coaching for beginners. The less the beginner is aware of details, the better. It occurs in sprinting, but as learning progresses, the demands of clearing a 3½-foot hurdle will tend to emphasize the forceful drive of this knee. (Note--I started to write "obstacle" in place of hurdle, then realized that is the wrong approach for beginners; obstacles, barriers, obstructions--all tend to block action and certainly, eagerness in the hurdler's mind.) A lead with the knee shortens the lever and so accelerates the forward action. A few hurdlers, whether naturally or by misinformed coaching, emphasize a forward-upward drive of the lead foot, but this for the opposite reason slows quickness of the leg lift.

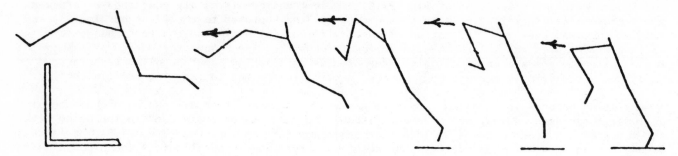

Fig. 27.7

This lead-leg action is not complex and so may be neglected in practice as needing no special emphasis. But read at the end of this Chapter of Nehemiah's clearance of four hundred hurdles in one session--that's 400 (4 sets of 10 x 10 hurdles). During his first year of serious hurdling, Nehemiah concentrated for weeks, even months, on this one phase of hurdling; concentrated, that is within the whole action of clearing five hurdles down and back 40 times! That's reaching for perfection and one more tenth of a second off hurdling time.

Action of the trail leg. As with the lead leg, the action of the trail leg is not complex, but to perfect its movements with no loss of forward lean or body balance and in the least possible time requires persistent practice--once again as demonstrated by Nehemiah.

The trail leg is, first, the driving leg. Full driving force from full extension of the ankle-foot is low-angled "into" the hurdle, not up-over it. That is, it comes through as close to sprint action as hurdle clearance will allow--flat as it approaches the hurdle (Fig. 27.5)

Fig. 27.8. Hayes Jones, Eastern Michigan, 1964 Olympic champion - 13.4. Jones was winner of an amazing 56 straight races indoors at from 50 to 70 yards, 1960-1964. Often won both dash and hurdles.

A trail-leg knee brought through high can have multiple adverse effects. It upsets over-all balance--a compensating lean away and straightening of the body angle. Its imbalance reduces the normal sprint movements of the arms. It tends to lower the trail foot so as to hit the hurdle with all the dire effects that follow. True, the trail knee, as shown clearly in Figs. 27.11 and 27.12 does remain relatively high as the foot swings through to a full stride off the hurdle, but not so high as to diminish forward lean at sprinting angles.

Action of the torso, head and arms. These actions all relate to overall body balance and continuance of a forward sprinting angle throughout. Careful study of all figures from Fig. 27.4 to 27.11 shows more clearly than any words: (1) good balance, (2) a forward lean of the torso low over the hurdle, (3) relaxed head in line with the torso, and (4) arm action as close to sprint action as clearing the hurdle will allow. A few great hurdlers have used a two-arms-forward style to ensure forward lean throughout. It worked well for them, but tends to be awkward and difficult to perfect. The arm actions shown in Figs. 27.9 and 27.10 illustrate common practice today.

Fig. 27.9. A long sprint stride, low over the hurdle.

Fig. 27.10. An overall impression of good balance, forward lean and relaxation over the 33" hurdle.

SPRINT BETWEEN THE HURDLES

A slight decrease in body momentum occurs while sprinting over each hurdle, a decrease which, by expert hurdlers, totals about 2 seconds for 10 hurdles. These changes in speed are shown by the stride lengths which average about as follows: landing beyond hurdle--3'6"; 1st stride--6'; 2nd stride--6'10"; 3rd stride--6'6"; distance of takeoff foot from hurdle--7'2". This pattern is very important as suggesting a relatively even momentum. Many less expert hurdlers take 4' coming off the hurdle and only 5' on the first stride. This forces over-striding on the 2nd and 3rd strides, a broken rhythm, and unreadiness for the next hurdle.

The entire action over the hurdle affects these strides, but especially forward lean, balance off the hurdle, the full reach of the trail leg, and the use of the arms coming off, as well as between the hurdles. In the Sprint Chapter, we have discussed the energizing effect of vigorous arm action on the speed of the legs. Such action is even more effective in high hurdling.

But mental attitude is at least as critical as mechanics. Nehemiah told an interviewer, "I try to anticipate hurdle action--pull the rear leg through before the lead foot touches the ground; it can't be done but it does speed up the action." That is, he tries to move faster, not by thinking of mechanics, but by centering on the muscle-feel of actions before they occur.

Fig. 27.11. Come off the hurdle sprinting.

Fig. 27.12. Two essentials of high hurdling technique are shown here--(1) forward body lean so necessary for continuous velocity, and (2) a flat trail leg which is reaching out for a full stride to the next hurdle.

THE FINISH

Fig. 27.13. The first and all-important tenet for finishing a high hurdle race is *first clear the last hurdle. How many a champion, intent on the finish line, has caught the hurdle with his lead or trail leg, and lost-- sometimes the BIG race of his entire career!* Assuming the hurdle has been cleared, then the methods shown here are valid. Both hurdlers are using a good body lean--chin and eyes down, arms extended down and back.

Fig. 27.14. Two styles of finish. The white figure simply maintains good forward lean and explodes through and beyond the finish line with no change in form. This style is conservative but sound. The black figure shows clearly the advantage of an exaggerated forward lean on the last stride. Many an Olympic decision has been in favor of the athlete using this method, since men are picked "in the order in which any part of their bodies (torso, as distinguished from head, neck, hands, feet) reach the finish line."

TOUCHDOWN TIMES FOR TEN HURDLES

A study[1] by Brent McFarlane, Ontario Provincial Coach, found that such Olympic hurdlers (men) as Guy Drut and Willie Davenport, and (women) Johanna Schaller and Grazyna Rabsztyn "had touchdown (TD) times of 2.4 and 2.5 off hurdle one, and maintained a consistent 1.0 to 1.1 throughout the race." Using these times as his base, McFarlane projected times for touchdown from each hurdle, using 10th seconds only. To smooth out his times, I have used 100th in estimating some figures.

TOUCHDOWN TIME CHART

MEN--110m Hurdles (42")

FT	H1	H2	H3	H4	H5	H6	H7	H8	H9	H10	Fin
13.0	2.4	3.4	4.4	5.4	6.4	7.4	8.4	9.4	10.5	11.6	13.0
14.0	2.5	3.55	4.6	5.65	6.7	7.8	8.9	10.05	11.2	12.4	14.0
15.0	2.6	3.75	4.9	6.05	7.2	8.35	9.5	10.7	12.0	13.3	15.0

WOMEN--100m Hurdles (33")

12.8	2.4	3.4	4.4	5.4	6.4	7.4	8.4	9.5	10.6	11.7	12.8
14.0	2.5	3.6	4.7	5.8	6.9	8.05	9.3	10.45	11.6	12.8	14.0
15.0	2.6	3.75	4.9	6.05	7.3	8.5	9.75	11.0	12.3	13.6	15.0

Actual times for slower, less perfect hurdlers would not have such regular increments, but these figures indicate a loss of velocity after five or six hurdles.

RELAXATION IN HURDLING

All the experts say, "Hurdling is sprinting." But more precisely, they should speak of hurdling as sprinting as released by relaxation. In describing great hurdlers such as Renaldo Nehemiah or Greg Foster, we use words such as "poise," "control," "fluid grace," "smooth and easy like Jesse Owens"--all words implying relaxation.

Such relaxation --like speed--is a natural talent of the great hurdler, but it is also the effect of practice related to relaxation--maximal speed with a sense of letting things flow, or of holding back one erg of effort.

Most world records in the hurdles have been set under low-stress conditions--lesser meets or hurdlers--that provide challenge but relative ease of mind. Only that of Rod Milburn (1972-13.24) was made in the Olympic Games. Nehemiah's amazing 13s-even was made in a lesser invitational meet, but certainly did not lack highest quality competition (Casanas 13.21WR, Foster 13.22, Cooper 13.72). As Nehemiah put it, "The names got the adrenaline going...If we had gotten out even, it would have been even faster." Maybe that's the answer-- enough adrenaline to make you try, not harder, but faster.

IAAF HURDLE SPACING

	Distance	H Hgt	To 1st H	Btwn Hs	To Finish
Men	110m	1.067m	13.72m	9.14	14.02
	120y	42"	15y	10y	15y
Women	100m	.84m	13m	8.5m	10.5m
	100m	33"	42'7 3/4"	27'10 5/8"	34'5 3/8"

---

[1]Brent McFarlane, "Touchdown Time Charts for the Hurdles," *Track Technique*, #67, March 1977, p. 2128.

WARMING UP FOR THE HURDLES.

Hurdling requires maximal-speed actions in the leg muscles, and a high degree of flexibility and overall stress in the upper body muscles and tendons. Total body warm-up is therefore essential. But to what degree, in what manner, or following what sequence of exercises has received little serious study in the United States. At the World Track and Field Championships in Helsinki, 1983, East German women in the 100m hurdles took 1st, 2nd and 7th, led by a 12.35w by Bettine Jahn, as compared with 12.84 by Benita Fitzgerald (U.S.) in winning the 1984 Olympic hurdles. Such preeminence did not just happen. The East Germans have researched every aspect of hurdling, including the warm-up.

Brent McFarlane,[1] National Hurdle Coach, Canada, observed and took notes of their warm-ups prior to the World Championships.

"For seven days I carefully observed a total of fifteen very sequenced and articulated warm-up series, which fell into what was (a single) design. Although...nothing new or startling happened...it seems these warm-ups do have a direct correlation with the results we saw on the track. Simply, the warm-up plan (1) does have a sequence, (2) does follow basic physiological principles, and (3) does the job...perhaps better than most hurdlers are accustomed to.

"The entire warm-up procedure took exactly one hour and ended exactly 30 minutes before race time. Qualifying rounds were completed without undue stress. The warm up procedure, timing and sequencing had minimal alterations between rounds. It seemed obvious that the GDR women were there for one purpose...to produce in the finals. For simplicity, the warm up will be broken into three parts.

"PART I (Total time 20 minutes)
    This initial series of exercises involve a tremendous amount of dynamic flexibility (swinging, bouncing type movements) that were done gradually and easily. Every body part, especially joints were continuously rotated and flexed in a specific pattern. No static (held movement) were observed in any of the warm ups.

1. easy jog on cinder track lane inside warm up track 6 x 100m turnarounds on the straight (very little warming up was done on the track)
2. 12 x easy ankle stretches (bounding in nature)
3. standing alternate toe touches (bounding movement), walk after a few reps
4. 5 x side steps facing different directions, with a few knee lift exercises
5. ankle extensions with bent knee while walking 100m, with easy jog
6. kicking a few bum kicks with jog over a 100m distance

7. upper body arm circles (10 reps)
8. hip (waist) circles (10 reps)
9. ankle stretches (bounding movement) in lunge position
10. achilles stretches (leaning against an object) (10 reps)
11. 5 x knee lifts to front of body and to the side of body
12. arm circles (rotations) while bent over and to the ground

13. leg shaking (standing and sitting)
14. hurdle stretch with trail leg to the inside of crotch (bouncing action)
15. leg shanking

---

[1] Brent McFarlane, "The First World Track and Field Championships, Helsinki, 1983," *Track and Field Quarterly Review*, Vol. 84 #2, Summer 1984, pp. 40-42.

16. hurdle stretch with bouncing movements lead knee, middle and trail leg shaking and then repeated to the other leg (alternated)
17. sit, pick of 1 leg into air and straighten knee (6x), leg shaking

18. lead leg swinging drill over the side of the hurdle (9 times)
19. stationary fast legs and short arm punch (5 times)
20. leg shaking

"PART 2 (in spikes; 40 minutes)
This second part of the warm up was very <u>specific</u> to the <u>exact skills</u> of the sprint hurdle event (or better known as second derivative exercises). All rehearsing was done with exactness to minimize any possible deviation or error.

1. 50m acceleration on the track with a walk back to the start x1
2. 50m acceleration; stand up start with an increase in speed after 20m (emphasis on short step frequency and fast hands...extremely fast) x1
3. 30m falling type start (hands in front of the body and fast frequency) 2x
4. 20m falling start (quick hands and feet) x1
5. easy run over 1 hurdle with a walk back recovery
6. 4 hurdles placed for 5 strides between hurdles (quick hands emphasis, fast downward action off the hurdle, fast leg turnover)

7. 2 minute rest
8. 4 hurdles with 5 strides between (using exaggerated running motion)
9. 4 hurdles with 5 strides (run off last hurdle hard; trail leg drops quickly after each hurdle; fast leg turnover)
10. sweats and rain pant put on; set up starting blocks using a measuring tape
11. sweats off; start over 1 hurdle
12. block start over 1 hurdle, hurdle 2 flat on the track but run over using 5 strides

13. block start over 2 hurdle with emphasis on fast hands and pulling of trail (5 strides between hurdles)
14. departure for competition stadium (40 mins. exactly) (1 hour total) for part 2

"PART 3 (Competition Stadium)
1. 3x hurdle 1 using blocks 3 times over the 1st hurdle
2. lots of leg shaking (while sitting)
3. start over 2 hurdles (5 strides between hurdles) x 1
4. RACE (Jahn 12.35; Knabe 12.42) (1st and 2nd) (World Championships)

"To look back at these results and to try to explain how or why they happened is virtually impossible. Much can be said for "results speak for themselves." Just prior to the sprint hurdles for women, I saw the same preciseness and rehearsal by two other women from the GDR...Marita Koch and Marlies Gohr who also placed first and second in the 100m final. This too was an education in itself. To some, the warm up may say nothing. To others, it says too much...judge for yourself. Nothing can be left to chance."

ORGANIZATION OF PRACTICE

The high hurdles require at least as careful planning or related training within whatever time per year, per month, per days as is available, as does any track and field event. Consider the great breadth of their requirements: (1) hurdling technique, (2) total body flexibility, (3) related speed-endurance, (4) velocity in sprint starts and between hurdles, (5) related speed-power.

This all adds up to practice--Practice--PRACTICE! Practice, that is, within the all-too-limited time that is available to a school-college athlete, and practice that follows a well-reasoned sequence of priorities as between the essentials of training just stated.

The following description of the two-year training of hurdler Renaldo Nehemiah by Coach Jean Poquette is based on such a carefully planned sequence. Poquette has two uncommon viewpoints, (1) "I honestly believe you can accomplish what is needed with no weight training." Nehemiah, greatest high school hurdler ever, did none at all. (2) "Another thing I didn't do was emphasize sprinting in practice." Nehemiah had great innate speed and thrived on such doubles as 2 x 220 or 10 x 65 yards with hurdles. Poquette trained his sprinters by a similar regimen.

Young men and women with different innate qualities, especially under a different coach, would use a different approach. But in all instances under all circumstances, the five essentials of technique, flexibility, hurdling endurance, sprinting speed, and specifically related power must be balanced within a training program in which each phase leads into the next, and all are related to the clear-in-mind goal of maximal velocity--minimal time from start to finish.

Specific Endurance in Hurdling. The following outline of methods of developing endurance specifically related to hurdling was excerpted by Jess Jarver[1] from the recommendations of V. Breizer and G. Ivkin, USSR. They make a different approach from that by Jean Poquette but one that is consistent with it:

"Observations indicate that specific endurance is decisive in hurdling performances. It can be developed by using the following training methods:

  1. Four series of repetition runs over 12 hurdles with 10-minute recoveries or five series over 10 hurdles with 8-10 minute recoveries.

  2. Four to five series over 10-12 hurdles with jog-back recoveries. The height of the hurdles and their distances apart are adjusted individually.

  3. Pendulum hurdling over two parallel lanes of 5-7 hurdles. Five to six series of three repetitions each with 8-10 minute recoveries.

  4. 80-120m runs, alternately over 8-12 hurdles and on the flat, employing the same intensity. Walk or jog-back recoveries.

  5. Hurdling imitation drills for the lead and trail legs with support at maximum speed. Three to six series of 15-20 seconds.

  6. Jumping series of 10 or more jumps, emphasizing either the distance or a fast forward movement. Up to 100 takeoffs in one training session.

  7. Bouncing 30-100m distances on one leg or alternate legs (stepping) and counting the number of takeoffs (less takeoffs indicates better specific endurance).

  8. Four to five series of 10-15 squats with 50% of body weight at a rate of 10 squats in 10 seconds.

  9. Repetition runs over 100-300m flat distances. The volume depends on intensity. It should not exceed 1000-1200m at a 90-100% intensity. If 80-90% intensity is employed the volume is increased to 1600-2000m. Recoveries in the first method are 10 minutes for 5-6 repetitions, decreased at 80-90% intensity to 6 minutes.

  10. Uphill running is employed to develop strength endurance, using the same principles applied to repetition runs. However, the volume is slightly reduced (30%) and recovery intervals are increased."

---

[1]Jess Jarver, "Specific Endurance in Hurdling," *Track Technique*, Vol. 86, Fall 1983, p. 2819. Also see pp 2743-2744.

FLEXIBILITY EXERCISES

Nehemiah's High School Training[1]

Renaldo "Skeets" Nehemiah was coached primarily by Jean Poquette. In high school, because of injuries during his sophomore year, his training was limited for the most part to his junior and senior years. Nehemiah went on to college and to post-college hurdling but from time to time he returned to his high school coach for fine tuning in technique but also for a little fatherly help in self-confidence and how to get along better with people--not easy when you're as great an athlete as was Nehemiah, with everyone clamoring for your services. The following material was written by Coach Poquette, though space limitations force my own summary of certain passages. Of the five essentials of hurdling--technique, flexibility, hurdling endurance, sprinting speed and related power--Poquette concentrated on the first two (technique and flexibility) during Skeets junior year, then, certain that sound technique had been established, on related endurance during his senior year. This decision was made carefully, in line with Poquette's view that technique is a first priority, plus his realization that Nehemiah had great innate speed and potential endurance. Poquette's remarks begin with the junior year when they moved outdoors in March:

The most important part of the technique was his lead leg....We thought that if we developed a very fast, snappy lead leg and got back down on the ground running as quickly as possible, that would account for about 65-70 percent of the total technique.

We worked on...leading into the hurdle with the knee, not letting the foot get ahead of the knee until almost over the hurdle, then snapping the leg right down onto the ground on the other side of the hurdle--never letting it get out in front, extended, and drifting down. It's all one continuous movement with no fault in the middle of it. We spent an awful lot of time just developing that snapping lead leg. Once that was accomplished-- and that took about two months--we could...start to work on the trail leg.

Our approach with the trail leg was that it should be one continuous motion from the time it leaves the ground until it returns to the ground, with no slowing or delay at the peak of coming through. We did things like not extending the lead leg, bringing the trail knee right up into the arm pit and getting a good rotation around and down.

Once the lead leg and the trail leg were one continuous motion, we worked on....(unifying them). We didn't want, first, a lead leg and then a trail leg. We fantasized that this unity would become so great that the lead and trail legs would hit the ground almost together....

Prior to the work on technique, an awful amount of time was spent on developing flexibility....This is as important to...hurdling as is technique. Instead of once a day....we worked three times a day for shorter periods. Skeets stretched every morning after he got out of bed and...every night before getting into bed. Also various stretching exercises as part of his warmup before the workout.

During his junior year, we practiced a minimum of three days a week, sometimes four times a week. (Poquette had three primary workouts.) One was a...shuttle-style workout, with five hurdles, ten yards apart, going down and five more, reversed, coming back, with 15 yards for each start....Once up and back we considered as one repetition, and initially he ran ten (such repetitions)....(100 hurdles in all). Eventually, we worked up to four such sets (400 hurdles in one day).

This workout accomplished two things. First, technique. (We might concentrate for the first couple of weeks and months, during an entire 400-hurdle workout on one aspect of his hurdling, say, on the lead leg.) Second, this workout....also functioned as a pretty tough conditioning workout....After we reached the point where the lead leg would go through the correct motion without thinking about it, where he was on his toes all the time....we went into the arm action, the forward lean, things like that.

The other workout we used...became much more important in his senior year. This time we placed four hurdles on the grass, 8½ yards apart, with the regulation 15 yards at the start....We had him run full speed; I mean really press him total full speed between

---

[1] Exerpted from Jean Poquette, "Nehemiah's High School Training," in Jess Jarver, THE HURDLES, Los Altos, CA: Tafnews Press, 1981. In my judgment, this paperback book, 123 pps. contains the most well-rounded and knowledgeable collection of articles by 29 authors on all aspects of 110m and 400m hurdling published to date.

the hurdles. This forced him (1) to get his knees up higher, (2) to chop his step a little, and (3) to turn over faster....

What happened is that he just wiped himself out. He'd smash into the hurdles. Partly for physical survival and partly to get him turning over faster, we jammed him. This helped him get a faster cadence between the hurdles....We were not concerned about the extra yard-and-one-half...in later competition. Adrenalin and everything else would compensate. (The theory was that once he was in a race with ten yards between hurdles, he'd run the same cadence and a faster time.)

The other thing we did during his junior year, primarily for technique, was to take starts with 15 yards to a single hurdle--some times two or even three to keep the drive going....

At no time throughout his entire high school career, did he ever run a full flight of hurdles in practice, not even in a time trial. (In practice they always worked on segments.) We knew that if he accomplished certain things on certain segments in practice, he should be able to meet certain standards in competition, and this proved accurate.

There was no emphasis at all during his high school career on weight training. (His training time was limited to two hours--3:30 PM to 5:30 PM.) I wasn't willing to sacrifice time on the track for time in the weight room....I honestly believe that....you can accomplish what is needed without the weight training.

Another thing I didn't do--that I thought was not that important in high school but becomes so in college--was to emphasize sprinting in practice....Our schedule called for two meets a week....I felt the competition served as the speed practice. (To take time for speed work would deemphasize conditioning work and, at least in high school, Poquette felt that technique-conditioning work achieves 90 percent of the needed development; speedwork, 10 percent. K.D.)

In his senior year, Skeets really only hurdled twice a week early season before competition. The workouts would be two days of back-and-forth maybe on Tuesday-Thursday or Tuesday-Friday. That way we could concentrate more on physical conditioning than on technique developments. In March, we only hurdled one day a week in the very early season and spent 4-days-a-week training on workouts which would be equivalent to what my ¼-milers or my ½-milers would be doing. He did 9 x 660 on Monday, in sets of 3. He'd run a 660 and jog a 220, run a 660 and bounce a 220, run another 660 for one set of 3 x 660s. Skeets would take a walking rest, then do two more sets of 3. Tuesdays, he might do sets of 8 x 220s or 4 x 220s. My philosophy on conditioning is rather than going out and busting 3 x 23-second 220s, have them run 16-24 x 220 @ 28-30s each. Once again, I think that speed is related to conditioning and many times, the stronger you are, the faster you are, and the speed is a result of strength, not a result of concentrating and practicing on speed work itself.

Speed becomes important prior to some big races, where you might want to do some speed work for 2 or 3 weeks, but primarily his was a strength-oriented workout schedule, along with 2-day-a-week hurdling workouts.

One of the workouts I liked contained 550s. All my sprinters trained primarily as ¼-milers and all served on legs of mile relays, because of my basic orientation towards strength work rather than speed work. And as a result, a Wednesday workout would be 6 x 550s, in which the sprinters would line up on the second turn, then bust at 110 yards, (13 or better), then settle down at the 330, and get back to the ¼-mark somewhere around 60 seconds. They would then sprint the final 110y and try to do that in 15 seconds or less, with the 550 in 75 seconds or under. After a ¼ or more of bouncing and jogging as a respite between, we did things like ladders or pyramids: A typical session might be some 110s, 3 x 220s, 2 x 330s, 1 x 440, 2 x 330s, 3 x 220s. Every workout totaled in distance between 2 and 3 miles of running on the track, not counting the bouncing and rest in between.

We didn't have set patterns week-in/week-out, thus offsetting boredom. Skeets might *do just a full set of 440s one day, or do 2 x 220s, 2 x 440s and 2 x 220s. As the season progressed, we'd start to go...more towards quality, and pick the pace up, so that we'd average about 60 seconds per quarter, (or faster 56-58) 30 per 220. Then we'd knock off one of the quarters, so that the set would be 2 x 220s, a quarter, 2 x 220s which equalled 3/4 of a mile in the set instead of a mile. The emphasis was still on strength with the competition being the speed work.*

In Skeets' senior year he did some work on the intermediate hurdling. And we per-mitted him once to compete in a 100-yard dash....In an event that wasn't his primary event, he ran 9.4--9.6 in a heat and a 9.4 final. (Absolutely amazing when one considers Poquette's lack of emphasis on speed work. K.D.)

One speed workout was to do 3 sets of 2 x 220 back to back. He'd go full speed and attempt to run 21.5 or 22, finish on the other side of the track, stay there and with a 30-second rest, run a second 220, trying to duplicate his time. We call them doubles and they're really tough. Skeets would do a walking-quarter recovery and come back and try to do another set....We also did a 4 x 550 workout...at 60-second per 440 pace, and then we'd do the 220 doubles. Usually that would be good preparation.

When I really knew in my heart that he was ready to break 13 in the high hurdles and challenge the national record in the intermediates was when Skeets ran a 46.5 400m leg on the 1600m relay at the Penn Relays, and when he ran a 20.8 220 on a turn.

Frankly I'm troubled by this account almost as much as I am impressed. "400 hurdles!" "9 x 660 on Mondays in sets of three!" And that's for a 120-yard hurdler, not a half miler; a hurdler that's still in high school, not a senior in college. And after such training, Skeets ran 09.4 for his first and only 100-yard dash! But we have the facts; it's up to each one of us to interpret them as our views on coaching decide. Nehemiah was one of the greatest talents, possibly the greatest, ever to take up hurdling. It's clear he could have been a great sprinter or, even more, a great quarter-miler.

1984 Olympic champion Benita Fitzgerald-Brown (left) and American record holder Stephanie Hightower in a 1982 high hurdles race in Berkeley./Photo by Bill Leung, Jr.

The incomparable Edwin Moses./Photo by Kevin R. Morris.

Chapter 28
THE 400-METER HURDLES

The 400-meter hurdles require toughness; not in some special awesome sense, as they have been viewed in the past through lack of familiarity, but toughness as is needed for the 880 or any speed-endurance distance. Of course it requires stamina, but that's a word to challenge men, not frighten them. On the contrary, this event, with its varied demand for speed, and endurance, and hurdling skill is the most exciting and challenging on the entire running program. No excuse for bordeom here; every reason for trying to do one's best.

I'm reminded of the comments of Josh Culbreath (5'7" tall, but 1955 world-record holder at 50.4 and third at Melbourne): "What I lack in stature and speed, I make up in determination and endurance!. . . Lift your knees, pump those arms . . . lean forward and *drive, drive drive!* Never give up; victory is always within your grasp--if you are a real fighter!" If you're looking for 440 hurdle prospects, look for such attitudes, as well as for height, speed, stamina, and hurdling skill.

A similar viewpoint was expressed by Mike Shine[1] who, despite relatively short legs that forced him to take 15 strides throughout, gained the silver medal at the 1976 Olympics with a fast time of 48.6.

Most of the people who describe the event that way (grueling) have never run the event...It is a tough race, but if you train properly for it and use a few mental tricks, it is just as easy as running the 120 (men) or 110 (women).

A BRIEF REVIEW OF PAST PERFORMANCES.
The First Olympic 400m Hurdles. Walter Tewksbury, winner of the 1900 Olympic 400-meter "hurdles" wrote me just prior to his death in 1970,

I note in your chart the wide discrepancy in times from 57.6 in 1900 to under 50 seconds today. You will be interested in the following details of the 1900 race. Ten men ran in the final, starting on a curve. The hurdles were 10 telephone poles, 6 to 8 inches in diameter, 30 feet long, stretched across the track. They were one meter high with boxes of brush beneath the poles. A water jump 5 meters wide was across the track halfway between the last hurdle and the finish. Figure my long legs saved the day for me.

No mention of lanes for there were none. In my library there are six histories of the Olympic Games. No explanation in any of them that telephone poles and water jumps might have influenced the time of 57.6. And to think that we sometimes speak of our modern laned race on a synthetic track over ten individual L-type hurdles as a "grueling" man-killer! Balderdash!

Four years later, 1904, at the Olympic Games, St. Louis, the 400 meters were run over individual hurdles 2'6" high in a time of 53 seconds by Harry Hillman, longtime Dartmouth

---

[1]Michael Shine, "400 Meter Hurdles," *Track & Field Quarterly Review*, Vol. 82, #2, Summer 1982, pp. 46-47.

TABLE 28.1

OUTSTANDING PERFORMANCES -- 400m and 300m HURDLES

OLYMPIC CHAMPIONS -- MEN

Date	Time	Name	Affiliation	Best Time 400m	Time Diff.
1928	53.4	Lord Burghley	G.Britain	46.7	6.7
1932	51.7	R.M.N.Tisdall	Eire		
1936	52.4	Glenn Hardin	Louisiana	46.8	5.6
1948	51.1	Roy Cochran	Indiana	46.7	4.4
1952	50.8	Charles Moore	Cornell	47.0	3.8
1956	50.1	Glenn Davis	Ohio State	46.5	3.6
1960	49.3	Glenn Davis	Ohio State		
1964	49.6	Rex Cawley	So.Cal.	46.2	3.4
1968	48.1	Dave Hemery	G.Britain		
1972	47.82WR	John Akii-Bua	Uganda		
1976	47.64OR	Edwin Moses	Morehouse St.	46.1	1.54
1980	48.70	Volker Beck	E. Germany		
1984	47.75	Edwin Moses	Morehouse St.		

OLYMPIC CHAMPIONS -- WOMEN (400m--10H--30")

1984	54.61	N. El Moutawakil	Morocco	(first time held)	

WORLD RECORDS OF SPECIAL INTEREST -- MEN

1958	49.2	Glenn Davis	Ohio State	45.7	3.5
1962	49.2	Salvatore Morale	Italy	47.6	1.6
1964	49.1	Rex Cawley	So.Cal.	45.7	3.4
1968	48.1	Dave Hemery	G.Britain	47.9	0.2
1972	47.82	John Akii-Bua	Uganda	47.2	0.62
1983	47.02	Edwin Moses	Morehouse St.	46.1	1.35

WORLD RECORDS OF SPECIAL INTEREST -- WOMEN

1980	54.28	Karin Rossley	E. Germany
1983	54.20	Ellen Fiedler	E. Germany
1983	54.14	Yeka Fesenko	USSR
1983	54.01	Anna Ambraziene	USSR

HIGH SCHOOL RECORDS -- BOYS (300m Hurdles)

1974	35.87y	Bill Blessing	Hillcrest, Dallas
1984	36.05	Arthur Blake	Haines City, FL
1984	36.25	George Porter	Cab.Lamp, CA

HIGH SCHOOL RECORDS -- GIRLS (300m Hurdles)

1981	41.91	Gayle Kellon	Walnut, CA (HS record)
1983	41.70	Leslie Maxie	Millbrae, CA
1983	42.26	Gail Devers	Sweetw, NC, CA

track coach and inventor of the Hillman L-type hurdle (1940s). His time (53s) was four seconds under the Olympic record but was disallowed since he knocked over the last hurdle. Also it probably was run out of the chute (as was the 400m dash), around only one curve, and perhaps without lanes with six hurdles abreast across the track.

An official world and Olympic record around two turns was first made at the 1908 London Games by Charles Bacon (Chicago) in 55s flat. It is not clear that they ran in lanes for "Bacon and Hillman ran almost abreast for the greater part of the race and took the last hurdle together."[1]

But lanes were definitely used in the 1924 Paris Games for second-place winner Charlie Brookins (Iowa) "was disqualified for failing to clear a hurdle cleanly and running out of his lane."[1]

The 400m hurdles in the United States. The 400m hurdles were not run in the U.S. Championships until 1914--a one and only competition. Except for each Olympic year, they did not appear in the College Championships until 1959 when concern for U.S. success took precedence over traditional college viewpoints. But at the Pennsylvania Relays they were run each year since 1915. Up to 1923, the hurdles were only 30 inches high, not in lanes and out of the chute. In 1924, the hurdles were raised to the present official 36 inches but the race was started outside the stadium, no lanes, and around one turn. Often as many as ten men would start, making quite a jam-up over the first few hurdles. I remember well the 1925 race won by Lord Burghley (54.8), winner of the 1928 Olympics, over Fordham's Johnnie Gibson, a later WR holder. Eight men started, but Burghley and Gibson were soon in the lead and so able to run the inside lanes around the turn.

NCAA 400m hurdles. In response to our felt need to improve United States Olympic performances, the NCAA Championships in 1959 were changed in a number of ways. Perhaps the most controversial of these was the shift from the 220y low hurdles on the straightaway to the 400-meters hurdles in lanes around two turns. The task of locating each of 60 hurdles in its proper lane--45 meters to the first, 35 meters between the 40 meters to the finish line--was both arduous and complex, even for the engineers that were usually called in. For the grounds-keeper or the coach, unused to the metric system, to measure 38¼ yards between 60 hurdles produced many a stiff back and broken tempers, to say nothing of mistakes to be discovered after the Big Race was over.

Then the problem for the sprinter-hurdlers to extend their endurance and their stride lengths was a tough one. The 1960 NCAA event was won, not by a hurdler, but by Cliff Cushman, Kansas, who according to *Track & Field News* "was once a great mile prospect and still prefers the mile." He alternated between 14 and 15 strides between hurdles, hit the 8th hurdle with his toe, but still ran 50.8.

A month later, the United States took the first three places in the 1960 Olympic 400m hurdles at Rome. First, Glenn Davis, Ohio, in 49.30R, 1956 NCAA 400m H champion; second, Cliff Cushman, Kansas, 1960 NCAA champion, in 49.6; third, Dick Howard, New Mexico, 1959 NCAA 400m H champion, in 49.7, certainly a great tribute to the U.S. college training program.

As a matter of interest, of the 14 Olympic Championships between 1924 and 1984 in the 400m hurdles, 9 were won by former U.S. college men; of the 42 winners of the first three places, college men won 19 places--that against the entire world of hurdling.

Edwin Moses, Morehouse College, (1976 Olympic IH Champion, 47.6 WR; age 20, 6'1¼", 162#), (1984 Olympic IH Champion, 47.75, age 28, 6'2", 170#). *Track & Field News* (April 1984) called him "the incomparable Edwin Moses, the peerless ruler of the event." Between Aug. 26, 1977 and Sept. 1, 1984 he had won 109 consecutive races, the most for any event in track and field history. According to *Sports Illustrated*, up to 1984, Moses had broken the world record four times with a best of 47.02, 1983, and had run 17 of the 18 fastest times in history. Furthermore he plans to continue hurdling in 1985 and who knows how far beyond that.

---

[1] "Olympic Track and Field," 1984 edition, Los Altos: Tafnews Press, p. 68.

Even more important, Moses has a B.S. in physics, and has worked as an aerospace engineer with General Dynamics. Also he's an officer on the advisory commission to the International Olympic Committee (IOC). Clearly a future that includes far more than hurdling.

Fig. 28.1. Edwin Moses at Montreal, 1976--47.64WR. Note foot placement well outside lane line; forward body lean with trail leg moving to a full stride beyond.

That's all in keeping with *Sports Illustrated's* comments that "Moses' workouts are planned, precise, always logical, never overburdening--then coded and correlated with his training sessions, past and future, on a computer terminal at home. His digital chest belt and digital watch are constantly beeping, flashing numbers, signalling lap times, pulse and heart rates, and playing who knows what other inspirational tunes for their master."

Add to such facts, Moses' background of training over long distances with his one-time room-mate, Henry Rono, great Kenyan distance runner; his best college HH time of 13.9, his 37-inch leg inseam, and his normal 9'9" stride when quartermiling, and you get an impression of the perfect talent, perfectly trained--and enjoying every minute of it--all within the liberal income allowed by the IOC for modern professional Olympians.

In an interview[1] by Jon Hendershott, Moses said he never ran the 400m hurdles until the Florida Relays, March 1976. In 1975, he usually ran the highs (13.9s), the quarter (46.1s), and the mile relay. Prior to the Florida meet "I had just been doing overdistance workouts-- 1000s and 600s, none of those special workouts for the IHs that coach came up with later... But once I started running them, I felt pretty comfortable. I ran 50.2 (2nd place) and I wasn't tired at all."

He then went on to win the Penn Relays IH (49.8s), the Final Olympic Trials (48.3s), and a world-record 47.64s in the Olympic Championships--not bad for a first-year effort by a man who previously had never won a major championship in any event.

In *Track & Field News*, March 1980, Hendershott wrote,

Moses learned early in his career to get along on his own, without the luxuries of training rooms or easily accessible facilities. He listened and learned, especially from his college coach, Lloyd Jackson..."Like training. You just have to get out there and do it. I mean, it hurts. I feel pain. But there are no secrets about the way I have run. Just a lot of hard work; more work than anybody realizes." Hard work plus talent, which is the same for any great athlete.

[1] Jon Hendershott, "Edwin Moses," *Track & Field News*, Sept. 1976, p. 33.

ESSENTIALS OF SOUND TECHNIQUE

The details of technical skill over the hurdles are adequately described in Chapter 27, the high hurdles. The three-inch difference in hurdle height does not make a significant difference. But the necessity of running counter-clockwise around two curves does give a definite advantage to those that lead with the inside (left) leg.

Measurements for Intermediate Hurdles. Distances are the same for men and women: 45m (147'7 5/8") to the first hurdle, 35m (114'10") between hurdles, 40m (131'2 3/4") from last hurdle to finish line. For men, hurdle height is .914m (39"); for women, .762 (30").

SPRINTING TO THE FIRST HURDLE. Take a natural number of strides. Put the first hurdle in place at 49 yards 7.65 inches. Now sprint from starting blocks in the lane next to the hurdle; sprint past it at such a relaxed pace as can be maintained for 400 meters. The coach should mark your strides. The last mark should be six feet or more from the hurdle; if not, adjust your strides. After repeated efforts over several weeks, you may decide to reverse your feet in the blocks. How many strides? That's not the crucial question. Whatever number works best for you is best for you, regardless of the experts. However, as a matter of interest, experienced hurdlers take 21 strides; others, 22; some of lesser ability, 23. Moses used only 20.

How fast? As fast as you are likely to be able to maintain over the distance. You should be able to maintain a pace within five seconds of your best 440 time; Ralph Mann did within 2.2 seconds! As a matter of interest, times to the first hurdle among champions have varied from 5.9 to 6.2; among women, from 6.2 to 6.6.

MEN'S TOUCHDOWN TIME CHART
400 METER HURDLES

Target Time	H1	H2	H3	H4	H5	200	H6	H7	H8	H9	H10	Run In
46.2	5.8	9.4	13.0	16.7	20.4	22.1	24.2	28.2	32.4	36.7	41.1	5.1
46.6	5.8	9.5	13.2	16.9	20.6	22.3	24.4	28.4	32.6	37.0	41.4	5.2
47.0	5.8	9.5	13.2	17.0	20.8	22.5	24.7	28.7	32.9	37.3	41.8	5.2
48.0	5.9	9.7	13.5	17.4	21.3	23.0	25.3	29.5	33.8	38.2	42.7	5.3
49.0	6.0	9.9	13.8	17.7	21.7	23.5	25.8	30.1	34.5	39.1	43.6	5.4
50.0	6.0	10.0	14.0	18.1	22.2	24.0	26.4	30.8	35.3	39.9	44.5	5.5
51.0	6.1	10.2	14.3	18.5	22.7	24.5	27.0	31.4	35.9	40.6	45.9	5.6

WOMEN'S TOUCHDOWN TIME CHART
400 METER HURDLES

Target Time	H1	H2	H3	H4	H5	200	H6	H7	H8	H9	H10	Run In
52	6.1	10.3	14.5	18.8	23.1	25.0	27.5	32.0	36.7	41.4	46.3	5.7
54	6.3	10.7	15.1	19.6	24.1	26.5	28.7	33.4	38.2	43.2	48.2	5.8
56	6.5	11.1	15.7	20.3	25.0	27.0	29.8	34.7	39.7	44.9	50.1	5.9
58	6.7	11.5	16.3	21.1	25.9	28.0	30.8	35.9	41.1	46.2	51.8	6.2
60	6.9	11.9	16.9	21.9	26.9	29.5	52.0	57.2	42.5	47.9	53.4	6.6
62	7.1	12.3	17.5	22.6	27.8	30.0	33.1	38.4	43.9	49.5	55.2	6.8
64	7.3	12.6	17.9	23.3	28.7	31.0	54.2	39.8	45.4	51.1	57.0	7.0

Table 28.2
These charts from Brent McFarlane,
"Hurdles Touchdown Charts," in Jess Jarver,
THE HURDLES, Los Altos: Tafnews Press, 1981
p. 34.

Fig. 28.2. Edwin Moses clearing last hurdle, 1984 Olympic Games; time--47.75.

   STRIDES BETWEEN HURDLES.   Most men with good hurdling technique and endurance can handle 15 strides throughout the full ten hurdles. (An even number forces a man to alternate the lead leg). Whether for lack of stride-length or of endurance, few men have been able to take 13 all the way. Charley Moore, 1952 Olympic winner, did it but he gave an impression of overstriding. In his first race, Ed Moses "ran 15 strides until the 6th hurdle, ran 14 strides for two because I wasn't sure of the pattern, and then 13 strides to the finish." But for the remainder of his career, he used 13 strides throughout. As a matter of interest, he experimented with 12 strides after the Games, and found he could do it comfortably.

   Mike Shine, 2nd at Montreal, used 15 strides for all hurdles, in part because of an outside lead leg. Akii-Bua, winner at Munich, used 15 strides to H5; 14 to H9; then 15 from H9 to H10. John Le Masurier reports[1] that Tziortsis of Greece (finalist at Munich; semi-finalist at Montreal), only 175 Cms (5-9) tall, ran his early hurdles with 15 strides, then used 16 and finally 17 at the end. Clearly, stride patterns do vary.

   Jon Hendershott[2] had an opportunity to interview a group of outstanding 400-meter hurdlers, and reported these comments on the matter of striding:

   Paramount to faster times, either over meters or yards, is the number of strides between hurdles. "If the athlete can take 13 steps for five or six hurdles, this is a great advantage," Vanderstock feels. Dave Hemery goes even further. "To really get the record down where it belongs, a fellow should work on striding 13s all the way," he says.

   Farmer pointed out some of the inherent advantages of "striding 13s," other than the speed factor. "At the start of any race, an athlete is a bundle of nervous energy, so why ask him to do anything but explode that energy at the very beginning of his race? Some people have said there is too much energy consumed in taking 13 strides for the first few hurdles, but there is even more energy used by putting on the brakes to chop stride. Competitively speaking, the most important reason for going 13s is that it applies pressure on the other hurdlers. Often you see a hurdler lose his concentration and rhythm as an opponent moves up on his inside after making up most of the original stagger.

   On the other hand, Cawley doesn't see much difference in using 13 or 15 strides. "I don't believe either method is inherently faster than the other," he says. "It depends on the man using it. A tall man chopping to 15 steps would tire quickly and look as ridiculous as a short man bounding along stretching to make 13. Whichever method is most comfortable and efficient for the athlete should be used. Sometimes a mixture of the two is best."

   Whitney adds another aspect to the stride controversy. "I used to think the 15-stride technique was the best," he comments. "With the advent of the Tartan track, though, I have to say 13 is the best. Just check the time differentials between dirt and Tartan. Hurdlers who have been no threat to us 15-striders on dirt turn around and run one or two seconds faster on Tartan. My difference is three-tenths.

   "Tartan gives you an elongated stride," Whitney continues. "I found myself too close to the hurdles on Tartan, even at the end of a race."

   Whitney brings up another requisite for faster times. "Left leg lead is essential," he says. "I am right, but I feel it makes at least a three to five-tenths difference. With a right leg lead you have to hurdle to the outside of the barrier, especially on the last turn when the staggers are being made up. I think every high school and college coach should demand that any hurdler with the slightest intention of becoming a medium hurdler use his left leg."

---

[1]John Le Masurier, "Olympic 400-Meter Hurdles (Men)--Mexico, Munich and Montreal," *Track & Field Quarterly Review*, Vol. 78 #4, Winter 1978, p. 39.

[2]Jon Hendershott, "Few US 440-Hurdle Specialists," *Track & Field News*, 1 May 1969, 16.

Whatever stride pattern is decided upon for this particular hurdler--the same throughout, alternating legs each hurdle, taking 15 for the first five and 16 or 17 for the last five-- that pattern must be mastered and certain in the mind of the hurdler. There is no time for uncertainty while racing, and no valid excuses for a mistake in judgment. A well-coached 400m hurdler makes plans ahead of time for weather conditions, lane drawings, track surfaces, whatever, and is tough in following that plan.

TABLE 28.2[1]
TOUCHDOWN TIMES
MEN'S 400-METER HURDLES
1976, 1972, 1968 OLYMPIC FINALS

Athlete	Yr	To H1 lead leg	H1	H2	H3	H4	H5	1st 200	H6	H7	H8	H9	H10	H10 to fin	2nd 200	Diff	Time
Moses USA	'76	20(L)	6.0	9.8 13(3.8)	13.5 13(3.7)	17.4 13(3.9)	21.4 13(4.0)	23.1	25.4 13(4.0)	29.6 13(4.2)	33.9 13(4.3)	38.2 13(4.3)	42.6 13(4.4)	5.04	24.54	1.44	47.64
Akii-Bua UGA	'72	21(R)	6.1	9.8 13(3.7)	13.6 13(3.8)	17.4 13(3.8)	21.3 13(3.9)	23.0	25.4 14.(4.1)	29.5 14(4.1)	33.7 14(4.2)	38.1 14(4.4)	42.6 15(4.5)	5.2	24.8	1.8	47.82
Hemery GBR	'68	21(L)	6.1	9.8 13(3.8)	13.6 13(3.8)	17.5 13(3.9)	21.5 13(4.0)	23.3	25.4 13(3.9)	29.6 15(4.2)	33.9 15(4.3)	38.3 15(4.4)	42.8 15(4.5)	5.3	24.8	1.5	48.1
Hemery BGR	'72	21(L)	6.1	9.8 13(3.7)	13.4 13(3.6)	17.2 13(3.8)	21.1 13(3.9)	22.8	25.1 13(4.0)	29.3 15(4.2)	33.6 15(4.3)	38.2 15(4.6)	43.0 15(4.8)	5.5	25.7	2.9	48.52
Mann USA	'72	22(L)	6.0	9.7 (3.7)	13.6 (3.9)	17.6 (4.0)	21.3 (3.7)	23.0	25.4 (4.1)	29.7 (4.3)	33.9 (4.2)	38.4 (4.5)	43.1 (4.7)	5.4	25.5	2.5	48.51
Seymour USA	'72	21(L)	6.1	9.9 (3.8)	13.8 (3.9)	17.7 (3.9)	21.7 (4.0)	23.4	25.9 (4.2)	30.2 (4.3)	34.5 (4.3)	39.1 (4.6)	43.5 (4.4)	5.1	25.2	1.8	48.64
Shine USA	'76	22	6.1	9.9 15(3.8)	13.8 15(3.9)	17.7 15(3.9)	21.7 15(4.0)	23.4	25.9 15(4.2)	30.2 15(4.3)	34.5 15(4.3)	38.9 15(4.4)	43.4 15(4.5)	3.29	25.29	1.79	48.69
Hennige GER	'68	21	6.0	9.9 (3.9)	13.8 (3.9)	17.8 (4.0)	21.9 (4.1)	23.8	26.1 (4.2)	30.5 (4.4)	34.9 (4.4)	39.4 (4.5)	44.0 (4.6)	5.0	25.2	1.4	49.0
Sherwood GBR	'68	21	6.0	9.8 (3.8)	13.7 (3.9)	17.7 (4.0)	21.8 (4.1)	23.7	26.4 (4.2)	30.2 (4.2)	34.7 (4.5)	39.4 (4.7)	43.9 (4.5)	5.1	25.3	1.6	49.0
Vanderstock USA	'68	22	5.9	9.7 (3.8)	13.8 (4.1)	17.8 (4.0)	21.8 (4.0)	23.7	25.9 (4.1)	30.2 (4.3)	34.5 (4.3)	38.9 (4.4)	43.5 (4.6)	5.5	25.3	1.6	49.0
Skomorokov USSR	'68	21	6.1	9.9 (3.8)	13.7 (3.8)	17.5 (3.8)	21.5 (4.0)	23.4	25.6 (4.1)	30.0 (4.4)	34.6 (4.6)	39.2 (4.6)	43.8 (4.6)	5.3	25.7	2.3	49.1
Whitney USA	'68	21	6.1	10.3 (4.2)	14.2 (3.9)	18.2 (4.0)	22.4 (4.2)	24.3	26.6 (4.2)	30.8 (4.2)	35.1 (4.3)	39.5 (44)	44.0 (4.5)	5.2	24.9	0.6	49.2
Schubert WG	'68	21(L)	6.0	9.8 (3.8)	13.7 (3.9)	17.7 (4.0)	21.8 (4.1)	23.7	25.9 (4.1)	30.3 (4.4)	34.8 (4.5)	39.3 (4.5)	44.0 (4.7)	5.2	25.5	1.8	49.2
Schubert WG	'72	21(L)	6.1	9.9 (3.8)	13.7 (3.8)	17.6 (3.9)	21.6 (4.0)	23.3	25.8 (4.2)	30.2 (4.4)	34.6 (4.4)	39.3 (4.7)	44.2 (4.9)	5.5	26.3	3.0	49.65
Tziortzis GR	'72	22(R)	6.2	9.9 (3.7)	13.8 (3.9)	17.7 (3.9)	21.8 (4.1)	23.5	26.1 (4.3)	30.3 (4.2)	34.8 (4.5)	39.4 (4.6)	44.2 (4.8)	5.5	26.2	2.7	49.66

TACTICS

In general, a man would do best to concentrate entirely on his own race and his own problems of proper stride, relaxation, and drive through to the finish. However, as experience and confidence are gained men learn to relax an infinitesimal degree "with their opponents" on the backstretch and going into the second curve. This is just enough to conserve their energies for the big drive to the tape. Glenn Davis was a master at this. He seldom had a lead until the seventh hurdle, but from then on he had his opponents "psyched out," for they knew how tough it would be to beat him over the last three.

It seems quite likely that Hemery established the pattern for the future in winning the 1968 Olympic final. Dick Drake[2] reported the race:

Schubert and Hemery were slightly ahead and Whitney already lagging by the

---

[1]This chart excerpted from Brent McFarlane, "Hurdles Touchdown Chart," in Jess Jarver, *THE HURDLES*, Los Altos: Tafnews Press, 1981.
[2]Dick Drake, "Hemery's 48.1 Cremates Field," *Track & Field News*, Oct/Nov, 1968, 23.

first hurdle. From there, Hemery pulled away startlingly--with remarkable technique that made the intermediates resemble low hurdles. Never have the first five hurdles been negotiated as quickly as Hemery was ripping over them. By the third, the 6' 1 1/2", 165-lb. Hemery had already made up the stagger on Whitney. He reached midway in the shocking 23.0, literally a half-flight ahead of his nearest competitors...

Powerfully but skillfully, Hemery left the field even further behind as he rounded the final curve and changed his steps from 13 to 15 after the sixth.

Hemery followed this same tactic at the 1972 Games, being timed by several observers in 20.8 at touchdown after the fifth hurdle (compared with 21.5 in 1968). At that point he had a yard or so lead over Ralph Mann, BYU 440y hurdle world-record holder, with Akii-Bua, in lane one, well under 21.5. Akii-Bua used 13 strides with an outside right leg lead for the first five hurdles, then shifted to 14 by alternating legs. (Six of the eight finalists led with the inside left leg.) The winner--Akii-Bua with a world-record time of 47.82, 1.2 seconds faster than his previous best but seemingly slower than his potential best. Ralph Mann was second in 48.51; Hemery third, in 48.52.

What were Edwin Moses's tactics during his 109 victories over a 7-year span? Primarily by being in superior condition, by using perfect technique, and by keeping relaxed throughout. By such means he simply out-ran his rivals, gaining slowly all the way. In race #60 in 1983 at the Mt SAC Relays, Moses actually had to come from behind after the 8th hurdle. But then, he was able to draw on superior condition and pull ahead. At the 1984 Olympics, he was gradually ahead all the way, holding a lead of three yards throughout the final straightaway.

THE ORGANIZATION OF PRACTICE

Planning a program of year-round training for the 400m hurdles should place first emphasis on basic endurance as would any 400m or 800m runner. Throughout the early months train with such men in doing fast-slow work (fartlek) off the track. Steady running over long distances may help in building basic endurance, but it is speed-endurance specifically related to the 400m IHs that is required. Work with the 440 and 880 men in doing interval training--repeat 200s, 300s, 400s, 600s--as developed in Chapter 21.

During the indoor season, train for and compete in the 400m, 600m or 800m runs. Most National and Olympic champions have developed by following this path. If, for whatever reason, competing in the 60m hurdles is necessary, then also train and compete on the 1600-meter relay team.

We are not decreasing the importance of technique for the 400m hurdles. To achieve a time difference between the 400 IHs and the 400 flat of three seconds or even less requires excellent technique, and such excellent technique requires persistent practice. But the more potential value in use of time during this early season lies in developing endurance.

As soon as outdoor conditions permit, emphasis should shift to use of the 3-foot hurdles, following such procedures as those devised for Nehemiah as described in the preceding Chapter. Coach Poquette emphasized technique--lead leg, trail leg, forward lean, arms--but he did so while developing related endurance: 4 x (10 x 10 hurdles), 400 hurdles in a single practice. That kind of workout can be used even better for the 400 IHs. For example, the following actions are my own version of those proposed by Michael Shine,[1] Penn State, and silver medallist in the 1976 Olympic IHs:

1. Run 600m--first 400m flat; last 200m over 5 IHs, being very conscious of technique.
2. 3 x 400m--(1) first 200 over IHs, second 200m flat; (2) reverse #1; (3) repeat #1.
3. 400m--run 3 IHs, middle-four distance (140m) on the flat, run last 3 IHs.
4. 3 sets of (2 x 200m with five IHs).
5. 6 x over 400m: (1) 2 x (3 IHs and finish 400m); (2) 2 x (Run 130m on flat, continue over middle four IHs, then final 130m on flat); (3) 2 x (run 295m on flat, then last three IHs).
6. Backoffs from 7 IHs (or from 6 or from 5 as seems best)--run 7 IHs, then 6 IHs, then 5 IHs, etc., dropping one hurdle each time.
7. Buildups to 7 IHs (begin over 3 IHs, then 4 IHs, then 5 IHs, etc.)

If it seems worthwhile, add incentive by timing some of these workouts, but maintain awareness of technique throughout, including avoidance of the inside lane line.

[1]Michael Shine, op. cit., pp. 46-47.

Carl Lewis./Photo by Paul J. Sutton/Duomo.

Appendix A
DYNAMICS OF SKILL

INTRODUCTION [1]

Any discussion of the dynamics of the skill events in track and field must focus on such fundamentals as "muscle sense," "whole-phase-whole learning," or "reinforcement," just as the dynamics of endurance must focus on such fundamentals as aerobic-anaerobic running, or those of power on overloading and relatedness. That is to say, in our modern and more scientific approach to coaching problems, we must understand and practice the basic knowledges that underlie our coaching of specific events. Such esoteric terms as "mental practice" or "feedback" may seem of little use when actually coaching a boy to throw the discus or hammer. But unless our modern coaching is consistent with the findings of related research, it will not be as effective and the athlete's performance will be decreased.

This is a hard fact which coaches of the pre-scientific decades find it agonizing if not impossible to swallow. As I write I just have to laugh a little as I think of the reaction to such gibberish by such excellent Olympic coaches as Lawson Robertson, Dean Cromwell, or Jim Kelley,--something comparable to "hogwash" or "horsefeathers"! And for their era, that's about what such an approach would have been, just as would heart-rate meters for coaching running or computers for coaching football. But today requires new and more scientific thinking and practice.

LEARNING A SKILL IS A HOLISTIC-DYNAMIC PROBLEM

In our introductory chapter we stated that the basic point of view of this book was "holistic-dynamic," a term coined by Abraham Maslow in his *MOTIVATION AND PERSONALITY*, 1970. By it, he emphasized wholes or systems in contrast to the separate elements of atomism.

The concept is of special value in coaching skills. Learning a skill is holistic in several ways. For example, the most valid unit of competitive performance is the whole person-situation in a time-place extensional sense. Skill is but one aspect of such performance and of the training behind it. Decades ago we assumed technique was a 90% factor in performance. If a man acquired proper technique, he needed only full motivation to achieve top performance. Thus, 90 percent of our practice time related to better technique. Today we know that high-level skill requires basic and related power, and that only a lesser portion of time-energy, say 50 percent or less, can be focussed on skill. As a second example of holism, we begin a skill with a vaguely grasped whole. We make a simple analysis of it by which we realize the unreality of our first grasp of the skill and try to create a better and more complete whole. Again this whole is analyzed; again we sense the skill at a higher level of wholeness and effectiveness. This process continues endlessly--and holistically.

Learning a skill is also a dynamic problem in that the athlete-situation (including the coach) is never static, never identical from any point of view. We say this in the Heraclitus sense that no one of us is ever twice the same, and that "we can never step in the same river twice." Thus we can never coach the same boy or the same skill in successive practice sessions. Everything changes: the athlete, the coach, their inter-personal attitudes, their

---

[1]This Appendix A was first written 15 years ago, but respected coaches have urged (1984) its continued publication.

mastery of learning and teaching, their awareness of goals, the social and physical surround within which they live and work--nothing is ever identical.

This suggests chaos and total breakdown of the learning-teaching process, that is, until we remember that endless change and diversity is but one side of the coin. The other equally valid side is a basic unity of all things. Even though "never the same river twice," there's "always the river."

If this discussion confuses more than it clarifies, read again the introductory chapter of this book. Succeeding sections on skill learning, especially "whole-phase-whole learning," and "mental practice," should be helpful. If specially interested in the problem, be sure to read Maslow but perhaps even more crucial the delightful book by Wendell Johnson, *PEOPLE IN QUANDARIES*, the semantics of personal adjustment. I know of no better mind opener or tension dropper. Now out-of-print, but worth searching for.

WHOLE-PHASE-WHOLE LEARNING IN FIELD EVENTS

Traditionally, the methods of motor learning as found in field events are presented from two points of view: that of "part learning" as developed by the "association" or stimulus-response schools of psychology, and that of whole-part-whole learning of the Gestalt or Organismic schools. These methods apply in our field as well.

PROGRESSIONS. By the stimulus-response theory of motor learning, the whole movement to be learned was divided into separate parts in a way that was meaningful logically (though not necessarily muscularly or organismically). Learning practice was then concentrated on each part in its logical order until each was learned well. Then the parts were re-joined as a basis for learning the whole movement.

Such coaching of parts has a definite validity in certain sports such as baseball, where for example the learning of batting skills has little relation to that of playing second base or pitching. But as a sport becomes less complex and more all-of-one-piece so to speak, such analysis and coaching of parts becomes less and less effective. I once observed an hour-long class in *discus throwing* (the italics are used with malice aforethought) in which the dozen or so prospects were taught: (1) to roll the discus around the first finger, (2) to toss it vertically while rolling it around the first finger, (3) to throw it from a standing position, and (4) to rotate the body without a discus. Considerable time and emphasis was given to perfecting each of these actions. These actions were called progressions, but progress occurred at such a slow rate and doubtful value as related to discus throwing that I wondered at the degree of acceptance by the students.

WHOLE-PART-WHOLE LEARNING. Effective coaching by whole-part-whole methods depends on a sound and precise understanding of the meaning of the concept. We do not wish to quibble over "mere words," as some might express it. But, as in every attempt at a more scientific approach, the precise meanings that are given to "whole" and "part" and their inter-relationships are basic to coaching that achieves a mastery of technique in the shortest possible time.

What degree of complexity should a teachable whole be? The most valid whole is the actual time-situation-action of the competition itself. And a strong case can be made for learning to perform in competition by performing in competition. At the other extreme, a coachable whole can be identified in almost any phase of movement, no matter how partial, as long as that phase is seen and used in its relationship to the whole movement of the event. Relatedness is the key to this method of motor learning.

Though such relatedness is implied by the hyphen in whole-part-whole, we prefer the word "phase" to that of "part." A part suggests a separate entity, as occurs in a machine such as a radio or automobile, in which the separate parts can be assembled to form the whole machine. This is never the case in human motor learning. In contrast, the word "phase" is always incomplete in its connotation, and always relative to its whole.

$WHOLE_1$-$PHASE_1$-$WHOLE_2$-$PHASE_2$-$WHOLE_3$ LEARNING. The wholes of a movement being learned are constantly changing. Only in the abstractions of our minds do they tend to remain the same. We can think of and speak of a movement such as high jumping as a fixed action. But each time we jump, that action changes--hopefully, it develops to a new and better whole (technique).

This is what is implied by the heading of this section. Think of whole$_1$ as a symbol for a first attempt to jump, in which we give special attention to phase$_1$, the upward thrust of the lead leg. Such attentive practice produces a change in skill, hopefully an improvement, so that we now have a new whole, as indicated by whole$_2$. Similarly, on our second effort, the action of the lead leg is not identical to that of the first effort, so we write it as phase$_2$.

This gives us the overall pattern of our preferred method of learning and coaching the skills of track and field. Each new phase emerges out of its precedent whole, and merges back into that whole at a different and, hopefully, more skilled level. At each new level of skill, the athlete feels, and may even yell, "I've got it!" He is experiencing what the Gestalt school calls a "perceptual reorganization" or insight that senses a closer approximation of the desired skill. "Closure" (Shaffer, 1956, 134) occurs, a restoration of equilibrium at a higher level. But the "it" that he feels probably recedes. He may even fall back to lower levels of skill for days or weeks. But with continued sound practice, there will come a new "I've got it!" at a new whole, and insight into a higher approximation of the goal. And so on, toward full mastery of "it."

The final goal is an all-out, uninhibited, perfect action. But with imperfect and finite men, such a goal, like that of Tennyson's Ulysses, "whose margin fades forever and forever as I move," constantly recedes with each new level of skill. After many years of striving, a Ralph Boston in the long jump or an Al Oerter in the discus feels that he is just beginning to grasp the real knack of his event. The only instance of perfect performance in motor learning is related by Eugen Herrigel (1953) in his autobiographical ZEN IN THE ART OF ARCHERY. The Zen Master is a coaching genius who demands, or better, assumes training and performance at the highest levels of non-effort. (If this is unclear, by all means read, or more likely, get lost in the book.)

USABLE WHOLES. Those who oppose the holistic approach to motor learning argue that sports are too complex to be learned as a whole, and must be divided into segments for separate practice. This certainly holds true for such actions as foul throwing in basketball or the backhand stroke in tennis. But it is our opinion that its application to field events should be limited as much as possible. As a rule of thumb, coach the largest whole, in terms of the event action, as can be used effectively. In most cases, this means the full action of the event performed at the highest usable speed.

When properly presented, field events are not so complex as to be unmanageable by the neophyte as a single undivided skill. The pole vault might be an exception, largely because of the danger of injury. But even in this event, once the beginner learns to grasp the pole firmly and swing into the air, we can take a "whole" though modified, approach. True the discus action is unique in sports, with its body rotation while holding the discus back in a power position, but boys well enough coordinated to be good prospects pick up the whole action quickly, even though imperfectly, of course.

Which reminds us to re-emphasize that holistic method does not require a perfect-or-not-at-all effort. It is enough that the learned whole (a) is acceptably satisfactory to the learner, and (b) is consistent with the whole skill that the coach is trying to teach.

In summary, learning by a whole-phase-whole method would proceed somewhat as follows:

a. A first emphasis upon the action as a whole, upon one thoughtless, unanalyzed, undivided movement. Such sense of the movement "as a whole" is initiated by watching and thus "getting the feel" of the action of expert throwers on the field, or on film, or by sequence drawings. Such a holistic feeling should precede all analytical coaching, and certainly, all teaching of so-called progressions in learning skills.

Some may prefer to reify this feeling of the whole action away from the coach, and even other throwers. Some coaches stay away from raw beginners on the first day or so. "You try it alone today, now that you've seen the champ in action; I'll see you tomorrow." This way the youngster gains a certain confidence, not in the sense of proper rhythm or skill, of course, but at least of having something positive, and of forming a base for interpreting the words of his coach.

Don't practice alone for long. It's amazing how the techniques of first learning tend to stay with a man; a wrong method learned early can be tough to break.

b. Now that you're back with the coach, relax, let yourself go, accept suggestions, ask questions. The coach isn't taking <u>you</u> apart; it's only your technique that concerns him. Naturally, you're going to feel unsure and off-balance when you try to focus your attention on holding your shoulder back while turning in the discus or shifting in the shot; everyone is--in the learning stage.

Gradually become aware of the parts of the whole event. For example, be conscious of the focus of your eyes while putting the shot. But maintain such awareness of parts as aspects of the whole, not as separate or unrelated entities. As separate entities, they disrupt what you are doing; they become a movement in themselves, rather than phases of the desired movement. For example, assume that your coach has called your attention to the focus of the eyes during the glide in the shot and then to their upward shift along a 75-degree plane during the final drive at the toeboard. Don't get into the circle yet. Take your time, think it through; or better, feel through the whole action of the put and the eye-focus as a phase of that action. Get the feel of it, out of the circle, not merely once but many times.

c. Now try it in the circle; try it as a whole but with an awareness of the phase, of the eye-focus. You did it!--or something like it. Now stop, and again think and feel through what you did, what you didn't do, and what you should have done. Now try it again, and again, and again. Not whole; then part; then whole as three distinct processes. But whole-phase-whole learning as one unified process.

MUSCLE SENSE IN LEARNING TRACK AND FIELD SKILLS

Muscle sense is the most crucial of all means to motor learning. In fact, Steinhaus[1] argues that it is man's most important sense organ, more vital to life than the eyes or the ears. This muscle sense, variously called the kinesthenic or proprioceptive sense, arises from stimulation of sensory organs by body movement, balance, and relation of the parts of the body.[2] Just as the eyes react only to light stimuli, and the ears only to sound stimuli, so the muscle-sense organs react only to sensory stimuli in the muscles and joints.

Movement, changes in muscle tension or stretch, changes in joint angles, pressures, resistances, all stimulate sense organs. These organs, including the muscle spindles, Golgi Tendon organ, Pacinian corpuscle, and Ruffini endings, give rise to sensations that report what the body is doing, and where it is as related to its parts, or to exterior objects where direct contact is made. Much of their effects helps to regulate movement and balance directly without reference to the cortex, but also there is a great deal of "feedback" into our consciousness. As Steinhaus tells us, "We can live without eyes, we can live without ears . . . but without the messages that come to us from our muscles and joint structures we could not talk, walk, breathe, find our mouth to feed it, or follow the printed line while reading--and probably we could not think."

Certainly, without these kinesthetic sense organs, the learning of track and field skills would be impossible, ignoring the fact that they would be meaningless as well.

Undoubtedly, men differ in their muscle-sense sensitivity, just as they do in the sensitivity of their eyes and ears and taste buds and olfactory organs. Some men are extremely high in their ability to discriminate sensations and interpret them muscularly, just as others have a similar ability in intellectual activities. Most men are predominantly "motor-minded," as related to motor learning. That is, they learn a movement best by doing that movement, or by simulating it at slower speeds or in related actions. But there is a wide range of difference among men in this respect. Some men seem to be visually-minded as related to motor learning. They are able to gain insights from watching others directly or in filmed action that are easily transmuted into the desired skill. Other men seem to be orally adept. They seem able to translate words into the action the words describe. Somehow they have trained themselves to

---

[1] Arthur H. Steinhaus, "Your Muscles See more Than Your Eyes," *Jour HPER,* September 1966, 38.

[2] E. A. Fleishman, "The Perception of Body Position in the Absence of Visual Cues," *J. Exp. Psychology,* 1953, 46, 261-270.

listen closely, feel the muscle-sense meanings of the words, then approximate the described skill quite closely. I've coached such men, and was often amazed at their ability to feel the meaning of my words, not merely as sound waves but as muscle movements.

Over 30 years of coaching have convinced me, though the related research is lacking, that this muscle sense or proprioception, to use the more scientific term, is present in each man within a range of potential use. Disregarding innate ability, a skilled performer is able to discriminate small differences between one effort and the next, differences that the unskilled does not detect. By intent awareness, the skilled performer feels such differences, much as the professional coffee or wine taster can, by both inborn talent and training, accept one product and reject another; or as the master violinist's muscle-sense organs detect infinitesimal differences in the movements of his bow.

It is also my experience that some so-called natural athletes, those that learn complex skills without apparent effort, sometimes have little conscious perception of how they do what they do. Skill seems to be acquired by muscle "insight," with little of the mental insight that the Gestaltists associate with learning. They seem to get "the feel" of action, with no conscious analysis on their part of how it is done. The ordinary athlete tends to repeat a movement many times, with awareness, before he learns it, so that there is a considerable involvement of the higher brain centers and therefore consciousness of the learned movements. In contrast, the natural athlete learns a new skill quickly, even at the first attempt, and the resultant skill becomes automatized within the cerebellum with comparatively little involvement of the cortex. In addition, this unawareness of the how of movement could be the effect of early coaching that seldom analyzed action, that instead emphasized doing the action without thought, imitating the techniques of others without taking them apart, so to speak.

Such men, highly effective as they may be as performers in competition, are likely to be less so as coaches. To be a competent teacher of techniques in sport, a man must have a highly developed awareness of the muscle senses. I emphasize the word "awareness." Muscle sense alone is not enough, for it functions primarily within the cerebellum. The effective coach needs the consciousness of the higher-brain centers if he is to have the feel of movement and be able to transmit that feel to others.

We accept the statement that one showing is worth a hundred sayings. It is equally true that one correct doing is worth a hundred showings. For example, it is very difficult to explain in words just how to tie a rather simple knot. It's far more effective to demonstrate how it is done. But one can teach even more quickly by helping the fingers manipulate the tieing. Once they get the feel of the action, learning is well under way. We hardly need to add that coaching requires a combination of all three methods (demonstration, active trying, and words) if it is to be most effective.

MENTAL PRACTICE
Mental practice, just as physical practice, is first of all a way of speaking. In reality there are not two separate practice methods--one physical, the other mental. Rather there are certain practices in which the physical is primary; others, in which the mental predominates. In both, there is a measurable flow of electrical impulses to the related muscles. In mental practice this flow is below the threshold of muscle sensitivity, so that no movement results. Actually I prefer not drawing even this sharp line of difference, for mental practice could also include a concentrated attention on the "how" of technique while moving very slowly through the action.

That there is such a measurable electrical flow was demonstrated by Jacobson (1932, 1934) who, studying relaxation, detected by very sensitive electromyography that mental states such as anxiety, fear, and tension do influence the muscle action potentials. Muscles are stimulated, even though below the threshold of movement. The converse of this was that complete muscle relaxation was achieved only when all such "mental" activity ceased.

Similarly, Shaw[1] measured muscle action potentials when weightlifters imagined, that is, concentrated attention on the simulation of the movements of lifting weights. The more

---

[1] W. A. Shaw, "The Distribution of Muscular Action Potentials during Imaging," *Psychological Record*, 1938, 2, 195.

concentrated the attention, the greater the electrical impulses. Lundervold[1] supported these findings when he reported increased electrical impulses to the muscles active in finger tapping, "when persons tested were sharply commanded to concentrate on the task," and conversely, fewer impulses when the subjects' thoughts were diverted from the tapping.

During my years of coaching, I have been impressed again and again by intelligent motor learners, notably Charles Fonville, former world-record holder in the shot. Sometimes he would come to me before starting a day's practice, saying "Coach, I think I've got it. I've been thinking about the action as the left foot hits the toeboard and I think I've got the hang of it." Then he'd go to the shot circle and immediately perform that phase of the action better than ever before. I asked Charlie several times just what he meant by "thinking." His answers were uncertain but tended to relate thought processes to action and the feel of action. He said that closing his eyes was helpful. He supposed that, even though he was lying in bed or sitting in a chair, his muscles did simulate the movements he was thinking about. Several times, sitting in the library, he found another student looking at him queerly and smiling, so he supposed that his "mental practice" was showing.

We must keep in mind that such men are highly talented, not merely in performing their events, but equally in their mind-muscle insight, their kinesthenic feeling of movement, and overall orientation to their events. Probably they can control their muscle action potentials, though well below the level of the threshold of muscle action, with much greater precision than can the beginner or the ordinary athlete. They're like the yogi who, according to recent observations by scientists, are able to control the autonomic nervous system including heart rate and blood pressure. Or, at a more feasible level, when in India in 1954 I observed and spoke at length with a man who had learned to make rippling movements of his pectorals and abdominals by just such concentrated mental practice.

In trying to decrease competitive tensions and improve skills in Olympic and University skiers, Richard Suinn[2] used a method he called "visuo-motor behavior rehearsal or VMBR" involving three steps: a version of Jacobsen's progressive relaxation, mental imagery as related to competitive performance, and mental imagery as related to improving skill. Results were strongly encouraging though of course still experimental and inconclusive.

MENTAL PRACTICE OFF AND ON THE FIELD. There is a tendency to assume that mental practice must occur away from the activity field, as when lying on one's bed, so that conscious perception and feeling of the desired movements can be undistracted and intently concentrated. Joel Sayre[3] reported that Parry O'Brien attempted such concentration in perfecting his style and his performances in meets,

> He [Parry] spends as much time just thinking about his shot as fondling it in the putting circle. Parry spent many of his nights alone in his ascetic bedroom, the lights dim, his weighty frame slack on the bed. From his tape recorder trickled the soothing sound of his own voice: "Keep low, keep back, keep your movement fast across the circle. Fast now! Fast! Fast! And beat them all! Beat them all!" Parry is convinced that this nocturnal rite adds inches to his toss.

But it is our view that mental practice is not an all-or-none method: all mental, no movement. Mental practice can occur also on the field when, between the regular practice efforts, the athlete reviews mentally what he has just done or is about to do. To refer again to O'Brien, he used to practice alone with but one shot. While walking slowly to and from the shot, he reviewed mentally and felt muscularly the many aspects of what he was doing. Call it thought-

[1] Arne Lundervold, "The Measurement of Human Reaction During Training," *Health and Fitness in the Modern World*, Chicago: *The Athletic Institute*, 1961, 125.

[2] Richard M. Suinn, "Body Thinking: Psychology for Olympic Champs," *Psychology Today*, July 1976, 38-43.

[3] Joel Sayre, "Parry's Power of Positive Thought," *Sports Illustrated*, March 21, 1955, 28.

ful practice if you prefer; the name is unimportant.

But it is important that the powers of the mind be added at their highest levels of concentration and reinforcement to the muscle senses of the body. A separate section emphasizes the crucial values of the muscle sense in motor learning. But to those values must be united the equally crucial values of conscious perception and control of movement.

MENTAL PRACTICE AND PHYSICAL SKILL RISE TOGETHER. The level of learning in mental practice is always proportioned to the level of skill in performing any given event. If performance is unskilled, the mental simulation of that action will be diffused, roughly approximate, vaguely related. That is, mental practice, as related to innervation of the related muscles (refer again to the research of Shaw and Lundervold), can be only slightly more skillful than actual performance. True, when watching a slow-motion movie of an expert performer, one may gain a mental concept of perfect skill, what might be called an eye-cortex concept in which the muscle sense would be at a minimum level. But to practice perfect skill mentally, so that a galvanometer would record electrical impulses to the related muscle groups, one's actual skill must be nearing perfection. Actually, mental practice and physical practice are verbal terms derived from the traditional dualism of mind and body; each focuses on only the extremes of the true range of action. In the human organism they are unified and cannot be separated.

MENTAL PRACTICE IS MORE THAN MENTAL INSIGHT. The concept of mental practice should not be confused with the Gestaltists' "insight," with its connotation of seeing or visualizing the solution of a problem. Kohler's (1925) ape saw the relationship between the stick and the previously unreachable banana. He learned the movement by visualizing relationships. Or to take a more recent example, yesterday I observed my eight-months old granddaughter as she watched her older brother spin a musical top by pumping its handle up and down. He then left the room. She crawled to the top, grasped the handle, dropped it; grasped the handle again, dropped it; then grasped the handle a third time and pumped it up and down in the correct way. I know she never had seen such a top before. There could have been no physical practice. By intent watching (mental practice?) she caught the idea. Gestaltists would call it insight, but such a term tends to ignore the crucial role of the muscle sense, and the unity of eye-cortex-muscle sense by which both Kohler's ape and my granddaughter achieved their goal.

But in the more complex movements of field and track events, mental practice does not produce immediate mastery of a skill, any more than does physical practice. We might gain a so-called mental insight of perfect skill, but actual insight in a mind-body sense can achieve only an approximation of such skill. At each stage, the learner feels again and again that he now has the knack of it, only to discover that the goal constantly recedes. This is so at even the highest levels, even at the level of a Warmerdam, a Brumel, or an O'Brien. Furthermore, one hardly needs the wisdom of a Zen Master to understand that, "he who has a 100 miles to walk should reckon ninety as but half the journey."

THE UNITY OF MENTAL-PHYSICAL PRACTICE. It may help to clarify our thinking if we consider sports practice as a parallelogram in which a diagonal line separates the physical aspect of practice from the mental (Figure A-1). No matter how automatized a skill may have become (AA), so that its actions are controlled entirely by the cerebellum, its improvement requires some degree of action in consciousness, that is, in the cortex. Similarly, no matter at how high a level of abstracting a certain insight of a skill might be, (CC), any attempt to "practice" that skill would result in low-level impulses to the muscles and stimulation of the muscle-spindle sensory organs.

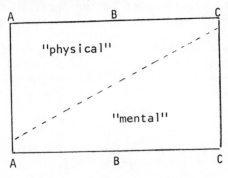

Fig. A.1 -- A crude representation of the mental-physical unity of sports action. Note that the dividing diagonal line never reaches zero -- all of one and none of the other.

Personally, I like much better the Chinese figure on the right, representing the yin-yang or unity-of-opposites principle.

HOW CLOSELY SHOULD MENTAL PRACTICE BE CONTROLLED BY THE COACH? A study by Jones[1] compared the values of two methods of mental practice in learning a new gymnastic skill: (1) controlled practice, and (2) individual freedom of practice. The first group had specific written instructions and close supervision of their mental practice. The second were free to discover their own insights and ways of procedure. Jones found that the undirected group learned more quickly, and reasoned that self-initiated methods led to better kinesthenic images and greater concentration in learning.

Such conclusions should not lead the coach to ignore mental practice altogether. They do caution us against over-coaching in all its forms, and suggest that the gist of coaching is to stimulate, encourage, and help the athlete to help himself.

TECHNIQUES OF MENTAL PRACTICE. Mental practice should not be thought of as some fanciful far-out method in which occult training of the mind produces some mysterious or magical effect on body training. Oxendine (1968, 238) states "there is research evidence to support the belief that a planned program of mental rehearsal might effectively supplement physical practice. . . . A planned program, and one in which some specific guidance is offered, seems more likely to result in useful conceptualization than will an informal or unstructured program." True, such research is scanty and its conclusions far from final, but it tends to support the basic tenets of mental practice. The following suggestions may be helpful in the development of method:

1. Mental Practice During Regular Practice on the Field. For example, in the high jump: (a) Think of the crossbar as at least six inches higher than your head; think-feel through in a mind-muscle sense the kind of run-jump that will clear such a bar--run velocity, rhythm, eye-head inclination, arm-leg actions, etc.--but emphasize the whole action, not its parts. (b) Think-feel through the particular phase of the jump you are now trying to improve; concentrate intently, so as to innervate the nerve-muscles of that phase. (c) Jump in terms of this phase-in-whole awareness, with special awareness of what happens during the phase being learned. (d) Immediately on landing, think-feel through the jump. What was the feeling of right action? Of wrong action? How will correct action feel on the next jump?

Repeat such a jump many times. Note that any one of these four steps can be emphasized by giving it more time and attention and concentration of awareness.

2. Immediate Playback and Review of One's Own Performance, Using Special Movie or Graphic Sequence Cameras. Correct action can be reinforced and incorrect inhibited by immediate reactions of approval or disapproval. Repeat the correct action kinesthetically.

3. Mental Practice with Movies. Loop films of expert performers can be of great value for mental practice. Various methods can be devised: (a) Attentive awareness, in a mind-muscle sense, of the whole action at normal speed, emphasizing rhythm and the skill as a whole; (b) Attentive awareness of a phase of action at slow speed; (c) Immediately following either "a" or "b" use mental practice to reinforce the desired skill; for better concentration, try closing the eyes and attend to the muscle cues of correct action. A coach or other athlete might add his personal cues to correct action, but concentrated attention is done best when alone. (d) Immediately following such a "mental" session, go to the field and practice what was seen and felt.

4. Mental Practice with Sequence Pictures. Once the beginner has gained a feeling for the wholeness of action, sequence pictures with detailed comments provide cues to the details of action that might not be seen in movies or in watching experts on the field.

5. The Laws of Learning Apply to Mental Practice. Since the main difference between physical and mental practice is merely one of degree of nerve-muscle innervation, the accepted laws of motor learning have their applications for mental practice. What will be written here about reinforcement, length and distribution of practice, specificity of learning, and so forth,

---

[1] J. G. Jones, "Motor Learning without Demonstration of Physical Rehearsal, under Two Conditions of Mental Practice," Unpublished Master's Thesis, University of Oregon, 1963.

has implications, though not full application, for mental practice. Of special importance is the maintenance of a close relationship, especially in time, of these two kinds of practice.

SUMMARY. 1. Mental practice in its various forms can be of practical use in track and field. It should not be confused with the illusory mind training of the now discredited faculty psychology. Actually so-called mental practice is as much training of the muscle sense as of the mind, depending on the method and degree of emphasis.

2. Related research in motor learning tends to confirm such practical use.

3. Mental practice is not a new approach to motor learning, though its precise method might be so described. Human learning of physical skills always has had a "mental" aspect. Even inattentive drill has a "mental" accompaniment, though below the level of awareness.

4. Though no related research has been reported, we can assume that the closer the relationship between mental and physical practice in time, method, and action, the greater the reinforcement of learning.

5. Mental practice is helpful for all stages of learning from beginner to expert. As mastery of skill progresses, crude approximations become more and more precisely controlled "movements."

6. The techniques of mental practice that will be developed in the future will be increasingly consistent with those of physical practice. Some will develop a mid-point method in which it would be difficult to say whether the practice is mental or physical. (As illustration, see Herrigel, Eugen, *ZEN IN THE ART OF ARCHERY*.)

REINFORCEMENT IN LEARNING TRACK AND FIELD SKILLS

The concept of reinforcement has been of increasing value in the psychology of motor learning over the past half-century or more. It was basic to Thorndike's "Law of Effect" which, oversimplified, stated that a response that satisfies, strengthens a modifiable connection; a response that annoys, weakens it. It was inherent in Pavlov's experiments in conditioning in which a reward (food for the dog) tends to connect two stimuli (food and the sound of a tuning fork); that is, contiguity led to reinforcement. Hull related reinforcement to a reduction of need or drive; Skinner, to "operants," the memory of reward for certain behavior in past situations. Most other schools of learning, including the Gestalt school (Kohler, 1947), Field Theory (Lewin, 1935), Organismic (Goldstein, 1939), and the Holistic-dynamics theory of Maslow (1954) have used and contributed to a more effective use of the reinforcement concept. Unfortunately, the limited space of this book permits only a very brief summary of its more everyday uses for track coaching.

KNOWLEDGE OF RESULTS (FEEDBACK). If successful response is to be reinforced, the outcome must be satisfying, must follow the response quickly, and must be directly related to the specific response desired. Other things being equal, the greater the feeling of satisfaction, the sharper and more related the awareness of the desired action, and the more immediate the resulting satisfaction, the more likely that response is to be repeated.

In field events and in track events involving skill, there are many criteria by which an athlete can judge a response as successful. Of these, distance is the most obvious and, unfortunately, the most commonly used. How far did it go? How high was the bar? What does the watch show? But this is an indirect and often erroneous way of judging success as related to skill. Many factors other than skill may produce distance: effort, relaxation, balance, throwing angle, speed of preliminary movements, and many more.

It all seems simple to follow Skinner's admonition, "Elicit the response you want and reward it," especially when applied to Skinner's pigeons and rats. But such a formula becomes most complex when applied to the many aspects and attitudes of response that occur in track and field. Of course there are some coaches who keep their coaching very close to the simple level of Skinner's pigeons. In fact, I've worked with two assistant coaches who had just such a tendency. Their desired response was simple, "Clear the bar. Throw for distance, Win!" When these things happened, the athletes were rewarded. Admitted, they had fun practicing and competing, with little of the frustrations of precise techniques. The athletes were likely to be good competitors, for this is what they practiced. But maximum performance as related to potentials? Never! A few men did acquire surprisingly correct technique, perhaps by observing others at meets or by loop films. They certainly had excellent team spirit and they did have fun, perhaps more fun than do the more seriously and technically trained track team members. Make of that what you will.

However, the method of this book is to proceed through complexity by relatively arduous efforts to the simplicity of mastery of skill. The truly simple technique is not that of the novice or untrained natural athlete, but rather that of the master athlete who has struggled with technique for years until he has perfected it, and now performs so easily and "naturally" that all complexity is gone. The action is simple, even though at a very high level of skill.

REINFORCEMENT METHODS. First concern should be for wholeness, for getting the overall feel, balance, rhythm of the whole event. Reinforcement should be directed in terms of each of these phases of the whole action, one at a time. But always with part-in-whole awareness. And always with an immediate "Yes!" for the desired action; the more enthusiastic the "Yes!" the greater the reinforcement.

At first, only the coach--or another knowledgeable athlete can give such affirmation. Some signal: "Right! That's it! Good!"--if given immediately while the feel of the action is still keen--produces reinforcement, strengthens the nerve-muscle channels of action. At first, an athlete's concentration on one phase of action may result in a degree of paralysis by analysis as happened with the fabled centipede,

> A centipede was happy, quite,
>   Until a frog in fun said,
> "Pray tell, which leg goes after which?"
> This worked her mind to such a pitch,
> She lay distracted in the ditch,
> And knew not how to run.

As long as the athlete is thinking in terms of segments of action, the whole action will not be smooth and won't feel good. If that is all he experiences, a weakening of the desired response will occur; inhibition, not learning, is likely to take place. But the trained observer, the coach, overcomes this disturbed feeling by the strength of his affirmative "Right!" How fortunate the learner whose coach can say "Right!" with the strong conviction of personal bone-muscle experience.

Few athletes take an analytical view of their own efforts on their own initiative. Such an attitude must be learned, usually by way of the coach but also from fellow athletes, and even then it requires time, perhaps years of time. Quite often an athlete will go through four years of high school, and even four years more of college, accepting the reinforcing approval of his coach, but with only incidental awareness of the kinesthetic cues within his own muscles. Though some of the best talks to coaches on techniques have been given by athletes, some of the least analytical have also come from athletes, despite their record performances.

Perhaps the best example of strong reinforcement occurs when a group of athletes get together on the field, or in the locker room, and talk-feel their way through the details of their event. Listen to, or rather, watch such a group sometime. You'll see more of muscle movements than you'll hear of words, and the words will be more related to action and the feel of action than they are to the theory and science of action. "I was watching the champ and saw him do this--" (Simulated action by A that is repeated by the others, actually or by an inner simulation of the movement.) "Yes, I saw him do it just that way, but he did it because his balance was like this--" (Simulated action by B, repeated by the others.) And so on until the point was clear--in their muscles as well as in their heads. It's a wise coach that encourages such group discussions. I remember how we used to accuse Coach Cromwell of USC of shirking his coaching duties, and leaving the job to his champion athletes. Yet we rarely saw a poorly coached USC field event man.

Under such a system, the athlete does not have to translate--no, that's too easy a word--transmute the words of the coach into the muscle ac tions of the event. Transmute means to change from one kind of form or nature to another, and that's not at all a simple process. Now, his own cues or feelings of action are the reinforcing agent. He learns to interpret these cues so that "it feels right," or "it feels wrong." Some men develop an amazingly sensitive muscle-sense of proper technique, often more sensitive than the eye-sense of the coach. Since such cues are simultaneous with the action, they tend to give maximum reinforment from a time standpoint.

But it is a very rare athlete that doesn't need the additional reinforcement of confirmation of correct action from others, whether those others be a coach, a fellow-athlete, or a playback of his own performance by a sequence or movie camera. Even at the Olympic level, athletes need and seek such confirmation. It's a primary function of an Olympic Coach.

REINFORCING APPROXIMATIONS OF SKILL. A beginner's first efforts tend to be rough approximations of the desired skill, and his awareness of his actions is vague, out-of-focus, not mentally separable into parts. If the approximation is an improvement, the coach says, "Yes!" but the tyro is likely to ask, "What do you mean? What did I do?" Gradually, these approximations begin to narrow, are channeled into the precise nerve-muscle patterns that we call a skilled effort. Our main point here is that approval does not wait for some desired perfect effort, but is given for improvement, for a closer approximation of such an effort. This applies to the whole action of a jump or throw, but equally important, to each small phase of action as it becomes the focus of coaching attention. A coach may direct attention on the movements of the left arm during the high jump take-off. If the athlete approximates the desired action, even though very imprecisely, the effort should be reinforced.

REINFORCING SPECIFIC PHASES OF SKILL. This book emphasizes a holistic approach to coaching. Whenever feasible, perform the whole action in throwing or jumping, with attention focussed on the particular aspect that is being learned. For example, in the high jump though attention might be on gradual acceleration of speed in the run, total learning will occur more effectively if actual jumps are taken, rather than running without jumping. But since reinforcement is greater when the affirming response is close in time-action, it will help if the coach yells "O.K.!" at the crucial moment during the run, rather than after the jump is completed. Loud enough of course for the jumper to relate approval while in action to the muscle-sense cues of that precise moment. If such approval comes some 15 or more seconds later when the jumper has walked back to the start of another effort, it has a lesser potential for reinforcement. My own coaching experience suggests that men vary greatly in their sensitivity to such cues, and in their power to recall their relevance.

Usually, when concern is with technique rather than with clearing the bar, the attempt ends with the bar on the ground. Despite all the disclaimers of the coach, this is easily interpreted as failure, with a resulting inhibition of the technique that produced it. The immediate and loud approval of the coach during the action helps prevent such a misinterpretation.

EXTINCTION OF ERRORS IN TECHNIQUE. The problem of how to eliminate so-called errors in technique is one of the most difficult, and crucial, or all aspects of coaching. After all, we coach men, not techniques, and some men are mighty sensitive to being analyzed (taken apart), even if only in the mind of a coach.

To understand the problem of errors best, they should be seen holistically in terms of the athlete's total attitude. A coach's knowledge of mechanics may cause him to judge a certain action as an error in technique. To the athlete, regardless of theoretical mechanics, his habitual way of performing an event has produced greater performance, a degree of success, and feels right! But this coach says it's not right; it's an error. That's both disturbing and confusing, not merely to the related muscle-nerve patterns, but to the athlete as a person.

When the athlete first does the mechanically-right action, though the coach yells "Right!" it feels wrong. At that stage, the "right" action is not integrated into his habitual way of jumping or throwing. His well-learned muscle-nerve cues cry out "Wrong!" and tend to inhibit further actions of the same kind. A coach has to be respected if his "Right!" is to achieve the dual task of strengthening the desired bond to correct action, and also disinhibit the effect of the athlete's cues that tell him "Wrong!" As long as the athlete is unable to integrate the technically sound action into his own individual style, his performance will be uncoordinated, tense, unsatisfying, and probably disappointing in height or distance. To serve as a positive reinforcement, a coach's approving signals must over-balance these negatives. We should emphasize that if a coach is critical and expresses disapproval of errors, he piles negatives on negatives. Small wonder the athlete often rebels inwardly, sometimes outwardly, and even quits the sport.

487

There are many ways of trying to solve the problem of extinguishing errors in technique; every coach and athlete with imagination will devise their own. Here we shall suggest three methods, all positive in their approach:

(1) In practice, encourage and reward attention to technique and the feel of correct technique; ignore or "punish" all concern for performance in terms of distance. Get rid of all measuring tapes or markers in practice. Keep the bar high enough to challenge the jumper, encourage him to make full efforts toward clearance as long as attention is on method, and to ignore the bar that falls to the ground. Remind them that the golfer who keeps his inner eye on distance can never keep his outer eye on the ball.

(2) Devise a major change in method, an entirely new total technique. In the high jump, change from the roll to the straddle or to the flop; in the javelin, change from a side-facing to a front-facing style. Now the attitude is toward learning something new, not on getting rid of the old.

(3) Ignore all direct reference to the error. Shift attention to some quite different phase of action that the coach knows can correct the error. Don't mention that there is such a relationship. Example: in the shot put, correct an "in-the-bucket" left foot by emphasizing the flexion of the right hip and the clockwise turn to the right by the right foot, shoulder, head and eyes. Make no reference to the left foot, but the coach will note that the left foot does not now drop "in the bucket."

The relative effectiveness of these methods will vary greatly with the teachability of the learner, but also the teaching skill of the coach. The latter is definitely a fine art in which imagination and a delicate touch are essential. Sometimes the technique the athlete learns first is very hard to change. For four years I coached a college athlete in a new, mechanically more effective, and very different style of high jumping. We thought he had learned it well. The old style was gone. But today, some 40 years later, I can still feel the shock of watching him in his senior-year Big 10 Conference meet, revert to his old style and clear the bar at a new record height!

Did this prove the old style was more mechanically "natural" for him, and that we had made a mistake in trying to change him? It's hard to say. But it did prove that the old style was more deeply anchored in his system so that when he dropped all inhibitions and all awareness of how he was jumping, he reverted to the style that had been more deeply reinforced over more years. I am reminded of my own experience in driving cars. For 20 years or more I drove gear-shift models. Even after five years or so of driving cars with automatic shifts, I often felt a strong urge in moments of semi-emergency to lift the left foot to the non-existent clutch and my right hand to the non-existent shift rod.

Throughout this discussion we have emphasized a positive approach, "elicit the response you want and reward it." But sometimes a fourth, more negative method may be helpful, if only to help the athlete compare the feel of doing it wrong with that of doing it right. Direct attention to the feel of the old "wrong" technique until the athlete senses that feeling as "wrong." Now try to associate the feeling of "right" with the new "right" technique. Rebuke and thereby inhibit what is "wrong"; reward (encourage, praise) what is "right." But also remember that the sooner the whole movement is "out of mind" and automatic, the better.

All of this becomes more difficult of course when, as happens occasionally, an athlete confuses the coach's criticism of technique as being a criticism of themselves personally. This produces a resistance to teaching techniques that even the most artful coach will find hard to overcome. Lack of space prevents fuller discussion; the reader will do well to study the chapter, "The Athlete Who Resists Coaching," (Ogilvie and Tutko, 1966, 26-45).

But in all such coaching, the emphasis should be strongly positive. As the old song goes, eliminate the negative by accentuating the positive. One could very well evaluate coaching skill on the degree to which this is accomplished.

FREQUENCY OF INDIVIDUAL COACHING. Should a coach be present each time an athlete practices, and give reinforcing approval of every correct effort? Disregarding the problem of being five places at one time, would such coaching be best? Most research suggests that learning occurs faster when other-person reinforcement is frequent, but not ever-present. There should be some opportunity for isolated self-evaluation. In fact, some effective coaches allow beginners a week or so of practice without any coaching so they can orient themselves to the event without the confusion of coaching analysis. Other coaches argue that errors in technique become embedded during that first week, and are hard to erase later. Take your choice.

In general, reinforcement is stronger and retained longer when it comes from the athlete's own muscle or kinesthetic sense. "That felt good! Let's see, what did I do? How did it feel? That was great!" It would take most enthusiastic praise from a respected coach to equal the strengthening effect of such a personal experience--assuming, of course, that what was interpreted as "right" was really right.

In our opinion, the evidence for maximum speed of learning and retention of correct technique suggests frequent reinforcement from the coach for the beginner, with a gradual decrease in frequency as the learner becomes aware of his own kinesthetic cues to correct action. Once the feel of action is gained, and especially if a small group of knowledgeable athletes will appraise each other, the frequency of adult coaching can be diminished. Above all, as someone once warned me, be aware of KISS--Keep It Simple, Stupid."

Obviously, individual differences would produce a different pattern of coaching for Johnny Milquetoast from that of a self-sufficient Roger Bannister (1955, 245) who insisted that "self-discovery is most rapid if we set out on the early stages alone. . . . The things a man learns for himself he never forgets . . . the things a man does by himself, he does best." On the other hand, we must consider that Roger was a runner whose skill was learned at the age of four, not a field-event man whose skill is usually learned at the age of 16 or later. The two problems are quite different.

EXTRINSIC REWARDS AND PUNISHMENTS. Prizes, awards, scholarships, travel do engender great enthusiasm and do motivate effort in general. When Jim Ryun was asked if his sacrifice of a normal social life had been worthwhile, he inquired as to how many of those boys who attended parties and dances regularly had ever seen Moscow and Helsinki? Such extrinsic rewards do ensure regular practice, do heighten attention and effort, and do urge conformance with training rules off the field. They are often attended by social recognition and a sense of self-importance.

But such material rewards are of lesser direct value in reinforcing improvements in skill in practice. First, there is a long separation in time between doing it right in practice and the reward following a meet performance. It would be a most retentive kinesthetic sense indeed that could relate the two in a degree that would strengthen the bonds of learning. Second, such prizes are for clearing the bar or for throwing farther than anyone else, not for the degree of technical skill. In competition, it's what you do that counts, not how you do it.

Some coaches use rewards in practice, from milk shakes to an invitation to the coach's home for dinner, but these are for measured performance, rarely for skill. The latter tends to be too subjective and immeasureable. In summary, when coaching for skill, rely on the intrinsic reinforcements that lie in the feel of action performed well. The inherent satisfaction aroused directly and immediately by such an action is enough to ensure its repetition. There's no need to reach outside for more tangible reinforcement.

COACHING FUNDAMENTALS AND DETAILS
A sound coach always emphasizes fundamentals in teaching the techniques of field events. But don't let that unqualified statement deceive you. For what is fundamental varies with the learner's natural ability, his expertness in this particular event, his understanding of the principles of mechanics, and of course, the entire approach of the coach in dealing with the problem.

As a matter of fact, it can be said that, though none disagree with our statement of the principle, each coach has his own unique interpretation of its meaning. I have known some "coaches" who, pleading the dangers of over-coaching details, have walked away from the problem altogether by making fun and competition in practice the main path to development. At the other extreme, some technical experts seem more concerned about verbalizing the details of their own theories than about advancing the performances of their athletes.

A group of experts could undoubtedly agree on a few fundamentals for each of the field events. But they could never agree on what is a fundamental for this particular athlete at this stage of his career. For to do so would necessitate a long-time and intimate coaching relationship with the boy, as well as with the manner in which he had been coached.

What is fundamental changes constantly with the technical development of each athlete. What would have been a disrupting detail to a beginner can become an entirely acceptable fundamental at a later stage of his development (Oxendine, 1968, 97). This suggests that a detail or non-essential of technique can be defined validly as one that tends to disrupt development more than it helps. What the athlete can ingest and use may not be a fundamental but it is quickly assimilated with what is fundamental. O'Brien's yogic exercises would be likely to disrupt the practice of a beginning shot putter; to him they were fundamental and in accord with his drive for maximum performance.

But also, the difference between what is fundamental and what is a disrupting detail depends on the coaching method. If the coaching follows a holistic pattern in which details are never presented separately but rather as they emerge out of fundamentals, then disruption will be minimal. In my own coaching, the use of the eyes was a fundamental in many phases of field e-vents. Change the eye direction or focus, and over-all balance or power will change with it. I've heard many coaches say that calling attention to the eye focus was disrupting, and in their experience, a non-essential detail. Of course I insisted on so-called mental practice during which one got the feel of the eye change before actually jumping or throwing, feeling it as inherent in the whole action. Disrupting? Oh, a little; all change is disrupting at first. But acceptably so, for it was soon integrated into the whole.

In other words, this problem is not so much one of distinguishing clearly between what is fundamental and what is a non-essential detail, as it is of coaching what is immediately relevant and in ways that make that relevancy clear to the learner. Elsewhere we have retold the story of the distracted centipede. The question of "which leg goes after which" just wasn't relevant to her continued smooth locomotion. A similar story is told by Charles Laughton about a fellow-actor, Charles Boyer, who had forgotten his lines--but good! What happened? "Suddenly, at the same moment I was saying it, I saw a certain word on the page. That word blanked me out on all the other words. It was as simple--and awful--as that!"

We began by advocating the coaching of fundamentals, but now there seems to be no clear distinction between fundamentals and details, at least in terms of what is essential to improvement, or of the size of the muscle groups involved. We tend to think of details as being related to fine muscle movements. But a fine muscle movement can be just as essential to improvement as a large one.

Whatever distinction is made between fundamentals and details should (1) be very flexible, and (2) be in terms of relevancy, especially in the learner's mind, to the particular phase of technique on which he is now centering his attention. Whatever is essential to mastery and relevant now can be viewed as fundamental. Whatever is essential to mastery but not now relevant to present practice can be viewed as a disruptive detail. Whatever seems non-essential at this moment should be ignored, but with an open mind that can accept it as a crucial coaching point next week or next year.

Coaching non-essential details is often associated with those who theorize or merely talk so much that their words distract from learning. Needless to say, words should be closely fitted to what is essential. Once an athlete closes his ears to the endless flow of words, even the most sound of coaching ideas will never gain acceptance. Coaching words should merge with movement, not distract from it.

Some coaches, whether from other busy-ness or merely laziness, never learn technique in full and detail. They then excuse their ignore-ance by claiming to coach only fundamentals. Their claimed fear of "overcoaching" leads them to underrate coaching. They give the boys a few "fundamentals," then allow them freedom to find their own way, to develop their own details of technique on a trial and--all too often--error basis.

In fact, some very successful coaches have followed this practice, have proclaimed its virtues at clinics and in journals. But somehow, at some time, by some one, the details must be taught--by an assistant coach, by a previous coach, by other athletes, by study of films and books. Details must be learned if mastery is to be gained. To be learned, they must be practiced. To be practiced, the learner must be aware of them--in specific detail. Such awareness comes best through sound coaching.

A RANGE OF TOLERABLE ERROR

Sound field event coaching recognizes that so-called perfect form cannot be described exactly and narrowly, but rather within a range of what industry calls "tolerance of error"--that is, within a range of error that does not make a significant difference. For example, in the shot put, the left foot at the toeboard should be placed with the toe in line with the heel of the right. But near-maximal puts can be made within a 3 to 4-inch range of this position. Any negative effect of an "error" at one extreme or the other can be balanced in various ways-- faster hip rotation and stretch reflex in related muscles, better bracing and upward thrust by the left leg, directing the put slightly to the left, and the like.

To use a different example, Charlie Dumas won the 1956 Olympic high jump (6-11½) after having jumped 7-½ in the Olympic Trials. In his approach run, he took five very slow and only three fast steps--an intolerable error if judged by the velocities gained by modern jumpers-- Yashchenko, Stones, Wszola. But for Dumas and his day, the error was quite tolerable--a world record and the first man ever over seven feet.

The first corollary to this principle is that one should select a style that is mechanically sound for the goal one has in mind. If the goal must be easily and quickly attained because of lack of time or low motivation then the style must be one that is quickly learned. For example one would select the hop style in throwing the javelin. But if one hopes to attain maximum performance, regardless of time and difficulty, then a more mechanically perfect style would be chosen.

The second corollary is that, having selected a style that can produce maximum performance, there should be perfection of the individual's variation of that style. For example, there is much discussion as to the merits of the longtime Feuerbach style of putting the shot as compared with the discus style with its faster hip rotation and shot momentum.   Each method has certain strengths and weaknesses. This corollary assumes that the crucial factor is not so much the style in general as it is the degree to which the individual has perfected all phases of his own unique style.

As one more example, the question as to which starting block spacing is best in sprinting can be answered (1) by deciding whether the spacing is within the range of tolerable error, mechanically, and (2) whether this sprinter has perfected a total pattern of starting that is best adapted to his unique block spacing.

In summary, this concept that there is a range within which error can be tolerated has many and valuable uses. It applies to overall technique, as indicated by the accepted range of high jump styles--western, straddle, Fosbury flop--each with its variations of the run-up, transition, take-off, clearance, but all acceptable.   It applies to individual differences in all related factors--height, weight, power, attitude, nutrition, you name it. It applies to the specifics of technique--angle of throw in the discus or javelin, speed in the high jump or long jump run-up, distance through which power is applied in the shot, and 101 other aspects. And always its significance depends on the level of excellence in performance; the closer performance is to human ultimates, the narrower the tolerance of error. To sharpen understanding, review the section in this book on "Coaching fundamentals and details."

ERRORS OF ANTICIPATION

Dyson (1962, 143) coined a most valuable phrase, "errors of anticipation," which is very useful in coaching field events, as well as the skill aspects of starting and hurdling on the track. Perhaps the most common example is the golfer who cannot keep his eye on the ball, in anticipation--or better, in apprehension--of its flight down the fairway. The same kind of error occurs in our sport. I've watched the great stylist, Al Feuerbach, anticipate the upward heave of the shot by rotating and lifting the eyes-shoulders-torso before landing his right foot at the center of the circle. I've watched Al Oerter, four-time Olympic discus champion, anticipate the final power drive by a too-early leading of the eyes-head-shoulders. I've observed Olympic pole vaulters, such as Dave Roberts or Earl Bell, anticipate the upward pull-push by turning their hips an instant too soon.

Almost no one is entirely free of this error; certainly not the beginner who anticipates the effects of action and so neglects the action itself. High jumpers anticipate the layout over the bar, and so neglect the takeoff actions that ensure full power upward. Long jumpers and triple jumpers lose running velocity just before the board as they anticipate too soon the upward leap.

The specific cause of such anticipation is specific to each individual and each situation, but in general it is a failure in proper concentration, or a failure to maintain the whole action when emphasizing a particular phase of that action. The solution lies in learning to inhibit the doubt or distraction, and in concentrating on how the action is done rather than on its effects.

Several decades ago, coaches tended to emphasize the importance of "follow-through" in field events. But later they found that such emphasis led to anticipation of the follow-through, that men were up-and-out before they had settled down and applied full force. Since then, follow-through has been taught as an inherent ballistic effect of proper precedent action, and so could be largely ignored as a coaching point.

A 1978 study by Gideon Ariel[1] compared the techniques of the top six shotputters at the Montreal Olympics with those of a group of national class U.S. putters. Among the latter, he found two examples of errors of anticipation.

Although the clinic throwers reached high accelerations in the stance phase, they attained these...too early...and were unable to maintain the high values. The Olympic throwers...started with lower accelerations and attained higher values in the middle of the stance phase....

In most cases the clinic putters raised the body prematurely during the gliding and transitional phases. The most efficient technique maintained the center of gravity low during the push-off phase, then raised it as rapidly as possible.

IMPROVEMENT IN CONSISTENCY OF SKILL AS WELL AS IN DISTANCE

In the throwing events, we usually judge improvement by distance. But exclusive concern for distance may lead to increased tension and defects in skill. Many sound coaches use a second criterion of improvement in the throwing events--a decrease in radius of the landing pattern of the implements. The pattern made by a beginner will be spread out over a relatively wide area. His distances will be both short and long, as well as wide to the left and to the right. This will be true even though some defect, such as a foot "in the bucket" may shift his pattern to the left. For example, after a large number of puts in the shot, the landing pattern may have a radius of six or more feet. There will be little centering of the pattern; many puts will lie near the circumference of the pattern.

In contrast, the pattern made by an expert will be much smaller. His skill will be channeled, will be in a certain groove as we say. Now, after a long workout in the shot, the landing pattern will tend to be along a single plane of power application. The distance may range widely, but because of differences in effort, not of skill.

This principle is of practical use. Sound coaching will encourage a man to make his throws in practice "for distance" but always within the pattern of consistent skill. How far the implement lands should be balanced with how skillfully it was thrown, that is, with how well it landed within the pattern of consistency. In my own coaching I used to place two lines on the ground. One was an arc at a distance less than maximum for the thrower; the other was a radius which set the line of throw. This radius varied with the event and with the athlete. Depending on various peculiarities of style, such as the placement of the left foot at the toeboard, a great putter might put just to the left or possibly to the right of the centerline.

Though not as obvious, this principle applies equally to the jumping events. Certainly it applies to the pattern of steps made in the run-up. But the discerning coaching eye can see it also in the various aspects of technique while airborne. The coaching method remains the same-- practice at near-maximum heights, if that seems best, but always within the pattern of consistency in skill.

---

[1] Gideon B. Ariel, Ph.D., Biomechanical Analysis of Shotputting," *Track & Field Quarterly Review*, Vol. 79 #4, Winter 1979, p. 27.

<u>PLATEAUS OF LEARNING MOTOR SKILLS</u>. Learners are less apt to become discouraged if they know about plateaus. Otherwise they tend to feel they have reached their limit of achievement, when actually they've hardly begun. I've always been fascinated by the implications for motor learning of the saying, "He that has walked 90 miles of a 100-mile journey is but halfway there."

Such slowdowns, especially in learning sports skills, have many possible causes, too numerous and complex to more than suggest here. Perhaps the technique being used is the limiting factor. The scissors style in high jumping has a lower maximum than does the straddle style. Perhaps a detail of technique is the limiting factor. A slow, uncertain run in the high jump can outweigh excellent technique in clearing the bar. Perhaps certain basic training has been neglected. Lack of related strength training limits performance in the high jump.

But there are also mental-emotional causes of plateaus. Over-training can produce chronic fatigue and disinterest. Failure or success in some other "unrelated" activity can reduce motivation in this activity. The distraction of other interests or other requirements may lead to a lower level of effort.

Obviously the method of breaking through these plateaus must be fashioned to the cause, rather than merely to the symptom. The traditional lay-off from activity is seldom a direct solution. It may work, but only if it brings about a fresh analysis of the problem which discloses the specific cause. One must hasten to add that in dealing with humans, there are often multiple causes, as well as multiple reactions to what seems to be the same cause.

Weight lifters speak of reaching a "sticking point," a stage at which no greater weight can be lifted. Suggestions given by most experts is that the overall conditions be changed in some way significant to the learner. Active-rest may refresh the energies. A new training partner may stimulate new insights and energies. The poundage can be reduced significantly with greater emphasis on explosiveness, so that a sense of "new beginning" is experienced. All such suggestions have reference to development in the field events.

Appendix B
DYNAMICS OF RELAXATION

THE DYNAMICS OF RELAXATION IN TRACK AND FIELD[1]

Agreement can be easily reached on the general meaning of relaxation as a loosening or release of tension, as a letting-go from contraction or anxiety or inhibition. But such "letting-go" can occur in a multitude of ways and at many degrees of release. Relaxation can be total when it seeks recovery from exertion or release from tension. Or it can relate to the short-time and limited area of the relaxation phase of repeated movement.

From a physical standpoint, a completely relaxed muscle is inert, electrically silent, with no muscle fibers in contraction. But in all live tissue, even though motionless, some electrical discharge is always present along with some degree of muscle tension (tonus), even though below the threshold of movement. Above this threshold there are gradations of muscle strength and speed of contraction. These gradations occur by varying the frequency of nerve excitation and thereby the number of muscle-fiber groups that are active. Each muscle-fiber group has its own precise threshold of excitation. At that precise level, the unit contracts and continues to contract until the excitation falls below its critical threshold (Åstrand, 1970, 79ff.).

It follows that the sports meaning of the expression "a relaxed muscle" is always relative to the ongoing action, whatever its degree of strength or speed. In a voluntary, all-out, dynamic contraction, no motor units would be inhibited, all would be active to their fullest extent, even though the movement can be validly described as relaxed. In relatively slow, repetitive movements, as occurs in running, relaxation is related primarily to the antagonistic muscles. In 1889 the great English physiologist, Sir Charles Sherrington, demonstrated that stimulation of a single point in the motor cortex of the brain excites the motoneurons which innervate the flexor muscles, and at the same time inhibits the motoneurons to the antagonistic extensors. In this case, a relaxed running action would maintain a precise alternation of innervation-inhibition. It seems reasonable to assume that tieing up while running is related to a breakdown of this alternation, as well as to increased contracture of muscle-fiber units within the running muscles.

But there are other uses of the word "relaxation." Relaxation is one way of looking at skill, for example, or at coordination, or power, or at self-control during physical effort. In sports, relaxation is inherent in the problems of hypertension and emotional stress that develop during the days and hours before important competition. In some events, such as the pole vault or discus throw, maintaining mental and physical relaxation (imperturbability) during the long waits between trials is a major problem, especially just prior to the final crucial efforts. In other events, reciprocal contraction-relaxation must be optimum, not merely of the leg and arm muscles but of many muscles of the torso as well. In all field events, certain maximum contractions can result only by "inhibiting the inhibitions," to use the expression of Ikai and Steinhaus (1963, 137), that is, by relaxing all inhibiting fibers.

Such a wide range of meaning for a single word may confuse as much as it clarifies, and we should be wary as to just which aspect of relaxation is being discussed. Of course, all this becomes even more complicated when we realize that no two competitive situations are ever exactly the same. What is effective in the way of achieving relaxation in one competition may be quite ineffective in another. What the gestaltists call the figure-ground or surround is always changing.

[1]This Appendix B was written some 15 years ago, but respected coaches have urged (1984) its continued publication.

This makes it clear that there can be no one definition of relaxation. The physiologist may argue that ultimately it all boils down to a nerve-muscle condition, but that over-simplifies the problem. Better understanding and use requires a multiple approach, both in definitions and methods of achievement. We shall suggest ten: (1) relaxation through skill learning, (2) differential relaxation, (3) holistic reorientation, (4) withdrawal and return, (5) progressive relaxation, (6) positive auto-suggestion, (7) relaxation by "emptying" the mind, (8) by repressing the negatives, (9) by underloading the action, and (10) by concentration on positive external factors. Actually there is an infinity of methods, limited only by our insights during analysis and abstraction. But these ten will suggest the range of possibility.

The first six of these methods tend to be related to general rest and recovery, and can be used throughout the year, though especially during the days and hours preceding competition. The last three methods seek to achieve relaxation while actually competing.

RELAXATION THROUGH SKILL LEARNING. First efforts at a skill, without spectators, coaching, or conscious analysis, tends to be relaxed. Later, coaching and attention to the "parts" of skill create uncertainty and self-doubt, and lead to tension and negative contractions. This is magnified when competition is impending and the learner is anxious about his lack of readiness. But as he masters skill and succeeds in competition, his inhibitions--in both a physical and mental sense--tend to fall away (Åstrand, 1970, 80). The useless, random, and counter movements cease; the positive movements become more deeply channeled. Somehow the muscles coordinate of themselves, without conscious direction. We can see this clearly in skilled piano playing, for example, in which any attempt at conscious control would be disruptive.

Progress will be facilitated if the beginner is made aware of this tendency of any new skill to be accompanied by both physical and emotional tensions, including wasteful efforts by unrelated and opposing muscles. If he feels certain that these negatives will disappear with practice, he'll relax much more quickly. For example, to tell beginners the story of Wendell Johnson's (1946) work with stutterers could be very helpful. Speech involves muscle control; stuttering is often the effects of psychic tension and uncertainty of control. When stutterers were asked to read in unison, they tended to drop their self-awareness and read quite normally. Whenever any stutterer was asked to read alone, he began to stutter again. Other methods, such as the use of headphones into which distracting noises could be directed, produced similar results. In summary, as the stutterers realized that their speech problems were quite ordinary, common, normal, they began to improve.

So with tension in field and track events. As long as the athlete is enmeshed in his own self-doubts, he cannot relax; as he realizes that early tension is normal to all athletes, he will begin to concentrate on the action rather than on himself.

DIFFERENTIAL RELAXATION. Relaxation through skill learning is really the same as that called "differential relaxation" by the foremost researcher in this field, Edmund Jacobson (1957, 124). By this method Jacobson taught his patients to differentiate between the muscles active in a given movement, and those unrelated or opposed to action. He did this by emphasizing pin-pointed awareness of each phase of movement, confirmed by sensitive voltmeters which recorded the tiny electric currents (.0000001 volt) produced in the muscles. With practice, his patients learned to detect even very slight muscle tensions that normally would be unnoticed.

Every athlete goes through some such re-learning process, though he tends to do it in terms of the event movement as a whole, and without the "abnormal" pin-pointed awareness of Jacobson's patients. For example, Nelson (1970, 124ff.) quotes Al Oerter, a true genius at achieving relaxation on crucial throws in crucial competition,

In the weeks before an Olympic competition, I mentally simulate every conceivable situation for each throw. For example, I imagine I'm in eighth place; it's my fifth throw, and it's pouring rain. What do I do? An inexperienced thrower might panic or be thinking, "Gees, I hope I don't fall down." I know ahead of time what I will do under every condition.

Faced with just such conditions at Mexico City, he knew just what to do. He kept on warming up in the rain; he eliminated certain preliminary movements in the throwing circle, started his spin slowly and carefully, and threw 212' 4½", a new personal record by almost five feet--and that after some 18 years of discus throwing.

Notice that Oerter said, "I mentally simulate--." The meaning of this in both a mind sense and a muscle sense may be clarified by reviewing the section in this book on "Mental Practice," or by reading Steinhaus's[1] article on the amazing "awareness" of the muscle spindles and the related organs. The words can never explain the action adequately, but they help.

But all great athletes learn to sense the effortless effort, are constantly practicing in terms of it, and learn ways of finding it in competition, not just in general but under the specific conditions that may arise in this particular competition. They may never be able to put it into words but they get the feel of it, and know it instantly when it happens. When Danielsen of Norway made his world-record throw (281' 2½") in the javelin at the Melbourne Olympics, he yelled excitedly while the javelin was still in the air. He knew that was it! His muscle spindles needed no steel tape. They sensed the ease, the rhythm, the relaxation of the throwing, and thus were their own accurate calculation of the distance.

RELAXATION BY HOLISTIC REORIENTATION. This third method, which I have called holistic reorientation, seeks to establish a sound relationship between the athlete and his total life situation, with emphasis of course on his competitive situation. Its full explanation would require a large volume, rather than a few paragraphs. In summary, until a sound relationship exists between the athlete and his surround, he is not likely to compete up to his potential. This surround has many aspects. It relates to his basic life needs (Maslow, 1954, 22-106): nutrition, activity, sex, safety, belongingness, etc. It relates to his culture. Yesterday I watched a basketball game between two teams with different life styles, so to speak--Pennsylvania with the traditional Establishment control, short haircuts, close discipline and all; and Harvard with its "mod" freedom as suggested by be-ribboned tresses. An athlete must achieve a relaxed attitude within the climate of his sports culture, whatever it may be.

Holistic re-orientation also relates to the conditions of practice and competition that are peculiar to each event and to each competitive situation. For example, this method seeks relaxation in endurance running by coming to terms with reality, by acceptance of hurt-pain-agony, to use Counsilman's term, as an inherent part of running that everyone must experience, and without the anxiety or fear with which our culture paralyzes such efforts. Similarly there must be realistic acceptance of victory and defeat, or of the facts of inequality among men. By such calm acceptance, a sense of holding oneself apart from the battle is gained, call it imperturbability, courage, fortitude, what you will. By such letting-go of self, both danger and the fear of danger lose much of their hindering power.

Emil Zatopek, the truly great Czech distance runner, has told of his habit in practice of holding his breath while walking or jogging from one tree to another. He did this so as to adjust to the feelings of low oxygen, not to build up his will power over such feelings, but to come to terms with them. He wrote, "I practiced holding my breath until will power was no longer a problem." This is quite a different approach from that of repressing them by power of will. By this approach, low oxygen held no dangers or fears for him. He could relax. Self-control was not an issue and "will power was no longer a problem."

To take a different example from Zatopek, his face in competition expressed the full gamut of fatigue from mere breathlessness to agony. Many criticized this as indicating a lack of self-control and relaxation. But Cerutty, Herb Elliott's coach, interpreted Zatopek's grimaces as a positive aid to effort with no inhibitions. He said that so-called relaxation by conscious control, by a determined maintenance of proper style or a certain decorum of facial expression is "a concept of weakly men and coaches." In his book, RUNNING WILD, Gordon Pirie (1961, 35) supported Cerutty in these views and accused British runners of keeping

> . . . *a stiff upper lip even in the agony of a race. They restrain their emotions not to show suffering. The free and relaxed runner shows in his face and gestures that it is torture and agony to give his last ounce of energy. How silly to pretend that it is not. . . . The restrained runner can never reach the greatest heights.*

Under this method of relaxation, we achieve ease of movement by coming to terms with the so-called negatives, whether physical or mental-emotional in nature, and so using them in every

---

[1] Arthur Steinhaus, "Your Muscles See More Than Your Eyes," *JOURNAL HPER*, September 1966, 38.

way possible. I think of the negative effects of lactic acid as an outcome of fatiguing activity and a deterrent to running, but also of its re-synthesis to glycogen for use again. True, the body does attempt to buffer against its negative acidity, but it also makes use of its positive values.

Herb Elliott (1961) wrote repeatedly of the two-phased need for tension-relaxation before a BIG race. "Better to be keyed up than relaxed before a race. . . . In races, I must let my body go--relax 100 percent. . . . Sometimes your mind is in such a jumble that it won't give your body a chance" (p. 51). "Sometimes we'd go to a quiet park a few hours before the race so that I could run spiritedly for twenty minutes or so and imagine myself winning. I became calm then and, back at the hotel, find no difficulty in sleeping for two hours before going to the stadium half an hour before the race" (p. 146). "Running should be free expression of the body; in the words of the song, ought to be doing what comes naturally" (p. 50).

Under holistic reorientation, every opposing force must be viewed as having a helpful quality also, even if it's only a challenge which draws forth a higher response. Endurance swimming affords an excellent illustration of this. Obviously water resistance to forward progress is an opposing force. But the expert swimmer uses that resistance in the actions of his legs and arms which push him forward. That is, instead of opposing force by greater force, he uses the water, merges himself within it, relaxes with it. Buoyancy aids relaxation of course, but that is not our point. The relaxation we are speaking of is that of a fish in his natural element, in contrast to that of a cat which, hating and fearing the water, fights its way out of it.

Another way of explaining this method is to emphasize the sheer joy of effort, of losing oneself in the fun of action, in the excitement of personal development and improving performance, in the anticipation of goals achieved. It's hard not to be relaxed when jumping or throwing or running because one enjoys it. Like so many other athletes, Jim Ryun quit track when endless pressures from others created inner tensions; he attempted a comeback when his reorientation to the sport allowed him to relax and enjoy his running.

RELAXATION BY WITHDRAWAL-AND-RETURN. There is another aspect of relaxation by holistic reorientation which is best explained by use of Toynbee's phrase, "withdrawal-and-return." Coaches and athletes have made use of the idea for decades, or even centuries. When the relationship between the athlete and his total life situation becomes over-filled with problems, tensions, anxieties, he should withdraw from that world for a time, then return to it, refreshed and eager.

The Greeks used this method, with or without awareness, when they required every Olympic prospect to spend ten months prior to the Games, away from the distractions and hindrances of the home situation, while concentrating on training in the gymnasium environment created for that purpose.

One of the happiest examples of modern times was the pioneer tourist camp established at Vålådalen, Sweden, by Gosta Olander. There, among the lakes and rivers and forests and hills, his guests from the city found quiet and slow-moving, and complete relaxation of the body and spirit. There, by following a training program called fartlek (speed-play), Gunder Haegg and many other Swedish runners found the ease of mind that could accompany even the most strenuous of physical exertions. Running became not so much a problem of will power over the pains of fatigue, as of the release of energy while enjoying the natural surroundings. Olander was once quoted[1] as saying,

Training is not only bodily exertion but mental preparation. The ultimate springs of physical performance are not in the muscles but in the mind. Exercise should be directed at helping nature. . . . Animals are always fit. The reason is that they stay relaxed--except when there is need for exertion, as in killing or escape. Their nerves never fight their muscles.

This was also the purpose behind Cerutty's move out of the tensions of Melbourne into the relative peace of a home along the sea coast at Portsea, where Herb Elliott and many others

---

[1] James Stewart Gordon, "Relax--and Get Fit!" *Today's Health*, August, 1964.

enjoyed the challenges of great sand dunes, of running naked along the beach and through the Australian bush. For a long weekend they would withdraw from their home tensions, relax for a time even though training strenuously, then return to the city with renewed vigor.

Many of us have experienced the excitement and joy of training during Spring Vacation. True, we worked out two or even three times a day, but the work was fun because we had dropped the tensions of normal living, and could achieve what might be called dynamic relaxation, that is, relaxation within strenuous action but without the life tensions that so inhibit full expression of our energies.

PROGRESSIVE RELAXATION. The term "progressive relaxation" was the invention of Dr. Edmund Jacobson (1957) who for over 25 years conducted research on relaxation and sleep. His methods have gained wide acceptance among therapists, physicians, mental hygienists, and others concerned with the conservation and restoration of human energies. His book for laymen, YOU MUST RELAX, is worth careful study by coaches. In brief, his method has two phases. (1) A muscle is first contracted hard, then suddenly relaxed, so that sharp awareness is gained of the contrasting feelings of tension and relaxation. (2) The subject relaxes one muscle group at a time in a systematic order from feet to head and head to feet. Gradually what Jacobson called "progressive relaxation" occurs throughout the body, and one might add, the mind as well.

The value of this method is for rest, recovery from fatigue, and prevention of wasteful tension during the days preceding competition, or during the rest periods of competition. With repeated practice an athlete learns to let go, to drop his tensions, instantaneously, by the cue of feeling tension and relaxing. It is possible to become very sensitive to this muscle sense, somewhat as a blind man's finger tips become sensitive to the raised dots of a Braille reader. Or as the actions of undressing, cleaning one's teeth, setting the clock, or reading in bed all serve as cues for falling asleep.

There have been many variations of Jacobson's methods. Steinhaus (1963, 306) suggests the following for schoolchildren sitting at a desk:

Keep your heads down; let your arms hang over the sides of your desk. Now imagine you are a large sack of flour that lies slumped over your desk. There is a tiny hole in each corner of the sack. Slowly, very slowly, the flour is running out of each hole; smoothly, smoothly, it is running out.

Feel it--just as if your arms and legs were running out of the sack. Slowly, steadily your arms are getting longer and longer and longer. You are getting limper and limper. You are lying heavily on your desk--slumped down--just like the sack of flour--flatter and flatter and flatter.

It works. Try it yourself, now. Soon you've let yourself go--all of you. Eddie Rickenbacher is reported to have followed just such methods in seeking relief from tension, and renewed energy for his strenuous life as flyer, aviation executive, public relations expert, you name it. But he used different analogies: a jellyfish completely limp in every part, a large burlap bag of potatoes, with holes out of which the potatoes are slowly rolling. Feel yourself deflate as each potato rolls away.

RELAXATION BY POSITIVE AUTO-SUGGESTION. Auto-suggestion is no longer an "in" word. Self-suggestion is now more easily accepted. Or, more commonly, relaxation by positive thinking, to use Norman Vincent Peale's term,[1] or relaxation by PMA (positive mental attitude), to use Napoleon Hill's term.[2] But auto-suggestion was in vogue in 1942 when psychologist Dorothy Yates first taught its values to Bud Winter, track coach at San Jose State. Winter became sufficiently enthusiastic about its potential for his track men, especially his sprinters, so that later, when the War brought him into the Navy, he sought Dr. Yates' help with the excessive nervous tensions of the men in pre-flight training school. Eventually, the Navy accepted mental conditioning by auto-suggestion as a regular part of its flight training program.

---

[1] Norman Vincent Peale, THE POWER OF POSITIVE THINKING, Englewood Cliffs, N.J.: Prentice-Hall, Inc., 1952.

[2] Napoleon Hill, SUCCESS THROUGH A POSITIVE MENTAL ATTITUDE, Englewood Cliffs, N.J.: Prentice-Hall, Inc., 1960.

Hubbard[1] summarized Dr. Yates' methods as follows:

First, in preliminary discussion, the athlete must be convinced the plan can be of assistance to him. Examples of success in concrete situations . . . are very helpful. At the same time, a non-technical description of the physical disturbances caused by nervous tension should also be given. Once the athlete understands the tremendous energy waste brought on by excess tension, the necessity for relaxation will become clear. . . .

Next, the athlete must be taught to relax--to rid himself of nervous tension. Dr. Yates tells her subjects to concentrate on a word of their own choice, such as "calm"--a word that signifies the exact opposite of tension. She explains that this chosen word will become the means for bringing back a state of relaxation in the future. Then she uses this word, and thoughts connected with it, in relaxing the subject.

The athlete lies on a couch or sits in a chair with a back high enough to support his head. He closes his eyes, and concentrates on the word he has selected as meaning the opposite of tension.

Dr. Yates talks to him slowly, reassuringly, asking him to picture in his mind a place of peace and tranquillity. She tells him to imagine he is there, to picture the calmness and contentment of the scene.

After about ten minutes of relaxation talk, Dr. Yates suggests that the athlete remain relaxed and quiet for a while, letting the thoughts of calmness and peace sink in. She allows him to spend at least five minutes in reflection.

At the end of this period she dismisses the subject, directing him to fall asleep each night thinking of his relaxation word. By so doing he will be able more quickly to cement the relationship between his word and a calm mental attitude. . . .

Usually in a very short time--perhaps two or three discussion periods with the psychologist--the athlete is able to relax without her guidance merely by forming a mental association between his chosen word ("calm" for example) and a relaxed condition.

Then, the subject must be taught what is called "set." For, while relaxation conserves energy, the employment of "set" enables an athlete to release that energy to the fullest and most productive extent when it is most needed--in action on the field, or in the ring. . .

While in the relaxed state, which he has been taught to attain, he sets his mind on being cool, or aggressive, or confident during a coming athletic event. At this point the "set," instead of being used to awaken the athlete, is used to give him confidence or whatever attribute he desires.

"Set," to Dr. Yates, is even more important than relaxation, and "set" and relaxation complement each other. The athlete employs "set" in learning to relax, and he uses the relaxed state to firmly implant "set" in his mind.

For this reason she combines the teaching of the two. In teaching "set" the first step is to have the subject accurately analyze his main difficulty. Is it lack of confidence? Is it an inability to remember the athletic skills he has learned?

Once the difficulty has been brought to the surface it is handled in this way: A short slogan is agreed upon--a slogan such as "I will be confident"--emphasizing a positive rather than a negative point of view.

Dr. Yates helps the subject relax, and then she repeats the slogan, amplifying its meaning to avoid monotony, but continually repeating the main theme.

---

[1] John M. Hubbard, "Autosuggestion--A New Formula in Mental Conditioning," *Scholastic Coach*, February, 1947, 14.

The athlete is told to go over his "set" slogan each night before falling asleep, along with his relaxation procedure.

Finally, the subject must be afforded an early opportunity to "try his wings," in order to prove to himself that this method of mental conditioning does work. "Nothing succeeds like success."

After the first few sessions, the athlete makes the entire method his own--the presence of an instructor is no longer required. Notice that the word "instructor" is used here, and not "psychologist."

That is because, as Dr. Yates points out, it is not necessary to resort to a trained psychologist, in implementing the formula.

Any coach who has gained the respect and friendship of his student athletes can achieve the desired results. His tutelage can be every bit as effective as that of a psychologist-- and any small mistakes in technique will not have a hindering effect if there is a basis of friendly trust.

Those having a special interest in this method will find other papers[1] by Dorothy Yates of value, as well as an excellent history of the entire movement in positive thinking by Donald Meyer,[2] including the viewpoints of William James, Emile Coué, Dale Carnegie, Henry Link, Harry Emerson Fosdick, and many others. What has been found helpful in other areas of life can be effective in sports.

RELAXATION BY "EMPTYING THE MIND." This method of relaxation can be interpreted and used as simply or as deeply as your interest in the subject may suggest. Viewed simply, it is a natural mental effect of Jacobson's progressive relaxation. As the muscles relax throughout the body, those related to speech and thought tend to relax also. We can only think of one thing at a time. As our attention concentrates on relaxing a particular muscle group, it shifts away from the doubts and anxieties that produce tension. Gradually, mental activity grows quiet; the mind, as we say, becomes empty. You may even fall asleep.

In his chapter, "Relaxing the Mind," Jacobson (1957, 160ff.) explains that electromyography has confirmed the presence of electrical stimuli to the speech muscles when a subject is thinking or worrying over a problem. He teaches that by relaxing the specific muscles related to speech, including the entire region of the lips, cheeks, jaws, and especially the eyes, the nervous excitation drops below the threshold, not only of speech but of thought as well. All mental imagery ceases. In support of such practice, Steinhaus (1963, 318) tells of his own ability to shut off the tuneful jingles that sometimes persist in the mind "by relaxing the muscles of my tongue and voice. Try it sometime. You can absolutely make such inner voices disappear."

Articles and books on the conservation of executive energies give many examples of high-pressure operators who, trained in some such method, gain a few minutes of complete mental relaxation, then snap back quickly with minds rested and cleared. For example, for 20 years I was associated with a man of tremendous energy, Dr. Joseph Maddy of the National Music Camp at Interlochen, Michigan. He had this remarkable facility to relax into nothingness for a few minutes, then to rise bubbling with vital energy. Steinhaus[3] has explained that the muscle sense is at least as sensitive as the visual sense, and that such men distinguish certain muscle-sense cues by which they relax and let their minds go empty. They don't try to relax; that's self-defeating. They simply let it all seep away.

But "emptying the mind" has a broader and deeper meaning than this, a meaning inherent in the word "holistic" as we have defined it, and in the relationship between the individual and the surrounding world. How can we find imperturbability in a time of trouble--of widespread social unrest, of war and violence, of growing awareness of inequality of opportunity based on irrele-

---

[1] Dorothy Yates, *Journal of Applied Psychology*, December 1943. *Journal of General Psychology*, April 1946.

[2] Donald Meyer, *THE POSITIVE THINKERS*, New York: Doubleday & Company, Inc., 1965, Paperback edition, 342 pages.

[3] Arthur H. Steinhaus, "Your Muscles See More Than Your Eyes," *Journal HPER*, September 1966, 38.

vant factors, of communication machines that bombard us with troubles even before they happen. I suddenly think of John Carlos at Mexico City who, at the potentially most happy moment of his life, carried his troubles with him on the victory stand, and raised his black-gloved fist. How could he have found inner relaxation?

Discussion of this difficult point is not within the scope of this book. In our Western culture it tends to be a religious problem, rather than a sports problem. Read Paul Tillich's *THE COURAGE TO BE*, or the writings of Kierkegaard. It creeps into the writings of psychologists, as in C. G. Jung's *THE UNDISCOVERED SELF*, or P. W. Martin's *EXPERIMENT IN DEPTH*, or Donald Meyer's *THE POSITIVE THINKERS*.

But for fuller understanding, we must turn to the East for enlightenment. There, anxiety is truly inherent, but men have learned to empty themselves of it. Read almost any of the books by Alan Watts, especially the chapters "Empty and Marvellous," and "Sitting Quietly, Doing Nothing," in *THE MEANING OF ZEN*, or his *PSYCHOTHERAPY EAST AND WEST*. But most fascinating of all such writings, as well as most relevant to sports, is Eugen Herrigel's *ZEN IN THE ART OF ARCHERY*. Even though the concept of competitiveness is unacceptable in Zen, the book describes relaxation-in-activity at a higher dimension than we can even dream of in sports. In teaching the artless art of archery, the Zen Master admonishes his pupil to stop thinking about the shot, to just let it happen (Herrigel, 1953, 71).

You only feel it (tension) because you really haven't let go of yourself. It is all so simple. You can learn from an ordinary bamboo leaf what ought to happen. It bends lower and lower under the weight of snow. Suddenly the snow slips to the ground without the leaf having stirred. . . . So indeed it is: when the tension is fulfilled, the shot must fall . . . from the archer like snow from a bamboo leaf, before he even thinks of it.

Admit that releasing an arrow is not at all the same as the powerful efforts of putting a shot or jumping high. But we must also admit that the athlete who has learned to free himself from all inner tension, physical or mental, who has learned how to "inhibit his inhibitions," who can release his full powers recklessly, with nothing held back--all within the channels of skill of course--has a tremendous advantage over the man who carries his and the world's tensions with him into the throwing circle or jumping runway.

One valid definition of relaxation is "the art of releasing power," not that of striving to use it.

RELAXATION BY REPRESSING THE NEGATIVES. "Relax! Go get 'em! Move up now! Relax!" How often I've listened to coaches, myself among them, urging our charges to lift themselves by their own bootstraps, so to speak, to run faster but easier, while a sharper and higher awareness of the anguish of fatigue threatens to overwhelm them. All too aften, the coach allows his own anxiety to raise the pitch of his voice, and this the runner hears, even though he may not hear the words themselves.

All such admonitions to deliberately repress our feelings actually tend to exaggerate the feelings, just as the old will-power psychology which sought to repress our lusts ended mainly in increasing them. It is hard to exaggerate the negative effects on young runners when writers, coaches, physicians, parents carelessly use such words as agony, suffering, torture, or man-killer as being related to endurance running. Young runners tend to look for such terrors, and find them even when they're really non-existent. After all, the process of training inhibits awareness of pain just as it reduces the negative physical effects of fatigue. The mind of an experienced runner becomes inured to what the layman calls "the agony of running" just as his body becomes inured to low oxygen and lactic acid.

This is the reasoning behind the "hurt-pain-agony concept" of training advanced by Jim Counsilman (1968, 338), Indiana swimming coach. By bringing such words into everyday parlance and using them as a natural and inevitable part of every swimmer's experience, they lose their power to paralyze action. They even become a stimulus to good-humored kidding within the team.

Without some such training of this kind, the mind of the young runner anticipates and exaggerates both pain and failure, becomes more sensitive to the dangers of pain and the competition than of its own power to control and repress them. At the first sense of uneasiness or mild ache while running, they tend to feel, "There it is!" and soon "THERE IT IS!" The expectation creates reality. The coach that expects such a mind to exert control when he yells

"Relax!" is certain to be frustrated. Unfortunately he tends to blame the boy rather than his own approach to the problem.

Related sciences use the term "psychoneurosis" to identify a fixation of attention on the possible negative aspects of action. The fear of failing to rise up to the expectations of others, or of undergoing the horrors of exhaustion overwhelms the mind. (Have you ever thought of the connotation of that word we use so casually, "exhaustion?" To exhaust anything is "to use up or consume completely." Such a term has no place in sports. Who can estimate its subconscious effects?) The runner feels that somehow he must try harder, while all the time convinced that it won't be hard enough. In the *NEUROTIC PERSONALITY OF OUR TIMES*, Karen Horney writes of the dangers of our competitive culture in creating "basic anxiety, the feeling of being isolated and helpless in a potentially hostile world." Such anxiety is inherent in our track and field world, whether we recognize it or not, and the concept of winning by will power and repression of the negatives increases its dangers.

RELAXATION BY UNDERLOADING THE ACTION. Underloading the action should be interpreted primarily in terms of speed more than of resistance or strength, especially the speed of the preliminary movements of each event. When Harold Connolly set his world record in the hammer throw in 1962, at 231' 10" he wrote that "People were beginning to think that I was all washed up. I had been experimenting with four turns. It worked well most of the time but it broke down under the pressure of the big meets. With three turns, I could just get in there and throw." Whether this meant lesser speed or lesser inner tension is not significant. It certainly meant an increase in throwing power by way of relaxation.

Jokl[1] explained Bob Beamon's superhuman long jump (29' 2½") at Mexico City, in part, by the "absence of the inhibitory component" of hitting the board without fouling, after a full-speed run. He spoke of Beamon as "an unsophisticated natural jumper who pays little attention to the organization of the run-up and its markings." He just ran-and-jumped with no inhibitions or reservations. He hit the board perfectly. "I was just lucky," Beamon remarked after the event.

To give a reverse example, John Thomas overloaded the action in 1963 when he attempted to match Brumel's speed in the early steps of his run-up. Lacking the strength-training work and the specific skill of so fast an approach, he was unable to relax, and slowed the last three steps as a matter of both physical and mental necessity.

A different kind of underloading occurs in baseball when the batter swings a weighted bat before stepping to the plate. The action of swinging the regular bat now seems underloaded, so that he swings easier, faster, more relaxed. He now has a muscle sense of quickness rather than of hard effort. For some reason this custom has not caught on in throwing events. It's altogether reasonable that a weighted shot, discus, hammer, or javelin, used just prior to performance, would aid relaxation.

Underloading can also occur by reducing the mental tensions during competition. Each athlete has a critical level of tension at which he performs best. If tension is lower, he is not properly "keyed up" for the competition; if higher, he is "tight," and unrelaxed. A precise optimum tension is what is needed. Such tension is sometimes gained by having an athlete compete against superior competition during the weeks preceding an all-important team meet. Superior competition serves the same purpose as the weighted bat.

In summary, the underloading to produce relaxation can be of many kinds, physical and mental: a slight slowing of velocity in the preliminary movements, a simplifying of technique in competition, an ignore-ance of technique, deliberate overloading prior to competition--anything to help the athlete drop his tensions just below the critical level of uninhibited action.

RELAXATION BY CONCENTRATION ON POSITIVE EXTERNAL FACTORS. Fatigue and hypertension have both mental and physical aspects. Without denying the physical brakes applied by fatigue, we emphasize that the greater danger lies in the mental awareness of the feelings of fatigue. It is doubt of success, distaste for the discomforts of fatigue, fear of all-out effort, that restrain

---

[1]Ernst Jokl, M.D., "A Report on Bob Beamon's World-Record Long Jump," *U.S.T.C.A. Quarterly Review*, October 1969, 39.

performance at least as much as physical inability.

Obviously then, relaxation-in-action is maintained by concentrating on the positive factors, especially those that are external to the athlete. He loses himself; he insulates his sensitivity to the negatives of action by attending to the more factual aspects of his surround. In endurance running, he concentrates on race tactics, on the changing positions of various runners, especially the main contenders, on pace and the voice of the timer.

Most runners would agree that their greatest performances came when they were least aware of their own feelings. When Bannister (1955, 213) wrote of his first-ever mile under four minutes, he said, "There was no pain, only a great unity of movement and purpose. The world seemed to stand still, or did not exist. The only reality was the next 100 yards of track under my feet."

Though fiction, Alan Sillitoe's excellent story "The Loneliness of the Long-Distance Runner" sticks to the facts of running. His main character says, "I put on a spurt, and such a fast spurt it is because I feel that up to then I haven't been running and that I've used up no energy at all. And I've been able to do this because I've been thinking; and I wonder if I'm the only one in the running business with this system of forgetting that I'm running because I'm too busy thinking." Every biography of great runners tells the same story, though of course, the kind of thinking will vary.

For example, when the New Zealand runner, Murray Halberg, (1963, 105) wrote about his Olympic race at Rome, he told of his difficulties in keeping relaxed before the race until finally he became aware of the strain on the faces of his competitors. Only then, "I began to enjoy myself and look forward to the race." As to the race itself, he wrote,

It wasn't like Melbourne. I wasn't running in a blur. I could see the distant faces of the crowd. I was aware of everything. . . .

In contrast to Melbourne, from the start of the race I ran dead last and let the rest of the field carry me around. I could see the fellows in the lead changing places, getting checked, striving for better pole positions. It was almost as though I was watching the race from a detached position on the terrace. . . . During the eighth lap I began working the plan Arthur (Lydiard) and I had talked over for so long before the race.

Here is a mind concentrated on the positives of action, on the problems of other runners, and on the positive plan.

<u>RELAXATION THROUGH WHOLENESS.</u> I have deliberately held back the surest and best way to relaxation--that of feeling and being whole, all of one piece, within oneself and among one's family and friends. If, as Erich Fromm contends in *MAN AGAINST HIMSELF*, individual isolation and separateness is the primary evil in modern society, it follows that a sense of unity, of mutual supportiveness, of wholeness within and without is our greatest need.

Only the rare individual has it. Among coaches I have known, I think of Brutus Hamilton, Bill Bowerman, Leroy Walker; among athletes, Roger Bannister, Brian Sternberg, Valeriy Brumel. There are others, but these indicate the type--men who are solid, inwardly relaxed, at home in their world.

Kenny Moore,[1] in an SI article on Sebastian Coe, portrayed him as such a person--self-possessed, natural in all sorts of situations, nerveless while racing, unimpressed by records or victory,

"How have you become so free of anxiety before competition?" Sebastian was asked. "In having to be awakened before the Oslo race (in which he set the 1500m world record--KD), I guess I gave the appearance of calm, but I get nervous....I don't know. I can't say I consciously mastered it. It's just something that evolved, being less and less nervous."
Sebastian glanced at his family. "Feeling I'd be well and truly supported in my efforts had to be a part of it."

---

[1] Kenny Moore, "A Hard and Supple Man," *Sports Illustrated*, June 20, 1980, p. 74ff.

BIBLIOGRAPHY

The text material makes specific references to all but a few of the following books. They include books in related fields that support the basic viewpoints of the author, as well as those directly related to track and field and to track and field coaching. Single references, especially to articles, are given at the bottom of each page.

Astrand, P. O. *Textbook of Work Physiology*. New York: McGraw-Hill, Inc., 1970, 669 pp.

Bannister, Roger. *The Four Minute Mile*. New York: Dodd, Mead & Co., 1955, 252 pp.

Blake, Robert R. & Jane S. Mouton. *The Managerial Grid*. Houston: Gulf Publishing Company, 1964, 338 pp.

Cerutty, Percy Wells. *Athletics. How to Become a Champion*. London: Stanley Paul & Co., Ltd., 1960, 189 pp.

_____. *Running with Cerutty*. Los Altos, CA: *Track & Field News*, 1959, 29 pp. paperback.

Clarke, Ron, and Alan Trengove. *The Unforgiving Minute*. London: Pelham Books, Ltd., 1966, 189 pp.

_____, and Norman Harris. *The Lonely Breed*. London: Pelham Books Ltd., 1968, 187 pp.

Costill, David L., Ph.D. *A Scientific Approach to Distance Running*. *Track & Field News*, P.O. Box 296, Los Altos, CA, 94022, 1979, paper, 128 pp.

Counsilman, James E. *The Science of Swimming*. Englewood Cliffs, N.J.: Prentice-Hall, Inc., 1968, 457 pp.

DeVries, Herbert A. *Physiology of Exercise*. Dubuque, Iowa: Wm. C. Brown Co., 1966, 422 pp.

Doherty, J. Kenneth. *Modern Track and Field*. Englewood Cliffs, N.J.: Prentice-Hall, Inc., 1963, 558 pp.

_____. *Modern Training for Running*. Englewood Cliffs, N.J.: Prentice-Hall, Inc., 1964, 281 pp.

_____. *Track and Field Movies on Paper*, 2nd edition, one set of 3 books, 1967, 248 pp.

_____. "Relaxation in All-Out Running," in *Proceedings Track and Field Institute*, ed. Allan J. Ryan, M.D. Madison: University of Wisconsin Extension Service, 1966, 2-28.

_____. "Holism in Training for Sports," in *Anthology of Contemporary Readings*, ed. Howard S. Slusher and Aileene S. Lockhart. Dubuque, Iowa: Wm. C. Brown Co., 1966, paper, 324 pp.

Dolson, Frank. *Always Young*. Mountain View, CA: World Publications, 1975, paper, 209 pp.

Dyson Geoffrey. *The Mechanics of Athletics*. London: University of London Press, 6th edition, 1974, 229 pp.

Ecker, Tom. *Track and Field Dynamics*. Los Altos, CA: Tafnews Press, 1971, paper, 112 pp.

Elliott, Herb, and Alan Trengove. *The Golden Mile*. London: Cassell & Co., Ltd., 1961, 178 pp.

Ferstle, Jim. *Dave Wottle Story*. Mountain View, CA: World Publications, 1973, paper, 44 pp.

Ganslen, Richard V., Ph.D. *Mechanics of the Pole Vault*. 1980 Olympic 9th edition, paper. 176 pp., available from author, 1204 Windsor Drive, Denton, Texas, 76201.

Gardner, John. *Excellence*. New York: W. W. Norton & Co., 1984, paperback, 150 pp.

Gilmour, Garth H. *A Clean Pair of Heels: The Murray Halberg Story*. London: Herbert Jenkins Ltd., 1963, 212 pp.

Goldstein, Kurt, M.C. *The Organism*. Boston: Beacon Press, 1963, paper, 531 pp.

Hannus, Matti. *Finnish Running Secrets*. Mountain View, CA: World Publications, 1973, paper, 93 pp.

Harris, Norman. *The Legend of Lovelock*. New Zealand: A.H. & A.W.Reed, 1964, 180 pp.

Henderson, Joe. *Thoughts on the Run*. Published by The Runner's World, P.O.Box 366, Mountain View, CA, 94040, 1970, 110 pp., paper.

_____. *New Views of Speed Training*. Mountain View, CA: The Runner's World, 1971, 48 pp.

Henry, Bill. *An Approved History of the Olympic Games*. New York: G.P.Putnam's Sons, 1948, 368 pp.

Herrigel, Eugen. *Zen in the Art of Archery*. New York: Pantheon Books, Inc., 1953, 109 pp.

Hewson, Brian and Peter Bird. *Flying Feet*. New York: Arco Publishing Col, Inc., 1962, 160 pp.

Horney, Karen. *The Neurotic Personality of Our Times*. New York: W.W.Norton & Co., Inc., 1937, 299 pp.

Ibbotson, Derek and Terry O'Connor. *The 4-Minute Smiler*. London: Stanley Paul & Co., Ltd., 1960, 175 pp.

Jacobson, Edmund. *Progressive Relaxation*. Chicago: University of Chicago Press, 1938.

_____. *You Must Relax*. New York: McGraw-Hill, Inc., 1957, 269 pp.

Jarver, Jess. *Sprints and Relays*. Los Altos, CA: Tafnews Press, 1978, paper, 128 pp.

_____. Editor. *Middle Distances*, Los Altos: Tafnews Press, 1979, 128 pp. paperback.

_____. *The Throws*. Los Altos: Tafnews Press, 1980, 158 pp. paperback.

_____. Editor. *Long Distances*. Los Altos: Tafnews Press, 1980, 136 pp., paperback.

_____. *The Jumps*. Los Altos: Tafnews Press, 1981, 128 pp., paperback.

_____. *The Hurdles*. Los Altos: Tafnews Press, 1981, 124 pp., paperback.

Jenner, Bruce & Phillip Finch. *Decathlon Challenge*. Englewood Cliffs, N.J.:Prentice-Hall, Inc., 1977, 210 pp.

Johnson, Wendell. *People in Quandaries*. New York: Harper, 1946, 532 pp.

Jordan, Tom. *Pre!*. Los Altos, CA: Tafnews Press, 1977, paper, 128 pp.

Kelly, Graeme. *Mr. Controversial--The Story of Percy Wells Cerutty*. London: Stanley Paul & Co., Ltd., 1964, 168 pp.

Kobayashi, Shigeru. *Creative Management*. New York: American Management Association, Inc., 1971.

Likert, Rensis. *New Patterns of Management*. New York: McGraw-Hill Book Co., 1961, 278 pp.

Loader, W. R. *Testament of a Runner*. London: William Heinemann Ltd., 1960, 170 pp.

Lydiard, Arthur and Garth Gilmour. *Run to the Top*. London: Herbert Jenkins Ltd., 1962, 182 pp.

_____. *Running Training Schedules*. 2nd edition. Track & Field News, Box 296, Los Altos, CA, 94022, 1970, 30 pp.

Martin, David E., Ph.D. *The High Jump Book*. Los Altos: Tafnews Press, 1982, 157 pp. paper.

Maslow, A. H. *Motivation and Personality*. New York: Harper & Row, 1954, 408 pp.

Matthews, Vince, with Neil Amdur. *My Race Be Won*. New York: Charterhouse, 1974, 396 pp.

McGregor, Douglas. *The Human Side of Enterprise*. New York: McGraw-Hill, Inc., 1960.

Menninger, Karl, M.D. *The Vital Balance*. New York: The Viking Press, 1963, 531 pp.

Murphy, Gardner. *Human Potentialities*. London: George Allen & Unwin Ltd., 1960, 340 pp.

Nelson, Cordner. *The Jim Ryun Story*. Los Altos, CA: Tafnews Press, 1967, 272 pp.

_____. *The Miler*. New York: S.G.Phillips, 1969, 158 pp.

_____. *Track and Field--The Great Ones*. London: Pelham Books, Ltd., 1968, 224 pp.

Noronha, Francis. *Kipchoge of Kenya*. Elimu Publishers, 1970. Distributed in U.S. by Tafnews Press, P.O.Box 296, Los Altos, CA 94022, paper, 160 pp.

O'Connor, Terry. *The 4-Minute Smiler: The Derek Ibbotson Story*. London: Stanley Paul & Co., Ltd., 1960, 171 pp.

Ogilvie, Bruce C. and Thomas A. Tutko. *Problem Athletes and How to Handle Them*. London: Pelham Books Ltd., 1966, 195 pp.

Oxendine, Joseph B. *Psychology of Motor Learning*. New York: Appleton-Century-Crofts, Inc., 1968, 366 pp.

Peters, J. H. and Joseph Edmundson. *In the Long Run*. London: Cassell & Co. Ltd., 1955, 216 pp.

Pirie, Gordon. *Running Wild*. London: W. H. Allen & Co., Ltd., 1961.

Raevuori, Antero and Rolf Haikkola. *Lasse Viren--Olympic Champion*. Portland, Oregon: Continental Publishing House, 1978, paper, 118 pp.

Reindell, Herbert, Helmut Roskamm, and Woldemar Gerschler. *Das Intervall-training*. Munich: Barth Publisher, 1962.

Rozin, Skip. *Daley Thompson*. London: Stanley Paul, 199 pp.

Schmolinsky, Gerhardt, ed. *Track and Field*. East Berlin: Sportverlag Berlin, 1978, 392pp.

Selye, Hans, M.D. *The Stress of Life*. New York: McGraw-Hill, Inc., 1956, 324 pp.

Snell, Peter and Garth Gilmour. *No Bugles No Drums*. Auckland, N.Z.: Minerva Ltd., 1965, 239 pp

Stampfl, Franz. *Franz Stampfl on Running*. London: Herbert Jenkins Ltd., 1955, 159 pp.

Tulloh, Bruce. *Tulloh on Running*. London: William Heinemann Ltd., 1968, 146 pp.

Tutko, Thomas A. and Jack W. Richards. *Psychology of Coaching*. Boston: Allyn and Bacon, Inc., 1971, 216 pp.

Track & Field News Editors. *Olympic Track & Field*. Los Altos: Tafnews Press, 1984, 152 pp.

Walker, Leroy T. *Championship Techniques and Track and Field*. West Nyack, N.Y.: Parker Publishing Co., 1969, 206 pp.

_____. *Track & Field for Boys and Girls*. Chicago: The Athletic Institute, 1983, 128 pp.

Walsh, Chris. *The Bowerman System*. Los Altos: Tafnews Press, 1983, 72 pp., paperback.

Williams, Roger J. *Biochemical Individuality*. New York: John Wiley & Sons, Inc., 1956, 214 pp.

Wilson, Harry. *Running Dialogue--A Coach's Story*. Foreword by Steve Ovett. London: Stanley Paul, 1982, 208 pp.

Wilt, Fred. *How They Train*. 2nd edition, 1973: Vol. 1--Middle Distances, 124 pp.; Vol. 2-- Long Distances, 124 pp.; Vol. 3--Sprinting and Hurdling, 96 pp. Tafnews Press, P.O. Box 296, Los Altos, CA, 94022. All paperback.

_____. *Run, Run, Run*. Los Altos, CA: Track & Field News, 1964, paper, 281 pp.

Winter, Lloyd C. ("Bud"). *So You Want to be a Sprinter*. San Francisco: Fearon Publishers, 2450 Fillmore St., 1956, paper, 48 pp.

_____. *The Rocket Sprint Start*. San Francisco: Fearon Publishers, 1964, 22 pp.

Zarnowski, Frank. *The Decathlon Guide*. Indianapolis: The Athletics Congress, 1984, 157 pp.

NAME INDEX

SUBJECT INDEX

CONVERTING ENGLISH-METRIC MEASUREMENTS

Meters into Feet and Inches

M.	FT.	IN.	M.	FT.	IN.
1	3	3⅜	51	167	3⅞
2	6	6¾	52	170	7¼
3	9	10⅛	53	173	10⅝
4	13	1½	54	177	2
5	16	4⅞	55	180	5⅜
6	19	8¼	56	183	8¾
7	22	11⅝	57	187	0⅛
8	26	3	58	190	3½
9	29	6⅜	59	193	6⅞
10	32	9¾	60	196	10¼
11	36	1⅛	61	200	1⅝
12	39	4½	62	203	5
13	42	7¾	63	206	8⅜
14	45	11⅛	64	209	11¾
15	49	2½	65	213	3
16	52	5⅞	66	216	6⅜
17	55	9¼	67	219	9¾
18	59	0⅝	68	223	1⅛
19	62	4	69	226	4½
20	65	7⅜	70	229	7⅞
21	68	10¾	71	232	11¼
22	72	2⅛	72	236	2⅝
23	75	5½	73	239	6
24	78	8⅞	74	242	9⅜
25	82	0¼	75	246	0¾
26	85	3⅝	76	249	4⅛
27	88	7	77	252	7½
28	91	10⅜	78	255	10⅞
29	95	1¾	79	259	2¼
30	98	5⅛	80	262	5⅝
31	101	8½	81	265	9
32	104	11⅞	82	269	0⅜
33	108	3¼	83	272	3¾
34	111	6⅝	84	275	7⅛
35	114	10	85	278	10¼
36	118	1⅜	86	282	1⅝
37	121	4¾	87	285	5
38	124	8⅛	88	288	8⅜
39	127	11⅜	89	291	11¾
40	131	2¾	90	295	3⅛
41	134	6⅛	91	298	6½
42	137	9½	92	301	9⅞
43	141	0⅞	93	305	1¼
44	144	4¼	94	308	4⅝
45	147	7⅝	95	311	8
46	150	11	96	314	11⅜
47	154	2⅜	97	318	2¾
48	157	5¾	98	321	6⅛
49	160	9⅛	99	324	9½
50	164	0½	100	328	0⅞

Centimeters into Feet and Inches

CM.	FT.	IN.	CM.	FT.	IN.
1		0⅜	51	1	8⅛
2		0¾	52	1	8½
3		1⅛	53	1	8⅞
4		1⅝	54	1	9¼
5		2	55	1	9⅝
6		2⅜	56	1	10
7		2¾	57	1	10½
8		3⅛	58	1	10⅞
9		3½	59	1	11¼
10		3⅞	60	1	11⅝
11		4⅜	61	2	0
12		4¾	62	2	0⅜
13		5⅛	63	2	0¾
14		5½	64	2	1¼
15		5⅞	65	2	1⅝
16		6¼	66	2	2
17		6¾	67	2	2⅜
18		7⅛	68	2	2¾
19		7½	69	2	3⅛
20		7⅞	70	2	3⅝
21		8¼	71	2	4
22		8⅝	72	2	4⅜
23		9	73	2	4¾
24		9½	74	2	5⅛
25		9⅞	75	2	5½
26		10¼	76	2	5⅞
27		10⅝	77	2	6¼
28		11	78	2	6¾
29		11⅜	79	2	7⅛
30		11¾	80	2	7½
31	1	0¼	81	2	7⅞
32	1	0⅝	82	2	8¼
33	1	1	83	2	8⅝
34	1	1⅜	84	2	9⅛
35	1	1¾	85	2	9½
36	1	2⅛	86	2	9⅞
37	1	2⅝	87	2	10¼
38	1	3	88	2	10⅝
39	1	3⅜	89	2	11
40	1	3¾	90	2	11⅜
41	1	4⅛	91	2	11⅞
42	1	4½	92	3	0¼
43	1	4⅞	93	3	0⅝
44	1	5⅜	94	3	1
45	1	5¾	95	3	1⅜
46	1	6⅛	96	3	1¾
47	1	6½	97	3	2⅛
48	1	6⅞	98	3	2⅝
49	1	7¼	99	3	3
50	1	7⅝	100	3	3⅜

Feet into Meters

FT.	M.
1	.31
2	.61
3	.91
4	1.22
5	1.52
6	1.83
7	2.13
8	2.44
9	2.74
10	3.05
20	6.1
30	9.15
40	12.2
50	15.25
60	18.3
70	21.35
80	24.4
90	27.45
100	30.5
110	33.55
120	36.6
130	39.65
140	42.7
150	45.75
160	48.8
170	51.85
180	54.9
190	57.95
200	61
210	64.05
220	67.1
230	70.15
240	73.2
250	76.25
260	79.3
270	82.35
280	85.4
290	88.45
300	91.5
310	94.55
320	97.6
330	100.65
340	103.7
350	106.75
360	109.75
370	112.8
380	115.8
390	118.85
400	121.9

Inches into Centimeters

IN.	CM.
¼	.63
½	1.27
¾	1.9
1	2.54
1¼	3.17
1½	3.81
1¾	4.44
2	5.08
2¼	5.71
2½	6.35
2¾	6.98
3	7.62
3¼	8.25
3½	8.89
3¾	9.52
4	10.16
4¼	10.79
4½	11.43
4¾	12.06
5	12.7
5¼	13.33
5½	13.97
5¾	14.6
6	15.24
6¼	15.87
6½	16.51
6¾	17.14
7	17.78
7¼	18.41
7½	19.05
7¾	19.68
8	20.32
8¼	20.96
8½	21.59
8¾	22.26
9	22.86
9¼	23.5
9½	24.13
9¾	24.77
10	25.4
10¼	26.04
10½	26.67
10¾	27.31
11	27.94
11¼	28.58
11½	29.21
11¾	29.85
12	30.48

tafnews books

A Scientific Approach to Distance Running, by David Costill. Our best-selling work analyzes scientific findings about distance training and racing. 1979. 128pp. $6.00

The Bowerman System, by Chris Walsh. Insights into the development of Bill Bowerman's training philosphies, with about 30pp. of middle and long distance training schedules. 72pp. 1983. $8.50

High School Cross Country, by Joe McLaughlin. A well-crafted basic guide for coach and athlete. 96pp. 1983. $6.00

The High Jump Book, by Dwight Stones, Greg Joy, Jacek Wzsola and Dr. David Martin. A great compilation of material on flop jumping from three masters of the genre. 1982. 160pp. $10.00

The Jumps: Contemporary Theory, Technique and Training, ed. by Jess Jarver. This collection of recent articles consititues a modern guide to the high jump, pole vault, long and triple jumps. 2nd ed. 1981. 128pp. $10.00

Middle Distances: Contemporary Theory, Technique and Training, ed. by Jess Jarver. 1979. 128pp. $10.00

The Throws: Contemporary Theory, Technique and Training, ed. by Jess Jarver. The four throws: shot, discus, javelin and hammer, with additional articles on strength training. 2nd ed. 1980. 160pp. $10.00

Sprints and Relays: Contemporary Theory, Technique and Training, ed. by Jess Jarver. Another great collection of articles. 2nd ed. 1983. 120pp. $10.00

The Hurdles: Contemporary Theory, Technique and Training, ed. by Jess Jarver. 1979. 128pp. $10.00

Long Distances: Contemporary Theory, Technique and Training, ed. by Jess Jarver. 1980. 160pp. $10.00

Running and Your body, by Bernie Dare. Exhaustive study of how to apply physiological principles to track training. Dozens of sample workout schedules. 1980. 160pp. $8.00

Computerized Running Training Programs, Gardner & Purdy. Still an immensely valuable book, with thousands of computer-generated workout schedules for runners at every level. 7th printing. 256pp. $8.00

Getting Started in Track & Field: A Coaching Manual, by R.S. Parker. The best guide for coaches of younger athletes. 1976. 128pp. $6.00

How High School Runners Train, ed. by Frank P. Calore. 2nd ed. 1982. 128pp. $7.00

How They Train: Long Distances, ed. by Jack Pfeifer. 1982. 160pp. $7.50

How Women Runners Train, ed. by Vern Gambetta. 1980. 128pp. $6.50

Basic Track & Field Biomechanics, Tom Ecker. Ready 2/85. A new complete introduction to the principles of biomechanics for track and field. $10.00

Track Management, by Andy Bakjian. Check lists for the official and meet director. 1982. 92pp. $5.00

How They Train: High School Field Events, ed. by Frank P. Calore. 160pp. $6.50

Add $1.50 per book for postage and handling. Calif. residents add 6% sales tax.

Tafnews Press, Book Division of Track & Field News, Box 296, Los Altos, CA 94022